RECENT AMERICA

*Conflicting Interpretations of the
Great Issues*

RECENT AMERICA

Conflicting Interpretations of the Great Issues

EDITED BY SIDNEY FINE

SECOND EDITION

The Macmillan Company · NEW YORK

Collier-Macmillan Limited · LONDON

© Copyright, The Macmillan Company, 1967

All rights reserved. No part of this book may be reproduced or utilized in any form or by any means, electronic or mechanical, including photocopying, recording, or by any information storage and retrieval system, without permission in writing from the Publisher.

First Printing

Earlier edition © 1962 by The Macmillan Company.

A portion of the text has been reproduced from *The American Past*, Volume II, by Sidney Fine and Gerald S. Brown, © 1961 by The Macmillan Company and © copyright 1965 by The Macmillan Company.

Library of Congress catalog card number: 67–10519

The Macmillan Company, New York
Collier-Macmillan Canada, Ltd., Toronto, Ontario

PRINTED IN THE UNITED STATES OF AMERICA

To Gail and Deborah

Preface to the Second Edition

The present edition retains the basic pattern of organization of the first edition. Ten of the selections and four of the topics included are new to this edition. The new selections, in addition to enhancing the teachability of *Recent America,* help to keep it abreast of the scholarship in American history that has been published since the first edition appeared.

The editor is pleased to express here his gratitude to both teachers and students for their helpful comments on the first edition.

S. F.

Preface to the First Edition

This volume, to repeat the substance of the preface to *The American Past,* is designed to bring into sharp focus some of the major issues of twentieth-century American history. For each of the topics selected, two historians present either directly conflicting interpretations or interpretations which illuminate the whole problem from complementary, but essentially different, approaches or emphases. Each historian is represented by a substantial piece of writing within the limits of which he could, so to speak, move around and develop his interpretation in some depth and with that degree of sophistication which characterizes the mature writing of history. The editor has deliberately avoided the snippets and shreds and the mélange of primary and secondary materials which so often typify volumes of this kind. It is hoped that it is history with style and meaning which is presented here.

Each pair of selections is preceded by a brief introduction which places the two interpretations in their historical and historiographical setting and which points up the nature of the conflict between them. It is expected that the selections will serve to stimulate discussion and thought concerning some of the principal themes of twentieth-century American history and will help to give the reader an appreciation of the nature of the historical process and of the variety and richness of the historical writing about our recent past.

S. F.

Contents

Contents

V

Prohibition:
Product of Hidden Urges or of Cultural Conflict?

VI

The Literature of the 1920's:
A Trivial Literature or a Literature of "Useful Innocence"?

VII

Herbert Hoover and the Great Depression:
Inflexibility or Innovation?

VIII

The New Deal and the American Reform Tradition:
How New Was the New Deal?

Contents

Contents

Theodore Roosevelt as Legislative Leader: Success or Failure?

INTRODUCTION

Whereas biographies of Theodore Roosevelt had previously been rather adulatory in tone, the publication in 1931 of Henry F. Pringle's charmingly written Theodore Roosevelt *ushered in a period during which historians either refused to take Roosevelt seriously or were highly critical of his actions. Pringle, Matthew Josephson, and others tended to minimize Roosevelt's accomplishments as President. His commitment to the cause of Progressivism was questioned, and he was pictured as a compromiser who was generally ready to settle for half a loaf when harder fighting might have gained the whole loaf.*

Thanks largely to the writings of George Mowry, John M. Blum, and Howard K. Beale and to the publication of The Letters of Theodore Roosevelt, *edited by Elting E. Morison, historians in the last two decades have begun to reappraise Roosevelt and to upgrade him in their evaluations. Today, Roosevelt the President is pictured as a leader who advanced the cause of Progressivism to a significant degree, who practiced the art of politics with consummate skill, who raised the office of the Presidency to a new stature, who asserted the supremacy of the national interest over any special interest, and who understood far better than most of his contemporaries both the nature of world politics and the role the United States would have to play in world affairs.[1]*

Both Matthew Josephson and John Blum, in the selections that follow, concentrate on Roosevelt's record as a legislative leader after his smashing triumph at the polls in 1904. The author and biographer Josephson argues that Roosevelt did not take advantage of the opportunity for positive leadership that his electoral triumph provided. Roosevelt, he contends, was not really devoted to the cause of reform and was bored by complex economic problems. In the crucial battle over the Hepburn Act, Roosevelt, according to Josephson, surrendered to the Old Guard and thus lost the fight for effective railroad regulation.

Blum, author of the brilliant The Republican Roosevelt *and associate editor of* The Roosevelt Letters, *takes direct issue with Josephson. The Yale history professor contends that Roosevelt was highly effective in his dealings with Congress and had a basic understanding of the problem of government control of business. In the fight for the Hepburn Act, Roosevelt, in Blum's opinion, maneuvered adroitly and ultimately secured from Congress precisely the sort of measure he wanted, a measure that "endowed the Interstate Commerce Commission with power commensurate with its task."*

---

[1] See, for example, Arthur S. Link, "Theodore Roosevelt in His Letters," *Yale Review*, XLIII (June 1954), 589–598.

2

The Politics of Reform

Matthew Josephson

The old Senators who still ruled Congress seemed surprisingly unhappy over the sweeping Republican party triumph of 1904.

"What is to be done now with our victory is a pretty serious question," wrote the canny Orville Platt of Connecticut to Aldrich.[1] It was a question that Theodore Roosevelt, too, asked himself continually.

Originally a political "accident," he had won more real power than any of the dreary Republican worthies who had preceded him in his office since Lincoln. He was not only the chief magistrate, but the unchallenged leader of his party organization, seated in the driving seat of the Steam Roller. The opportunity for positive leadership lay open for him, with the Presidential power less restricted by indirect controls than ever before, as a similar opportunity fell one day to a later Roosevelt after re-election in 1936.

Moreover he could say, in this great hour, that his re-election, which vindicated his principles, was owing

> not to the politicians primarily, although I have done my best to get on with them; not to the financiers, although I have staunchly upheld the rights of property; but above all to Abraham Lincoln's "plain people"; to the folk who worked hard on farm, in shop, or on the railroads, or who owned little stores, little businesses which they managed themselves. I would literally, not figuratively, rather cut off my right hand than forfeit by any improper act of mine the trust and regard of these people.[2]

No one could utter braver sentiments than T. R., nor with firmer conviction, at a given moment. His second inauguration, celebrated by a crowd of 500,000 persons who streamed into the capital, witnessed his liberation from pledges to the dead man he had succeeded. "I am glad to be President in my own right," he said to John Hay.[3]

From Matthew Josephson, *The President Makers* (New York: Harcourt, Brace and Company, 1940), pp. 175–182, 219–221, 226–236. Reprinted by permission. Although extracts from both Chapters VI and VII of the Josephson book are included in the selection, the title is that of Chapter VII.

[1] Stephenson, *op. cit.*, p. 250.
[2] Bishop, *op. cit.*, T. R. to Wister, Nov. 19, 1904, Vol. I, p. 345.
[3] Hay, *Diaries*, Vol. V, Nov. 8, 1904.

There is evidence that he weighed the trend of the recent elections, and the popular emotions that accompanied it, in serious spirit. One perhaps important symptom was the sharp rise of the tiny Socialist party, led by Eugene Debs, from 100,000 votes in 1900 to 400,000 votes in 1904. Roosevelt duly noted this when he remarked privately in February, 1905, that the growth of the Socialist party was "far more ominous than any Populist or similar movement in the past." [4] William Jennings Bryan, who also watched the popular pulse most carefully, told friends that he now feared the coming of socialism. The new party's rapid growth might lead soon to the capture of one of the older parties, as the Populists had managed to do in 1896. It was proof also "that the Democratic party has been too conservative to satisfy the reform element of the country." [5]

In serious vein, Roosevelt also pondered over the labor problem, though only a minority of American workers were Socialists, while the great majority pinned their hopes upon the economic action of the federated craft unions led by Samuel Gompers. In a long letter, written two days after the election to his Attorney General, Philander C. Knox (retiring now to enter the Senate), Roosevelt explored the possibilities of a Square Deal to labor. Hitherto, with Knox's aid, he had grappled chiefly with the great problems of the day that were connected with organized capital. To Knox, the conservative attorney for Carnegie, Roosevelt gave credit handsomely for having given shape to policies which were only "half-formulated" in his own mind. But once in the Senate, there would be occasion for Knox to give as deep thought to the problem of labor as he had given to that of capital.

> More and more the labor movement of this country will become a factor of vital importance. . . . If the attitude of the New York *Sun* toward labor, as toward the trusts, becomes the attitude of the Republican party, we shall some day go down before a radical and extreme democracy with a crash which would be disastrous to the nation. We must not only do justice *but we must show the wage-worker that we are doing justice.* We must make it evident that while there is not any weakness in our attitude, while we unflinchingly demand good conduct from them, yet we are equally resolute in the effort to secure them all just and proper consideration.

Here we see in this confidential, artless letter how Roosevelt still never falters in his desire to play the Great Mediator. His hope of upholding the democratic doctrine of "equality before the law" in the conflicts of capital and labor corresponded significantly with the English and European political reform movements of this time, which conceived of social legislation as concessions to be made in time, as a form of "ransom" paid in order to safeguard society and its prosperity. The concessions might be costly; yet, as a

---

[4] Pringle, *Roosevelt*, p. 368.
[5] E. E. Robinson, *American Political Parties*, p. 289.

Joseph Chamberlain intimated, their costs could be paid out of future profits, and would be outweighed by the gains in security from tragic upheavals.

Roosevelt argued:

> It would be a dreadful calamity if we saw this country divided into two parties, one containing the bulk of the property owners and conservative people, the other the bulk of the wage-workers and less prosperous people, generally; each party insisting upon, demanding much that was wrong, and each party sullen and angered by real and fancied grievances.

And what was the answer, what were the measures which, taken in time, would prevent such a fearful outcome? Roosevelt like the corporation lawyers Knox and Root wished to preserve the existing balance of property relations. Further than this he had no definite measures in mind, no timetable, no program. He seemed to offer only a standard, a kind of "moral" imperative, which his conservative colleagues often accepted, but as often wavered from, as it suited their material interests: ". . . Here in this republic, it is peculiarly incumbent upon the man with whom things have prospered to be in a certain sense the keeper of his brother with whom life has gone hard." For "the surest way to provoke an explosion of wrong and injustice is to be short-sighted, narrow-minded, greedy and ignorant. . . ." [6]

Yet vague as was the plan, and wavering the leader, it is true, as Herbert Croly later reflected, that Roosevelt groped in sound directions. His "new Nationalism" or "new Hamiltonianism," while strongly centralizing the government authority, made this augmented authority appear to be more responsive to the popular will; it served not as a bulwark against the rising tide of democracy, but as an effective instrument of the common national welfare. Even in compromise and failure, Rooseveltian leadership gave signs of what could be done; pointed to the "promise of American life."

"In internal affairs, I cannot say that I entered the Presidency with any deliberately planned and far-reaching scheme of social betterment," Roosevelt recollected in writing his autobiography. The more was the pity. What is remarkable at this stage is that, with a record-breaking victory to his credit, and holding an unchallenged position of leadership, Roosevelt confined himself so severely in his actual domestic policies.

While he wondered what to do with his victory, strong influence was brought to bear upon him to see to it that any reform or trust control activities should work, as he put it, "without paralyzing the energies of the business community." [7] From the West came two spokesmen of progressive measures, Governors Cummins and La Follette, with whom he held a long conference. La Follette advocated strong measures to control railroads and

---

[6] *T. R. Papers*, T. R. to P. C. Knox, Nov. 10, 1904.
[7] *T. R. Papers*, T. R. to Sir George Trevelyan, Mar. 9, 1905.

fix the rates they charged; Cummins urged a reduction of the tariff rates that would help, as he thought, to curb the trusts and lower the cost of living. Cummins, on leaving, expressed himself as satisfied with the interview, and counted upon Roosevelt's adherence to tariff reform. He recalled in later years that the President had shown him a passage in his forthcoming Message to Congress indicating as much.[8]

However, something very powerful moved Roosevelt at this juncture, and at almost the last hour before making public his message he veered and changed his mind. Senator Aldrich came to see him; Senator O. H. Platt likewise; and Speaker "Joe" Cannon also came to his desk. To Roosevelt's proposal to do something about tariff reform in the early future, Aldrich coolly answered: "Possibly." Senator Platt may well have reminded the President of the wisdom of holding to the "gentleman's agreement" of 1902 * to avoid forbidden subjects. Cannon was even more forthright, according to his own later account. A struggle over the tariff would probably end in failure, and would moreover prevent enactment of the railroad bill Roosevelt had set his heart upon. By telegram, the sentences in the Message of December, 1904, referring to tariff reform, already given out to the press, were "killed." [9]

The Message to Congress of December, 1904, which was to announce a Roosevelt who had "come into his own," and which had been awaited with burning curiosity, proved to be a most moderate document. In a spirit of humanity it recommended laws fostering workmen's compensation and restricting child labor. It was silent upon the tariff issue. Its proposals for the extension of government control over the railroads were the most important ones. Responding to bitter criticisms of existing freight rates, Roosevelt urged that Congress must accord a genuine power to the Interstate Commerce Commission—when complaints were brought—"to decide, subject to judicial review, what shall be a reasonable rate. . . ."

The terms of the Message were conciliatory. Great corporations, the President said, were "necessary," and for their "great and singular mental powers" the masters of corporations were entitled to large rewards. However, they must give due regard to the public interest.

Instant relief was felt now by the anxious railroad lobbyists and "railroad Senators" in Washington. Soon it became plain that, although an administration railroad bill was to be introduced in Congress, nothing would be done during the "Lame Duck" session, and that Roosevelt would not care to

---

[8] Stephenson, *op. cit.*, p. 235, citing memorandum of A. B. Cummins.

* Editor's note: The reference is to an agreement Roosevelt is alleged to have made with Senators Nelson Aldrich and Mark Hanna by which the President promised not to tamper with the tariff or the currency in return for a free hand in dealing with other problems.

[9] *Ibid.*, p. 462, memorandum of L. W. Busbey; cf. also L. W. Busbey, *Cannon*, pp. 208–209.

call a special session of the new, more liberal Congress, which would normally convene at the end of 1905. It was evident also that Roosevelt had as yet won no agreement of definite support for his bill from Aldrich and Cannon, who controlled Congress still with an unshaken grip. These men waited, and worked to gain time.

It was less well known that the great railroad master Edward H. Harriman, accompanied by his lawyer, quietly visited Washington several times in the winter of 1904–1905, and also in December, 1905, at the time of the new session of Congress. It is evident that in keeping with the friendly alliance between Harriman and Roosevelt, during the late campaign, Harriman was being "consulted" by those who advised the President in framing the proposed law. Yet Harriman disapproved of everything in the way of railroad legislation. He was not an easy man to please, and strain arose between the two aggressive men, more than a year before their public quarrel, almost immediately after the election to which Harriman had given such signal help.

The difficult course of Roosevelt's negotiations with both the railroad magnates and the Standpat leaders in Congress is reflected in certain letters to his Boswell, Joseph B. Bishop, and to Lodge. After a snarl of debate, the railroad reform bill, which had passed the House, died in the committee rooms of the Senate. It was evident that Roosevelt did not press the issue strongly and was easily resigned to waiting for another year, when perhaps the force of public opinion would come to his aid more strongly.

> My chief fear is lest the big financiers who, outside of their own narrowly limited profession, are as foolish as they are selfish, will force the moderates to join with the radicals in radical action, under penalty of not obtaining any at all. *I must prefer moderate action:* but the ultraconservatives may make it necessary to accept what is radical.[10]

In a similar vein he wrote to his old political mentor Lodge, saying that the railroads were opposing his reform bill vigorously and hoped to beat it. ". . . I think they are very short-sighted not to understand that *to beat it means to increase the danger of the movement for government ownership of railroads.*" [11]

These are scarcely the tones of one who, by a tremendous personal victory, had made himself the master of his party. Roosevelt's ventures in legislative leadership (actually very few) show instead that he accepted strict limitations of his power in this field; that he dreaded the wearisome, perplexing task of driving a definite program of legislation through Congress; that he feared the machinelike control of the Senate and the autocratic rule of Speaker Cannon, in the House, would be immune to direct attacks. This machine

---

[10] Bishop, *op. cit.,* Vol. I, p. 428, Mar. 23, 1905; italics mine.
[11] *T. R. Papers,* T. R. to Lodge, May 24, 1905; italics mine.

like control, especially in the lower House, remained unchallenged by both Roosevelt and Taft, until the insurrection led by Congressman Norris of Nebraska in 1910 suddenly overthrew it.

It was true that the President sought to rally public opinion to his side by making certain fighting speeches, such as that at Philadelphia, January 30, 1905. Here, waving his Big Stick a little, he declared that our free people would not tolerate longer the vast power of corporate wealth, unless "the still higher power" of controlling this wealth in the interests of the whole people were lodged "somewhere in the Government." He asked for "justice" in the way of submitting the railroads to more rigorous supervision by the Interstate Commerce Commission, and gave warning once more that, without such measures, our republic might founder like republics of olden times amid the destructive contests of the Haves and the Have-Nots, the Poor and Rich.

Yet it was all too plain that his mind was distracted by the pernickety controversies that arose over the terms and details of a new empowering act for the Interstate Commerce Commission. Complex economic or financial problems always ended by boring him, for his mind, as his friends knew, was wanting in the spirit of orderly logic necessary to a law-making program. His heart, his emotions, were turned elsewhere in 1905—during this time of painful domestic controversy, financial scandal, and popular unrest—to more distant fields, abroad, where a role of glory, infinitely simpler and more attractive to his nature, beckoned him. . . .

Theodore Roosevelt's sharp veerings, his lapses into reform, so to speak, can be understood only in relation to the growing pressure brought upon him by the radicals. Left to his own devices, he tended to wait, to hesitate, to temporize, like so many other professed reformers who were ready to believe that the mere occupation of office by themselves meant the winning of the battle. But the arrival of a La Follette, fresh from his provincial successes, to a leading place in national politics was a portent and a reminder.

Now Bryan, the "peerless leader" of the opposition party after 1904, began to urge radical policies for the Democrats. His influential weekly newspaper, The Commoner, kept up a constant fire of criticism upon Mr. Roosevelt, pointing out week after week the compromising features of his tactics. According to the indefatigable adversary, Roosevelt was dangerously "Hamiltonian" and believed that "the well-born were born to rule"—a very accurate judgment of the President's convictions. Great opportunities lay before the powerful President, said Bryan, but his own instincts led him to protect the "plutocracy," whatever he might say in his set speeches year after year. Bryan challenged him on a series of issues. What was President Roosevelt doing (1) to advance the Eight-Hour Day, even to the extent of enforcing it in the District of Columbia on government contracts? (2) What was he doing to bring about a constitutional amendment permitting "more democracy" through the Direct Election of Senators? (3) What of more vigorous prosecution of monopolies? Why were horse-thieves who broke the law given criminal punishment, while trust magnates who broke the law went unpunished? (4) Why was nothing done about the infamous court injunction used in labor disputes? (5) Why was there still no strict regulation of the railroads, after all these years? Why did President Roosevelt still oppose giving to the Interstate Commerce Commission the real power to initiate and fix railroad rates? What truth was there after all in the legend of the "iron man in the White House"? Bryan's organ asked.[12]

Thus after years of good fortune and comparatively smooth sailing Theodore Roosevelt faced an increasingly troubled and critical public opinion at home after 1904. Though he stood at the zenith of his power and glory, thanks chiefly to foreign exploits, his hesitations were noticed, his compromises were measured by would-be rivals for popular leadership.

The danger of party cleavage was always perfectly real to him. In the northwestern tier of states, hitherto staunchly Republican, he felt the constant clamor for downward revision of the tariff and increased trust prosecution. The clamor for more effective railroad regulation, led by La Follette and others, threatened to become a veritable "prairie fire." Yet for nearly two years, up to 1906, the clique of Aldrich and Cannon that still ruled Congress had warily forestalled legislative action.

The essence of Roosevelt's diplomacy, as Professor C. E. Merriam has pointed out, lay in pursuing tactics of combination, and in avoiding the "permanent consolidation of any one group against him. . . ." His "on the one hand" and "on the other hand" policy enabled him to hold the middle class, and alternately to attract and repel the labor group and the business group. "Broadly speaking . . . he was always detaching part of a group, commercial, labor or otherwise, and preventing solid opposition against him." [13] It was in very fear of a rupture within his party and of a combination of militant sectional and class movements, including Bryan, La Follette, and even Debs, that the Square Deal President now turned resolutely to the unpleasant business of writing large reforms into the statutes. For more than four years he had preached the Ten Commandments, yet no signal legislative achievements were credited to his name. . . .

By strenuous fighting for conservation, for pure-food and meat-inspection laws, and by frequent indictments of trusts, Roosevelt appeared to wage the struggle for reform with increasing vigor. His main objective, however, was still the passage of stronger laws regulating the railroads. To the press he stated frankly that the hour was late, that the people must have relief from the burdensome rates of the railroads. Yet in this contest he feared the outcome. The railroads, he felt, were "crazy" in their hostility. In the winter of 1906, while the railroad bill was being debated, Mr. Harriman and his

---

[12] *The Commoner*, Nov. 18, 1904; Dec. 9, 1904; Apr. 13, Apr. 20, 1906.
[13] Merriam, *Four American Party Leaders*, p. 34.

lawyer, Sidney Webster, came several times to Washington and expressed the strongest objection, not only to the railroad bill but to investigations of the Harriman lines being made by the Interstate Commerce Commission. It was plain that Harriman, who had raised $250,000 for the campaign of 1904, was becoming alienated, although in endeavoring to learn what he desired the President could get nothing but "general allegations or sweeping accusations" from him.[14]

In a public address on October 19, 1905, Roosevelt had already hinted that he would willingly accept *only a part* of the power he sought in order to regulate the railroads; it was a hint of compromise. His Message to Congress of December 9, 1905, whose main feature was the appeal for railroad control, also reiterated his prudent position of the year before: "My proposal is not to give the Interstate Commerce Commission power to initiate or originate rates generally, but to regulate a rate already fixed or originated by the roads, upon complaint and after investigation." The new rates to be established were to be, of course, "subject to review by the courts." Full publicity for the accounts of the railroad was another condition he favored.

The remarkable thing was that twenty years after the Interstate Commerce Act had become law, the Commission it established had almost no power to interfere with the activities of railroads. One of the members had even resigned lately, making public protests at the impotence of this regulatory body. Even its limited power had been stripped away—chiefly on the Constitutional ground of "due process"—by the remorseless reasoning of the Supreme Court, the court which Senator Aldrich was said to trust in as he trusted in Providence. The Commission could not of its own authority fix rates for the railroads, for such action might result in "confiscation." On the other hand, if a fair valuation of the railroad properties could once be established, as La Follette urged, then "reasonable" rates permitting fair profits might be fixed. But the very mention of government appraisal of the railroad properties and fixing of their rates aroused terror of a red Socialist revolution in Senatorial breasts.

In January the act enlarging the powers of the Interstate Commerce Commission, in line with the President's moderate views, was introduced in Congress by Representative Hepburn of Iowa. After brief debate, the bill was quickly passed by the Lower House—Speaker Cannon evidently offering no resistance—and committed to the charge of a committee of the Senate for consideration. Here, the leader of the "Railway Senators," the multi-millionaire Elkins of West Virginia, was chairman; beside him stood Nelson Aldrich, the "dictator," with divers faithful Republican followers. Tillman, on behalf of the Democratic minority in the Senate's Committee on Interstate Commerce, it was expected, would be able to accomplish nothing, and the bill would either be strangled by amendments or altogether killed.

---

[14] *T. R. Papers,* T. R. to Sidney Webster, Jan. 31, 1907.

The Old Guard was willing to grant power to the government commission, ostensibly to fix rates, upon complaints brought before it; provided, first, that complaint could be made difficult, costly, and infrequent. That is, a grain shipper with a grievance would be obliged to retain a lawyer and send him to Washington to defend his petition. In the second place, rate cases were to be reviewed after considerable delays, and judged before Federal courts, involving further costly legal process and (probably) very conservative judgment. This was what was meant by allowing for "broad court review" of railroad rate cases. Now the trouble with Hepburn's bill, as sent from the Lower House, was that it provided for no special intervention by the Federal courts, save those normally offered under the Constitution. Aldrich therefore prepared to amend the Hepburn Bill; it was rumored also that rather humorous, dilatory tactics were planned in the shape of a long series of "joke" amendments. Suddenly, to the astonishment of the Senate leader, one of the "regular" Republican members, Jonathan Dolliver of Iowa, rebelled, and with two other Republicans joined the Democratic minority to report the bill favorably.

Dolliver, the genial, studious giant with a pleasing gift for Lincolnesque oratory, long a popular and useful ornament in the conservative organization, had for several years, since 1903, shown signs of wishing to break from the leash. Like Governor Cummins of Iowa, who was soon to enter the Senate in place of the ancient Allison, Dolliver was sensitive to the strong current of discontent running again through the Granger states. Allison, who had reared him as his protégé since the '80's, and raised him to the party's Inner Circle, had often stayed Dolliver's hand when he thought to revolt, saying: "Don't do it now. Wait until I'm gone. I know it is wrong. . . . I have only a little while left, and I haven't got the strength to break away. But wait until I am gone. . . ." [15] Yet Dolliver now took a leading hand in the railroad bill, and prepared to issue a report in defiance of the Standpat dicta, saying nothing of "broad court review" and leaving the disposition of railway rate cases as the Lower House had voted it.

On the 15th of February, 1906, Aldrich had an interview with the President—possibly a stormy one—of which neither divulged anything to the public. Aldrich fought for delay, and even turned for aid to certain friends on the Democratic side of the Senate. Meanwhile Dolliver worked in close collaboration with Roosevelt to advance the new bill.

When the Senate's Committee on Interstate Commerce reported out the bill, it was seen that the Republican majority had split its vote. The Eastern faction, among them Aldrich, Foraker, Elkins, and Kean, opposed the Hepburn Bill; the Western Republicans, Dolliver and Clapp, joined with the Democratic minority under Tillman to bring about favorable recommendation. This development, undoubtedly forced by the crafty Aldrich, gave him

---

[15] La Follette, *Autobiography*, pp. 432–433.

the occasion for his astonishing maneuver by which "Pitchfork Ben" Tillman, the Southern radical Democrat, was designated to report the bill out of committee without the official indorsement of the Republican party. Thus if the bill came to grief or created evil consequences it would not be a Republican affair. Moreover Dolliver, who had hoped to sponsor the bill, was out-flanked, while the President would be placed in an awkward position. For not long ago Mr. Roosevelt had had a resounding personal quarrel with the irascible Southerner Tillman and had barred him from the White House.

Yet Tillman accepted his mission in good faith. As in the stirring campaign of '96, beside Bryan and Altgeld, he girded himself for a general onslaught upon entrenched corporate wealth and privilege, eager to garner what credit he could for the Democratic party. The President, meanwhile, after enjoying Aldrich's strange pleasantry, made conciliatory statements to the press, declaring that he "did not care a rap" for personal difference, and, in the interests of railroad reform, would co-operate unstintedly with the Democratic leader, "Pitchfork Ben."

For sixty days, during the months of March and April, the Senate chamber rang with a great "Constitutional debate" over railroad control. One by one the conservative Republican orators arose and attacked a measure which ostensibly had the support of their own administration. Foraker of Ohio, the grey-haired hero of the Civil War, condemned the Hepburn Bill as "Democratic" in its inspiration. This old politician, not yet known as the "hireling" of the Standard Oil Company that he was, was heard with respect when he pleaded passionately for liberty to railroad owners. The policy of centralized control that was embodied in the Hepburn Bill, he argued, would "feed on itself . . . and spread like a conflagration until in some form or other it comprehended and applied to every other kind of business, for such were the teachings and plans of Socialism." [16]

Senator Philander Knox of Pennsylvania, formerly Attorney General in Roosevelt's Cabinet, pointed out that the bill placed some ten billions of railroad property under the arbitrary control of government agencies, "beyond the protecting clauses of the Constitution." He urged the inclusion of an amendment providing for "broad judicial review" of all railroad rate cases (which would be, in effect, an invitation to endless court suits). Otherwise, sacred rights, "painfully won from the tyrannies of the past, rights adhering to the rich as well as to the poor, would be forfeited. . . . The courts," cried Knox, in a ringing peroration, "are the guardians of our rights and liberties." [17] Thus the theme of the opposition was the danger of a tyranny of the poor over the rich!

While Aldrich and his Senatorial lawyers fought to defeat the Hepburn Bill by ingenious constitutional arguments, or sniped at it with a series of

---

[16] *Congressional Record*, May 18, 1906.   [17] *Ibid.*, Mar. 28, 1906.

amendments, a crowd of Democratic and Republican "Granger" Senators, led by Tillman and Dolliver, defended the bill in torrents of words. They fought for "narrow court review," limiting the injunctive power of the Federal courts to suspend the government's action in railroad-shipper disputes; else, they contended, the floodgates of litigation would be opened. The issue was, simply put: should the Interstate Commerce Commission be given veritable power over the railways, or illusory powers that would be haltered in the courts?

The President for a time pursued the fight with uncommon force and resourcefulness, though Aldrich held the votes of forty Senators in his hand. As Mark Sullivan has recalled it, Roosevelt arranged with his admirers among the newspaper correspondents that a series of vigorous articles on the railroads and on Senators sympathetic to them should appear during the debate over the railroad control bill. In January, 1906, there appeared in the *World's Work* a powerful attack upon Senators Aldrich, Hale, Spooner, Elkins, Penrose, Foraker, Depew, and Kean, as "representatives of corporate business everywhere. . . ." In *McClure's Magazine* for March, 1906, Ray Stannard Baker published a careful, documented study of the evil tendencies of the railroads and their abuse of political privilege.[18] Rumors were circulated in the press, evidently inspired, that the President even hoped to send a few railroad presidents to jail, believing that it would have a wholesome effect on the situation.

News of sensational charges against the Standard Oil and the American Sugar Refining companies, developing from current investigations, was hinted at, as if held over the heads of the opposition. Also, in a series of public addresses during the early spring of 1906, Roosevelt made what then seemed radical proposals—proposals for an inheritance tax that would gradually level wealth, and for Federal laws regulating insurance companies within the District of Columbia. These were the days when Roosevelt thundered most heavily against the "malefactors of great wealth." Yet, whatever the popular effect of these broadsides, votes were still lacking in the Senate to encompass the passage of the Hepburn Bill, which he had made the spearhead of his program of economic reform.

In the early stages of the Senate deadlock, Roosevelt made great efforts to gather together a Senate majority. Through an intermediary he communicated privately with Senator Tillman, the Democratic floor leader, and made an "arrangement" for collaboration between the Democrats and himself. Tillman reported that he could count upon the aid of from twenty-six to twenty-eight of the Democratic contingent of thirty-three Senators. In addition, Dolliver promised the support of between twenty and twenty-two Western Republicans, making a majority of from forty-six to fifty votes out of ninety. The delicate negotiations for a coalition with the Democrats—

---

[18] Sullivan, *op. cit.*, Vol. III, p. 241.

a rather bold undertaking for a Republican President—were completed at a conference on April 14, 1906, in Attorney General Moody's office, both Tillman and Dolliver being present. Roosevelt, as Tillman declared, promised to "stand by" the coalition and contribute executive pressure in support of the bill, whose terms, providing for "narrow court review," were agreed upon.[19]

Roosevelt's public struggles with Aldrich often partook of the character of mock warfare. He respected and bowed before Aldrich's power. "My experience . . . has made me feel respect and regard for Aldrich," he told Taft in 1903, "as one of that group of Senators, including Allison, Hanna, Spooner, Platt of Connecticut, Lodge, and one or two others, who . . . are the most powerful factors in Congress." Though he disagreed with them radically on many questions they were "the leaders, and their great intelligence and power, and their desire . . . to do what is best for the government, makes them not only essential to work with but desirable to work with." [20]

To work instead with the Democrats, in order to pass a bill which Aldrich opposed, meant not only a break in the party harmony, but final departure from the President's tacit "gentleman's agreement" with the Standpatters. It was a decision before which Theodore Roosevelt hesitated deeply. Fortunately, conciliators were there to devise a compromise between the "narrow" and "broad" court review positions, difficult as that seemed. And then the magic of Aldrich accomplished the rest: subjection of the dynamic President, in his first large battle to lead Congress.

Aldrich's magic consisted at this time simply in his subterranean connection with friendly "Railway Senators" among the Democrats. The veteran Joseph Bailey of Texas, a florid, old-fashioned orator, with large black hat, sedate black suit, and string necktie, was at that time the real leader of the Democrats in the Senate. Though he publicly appeared to be sponsoring the "narrow" review clauses of the Hepburn Bill, as well as other popular measures urged by the Democracy, public scandal not long afterward stamped him as a partner in certain dubious oil enterprises that eventually came under the control of the Rockefeller clan. Legend also has pointed to him as the secret lieutenant of Aldrich on the Democratic side, who brought about, when needed, the sudden switch of two or three vitally necessary Democratic votes to the conservative side. For example, one of the amendments that Bailey proposed, an "anti-injunction" clause, had the air of being so radical that the Supreme Court would certainly nullify the whole railroad act.[21]

Tillman himself, according to his memorandum of the proceedings, "sus-

---

[19] Tillman's account, *Congressional Record*, May 12, 1906; Stephenson, *op. cit.*, pp. 307–308.

[20] *T. R. Papers*, Roosevelt to Taft, Mar. 13, 1903.

[21] S. H. Acheson, *Joe Bailey, The Last Democrat*, p. 201.

pected the Texan [Bailey] . . . of holding secret conferences with Aldrich," and, as he reported to Roosevelt, kept a close watch on his colleague, lest he "sell out." [22]

Just when victory over the Standpatters seemed assured—though with the dangerous help of a coalition of Democrats and Western Republicans of the La Follette type—the game passed from the President's hands. For at the Democratic caucus, on April 18, 1906, when noses were counted, to everyone's surprise it was found that several recruits were missing. This was all that Aldrich needed.

For Roosevelt the deadlock had been wearying, and the adventure of working with the Democrats, who would seek credit for railroad reform, politically hazardous. He pressed the distraught Tillman to produce the missing Democratic votes; but though Tillman pleaded for time, they were not found in the last two weeks of April. After having held the threat of a coalition with the Democrats over Aldrich's head, Roosevelt was now ready to abandon the comedy of intrigue, and to "trade" or compromise. He wished, as both Lincoln Steffens and La Follette complained, simply to "get something through"; he would content himself in the end with "half a loaf," when half a loaf was worse than none.

On May 4 Nelson Aldrich called at the White House. Reports of this secret interview held that the "dictator" of the Senate was suave and gracious in victory. Roosevelt, judging from his letter to Lodge, acknowledged his defeat in "sporting" fashion, and vowed that Aldrich, who represented only "ten per cent of the people," would be vanquished the next time. Meanwhile an election was approaching, and they must think of the fortunes of their party.[23]

A compromise amendment, made ready by the practiced Senator Allison, was now quickly produced. It had the language of strong railroad reform, but it offered the legal realities of *broadest court review* and restraint in favor of the railroads, in the shape of occult clauses permitting "interlocutory injunctions" and other court interventions which would limit government control. On the morning of May 4, 1906, it was understood in Washington that the harassed President had yielded suddenly and given his approval to the "Allison amendment," abandoning the Tillman-Dolliver reform coalition. When the Republican compromise terms were made known a week later, they were universally described as a "gold brick."

The vociferous Tillman and his fellow Democrats were outraged by the bad faith, and even "betrayal," they had suffered at the hands of the President. Roosevelt, they cried, had ended by yielding to Aldrich. He was "so constituted," as Senator Rayner of Maryland remarked, "that he cannot look at a trap without fooling with the spring." [24] The Hepburn Act emerged,

---

[22] Roosevelt to Allison, the New York *Tribune,* May 16, 1906.
[23] Lodge, *Correspondence,* Vol. II, p. 370.   [24] The New York *World,* May 12, 1906.

however, as a simon-pure Republican party measure, supported by the Old Guard. The embittered Tillman then disburdened himself of a remarkable "confession" on May 12, 1906, before the Senate, relating how the President had sought him out and agreed to use his services as leader of the opposition party, then cast him aside in order to effect a compromise with his own party leaders. Roosevelt issued angry denials from the White House; charges and countercharges filled the air with confusion as the memorable session of Congress drew to its close in June.

Roosevelt had been on the verge of forcing through Congress a measure that would have substantially increased the power of the Interstate Commerce Commission over railroad rates. It would have meant a bitter conflict within his own party, the possibility of overthrowing the old leaders and creating a new political alignment upon progressive and conservative beliefs. Instead he had recoiled, accepted a half-measure that brought no relief from the abuses that agitated a large part of the public. In defending himself, he argued that the bill he signed was the "same thing" that he had asked for; yet few believed him.[25]

As if to conceal his embarrassment, on May 4, 1906, the day when his compromise with Aldrich was announced, Roosevelt delivered his fiercest broadside against the industrial trusts in a message to Congress which laid bare the secret practices of the Standard Oil and sugar-refining trusts and the coal-carrying combination. He promised that his Attorney General would institute prosecutions against all these wrongdoers at an early date.[26] But one of the newspaper men present continued to question the President concerning the Hepburn Act amendments, and his explanations appeared labored. Finally, the reporter who had admired him exclaimed bluntly: "But Mr. President, what we want to know is why you surrendered." To this Roosevelt made no direct reply.[27]

---

[25] The Hepburn Act extended the authority of the Interstate Commerce Commission over pipe lines, express companies, sleeping-car companies, and railway terminals; it was given the power not to fix rates, but to nullify rates found unreasonable, on complaints of shippers. "Far from satisfying agrarian demands, the Hepburn Act only stimulated the progressive surge which was soon to induce a political earthquake. . . ." (C. A. and M. R. Beard, *The Rise of American Civilization*, Vol. II, p. 568.)

[26] The New York *World*, May 5, 1912.

[27] Stephenson, *op. cit.*, pp. 314–315, citing memorandum of Richard Hooker.

President, Congress, and Control

John Morton Blum

At no time was Theodore Roosevelt more intent on achievement, more attuned to opinion, or more conscious of the nice relationships within his party than in November 1904 when he had at last become President in his own right. "Stunned" though he may have been "by the overwhelming victory" he had won, he nevertheless turned at once to fashion a program for Congress. His pursuit of the objective in that program he most valued —a measure to regulate the railroads—demonstrated perhaps better than any other episode in his Presidency both his facility in dealing with Congress and his mature evaluation of the kind of public arrangement which would best permit necessary government control over industrial operations.

Roosevelt was never a speculative man. Thinking as he did primarily about specific issues, he understood and judged large problems in terms of their more limited parts. By his intent, furthermore, his actions spoke for him better than did his words. He made his points most convincingly when he dealt with situations instead of theories. His talents and his purpose are best understood, therefore, by examination of those activities he counted most significant. This was the importance of his railroad program. For it he exercised those qualities of executive leadership upon which successful Presidents must depend; with it he expected to provide the devices upon which the governing of an industrial society might depend.

On various occasions Roosevelt overcame the obstacles imposed by the American Constitution and party system. Again and again he arranged that his recommendations should embody or win the concern of party leaders who, reflecting conflicting regional and economic demands, often had little in common other than the desire to retain office. He maneuvered legislation past the gamut of committee hearings and congressional debates where powerful chairmen and adroit parliamentarians knew how to delay and divert, sometimes defeat, the consensus of the party. Prepared as he was to influence his party and Congress by mobilizing public opinion, careful as he was never to press his program beyond the limits he calculated as practi-

Reprinted by permission of the publishers from John Morton Blum, *The Republican Roosevelt*. Cambridge, Mass.: Harvard University Press, Copyright, 1954, by The President and Fellows of Harvard College. Pp. 73–105.

cable, he nurtured bills for the inspection of meat-packing, for the definition and enforcement of pure food and drug standards, for the expansion of the navy. But of all the legislation Roosevelt proposed, he had to work hardest and most skillfully for his railroad program.

Conspicuous inequities in American industrial life drew Roosevelt's concentration to railroad regulation. Existing laws had failed to affect the practices by which railway managers, usually unwillingly, often solely to protect their properties, favored the largest, most ruthless industrial corporations. Faced, as they were, with enormous fixed costs—interest on huge bonded debts, depreciation on large and expensive equipment—railroads, to insure enough business to meet their overheads, acceded to the demands of such corporations as the Standard Oil Company, the Armour Company, and the American Sugar Refining Company for freight rates below those accorded to smaller shippers. Although the Elkins Act of 1903 forbade these discriminations, the law was continually violated outright. These violations the offenders could usually obscure by bookkeeping methods over which the Interstate Commerce Commission had no control. The Elkins Act, furthermore, was continually circumvented. Standard Oil and Armour, among many others, besides seeking rebates, obtained discriminatory favor by arranging to receive inordinately large fees from railroads for the use of private cars—such as oil or refrigerator cars—and private sidings and terminals which the corporations owned. Practices such as these helped large shippers to grow wealthier, to absorb their less-favored competitors, to increase thereby their control over markets, and consequently to set prices for their products higher than those that might otherwise have obtained. If the railroads suffered, they too often compensated for their losses by establishing seemingly excessive freight rates either on commodities—like grain and carbon black—whose producers were in no position to demand favors, or over routes where there was no competition for transportation services.

Determined to remedy these conditions, Roosevelt proposed that Congress give the Interstate Commerce Commission effective power over railroad accounts, over private railway equipment, and—most important—in modest degree, over railroad rates. To translate this recommendation into legislation, Roosevelt first created a controlled environment within his party and then adapted his views to parliamentary conditions. He established by his tactics a productive relationship between the executive and Congress. While his program was debated in the Senate, in the session of 1905–1906, Roosevelt defined explicitly the concepts of executive control essential to his more elaborate theses on political economy. During and immediately after the lame duck session of 1904–1905, by strategy as revealing of his purpose as was his later, more explicit definition, he committed the Republicans to railroad regulation and twice got through the House bills that embodied his policy.

Roosevelt's first negotiation necessitated the sacrifice of his announced intention to direct a revision of the tariff. It depended, however, on the continuing threat of tariff revision. The manner in which Roosevelt used tariff revision to advance railroad regulation and the reasons for which he subordinated the one issue to the other have meaning both as a revelatory instance of executive leadership and as an important indication of the central purpose of Roosevelt's political action.

Only two days after the election of 1904 Roosevelt informed Nicholas Murray Butler that he had "already begun the effort to secure a bill to revise and reduce the tariff." The President well understood the dimensions of this task. In his first term he had almost lost to the Republican standpatters his prolonged fight for reciprocity with Cuba. Yet even as his second term began he raised the whole tariff issue, because, he suggested in a heated moment, "we beat the Democrats on the issue that protection was robbery, and that when necessary we would amend or revise the tariff ourselves." This explanation, as Roosevelt knew, did violence to the facts. If the Republicans had any effective national issue in the campaign of 1904 other than Theodore Roosevelt and the Square Deal, it was certainly not tariff revision. The President had accepted a platform that complacently praised Dingleyism; he had strongly endorsed the principle of protection, chastised his Secretary of War for favoring tariff reduction in a campaign speech, and denounced the Democrats for their insistence that protection was robbery.

In his more candid and quiet moments, Roosevelt explained his position with less hyperbole and more effect. "I am convinced," he wrote, "that there is, among the good Republicans and among the masses of independent Democrats who supported us . . . , a very strong feeling in favor of what I prefer to call an amendment rather than a revision of the tariff laws." "My own judgment," Roosevelt confessed, "is that it is dangerous to undertake to do anything, but that it is fatal not to undertake it . . ."

This assessment of political sentiment had some validity. The Republican differences on the tariff were major and real. A considerable minority, primarily composed of Western agrarians, favored a general reduction of schedules. Others, for the most part representing Minnesota and Massachusetts shoe, woolens, and flour manufacturers, advocated reciprocity agreements, particularly with Canada, under which their constituents would benefit by cheaper raw materials and larger export markets. These revisionists contended that the party had promised the voters adjustment, though not abandonment, of the protective system. Failing this, they warned, the Democrats as they had in Massachusetts in 1904, would profitably exploit the tariff issue. They urged Roosevelt, therefore, to summon an extra session of Congress to deal with the tariff, preferably in the spring of 1905. Most Republican leaders, including the most powerful members of Congress, however, opposing any changes in the tariff and jealously guarding the principle of protection, asserted that the election returns evidenced popular satisfaction with the Dingley rates.

Sympathetic to the revisionists, Roosevelt also recognized their strength, but he lacked their conviction and, conscious of the greater strength of their opposition, he feared the divisive hostilities and probable futility that characteristically attended tariff debates. For him the tariff was a matter of expediency. Never willing to risk a division of his party that would endanger his favored measures on an issue about which he did not feel strongly, Roosevelt, in spite of his occasional hyperbole, approached revision with consummate caution. Yet because of the articulate minority support for revision, Roosevelt seized upon tariff discussions as a useful weapon. The prospect of revision, even of a tariff debate, alarmed the standpatters sufficiently to provide an effective disciplinary tool. For Presidential coöperation on the tariff, they were ultimately willing to reach an understanding with Roosevelt, perhaps even to strike a bargain, on railroad regulation.

To that end Roosevelt maneuvered skillfully. His problem was to talk of tariff revision firmly enough to frighten the Old Guard but gently enough not to alienate them. If in the process of negotiation and legislation he could arrange tariff modifications, the achievement would be welcome, but he considered it always incidental. From the very beginning the form of his tariff negotiations suggested that they were less an objective than a device. Roosevelt did not demand; he consulted. "When I see you," he informed the Republican whip in the House, "I want to take up the question of the tariff . . . It seems to me that our party ought to revise the tariff now, but of course I do not want to say anything about it unless the leaders of the House approve, because I realize thoroughly that the matter is primarily one for you all in the House." A week later he added that "an extra session, even if it was not held until the 1st of September [1905], would be most desirable," for, he feared, "if we wait until the regular session, . . . the Democrats will talk the matter over for a year and then we shall be swamped at the Congressional elections." Yet he acknowledged to one senator that "there should be only a few and moderate changes"; and even as he labeled protection "robbery," he assured the president of the American Iron and Steel Institute that he intended "of course, to abide by the general judgment of the party." Meanwhile Roosevelt's personal secretary had announced on November 19 that the President's forthcoming State of the Union message would not mention the tariff.

Clearly Roosevelt never considered the tariff worth a fight. Three weeks after telling Butler he had begun his "effort to secure" a revision, he confessed privately that the issue was practically dead. "The trouble," he explained, "is that there are large parts of the country which want no tariff revision, and of course their representatives are hostile to any agitation of the subject. They say, with entire truth, that neither in the platform nor in any communication of mine is there any promise whatever that there shall be tariff revision. They also say, with equal truth, that the tariff changes should not be great, and that those clamoring for tariff changes are certainly to be disappointed at whatever is done . . . I am going to make every effort to get something of what I desire . . . ; but I shall not split with my party on the matter . . ." Having shed all pretense that the party had a mandate for revision, Roosevelt several days later, again privately, admitted that he had no intention of tackling the tariff in the immediate future. "At present, . . ." he wrote Butler, "there is a strong majority against [amendment or reduction] . . . The minority . . . is entirely split up as to the articles on which the amendment should come . . . This means that unless circumstances change in the next sixty days it will be . . . worse than idle to call the extra session early."

It was not that Roosevelt had retreated. He had never really attacked. But before making his candid admissions to Butler, he had, with less candor, begun to bargain. Just before leaving Illinois for Washington, that archpriest of protection, Speaker of the House Joe Cannon, had received from Roosevelt a disturbing draft, dated November 30, of a special message on the tariff that the President proposed sending to Congress. "While it is above all things desirable that the present tariff law should be kept in its essence unchanged," the draft read, "there may well be certain points as to which it can be amended. There may be some schedules that . . . should be changed . . . If it were possible to provide for reciprocity by a maximum and minimum scale to be applied in the discretion of the Executive, this should be done . . . In any event some of the schedules should now be examined . . ." If these modest proposals could not alarm the Speaker, they were certain at least to worry him. Carefully Roosevelt mitigated even worry, observing that he sent the draft "merely for the sake of having something which can be worked out, after you have consulted the men fresh from the people . . ."

Roosevelt timed the dispatch of the draft nicely. The Speaker was not to be allowed to forget that the tariff issue remained, even though the annual message, opening the last session of the Fifty-eighth Congress, said nothing of revision. He could not be allowed to forget, for that message voiced aggressively Roosevelt's demand for railroad regulation. "The government," Roosevelt instructed Congress, "must in increasing degree supervise and regulate the workings of the railways engaged in interstate commerce; and such increased supervision is the only alternative to an increase of the present evils on the one hand or a still more radical policy on the other. In my judgment, the most important legislative act now needed as regards the regulation of corporations is this act to confer on the Interstate Commerce Commission the power to revise rates and regulations."

With these words Roosevelt set off the battle over railroad regulation. On this issue the party was as divided as on the tariff. And the division, to Roosevelt's advantage, followed similar personal and sectional lines. The advocates of revision and reciprocity were also the proponents of regulation. Speaking for Western agrarians and grain dealers and for Massachusetts manufacturers, they wanted federal review of freight rates which had been, from their point of view, increasingly discriminatory. On the other hand, the standpatters, speaking either for or with the big business interests, had long resisted any departures from nineteenth-century *laissez faire*.

For the railroad program, to which there was strong Republican opposition, Roosevelt had genuine concern. He consulted Congress less and demanded more. It was "unwise and unsafe from every standpoint," he had concluded, "to fail to give the Interstate Commerce Commission additional power of an effective kind in regulating . . . rates." This, he believed, was an essential ingredient for his basic determination "that the Government should effectively shape the policy [of the] . . . Square Deal."

Thus fervently committed, but confronting a powerful opposition, Roosevelt capitalized on the divisions in Congress produced by regional and economic self-interest. The low-tariff, antirailroad group was to have one reform, the high-tariff, prorailroad group to hold one redoubt. Saving what he considered vital by sacrificing what he considered marginal, Roosevelt for the sake of railroad regulation jettisoned the draft of the special message on the tariff that had worried Cannon.

Toward this decision Cannon, by his own account, exercised his influence. The Speaker, and perhaps also Senator Nelson Aldrich, may have struck a bargain with Roosevelt on railroad regulation. The circumstantial evidence that there was some bargain or understanding is overwhelming. The alignments of economic self-interest provided fertile ground which Roosevelt had cultivated for such an understanding. The diminuendo in Roosevelt's private letters to Butler on tariff revision suggests that the President had settled his course in early December. Roosevelt's tariff conferences continued through the first week of January when, according to Cannon's account, he told the congressional leaders that revision would await the election of his successor. Cannon exaggerated, but shortly after that conference Roosevelt defined his position to a friend. "I am having anything but a harmonious time about the tariff and about the interstate commerce . . . ," he wrote. "On the interstate commerce business, which I regard as a matter of principle, I shall fight. On the tariff, which I regard as a matter of expediency, I shall endeavor to get the best results I can, but I shall not break with my party." And for the time being, with regard to the tariff, Cannon and the party were one. Two days later Roosevelt wrote Cannon: "Stop in here as soon as you can. I care very little for what the newspapers get in the way of passing sensationalism; but I do not want the people of the country to get the idea that there will be any split or clash between you and me on the tariff or anything else."

Roosevelt permitted no clash. He made no recommendation for specific or general revisions. Although he encouraged efforts for reciprocity arrangements with Canada and Newfoundland, he gave those efforts only desultory support in his dealings with Congress. At the other end of Pennsylvania Avenue, Cannon gave railroad legislation a clear track. The Speaker, it has been argued, saw to it that no bill passed until so late in the session that the Senate could not act. Actually Cannon had no need for such a scheme. The hearings of the House Committee on Interstate Commerce, as much as the debates on the floor, delayed approval of the bill. When it did finally come to a vote, it passed with a decisive majority of 309. Had it passed earlier, judging by the course of the railroad bill at the following session, it would have failed to get through the Senate before adjournment. And during the following sessions Cannon again presented no obstacles to railway regulation.

In the months following the expiration of the Fifty-eighth Congress, Roosevelt continued to rely on the threat of tariff revision. During that Congress the Senate Committee on Interstate Commerce began to hold hearings that continued through most of May 1905. Railroad executives, mobilized by Samuel Spencer, the chief of J. P. Morgan's railway division, and encouraged by sympathetic senators, used these hearings as a sounding board for opposition to Roosevelt. Outside of the committee room the railroads underwrote an expensive publicity campaign in which various business organizations, including the National Association of Manufacturers, came to their aid. With increasing fervor they rehearsed the dangerous folly of the President's proposals. As this propaganda received wide dissemination in the press, the enemies of regulation seemed to be gaining an upper hand.

Yet Roosevelt in this period displayed a measured optimism. Perhaps he suspected that the railroads would, as they did, overreach themselves. Doubtless he foresaw that investigations of the Standard Oil Company and the beef trust then under way would furnish much evidence to sustain him. Surely he had confidence that his speeches and those of his advisers would counteract the railroad propaganda. The President was continually at the hustings. In the winter at the Philadelphia Union League Club, later in Texas and Colorado, at Chautauqua and Chicago, along the southeastern seaboard, he spoke to adulating audiences of the righteousness, and yet the reasonableness, of his cause. If, in part, the prestige of his office drew them to hear him, the fervor in his falsetto persuaded them to listen. The overdrawn counterpropaganda of the railroads, whatever its merit in logic, could scarcely compete in a society primed by the muckrakers with the explosive personality of the President. Assertively he equated his view of rate-making with his then regnant dictum of a square deal for every man. He would restrain the perverters of privilege who by their manipulations of rates and rebates purloined the just profits of their honest competitors and threatened to provoke by their excesses the menace of socialism. This was a crisis (Theodore Roosevelt coped constantly with crises), but he would shackle greed and, routing the proponents of nationalization, save the railroads from themselves.

But Roosevelt did not confine his energies to the podium. In May he reminded the Old Guard that the tariff could still be an issue. To emphasize the tariff-railroad understanding that the battle of propaganda might otherwise have obscured, Roosevelt thrust at the standpatters' most sensitive spot. One guardian of protection had admitted the previous fall that the "strongest argument" for revision was that American manufacturers sold goods in foreign markets for less than they received at home. This condition, he then pointed out, while perhaps inequitable, was irremediable, for "no revision of the tariff which still left a protective margin could prevent" it. To challenge the differential in the export and domestic prices of protected commodities was to challenge the whole principle of protection. This was precisely what Roosevelt did.

On May 16, 1905, while the railroad propaganda was at its peak, an announcement that the Isthmian Canal Commission had decided to purchase supplies for the construction of the canal in foreign markets immediately staggered the standpatters. They were further shocked when Roosevelt flatly assumed all responsibility for the adoption of this "cheapest-market" policy. The New York *Times* called the announcement the "doom of Dingleyism." The steel industry's most active lobbyist and his reliable congressional echoes shared the view of the New York *Press* that the cheapest-market policy, repudiating the high-tariff mandate of 1904, was "a faithless service of outrage." The president of the National Association of Manufacturers and the secretary of the American Protective Tariff Association tersely labeled Roosevelt's action "un-American."

Less emotional observers noted that Roosevelt probably intended not to abandon protection but to call the attention of Congress to the whole subject of tariff adjustment. They were correct, for after succeeding admirably in just that, the President was satisfied. Three days after the announcement was made, Cannon conferred with Secretary of War Taft, who then rescinded the cheapest-market order, referring to the next Congress the question of canal purchases. Responsible, according to his own statement, for the order, Roosevelt must also have been responsible for the reversal.

The dramatic episode of the canal purchases served as Roosevelt's most forceful but not as his final reminder to the standpatters that the tariff remained a potential issue. In August, White House "leaks" inspired newspaper reports that the President contemplated calling an extra session of Congress to consider tariff revision. If he did not plant these rumors, Roosevelt at least used them. To his Secretary of the Treasury, an uncompromising protectionist, he wrote in the tone he had long used: "I entirely agree with all you say as to the dangers which accompany tariff revision— or any attempt at it, but as yet I am not sure whether there are not at least equal dangers in avoiding [it] . . . I want to go over the entire matter very carefully with all of the Congressional leaders before we decide which set of risks to take." Roosevelt quickly decided. It was scarcely necessary for him to consult his congressional leaders—they had understood each other for months. In mid-August, Taft, then in the Philippines, released a message from the President that there would be no extra session of Congress. The regular session, Roosevelt had already implied at Chautauqua and stated in private, would be, insofar as he could control it, devoted to rate regulation.

In December 1905, the Fifty-ninth Congress convened. During the fall, the campaigns in Massachusetts and Iowa had kept the tariff issue alive while Roosevelt, in the South, had focused on the railways. The President's annual message, silent, as it had been in 1904, on the tariff, made railroad regulation the central objective of the Administration. In the long struggle that ensued, the tariff once more provided a lever. In the House, a combination of Democrats and Administration Republicans passed a bill reducing the rates on Philippine products. Intended as an instrument of colonial policy, the measure was nevertheless considered by standpat Republicans to breach the principle of protection. Administration leaders in the Senate by their lassitude permitted it to die in committee while, like Roosevelt, they concentrated their energy and their power on the railroad bill. For this division of labor no explicit bargain need have been made, for all matters pertaining to the tariff continued in 1906 to be, as they had been since 1904, useful whips rather than real targets. By 1906 Roosevelt had abandoned all effort for tariff revision, yet essentially he abandoned only a bargaining instrument. At no time in his long public career did tariff revision much concern him. For eighteen months, however, he employed adroitly the specter of tariff agitation.

By defining tariff revision as a matter of expediency and railroad regulation as a matter of principle, Roosevelt established his own position. His life, he felt, was a quest for the moral. What he meant by morality was not always clear, but the concept had obvious components. In some cases, that which was moral was that which could be accomplished. Given two paper trusts to bust, Roosevelt had attacked the less offensive but legally vulnerable pool and ignored the more oppressive but legally secure holding company. By this criterion, railroad regulation was in 1904 more moral than tariff revision, for public and political opinion on the railways divided on nonpartisan lines and the Republican party was less committed to the Elkins Act as a line of defense than to the Dingley Act. That which was moral was also often that which was popular. In making a crucial test of the Sherman Antitrust Act, Roosevelt had prosecuted neither the largest nor the most monopolistic holding company. He had chosen, rather, a railroad merger that had been born of a discreditable stockmarket battle, that consisted of units long unpopular with shippers in the areas in which they ran, that had already been challenged by state authorities. Unlike Justice

Holmes, Roosevelt wanted to bring the voice of the people to bear on decisions. Showered as they were in 1904 by private and official disclosures of the iniquities of rebates, the evils of Armour, the machinations of Standard Oil, most of the people, particularly middle-class people, were less interested in the tariff than in direct controls of big business, especially the railways.

But Roosevelt's morality was not simply opportunistic. He felt that the central issue of his time pivoted on the control of business because this control determined conduct, and morality was for him a matter of conduct. He feared not the size but the policies of big business. He cared not about profits but about the manner of earning profits. This was the essence of the Square Deal. Roosevelt fought for railroad regulation because it was designed to control process. By his standard, tariff schedules—static matters —were as unimportant as an administrative agency overseeing day-by-day business arrangements was essential.

These dimensions of morality—practicability, popularity, and especially preoccupation with process—characterized Roosevelt's emergent progressivism. They permitted him to yield, when necessary, on details in order to advance his favored measures. They also persuaded him for reasons of policy as well as of tactics to arrange the understanding on tariff revision and railroad regulation that prepared the way for perhaps the most significant legislation of his Presidency.

Railroad rates could not be regulated, however, until Roosevelt, having committed the House to his policy, slowly brought the Senate also into line. In that second task, as in the persuading of the House, he exercised artfully the resources of office and person by which a President can lead Congress, in spite of the separation of powers imposed by the Constitution, to consummate his policies. Roosevelt's impressive ability to work within the structure of government, like his facility in managing the party, depended less on his arresting manner than on his appreciation of the institutions that shaped American political life. Like Edmund Burke, perhaps the greatest of British conservatives, Roosevelt valued the long wash of historical development, sometimes controlled, sometimes accidental, that had given form to the political society in which he lived. Both were wisely careful never to set up a system of their own. Like Burke, Roosevelt delighted in the processes by which political achievement and further institutional development were made possible. Both considered political peace the breathing-time which gave them leisure further to contrive. As he guided his railroad program through the Senate where formidable obstacles blocked his way, Roosevelt needed and took his daily gladness in situations "of power and energy," in government—as Burke described it—"founded on compromise and barter."

Behind all the political manipulation, beneath all the legalistic forensics, the issue was control. Theodore Roosevelt intended that an administrative agency should have the authority to rectify the inequities in the business of transportation. Nelson Aldrich, the resourceful leader of the President's opposition, intended that it should not. Roosevelt demanded that the Interstate Commerce Commission be invested with power to revise railroad rates. Here, he felt, lay the key to control. Aldrich, when he drew his lines, sought to transfer the final decision on rates from the commission to the courts, to leave the judiciary in its traditional, ineffectual, disorderly role of monitor of the price of transportation. President and senator, sensitive always to each other's strength, delighting in the test, came slowly to a crisis.

"I am well aware," Roosevelt stated in his annual message to Congress of 1905, "of the difficulties of the [railroad] legislation that I am suggesting, and of the need of temperate and cautious action in securing it. I should emphatically protest against improperly radical or hasty action . . . [But] the question of transportation lies at the root of all industrial success, and the revolution in transportation which has taken place during the last half-century has been the most important factor in the growth of the new industrial conditions . . . At present the railway is [the highway of commerce] . . . and we must do our best to see that it is kept open to all on equal terms . . . It is far better that it should be managed by private individuals than by the government. But it can only be so managed on condition that justice is done the public . . . What we need to do is to develop an orderly system, and such a system can only come through the gradually increased exercise of the right of efficient government control."

A year earlier Roosevelt had sent Congress only a paragraph on railroad legislation. Now he spelled out the elements of what he considered an orderly system of control. These he had derived from the accumulated findings of the Bureau of Corporations and the Interstate Commerce Commission and from the expert advice of the lawyers and railroad men in his Cabinet. Their recommendations, embodied in the Hepburn Bill with Administration guidance substantially as Roosevelt had announced them, covered every aspect of the railroad problem then recognized by the foremost authority on railroad economics in the United States. Grounded as it was on thorough study by essentially conservative men, much of Roosevelt's program provoked little congressional dissent.

The area of agreement was large. The Elkins Antirebate Act of 1903 had failed utterly to prevent the discriminations it explicitly forbade. Alive to this, and to the public's growing displeasure over the outrageous practices of Armour and Standard Oil, practices as harmful to the railroads as to the competitors of the favored, Congress shared the President's opinion that "all private-car lines, industrial roads, refrigerator charges, and the like should be expressly put under the supervision of the Interstate Commerce Commission . . . ." Conscious of the experience of the government in investigating both railways and industrial concerns, Congress, like Roosevelt, had reached the commonsense conclusion that standardized records open to official inspection were a prerequisite for the determination of adequate policies of regulation as well as for the prevention of familiar abuses in corporation management. Congress was also willing, by providing for expeditious action in cases arising under the commerce act, to destroy "the weapon of delay, almost the most formidable weapon in the hands of those whose purpose is to violate the law." [1]

Had Roosevelt recommended and Congress agreed to nothing else, these provisions would in themselves have been worth-while but inadequate achievements. They did not fundamentally alter the existing relationship between the federal government and the railroads. They established no new device of regulation. The restriction of rebats, now strengthened, had earlier existed; the inspection of records, now facilitated, had long since begun; the expedition of trial for suits involving infractions of the Interstate Commerce Act had already been provided for suits arising under the Antitrust Act. Roosevelt's orderly system of efficient government control depended not on these precedents but on an innovation to which many in Congress were still openly hostile. The President proposed that the I.C.C. be given limited authority to make rates. As he carefully defined it, this was his central objective.

Roosevelt took his first and final position on rates in his annual message of 1904. He there considered it "undesirable . . . finally to clothe the commission with general authority to fix railroad rates." "As a fair security to shippers," however, he insisted that "the commission should be vested with the power, where a given rate has been challenged and after full hearing found to be unreasonable, to decide, subject to judicial review, what shall be a reasonable rate to take its place; the ruling of the commission to take effect immediately." The "reasonable rate," Roosevelt implied by his reference to the Supreme Court's interpretation of the Interstate Commerce Act, was to be only a maximum rate. This meaning he made explicit in 1905 when he requested that the commission receive power "to prescribe the limit of rate beyond which it shall not be lawful to go—the maximum reasonable rate, as it is commonly called."

Roosevelt's Attorney General had advised that legislation empowering the commission to set definite rate schedules—the objective of many Democratic and some Western Republican senators—might be declared unconstitutional. "The one thing I do not want," Roosevelt explained to one critic, "is to have a law passed and then declared unconstitutional." Furthermore, he argued, the authority to prescribe a maximum rate, while perhaps short of the ultimate ideal, promised immediate, substantial improvement in existing conditions. "If the Commission has the power to make the maximum rate that which the railroad gives to the most favored shipper, it

---

[1] Without Presidential prodding, the Senate added to the Hepburn Bill two important clauses, one imposing criminal penalties for certain violations, another, more significant, forbidding corporations producing such commodities as coal from owning the railroads that transported them.

will speedily become impossible thus to favor any shipper . . ." If, after a test, it should prove inadequate, he would then be willing to try to secure a definite rate proposition. "I believe," he explained to the impatient, "in men who take the next step; not those who theorize about the two-hundredth step."

Roosevelt intended primarily to protect individual shippers from excessive or discriminatory rates. He agreed that the maximum rate provision would afford little remedy for discrimination between commodities or between localities, but such discriminations seemed to him relatively impersonal. He cared less about freight classification and long and short haul differentials because he could not readily associate those matters with a doer of evil and a victim. Discriminations against a small shipper or exorbitant rates the President understood and despised. They were, he was sure, immoral. His interest had also political meaning, for the spokesmen of the shippers' organizations concentrated on the problems that a maximum rate provision could begin to resolve. They neglected to mention, and Roosevelt did not apparently recognize, that no recommendation in the annual messages or provision in the Hepburn Bill prevented shippers or their consignees from passing on rate burdens originating in any discriminatory devise to the still unorganized, essentially undiscerning consumers.

The maximum rate proposal, in many respects inadequate, properly labeled so by liberals of the time, nevertheless earned for Roosevelt the opprobrious criticism of a large part of the business community and the tenacious opposition of a near majority of the United States Senate. Modest as the proposal was, it challenged the most cherished prerogative of private management, the most hoary tenet of free private enterprise—the ability freely to make prices. This threat gave Roosevelt a reputation, persisting still among railway executives, of being a scandalous advocate of something closely akin to socialism. A more radical proposition, the President well knew, would have had no chance for success.

Roosevelt had constructed the Hepburn Bill with practiced care. Including as it did just enough to satisfy his purpose, it contained nothing that would alarm the marginal supporters without whom it could not survive. This was the last in a series of calculated tactics by which Roosevelt had prepared the parliamentary environment for his railroad program. "I have a very strong feeling," he acknowledged, "that it is a President's duty to get on with Congress if he possibly can, and that it is a reflection upon him if he and Congress come to a complete break." Avoiding a break, understanding his situation, he made the powers of his office and the talents of his person the instruments of viable leadership.

He had begun by trading tariff reform for railroad regulation. He had continued, after the adjournment of the lame duck session of the Fifty-eighth Congress, by taking his railroad issue, then the foremost national political problem, to the people. At the hustings his vigorous pleading won enthusiastic acclaim. His "plain people," for the most part, heard only the voice of their champion. Significantly, however, more careful, more cautious listeners, disregarding his dramatic allusions, at once could ascertain the moderation of his demands. Roosevelt's message was simple. His demands were not new. Indeed, Roosevelt added nothing to the principles or to the histrionics of the Granger and Populist railroad regulators of years gone by. But he did bring to their long-rejected national program a new respectability, an incomparable personal vitality, and assurances, impressive to thoughtful conservatives, that he, unlike his predecessors, would direct regulation to constructive ends.

The last was particularly important. By the fall of 1905 such reliable Republican senators from the West as Allison of Iowa and Spooner of Wisconsin, traditionally conservators of the status quo, now sensitive to the growing complaints of the farmers and shippers whose protests had preceded and exceeded Roosevelt's, realized that their political life rested upon an unprecedented capitulation to their constituents. In the President they recognized a safe sponsor for reform. If his language seemed at times extravagant, if his central purpose was a genuine departure from the past, he nevertheless, they knew from experience, guarded their party and, in the largest sense, their principles. This knowledge may also have comforted others who deeply distrusted the emotions Roosevelt evoked. Before the Fifty-ninth Congress convened, the roar of the President's crowds penetrated, perhaps, the cold quiet where Nelson Aldrich, by preference undisturbed, made policy. That master of the Senate, in any case, was thereafter willing to make a conciliatory gesture toward Roosevelt and his allies.

The President had set his stage. Reminded of the arrangements by which the tariff remained inviolate, the new House in February 1906, with only seven adverse votes, passed the Hepburn Bill. It provided for every objective of the Administration. The most thoughtful member of the I.C.C., Commissioner Prouty, told Roosevelt that it represented "an advance so extraordinary that he had never dared to suppose it would be possible to pass it." The President judged that it was "as far as we could with wisdom go at this time." Politically he was surely correct. Although an aroused constituency cheered the champions of the bill in the Senate, Nelson Aldrich, as debate began, had yet to surrender command of the chamber he had so long dominated. Roosevelt, until this time the aggressor, had now to adjust to the strength and the tactics of a talented oppositionist.

How unlike the President in many ways his adversary was: so urbane, so controlled, so indifferent to manifestations of approval, so patently disdainful of the string-tie statesmanship surrounding him; but, like Roosevelt, so bemused by the endless adventure of governing men! Did his friend Allison have, of a summer, to explain himself in ponderous periods from a rural podium? How dreary for Allison. Aldrich preferred the politics that the caucus controlled, the constituents one met graciously over liqueurs, the measured exchanges between mutually respectful equals who understood the manners and the meaning of their power. For all that, Aldrich was not the less discerning, not the less tenacious. Many of the dreadful things that Theodore did, the senator knew, he had to do. The people, after all, could vote. The railroads were unpopular. Roosevelt could have his bill, but not the way he wanted it. A gesture now, a delaying action—then, perhaps, the worst would pass. Perhaps, again, it would not pass, the comfortable world was changing. In that case, delay had of itself some value. And the means to resist were familiar and strong.

Aldrich had a corps of allies: among the Republicans, the intractables, all reliable, some expert parliamentarians, some outstanding men. There were also among the Democrats those who regularly resisted any reform and others, bound by quixotic tradition confounded with visions of miscegenation, who could be made to shy at any extension of the federal executive power. These were less reliable. Yet Aldrich in the past by prestige and by persuasion had combined these parts into a solid phalanx to front, unbudging, the bills that carried change.

Aldrich, disingenuous, moved quietly to bring the Hepburn Bill with its objectionable clause on rates into the arena where he and his allies had long had their way. While the measure lay before the Committee on Interstate and Foreign Commerce he labored at a disadvantage. There, with few exceptions, his trusted assistants had no seat. There Roosevelt's friends, making the President's moderation their own, seemed capable by coöperation with the Democratic committeemen of carrying crucial votes. There Jonathan Dolliver, the junior senator from Iowa, then beginning the progressive period of his career, ably pleaded the case of the Administration. Dolliver's continuing intimacy with Roosevelt and Attorney General Moody made him as informed as he was ardent. If Dolliver could with the Democrats model the bill to Roosevelt's satisfaction and then bring it out of committee as a party measure, he would have thereafter a tactical advantage. In these parts, Aldrich did not try to shape the bill in committee. He could not have persuaded a majority to go his way, but he could and did persuade a majority to ease his way. Seeming to yield, disarming Dolliver, Aldrich permitted the Hepburn Bill to be reported unamended. Then, supported by Democratic votes on which Dolliver had counted, he secured a motion reserving to each committee member the right to propose amendments from the floor. The issue, still unresolved, was now before the whole Senate.

The same Democratic votes sustained Aldrich's next move. Had Dolliver, as he expected, been designated to guide the measure on the floor, he would still have been an asset to the President and the bill might still have been presented as the party's. Almost the senator from Iowa could see the "Hepburn-Dolliver Act" engraved in history. The Democrats, however, desiring some credit for regulating railroads, preferred that half that title belong to them. This preference Aldrich exploited. He had won the Democrats in the committee to reporting the bill for amendment from the floor by arranging to name as its floor leader one of their party, Benjamin Tillman of South Carolina. With that serpent-tongued agrarian as its guide, the bill could not be labeled "Republican." For Dolliver this was a staggering personal blow; for Aldrich, a beguiling triumph; for Roosevelt, an embarrassing problem in communication. The President and Tillman had long loathed each other. Only recently the senator had made one of his calculated, insulting attacks on Roosevelt's character. For years they had not spoken. Now Aldrich had forced them either to coöperate or to endanger the policy they both espoused. Whatever their course, furthermore, Aldrich had moved the bill into a position where he and his collaborators had an excellent chance of neutralizing it by amendment. "Aldrich," Roosevelt concluded irritably, had "completely lost both his head and his temper." The President had lost the first round.

Well before the Hepburn Bill reached the Senate, Aldrich and his associates had determined on the nature of their attack. Perhaps out of deference to the electorate, they refrained from a direct assault on the maximum rate clause. Instead, they concentrated on amendments by which they intended to endow the judiciary, the least mobile of the branches of government, with the authority to nullify and to delay the rate rulings of the I.C.C. In behalf of these amendments they debated not the economics of rate-making or the proprieties of privilege, but the constitutionality of the regulatory process, the orderly system that the President proposed to create.

Roosevelt had noted with care that the I.C.C. or a substitute commission "should be made unequivocably administrative." To an administrative body as opposed to an executive department, Congress could, he believed, within the meaning of the Constitution on the separation of powers, delegate the authority to fix maximum rates. This has become a commonplace assumption, the basis of a proliferation of alphabet agencies, but in 1906 men of disinterested conviction as well as those who were sheer obstructionists questioned the legality of combining in one body the quasi-legislative power of determining rates, even maximum rates, the quasi-judicial authority of deciding upon the validity of rates, and the quasi-executive function of investigation and enforcement. The unsuccessful railroad bill of 1905, attempting to resolve this constitutional difficulty, had included a clause, briefly resuscitated in 1910 by the Mann-Elkins Act, establishing a special court of commerce to review the rate decisions of the I.C.C. The Hepburn Bill as it emerged from the House, however, made no similar provision. Dodging the whole issue of judicial review, it said nothing at all about jurisdiction in cases arising under it.

On the question of judicial review, the proponents and the opponents of Roosevelt's program drew their lines. Contrasted to the large and varied significance of the whole railroad measure, this deployment seems at first almost chicane. Yet since the debates on Hamilton's reports, American legislators had persisted in clothing their differences in constitutional terms. Nor, in the case of the Hepburn Bill, was this lawyers' legacy meaningless. Roosevelt envisioned a new kind of federal executive power to control the complex processes of an industrialized state. He anticipated the methods of the future. His opponents in the Senate, seeking to perpetuate the method or lack of method of the past, relied upon the prevailing dicta of the American courts to prevent the executive from interfering in the day-by-day operations of American business. In government based on law, this was in 1906 still a legal as well as an economic issue. Both sides assiduously spoke the Constitution fair.

The President by no means denied the right of judicial review. He did not believe that any legislation could "prevent . . . an appeal" from a ruling of the I.C.C. "The courts will retain, and should retain, no matter what the Legislature does," he had asserted, "the power to interfere and upset any action that is confiscatory in its nature." Yet Roosevelt also preferred that judicial review should be limited essentially to procedural questions— to a determination, in any mooted case, of whether the commission's method of reaching the decision had been fair to the carrier. His opponents, on the other hand, hoped to emasculate his program by providing explicitly for broad judicial reinterpretation of the facts of each case. This would have given the courts, considered friendly by the railroads, rather than the commission, which the railroads feared, the real authority over rates.

By its reticence on the matter, the House's version of the Hepburn Bill left to the courts themselves the determination of the scope of review. Roosevelt expressed his satisfaction with this evasion. Attorney General Moody, however, advised him that the measure, in order to pass the test of constitutionality, needed an amendment affirming the right of the railroads to have the courts review the commission's decisions. Roosevelt then considered it only desirable but not essential that the bill provide narrow review. As he began negotiations with the leaders of the Senate, he sought not a limitation to procedural review but only an ambiguous declaration, consonant with the evasion in the unamended version, of the right of review.

Inherent in, but in Roosevelt's opinion subordinate to, the problem of the scope of judicial review was the question of the time at which the rate decisions of the I.C.C. should become effective. Roosevelt had asked that they take effect "immediately," a stipulation the Hepburn Bill fulfilled to his satisfaction by making them effective in thirty days. But if the railroads took to court a decision of the commission, the long process of litigation would postpone indefinitely the application of the revised maximum rate. The House had avoided this problem. In the Senate, while the friends of the railroads wanted just such a delay, the advocates of regulation endeavored to construct some amendment that would prevent the use of injunctions to suspend, pending the outcome of litigation, the rulings of the commission. Roosevelt when debate began preferred, but, as on the question of narrow review, did not insist that the use of injunctions be restricted.

Against the President's moderate, almost uncertain, position the prorailroad senators launched an offensive. Philander Chase Knox, who had while Attorney General seemed to endorse Roosevelt's program refused in a conference with Moody to reach an agreement on an amendment pertaining to judicial review. Moody's draft, supported by the President, protected the constitutionality of the Hepburn Bill without increasing the appellate jurisdiction of the courts. This was not enough for Knox. In conference he stated that he preferred the House's bill to Moody's amendment. To the Senate he proposed in February that the courts pass on the "lawfulness" of the commission's orders—a term Moody considered so vague as to invite continuing litigation on the economic details and constitutional implications of each rate order. Knox's broad definition of review, carrying as it did the prestige of its author, provided in compelling form precisely the objective of Aldrich and his allies. To graft upon the Hepburn Bill Knox's amendment or one just like it, Aldrich had maneuvered the measure out of committee and onto the floor.

Roosevelt, while Aldrich deployed, had not been idle. From the time the Hepburn Bill reached the Senate, even as it lay in committee, the President had begun to confer with his Republican associates about amendments. Like Aldrich, he had able collaborators. Most helpful of these were William B. Allison of Iowa and John C. Spooner of Wisconsin who, in other years, had with Aldrich and the now deceased O. H. Platt composed the Senate's inner council of control. Allison, of that Four the most sensitive to the tolerances of public opinion and the most skillful negotiator, "rendered," Roosevelt later recalled, "unwearied and invaluable service in the actual, and indispensable, working out of legislative business." Spooner, scarcely less gifted, had a large personal stake in the satisfactory resolution of the problem of regulation, for his home bastion rattled before the guerrillas of the insurgent La Follette. Allison and Spooner brought with them a loyal corps of lesser Western Republican veterans for whom freight rates had assumed pressing political importance. The President could also rely upon, though he would not confide in, the intense Republican left. Could these men clearly demonstrate their strength, others in the party would reluctantly go their way. Finally, there were the Bryan Democrats, Tillman, Bailey of Texas, and a few more cautious in thought and less erratic in deportment who would probably damn Roosevelt's bill but give it their votes.

So positioned, Roosevelt planned at first to carry the bill by sponsoring amendments which would attract the Republican center without alienating the bipartisan left. Throughout February and much of March, while the bill lay in committee, he sought only to perpetuate explicitly the ambiguities implicit in the House's version. The plan seemed feasible so long as the committee might fashion a party measure. But Aldrich's coup, preventing this, also permitted the senator to vitiate Roosevelt's influence with the uncertain. Naturally like Aldrich disposed to trust the judiciary to brake change, the Republican center, relieved of party discipline, now looked more favorably on broad review. Tillman as floor leader for the bill was scarcely fit by temperament or inclination to dissuade them. The President, consequently, had to adjust his strategy to Aldrich's *démarche*.

Roosevelt acted at once. As his personal, unofficial representative in the Senate he selected Allison, who could reach and convince a larger number of Republicans than could have any other possible agent. He arranged also to communicate with Tillman through ex-Senator William E. Chandler, a mutual friend and advocate of regulation. By this clumsy device, with Tillman's help and through Allison's negotiations, Roosevelt then set out to construct a new coalition. "Inasmuch as the Republican leaders have tried to betray me . . . ," he explained, "I am now trying to see if I cannot get . . . [the bill] through in the form I want by the aid of some fifteen or twenty Republicans added to most of the Democrats." For this purpose, involving as it did both the enthusiasm of Tillman and the loyalty of Allison, Roosevelt had to move cautiously but clearly to the left of his original position.

Largely to Allison fell the difficult task of seeking a formula which would solve the problems of judicial review and the use of injunctions to the satisfaction of the divers partners to the potential coalition. Aldrich, if not surprised, must have been a little hurt to find his friend working the other side of the aisle. The work was tedious. Senator after senator contributed to the dozens of amendments under consideration. Three of these sufficiently reveal the nature of Allison's predicament. That of Senator Long of Kansas, the well-advertised product of a White House conference held just at the time Roosevelt decided to rely upon a coalition, prevented, according to the consensus of the Senate, judicial reconsideration of the facts of a case. In endorsing it, the President, no longer equivocal, won the favor of the coalition's Republicans and populist Democrats. Yet this was not enough. Senator Bailey of Texas, Tillman's closest associate, and other persistent Jeffersonians opposed the amendment, as Aldrich expected they would, because it seemed to them an unwarranted extension of executive power. Both Tillman and Bailey, moreover, considered the injunction issue more important than judicial review. The Texan had introduced an amendment, endorsed by most Democrats, which deprived the courts of authority to issue temporary writs suspending rate orders. Although this proposal effectively prevented delay in the application of rate rulings, it seemed to Roosevelt and his harassed lieutenants to be clearly unconstitutional. As negotiations proceeded, the President feared that Aldrich might adopt Bailey's plan or any of several like it in order with Democratic support to write a law that the courts would promptly nullify. Roosevelt and Allison therefore sponsored as an alternative an amendment drafted by Spooner. It provided that whenever a court suspended a rate order the amount in dispute between the carrier and the commission should be placed in escrow pending the outcome of litigation. Spooner's plan at once prevented confiscation of railroad property without due process of law, protected the shippers, and eliminated any advantage for the railroad in seeking litigation simply to cause delay.

Had Roosevelt and Allison been dealing only with resilient men, such ingenuity as Spooner's might, in time, have permitted them to devise a winning compromise. Bailey, for one, began to trim toward Allison. But a few Republicans and Tillman Democrats remained so adamantly for narrow review, many other Democrats so firmly for broad review, that Spooner's promising solution for injunctions never commanded the serious attention of either extreme. Before Allison had a chance to homogenize these stubborn parts, Aldrich precipitated crisis. He, too, had been active across the aisle. On April 18, as he predicted, the Democratic caucus refused to follow Tillman and Bailey. Roosevelt's attempt at coalition had failed.

Aldrich, the second round his, doubtless hoped that Roosevelt would either capitulate or, as he had a few weeks earlier, move further left. The President could have consolidated a noisy defense by throwing in his lot with the La Follette Republicans and Tillman Democrats. He could with them have swelled the rising voices of protest. He might, by such a move, have earned a popularity beyond even that already his. But he would have lost his bill. Seeing this as clearly as did Aldrich, Roosevelt had already prepared once more to redeploy.

Six days earlier, sensing defeat, the President had begun to hedge. If he could not win with Tillman, he might still win on his own original terms without the Democrats. "I am not at all sure," he then wrote Allison, "but that the easy way will be to come right back to the bill as it passed the House, and with very few unimportant amendments to pass it as it stands." On April 22 Roosevelt told Knox, again his confidant, that this opinion was "evidently gaining ground." Indeed it was, for Nelson Aldrich turned toward Roosevelt after the Democrats turned away. The leaders of the President's Republican opposition by early May ceased to insist on an explicit statement for broad review. Perhaps Aldrich became impatient with the continuing delay in the work of the Senate brought about by the everlasting debate on regulation. Perhaps he decided that Republican solidarity was more important than Roosevelt's purpose was dangerous. Probably, however, he saw that he had miscalculated. When Roosevelt, refusing to list with the left, reverted doggedly to the ambiguous center where he had first stood, he impelled Tillman, La Follette, and their likes, his erstwhile allies, into embittered opposition. Their protestations, couched in their inevitable vocabulary of revolt, attested to the safe reasonableness Roosevelt had ever claimed as his own. The uncertain minds of the wavering Republican center might now hear Allison out—might now, as Allison and Spooner had, see in Roosevelt safety. By some new alignment, like that he had hoped Dolliver would muster, the President with Time in *Thermidor* might triumph. At least, so Aldrich may have reasoned. In any case he retreated.

He may also have drafted the amendment which, introduced by Allison, won a majority vote and thereby secured the enactment of the Hepburn Bill. Whether or not Aldrich drafted it, Allison's amendment, leaving the bill in effect as the House had written it, gave Roosevelt what he had started out to get. The authorship of the amendment, like the working of Aldrich's mind, remains obscure. Whoever wrote it, Allison guided it. His activities in the two weeks following the Democratic caucus may be accurately surmised. Leaving no records, the "unwearied and invaluable" senator from Iowa, camped in the cloakroom where he excelled, had fashioned for the President a compromise that satisfied enough Republicans to save the bill.

The Allison amendment covered both judicial review and the use of injunctions. With purposeful obscurity, it granted jurisdiction in cases arising under the Hepburn Act to the circuit courts but left the definition of the scope of review to the courts. In a flood of oratory over the meaning of the amendment, each senator interpreted it to suit himself and his constituents. Both sides claimed victory. Insofar as the amendment was described as a victory for either narrow or broad review, the claims were nonsense. The question of review remained in May as unsettled as it had been in February. Roosevelt had then asked for no more. Ultimately the Supreme Court, which he trusted so little, in the first decision involving rate rulings made his preference law by refusing to review the facts of the case.

The Allison amendment did affirmatively settle the matter of injunctions by empowering the courts to "enjoin, set aside, annul, or suspend any order" of the I.C.C. It also prescribed that appeals from the orders of the I.C.C. were to go directly to the Supreme Court with the calendar priorities of antitrust cases. The amendment did not, however, specify the grounds for suspension or establish an escrow scheme. There remained, consequently, the possibility of considerable delay before rate rulings took effect. Roosevelt had constantly expressed his preference for an arrangement less favorable to the railroads, but he had also continually indicated that he would accept a solution like that of the Allison amendment. On this matter Tillman and Bailey, but neither Aldrich nor Roosevelt, had been defeated.

Roosevelt was "entirely satisfied" with the Allison amendment, he pointed out, because he was "entirely satisfied with the Hepburn bill." The amendment, he informed a less satisfied representative of midwestern shippers, was "only declaratory of what the Hepburn bill must mean, supposing it to be constitutional . . . I should be glad to get certain [other] amendments . . . ; but they are not vital, and even without them the Hepburn bill with the Allison amendment contains practically exactly what I have both originally and always since asked for."

Characteristically, Roosevelt overstated his case. "Always since" did not apply, for in his maneuvers of late March and April, although only at that time, the President had asked for more. Tillman and Bailey, who had joined him then, with rankling disappointment attacked him for returning to what he had originally requested. Their attacks, often repeated by their friends, have persuaded two generations that Roosevelt, irresolute and insincere, deserting his friends, yielding to Aldrich, lost the battle for regulation. Surely his detractors felt this, but they erred. Roosevelt had made overtures to Tillman and Bailey only for tactical reasons. He had, temporarily and for parliamentary support, enlarged his earlier demands. When this did not produce sufficient support, he reverted for tactical reasons to his first position. In so doing he deserted his temporary allies, but he did not compromise his policy. Tillman and Bailey, proud veterans of the Senate, perhaps resented most the knowledge that they had been used. Doubtless their pain gave Aldrich, who had made Roosevelt woo them and leave them, some amused satisfaction.

His objective attained, Roosevelt exulted. "No given measure and no given set of measures," he believed, "will work a perfect cure for any serious evil; and the insistence upon having only the perfect cure often results in securing no betterment whatever." The Hepburn Act was not perfect. But, Roosevelt maintained, it represented "the longest step ever yet taken in the direction of solving the railway rate problem." This was a fair assessment. With his clear perception of political situations, Roosevelt had set the highest practicable goal. By his mastery of political devices, in contest with another master, he had reached it. The Senate, in the end, supplied the federal executive with authority beyond any antecedent definition to mitigate the maladjustments of a growing industrial society.

The Hepburn Act endowed the Interstate Commerce Commission with power commensurate with its task. By informed, expert decisions, it could at last alter the artificial configurations of a market that had long since ceased, in the classic sense, to be free. The courts inexpertly had judged transportation by criteria which, however precious in jurisprudence, bore little relation to the economics of the process. Released from the inhibition of judicial reinterpretations (the bond that Aldrich had sought to supply), endowed with weapons the carriers respected, the I.C.C. began to develop after 1906 the techniques of effective supervision. The need for further change of course remained. But the Hepburn Act provided the precedent, accepted by the courts and enlarged by later Congresses, by which federal regulatory agencies have promoted the national welfare. Now vastly ramified, the government by administrative commission remains, though somewhat shabby, a useful part of American political arrangements.

For a troubled people in a complex time perhaps only the executive could have become steward. Aldrich, in that case, fought history and Roosevelt only accelerated what no man could have prevented. But Roosevelt's reputation rests securely even in acceleration, for the inevitable sometimes takes too long, and he knew just what he did. His efforts in behalf of the Hepburn Act—a measure meaningful but moderate—demonstrated his skilled concern for creating the instruments he thought the nation needed. For an orderly administrative system, for the right of efficient federal controls, for the positive government of an industrial society, he mobilized in a crucial first skirmish the full powers of his office. And he won. . . .

II

Woodrow Wilson and
Progressivism:
Did the South Help Make
Wilson an Advanced
Progressive?

INTRODUCTION

In terms of ideas, the significant aspect of the election campaign of 1912 was the struggle between two types of progressivism, the New Freedom of Woodrow Wilson, with its plea for regulated competition and the restoration of the economic individualism of days gone by, and the New Nationalism of Theodore Roosevelt, with its advocacy of regulated monopoly and advanced welfare legislation. Upon assuming the Presidency, Wilson sought to persuade Congress to adopt a legislative program consistent with the principles of the New Freedom, and he specifically opposed certain legislative measures that comported better with the philosophy of the New Nationalism than with that of the New Freedom. Within a short time, however, Wilson was forced to modify his position somewhat, and eventually he espoused virtually the whole of the New Nationalist program. What accounts for this change in Wilson's policy?

In the first of the two selections that follow, Professor Arthur S. Link, the foremost Wilson scholar of our day, contends that a "Southern Agrarian" faction in Congress "helped to make Wilson an advanced progressive and helped to commit his administration to a broad program of welfare legislation." The contributions of this Southern group, Link declares, were "in many ways decisive" in pushing the Wilson administration away from the New Freedom and toward the New Nationalism.

Challenging Link on this point, Richard Abrams, who at the time the article here reprinted was written was a member of the research staff of the Dictionary of American Biography, *argues largely on the basis of an analysis of the votes of Southern members of Congress that there was no "coordinated" Southern radical faction in Congress, that the radicalism of the Southern group and the conservatism of Wilson have been exaggerated, and that in so far as Southerners deviated from administration policies, it was generally in the direction of conservatism rather than of radicalism.*

The South and the "New Freedom":

An Interpretation

Arthur S. Link

The election of Woodrow Wilson and Democratic majorities in the House and Senate in 1912 confronted the Democrats of the South with their most serious challenge since before the Civil War. They had come to power more because of the disruption of the Republican party than because their party now represented the majority opinion of the country, and the future of the Democratic party for many years to come would depend upon their performance during the next two years. But the question whether they were not too much rent by personal factionalism and too sectionally conscious to govern in the national interest remained yet to be answered.

Southern Democrats in 1913 controlled practically all important congressional committees; they had a large majority in the Democratic caucuses in both houses; they had a president apparently responsive to their wishes, and they had a goodly representation in the cabinet. Judged by all superficial appearances, at least, the South was "in the saddle." These, however, were only the outward signs of control. The fact that Southerners happened to be chairmen of certain committees may or may not be important. The important question is whether they used the power they possessed to achieve political and economic objectives that the South especially desired, and whether they helped to shape the character of Wilsonian reform.

Wilson came to the presidency in 1913 with a clear conception of what the Democratic party should do to right the wrongs that special privilege had allegedly perpetrated through the Republican party. He would have the Democrats revise the tariff to eliminate all features of special privilege to domestic industries, bring the national banks into effective cooperation and control, and work out a new code for business in order to restore competition and make impossible the misuse of power by the giant corporations. This was the sum and substance of the "New Freedom." The political and economic millennium was to be achieved by these simple expedients, all of

Reprinted from *The American Scholar*, Volume XX, Number 3, Summer 1951. Copyright © 1951 by the United Chapters of Phi Beta Kappa. By permission of the publishers. Pp. 314–324.

which were based upon the assumption implicit in Wilson's campaign addresses of 1912, namely, that the limits of federal authority under the Constitution would not permit, and wise statesmanship would not desire, the extension of federal authority directly into business operations or the use of that authority to change the social and economic relationships then existing among the various interest groups.

Wilson originally conceived of the New Freedom as the political means of implementing the doctrines of laissez-faire, by removing all kinds of special class legislation. It was, therefore, a program intended to meet the needs primarily of the business community. There was nothing in it for the farmers or laborers directly, although these groups presumably would benefit from lower tariff rates and the restoration of competition in business. But Wilson had no more idea of legislating to advance the interests of these particular groups than he did of granting subsidies to American manufacturers. It can be said, in brief, that the Wilsonian program had the one supreme objective of taking the government out of the business of subsidizing and directly regulating economic activity and of taking the country back to some mythical age when there was a perfect natural identification of economic interests.

The most significant fact about the first Wilson administration is that the New Freedom, as it was originally conceived by its author, survived for only a few months. It required only short contact with reality to convince Wilson that his elaborate doctrines of 1912 were inadequate to deal with such great concentrations of economic power as existed at the time. More important as a factor in moving him away from his laissez-faire position, however, were certain powerful political forces over which Wilson and his administration had no control and which, as it were, seized control of administration policy and pushed it far beyond the bounds that Wilson and his advisers had originally thought desirable. In effect, what occurred from 1913 to 1917 was that Wilson adopted many of the assumptions and almost the whole platform of Theodore Roosevelt's New Nationalism.

This metamorphosis in the Wilsonian program is the key to understanding the first Wilson administration. The Southern contribution toward bringing the administration to an advanced position with regard to the exercise of federal authority was considerable, but the character of this contribution was different from what has been generally assumed. The Southern Democrats in Congress were divided roughly into two factions. First, there was what might be called the administration faction, consisting mainly of committee chairmen like Oscar W. Underwood and Carter Glass, who, by and large, represented a political tradition and constituencies whose interests were more or less divergent from those of the more numerous Southern group. Members of the administration faction were for the most part conservatives, although most of them had no fundamental political principles, were loyal party men, and would follow Wilson's lead. Secondly, there was a larger faction that represented more accurately the political traditions and economic interests of the South—the spokesmen for the agrarian interests of the South, men like Claude Kitchin, Otis Wingo, James K. Vardaman and Robert L. Henry.

The Southern Agrarians of the Wilson period were the direct inheritors and now the prime articulators in the Democratic party of the philosophy underlying the Agrarian crusade—namely, that it was government's duty to intervene directly in economic affairs in order to benefit submerged or politically impotent economic interests. As it turned out, the existence and power of the Southern Agrarian group had important consequences for the Democratic party, the Wilson administration, and the nation. Whereas the administration faction usually followed the regular party line, the Southern Agrarians were often far to the left of it; and in the end they helped to make Wilson an advanced progressive and helped to commit his administration to a broad program of welfare legislation.

The program of the Southern Agrarians was aimed at benefiting the farmers almost exclusively. Although this had been true also of the Democratic program in 1896, Bryan and progressive Democrats in the North and West had moved beyond the almost pure agrarianism of 1896. There was a growing concern for the plight of submerged groups from about 1890 to 1913 and a consequent rise of a great movement for social justice. This phase of progressivism had not been totally absent in the South, but the Southern states were still overwhelmingly rural, and most Southerners had no conception of the grave social and economic problems raised by industrialization and urbanization.

Hence Southern progressives were more concerned with strengthening the political and economic position of the farmers, through regulation of railroads and corporations, a low tariff, the direct primary, and the like, than with tenement reforms, minimum wage legislation, or workmen's compensation legislation. But the important point about the Southern Agrarian program is not that it was limited in scope, but that its advocates were an important element in the Democratic party and that they were now in a position to give voice to their own demands.

The brief period when the philosophy of the New Freedom had any real authority was the few months in 1913 when the Underwood tariff bill was under discussion in Congress. There was little disagreement among Democratic congressmen, progressive or conservative, over the provisions of the bill, except for minor differences on the wool and sugar schedules. There was a much greater difference of opinion between the conservatives and the agrarian radicals, however, on the question of the reorganization of the banking system and the control of the money supply. It was here that the Southern Agrarians, acting with their colleagues from the West, first helped to move their party away from laissez-faire toward a dynamic concept of government.

In line with his New Freedom principles Wilson was inclined to favor the banking and monetary system proposed by the National Monetary Commission, one providing for a reserve association or associations owned and controlled by the bankers themselves. The original Glass bill, which had the tentative endorsement of the administration, provided for such an arrangement. But even before the federal reserve bill emerged from the House Banking Committee, there occurred a momentous struggle within the party councils that was not ended until the Agrarian leaders had won all their important demands. Secretary of State Bryan and Louis D. Brandeis persuaded the President that a banking bill which did not provide for exclusive governmental control, on the top level, was not only unwise but also would never be approved by the House caucus. This was true, incidentally, regardless of the position Bryan might have taken in the controversy.

Wilson was won over by the persuasive arguments of Bryan and Brandeis and the threats of the radicals. Thus the Glass bill, as it finally emerged from the House committee, provided for a decentralized reserve system, for government issue of federal-reserve currency, and for an over-all supervision and limited control of the new system by a central reserve board composed exclusively of presidential appointees. It marked, to all practical purposes, the demise of the New Freedom and the beginning of the rise to dominance of the progressives in the Wilson administration.

Bryan and the Western Democrats were now satisfied, but not the Southern Agrarian leaders. In spite of the radical changes that had been effected, the new banking system still would operate exclusively for the benefit of the business community. Here was the rub, as far as the Southern radicals were concerned. After tariff reform had been accomplished, their main objective was the establishment of a system by which farmers could obtain easier and cheaper credit. When the Glass bill was published, and the Southern Agrarians discovered that it included no provision for agricultural credit, they rose in rebellion and declared that they would help the Republicans defeat the measure if the administration did not concede their demands. The fight between the administration forces and the Southern Agrarians was bitter, and for a time threatened to defeat banking reform altogether. Suffice it to say that, in spite of the ridicule of the Eastern press and in spite of the opposition of the administration and of Wilson's spokesmen in the House, the Federal Reserve Bill as finally passed by Congress contained ample provisions for short-term agricultural credit. And this was true because Wilson realized that he must give in to the demands of the Southerners.

The philosophic foundations of the New Freedom were dealt another heavy blow during the formulation of an antitrust policy by administration leaders. It was Wilson's original idea that all that was required was to define precisely what constituted an unfair trade practice or illegal restraint of trade, so as to remove all element of doubt from the laws. The enforcement of the antitrust laws would be delegated, as before, to the Justice Department and the courts. Some of the Southern radicals proposed more drastic remedies, such as prescribing by law the percentage of the total production of a field of industry which one corporation would be allowed to control, or a high excess profits tax which would increase in direct proportion to the size of the industry; but they made no determined fight for these proposals. Wilson, therefore, gave the job of drawing up the measure to Representative Clayton of Georgia, chairman of the Judiciary Committee, and the bill that came out of his committee was simply a synthesis of current ideas, most of which were already embodied in the laws of many states. In addition, Representative Covington of Kentucky drew up at Wilson's request a bill providing for an interstate trade commission, which was to be an enlarged Bureau of Corporations and without any real authority over business practices.

Thus far Wilson had proceeded in line with his New Freedom concepts. At this point, however, an important turn in administration policy occurred. Brandeis, George L. Rublee, and Representative Stevens of New Hampshire visited the President and persuaded him to change the character of his antitrust program entirely. Under their direction, the Clayton bill was rewritten so as to provide for greater flexibility in defining an unfair trade practice and, more important, the interstate commerce commission was reconstituted as the Federal Trade Commission and given apparently vast authority over the day-to-day operations of the business world. The Covington bill had provided for nothing more than an investigatory body to serve as an adjunct of the Justice Department. In the revised bill, the Commission was established as an independent regulatory agency, empowered to supervise business practices and to issue cease and desist orders when it found that corporations were engaging in unfair practices. This last change marked the complete adoption by the Wilson administration of Roosevelt's program for the regulation of business.

The Southern leaders in Congress had nothing to do with bringing about this profound change in Wilson's antitrust policy. The Southern and Western Agrarian radicals, acting with a small Labor bloc in the House, worked hard, however, to have a provision inserted in the Clayton bill exempting farm and labor unions from the operation and application of the antitrust laws. This had been one of the major objectives of the American Federation of Labor since 1906 and had been given Democratic approval in the platforms of 1908 and 1912. Although Wilson was rapidly abandoning his New Freedom assumptions, he was not yet ready to go so far as to approve what was obviously legislation in the interest of particular classes. Since the first days of his administration he had resisted bitterly this move, and a bill specifically exempting farm and labor unions from antitrust prosecutions, which had been passed by the House in the previous session, was blocked by administration pressure. When the Clayton bill was under discussion in the House committee, however, the Agrarian and Labor bloc declared that they would guarantee its defeat unless Wilson gave in to their demands.

Thus faced with another major revolt within his party, Wilson resolved his dilemma by resorting, it must be admitted, to one of the most artful dodges in the history of American politics. The famous labor provisions of the Clayton bill were drawn by Representative E. Y. Webb of North Carolina, who had succeeded Clayton as chairman of the Judiciary Committee, and represented Wilson's attitude perfectly. On the face of it, the new provision did indeed seem to give the exemption and immunity from antitrust prosecutions that the farm and labor spokesmen were demanding. Actually, this was not the case at all. Farm and labor organizations were not to be construed by the courts as being, *per se,* combinations in restraint of trade, but they were in no way freed from the threat of prosecution if they violated the antitrust laws.

Wilson had completed his program of domestic reform by the fall of 1914. In his letters and public statements at the time, he made it clear that he thought everything had been done that was necessary to clear away special privilege and put all classes on an equal footing. Under the operation of the beneficient new laws, Wilson was sure that the nation would enjoy a long period of prosperity and economic freedom. As we have seen, he had been forced partially to abandon his earlier position and to make important concessions in order to get his program across. He was reconciled to the concessions he had been compelled to make, but he was absolutely determined to draw the line at the point it had reached by the fall of 1914.

In fact, a pronounced reaction against progressive policies had set in among Wilson and his advisers during the spring of 1914, and relations between the President and progressive leaders became exceedingly strained at this time. The following year, 1915, was practically barren of progressive accomplishments, except for . . . La Follette's Seamen's Act, which the administration had opposed and which Wilson almost vetoed. There were, however, several great political forces at work which were so strong that Wilson would be compelled to accommodate his program to satisfy their demands. One was the well-organized Agrarian movement for the establishment of a federal system of long-term rural credits. Another was the movement in behalf of federal social legislation, which was rapidly gaining momentum during this period. Another was the movement for women's suffrage, which was becoming so powerful that it would soon be dangerous for any politician to oppose it. Finally, there was the fact that the Progressive party was obviously disintegrating after 1914 and that the only hope the Democrats had of obtaining a national majority in 1916 was in winning a large minority of the former Bull Moosers to the Democratic side.

Wilson resisted this movement to extend the intervention of the federal government into the fields mentioned here as long as he could do so safely.

Then, when it became evident that the Democrats could win the election of 1916 only by adopting the New Nationalism, lock, stock and barrel, Wilson capitulated and supported the very demands he had so long opposed, as strongly as if he had been their originator. We do not have the space to discuss this last and most important phase of Wilsonian reform in any detail, except to consider the extent to which the Southern leaders contributed to the administration's final, complete surrender to the New Nationalism.

The main objective of the Southern Agrarian progressives after 1914 was the adoption of a federal rural credits bill. The first nationwide movement for long-term federal rural credit facilities had been inaugurated by the Southern Commercial Congress in 1913, and during the next year or two there was widespread discussion of the subject all over the country. In the spring of 1914 a joint subcommittee drew up the bill which was finally passed in 1916 and which would have passed in 1914 had not Wilson let it be known that he would veto the bill if Congress enacted it. Both Wilson and the Agrarian leaders proclaimed themselves advocates of a rural credits measure. What, therefore, was the root of the difference between them? Wilson would not agree to the establishment of a system involving direct subsidies or financial support by the government, and Wilson, Secretary of Agriculture Houston, and Carter Glass were insistent that the government should do no more than provide for the structure of a rural credits system, with capital and management to be provided by private sources. The Agrarian spokesmen, on the other hand, contended that any system which was not operated and financed by the government was bound to fail. But as this involved the direct intervention by the government in behalf of a special class, Wilson was absolutely adamant against it. The result was an impasse, with both sides holding out stubbornly for their own proposals until 1916, when Wilson accepted the Agrarian proposal for reasons of political expediency.

It was, in fact, in agricultural legislation that the Southern Agrarians had the greatest influence in the shaping of the later Wilsonian program. Their greatest contribution was undoubtedly the forcing of the Rural Credits Act of 1916, but they were also able to obtain the adoption of the Lever Warehouse Act in 1914, the Smith-Lever Act for rural extension work of the same year, the Smith-Hughes Act for vocational education, and the program of federal subsidies for highway improvement in 1916.

Southern influence was practically negligible, however, in the formulation of the remaining great social and economic legislation of 1916—the federal Workmen's Compensation Act, the Child Labor Law, the Adamson Act, and the act establishing the Federal Tariff Commission. But there still remain three other areas of legislation in which the influence of the Southern Agrarians was decisive and which merit notice here.

The first involved the question of what sort of military and naval bills Congress should enact in 1916. On this controversial subject the Southern progressives joined with radicals throughout the country in resisting the administration's designs greatly to increase the navy and to establish a large volunteer army. They were not successful in blocking the movement for a large navy, because the pressure here was too great. But they were signally successful in blocking Wilson's plans for military preparedness, indeed, in emasculating them.

The second field of legislation in which Southern progressive influence was decisive was the area of federal fiscal policy. Before the outbreak of the World War, Wilson and McAdoo were able to keep a firm grip on the formulation of tax policies, and their influence was conservative indeed. The tax structure that the Republicans had erected and which was weighted so heavily in favor of the upper classes was left practically undisturbed by the Wilson administration. An income tax provision was included in the Underwood Tariff Law, to make up the anticipated deficit resulting from the lower duties, but the rates were very low and the administration was quick to make it clear that it had no intention of using the income tax to effect a redistribution of wealth.

The outbreak of the war in Europe in the summer of 1914 caused a temporary disarrangement of the finances of the United States and resulted in a sharp decline in imports, which meant that the administration was faced with an alarming decline in revenues. To meet this emergency, Mc-Adoo proposed a series of new excise taxes and a tax on freight shipments, such as had been applied during the Spanish-American War. The Southern and Western Agrarians rebelled at the administration's emergency tax program, claiming that it would throw the whole burden of carrying the country through the crisis on the masses and demanding instead an increase in the income tax. They were successful in eliminating the tax on freight shipments and in getting most of the new taxes put on alcoholic beverages and other luxuries. Even so, they did not like the emergency tax law and vowed that they would continue to fight all such consumption taxes.

With the opening of Congress in December, 1915, the Southern progressives found themselves virtually in control of the House Ways and Means Committee. Long before the new session convened, a majority of the committee declared in writing to the new chairman, Claude Kitchin of North Carolina, their determination to overhaul the tax structure and make it more democratic. The result was that during the winter and spring of 1916 the control of federal tax policy was literally taken out of the hands of the administration leaders and assumed by these Southern Agrarians and their Western allies. It was obvious by this time that some kind of preparedness measures would be adopted, and that either the government would have to find new sources of revenue or else resort to borrowing. The Republicans proposed a bond issue; the administration proposed new consumption and excise and increased income taxes. The Ways and Means Committee, however, replied with one of the most startling and significant tax bills in the history of the country. The Southern Agrarians, who had bitterly resisted the preparedness movement, saw now that new defense measures were inevitable; but they were determined that the people of the East, who had been most vociferous in support of preparedness, should pay for it. Kitchin said as much, in fact, before the House caucus when he explained the new tax bill, which greatly increased the income tax, levied the first federal inheritance tax in our history, and placed an excess profits tax on munitions manufacturers.

The last area in which Southern influence was decisive in determining the policies of the Wilson administration was the federal government's policy toward Negroes. Here the Southern contribution was definitely retrogressive and proved that it was impossible for white Southerners of all shades of opinion to get much beyond the rationale of slavery. Suffice it to say that Wilson practically sacrificed the Negroes on the altar of political expediency, by allowing segregation in the government departments, dismissal and downgrading of Negro civil servants in the South, and the like, in order to win Southern support for his program.

Yet in spite of this and other blind spots in the Southern progressive program, it must be concluded that the contributions of the Southern Agrarians were undoubtedly in many ways decisive in moving the Wilson administration away from a static laissez-faire program, to which it was originally dedicated, toward a dynamic, positive program of federal action. Although their program was limited in scope and motivated largely by class interests, the Southern progressives could claim as much credit as could several other major groups for the amazing metamorphosis in Democratic policy that occurred from 1913 to 1916. That is the real significance of their contribution.

Woodrow Wilson and the Southern Congressmen, 1913–1916

Richard M. Abrams

During the Presidential campaign of 1912, Woodrow Wilson, in conjunction with Louis D. Brandeis, outlined the principles on which Wilson proposed to base a legislative program. As originally conceived, these principles— which have come to be known as the New Freedom—appeared to follow traditional assumptions of free enterprise and economic individualism. According to the New Freedom, the purpose of government was to remove all obstacles to the smooth operation of the mechanisms of the free market; logically this implied proscription of special privileges or favors which the government might extend to any interest or group. In a word, the New Freedom aimed to make *laissez faire* a practicable and just principle of government.

On the other hand, Theodore Roosevelt set forth a program of industrial progress and social welfare requiring active governmental intervention in the economic affairs of American society. According to the New Nationalism, as this program was called, business, farm, and labor consolidations were to be encouraged, underprivileged elements in society were to be given direct government benefits, and the government was to act in general as a mediator among the various contending interests. In brief, while the New Freedom emphasized decentralization of power in politics and economics, the New Nationalism emphasized concentration of power, in the name of efficiency, science, and progress.

The problem for the historian has been to understand how, if Wilson was committed to the New Freedom, so much legislation was passed during his first administration which does not appear to fit within the New Freedom's principles. Professor Arthur S. Link, the foremost student of the Wilson era, has been one of the first to attempt to resolve this problem.[1] He contends

---

From *The Journal of Southern History*, **XXII** (November 1956), 417–437. **Copyright 1956 by the Southern Historical Association. Reprinted with permission of the Managing Editor.**

[1] See especially Arthur S. Link, "The South and the 'New Freedom': An Interpretation," in *American Scholar* (New York, 1932–), XX (1951), 314–24; and *Woodrow Wilson and the Progressive Era, 1910–1917* (New York, 1954).

that although the "sum and substance" of Wilson's New Freedom was the elimination of special privilege by means of a thorough revision of the tariff system, the banking system, and the trust laws, before long certain radical forces compelled Wilson to use the powers of the government along lines prescribed by the New Nationalists. Prominent among these radicals was a large congressional faction of Southern agrarians, representing the true political traditions and economic interests of the South.

> The Southern Agrarians of the Wilson period were the direct in-
> heritors and now the prime articulators in the Democratic party of the
> philosophy underlying the Agrarian crusade—namely, that it was gov-
> ernment's duty to intervene directly in economic affairs in order to
> benefit submerged or politically impotent economic interests. . . . in
> the end they helped make Wilson an advanced progressive and helped
> to commit his administration to a broad program of welfare legislation.

By 1916, Professor Link concludes, Wilson had adopted the New National-ism "lock, stock and barrel." [2]

The purpose of this paper is to investigate the role of the Southern con-gressmen in the enactment of the domestic legislative program of Wilson's first administration; in part, perforce, it is to discover exactly who were the Southern agrarians to whom Professor Link refers. Were they a definite group or faction with a specific philosophy or program? What specifically did they accomplish? Were they indeed "radicals" or "progressives" in the sense understood by contemporary Americans?

To open the war on "privilege," President Wilson, in his inaugural ad-dress, summoned a special session of Congress to enact a tariff protecting no interests and earning only the revenue needed for normal governmental functions. Almost unanimously, the Southern congressmen (who comprised about 35 per cent of all congressional Democrats and commanded nearly all positions of power in Congress) co-operated fully with the administration in passing the Underwood Tariff Act.

Serious insurgency within the Democracy first arose during the contest over the bill to reform the national banking system, which the House took up while the Senate debated the tariff measure. Although the American business community had long recognized the need for a thoroughly reformed banking system, few agreed upon a definite plan. The principles of the New Freedom required a bill which, like the tariff measure, extended no govern-mental favors to any interest. It was natural, however, that whatever scheme the administration might choose, it would meet with heated opposition, not the least of which would be from the bankers and businessmen who had the most immediate material interest in the nation's financial structure.

---

[2] Link, "The South and the 'New Freedom,'" 316, 321. It is not clear just what states Professor Link includes in the "South." For the purposes of this paper, the "South" will be used to designate the eleven states of the Confederacy.

The bill initially drafted by Representative Carter Glass of Virginia, and used by the administration as the foundation for subsequent alterations, was essentially a conservative one, but the conservative banking community, unwilling to accept any reform it could not itself write, immediately protested to Washington. The chief opposition in Congress, however, came from those seeking a *less* conservative measure—a measure which would, through governmental intervention, provide easier credit for particular interests. Secretary of State William Jennings Bryan indicated that he and his congressional followers would oppose any plan not providing for federal control over the issue of currency, while Robert L. Owen of Oklahoma, chairman of the Senate Banking Committee, suggested that the Treasury Department directly control the entire banking system.[3] Hostility in Congress mounted among those who resented the "private" fashion in which the administration had drafted the bill, as well as among those who viewed the bill as "legalizing the money-trust" by leaving credit and the currency in bankers' control. In response to this hostility, the President called for advice from Louis D. Brandeis, on whom he had depended so often in the past campaign.

Brandeis persuaded Wilson to vest the power to issue currency in the government, and to limit the bankers to an advisory capacity. He pointed out that while it was desirable to pass a measure quickly, until then the only discussion of the issue had been "that organized by the bankers," so that the bill was too heavily influenced by this single source. Brandeis urged that time be allowed for the business and agrarian interests to make their suggestions. He added: "Nothing would go so far in establishing confidence among businessmen as the assurance that the Government will control the currency issue"—a sentiment which he shared with Owen.[4]

Although Wilson forced Glass to accept Brandeis' suggestions, an extremist element remained hostile. For the bill still omitted prohibition of interlocking directorates among national banks (one of the two major recommendations of the Pujo Committee of 1911–1912), it left the private bankers with considerable influence within the proposed Federal Reserve System, and it omitted provisions for long-term agricultural credit. When Glass made public the "compromise" bill on June 14, 1913, Robert L. Henry of Texas, chairman of the House Rules Committee and leader of the "radical agrarians" (as Professor Link refers to them), publicly blasted the measure.[5] The bill was formally introduced June 26, three days after the President addressed Congress declaring: "The control of the system of banking and of issue which our new laws are to set up must be public, not private, must be

---

[3] New York *Times*, April 30, 1913.

[4] Louis D. Brandeis to Woodrow Wilson, June 14, 1913, in Wilson Papers (Manuscripts Division, Library of Congress). Wilson had asked Brandeis to put in writing the major points of their discussion on June 12.

[5] New York *Times*, June 15, 1913; Ray Stannard Baker, *Woodrow Wilson, Life and Letters* (8 vols., Garden City, 1927–1939), IV, 164–65.

vested in the Government itself, so that the banks may be the instruments, not the masters, of business and of individual enterprise and initiative." [6]

While the bill was in committee, administration leaders conceded to insurgents only a few amendments, among which were prohibition of interlocking directorates and of loans by national banks in which their officers were interested.[7] The most serious challenge to the administration measure developed July 24, when J. Willard Ragsdale of South Carolina, following Robert Henry's lead, prepared a drastic substitute bill providing for an issue of currency based on warehouse receipts for cotton, corn, and wheat.[8] At this point, Wilson intervened, persuading Otis Wingo of Arkansas, leader of the committee rebels, to have proposals for agricultural credit introduced as a separate bill, and to take the banking bill into caucus where proceedings could be more confidential.[9]

On July 28 the Democrats on the committee voted 11–3 to send the bill to caucus beginning August 11—from where it emerged August 28 substantially unchanged. Before the Democrats caucused, however, the major accomplishment of the committee insurgents—banning interlocking directorates—was stricken from the bill (August 1), and August 22, in caucus, it was rejected again, 60–143. On the twenty-third Wingo's amendment, to limit the voting power of banks owning other banks in the election of regional reserve boards, was defeated 46–95. Henry's proposals for an "agricultural currency" based on warehouse receipts or liens on agricultural products, and to extend the maturity period of agricultural and commercial paper to six months, were repeatedly rejected; the only "concession" to the insurgents on this issue was an amendment adopted August 25 establishing the equality of agricultural and commercial paper.[10] Rebel strength slowly crumbled after Bryan (August 11) urged his supporters to end their opposition to the bill, and after the President issued a statement two days later promising that an agricultural credits bill would be introduced during the next session.[11] On the final day (August 28) the caucus voted 163 to 9 to reintroduce the bill into Congress.[12]

It is noteworthy that although during the caucus sessions the hostile press

---

[6] Quoted in Link, *Wilson and the Progressive Era*, 48.

[7] New York *Times,* July 13, 24, 1913; *American Year Book* (New York, 1911–), *1913,* p. 44.

[8] New York *Times,* July 25, 1913.

[9] *Ibid.,* July 26, 1913. Wilson feared that the intracommittee haggling would lead to an open breach among Democrats, and that the day-to-day decisions and reversals were jeopardizing business conditions, which showed signs of serious deterioration.

[10] *Ibid.,* August 29, 1913; *American Year Book, 1913,* p. 45; *La Follette's Weekly* (Madison, Wis., 1909–1929), March 21, 1914, p. 4. After the August 25 session the Henry-Ragsdale-Wingo forces contended they had won a victory, while the Glass supporters just as stoutly contended they had successfully resisted the insurgents. New York *Times,* August 26, 1913.

[11] Baker, *Wilson, Life and Letters,* IV, 174; *American Year Book, 1913,* p. 45.

[12] The nine were: Robert L. Henry, Joe H. Eagle, and Oscar Callaway of Texas, Thomas W. Hardwick of Georgia, George N. Neeley of Kansas, Thomas U. Sisson of Mississippi,

rang with reports of "open rebellion" and irreparable cleavages within the Democratic ranks, the opposition mustered on no occasion more than 35 per cent of the Democrats voting, and usually less than 25 per cent, of which a large number were from the Midwest. The one issue on which they showed the greatest strength, in and out of the caucus, was on a clause re-affirming the gold standard. Faced with last-minute pressure from Northern Democrats, Progressives, and Republicans, and with possible complications involving the Standard of Value Act of 1900, Glass had reluctantly accepted the clause on the final day of debate (September 18). Although some Demo-crats declared that the provision would be "a slap in the face" of the many silverites among them, it passed 299–68. Only 32 of the 68 were Southern Democrats.[13]

The roll call on the gold standard was one of the few in which the Demo-crats were not committed to a caucus pledge of party regularity, and, except for deference to the wishes of Carter Glass, were free to vote their convictions and interests. Significantly, several of those who persistently fought with the Henry-Ragsdale insurgents voted for the gold standard.[14] Thus, it appears that the composition of the insurgents was not only always small, it was con-tinually shifting; so that it is inaccurate to talk of a "radical" *faction* within the party threatening the stability of the administration.[15] This conclusion is supported by the only other important roll call available on the Glass Act in which the Democrats were not entirely bound by a caucus pledge: on a motion, December 20, to concur in a Senate amendment which in effect rewrote the Glass bill.

The Senate version contained two important additions to the bill received from the House on September 18: (1) a bank deposit guarantee clause; (2) an extension of the maturity period of loans on agricultural paper, from three to six months. The second was something for which agrarians had been striving since the early days of the Populists. Two wheat representatives from the Midwest and one cotton representative from the South[16] led the efforts for acceptance of the Senate measure, pointing out that a vote against

---

Charles O. Lobeck of Nebraska, and Frank Buchanan and H. Robert Fowler of Illinois. *La Follette's Weekly,* September 6, 1913, p. 9. Wingo's vote indicates that he was ap-parently reconciled with the administration leadership.

[13] *Cong. Record,* 63 Cong., 1 Sess., 5127–28. Significantly, the Progressives and progres-sive Republicans in the House voted 21–1 for the clause.

[14] For example, Hardwick of Georgia and Robert L. Doughton of North Carolina, to name but two.

[15] The jargon of contemporary observers made a "radical" out of every Democratic opponent of the administration during the banking and currency debates. Without defining terms any more carefully, these observers, and some historians, continued to use the epithet whenever referring to Democratic opposition to Wilson's policies. In most cases, however, the only sense in which most individual opponents might be considered radicals is in their occasional violation of party regularity.

[16] William H. ("Alfalfa Bill") Murray of Oklahoma, George A. Neeley of Kansas, and Hardwick of Georgia.

concurrence was a vote against long-term loan benefits for farmers. Glass meanwhile pleaded to be allowed to go into joint conference with a free hand.

The House defeated the motion for concurrence 59–295, with the Southern Democrats voting 22–68 against it, and with those previously among the insurgents badly split; for example, Wingo of Arkansas, Oscar Callaway and Joe H. Eagle of Texas, and J. Thomas Heflin of Alabama opposed the Senate measure, while Ragsdale of South Carolina, James L. Slayden of Texas, and Thomas U. Sisson and Samuel A. Witherspoon of Mississippi voted for it. Among the 22 Southerners voting for the Senate bill, moreover, were such stalwart conservatives as Martin Dies of Texas and Robert N. Page of North Carolina.[17]

Who, then, were the Southern "radicals" to whom contemporary observers (and many historians) frequently referred? If we consider them to have been those who voted differently from Carter Glass on either the Senate concurrence or the gold standard issues (thus taking in the maximum number of dissenters), they totalled 44, or about 40 per cent of all the Southerners. Included in this group, however, were many old-line conservatives, such as Dies, Page, Charles R. Crisp (Georgia), and William Adamson (Georgia). Had they been a real faction, with a program or a philosophy, had they acted together consistently under any pretext, these forty-four might have forced the administration to make major concessions. Instead, the "radicals" failed in their three prime goals: to ban interlocking directorates among national banks, to obtain long-term credits for farmers, and to have the government issue currency based on crop warehouse receipts; they even failed in their mightiest united effort—renunciation of the gold standard (and in this they encountered the almost unanimous opposition of the Northern and Western progressives).[18]

To say that before Glass introduced his revised bill in late June 1913, the "radicals" succeeded in forcing the administration to accept the responsibilities of directly controlling the national banking and currency system is to assume that the administration had, at that time, rather precise ideas on the details of its banking program.[19] The contrary is more likely true. Wilson sought a balanced measure which would be tolerable to both Congress and

---

[17] *Cong. Record*, 63 Cong., 2 Sess., 1307. In conference, as expected, Glass reduced the period of maturity for discountable paper to three months and eliminated the guarantee of bank deposits. H. Parker Willis, "The Federal Reserve Act," in *American Economic Review* (Ithaca, N. Y., 1911–), IV (1914), 12.

[18] By progressives I mean those non-Democrats who were elected to Congress in 1912 with Progressive party support, as well as some who were commonly recognized as progressives although, for various reasons, they kept the Republican party label (for example, Senators Robert M. La Follette and George Norris and Congressmen Charles A. Lindbergh and Irvine L. Lenroot). I count twelve such senators and twenty-seven such members of the House in the Sixty-Third Congress.

[19] See New York *Times,* June 14, 1913, on this point.

to the banking community (on whose co-operation success so largely depended). Once he decided on a specific measure and was content with its fairness, once he determined to fight for it through his congressional leaders, he won every major point.

On the subject of who was pushing whom into "advanced progressivism," the contest over the Federal Trade Commission is significant. If there was little agreement in 1913 on the kind of banking legislation needed, there was considerably less on exactly how to reform the trust laws. In fact, the progressives themselves were divided on fundamental policy. In the presidential campaign of 1912 the programs of the two major candidates differed significantly on how to cope with the problem of large aggregations of capital. Theodore Roosevelt proposed that government ought to regulate business consolidations in the public interest only by means of a strong commission; he decried antitrust acts as reactionary. Wilson denounced Roosevelt's program because he saw the likelihood of the corporations controlling the commission rather than the reverse, and because the entire scheme tended toward a paternalistic society dominated by the giant trust; he preferred to "regulate competition" (Louis Brandeis' phrase) rather than to "legalize the trusts"—to maintain competition by removing the conditions leading to trust formation.

As it developed, probably a majority of progressives, including those who joined Roosevelt's Progressive party, sought stronger *anti*trust laws. For example, "Bull Moose" Senator Joseph L. Bristow of Kansas wrote to Roosevelt on July 15, 1912, protesting against his New Nationalist program: "Many Progressives contend for a restoration of competition, believing that it would be better for the country and more conductive to industrial progress." Bristow had the hearty support of such progressive Republicans as Albert B. Cummins of Iowa, Moses E. Clapp of Minnesota, and William E. Borah of Idaho.[20]

Nevertheless, although Wilson had opposed the idea of a regulatory commission during the campaign, in June 1914 (in part because he was faced with a serious economic recession) he accepted a plan proposed by Brandeis and George L. Rublee for a commission which would define, investigate, and set governmental machinery in motion against unfair competition.[21] In doing so, Wilson actually surrendered no principles because the bill was designed to preserve competition and was not concerned with regulating monopoly or punishing fraudulent practices.[22]

The new bill consisted fundamentally of the old Covington bill, which

---

[20] George E. Mowry, *Theodore Roosevelt and the Progressive Movement* (Madison, Wis., 1946), 270.

[21] W. H. S. Stevens, "The Trade Commission Act," in *American Economic Review,* IV (1914), 840–55; Link, *Wilson and the Progressive Era,* 71–72.

[22] E. Pendleton Herring, "Politics, Personalities and the Federal Trade Commission," in *American Political Science Review* (Baltimore, 1906–), XXVIII (1934), 1016–29.

proposed an investigatory interstate trade commission to replace the Bureau of Corporations; it added, however, the notorious "Section 5," authorizing a Federal Trade Commission "to prevent the use of unfair methods of competition in interstate commerce." The provisions were made deliberately vague, in order to give the commissioners wide discretionary powers in determining unfair competition. In thus establishing a "quasi-judiciary" executive department, Wilson made his one real concession to [the] New Nationalism; and in doing so he drew the fire of many progressives as well as the Southerners in Congress.

On August 5, 1914, Democratic Senator James A. Reed of Missouri, an avowed enemy of the FTC, introduced a motion to define "unfair competition" in the bill. The motion was defeated 29–33, with five Southerners (including the radical James K. Vardaman of Mississippi) and two progressives for the motion.[23] Since the bill was a party measure, the Democratic vote for Reed's crippler indicated only those most strongly opposed to the idea of an FTC.

Better evidence for determining the Southerners who really favored the Trade Commission and were not merely deferring to administration policy, is provided by a roll call taken June 27, 1916. When Senator Henry F. Hollis of New Hampshire, who had led the pro-FTC forces in 1914, proposed an amendment reapportioning funds to increase the efficiency of the Commission, 14 out of 17 Southerners voted against Hollis, endorsing the claim of Senate Leader Thomas S. Martin of Virginia that the FTC was totally useless, inefficient, and extravagant. The amendment failed, 28–42.[24]

In May 1916 the Senate rejected the nomination of George Rublee to one of the five posts on the FTC. One of the principal issues of the nomination was Rublee's role in writing Section 5. Ten Southerners voted to approve the President's nominee, but nine opposed. Six of those who opposed strengthening the FTC would not oppose their leader's nomination, while only the inexplicable Vardaman voted for Hollis' amendment but against Rublee.[25]

The principal objections to the FTC Act centered on Section 5, one of the few parts of Wilson's entire trust program which offered something to the New Nationalists in the country. Not only did the Southerners have "noth-

---

[23] *Cong. Record,* 63 Cong., 2 Sess., 13314, 13319. James K. Vardaman is one of the very few Southerners who indeed deserves the label "radical" even apart from his role in the Glass Act debate; he may be called a radical because, like many progressives, he sought to commit the government to a program of welfare legislation.

[24] *Ibid.,* 64 Cong., 1 Sess., 10050, 10062. Vardaman (perverse as usual!), Luke Lea of Tennessee, and Morris Sheppard of Texas were the only three Southerners with Henry F. Hollis. Progressives William E. Borah of Idaho, Asle J. Gronna of North Dakota, Wesley L. Jones of Washington, and John D. Works of California opposed the amendment. Borah once declared: "I am opposed to it [the FTC] now, and I expect to be opposed to it so long as I retain my right mind." *Ibid.,* 63 Cong., 2 Sess., 14414.

[25] *Ibid.,* 64 Cong., 1 Sess., 7962, 8510. There was a direct correlation between the progressives' votes on Hollis' amendment and their votes on Rublee.

ing to do with bringing about this profound change in Wilson's antitrust policy," [26] but Wilson also had to face the opposition of many congressional progressives.[27]

If the southerners were reluctant to support the administration's "radical" FTC which put limits on "free competition," they were no more anxious to strengthen the antitrust laws. Charles A. Culberson of Texas, chairman of the Senate Judiciary Committee, successfully resisted all efforts to include in the Clayton Act (1) a provision making the settlement of a federal suit against a corporation for violation of the trust laws conclusive evidence in personal damage suits against that corporation, (2) penalties for conviction of price discrimination, rebates, and similar unfair trade practices, (3) effective prohibition of interlocking directorates, and (4) prohibition from interstate commerce of all corporations, except common carriers, capitalized at more than $100,000,000. Only four Southerners opposed Culberson with any consistency.[28]

Led by Culberson, Southerners also played a major role in crippling the efforts of labor to include in the Clayton Act explicit recognition of labor's claimed rights under the law. When Culberson's committee received the Clayton bill from the House it contained clauses (1) clearly limiting the issuance of restraining orders in labor disputes, (2) precluding a court interpretation of labor organizations *per se* as "conspiracies in restraint of trade," [29] and (3) prescribing trial by jury in contempt proceedings. When the committee released the bill, the first two clauses had been emasculated and the last had been omitted entirely. In the only roll call recorded in the

---

[26] Link, "The South and the 'New Freedom,' " 319.

[27] This is not the only evidence of the progressives' and the Southerners' reluctance to accept the New Nationalism. In an effort to exempt labor and farm organizations from the Sherman Antitrust Act, Congress attached a rider to the Sundry Civil Appropriations Bill of 1913 prohibiting the use of any money for prosecution of labor groups organized for the purpose of obtaining better wages or working conditions, or for anything "not in itself unlawful"; or of farm associations organized to maintain price levels. President Taft vetoed the bill, but it was reintroduced and passed almost immediately in the next Congress. Before passage in the Senate, a motion by Senator Jacob H. Gallinger, Republican of New Hampshire, to strike out the rider was defeated, 32–41; the progressive Republicans voted 8–3 for the motion. In the preceding debate Senator Norris of Nebraska pleaded that the measure was "an attempt . . . to differentiate between good trusts and bad trusts"; but his progressive colleague Borah replied with a sharp denunciation of price-fixing farm organizations and warned that it was "a very difficult matter" to determine when a trust became bad, and that creating supervisory federal bureaus to determine such matters invited a cumbersome, meddling government. In the end only La Follette, Norris, and Jones, among the progressives, voted against the Gallinger motion. *Cong. Record,* 63 Cong., 1 Sess., 1271, 1292.

[28] *Ibid.,* 63 Cong., 2 Sess., 13858, 13907, 14273, 14420–21, 14527.

[29] *American Year Book, 1914,* p. 16. Charles C. Carlin of Virginia, of the House Judiciary Committee, expressed his view to the President that the clause still did not exempt labor *acts* from such interpretations. Carlin to Wilson, about May 26, 1914, in Wilson Papers.

Senate only two Southerners joined with the progressives and some Northern Democrats in a vain attempt to replace the jury trial provision.[30]

Government control and operation of railroads had been one of the major demands of the agrarian rebels of the 1880's and 1890's, and had maintained its popularity among many progressives. On May 29, 1913, President Wilson wrote to Majority Leader Oscar W. Underwood of Alabama: "I am deeply interested in the passage of a bill authorizing the government to build a railroad in Alaska, and so soon as the pressure of Ways and Means work is off, I would very much value a conference with you." [31] Here was a measure close to the hearts of progressives and the "direct inheritors and . . . prime articulators in the Democratic party of the philosophy underlying the Agrarian crusade." [32]

In his first annual address Wilson requested an Alaskan railway system which "the Government should itself build and administer, and . . . ports and terminals [which] it should itself control in the interest of all who wish to use them for the service and development of the country and its people." [33] The bill was not a party measure, and so the Democrats were bound to no caucus pledge; although it still must be assumed that many simply followed the President's lead, those opposing the bill most probably expressed their genuine convictions on the role of the government in society. The issue of government participation in the railroad business was clearly drawn during the debate.

The bill passed the Senate 46–16, with 7 out of the 16 Southerners voting opposing it. The House passed the bill 232–86, with 49 of the 90 Southerners voting opposed. (The progressives in each house unanimously supported the act.) Of the 44 Southerners who harassed the administration in the Glass Act contest, 23 opposed the Alaska Act, only 11 favored it, and 10 abstained. Of the 11 for the act, only J. L. Eagle (Texas), Robert Henry (Texas), and P. E. Quin (Mississippi) had been consistently among the insurgents in the Glass Act fight, whereas a majority of the leading "radicals," including Slayden, Sisson, Wingo, Callaway, and Elder, opposed.[34]

By the end of 1914 the banking system, the tariff, and the trust laws had been drastically revised; the European war was contributing to the confusion and anxiety of depressed business; the President's patronage weapon was virtually exhausted so that his hold on Congress was considerably weakened; finally, the European conflict and a troublesome Mexican situation were absorbing more and more of Wilson's energy. Each or all of these facts may have led Wilson to indicate that he considered his major commitments to

---

[30] *Cong. Record*, 63 Cong., 2 Sess., 14417. Nathan P. Bryan of Florida and Vardaman were the two Southerners.

[31] Wilson to Oscar W. Underwood, May 29, 1913, in Wilson Papers.

[32] Link, "The South and the 'New Freedom,' " 316.

[33] *Cong. Record*, 63 Cong., 2 Sess., 45.   [34] *Ibid.*, 2250, 3646–47.

the electorate fulfilled and that he did not expect to push further domestic reforms.

With the President relinquishing the leadership of reform, only one major progressive bill passed Congress in 1915: La Follette's Seamen's Act. While the act was highly complex, causing serious international difficulties which would have killed any other bill and had already delayed this one several years, its popular human appeal served to dampen the opposition. Significantly, although the bill passed Congress with heavy majorities,[35] the only important opposition came from the South. From an examination of the debates on the bill and the roll calls on various motions and amendments, it is evident that eight Southern senators consistently opposed the popular measure, while eight supported it.[36] President Wilson signed the bill one day before the Sixty-Third Congress ended. Although it is true that he contemplated pocket-vetoing it, it is also true that until Secretary of State Bryan advised him that its safety provisions violated treaties with eighteen foreign powers, Wilson gave La Follette hearty encouragement.[37]

As the European war moved into its second year the Wilson administration came under increasingly heavy fire from Republicans and some non-office-holding Progressives (for example, Roosevelt and Albert J. Beveridge) for failing to take a firmer stand against German militarism; on the other hand, a large number of Democrats (especially from the South and the West) and the congressional progressives assailed the President for being "Anglophile" and for behaving too belligerently toward Germany. That year, nevertheless, Wilson regained both his will for leadership in domestic affairs and the power to enforce his will; for 1916 was an election year, and the mass of Democrats well knew that without President Wilson they had no hope of maintaining national power.

If the desire for victory kept the Democrats behind the President, Wilson's desire for re-election led him to make a series of moves designed to appeal to progressive-humanitarian interests. Wilson knew that unless he could capture the votes of the independent progressives, with whom labor and some farm interests had become associated in politics, his bid would fail. At the same time, the European war indirectly extended both the motive

---

[35] It passed both houses without a roll call—the Senate on October 23, 1913; the House on August 27, 1914, where at least a two-thirds vote was first necessary to suspend the rules in order to act on the motion for passage. *Ibid.*, 63 Cong., 1 Sess., 5791; *ibid.*, 63 Cong., 2 Sess., 14362.

[36] Various versions of the act had been pending for several years. *La Follette's Weekly*, March 29, 1913, pp. 14–15, contains three vote tabulations on the bill President Taft pocket-vetoed. See *Cong. Record*, 62 Cong., 3 Sess., 4587; *ibid.*, 63 Cong., 1 Sess., 5790, 5791; *ibid.*, 63 Cong., 3 Sess., 4817, for other roll calls especially the last, which records a vote on a last-minute crippler.

[37] For a fine brief statement on this matter see Link, *Wilson and the Progressive Era*, 61–63. Also cf. Baker, *Wilson, Life and Letters*, IV, 213, 364; Paul McKown, *Certain Important Domestic Policies of Woodrow Wilson* (Philadelphia, 1932), 82–83; Robert M. Lansing to Wilson, June 19, 1916, in Wilson Papers.

and the power of the administration to satisfy progressive demands, as the President found it necessary to center increasing power in the federal government.

President Wilson's nomination of Louis D. Brandeis to the Supreme Court on January 26, 1916, was the first of six major acts that year which appealed to progressive sentiment. For four months the Senate held up confirmation of the appointment while it conducted an unprecedented personal and professional inquiry. Leading the opposition among the Democrats were the Southerners, rebelling because Wilson had not consulted them in making the appointment, because they suspected it was a political appeal to the progressives (who currently were harassing the South on the child-labor issue), and because parts of the South, especially Georgia, had been whipped into an anti-Catholic and anti-Semitic frenzy, led by the old radical Tom Watson.[38] Party regularity ultimately prevailed, and on the final vote only one Democrat went on record against the President's nomination.

Wilson's nomination of the "radical" Brandeis marked no change in his attitude, for in 1913 he had to be dissuaded by his political advisers from naming Brandeis to his cabinet; if anything, the nomination indicated that Wilson's advisers had decided at last that, despite the South, in 1916 the Northern progressive vote must have prime consideration. On child-labor legislation, however, Wilson did reverse himself; as late as 1914 Wilson noted privately to his secretary, Joe Tumulty: ". . . in all frankness . . . no [federal] child labor law yet proposed has seemed to me constitutional." [39] Although, because of Southern opposition, a child-labor bill had languished in the Senate for almost four years, in 1916 it passed quickly once the President assumed leadership.

Southern representatives voted 41–43 against the bill that Wilson signed in 1916. Of the "radicals" of the Glass Act contest, 18 opposed child-labor legislation, while only 17 favored it. (Another four voted for the 1916 measure probably only because Wilson had demanded it; for previously they stubbornly opposed all federal legislation, including a 1913 bill designed simply to establish an investigatory Federal Children's Bureau.) Texas and Arkansas accounted for 76 per cent of those Southerners for federal legislation, although leading insurgent Oscar Callaway of Texas opposed all bills. In the Senate, four Southern textile states—North Carolina, South Carolina,

---

[38] Edward F. McClennen, Brandeis' law partner, wrote to Brandeis Attorney-General Thomas W. Gregory's advice "that no effort should be made by anyone which might arouse any suspicion that this appointment sprang from any 'Progressive' source or any other except purely Democratic. The strength is in Democratic party loyalty. . . . he believes activity by the Jews is not likely to help with Bourbon [Southern] Democrats. They know what this support means in the coming elections, without having it called to their attention." Alpheus T. Mason, *Brandeis: A Free Man's Life* (New York, 1946), 467–68. John K. Shields of Tennessee, Hoke Smith of Georgia, and Lee S. Overman of North Carolina led the Southern opposition.

[39] Link, *Wilson and the Progressive Era*, 59 n.

Georgia, and Alabama—plus Florida and Mississippi voted as a unit against all measures, although on the final vote in 1916 Underwood and Vardaman acquiesced. Only Thomas S. Martin and Claude A. Swanson of Virginia, Luke Lea and John K. Shields of Tennessee, Joseph T. Robinson of Arkansas, and Morris Sheppard of Texas consistently supported the reform.[40]

In his first annual address to Congress in December 1913 Wilson declared:

> The farmers, of course, ask and should be given no special privilege, such as extending to them the credit of the Government itself. . . . And yet the farmer does not stand upon the same footing with . . . [others] in the market of credit. He is the servant of the seasons. . . . He may give his note, but the season of its maturity depends upon the season when his crop matures. . . . And the security he gives is of a character not known in a broker's office or as familiarly as it might be on the counter of the banker. . . . Systems of rural credit have been studied and developed on the other side of the water while we left our farmers to shift for themselves in the ordinary money market.[41]

As we have seen, following the leadership of Carter Glass, Congress refused in 1913 to provide for long-term credits. Subsequent efforts to embody such provisions in a separate bill also failed—for which Wilson must bear heavy responsibility. For with the onset of the European war, the Mexican difficulties, and the business recession in 1914, the administration shied from further innovations and thus refused aid to the still vital reform currents. In the fall of 1914, however, Wilson did sign the Cotton Warehouse Act, which purported to facilitate better distribution of warehouses for (1) safer storage of crops throughout the nation and (2) better business methods in the handling of stored crops under license from the government, in order that warehouse receipts might be more readily acceptable as collateral for loans by banks.

If, in signing the bill, Wilson was yielding to the philosophy of the New Nationalism, the Southerners who pushed the bill were of a different mind. "It is emergency legislation," insisted Tom Heflin. "If the South were not in the distressed condition that she is [caused by the temporary shrinkage of the European market], and if the legislatures of the States were in session, we might go to the States and get this legislation." Although Heflin eventually won his point, he did not convince a large minority of the Southern "radicals" who voted against the bill because, as Robert Henry declared, it was "saturated, reeking, unduly intoxicated with rank federalism." [42]

In January 1916 Wilson was willing to go further than the warehouse

---

[40] There is no space here to present the roll calls and their significance on the various child-labor measures from 1912 on. See *Cong. Record*, 62 Cong., 2 Sess., 1578; *ibid.*, 63 Cong., 3 Sess., 3836; *ibid.*, 64 Cong., 1 Sess., 698, 2035, 12311, 12313.

[41] *Ibid.*, 63 Cong., 2 Sess., 44. One fourth of the entire message Wilson devoted to rural credits.

[42] *Ibid.*, 16204, 16210. Among the "radicals" who opposed the Warehouse Act were

measure provided—even to extend to the farmers "the credit of the government itself." Summoning Senator Hollis and Congressman Asbury F. Lever of South Carolina to the White House, he announced his support of their rural credits bill which had floundered in Congress for almost two years without administration support. The bill provided for the establishment of twelve farm loan banks, with the government purchasing up to $750,000 in bonds for the initial capital of each bank. What caused Wilson to endorse such a measure after insisting for years that it was "class legislation"?

One answer is provided by Wilson himself. In his third annual address the President declared that in order to prepare the country for mobilization, it was necessary to provide extensive borrowing facilities for farmers beyond those already provided by the Glass Act.[43] An equally important answer, however, is Wilson's desire for re-election and his need for the Western farm vote. Indeed, Wilson's summons to Hollis and Lever followed almost immediately a speech on January 9, 1916, by Frank G. Odell, secretary of the American Rural Credits Association, in which Odell stated: "The support of the farmers, which would be engaged by rural credits legislation, is necessary to the Democratic Party in the Middle West." [44]

Pressure from Southern interests could not have been crucial in Wilson's decision to press for rural credits act. He could hardly have feared the loss of Southern electoral votes. Moreover, if the Southerners had combined with the Western farm representatives any time before 1916, they might easily have forced Wilson to accept a rural credits system; instead, the project had to await administration leadership before it succeeded.

Another of Wilson's 1916 policy changes appealed to the Western farmers, while it antagonized the Southern agrarians. For years Western insurgents and Democrats in general, hoping to reduce the high and discriminatory tariff rates of Old Guard Republican design, had urged the creation of a nonpartisan tariff commission which could determine rates on a nonpolitical basis. Western farmers and progressives were nevertheless protectionists,[45]

Robert L. Henry, James L. Slayden, Thomas U. Sisson, and Samuel A. Witherspoon. By "radicals" I mean, as I have consistently meant in this paper in reference to the Southern congressmen, those who harassed the administration leaders on behalf of agrarian interests during the Glass Act debate.

[43] *Ibid.*, 64 Cong., 1 Sess., 99. Secretary of Agriculture David F. Houston, in his book *Eight Years with Wilson's Cabinet, 1913–1920* (2 vols., Garden City, 1926), I, gives the impression that the war emergency was principally responsible for the extension of the government's credit to the farmers.

[44] New York *Times*, January 10, 1916. William E. Gonzales, one of the leaders in Wilson's successful primary fight in South Carolina in 1912, wrote to Joseph P. Tumulty about the coming campaign: "Right now, it seems to me, is the time to catch the Progressives while their minds are open. . . . The National Committee should limit its efforts in the South to urging the newspapers to raise money; don't spend a stamp for anything else there." Gonzales to Tumulty, June 28, 1916, in Wilson Papers.

[45] See, for example, Robert M. La Follette's defense of the McKinley Tariff (which he had helped to write) in "The Farmer and the Tariff Bill," in *La Follette's Weekly*, December 14, 1912, pp. 1–2.

because they dealt largely in the domestic market. Southern cotton producers, on the other hand, depending chiefly on a foreign market, favored free trade. When the Old Guard fell in 1912, the triumphant Democrats bypassed demands for a commission; for President Wilson and the Democratic leaders favored a tariff for revenue only, and consequently had no use for a commission to adjust rates according to the marketing needs of American producers.

Although Wilson's sudden advocacy of a commission in January 1916 appealed to the progressives and Western farmers (as well as to Samuel Gompers and organized labor), and therefore may be considered a concession to them, we must not discard Wilson's own explanation that world conditions were changing so rapidly and unpredictably that a fact-finding and rate-adjusting commission was essential to carry out national policy.[46] Administration leaders feared that the commercial boom would collapse with the return of the European mercantile nations to peacetime trade and that Europe's surplus products would be "dumped" in the United States. In other words, Wilson's policy was not simply an election-year sop to the special interests of the West.

The European war (as well as the election campaign of 1916) created many circumstances with which the New Freedom, as originally conceived, proved inadequate to cope. With the disruption of international commerce in 1914, the revenue raised by the Underwood Tariff of 1913 could not meet government expenses; in the autumn Wilson called on Congress for an emergency revenue measure, suggesting traditional indirect taxes to raise the needed funds. The agrarians, especially the Southerners (who held the major committee posts), objected that additional excise taxes would hit hardest those who could least afford to pay, but since an income tax could not raise the money needed in the time required, Congress passed the administration's bill with no basic change.

It was natural for the South, where real estate still provided the major source of revenue, to lead in the drive for taxes on "intangible" wealth; not only had agrarians such as Claude Kitchin long fought for a national income tax, but many old-line Southern conservatives, from Joseph W. Bailey to John Sharp Williams, had been in the forefront of the fight. Although it is correct to say that the South led in the fight to increase income taxes during the first Wilson administration, it would be incorrect to mark Wilson as distinctly hostile to the idea. It is important to remember that Wilson had just forced through three great reform measures (plus the Alaska Railway Act, and repeal of the Panama Canal Tolls Act of 1911 in which he faced the opposition of almost every congressional leader); in addition, busi-

---

[46] See, for example, Wilson's explanation to the hostile Claude Kitchin of North Carolina, House majority leader. Wilson to Kitchin, January 26, 1916, in Wilson Papers. Pro-tariff business interests, of course, were quite as pleased as the Western farmers.

ness conditions were bad. The President preferred to consolidate his gains against the growing hostility and suspicion of conservative business.

In his third annual address, at the end of 1915, President Wilson again asked for additional revenues, this time advising: "We should be following an almost universal example of modern governments if we were to draw the greater part or even the whole of the revenues we need from the income taxes." [47] Congress responded by passing a bill in September 1916 which went far beyond the still conservative tax plan outlined by the administration. Instead of lowering the exempted income and surtaxable income levels, as Wilson requested, Congress doubled the tax rates and imposed a graduated estate tax. The revenue bill marked the first time the agrarians of the South and West (together with Northern labor representatives) successfully combined to press beyond the bounds set by the Wilson administration.[48]

Like the extended use of the income tax and other progressive innovations, the Adamson Act probably would not have passed except for the war in Europe. The act established the first federal eight-hour day law applying to nonfederal employment. In the summer of 1916 the four major railroad brotherhoods threatened to tie up the nation's railroad system unless demands for an eight-hour day and time and a half for overtime were met. Wilson stepped in to mediate a settlement. When the railroad managers refused Wilson's terms, the President went to Congress to enforce his settlement by legislative act. The act passed by almost a straight party vote.[49]

The Adamson Act was the last important domestic measure passed before the elections of 1916. It was symbolic of how far the Wilson administration had drifted from the original principles of the New Freedom. Apparently founded on principles requiring government abstinence in the unending struggle among contending interests in a free-market economy, the first Wilson administration culminated in a series of acts gauged to aid particular interests in their individual contentions. This paper has been devoted to the evolution of the change and to an analysis of the Southern contribution to it.

From the evidence, it is clear that both the radicalism of the Southern congressmen and the conservatism of Woodrow Wilson have been overestimated. It is also clear that the Southerners played a subordinate role in the Wilson administration's drift toward New Nationalism from 1913 to 1916.

As a group locally secure but long out of power nationally—and in low national repute—the Southern Democrats generally would not cross the one man who had a maximum of national respect and could give them the

---

[47] *Cong. Record,* 64 Cong., 1 Sess., 98.

[48] *Cf.* Link, *Wilson and the Progressive Era,* 192–96; Sidney Ratner, *American Taxation* (New York, 1942), 342–61.

[49] *Cong. Record,* 64 Cong., 1 Sess., 13655. The brotherhoods gave up their demands for time and a half for overtime.

rewards of national power.[50] Those Southerners who did oppose administration policies usually did so out of conservatism rather than radicalism. In one of the two most noteworthy exceptions to this fact—the opposition to the Glass bill—the "radical" Southerners won no important concessions from the administration; in the case of the income tax the Southern "radicals" successfully forced a progressive innovation upon a reluctant administration. In both cases, however, the term "radicals" must include many who were conservative and reactionary in all other instances. The term is justifiable only when it is understood that it does not necessarily represent a co-ordinated group within Congress, but simply those elements which, on various measures, favored further reforms. In fact, it is clear that whatever there was of a co-ordinated radical faction, its stable core was very small (perhaps fifteen or twenty congressmen), its periphery of drifters was highly mobile, and its political position was not consistently progressive.

Rather than being the masters of the administration's changing policy, the Southern congressmen were usually little more than the instruments of that policy. In almost every case, the immediate impulse for extending the government's power, authority, and credit on behalf of particular groups came from the administration in response to the exigencies of an impending national election and a world war. Wilson always subordinated his commitment to the New Freedom to his obligation—owed to himself, his country, and his party—to come out on top in both the international crisis and the election campaign of 1916. It was to fulfill this obligation that Wilson moved toward a more advanced progressivism during the years 1913–1916.

---

[50] The best example of this is the contest in 1913 over the repeal of the Panama Tolls Act, in which the mass of Southerners reversed themselves in deference to Wilson's wishes.

III

*The United States and
World War I, 1914–1917:
Did the Wilson Administration
Pursue a Policy of Neutrality?*

INTRODUCTION

Few aspects of American history since 1865 have been as productive of bitter argument among historians as the question of American entry into World War I and World War II. The debate has raged between those who have in the main defended the policies of the administrations in power when the United States became a belligerent in the two great wars and the so-called revisionists, who have been highly critical of the official version of how the nation became involved in war.

Following World War I the initiative in the evaluation of American neutrality between 1914 and 1917 was seized by the revisionists. Such writers as John K. Turner, Harry Elmer Barnes, and C. Hartley Grattan penned accounts of the American involvement in the war that were condemnatory of administration policy. (Professor Barnes' book, The Genesis of the World War, *was primarily concerned with the European origins of World War I, but Barnes also included a chapter on American intervention.) In the 1930's the revisionist case was most notably argued in books by Walter Millis, Edwin Borchard and William Potter Lage, and Charles C. Tansill.*

What has been called "the first historian's history of intervention" [1] *appeared in 1934, when Professor Charles Seymour's* American Diplomacy during World War I *was published. Seymour took issue with the revisionist position and pointed to the submarine as the chief cause for American entry into the war. Although new documentation has become available since Seymour wrote and although his view of American neutrality is regarded as too narrowly focused, Seymour's interpretation is considered to be basically sound by such recent defenders of Wilson's position as Professors Arthur S. Link and Ernest R. May.*

The revisionist position in the selections that follow is represented by Harry Elmer Barnes in a 1940 restatement of the thesis that he first presented in 1926. Barnes contends that the administration was far from neutral between 1914 and 1917, and he lays heavy stress on economic factors as the explanation for American entry into the war. Professor Link, by contrast, finds that Wilson was "substantially neutral in attitude" and that he strove desperately to the very end to keep the United States out of the war.

---

[1] Richard W. Leopold, "The Problem of American Intervention, 1917: An Historical Retrospect," *World Politics,* II (April 1950), 411.

The United States and the First World War

We may now consider the forces, factors, and personalities which brought the United States into the war.

The United States could not have been more perfectly set up for neutrality than it was in July and August, 1914. President Woodrow Wilson was a lifelong and deeply conscientious pacifist. His convictions in this matter were not emotional or impressionistic, but had been based upon deep study and prolonged reflection. Moreover, he was married to a woman noted for pacific sentiments and firm convictions on such matters. She strongly backed up her husband in his pacific beliefs and policies. As Secretary of State, we had in William Jennings Bryan the world's outstanding pacifist. His pacifism was notably courageous; he was willing to stick by his guns even in the face of malicious criticism.

Moreover, Wilson was almost uniquely well informed as to the essentials of the European situation before war broke out in the summer of 1914. He had sent his personal representative, Colonel Edward M. House, to Europe to study the international situation and to report to him upon it. Whatever his later mistakes, Colonel House sized up matters in Europe with almost perfect sagacity and understanding in May, 1914. He concluded his observations with the statement that "whenever England consents, France and Russia will close in on Germany."

If one were to summarize, as briefly as this, the outcome of the years of scholarly study since 1918, with respect to responsibility for the World War, a more perfect estimate and verdict than Colonel House's phrase could not be rendered in the same number of words. Further, the Colonel pointed out that, whatever the Kaiser's emotional shortcomings, he wished for European peace. On the other hand, he stated candidly that George V of England was "the most pugnacious monarch loose in these parts."

When war broke out, President Wilson's statements were a model of neutral procedure. He issued a formally correct neutrality proclamation and

From *War in the Twentieth Century*, Willard Waller (Editor), Copyright © 1940. Reprinted by permission of Holt, Rinehart and Winston, Inc., publishers. Pp. 71–82.

went on to exhort his countrymen to be neutral in thought as well as in action. There is no doubt that he was completely neutral at heart in August, 1914. Less than three years later, however, in April, 1917, he went before Congress and told its members that "God helping her," this country could do no other than make war on Germany. Moreover, he returned from the Capitol to the White House and made statements to his secretary, Joseph P. Tumulty, indicating that, at the time of his war message, he had so far changed his attitude that he could not believe he ever had been neutral. He cited with approval an article by the correspondent of the *Manchester Guardian* stating that Mr. Wilson had always been sympathetic with the Allies and had wished to throw this country into war on their side just as soon as circumstances would permit.

We shall first briefly consider some of the reasons why Wilson altered his point of view, since no other set of circumstances could alone have forced us into the war, if Wilson had not been favorable to our entry by the spring of 1917.

First and foremost, we must take into account the fact that Wilson's intellectual perspective was predominantly Anglo-Saxon. He had little knowledge of, or sympathy with, continental European culture and institutions. His great intellectual heroes were such English writers as John Milton, John Locke, Adam Smith and Walter Bagehot. He did his graduate work in the Johns Hopkins University Seminar under Herbert Baxter Adams, where the "Anglo-Saxon Myth" [1] reigned supreme. Wilson was a persistent student and admirer of the English constitution and frankly regarded the British system of government as superior to our own.

Then Wilson had in his cabinet and among his ambassadors men who were intensely pro-English or pro-Ally in their sympathies. Such were Secretaries Lindley M. Garrison and David F. Houston. Walter Hines Page, our ambassador in London, was even more intensely pro-English than Wilson. Indeed, he frequently went to such excesses as to annoy the President. When Bryan was succeeded by Robert Lansing, the most crucial post in the cabinet went to another vehemently pro-English sympathizer. The biases of Page and Lansing made it difficult to pursue forthright diplomacy with Great Britain.

Another major difficulty lay in the fact that President Wilson and Secretary Lansing did not formulate and execute a fair and consistent line of diplomatic procedure. They had one type of international law for England and the Allies, and quite another for Germany. They all but allowed Great Britain to run wild in the violation of international law and of our neutral rights, while they insisted on holding Germany "to strict accountability."

England started out in 1914 by making a scrap of paper out of the Decla-

---

[1] *I.e.*, the idea that American political ideals and liberties are a heritage from a racially pure Anglo-Saxon England.

ration of London governing contraband in wartime. Next, we proceeded to allow her to make use of armed belligerent merchantmen as if they were peaceful commercial vessels. England violated our neutral rights far more extensively between 1914 and 1917 than she did before the War of 1812, even to the point of flying the American flag.

Wilson came to believe, however, that Great Britain was fighting for civilization and that so trivial a thing as international law must not be allowed to stand in her way. Wilson's Attorney-General, Thomas W. Gregory, tells of the rebuke which the President administered to certain cabinet members when they protested over the flagrant British violation of our neutral rights: "After patiently listening, Mr. Wilson said, in that quiet way of his, that the ordinary rules of conduct had no application to the situation; that the Allies were standing with their backs to the wall, fighting wild beasts; that he would permit nothing to be done by our country to hinder or embarrass them in the prosecution of the war unless admitted rights were grossly violated, and that this policy must be understood as settled." Bryan protested against our unfair and unneutral diplomacy and ultimately resigned because he could not square his conscience with it.

Secretary Lansing admits in his *Memoirs* that he made no real pretense of holding England to the tenets of international law. He tells us that after the sinking of the *Lusitania* he thought we should be fighting on the side of the Allies and that he was determined to do nothing which would prove embarrassing to us when we later took up our position as a military comrade of the Allied powers. He persisted in this attitude, even though he was honest enough to write after the war that in 1917 we had as good, if not better, legal grounds for fighting Britain as for fighting Germany.

Ambassador Page even went so far as to collaborate with Sir Edward Grey in answering the protests of his own government, an unparalleled procedure which, when revealed, outraged even so pro-Ally a journal as the *New York Times*.

We thus encouraged and perpetuated the illegally extensive British blockade, which provoked the German submarine warfare. In time, we made war on the latter, though it was our unneutral diplomacy which contributed, in large part, to the continuance of both the British blockade and the German submarine activities.[2]

Wilson was deeply affected by the criticisms to which he was subjected by prominent Americans sympathetic with the Allies and in favor of intervention on their side. He was stung by the famous speeches of Theodore Roosevelt on "The Shadows of Shadow Lawn," and by the latter's reference to Wilson's diplomatic statements as examples of "weasel words." He was par-

---

[2] From the studies of Professor Charles C. Tansill and others, it would seem that on the rare occasions when President Wilson and Secretary Lansing became outraged over the grossest British violations of our neutrality, Colonel House invariably appeared on the spot to prevent even a show of firmness on the part of our State Department.

ticularly annoyed by the statement of Elihu Root that "first he shakes his fist and then he shakes his finger."

On the other hand, Wilson was human enough to take note of the praise which was showered upon him by the press when he made a bellicose statement or led a preparedness parade. This contrasted sharply with the bitter criticism he evoked when he made a statesmanlike remark, such as that a country might be "too proud to fight," or that the only desirable peace would be "a peace without victory."

Wilson was also profoundly moved by the British propaganda relative to German atrocities and territorial ambitions. This was particularly true after Lord Bryce lent his name to the prestige and veracity of the propaganda stories as to German savagery. Of all living Englishmen, Bryce was probably the man whom Wilson most admired and trusted. When Bryce sponsored the propaganda lies, Wilson came to believe that they must have a substantial basis in fact. This helped on his rationalization that England was fighting the battle of human civilization against wild beasts.

Personal matters also played their rôle in the transformation of Wilson's attitude. His first wife died and a strong pacific influence was removed. He then courted and married a dashing widow who was sympathetic with the Allied side and friendly with Washington military and naval circles. She was also bitterly resentful of the criticism to which Wilson was subjected on account of his refusal to be stampeded into intervention. She appears to have wished him to take a stronger stand for intervention. The domestic influence on the President was, thus, completely transformed in character as a result of his second marriage. The publication of Mrs. Wilson's *Memoirs* does not make it necessary to modify this statement.

When, as an outcome of these various influences, Wilson had been converted to intervention, he rationalized his change of attitude on the basis of a noble moral purpose. As he told Jane Addams in the spring of 1917, he felt that the United States must be represented at the peace conference which would end the World War if there was to be any hope of a just and constructive peace. But Wilson could be at the peace conference only if the United States had previously entered the World War.

It is still asserted by many writers, such as Professor Charles Seymour, that the resumption of submarine warfare by Germany was the sole reason for Wilson's determination to enter the war on the Allied side. But we know that he had been converted to intervention long before January, 1917. A year earlier, he had sent Colonel House to Europe with a plan to put us in the war on the side of the Allies if Germany would not accept peace terms obviously unfavorable to her. But even such peace terms for Germany were rejected by the British leaders, who felt sure of American aid anyway and were determined to crush Germany. Yet this British rebuff did not lead Wilson to lose heart in his efforts to put this country into the war.

His next step was taken in this country. Early in April,[3] 1916, Wilson called into consultation Speaker Champ Clark of the House of Representatives and Congressional leaders Claude Kitchin and H. D. Flood, and sounded them out to see if they would support him in a plan to bring the United States into the war on the side of the Allies. This was the famous "Sunrise Conference" described later by Gilson Gardner in *McNaught's Monthly* of June, 1925. These men sharply refused to sanction any such policy, and Wilson allowed the campaign of 1916 to be fought out on the slogan, "He kept us out of war." Wilson did not dare to risk splitting the Democratic Party over entry into the war before the campaign of 1916 had successfully ended. The existence of the "Sunrise Conference" has been fully verified by Professor A. M. Arnett in his scholarly book on Claude Kitchin.[*]

Wilson was convinced after the failure of the "Sunrise Conference" that there was no hope of getting the country into war until after the election. The sentiment of the nation was for peace. If he was elected as an exponent of peace and then went into war the country as a whole would believe that he had done his best to "keep us out of war." He would have a united country behind him. Hence, he and Colonel House sent Governor Martin Glynn of New York and Senator Ollie James of Kentucky to the Democratic National Convention at St. Louis, in June, 1916, with instructions to make keynote speeches emphasizing Wilson's heroic efforts to keep us out of war.[†]

Thus was fashioned the famous slogan "He kept us out of war," which re-elected Woodrow Wilson to the presidency almost a year after Colonel House, following Wilson's directions, had declared that: "The United States would like Great Britain to do whatever would help the United States to aid the Allies." [4]

The campaign and election of 1916 were very really a referendum on war, and the people voted against war. This is illuminating as an illustration of the fallacy that a war referendum, such as the Ludlow Amendment,[‡] would,

---

[3] Professor Tansill believes that this conference was probably held in February rather than April. I still incline to credit the April date.

[*] Editor's note: Arthur S. Link has made it clear that the date of the conference was February 25. He insists that there is no "reliable" evidence that the President suggested that he desired American entry into the war. Wilson, in reply to questioning, simply declared that if an armed ship were torpedoed with a loss of American life, he would break relations with the Central Powers, and he had been told that this might lead to war. He indicated, however, that it was peace, not war, that he sought. Link, *Woodrow Wilson and the Progressive Era, 1910–1917* (New York: Harper & Brothers, 1954), pp. 212–13.

[†] Editor's note: The emphasis on the peace theme at the convention was not the result of Wilson's planning, according to Arthur Link. Link, *Wilson and the Progressive Era*, pp. 233–34.

[4] Grey of Fallodon, *Twenty-five Years*, Vol. II, p. 127; and B. J. Hendrick, *The Life and Letters of Walter Hines Page*, Vol. III, p. 279.

[‡] Editor's note: The Ludlow Amendment, a proposed amendment to the federal Constitution sponsored in the mid-1930's by Representative Louis Ludlow of Indiana, pro-

by itself alone, suffice to keep us out of war, but the election of 1916 does offer definite proof that Wilson was not pushed into war by popular demand.

The influence exerted by American finance upon our entry into the World War has been revealed in Ray Stannard Baker's *Life and Letters of Woodrow Wilson,* in the volumes of the Nye armament investigation, and in Professor C. C. Tansill's *America Goes to War.*

At the outset, the international bankers were not by any means all pro-Ally. Some, like the Morgan firm, were pro-British, and had been for years, while others, like Kuhn, Loeb and Company, manned chiefly by men of German derivation, were pro-German. But the financial interests of all the bankers soon came to be pro-Ally, for credit and loans to Germany were discouraged, while large loans were presently being made to the Allied powers.

On August 15, 1914, at the beginning of the war, Bryan declared against loans to any belligerent, on the ground that credit is the basis of all forms of contraband. President Wilson backed him up. For the time being, this position did not operate seriously against the Allies, for the balance of trade and investment was against the United States, and the Allied countries could pay for their purchases by cancelling the debts owed abroad by Americans. This situation took care of matters for a few months. But Allied war purchases became so great that, by the autumn of 1914, there was a credit crisis. The National City Bank addressed Robert Lansing, then Counsellor of the State Department, on this matter on October 23, 1914. Short-term credits to European governments were advocated. Lansing talked the matter over with President Wilson at once, and the latter agreed that the government would not interfere with such an arrangement. This information was transmitted orally to Willard Straight of J. P. Morgan & Company at the Metropolitan Club in Washington on the same night.

Shortly afterwards, H. P. Davison of the Morgan firm went to England and signed a contract to become the British purchasing agent in America. A similar contract was soon made with France.

The short-term loans sufficed for some months, but by the summer of 1915 Allied buying had become so extensive that the bankers saw that they must float loans here for the Allied countries if the latter were to continue to buy American munitions on a large scale. So they made strong representations to Colonel House and to the Secretary of the Treasury, W. G. McAdoo.

On August 21, 1915, McAdoo wrote a long letter to President Wilson, pointing out that great prosperity had come to the country as a result of the sale of munitions to the Allies, but that this prosperity could not continue unless we financed it through open loans to the Allies—i.e. selling Allied bonds in our own financial markets.

---

vided that Congress could not declare war, unless the United States or its possessions had been invaded, until a nation-wide referendum on the subject had been approved by majority vote.

On September 6, 1915, Secretary Lansing argued similarly in a letter to President Wilson, stressing the crisis that faced American business if the earlier ruling of Bryan and the President on American loans to belligerents was not rescinded. Colonel House supported this position. McAdoo and Lansing won their point. On September 8, 1915, Wilson assented to loans and the Morgan firm was once more given oral information. Very soon, the first public loan, the $500,000,000 Anglo-French loan, was floated.

The formal loans to the Allies—over $2,500,000,000 in all—financed their purchases for a little over a year, but their buying was so heavy that even the great investment banking houses could not take care of their needs. By January, 1917, the Allies had overdrawn their credit by nearly $500,000,000. Only Uncle Sam could save the great banking houses and the Allies. And Uncle Sam could help only if the United States were at war with Germany. We could not, as a government, lend money to a belligerent, unless we were at war with its enemy.

Just at this time the Germans renewed their unrestricted submarine warfare. The United States could now be led into the war, and the bankers would be repaid. They were repaid to the last cent. When the war was over, Mr. Thomas W. Lamont, of J. P. Morgan and Company, stated the facts relative to the attitude of his firm toward the World War and the belligerent powers:

> At the request of certain of the foreign governments the firm of Messrs. J. P. Morgan and Company undertook to co-ordinate the requirements of the Allies, and then to bring about regularity and promptness in fulfilling these requirements. Those were the days when American citizens were being urged to remain neutral in action, in word, and even in thought. But our firm had never for one moment been neutral: we didn't know how to be. From the very start we did everything we could to contribute to the cause of the Allies. And this particular work had two effects: one in assisting the Allies in the production of goods and munitions in America necessary to the Allies' vigorous prosecution of the war; the other in helping to develop the great and profitable export trade that our country has had.[5]

Most American industrialists naturally shared the attitude of the bankers. Since England controlled the seas, our sales were mainly to the Allied powers. We wished to see the Allies continue the war and win it. Upon their purchases depended most of our sales and prosperity, and upon their success and solvency depended the prospect of their being able to pay us in the end. The trade in munitions carried us from a depression in 1914 to boom years in 1915 and 1916.[6]

---

[5] *Manchester Guardian,* January 27, 1920.

[6] There has been much dispute as to whether we were forced into war by the loans and sales to the Allies or by the resumption of German submarine warfare early in 1917. In an important article in *Science and Society* (Spring, 1939) on "Neutrality and

By abandoning his neutral financial and industrial policy in favor of the Allies, President Wilson made it possible for the Entente Powers to enjoy an enormous advantage over the Central Powers in getting war supplies. The only way for the Central Powers to overcome it was to resume unlimited submarine warfare and try to sweep from the seas the ships that were carrying these supplies to the Allies.

It was our unneutral financing of the Allies that led to the resumption of German submarine warfare, and it was the resumption of this warfare which furnished the "incident" that enabled the war party in this country to put us into the conflict. It is, thus, perfectly clear that economic and financial pressure was the crucial factor which led us into war in 1917.

But no one need hold that President Wilson was moved primarily by any tender sentiments for the bankers. Both McAdoo and Lansing argued that it was essential to American prosperity to finance the Allies.

It was this general consideration of continued prosperity in 1915–16, and the relation of this to the prospects of the Democratic Party in the election of 1916, rather than any direct banker pressure on the White House, that bore in on Wilson's consciousness in the late summer of 1915, when he let down the gates to financing the Allies.

Yet, it is downright silly to contend that the bankers had no influence on Wilson's policy. If he did not listen to the bankers himself, he did listen very attentively to those who did heed banker pressure, namely, McAdoo, Lansing and House.

The active campaign for American preparedness and intervention was engineered by leaders of the war cult in the United States, such men as Theodore Roosevelt, Leonard Wood, Henry Cabot Lodge, "Gus" Gardiner, and the like. They led in the preparedness movement, the Plattsburg camp episode, and other steps designed to stimulate the martial spirit in America. The newspapers warmly supported this movement because of the circulation appeal which preparedness material supplied.

While there were notable exceptions, the majority of our newspapers were pro-Ally and pro-interventionist. Many of them were honestly sympathetic with the Allies. Others were deeply influenced by Allied propaganda. Some were heavily subsidized by the Allies. Still others were bought outright by Allied interests. Moreover, the Allies supplied all American newspapers with a vast amount of war-news material always favorable to the Allied cause. The newspapers also had a natural affinity for the bankers and industrialists who were their chief advertising clients. Finally, the newspapers were not unaware of the enormous circulation gains and increased advertising revenue which would follow our entry into the World War.

In the matter of propaganda the Allies had a notable advantage. They

Economic Pressures, 1914–1917" Professor Paul Birdsall shows that the two were inseparably tied together.

controlled the seas, the cables, and other means of communication. The Germans had only one crude and temporary wireless contact with the United States. Further, Allied propaganda was far better organized and more lavishly supported. It was also much more adroit than the German. As a result, a majority of Americans were led to believe in the veracity of the great batch of atrocity lies relative to the German invasion of Belgium, submarine warfare, and the like. This was particularly true after Lord Bryce put the force of his name and prestige behind the authenticity of such tales. Lord Northcliffe, who was in charge of British propaganda, in moments of unusual candor, stated that the Americans proved more gullible in such matters than any other people except the Chinese and called us "a bunch of sheep."

The ministers of the gospel also joined heartily in the great crusade to put us into the World War. Lining up behind such a stalwart as Newell Dwight Hillis, they preached a veritable holy war. They represented the Allies as divinely-anointed promoters of international decency and justice and the Central Powers as the servants of evil and the agents of savagery.

The net result of all this was that we entered the World War in April, 1917. We did so, even though there was no clear legal or moral basis for our so doing. If there ever was an instance in which the facts were clearly in accord with a neutrality policy it was in the spring of 1917. We should have fought both Germany and Britain or else neither. But the country went into war, with most of the citizens of the United States feeling that our self-respect and national honor demanded it. No other course seemed open to us.

Wilson and American Neutrality, 1914–1917

Arthur S. Link

WILSON AND THE PROBLEMS OF NEUTRALITY

For Woodrow Wilson and the American people, who had a positive disinclination to play the game of power politics, events on the international

From Arthur S. Link, *Wilson the Diplomatist* (Baltimore: The Johns Hopkins Press, 1957), pp. 31–90 *passim*. Reprinted by permission. The over-all title for the two chapters from this book was supplied by the editor.

stage intruded in an ironic if fateful way from 1914 to 1917. By the spring of 1915 the United States was the only great power not directly involved in the war then raging from western Europe to the Far East. Desiring only to deal fairly with both sides and to avoid military involvement, the President soon found that neutrality, as well as war, has its perplexities and perils.

The way in which Wilson met the challenges to America's peace and security raised by the death grapple between the opposing alliances has never been fully explained, notwithstanding scores of books and articles. Too often, historians, in company with public men, have looked for culprits instead of facts. Too often they have misunderstood the facts even when they found them. Too often they have written as if Wilson and his advisers made policy in a vacuum independent of the interplay of conflicting pressures. If we can see the President's policies of neutrality in the light of his convictions and objectives, the pressures and events (both domestic and foreign) that bore constantly upon him, and the alternatives between which he was often forced to choose—if we can do this, then perhaps we will see that his task in foreign policy at this juncture was not as simple as it has sometimes been described.

Among the most pervasive pressures controlling Wilson's decisions throughout the period 1914–1917 were the attitudes and opinions of the American people concerning the war and America's proper relation to it. Few presidents in American history have been more keenly aware of risks that the leader runs when he ceases to speak for the preponderant majority. "The ear of the leader must ring with the voices of the people. He cannot be of the school of the prophets; he must be of the number of those who studiously serve the slow-paced daily need." Thus Wilson had written in 1890;[1] thus he believed and practiced while formulating his policies toward the belligerents in the First World War.

The dominant American sentiment throughout the period of nonintervention can be summarily characterized by the single adjective "neutral." This is not to say that Americans had no opinions on the merits of the war and the claims of the opposing alliances, or that there were no differences among the popular reactions. It is simply to state the fairly obvious fact that the preponderant majority, whose opinions played a decisive role in shaping Wilson's policies, did not believe that their interests and security were vitally involved in the outcome of the war and desired to avoid participation if that were possible without sacrificing rights that should not be yielded. The prevalence and astounding vitality of neutralism, in spite of the severest provocations and all the efforts of propagandists on both sides, formed at once the unifying principle of American politics and the compelling reality with which Wilson had to deal from 1914 to 1917.

On the other hand, it would be a large error to imply that Wilson was a

---

[1] T. H. Vail Motter (ed.), *Leaders of Men* (Princeton, N. J., 1952), p. 43.

prisoner of the public opinion of the majority, and that his will to adopt sterner policies toward one group of belligerents or the other was paralyzed by the stronger counterforce of neutralism. Actually, the evidence points overwhelmingly to the conclusion that Wilson personally shared the opinions of the majority, in brief, that he was substantially neutral in attitude, and that his policies were controlled as much by his own convictions as by the obvious wishes of the people. . . .

It followed in Wilson's mind . . . that all the belligerents shared to some degree in the responsibility for the war and that one could not ascribe all blame to one side or the other. Nor could one use simple explanations in talking about conflicting war objectives. It was clear to Wilson that all the belligerents sincerely believed that they were fighting for their existence, but that all of them desired a smashing victory in order to enhance their power, win new territory, and impose crushing indemnities upon their enemies. Because this was true, Wilson reasoned, the best kind of settlement would be a stalemate in which neither alliance would have the power to impose terms upon the other.

In his fundamental thinking about war in general, moreover, Wilson shared in a remarkable way the assumptions of the majority of Americans. Like most of his fellow-citizens, he abhorred the very thought of using violence to achieve national objectives; indeed, he was reluctant to use even the threat of force in diplomacy. Like the Socialists, independent radicals, and a large majority of southern and western farmers, he suspected that the financiers and industrialists favored preparedness and a strong foreign policy in order to increase profits and provoke a war that would end the reform movement at home. Like the majority of Americans, he was willing to think of fighting only as a last resort and then only as a means of defending rights that no civilized nation could yield.

Fortified by these convictions, Wilson struggled hard and on the whole successfully to be impartial in thought as well as in deed, as he had asked the American people at the outbreak of the war to do. In fact, he succeeded in this impossible undertaking far better than most of his contemporaries and his historical critics. His method was to rely upon the general assumptions that he was sure were sound and then virtually to seal himself off from the passionate arguments and indictments of partisans of either alliance, by simply refusing to listen to them. "I recall," Secretary Lansing afterward wrote, for example, "that . . . his attitude toward evidence of German atrocities in Belgium and toward accounts of the horrors of submarine warfare . . . [was that] he would not read of them and showed anger if the details were called to his attention." [2]

This does not mean that Wilson was able completely to subordinate emotional reactions and personal feelings. Like the majority of Americans, he

---

[2] The Diary of Robert Lansing, November 20, 1921, MS in the Library of Congress.

was to a degree pro-British; on two, perhaps three, occasions during the two and a half years of American neutrality he avowed to close friends his personal sympathy for the Allied cause. But it would be a difficult task to prove that Wilson's pro-British sympathies were ever controlling or indeed even very strong. At no time did he act like a man willing to take measures merely to help his supposed friends. On the contrary, all his policies were aimed either at averting American participation on Britain's side or at ending the war on terms that would have denied the spoils of victory to Britain and her allies. If this is too big an assertion to be taken on faith, then perhaps the reasons for making it will become apparent as we see the way in which Wilson executed policies toward the two leading antagonists.

All authorities, whether friendly or hostile to Wilson, would agree that the acid tests of his neutrality were the policies that he worked out and applied vis-à-vis the British from 1914 to 1917. He has been most condemned by that group of historians highly censorious of his policies, generally known as revisionists, on this score—for becoming the captive of pro-Allied influences within his administration, for condoning such sweeping British control of neutral commerce that the Germans were forced to resort to drastic countermeasures, for permitting American prosperity to become dependent upon loans and exports to the Allies, in short, for permitting a situation to develop that made it inevitable that the United States would go to war if the success of Allied arms was ever seriously threatened.

Like most fallacious arguments, this one contains a certain element of plausibility. Wilson did condone a far-reaching British maritime system. American neutrality did work greatly to the benefit of the Allies. The error arises in saying that these things occurred because Wilson and his advisers necessarily wanted them to occur.

Perhaps the best way to gain a clear understanding of why Anglo-American relations developed as they did from 1914 to 1917 is to see how the policies that decisively shaped those relations emerged in several stages in response to certain pressures, events, and forces. The first stage, lasting from August, 1914, to about August, 1915, was in many ways the most critical, because the basic American response to the war and to the British maritime system was formulated then. That response was governed in the first instance by two domestic realities: the overwhelming, virtually unanimous, American desire to be neutral, and the pressures in the United States for a large measure of free trade with Britain's enemies.

In view of the prevailing American sentiment at the outbreak of the war, a policy of strict official neutrality was the only possible course for the United States government. This fact prompted the President's official proclamations of neutrality, supplemented by his appeal to the American people for impartiality in thought; the subsequent working out by the State Department of the elaborate technical rules to preserve American neutrality;

and the establishment of a Joint State and Navy Neutrality Board to advise the various departments upon the correct interpretation of international law.

One cannot read the records revealing how these policies were formulated without being convinced that their authors were high-minded in their determination to be fair to both sides. Indeed, Wilson and the man who chiefly influenced him in the formulation of the rules of neutrality, Secretary of State Bryan, were so intent upon being fair to the Germans that they adopted policies during the first months of the war that were highly disadvantageous to the British, if not unneutral. One was to prevent the sale of submarine parts, and hence parts for any naval craft, by a private American firm to the British government, on the ground that such a sale would be "contrary to . . . strict neutrality." Wilson persisted in supporting Bryan in this matter, in spite of advice from Counselor Lansing and the Joint Neutrality Board to the effect that their position was contrary to international law.

Infinitely more damaging to the Allies was the administration's second effort to lean over backward in being "strictly" neutral—the ban of loans by American bankers to the belligerent governments that the President permitted Bryan to impose in August, 1914. From a technical viewpoint, the ban was not unneutral, but it was highly prejudicial to the Allies because its effect was potentially to deny them their otherwise legal right to purchase supplies in the American market. These two incidents are not to be understood as revealing any anti-British bias on the part of Wilson and Bryan, although British officials at the time were convinced that they did. I mention them only to show what an important role the administration's desire to be impartial played in the formation of policies vis-à-vis the British during the early period of American neutrality.

The other pressure shaping American policies at this time was the force of combined demands at home for the virtually free transit of American ships and goods to the European neutrals and the belligerent Central Powers. So powerful were these demands, especially from cotton growers and exporters and their spokesmen in Congress, that Wilson personally sponsored two measures highly disadvantageous to the British and unneutral in fact as well as in spirit. One was a change in the ship registry law, put into effect by an act approved August 18, 1914, which made it easy for German or other foreign shipping firms to take out American registry for their vessels. The other was a plan to establish a federal corporation to purchase German ships in American ports and to use them to carry supplies to the belligerents, particularly to Germany. Wilson applied heavy pressure to obtain congressional approval of this, the so-called ship-purchase bill, during the short term from December, 1914, to March, 1915; he failed only because of a stout senatorial filibuster.

In negotiations with the British government during the early months of the war, Wilson fought hard in response to domestic pressures to keep the channels of international commerce open to American ships and goods. He did not go as far in defense of neutral rights as some of his predecessors, but he did suggest a code so sweeping that an enforcement of it would have meant almost total destruction of the British system of maritime controls. Specifically, the President first proposed on August 6, 1914, that the belligerents adopt the rules of naval warfare laid down in the Declaration of London of 1909, a convention never ratified by Great Britain or the United States, which permitted the free transit of all goods except those obviously contraband. When the British rejected this suggestion, the President came back on October 16, proposing a compromise that would have still seriously impaired the effectiveness of British sea power. When this effort also failed, Wilson then announced that his government would assert and defend all its rights under international law and treaties.

I have described these policies and proposals because they so clearly reveal Wilson's neutral intentions and what he would have done in matters of trade had he been able to make the rules himself. But he obviously could not follow his personal preferences alone or respond only to domestic pressures. In seeking to assert and defend American neutral rights he ran head-on into a reality as important as the reality of the pressures at home. It was the British determination to use sea power to prevent American ships and goods from going to the sustenance of the German economy and military forces.

British assumption of a nearly absolute control of the seas washing western Europe began with relatively mild measures in August, 1914, and culminated in the suppression of virtually all commerce to the Central Powers in March, 1915. For the British, this was not a question of adhering to the laws of blockade or of violating them, or of doing things merely to be nice to American friends. It was a question of achieving their supreme objective, to deprive their enemies of vital raw materials and goods, without risking the alienation of the United States. The controlling fact for the British was the necessity of preserving American friendship, in order to assure the uninterrupted rhythm of the North Atlantic trade. As the British Foreign Secretary at the time frankly put it:

> Blockade of Germany was essential to the victory of the Allies, but the ill-will of the United States meant their certain defeat. . . . It was better therefore to carry on the war without blockade, if need be, than to incur a break with the United States about contraband and thereby deprive the Allies of the resources necessary to carry on the war at all or with any chance of success. The object of diplomacy, therefore, was to secure the maximum of blockade that could be enforced without a rupture with the United States.[3]

---

[3] Viscount Grey of Fallodon, *Twenty-Five Years, 1892–1916* (2 vols.; New York, 1925), II, 107.

The crucial question all along, therefore, was whether the United States, the only neutral power strong enough successfully to challenge the British measures, would acquiesce or resist to the point of threatening or using force. The American response during the formative period of neutrality was, in brief, to accept the British system and to limit action against it to a vigorous assertion of American legal rights for future adjudication. All this is too well known to require any further exposition. What is not so well understood are the reasons why Wilson and his advisers acquiesced in a solution that denied the objectives that they and a large segment of the American public demanded. These reasons may be briefly summarized, as follows:

First, the British maritime system, in spite of American allegations to the contrary, enjoyed the advantage of being legitimate and usually legal, or nearly so, by traditional criteria. It was legitimate rather than fraudulent, and legal rather than capricious or terroristic, in its major aspects because the British did in fact hold undisputed sea supremacy and were therefore able to execute their controls in an orderly fashion. In asserting their own rights, the Americans could not well deny the advantages that accrued to the British by virtue of their sea power. The British, for example, had an undoubted right to establish a blockade of the Central Powers, and the American attempt to persuade the London government to use techniques effective only in the days of the sailing ship did not have much cogency in the twentieth century.

Second, much of the success of the British in establishing their control depended upon the way in which they went about it. Had they instituted their total blockade at the outset of the war, the American reaction would undoubtedly have been violent. Instead, the British applied their controls gradually, with a careful eye upon American opinion, using the opportunities provided by recurrent crises in German-American relations to institute their severest measures.

Third, the British were careful never to offend so many American interests at one time that retaliation would have been inevitable, or any single interest powerful enough by itself to compel retaliation. There was the case of cotton, which the officials in London were determined to prevent from going to Germany because it was an ingredient of gunpowder. Not until a year after the war began did they put cotton on the list of absolute contraband; even then they went to the extraordinary length of underwriting the entire American cotton market in order to avert an irresistible southern pressure in Congress for retaliation.[4] In addition, although they were ruthless in enforcing their blockade, the British took careful pains to avoid any serious injury to American property interests. They confiscated only the most obvious contraband; in all doubtful cases they paid full value for

---

[4] For a full discussion, see my "The Cotton Crisis, the South, and Anglo-American Diplomacy, 1914–1915," in J. C. Sitterson (ed.), *Studies in Southern History in Memory of Albert Ray Newsome, 1894–1951* (Chapel Hill, N. C., 1957), pp. 122–38.

cargoes or ships seized. Their objective was to control, not to destroy, American commerce.

Fourth, there was great significance in the language and symbolism that the British Foreign Office used in defending the measures of the Admiralty and Ministry of Blockade. By justifying their maritime system in terms of international law and the right of retaliation, and (at least before the summer of 1916) by making an honest effort to meet American objections half way when possible, the British made it almost inevitable that the Washington authorities would have to reply in the same language, thus giving a purely *legal* character to the issues involved and for the most part avoiding raising the issues of sovereignty and inherent national rights. The significance of this achievement can be seen in the conviction of Wilson and the majority of Americans that the Anglo-American disputes did involve only property rights, which should be vindicated only by an appeal to much-controverted international law. Moreover, by appealing to the American government and people in the name of friendship and by always professing their devotion to the cause of humanity, the British succeeded in evoking strong feelings of sympathy and understanding on the other side of the water.

Finally, the British were able partially to justify their own blockade measures as legitimate adaptations to a changing technology by pointing to precedents established by the Washington government itself during the American Civil War. To be sure, the British drew some incorrect analogies (as Lansing pointed out) between American and British practice; even so, their main contention—that the American government had also stretched the rules of blockade to allow for technological changes—was essentially correct.

Wilson's refusal to challenge the British maritime system, in short, to break the British blockade, was almost inevitable in view of the facts we have just reviewed, *if the President's objective was simply to maintain as best he could the neutral position of the United States.* An absolute neutrality was in any event impossible because of the total character of the war and America's importance in the world economy. It often happened that any action by the United States inevitably conferred a benefit on one side and thereby injured the other, at least indirectly. In these circumstances, neutrality often consisted of doing the things that would give the least unwarranted or undeserved advantages.

By this standard, it would have been more unneutral than neutral for Wilson to have broken the British maritime system by enforcing highly doubtful technical rights under international law. Judged by practical standards rather than by the often conflicting criteria of neutrality, Wilson's acceptance of the British system seems realistic and wise—indeed, the only choice that he could have made in the circumstances. This is true because the results of destroying the British blockade would have been the wrecking of American friendship with the two great European democracies and the probable victory of the Central Powers, without a single compensating gain for the interests and security of the United States. Only the sure achievement of some great political objective like a secure peace settlement, certainly not the winning of a commercial advantage or the defense of doubtful neutral rights, would have justified Wilson in undertaking a determined challenge to British sea power.

The second stage in Anglo-American relations, lasting from the summer of 1915 to the late spring of 1916, saw the development of the natural economic consequence of the American adjustment to tightening British control of the seas. That consequence was the burgeoning of an enormous war trade between the United States and the Allies. The United States became the storehouse and armory of the Allies neither because there was any conspiracy on the part of certain pro-Allied leaders in Washington to make American prosperity dependent upon an Allied victory, nor because American businessmen and bankers were willing to incur the risks of war in order to increase their profits. The United States became the storehouse of the Allies for the simple reason that Great Britain and not Germany controlled the seas.

The war trade itself was entirely neutral. Indeed, any action by the United States government to impede it, unless undertaken for overriding political motives, would have been grossly prejudicial and unneutral. If it had been permitted to develop in a normal way, this commerce would have raised no important problems in the relations of the United States with the Allies. A problem of the first magnitude did arise, however, because the President, in the summer of 1914, had permitted Secretary Bryan to enforce his own private moral views by imposing a ban on loans by American bankers to the belligerents.

There was no difficulty so long as the British and French governments could find gold and dollars to settle their adverse trade balances. By the summer of 1915, however, Allied gold and dollar resources were near the point of exhaustion; and American insistence upon a continuation of cash payments could result only in gravely damaging the Allied economies and ending the North Atlantic trade altogether. Credit could be found only in the United States, but credit meant floating loans, and loans to the belligerents were as much a political as an economic question because of the existence of Bryan's ban.

It is well known that the State Department under Bryan's direction substantially relaxed its credit embargo during the spring of 1915 and that Wilson and Bryan's successor, Lansing, lifted the ban altogether a few months later, at a time when the credit needs of the Allied governments were demonstrably acute. Even though the full facts bearing upon this matter have been available to scholars for more than twenty years, the reasons for the administration's reversal are still not properly understood.

Bryan's ban could not survive the development of the war trade on a large scale because, in the first place, it (like the Embargo of 1808) was potentially nearly as disastrous to the United States as to the Allies. American material well-being was in large measure dependent upon foreign trade, and particularly upon trade with the Allied world. Such trade was possible during wartime only if American businessmen were willing to do for the Allies what they always did for solvent customers in temporary straits, namely, sell them goods on credit.

The most important reason that Bryan's embargo could not survive, however, was that it was an essentially unneutral policy that impeded the growth of the chief economic consequence of American neutrality, the legitimate war trade. The credit embargo and the war trade could not both survive. The former gave way because Wilson finally realized that it would be as unneutral to interfere with the extension of credit as it would be to stop the flow of goods. Bryan's ban was in a sense, therefore, a casualty chiefly of American neutrality. . . .

The second stage in Anglo-American relations also witnessed the apparent convergence of the diplomatic policies of the two countries on the high level. During the summer and autumn of 1915 Colonel Edward M. House, Wilson's confidant and principal adviser on foreign policy, conceived a plan by which the American and British leaders would join hands to press for an end to the war through Wilson's mediation. The British Foreign Secretary, Sir Edward Grey, replied that his government would cooperate only if the Washington administration were willing to go beyond simple mediation and would agree to join a postwar international organization established for the purpose of effecting disarmament, maintaining freedom of the seas, and preserving peace. Wilson hopefully consented, and House went to Berlin, Paris, and London in January, 1916, to lay the diplomatic basis of mediation.

In London, House worked out in documentary form with Grey and the other members of the British Cabinet the specific terms of Anglo-American co-operation. Initialed by House and Grey on February 22, 1916, and known as the House-Grey Memorandum or Agreement, this document declared that President Wilson was ready, upon hearing from England and France that the time was ripe, to propose that a conference be called to end the war. Should the Allies accept and Germany refuse the invitation, the United States would "probably" enter the war against Germany. Should the conference meet and Germany refuse to accept a reasonable settlement, then the United States would also "probably" enter the war on the Allied side.

To the so-called revisionists the conclusion of the House-Grey Agreement is irrefutable proof that Wilson had abandoned neutrality and meant to take the country into war at the first opportunity. To remove all doubt that this was true, they point to what happened during the weeks immediately following the initialing of the agreement.

While House had been carrying his negotiations in London to a success-ful conclusion, Wilson and Lansing had undertaken to avert the possibility of conflict with Germany over the issue of submarine attacks against armed merchantmen by proposing that the Allies disarm their merchant ships and that U-boats follow the old rules of cruiser warfare in attacking them. Using the President's suggestion as a pretext, the German authorities announced on February 10, 1916, that submarines would attack *armed* enemy merchant-men without warning after February 29. Then without warning Wilson and Lansing reversed themselves and announced that the American government would insist upon the right of Americans to travel on ships defensively armed and would hold the German government to strict account for the loss of any American lives on armed merchantmen. Adhering doggedly to this position in the face of a threatened rebellion in Congress, the President pro-ceeded to use the opportunity afforded by the torpedoing without warning of the French Channel packet *Sussex* by a German submarine, "in contra-vention of earlier pledges," to threaten a break in diplomatic relations with Germany and to force the Imperial government to make sweeping conces-sions in its conduct of submarine warfare.

To the revisionist critics, the case is so clear that it needs no further proof. The House-Grey Agreement, they say, was conceived and concluded for the purpose of promoting early American intervention. Wilson at once sought to accomplish this goal by taking a position on armed merchant ships that was bound to provoke a crisis with Germany, and by pressing the German government so hard during the *Sussex* controversy that a break in relations would probably ensue. The plan failed, the revisionists explain, only be-cause the violent opposition in Congress convinced the President that the lawmakers would never approve a declaration of war to uphold the right of Americans to travel on belligerent armed merchant ships, and only because the German authorities proved to be more conciliatory than Wilson had expected.

The revisionists are correct in asserting that the conclusion of the House-Grey Agreement marked the beginning of a new and epochal phase in Wil-son's policies toward the belligerents. Otherwise they have missed the entire meaning of the affair, for the House-Grey Agreement was in Wilson's pur-pose *not an instrument of intervention, but a means of averting American involvement*. The truth of this important generalization will perhaps be-come evident when we recall the realities of the American diplomatic situa-tion during late 1915 and early 1916, and when we understand Wilson's motives and intentions in devising a solution.

The overshadowing reality confronting the makers of American foreign policy at this time was the grave possibility of war with Germany over the submarine issue. It caused Wilson and Lansing, for example, to abandon ambitious plans for further intervention in Mexico. It speeded the Amer-ican acquiescence in the British maritime system. Most important, it prompted the President and his advisers to search for ways to avert the rupture that might draw the United States into the maelstrom.

One way out of the predicament was to come to a full understanding with the German government over the issues involved in the submarine controversy. This is what Lansing attempted to do and almost succeeded in accomplishing during his negotiations over the *Lusitania* affair. Another way out and a surer means of averting the peril of American involvement in the future was to bring the war itself to an end through Wilson's mediation. It seemed at the time that the best hope of peace lay in Anglo-American co-operation for a peace of compromise, specifically in the kind of co-operation detailed in the House-Grey Agreement.

Thus Wilson approved this plan of mediation, but with a full realization that certain obligations and risks were involved. There was the necessity of giving positive assurances to the Allies, for they would have been at a fatal disadvantage in a peace conference without American support, in view of the strategic advantages that the Germans then enjoyed on the Continent of Europe. There was, moreover, the risk of war if the Germans refused to approve an armistice or proved to be unreasonable at a peace conference after agreeing to end the fighting. However, Wilson gave the necessary assurances in the belief that the risk of war involved was insignificant as compared to the greater danger of hostilities with Germany if he could not somehow bring the war to an end. This, then, was his dominant motive in sending House to Europe in January, 1916, and in approving the House-Grey Agreement at the cost of Lansing's proposed compromise for submarine warfare.

In the final analysis, our judgment of Wilson's mediation plans must depend upon the kind of settlement that he had in mind and for which he was willing to run the risk of war in order to achieve peace. It is clear that Wilson envisaged a "reasonable" settlement based upon recognition that the war was a stalemate and upon a return for the most part of the *status quo ante bellum*. It meant, Wilson also hoped, the kind of settlement in which all the belligerents would forego annexations and indemnities, put aside past differences, and joins hands with the United States to create a new international order. In his final discussions with the British Cabinet, Colonel House made it clear that this, and this only, was the kind of settlement that Wilson was prepared to use the House-Grey Agreement to achieve. In other words, as House told the British leaders, the President would "throw the weight of the United States on the side of those wanting a just settlement—a settlement which would make another such war impossible." [5]

Granted that Wilson's purpose was a genuinely neutral mediation, we can almost hear the critics say, how can one explain his seemingly provoca-

---

[5] The Diary of Edward M. House, February 14, 1916, MS in the Yale University Library.

tive stand during the crises over armed merchantmen and the *Sussex?* Was he not making such a bold assertion of American rights in the hope that the German government would deny them and thereby give him an excuse for going to Congress for a declaration of war?

The answer, again, is that Wilson was trying desperately to prepare the way for peace and not for war. He and Lansing had proposed the disarming of merchant ships in the hope that this would facilitate a definitive understanding with Germany. But, as House and Page pointed out in urgent telegrams from London, such a proposal was unneutral in spirit and if implemented might mean the destruction of the British merchant marine; and Wilson's insistence upon it would assuredly disqualify him as a mediator acceptable to the Allies. Wilson suddenly reversed himself on the armed ship issue, therefore, primarily in order to restore his neutral standing. Then, following the conclusion of the House-Grey Agreement, the President pressed the Germans for guarantees of good behavior in the conduct of their submarine operations. But he did this with agonizing reluctance because of the risk of war involved and only in order to create a situation in which he might begin to move for peace.

All of Wilson's actions during the third and final stage in American neutrality, lasting from early May, 1916, to early February, 1917, confirm these conclusions. I will discuss his efforts to avert American involvement and his plans for peace in the next . . . [chapter]. Let us now see how he had meanwhile worked out his response to the continuing challenge of the submarine, and why.

So long as the British controlled the seas and the Germans commanded the strategic territories and resources of Europe, the American task of neutrality was the relatively easy one of accepting a *de facto* situation and of pursuing the most impartial policies possible within this framework of power. Thus Wilson permitted the German invasion of Belgium to pass without protest, even though some Americans contended that he was morally obliged to denounce such a gross violation of international law; thus he accepted the British maritime system. In this situation of actual stalemate, there was little likelihood of an Anglo-American rupture and no possibility of a German-American conflict, because there were no points of friction between the two governments. But the German decision to attempt to break the stalemate by using an untried weapon, the submarine, created a situation of great peril for the United States because it raised the issue of fundamental national rights and made it exceedingly difficult for the President to continue to steer a neutral course. Before we see how he struggled to find some adjustment to this new situation, let us consider for a moment some of the underlying factors that helped to govern German submarine policy and Wilson's response.

First, German decisions regarding the use of the submarine were determined almost exclusively by internal and objective considerations—the number of submarines on hand and their calculated effectiveness, the military situation in Europe and how it might be affected by American intervention, and the like—and in no essential way by American policies vis-à-vis the British, or by the rules of international law for cruiser warfare. . . . That is to say, calculations of sheer military advantage or disadvantage and not American or even British maritime policies dictated the way in which the Germans would prosecute their underseas campaign.

Second, the submarine was in 1915 a new weapon of naval warfare. This was an important fact, for it meant that there was no special international law to govern its use when the rights of neutrals were involved. The only laws that could be applied were the rules of cruiser warfare, which required attacking warships to warn merchant ships before sinking them and to make provision for the safety of passengers and crew. The trouble was that the submarine was not a cruiser, but a frail craft that had to rely upon deception and quick striking power for safety and effectiveness. If its use had been an issue only between the belligerents, then international law would not have been much involved. But international law was directly involved, because its provisions defined not only the rights of neutrals, but their obligations to the belligerent powers as well. Having chosen a course of neutrality under international law, Wilson had to work within accepted rules in formulating his response to the submarine challenge insofar as American rights were concerned. The Allies, understandably, would not consent to modifications to permit enemy submarines to operate at their peak deadly efficiency; their refusal made it difficult for Wilson to insist upon changing the rules without seeming to be unneutral in spirit and without in fact conferring enormous advantages upon the Germans.

Third, all questions of international law aside, a great power like the United States could not view the submarine blockade as a legitimate weapon, one that should be considered and perhaps accepted on grounds of expediency or necessity. This was true because at the time of its inauguration in February, 1915, the submarine blockade was actually a sham, since the Germans were then able to keep at most only seven U-boats at one time in all the waters surrounding the British Isles. The Germans, in fact, inaugurated the "blockade" with four submarines in service in the area. A year later, at the time of the *Sussex* crisis, the German Admiralty could send only eleven or twelve submarines into western waters at one time. Knowledge of these facts decisively influenced the way in which Wilson and his advisers viewed the so-called blockade and formulated policies regarding it, for it was one of the oldest and most generally recognized rules of international law that a blockade must be effective in order to be legal.

Fourth, unlike the Anglo-American disputes over trading rights, which involved only property interests, the German submarine campaign as it was often prosecuted raised an issue which no great power should ever evade or arbitrate—the safety and welfare of its people in pursuits and areas where they have a right to be. It is almost inconceivable that Wilson and the American people could have thought of going to war with the British over issues of search and seizure or of blockade. It is also inconceivable that they would not have been willing to think in terms of war with a government that permitted, indeed, instructed, its naval commanders to slaughter Americans indiscriminately upon the high seas.

It would, however, be a mistake of almost fatal magnitude to conclude, as so many writers have done, that Wilson's response to the submarine challenge was a simple and automatic reaction governed entirely by these factors. Although they played an important role, Wilson actually formed and executed, not a single consistent submarine policy, but a series of policies in response to changing issues and circumstances and in response to his own larger diplomatic objectives.

His first policy was formed in answer to the original German proclamation of submarine warfare. Avoiding the more difficult issue raised, the one involving the right of Americans to travel in safety on belligerent ships, Wilson replied by simply but strongly affirming the right of American vessels to use the seas subject to limitations permitted by international law, and by warning that the United States would hold Germany to a "strict accountability" (Counselor Lansing's words) for lives and property lost as a consequence of illegal submarine attacks against *American neutral* shipping. It was the only position that the President could have taken without abandoning the pretense of neutrality and national dignity, and the Germans soon retreated and gave such sweeping guarantees regarding American ships that this issue was never again a point of conflict between the two governments before 1917.

There still remained the necessity of devising a policy to deal with the more controversial issue of the right of American citizens to travel and work on *belligerent* merchant ships under conditions of safety specified by international law. When a German submarine sank the British liner *Falaba* without warning in March, 1915, killing an American citizen, Wilson's advisers in the State Department squared off in a momentous debate over the formulation of a proper response. One group, headed by Secretary Bryan, argued that American interests were not sufficiently involved to warrant a stern protest against submarine attacks on Allied ships, even when Americans were traveling on them, and that the spirit of neutrality demanded that the United States condone German violations of international law as it had done with British violations. The other group, headed by Counselor Lansing, replied that the attack on the *Falaba* had been such a flagrant infraction of international law that the United States must protest uncompromisingly in order to defend its neutrality and honor.

The records reveal that Wilson would have preferred to avoid any involvement while the two giant belligerents fought it out on the seas. In legal theory he agreed with Lansing, but he was so strongly moved by Bryan's pleading that he had apparently decided by the end of the debate over a *Falaba* note to make no protest at all. This is the course that he would probably have followed in the future if the Germans, by confining their underseas campaign to attacks against Allied cargo ships and by showing a desire to avoid the loss of American life, had made it possible for him to find a means of adjusting to the new situation.

A policy of noninvolvement, however, became impossible when a German U-boat sank the British passenger liner *Lusitania* without warning on May 7, 1915, with the loss of almost 1,200 civilians, including 128 Americans, men, women, and children. Wilson had to make some positive response now, so atrocious was the deed in the eyes of the American people, so flagrant was the violation of elemental national rights, so unneutral and degrading would be an acceptance of the terror campaign against the North Atlantic passenger liners.

The strategic facts of the situation—the German inability to maintain any effective blockade of the British Isles and the consequent serious dangers to Germany from a break with the United States—would have justified the President in peremptorily demanding prompt disavowal and guarantees. Wilson's response, however, reflected his own desire and that of the majority of Americans to preserve neutrality and to avoid taking any position short of yielding essential rights that might lead to hostilities with Germany. Thus all during the summer of 1915 Wilson pounded out notes on his typewriter, for the sole purpose of persuading the German government to disavow the sinking of the *Lusitania* and to abandon its campaign against unarmed passenger vessels. Threatening to break relations after a U-boat sank the liner *Arabic* on August 19, 1915, Wilson finally won the promise that he demanded.

By the end of the summer of 1915 the President had thus worked through two stages of policy and had won immunity from ruthless submarine attacks on American neutral ships and unarmed belligerent passenger liners. Up to this time, at any rate, Wilson had been patient, conciliatory, and firm only in his demand that the Germans give up measures that had already taken American lives and threatened untold others.

The third stage in the formulation of Wilson's policies toward the submarine, lasting from the early autumn of 1915 through the *Sussex* crisis in the spring of 1916, saw the President attempting to reach a definitive understanding with the Berlin authorities over all phases of submarine warfare against merchant shipping. The issue was daily becoming more difficult to solve by the application of traditional law, because the Allies since March, 1915, had been arming some passenger and cargo ships and ordering them to attack submarines that showed "hostile intent." But Wilson and Lansing persisted in trying to find a solution in spite of the obstacles because they (or Wilson, at any rate) and the majority of Americans still earnestly desired to avoid conflict over merely technical issues.

By patient negotiation Lansing finally won something resembling a German apology for the loss of American lives on the *Lusitania* and an implicit reaffirmation of the *Arabic* pledge. In order to hasten this German concession and to avert even the possibility of future contention, Lansing proposed his *modus vivendi* of January 18, 1916 (already mentioned), designed to provide a new code to govern the German underseas campaign against maritime commerce. This was the proposal that the Allies disarm their merchant ships and that the German submarines observe the rules of cruiser warfare in attacking them.

Adoption of the proposal by the opposing belligerents, or by the United States and Germany alone, would have achieved Wilson's objective of a comprehensive settlement of the submarine issue. And yet, for reasons that we have already seen, Wilson jettisoned the *modus vivendi* in order to save the House-Grey Agreement. Soon afterward, during the *Sussex* controversy (as we have also seen), he launched a new campaign to force the German government to conduct submarine operations against all merchant ships, armed and unarmed, within the rules of cruiser warfare.

Wilson's rejection of the opportunity to come to a seemingly definitive understanding with Germany seems altogether logical and wise when we remember his objectives and the circumstances in which he made these decisions during the third stage in German-American relations. Wilson's supreme objective now was peace through his own mediation. Mediation seemed possible at this time only through the co-operation of the British government. But the British would co-operate only if they believed that the President was genuinely neutral, and certainly not if he insisted upon a code of submarine warfare that minimized the risks to Americans at the expense of British sea power to the advantage of an essentially illegitimate weapon.

Mediation was a noble objective with such great benefits to the United States that it justified taking a few risks to achieve. But Wilson could have followed no other course than the one he followed during the crises over armed merchantmen and the *Sussex,* even if his objective had been merely to maintain American neutrality. In the circumstances prevailing in the late winter of 1916, Wilson had to choose between continuing to accept the British maritime system, mooted by American Civil War precedents, or acquiescing in the challenge to that system, the German submarine blockade. The first was legitimate because it was based upon *de facto* power as well as legal precedent; the second was not legitimate because it was still a paper blockade without any power of effective enforcement. By insisting upon adherence to traditional rules insofar as the rights of Americans were concerned, Wilson was not at this time depriving the Germans of a weapon essential for their survival or one the free use of which would bring them victory at this time. This, essentially, was the reason that they yielded (for the time being) to Wilson's demands in the *Sussex* crisis. By insisting upon the adoption of Lansing's *modus vivendi,* on the other hand, Wilson in effect would have changed the traditional rules and aimed a heavy blow at the British maritime system, and only for the illusory purpose of averting the possibility of a conflict with Germany.

The final test of any foreign policy is whether it serves the national interest. If it was to the interest of the United States to avoid participation in the war at any cost, regardless of its outcome, and if implementing the *modus vivendi* would have averted all possibility of American involvement, then Wilson's policies at this time were unwise. This generalization, however, is faulty in all its assumptions. To begin with, American interests would be best served by a stalemate and by a peace of reconciliation through Wilson's mediation, not by driving the Allies into sullen opposition, thereby making mediation impossible, and not by promoting a German victory. More important was the fact that implementing the *modus vivendi* would not have prevented the conflict with Germany that Wilson wished to avoid. As we now know, and as Wilson did not know, conflict would come inevitably when the Germans had enough submarines to institute an effective blockade. In that event neither right nor law nor concessions by the United States would dissuade the Germans from making an all-out bid for victory through a devastating attack upon all maritime commerce to the Allied nations.

With the conclusion of the *Sussex* crisis, Wilson's task of erecting a solid structure of neutral policies to govern relations with Britain and Germany was complete, and the next great effort of American foreign policy would be aimed at the higher goal of peace. Operating within the limitations imposed by American public opinion, external realities, and his own conception of the right role for the United States to play, Wilson had made the only kind of adjustments possible in view of American rights and duties as the leading neutral power. He was now in a position from which he could launch his peace campaign. Thus by virtue of Wilson's leadership, American neutrality was not merely a fact in the spring of 1916, but the most important and the most hopeful fact of international life at the time. . . .

WILSON AND THE DECISIONS FOR WAR

The interval between May 1, 1916, and February 1, 1917, was one of the fateful turning points of modern history, because the decisions that the leaders of the great powers made during this brief period determined the future of mankind for generations to come. It was a time of gloom, because by the spring of 1916 the war had become a bloody stalemate in the trenches and upon the seas, and its futile continuation could mean only the attrition and perhaps the ruin of Western civilization. It was also a time of hope, for, as events turned out, statesmen had the opportunity to end the war on terms that might have promised a secure and peaceful future. . . .

Wilson made the first decision during the period under review. It was to press for mediation under the terms of the House-Grey Agreement, a choice almost foreordained by developments that I described in the preceding chapter. Indeed, he began even before the end of the *Sussex* crisis, only to encounter a firm refusal by Sir Edward Grey, the British Foreign Secretary, who made it plain that he preferred American belligerency and that he did not have much hope for the President's mediation in any event.

Undaunted by these early rebuffs, Wilson, assisted by Colonel House, returned to the task with a new zeal born of the hope engendered by the happy resolution of the *Sussex* affair and his and House's still strong belief that the British leaders sincerely wanted peace. From May 10 through July 15, 1916, the two American leaders applied a mounting pressure upon the British Foreign Office, appealing, pleading, and warning that British refusal to co-operate with the President would drive the United States into complete isolation and compel the Washington government to re-examine its attitude toward British maritime measures. As Wilson put it:

> We are plainly face to face with this alternative, therefore. The United States must either make a decided move for peace (upon some basis that promises to be permanent) or, if she postpones that, must insist to the limit upon her rights of trade and upon such freedom of the seas as international law already justifies her in insisting on as against Great Britain, with the same plain speaking and firmness that she has used against Germany. And the choice must be made immediately. Which does Great Britain prefer? She cannot escape both. To do nothing is now, for us, impossible.[6]

In the beginning Grey tried to avoid a plain refusal by saying that the time for calling a peace conference was not yet ripe, and by urging the President to raise the question with the French government, which he knew would reject outright any suggestions of peace. But when pressed for a direct answer, the Foreign Secretary finally had to reply frankly that the Allies, and not the United States, would decide when the time for peace talks had come, and that there was no chance of implementing the House-Grey Agreement so long as the Allies had any hope of winning a military decision. In addition, other spokesmen of the British and French governments, who were not as much personally involved as Grey, made it plain by private conversation and public statement that the Allies would regard any mediation move by the President as a hostile act designed to deprive them of their chance of victory. . . .

Wilson's response was a decision with momentous possibilities for good or for ill—to strengthen American neutrality and then to press forward in his own independent campaign for peace. It was the grand culmination of American neutrality and the almost inevitable outgrowth of pressures and

---

[6] Wilson to E. M. House, May 16, 1916, the Ray Stannard Baker Collection of Wilson Materials, Library of Congress.

events at home and abroad that were converging during the summer and autumn of 1916 to cause a radical shift in American foreign policy.

One of these events was Wilson's mounting anger with the British and his growing disillusionment about the merits of the whole Allied cause as a consequence of the British rejection (as he saw it) of his right hand of fellowship. Going far beyond mere irritation, this anger and disillusionment culminated in convictions powerful enough to affect national policy—that the Allies were fighting for selfish motives and domination, and that they would prolong the carnage rather than consent to a fair and liberal settlement.

Developments in the official relations of the United States and Great Britain during the summer and autumn of 1916 also speeded the disillusionment in Washington and prepared the way for a change of American policy. To state the matter briefly, the Admiralty and Ministry of Blockade tightened the British maritime system to the point of denying the last vestiges of the freedom of the seas. This they did by such measures as the search and seizure of American mail, carrying the economic war to America by forbidding British subjects to have any dealings with neutral individuals and firms suspected of trading with the Central Powers, and attempting to bring all American shipping under British control by denying shipmasters the right to purchase coal in distant British ports if they refused to submit to the Admiralty's control.

A force of even greater power propelling Wilson toward policies of stern neutrality and independent mediation was the extraordinary growth of American neutralism following the settlement of the *Sussex* affair. In part it was the result of a sharp increase in anti-British sentiment as a consequence of the tightening of the maritime system and the American revulsion against the ruthless way in which the British army suppressed the Irish Rebellion in April, 1916. In larger measure it was a reflection of the overwhelming desire to avoid participation in a war the outcome of which did not concern most Americans. Whatever the causes for its spectacular increase, neutralism became the reigning passion during the summer and autumn of 1916. . . .

There was a final and irresistible force propelling Wilson toward a new diplomatic course at this time—his fear that the war was entering a new and more desperate stage in which the aggressions of the belligerents might drive the American people to war in sheer anger. If this happened, then Americans would be fighting in blind defense of national rights, not knowing really why they fought, and only to the end that one side might win a smashing victory and thus be able to impose a peace that could not endure. . . .

It was to avoid being caught in such a predicament as this that Wilson embarked upon the policies that I will now describe.

First, he began to move in a really menacing way to defend alleged American neutral rights in the face of the new British maritime measures. No longer couched in friendly terms, the State Department's protests now accused the London government of "lawless" conduct and warned that the United States would not tolerate the continuation of "repeated violations of international law." To give teeth to these warnings, Wilson obtained legislation from Congress in early September empowering him to deny clearance and port facilities to ships of any nation that discriminated against American commerce, and to use the armed forces to enforce the prohibition. In addition, he persuaded the Federal Reserve Board to warn American bankers to exercise caution in financing the war trade with the Allies.

The consequences of this new sternness—a sharp increase in Anglo-American tension and vigorous protests from London—were also a calculated component of Wilson's plan. His grand objective was independent mediation, and such mediation would be possible only from a posture of severe neutrality. In other words, mediation could succeed only if the President convinced the British that he meant to use his powers of retaliation to force them to co-operate, and the Germans that he was determined to compel as much respect for American rights from their enemies as he had from them.

Wilson proceeded with his preparations for a climactic peace campaign once the voters had decreed that he should have charge of foreign relations for another four years. Protracted discussions among Wilson, Lansing, and House during late November, 1916, pointed up the possibilities and dangers of the situation. The Allies were now even more violently opposed to peace talk of any kind than they had been during the preceding summer. The German leaders, on the other hand, were not only increasing their pressure on Wilson for a peace move, but were now even promising (at least so the German Ambassador in Washington said) to evacuate Belgium and France if the Allies consented to an armistice. There was the danger, therefore, as House and Lansing pointed out, that Germany would respond favorably to a call for peace and that the Allies would reject it. If this happened, the President's advisers further warned, then the United States might drift into a sympathetic alliance with Germany and into a naval war with England and Japan. Would it not be safer, House asked, to attempt to revive the House-Grey Agreement and to move for mediation under its terms?

These were weighty issues, and in dealing with them Wilson revealed for the first time his innermost thoughts about the war and America's duty toward the belligerents. Old plans like the House-Grey Agreement based upon the assumption of intimate Anglo-American co-operation were, he exclaimed, out of date. He must stand for peace alone, free and compelling, no matter what the risks might be. If the Germans responded favorably, he would work with them. If the Allies resisted, he would attempt to coerce them. There was the risk of a rupture and war, but he did not think that it was great.

"This morning in discussing these matters with the President," House wrote in his Diary on November 15, 1916,

> he went so far as to say that if the Allies wanted war with us we would not shrink from it. . . . He thought they would not dare resort to this and if they did, they could do this country no serious hurt. I disagreed with him again. I thought Great Britain might conceivably destroy our fleet and land troops from Japan in sufficient numbers to hold certain parts of the United States. He replied they might get a good distance but would have to stop somewhere.

Neither these somber warnings, which he did not take seriously, nor the call by the German government for a peace conference, issued on December 12, diverted Wilson from the course that he had decided to pursue, and he sent a message to the belligerent capitals on December 18, 1916. In order to avoid the appearance of supporting the German maneuver, the President eliminated a demand for the assembling of a peace conference and simply asked the belligerents to say frankly what they were fighting for and upon what terms they would consent to end the war. The whole world knew, however, that it was merely the first step in a bold campaign.

The time was now at hand when the belligerent leaders had to choose between peace and prolonging the war at the risk of incurring American intervention. To provide the opportunity for frank discussions, Wilson opened secret negotiations through Colonel House with the British Ambassador in Washington, with Sir William Wiseman, an agent accredited to the British Embassy, and with the German Ambassador to the United States. While waiting for their replies, moreover, the President went before the Senate on January 22, 1917, to describe the kind of settlement that he hoped to achieve.

The British gave their answer first, on January 26, 1917, when Wiseman told House that his government would agree to the meeting of an early peace conference, provided that the Germans returned a favorable reply to the President's appeal. It was a startling announcement in view of the hitherto bitter opposition of the British Cabinet to any suggestion of mediation and the Allied public answer of January 10, 1917, to Wilson's peace note, which had revealed ambitions so sweeping that they could be realized only by the defeat of Germany. . . .

At this point, however, it mattered comparatively little what the British said, or why they said it. Wilson had the power of life or death over the Allies and was prepared to use it to force them to the peace table, provided that the Germans approved his objectives and accepted his leadership. As he put it:

> If Germany really wants peace she can get it, and get it soon, *if she will but confide in me and let me have a chance.* . . . Feelings, exasperations are neither here nor there. Do they want me to help? I am

entitled to know because I genuinely want to help and have now put myself in a position to help without favour to either side.[7]

. . . The High Command had already made the decision by late December; it was confirmed by a conference of all leaders at Pless Castle on January 9, 1917. That decision was, in brief, to begin unrestricted submarine warfare against all shipping, belligerent and neutral, in the approaches to the British Isles and the eastern Mediterranean after January 31.

It was easily the most fateful decision made by any government during the course of the war, and the German records fully reveal the reasons for its adoption . . . on a basis of elaborate calculations the Admiralty spokesmen guaranteed absolutely to reduce the British to actual starvation within five months after the submarine blockade began. If this were possible, then Germany had it within her power to win a total victory and a settlement that would establish the Reich in an unassailable position. To the military leaders, who had despaired of winning the war in the trenches, it was an opportunity that could not be refused.

Fear of American belligerency no longer had any effect on German policy in such an atmosphere of confident expectation. The German leaders all assumed that a wholesale attack on American maritime commerce would drive the United States into the war. These same leaders also concluded that American belligerency would not make any difference. On the contrary, American participation would have certain positive advantages, for it would mean the diversion of huge quantities of food and matériel to an American army in training during the very period when the U-boats would be winning the war on the seas. But in any event, American participation was in the circumstances necessary to the success of the German plans, because the submarine blockade could succeed only if it were total, that is, only if American as well as British ships were prevented from carrying life-giving supplies to the beleaguered British Isles. Of course, no German leader wanted recklessly to provoke an American declaration of war; all Germans, however, were prepared to incur American belligerency if they could win the war by so doing. . . .

There remains only one further question, whether the Germans decided to go the whole length and to attack American shipping because they believed that the United States would enter the war in any case if they violated the *Sussex* pledge. In other words, did the Germans conclude that there was little point in confining unrestricted attacks to armed merchantmen or to *belligerent* shipping, armed and unarmed, because any deviations from the rules of cruiser warfare would provoke American intervention? This is an academic question, but an important one, because the answer to it sheds additional light upon Wilson's intentions and the German choice of alternatives.

---

[7] Wilson to E. M. House, January 24, 1917, R. S. Baker Collection, Library of Congress.

There is much evidence that by the end of 1916 Wilson was prepared to effect a sharp diplomatic withdrawal if both belligerent groups refused to heed his peace appeal. . . . It seems almost certain that he would have accepted unrestricted submarine attacks against *armed* merchantmen. On January 10, 1917, the German government informed the State Department that its submarines would hereafter attack armed merchant ships without warning, because these ships had all been offensively armed and instructed to attack submarines. The German proclamation was, technically, a violation of the *Sussex* pledge, but Wilson's only response was to indicate that he doubted that his earlier position on armed ships had been sound.

We can go further and say that it seems also possible that Wilson would not have broken diplomatic relations over unrestricted submarine attacks against all *belligerent* merchantmen, exclusive, perhaps, of passenger liners. . . .

The Germans never seriously considered adopting these limited alternatives, not because they believed that any infraction of the *Sussex* pledge would automatically provoke American intervention, but because they thought that they could win only by enforcing a total blockade. . . .

President Wilson's response to the German blockade proclamation lends additional evidence to my theory that the United States might not have broken diplomatic relations if the Germans had exempted American shipping from the wrath of their underseas campaign. The German Ambassador delivered copies of the German blockade announcement to Lansing and House on January 31, 1917. Wilson did not act like a man who had a predetermined course of action in mind. Even in the face of a German declaration of war against American commerce, he hesitated to take any step that might lead to war. He was willing, he told Lansing, to go to almost any lengths "rather than to have this nation actually involved in the conflict."

There was, however, only one decision that Wilson could now make. No great power could continue to maintain diplomatic intercourse with a government that promised to destroy its shipping and slaughter its citizens in violation of national and treaty rights and solemn pledges. . . . The remarkable thing is not that Wilson severed diplomatic relations as he did on February 3, but that he hesitated at all.

To engage in a debate at this point over the reasons for Wilson's severance of diplomatic relations with Germany would obscure a development that was vastly more important than the handing of passports to the German Ambassador. It was Wilson's announcement, made in an address to Congress on February 3, 1917, that the United States would accept the new submarine blockade and would not go to war, in spite of the break in relations, provided that the Germans did not carry out their threat to destroy American ships and lives. . . .

In short, Wilson was saying that he would follow a policy of watchful waiting and govern his future policies in response to what the Germans did.

If they spared American ships and lives, presumably upon American ships of all categories and upon belligerent unarmed passenger vessels, then he would do nothing. If they attacked American ships, then he would defend them by an armed neutrality. This, obviously, was not the language of war, such as Lansing had urged the President to use. It was the language of a man determined to avoid such full-fledged commitment as a war declaration would imply, willing in the worst event only to protect "our seamen and our people in the prosecution of their peaceful and legitimate errands on the high seas."

. . . As the days passed, however, the pressures for an end to watchful waiting and for the adoption of at least an armed neutrality mounted almost irresistibly. Members of the Cabinet, shipowners, a large majority of the newspapers, and a growing body of public opinion combined in the demand that the President either convoy merchantmen or arm them with naval guns and crews. Still protesting that the people wanted him to avert any risk of war, Wilson gave in to their wishes on about February 25. Going to Congress the following day to request authority to arm merchantmen and to "employ any other instrumentalities or methods that may be necessary and adequate to protect our ships and our people in their legitimate and peaceful pursuits on the seas," he carefully explained that he was not contemplating war or any steps that might lead to war. . . .

Although a small group of senators prevented approval of a bill authorizing Wilson to arm merchantmen, the President took such action anyway on March 9, 1917. . . .

By the middle of March, therefore, it seemed that Wilson had made his decision in favor of a limited defensive war on the seas. "We stand firm in armed neutrality," he declared, for example, in his second inaugural address on March 5, "since it seems that in no other way we can demonstrate what it is we insist upon and cannot forego." Yet on April 2 (he had meanwhile convened Congress for this earlier date), scarcely more than a month after he had uttered these words, he stood before Congress and asked for a declaration of full-fledged war. What events occurred, what forces were at work, what pressures were applied during this brief interval to cause Wilson to make the decision that he had been trying so desperately to avoid? We should perhaps put the question in a less positive way, as follows: What caused the President to abandon armed neutrality and to *accept* the decision for war?

There was first the fact that from the end of February to the end of March the Germans gave full evidence of their determination to press a relentless, total attack against all ships passing through the war zones that enveloped western Europe.

. . . the *immediate* reason why Wilson made his decision of war . . . was simply that the German assault upon American lives and property was so overwhelming and so flagrant that the only possible way to cope with it was to claim the status of a belligerent in order to strike at the sources of German power. "I would be inclined to adopt . . . [armed neutrality]," the President wrote only two days before he delivered his war message,

> indeed, as you know, I had already adopted it, but this is the difficulty: . . . To make even the measures of defense legitimate we must obtain the status of belligerents.[8]

Certainly Wilson had convinced himself that this was true, but I have a strong suspicion that he would have stood doggedly by his first decision to limit American action to a defense of rights on the seas if this decision had not been overridden by convictions, events, pressures, and ambitions that were themselves decisive in Wilson's final shift from armed neutrality to war, in forcing him to the conclusion that the *immediate* circumstances left the United States with no choice but full-scale participation.

One of the most important of these factors was the subtlest and the one for which the least direct evidence can be adduced. It was Wilson's apparent fear that the threat of a German victory imperiled the balance of power and all his hopes for the future reconstruction of the world community. We must be careful here not to misinterpret his thoughts and motives. There is little evidence that he accepted the decision for war because he thought that a German victory would seriously endanger American security, because he wanted to preserve Anglo-American control of the North Atlantic sea lanes, or because he desired to maintain the traditional balance of European power because it served American interests. Nor is there any convincing evidence that Wilson's attitude toward the objectives of the rival alliances had changed by the time that he made his final decision.

On the other hand, there was now a great and decisive difference in the relative position of the belligerents: The Allies seemed about to lose the war and the Central Powers about to win it. This, almost certainly, was a governing factor in Wilson's willingness to think in terms of war. Germany, he told Colonel House, was a madman who must be curbed. A German victory meant a peace of domination and conquest; it meant the end of all of Wilson's dreams of helping to build a secure future.

As the President pondered America's duty at this juncture in history, the answer must have seemed obvious to him—to accept belligerency, because now only through belligerency could the United States fulfill its mission to insure a just and lasting peace of reconciliation. This could be accomplished only by preventing a German victory and only by the assertion of such power and influence among the Allies as would come to the United States by virtue of its sacrifice of blood and treasure.

If the immediate events made a war resolution necessary, then the goal of a righteous peace was the objective that justified full-scale participation in Wilson's mind and raised that effort to a high and noble plane. It was, there-

---

[8] Wilson to Matthew Hale, March 31, 1917, Wilson Papers, Library of Congress.

fore, not war in anger that he advocated, not war sheerly in defense of national rights, but, as he put it in his war message,

> [war] for democracy, for the right of those who submit to authority to have a voice in their own governments, for the rights and liberties of small nations, for a universal dominion of right by such a concert of free peoples as shall bring peace and safety to all nations and make the world itself at last free.

The combined weight of official and public opinion was another pressure meanwhile driving Wilson toward acceptance of the decision for war. It was a fact of no little consequence that by the end of March every important member of the administration, including those members of the Cabinet who had heretofore opposed any bellicose measures, urged the President to admit that a state of war with Germany in fact existed. Public opinion had remained stubbornly pacific until near the end of February, 1917. Then the publication of the Zimmermann telegram, in which the German government proposed to Mexico a war alliance against the United States, the sinking of the *Laconia,* and, above all, the destruction of American ships in the war zones after mid-March generated a demand for war that grew with mounting crescendo in all sections and among all classes, until it seemed beyond doubt to be a national and a majority demand. It was further stimulated by news of the downfall of the czarist regime and the establishment of a provisional republican government in Russia—news that convinced many wavering Americans that the Allies were indeed fighting for democracy and also changed overnight the large and influential American Jewish community from a position of strong hostility toward the Allies to one of friendship.

This was all a development of profound importance for a leader as keenly sensitive to public opinion as was Woodrow Wilson. He could have joined forces with the large antiwar minority to resist the demand for war; indeed, he probably would have done so had he been convinced that it was the wise and right thing to do. The point is not, therefore, that public opinion *forced* Wilson to accept the decision for war, but that it facilitated doing what Wilson for other reasons now thought was necessary and right to do.

All this is said without any intention of implying that Wilson ever *wanted* war. The agony of his soul was great as he moved through the dark valley of his doubts. He had no illusions about the merits of the conflict into which he and his people were being drawn. He saw the risks of intervention, both to his own nation and to the world, with remarkable clarity. But he could devise no alternative; and he set aside his doubts in the hope that acting now as a belligerent, with all the power and idealism of the American people sustaining him, he could achieve objectives to justify the misery of mankind.

IV

*The Defeat of the
Versailles Treaty:
Who Was Responsible,
Wilson or Lodge?*

INTRODUCTION

Following the conclusion of the armistice in November, 1918, Woodrow Wilson journeyed to France to play the role of peacemaker. He insisted that the covenant of the League of Nations be made an integral part of the Treaty of Versailles, and it was a treaty with the covenant included that the United States Senate was eventually asked to approve. The Senate, however, did not supply the two-thirds majority required for ratification of the treaty, with the result that the United States failed to become a member of the League.

Because the chief protagonists in the struggle for the ratification of the Versailles treaty were President Woodrow Wilson and Senator Henry Cabot Lodge, it is not surprising that there should be interest in the question as to which of the two was primarily responsible for the defeat of the treaty. Of course, it is perfectly clear that had Wilson not dissuaded his loyal followers in the Senate from voting for the Lodge reservations, particularly in the vote of March 19, 1920, the treaty would have been approved. In this tactical sense, Wilson, who thought that the electorate would ultimately compel the Senate to approve the treaty in a form acceptable to the President, was responsible for the defeat of the treaty (with the Lodge reservations appended). This still leaves unanswered, however, the question of Lodge's motivation during the treaty fight. Was Lodge really an irreconcilable on the League issue who added reservations to the treaty as the most likely way of securing its defeat and of thus blocking American entry into the League; or did Lodge wish to see the treaty approved and the United States enter the League, provided, of course, that his reservations were accepted?

Although not unmindful of Wilson's refusal to compromise, Professor Walter Johnson, writing in the midst of World War II, when thoughts were turning to the creation of a new world organization, concentrates his attention on Lodge. He pictures the Massachusetts senator as an irreconcilable at heart who used reservations as the means of preventing approval of the treaty. Professor Thomas A. Bailey, focusing in the selection that follows on the treaty vote of March 19, 1920, absolves Lodge of primary responsibility for the defeat of the treaty and directs his main shafts at Woodrow Wilson. "In the final analysis," he asserts, "the treaty was slain in the house of its friends rather than in the house of its enemies."

Senatorial Strategy, 1919–20 . . .

Walter Johnson

When, on September 1, 1939, the world was plunged into war for the second time in twenty-five years, many people turned their thoughts to the problem of creating some agency that in the future would have sufficient power to maintain world peace. Shortly after the United States entered the war, President Roosevelt told Congress that the American people were not going to be satisfied with just winning the war, but that they wanted to "maintain the security of the peace that will follow." Increasingly, more and more people have felt that if the United States had joined the League of Nations in 1919 or 1920 there would have been a strong possibility that now [1943] there would not be a war ravaging the earth. In a very blunt fashion Prime Minister Winston Churchill told the American Congress on December 26, 1941, that this war need not have happened had the peace-loving nations worked together during the past twenty years. In the light of this statement, why did the United States abstain from the league? Why did the United States shirk its responsibility as a major power and generally follow an irresponsible course in world affairs?

Unfortunately the Versailles Treaty, in which the League of Nations was incorporated, was not debated in the United States Senate purely on its merits. Instead of a reasonable atmosphere to discuss this proposed method of ending wars, the air of the Senate was one of bitterness, partisanship, and hostility. Some Senators, like Henry Cabot Lodge, had a deep personal hatred for Woodrow Wilson; some Senators were personally piqued that the President had not included any members of their body on the Peace Commission; some partisan Republicans did not want to pass a peace treaty drawn up by a Democratic President since this might insure a Democratic victory in 1920. Then, of course, certain Senators were influenced by their constituents: many German-Americans were opposed to the treaty because in their opinion it was too severe on Germany; many Italian-Americans were against the treaty because Italy had not been given Fiume; many Irish-Americans looked upon the treaty as an English plot to control the world and were particularly furious at England at that moment because of Eng-

From *The Antioch Review*, III, No. 4 (Winter 1943), 512–529. Reprinted by permission.

land's suppression of the Irish revolution; reactionaries were opposed to the treaty because it was not severe enough toward Germany; and, on the other hand, a number of liberals opposed the treaty because they felt that it was too harsh toward Germany.

When President Wilson presented the Versailles Treaty to the Senate on July 10, 1919, the Senate did not divide into two groups, one for the treaty and the other against. Instead, four groups were formed: (1) a protreaty group, composed of 43 Democrats and one Republican, who were for ratification without any qualifications; (2) the "mild reservationists," made up of about 15 Republicans, who were warmly for the treaty but desired reservations of a mild character; (3) the "strong reservationists," consisting of about 20 Republicans, who favored ratification but with "strong" reservations; and (4) the "irreconcilables," 12 Republicans and 3 Democrats, led by William E. Borah, who were opposed to ratification under any conditions.

The vast majority of the Senate, 80 out of 96, were for the treaty, although groups two and three wanted certain reservations. The problem of strategy was to present the question in such a way that the three groups favorable to the treaty could unite. The tragedy was that the treaty "failed of ratification not because a constitutional majority desired to reject the treaty but because the different groups in favor of the treaty were unable to agree on the conditions of ratification." When the two votes on ratification occurred (November 19, 1919,* and March 19, 1920) the treaty was defeated not by its enemies, the "irreconcilables," but by its most ardent friends. On both occasions when the treaty with reservations came to a vote, the reservationists voted for it and the "irreconcilables," in combination with the administration Democrats (group 1), voted against it. The administration Democrats did not want to defeat the treaty. They only wanted to defeat the treaty with reservations in order that a vote could be had under more acceptable conditions. In so doing they were acting on the advice of President Wilson, who wrote to Senator Hitchcock just before the first vote was taken: "I sincerely hope that the friends and the supporters of the treaty will vote against the Lodge resolution of ratification. I understand that the door will then probably be open for a more genuine resolution of ratification."

A majority of the Senators, then, desired to accept the treaty, but they could not devise the strategy necessary to bring this majority together on the vote. This favorable majority was backed up by a majority of the American public who, too, wanted to accept the treaty and entrance into the League of Nations. The *Literary Digest* conducted a poll of newspapers in April, 1919, and found that 718 were for ratification, 478 were for ratification with conditions, and only 181 were against ratification. For a long time,

---

* Editor's note: There were three separate votes on the treaty on November 19, 1919, two on the treaty with reservations and one on the treaty without any reservations. The treaty did not command a simple majority on any of these votes.

the idea of a league of nations had been growing in the United States. Theodore Roosevelt, speaking before the Nobel Prize Committee in 1910, advocated a League of Peace to prevent war from breaking out. After the outbreak of the World War, he wrote that "the great civilized nations of the world which do possess force, actual or immediately potential, should combine by solemn agreement in a great world league for the peace of righteousness." President Wilson was also thinking along the same lines in the fall of 1914. He told a friend that "all nations must be absorbed into some great association of nations whereby all shall guarantee the integrity of each so that any one nation violating the agreement between all of them shall bring punishment on itself automatically." Ex-President Taft expressed much the same opinion in October, 1914.

So many Americans were in agreement with these distinguished leaders that there was formed on June 17, 1915, a Committee for a League to Enforce Peace. Within a year the league had branches in almost every congressional district in the country. The organization felt that it was desirable for the United States to join a league of nations. Senator Lodge publicly gave his support to the proposal in 1916, as did Woodrow Wilson. On January 22, 1917, President Wilson told the Senate that one of the things necessary for permanent peace was a league of nations. On January 8, 1918, in his message to Congress setting forth the fourteen points on which he thought that the peace should be based, Wilson included a general association of nations to give "mutual guarantees of political independence and territorial integrity to great and small states alike" as the last point.

When Wilson sailed for Europe in December, 1918, to attend the peace conference, he did not have, however, a completely united country behind his desire to make a peace that would be permanent. In the mid-term Congressional elections, the Republicans had gained control of the Senate by a majority of two. Wilson, on October 25, 1918, had publicly asked the voters:

> . . . If you have approved of my leadership and wish me to continue to be your unembarrassed spokesman in affairs at home and abroad, I earnestly beg that you will express yourselves unmistakably to that effect by returning a Democratic majority to both the Senate and the House of Representatives. . . .

He pointed out that he wanted this because a Republican Congress would divide the leadership of the nation. The Republicans in Congress had been prowar but antiadministration, and this was no time for divided leadership. Furthermore, the election of a Republican majority in either house of Congress would be considered abroad to be a repudiation of his leadership. Theodore Roosevelt denounced this appeal and repudiated Wilson's Fourteen Points. Other Republicans like Charles E. Hughes, William H. Taft, and Will Hays, chairman of the Republican National Committee, stated they did not agree that Wilson's control of the government should be unhampered nor was it necessary for the country's welfare. In the months that followed, when Taft fought shoulder to shoulder with Wilson against the leadership of his own party in the Senate for the Versailles Treaty and the League of Nations, one leading writer has pointed out that Taft "must have wondered whether it might have been better to have given Wilson the continued control for which he asked. Wilson was destroyed in the conflict with a Republican Congress which followed the election of 1918. . . ." [1]

The election of a Republican Senate in 1918 should not necessarily be taken as evidence that the nation thereby repudiated Wilson's leadership. A majority of the people had long been Republican and Wilson had been elected in 1912 when the Republican party had split into two wings. In each of the elections from 1914 to 1918 the Republicans had slowly regained seats in Congress. When it is remembered that there is usually a reaction against the party in power at a midterm election when the Presidency is not at stake, the election of 1918 was not a great victory for the Republicans nor a great defeat for the President.[2]

As soon as the Armistice celebration had quieted, Senators Knox, Poindexter, and Reed attacked the proposal of a league of nations. Former Senator Albert Beveridge of Indiana had through his correspondence been urging the defeat of a league of nations for some time. He wrote Theodore Roosevelt and Will Hays that the Republican Party would be injured if Wilson's plans were not opposed. He wrote Henry Cabot Lodge, Republican majority leader and Chairman of the Senate Committee on Foreign Affairs, that the future of the party was in his hands and that its prospects would be "seriously, perhaps fatally, injured by the acceptance of Mr.

---

[1] Page 37 of D. F. Fleming, *The United States and the League of Nations 1918–1920* (G. P. Putnam Sons, 1932), upon which I have drawn for a number of details stated above.

Appeals similar to Wilson's had been made before. Lincoln in 1864 had warned the people against "swapping horses in midstream"; McKinley on October 11, 1898 had asked for the election of a Republican Congress as had Governor Theodore Roosevelt and H. C. Lodge (Fleming, pp. 48–49).

[2] Charles P. Howland, *American Foreign Relations* (New Haven: Yale University Press, 1928), pp. 239–246, in analyzing the result in each of the thirty-seven senatorial contests writes:

"The forces which determined the several elections were sometimes local, sometimes general. They included support for or hostility to prohibition; the tendency of the business interests, large and small, to back the Republican party; pressure for a high tariff in industrial districts; objection on the part of food producers and distributors to the fixing of food prices, especially as the South had profited enormously from unregulated cotton prices; resentment in the states where General Leonard Wood was popular that the administration had not permitted him to go to France; the attitude of the Non-Partisan League or of its anti-agrarian opponents, and the enthusiastic support by the women of those who had appealed for their new suffrages. There was virtually no issue contested and properly discussed which arose out of the policies that were the cause of our entering the war, of the degree of efficiency with which it was conducted, of the aims announced for the United States by its official spokesman, or of the effort which the United States was to put forth in the making of a durable peace."

Wilson's international plan, or any variation of it." With the Democrats winning prestige for the successful prosecution of the war, some Republican politicians felt that they could not permit that party also to write a successful peace, or victory for the Republicans in 1920 would be impossible.

When Congress reassembled in December, partisan attacks were made on the way the war had been conducted and on Wilson's decision to attend the peace conference in person. Wilson's failure to include any Senator in his peace commission rankled in the breasts of some Senators. In the next three months, the small group of irreconcilables, unalterably opposed to the League of Nations, seized the initiative in the Senate and assailed the idea of internationalism. The majority of Republicans who favored the league in some form or other remained quiet, and the country at large gained the impression that the peace was becoming a partisan issue.

Just what the role that Henry Cabot Lodge was playing in these months and those to come is not entirely clear. His apologists claim that he was honestly for a league of nations, with reservations. There is evidence, however, to demonstrate that he was out to kill the league under any circumstance, and that he considered the best way to accomplish this was through attaching reservations to the covenant. Lodge was a partisan Republican willing to sacrifice ideals or anything else to party loyalty. From 1893 to 1924, as a member of the Senate, he never departed from strict party regularity. In addition to party regularity, he hated Woodrow Wilson. Until Wilson's entrance into politics, Lodge had been known as "the scholar in politics," but this title, probably much to the bitterness of Lodge, then passed to Wilson. According to the estimate of Nicholas Murray Butler, "The figure that made the least appeal throughout all these years was that of Henry Cabot Lodge. He was able, vain, intensely egotistical, narrow-minded, dogmatic, and provincial."

Lodge was a master of parliamentary technique. By 1919 no one knew better than he the devices to be used to kill a treaty in the Senate. That Lodge would oppose a treaty drawn up by a Democratic President, and one whom he personally hated, seems obvious. In his public statements on the treaty, Lodge avoided any evidence of hostility toward the President. As Republican leader, it would have been unwise to have attacked the President. But in the book that Lodge wrote in 1925, justifying his conduct against the league, "his hatred for Wilson shines forth in its full intensity." [3]

Some of Lodge's personal associates, including a grandson, believe that Lodge sincerely was for the United States entering the league with reservations. Yet his daughter, who claimed to be close to him during the struggle, has stated:

---

[3] W. S. Holt, *Treaties Defeated By the Senate* (Baltimore, The Johns Hopkins Press, 1933), p. 263.

My father hated and feared the Wilson league, and his heart was really with the irreconcilables. But it was uncertain whether this league could be beaten straight out in this way, and the object of his reservations was so to emasculate the Wilson pact that if it did pass it would be valueless. . . . My father never wanted the Wilson league, and when it was finally defeated, he was like a man from whom a great burden had been lifted.[4]

Lodge, in his book, *The Senate and the League of Nations,* admitted that he had told Senator Borah, the leader of the irreconcilables, that "any attempt to defeat the treaty of Versailles with the league by a straight vote in the Senate, if taken immediately, would be hopeless, even if it were desirable" and that the thing to do was "to proceed in the discussion of the treaty by way of amendment and reservation."

There is other information to indicate that Lodge used reservations as a method of killing the league. According to Senator James E. Watson, Lodge planned to defeat the league through this technique. Watson said to Lodge, when the latter was planning the fight against the league:

"I don't see how we are ever going to defeat this proposition. It appears to me that eighty per cent of the people are for it. Fully that percentage of the preachers are right now advocating it, churches are very largely favoring it, all the people who have been burdened and oppressed by this awful tragedy of war and who imagine this opens a way to world peace are for it, and I don't see how it is possible to defeat it." He turned to me and said, "Ah, my dear James, I do not propose to try to beat it by direct frontal attack, but by the indirect method of reservations." "What do you mean by that?" I asked. "Illustrate it to me." He then went on to explain how, for instance, we would demand a reservation on the subject of submitting to our government the assumption of a mandate over Armenia, or any other foreign country. "We can debate that for days and hold up the dangers that it will involve and the responsibilities we will assume if we pursue that course, and we can thoroughly satisfy the country that it would be a most abhorrent policy for us to adopt." . . . Senator Lodge then went on for two hours to explain other reservations, and went into the details of the situation that would be thus evolved, until I became thoroughly satisfied that the treaty could be beaten in that way.[5]

There is also evidence that Lodge desired to kill the treaty by attaching reservations unacceptable to Wilson, in order that the responsibility for the defeat would then fall upon the President. Lodge wrote later:

There was another object which I had very much at heart, and that was that if we were successful in putting on reservations we should create a situation where, if the acceptance of the treaty was defeated,

---

[4] *The New York Herald Tribune,* March 7, 1930.
[5] James E. Watson, *As I Knew Them* (Bobbs-Merrill, 1936), pp. 190–191.

the Democratic party, and especially Mr. Wilson's friends, should be
responsible for its defeat, and not the opponents of the treaty who
were trying to pass it in a form safe for the United States.

As yet, evidence in the form of letters or memoirs, has not come to light
which would definitely indicate that the irreconcilables knew that Lodge
was fighting for them from the camp of the reservationists. However, Lodge
was close to them during the fight and consulted with them on most major
decisions. When former Senator Beveridge urged a more aggressive policy
on Lodge to defeat the league, he replied agreeing with the ends sought
but differing as to the method to obtain them.

The initial plans to attack the league were made by Lodge and Theodore
Roosevelt in December, 1918. Although no draft of the league covenant had
as yet been published, these two men planned to attack whatever league
proposal the President brought home. On the floor of the Senate on December
21, Lodge made a speech, intended for the ears of the Allies, in which
he warned that if certain "extraneous provisions"—i.e. The League of Nations—were to be found in the treaty of peace, then they would be struck
out or amended by the United States Senate.

The text of the covenant of the league was first published in American
papers on February 15, 1919. Immediately, the small minority of irreconcilables rallied to the attack. There can be no question that the majority of
Republican Senators wanted the United States to join the league. They saw
some shortcomings in it, but they felt that it was bigger than the shortcomings. The most active Senators in debate, however, were the opponents of
the league. Lodge, as Republican leader, had a difficult time in preserving
party unity, but he struck upon a device to accomplish this. On March 3,
in the Senate, he introduced a resolution signed by thirty-seven* Republican Senators and Senators-elect of the next Congress to the effect that the
peace treaty should be signed immediately and that the question of a
"league of nations to insure the permanent peace of the world should
then be taken up for careful and serious consideration." The real purpose
of the round robin was to commit more than one-third of the Republican
Senators to a policy of united, partisan action on the treaty. This policy was
a victory for the irreconcilables, since one of them, Senator Brandegee, had
first suggested it to Lodge. Although this was a victory for the irreconcilables, it was not a complete one. In order to gain the signatures of many
Republican Senators, a statement had to be inserted in the resolution that
the signers could not accept the constitution of the league "in the form
now proposed." If changes were made, many of the signers were still free
to accept the league.

When Lodge was discussing future plans, shortly after this round robin,
with Borah, he had to admit that "the vocal classes of the community,

---

* Editor's note: The resolution was eventually signed by two additional Senators.

most of the clergymen, the preachers of sermons, a large element in the teaching force of the universities, a large proportion of the newspaper editors, and finally the men and women who were in the habit of writing and speaking for publication, although by no means thoroughly informed, were friendly to the league as it stood, and were advocating it." A month later Lodge admitted that a majority of the people favored the league. Outstanding Republicans outside the Senate, like former-President Taft and A. Lawrence Lowell, were actively campaigning for the league. When the covenant of the league was changed by the peace conference to meet the principal American objections, it was possible for the signers of the round robin to accept the league. Senator Hitchcock, the acting Democratic leader, had written Wilson: "A number of Republican Senators who signed Lodge's manifesto on the League of Nations will, in my opinion, vote for it nevertheless, if it is a part of the peace treaty. A still larger number will give it support if certain amendments are made." Taft and Lowell wired Wilson along the same vein, and the American delegation at Paris secured the consent of other nations to changes on certain points. These points were: (1) a recognition of the Monroe Doctrine by name; (2) exclusion of domestic questions like immigration and the tariff from the league's jurisdiction; (3) right of withdrawal from the league; (4) right to refuse to accept a mandate over territory.

When the new Congress met in special session on May 19, 1919 the irreconcilable Republicans gained a great advantage. The Republicans controlled the Senate by a majority of two, and thus they would have a majority on each committee. In control of the Committee on Foreign Relations, they could delay or hasten action on the treaty. When the composition of the committee was announced, of the ten Republican members six were openly irreconcilable. The other four were Lodge, the chairman, who was really irreconcilable; McCumber, the most outspoken Republican for the league; and two party regulars, Harding and New, who would follow the party leaders. Lodge seems to have deliberately packed the Republican membership of the committee with men hostile to the League. Thus he gained the power to keep the treaty in the committee's hands, while a campaign was launched to arouse public sentiment against the league. Millionaires H. C. Frick and Andrew W. Mellon contributed money, and a propaganda campaign consisting of mailings and speaking tours was started. The following advertisement is an example of their propaganda campaign:

Americans, Awake!
Shall We Bind Ourselves to the War Breeding Covenant?
It Impairs American Sovereignty!
Surrenders the Monroe Doctrine!
Flouts Washington's Warning!
Entangles Us In European and Asiatic Intrigues!
Sends Our Boys To Fight Throughout the World by Order of a League!
The Evil Thing With a Holy Name!

While this minority was working against the league, evidence continued to pile up of the great support that the league had among the people. Thirty-two state legislatures endorsed the league and two others made a conditional endorsement. Thirty-three governors of states, also, had endorsed a league of nations.

On July 10, the day after he returned from France, Wilson presented the treaty of peace to the Senate. The Committee on Foreign Affairs kept it in their hands for two months. They had to delay in this way in order to defeat the treaty, because, as one of the irreconcilables, Senator Moses, later said, if the rules of the Senate had permitted a quick vote, "the Versailles Treaty would have been ratified without reservation." In order to stall, the committee read the treaty aloud line by line. This required two weeks. Then, the next six weeks were devoted to permitting representatives of national groups that felt that the treaty was not fair to their homeland to vent their rage. It was natural for the irreconcilables to stir up this opposition to the treaty among foreign elements in the United States.

On September 10, the Committee on Foreign Relations presented its majority report to the Senate. The irreconcilables realized by now that they could not persuade the majority of the Republicans in the Senate to reject the treaty. Not one of the irreconcilables signed a report calling for rejection. Instead, they followed the advice of Lodge and proceeded "by way of amendment and reservation." With Lodge, Harding, and New, they recommended forty-five amendments and four reservations to the covenant of the league. The minority report, filed by six of the seven Democratic members, urged acceptance of the treaty without change. Senator McCumber, the tenth Republican on the committee, filed his own minority report in which he rebuked the partisanship of the majority:

> . . . Not one word is said, not a single allusion made, concerning either the great purpose of the League of Nations or the methods by which those purposes are to be accomplished.
>
> Irony and sarcasm have been substituted for argument and positions taken by the press or individuals outside the Senate seem to command more attention than the treaty itself. It is regrettable that the animosity which centers almost wholly against the League of Nations provisions should have been engendered against a subject so important to the world's welfare. It is regrettable that the consideration of a matter so foreign to any kind of partisanship should be influenced in the country, as well as on the floor of this Senate, by hostility toward or subserviency to the President of the United States. No matter how just may be any antagonism toward President Wilson, the aspirations and hopes of a wounded and bleeding world ought not to be denied because, under the Constitution, the treaty must first be formulated by him.

The majority report did not reflect the sentiment of the Senate. While the treaty was in committee, the debates on the floor of the Senate had demonstrated that the majority of the Republicans were going to vote for entrance into the league. Some wanted strong reservations, others mild, but both groups wanted acceptance of the treaty. The irreconcilables had failed to hold a majority to rejection, and admitted this in their majority report. Now their approach was to hold all Republicans together by a program of amendments or reservations. The Wilson Democrats had two courses of action. They might reach an agreement with the mild reservationists and detach them from the other Republicans, or they could refuse any concessions and possibly win some Republican Senators who would be willing to give up any reservations rather than have the treaty rejected.

It was this last course of action that they decided to follow. Wilson publicly made no suggestion that he might accept mild reservations. To his Senate leader, Hitchcock, he gave a list of reservations that he would accept if necessary, but Wilson took no public step to win the support of the mild reservationist Republicans. Wilson apparently felt that either it was not necessary to accept any reservations, or he was afraid that concessions so early might lead to further demands. In September, the President started on a tour of the nation to arouse the people to vigorous support of the league. On this tour he collapsed and returned to Washington, broken and paralyzed. With his collapse, the most powerful protagonist of the league could fight no more.

The debate in the Senate, following the reports of the Committee on Foreign Relations, was one replete with a great deal of demagoguery. The opponents of the league pandered to popular and national prejudices. They stated that the United States would become entangled in the broils of Europe; that the United States would lose its national sovereignty; that the league was a device for the British Empire to rule the world, since the Dominions as well as Great Britain had a vote; that the majority of countries in the league would be Catholic and thus the league would be under the Pope. They also tried to rally support by denouncing English activities in Ireland and the wrongs done to China in Shantung.

In October the voting began on the amendments. The mild reservationists joined with the almost solid Democratic membership, and all the amendments were defeated. On November 7, the voting began on the reservations, and then the mild reservationists joined with the rest of the Republicans to attach these to the treaty. When the treaty with fourteen reservations came to a vote on November 19, it was rejected by a vote of 39 to 55. Ratification was supported by the reservationist Senators and was opposed by the irreconcilables in combination with the Wilson Democrats, who voted for rejection in hopes of getting final ratification later on just the question of the league as it stood in the treaty of peace. McCumber, just before the vote was taken, pled with the administration Democrats to accept what could be obtained rather than lose everything, but Wilson sent a letter to them to vote against the treaty with reservations. Wilson did this in expectation that a favorable vote could be obtained without any reservations, and also that if the United States placed conditions on its entrance to the league, other nations might do the same and the league would be greatly weakened.

The Senate's action came as a shock to the nation. As one authority has written, "It seemed absurd that the national policy adopted should be the one advocated by only seventeen Senators. Common sense revolted at seeing the votes of seventy-eight Senators to enter the League nullified because they could not agree among themselves on the terms of entry." Immediately the Senate voted to reconsider the question in the next session. The bewilderment of the people at the action taken by the Senate can well be imagined from the observations of Ida Tarbell, who made a speaking tour of the west in the interests of the league in the summer of 1919:

> As the days went by, I sensed a growing bewilderment at the fight against the league. These people had listened for years to people they honored urging some form of international union against war. They had heard Dr. Jordan and Jane Addams preaching a national council for the prevention of war, President Taft advocating a league to enforce peace. In many of these towns there had been chapters of these societies. . . . With such a background, was it strange that many people in the Northwest should have been puzzled that the Congress of the United States was seemingly more and more determined that we should not join this first attempt of the civilized world to find substitutes for war in international quarrels?

When the demand swept the country for a compromise between the league Democrats and the reservationists even Lodge felt compelled to go into a conference on the question. He did so, however, from his own admission with no idea of compromising. He refused to admit that the treaty had been defeated because of verbal differences between the pro-league groups. According to Lodge, the difference between those who supported the treaty and those who opposed it was "not verbal, but vital and essential." By this he could only have meant that the difference between the irreconcilables (of which he really was one) and the administration Democrats was vital, because the difference between the reservationists (strong and mild) and the administration Democrats was one only of a verbal nature or at least of strategy.

A bipartisan conference met to discuss a method of common action between the reservationists and the Wilson Democrats. This conference failed, however, to work out a plan of action. The irreconcilables and the reservationists voted together to add reservations to the treaty, which were without essential changes from those of November 19. In spite of the fact that they voted for adding reservations to the league, on the question of ratification of the treaty with these reservations, there was no doubt but that the irreconcilables would vote against. The question was whether enough

Democrats would realize that there was no alternative but to vote for reservations or the treaty would be defeated. Again, however, Wilson wrote a letter from his sickbed urging his followers to oppose the treaty with the reservations. He still had faith that the public wanted the league, and he was willing to wait for the approaching presidential election to serve as a popular referendum on the subject.

The vote on March 19, 1920, on the question of ratification of the treaty with reservations, resulted in a majority of the votes cast being for the ratification, but not the requisite two-thirds majority, forty-nine being in favor and thirty-five being opposed. Some Democrats who had voted against in November voted *for* this second time, but there were still enough administration Democrats who carried out Wilson's desire that they vote against, and the treaty was defeated. For the second time, the responsibility for the defeat lies not alone with the irreconcilables but with the league's warmest friends. If Wilson had not been quite so uncompromising in his position, the treaty with reservations could easily have passed.

This possibility greatly disturbed some of the irreconcilables. One of them mentioned to Lodge that Wilson might accept the reservations and then the country would be in the league. Lodge's reply was:

> ". . . you do not take into consideration the hatred that Woodrow Wilson has for me personally. Never under any set of circumstances in this world could he be induced to accept a treaty with Lodge reservations appended to it!" "But," I replied, "that seems to me to be rather a slender thread on which to hang so great a cause." "A slender thread!" he answered. "Why, it is as strong as any cable with its strands wired and twisted together." [6]

That Lodge carefully estimated and studied Wilson at every step can be seen from Lodge's own book. After admitting that there was a possibility that the treaty might pass with the reservations, he observes that ". . . I also felt convinced that President Wilson would prevent the acceptance of the treaty with reservations if he possibly could. I based this opinion on the knowledge which I had acquired as to Mr. Wilson's temperament, intentions, and purposes." On the final page of his book Lodge repeats this same thought: "As the strenuous days which were filled by the contest over the League of Nations passed by, almost every one bringing its difficulty and its crucial question, I made no mistake in my estimate of what President Wilson would do under certain conditions."

Although President Wilson called for the presidential election of 1920 to serve as a great national referendum on the question of the league, it did not serve this purpose. The league was actively debated during the campaign, but the majority of seven million for Harding cannot be translated into a majority of seven million against the league. The Republican plat-

[6] James E. Watson, *op. cit.*, p. 200.

form was ambiguous, but it did advocate entrance of the United States into an international association of nations. In the platform committee there was a spectacular fight between the proleague Republicans and the irreconcilables. There was a move to adopt a plank favoring the league with the Lodge reservations, but Lodge prevented this plank from being included. This action of Lodge's tends to prove that he always had been an irreconcilable and had used reservations only as a technique to defeat the league.

During the campaign, Harding interpreted the plank on some occasions to be proleague and on other occasions to be antileague. This equivocal stand was, of course, designed to confuse the voters and muddle the issue. Near the end of the campaign Harding seemed more and more to favor an international league. All this time the Democrats were campaigning for the League of Nations without reservations. Outstanding Republicans like former-President Taft and Herbert Hoover campaigned for Harding and made it plain that they considered support for Harding equivalent to support of the League of Nations. On October 14, 1920, thirty-one leading Republicans, including Elihu Root, Charles E. Hughes, Henry L. Stimson, Herbert Hoover, and William Allen White, issued a public statement that a vote for Harding would be the surest way of indicating that the citizen favored joining the league.

Probably thousands of voters took these men at their word. In the light of their statement and the, at times, proleague stand of Harding, many proleague citizens undoubtedly voted for the Republican candidate. Calvin Coolidge, in a post-election statement, observed:

> I doubt if any particular mandate was given at the last election on the question of the League of Nations and if that was the preponderant issue. In the South, where there was decided opposition to the league, they voted the Democratic ticket. And as far as the League of Nations was concerned in the North, the vote was with equal and even greater preponderance in favor of the Republican ticket. Of course, many men voted thus who were in favor of the league. With them it became simply a question of supporting the Republican or Democratic party. So you can't say that there was a preponderance of votes against the League of Nations.

The entire story of the fight in the Senate and in the campaign of 1920 demonstrates that the American people never had the opportunity squarely to vote for the League of Nations. . . .

The Supreme Infanticide

Thomas A. Bailey

As a friend of the President, as one who has loyally followed him, I solemnly declare to him this morning: If you want to kill your own child because the Senate straightens out its crooked limbs, you must take the responsibility and accept the verdict of history.

Senator Ashurst of Arizona (Democrat),
March 11, 1920

I

The treaty was now dead, as far as America was concerned. Who had killed it?

The vital role of the loyal Democrats must be reemphasized. If all of them who professed to want the treaty had voted "Yea," it would have passed with more than a dozen votes to spare. If the strait-jacket of party loyalty had not been involved, the necessary two-thirds could easily have been mustered.*

In the previous November, the Democrats might have voted against the treaty (as they did) even without White House pressure. But this time pressure had to be applied to force them into line, and even in the face of Wilsonian wrath almost half of them bolted. On the day of the final balloting the newsmen observed that two Cabinet members (Burleson and Daniels), possibly acting at the President's direction, were on the floor of the Senate, buttonholing waverers. The day after the fateful voting Hitchcock wrote Wilson that it had required the "most energetic efforts" on his part *to prevent a majority of the Democrats from surrendering to Lodge.*

Desertion of the President . . . is no light offense in the political world, especially when he has declared himself emphatically. Senators do not ordinarily court political suicide. Wilson still had the patronage bludgeon in his hands, and having more than a trace of vindictiveness, he could oppose renegade senators when they ran again, and in fact did so.

Reprinted with the permission of The Macmillan Company from Thomas A. Bailey, *Woodrow Wilson and the Great Betrayal* (New York: The Macmillan Company, 1945), pp. 271–287. Copyright 1945 by Thomas A. Bailey.

* Editor's note: The reference is to the vote on the treaty of March 19, 1920.

Many of the loyal Democrats were up for reelection in 1920. They certainly were aware of the effects of party treachery on their political fortunes. They knew—or many of them knew—that they were killing the treaty; they made no real effort to revive it; they must have wanted it killed—at least until after the November election.

One striking fact stands out like a lighthouse. With the exception of Hitchcock of Nebraska, Johnson of South Dakota, and Thomas of Colorado, *every single one of the twenty-three senators who stood loyally with Wilson in March came from south of the Mason and Dixon line.* Only four of the "disloyal" twenty-one represented states that had seceded in 1860–61. At the polls, as well as on the floor of the Senate, decent southern Democrats voted "the way their fathers shot." As between bothersome world responsibility on the one hand, and loyalty to President, party, section, and race on the other, there was but one choice. Perhaps world leadership would come eventually anyhow.

Democratic senators like Walsh of Montana and Ashurst of Arizona were not from the South. When the issue was clearly drawn between loyalty to party and loyalty to country, their consciences bade them choose the greater good. Ashurst had gone down the line in supporting Wilson; but several days before the final vote he declared, "I am just as much opposed to a White House irreconcilable as I am to a Lodge irreconcilable."

II

A word now about public opinion.

In March, as in November, more than 80 per cent of the senators professed to favor the treaty with some kind of reservations. All the polls and other studies indicate that this was roughly the sentiment of the country. Yet the senators were unable to scrape together a two-thirds vote for any one set of reservations.

The reaction of many newspaper editors, as before, was to cry out against the shame of it all—this indictment of the "capacity of our democracy to do business." We had astonished the world by our ability to make war; we now astonished the world with our "imbecility" in trying to make peace. How could we blame other countries for thinking us "a nation of boobs and bigots"? The Louisville *Courier-Journal* (Democrat), referring to our broken promises to the Allies, cried that we stood betrayed as "cravens and crooks," "hypocrites and liars."

Partisan Republican newspapers loudly blamed the stiff-backed Wilson and his "me-too" senators. Two wings of "irreconcilables"—the Wilsonites and the "bitter-enders"—had closed in to execute a successful pincers movement against the treaty. The New York *Tribune* (Independent Republican) condemned the "inefficiency, all-sufficiency and self-sufficiency of our self-named only negotiator," Woodrow Wilson. If the treaty died, said the

Tribune, the handle of the dagger that pierced its heart would bear the "initials 'W. W.'"

If Republicans scolded Democrats, Democrats scolded Republicans. Lodge and his cheap political tricks were roundly condemned, and the general conclusion was that "the blood of the Treaty stains the floor of the Republican wigwam." A few of the less partisan Democratic journals openly conceded that Wilson's obstinacy had something to do with the final result. William Jennings Bryan asserted from the platform that this "most colossal crime against our nation and the civilized world in all history" made his "blood boil." He began a vigorous campaign against the two-thirds rule in the Senate. "A majority of Congress can declare war," he cried; "it ought to be as easy to end a war as to begin it."

The leading liberal journals, as before, were sadly happy. They rejoiced that the result would clear the way for a renovation of the treaty, but they regretted that the pact had been defeated as a result of partisanship rather than as a result of the betrayal of Wilson's promises.

An impressive number of the more discerning editors deplored the fact that the issue was now in the dirty hands of politicians. An electoral referendum, it was felt, would merely confuse the issue; such a canvass could not possibly reveal anything more than was already known, namely, that *an overwhelming majority of the people wanted the treaty with some kind of reservations.*

III

Is it true that the invalid in the White House really strangled the treaty to death with his own enfeebled hands?

It is seldom that statesmen have a second chance—a second guess. They decide on a course of action, and the swift current of events bears them downstream from the starting point. Only rarely does the stream reverse itself and carry them back.

In November, Wilson had decided that he wanted deadlock, because he reasoned that deadlock would arouse public opinion and force the Senate to do his bidding. The tidal wave of public opinion did surge in, and Wilson got his second chance. But he threw it away, first by spurning compromise (except on his terms), and then by spurning the Lodge reservations.

There had been much more justification for Wilson's course in November than in March. In November he was sick, secluded, was fed censored news, and was convinced by Hitchcock that the strategy of deadlock was sound. In March, he was much improved in health, far less secluded, more in touch with the press and with the currents of opinion, though probably still not enough. He consulted even less with the Senate, presumably because he had made up his mind in advance to oppose the Lodge reservations. In November, there was a fair possibility of reconsideration; in March, it was clear that the only possibility lay in making the League an issue in the coming campaign. Wilson, with his broad knowledge of government and politics, should have seen that this hope was largely if not completely illusory. Perhaps he would have seen it had he not been blinded by his feeling for Lodge.

The evidence is convincing that Wilson wanted the issue cast into the hurly-burly of politics. He could not accept Lodge's terms; Lodge would not accept his terms. The only possible chance of beating the senator—and this was slim indeed—was to win a resounding mandate in 1920.

Yet this strategy . . . meant further delay. At Paris, the feeling at times had been, "Better a bad treaty today than a good treaty four months hence." Europe was still in chaos, and increasingly in need of America's helping hand. Well might the Europeans cry, "Better a treaty with the Lodge reservations today than a probable treaty without reservations after the election." Or as Dr. Frank Crane wrote in *Current Opinion,* "It is vastly more needful that some sort of League be formed, *any sort,* than that it be formed *perfectly.*" (Italics Crane's.)

Yet Wilson, for the reasons indicated, could not see all this clearly. Four days after the fatal vote he wrote Hitchcock, praising him for having done all in his power to protect the honor of the nation and the peace of the world against the Republican majority.

Mrs. Wilson, no doubt reflecting her husband's views, later wrote, "My conviction is that Mr. Lodge put the world back fifty years, and that at his door lies the wreckage of human hopes and the peril to human lives that afflict mankind today."

IV

To the very end Wilson was a fighter. When the Scotch-Irish in him became aroused, he would nail his colors to the mast. He said in 1916 that he was "playing for the verdict of mankind." His conception of duty as he saw it was overpowering. He once remarked that if he were a judge, and it became his duty to sentence his own brother to the gallows, he would do so—and afterwards die of a broken heart.

It is well to have principles; it is well to have a noble conception of duty. But Wilson, as he became warmed up in a fight, tended to get things out of focus and to lose a proper sense of values.

The basic issue in 1920 was the Hitchcock reservations* or the Lodge reservations. Wilson accepted those of Hitchcock while rejecting those of Lodge,

---

* Editor's note: Four of the five so-called Hitchcock reservations were drafted by President Wilson; the fifth was added by Senator Hitchcock. For the text of these reservations, see Bailey, *Woodrow Wilson and the Great Betrayal,* pp. 393–394.

which, he said, completely nullified the treaty and betrayed his promises to the Allies and to the American dead.

This . . . was a gross exaggeration. Minds no less acute than Wilson's, and less clouded with sickness and pride, denied that the Lodge reservations completely nullified the treaty. To the man in the street—in so far as he gave the dispute thought—there was little discernible difference between the two sets of reservations. How could one decry statements which merely re-affirmed the basic principles of the Constitution and of our foreign policy? To a vast number of Americans the Lodge reservations, far from nullifying the treaty, actually improved it. This was so apparent to even the most loyal Democrats in the Senate that Wilson could barely keep them in line.

In the final analysis the treaty was slain in the house of its friends rather than in the house of its enemies. In the final analysis it was not the two-thirds rule, or the "irreconcilables," or Lodge, or the "strong" and "mild reservationists," but Wilson and his docile following who delivered the fatal stab. If the President had been permitted to vote he would have sided with Borah, Brandegee, Johnson, and the other "bitter-enders"—though for en-tirely different reasons.

Wilson had said that the reservation to Article X was a knife thrust at the heart of the Covenant. Ironically, he parried this knife thrust, and stuck his own dagger, not into the heart of the Covenant, but into the entire treaty.

This was the supreme act of infanticide. With his own sickly hands Wilson slew his own brain child—or the one to which he had contributed so much.

This was the supreme paradox. He who had forced the Allies to write the League into the treaty, unwrote it; he who had done more than any other man to make the Covenant, unmade it—at least so far as America was concerned. And by his action, he contributed powerfully to the ultimate undoing of the League, and with it the high hopes of himself and mankind for an organization to prevent World War II.

V

The preceding dogmatic observations are of course qualified by the phrase, "in the last analysis."

Many elements enter into a log jam. Among them are the width of the stream, the depth of the stream, the swiftness of the current, the presence of boulders, the size of the logs, and the absence of enough lumberjacks. No one of these factors can be solely responsible for the pile-up.

Many elements entered into the legislative log jam of March, 1920. Among them were isolationism, partisanship, senatorial prerogative, confu-sion, apathy, personal pride, and private feuds. No one of them was solely responsible for the pile-up. *But as the pile-up finally developed, there was only one lumberjack who could break it, and that was Woodrow Wilson.*

If at any time before the final vote he had told the Senate Democrats to support the treaty with the Lodge reservations, or even if he had merely told them that they were on their own, the pact would almost certainly have been approved. So "in the last analysis" the primary responsibility for the failure in March rested with Wilson.

What about Lodge? If the treaty would have passed by Wilson's surrendering, is it not equally true that it would have passed by Lodge's surrendering?

The answer is probably "Yes," but the important point is that Lodge had far less responsibility for getting the treaty through than Wilson. If Lodge had yielded, he probably would have created a schism within his ranks. His ultimate responsibility was to keep the party from breaking to pieces, and in this he succeeded. Wilson's ultimate responsibility was to get the treaty ratified, and in this he failed. With Lodge, as with any truly partisan leader, the party comes before country; with the President the country should come before party, though unhappily it often does not.

It is possible that Wilson saw all this—but not clearly enough. He might have been willing to compromise if his adversary had been any other than Lodge. But so bitter was the feeling between the two men that Wilson, rather than give way, grasped at the straw of the election of 1920.

Lodge did not like Wilson either, but he made more of a show of compromising than the President. He actually supported and drove through amendments to his original reservations which were in line with Wilson's wishes, and he probably would have gone further had the "irreconcilables" not been on his back. He fought the crippling Irish reservation, as well as others supported by the "bitter-enders." Finally, he gave the Democrats a fair chance to reconsider their vote and get on the bandwagon, but they spurned it.

If Lodge's words mean anything, and if his actions were not those of a monstrous hypocrite, he actually tried to get the treaty through with his reservations. When he found that he could not, he washed his hands of the whole business in disgust.

The charge is frequently made that, if Wilson had yielded to his adversary, Lodge would have gleefully piled on more reservations until Wilson, further humiliated, would have had to throw out the whole thing.

The strongest evidence for this view is a circumstantial story which Secretary Houston relates. During a Cabinet meeting Wilson was called to the telephone, and agreed to make certain concessions agreeable to Lodge. Before adjournment the telephone rang again, and word came that Lodge would not adhere to his original proposal.

This story is highly improbable, because Wilson attended no Cabinet meetings between September 2, 1919, and April 13, 1920. By the latter date, all serious attempts at compromise had been dropped; by the earlier date the treaty was still before the Senate committee, and the Lodge reservations, though in an embryonic stage, were yet unborn. But, even if the story is true, it merely proves that Lodge veered about, as he frequently did under "irreconcilable" pressure.

In March, as in November, all Wilson had to do was to send over Postmaster General Burleson to the Senate a few minutes before the final vote with the quiet word that the Democrats were to vote "Yea." The treaty would then have passed with the Lodge reservations, and Lodge could hardly have dared incur for himself or his party the odium of moving to reconsider for the purpose of screwing on more reservations. Had he tried to do so, the "mild reservationists" almost certainly would have blocked him.

VI

A few days after the disastrous final vote, Wilson's only comment to Tumulty was, "They have shamed us in the eyes of the world." If his previous words said what he really meant, he was hardly more shamed by the defeat of the treaty than by the addition of the Lodge reservations. In his eyes it all amounted to the same thing.

If the treaty had passed, would the President have been willing to go through with the exchange of ratifications? Would he not have pocketed it, as he threatened to do prior to the November vote?

Again, if Wilson's words may be taken at their face value, this is what he would have done. He had not backed down from his pre-November position. His Jackson Day message and his letter to Hitchcock made it unmistakably clear that he preferred the uncertainties of a political campaign to the certainties of ratification with the Lodge reservations. The addition of the indefensible Irish reservation provided even stronger justification for pocketing the entire pact.

It is probable that some of the loyal Democrats voted as they did partly because they were convinced that Wilson was going to pigeonhole the treaty anyhow. From their point of view it was better that the odium for defeat should seemingly rest on Lodge rather than on their President. It also seems clear that Wilson preferred, as in November, to have the blood of the treaty on the Senate doorstep rather than on his. As he wrote to Secretary Colby, on April 2, 1920, the slain pact lay heavily on the consciences of those who had stabbed it, and he was quite willing to have it lie there until those consciences were either awakened or crushed.

Yet it is one thing to say, just before Senate action, "I will pocket the treaty." It is another, after the pact is approved and sent to the White House, to assume this tremendous responsibility. The eyes of the world are upon the President; he is the only man keeping the nation out of the peace which it so urgently needs; he is the one man standing in the way of the rehabilitation which the world so desperately demands. Public pressure to ratify in such a case would be enormous—probably irresistible.

Some years later Senator Hitchcock said that in the event of senatorial approval Wilson would possibly have waited for the November election. If he had won, he would have worked for the removal of the Lodge reservations; if he had lost, then the compulsion to go through with ratification would have become overpowering. By November more than six months would have passed, and by that time Wilson might have developed a saner perspective.

But this is all speculation. Wilson gave orders that the treaty was to be killed in the Senate chamber. And there it died.

VII

One other line of inquiry must be briefly pursued. Is it true, as some writers allege, that the thirty-odd Allied signatories of the original treaty would have rejected the Lodge reservations when officially presented? We recall that under the terms of the preamble these nations were privileged to acquiesce silently or file objections.

One will never know the answer to this question, because Wilson denied the other signatories a chance to act. But it seems proper to point to certain probabilities.

One or more of the Latin American nations might have objected to the reservation regarding the then hated Monroe Doctrine. Yet the Monroe Doctrine would have continued to exist anyhow; it was already in the Covenant; and these neighboring republics might well have swallowed their pride in the interest of world peace.

Italy probably would have acquiesced, and the evidence is strong that France would have done likewise. The Japanese could not completely overlook the Shantung reservation, but it was generally recognized in their press as meaningless, and for this reason it might have been tolerated, though not without some loss of face. It is noteworthy that the most important Japanese newspapers regretted the Senate stalemate as an encouragement to world instability, particularly in China.

Great Britain probably would have been the chief objector. The reservation on Ireland was highly offensive but completely innocuous, for the British lion had long endured Irish-American tail-twistings in pained but dignified silence. The reservation on six-to-one was a slap at the loyal and sacrificing Dominions, but it did not mean that their vote was to be taken away. Moreover, the contingency envisaged by this proviso was unlikely to arise very often, and in the long run would doubtless have proved inconsequential.

In sum, there were only two or three reservations to which the outside powers could seriously object. If they had objected, it is probable that a satisfactory adjustment could have been threshed out through diplomatic channels. For when it became clear that only a few phrases stood between the United States and peace, the dictates of common sense and the pressure of public opinion probably would have led to an acceptable compromise. If the Senate had refused to give ground in such a case, then the onus would have been clearly on it and not on Wilson.

The World Court is a case in point. In 1926 the Senate voted to join, but attached five reservations, four of which were accepted by the other powers. By 1935 a compromise was worked out on the fifth, but an isolationist uprising led by William Randolph Hearst and Father Coughlin turned what seemed to be a favorable vote in the Senate into a narrow defeat for the World Court. The one-third minority again triumphed, with the aging Borah and Johnson and Norris and Gore still voting their fears and prejudices.

But the World Court analogy must not be pressed too far. In 1920 Europe was in a desperate condition; the only real hope for a successful League lay in American cooperation. Unless the United States would shoulder its obligations the whole treaty system was in danger of collapse. In 1926 the powers could afford to haggle over the World Court; in 1920 there was far less temptation to haggle while Europe burned. The European nations were under strong compulsion to swallow their pride, or at the very worst not to drive too hard a bargain in seeking adjustment.

But this again is pure speculation. Wilson never gave the other powers a chance to act on the reservations, though Colonel House and others urged him to. He assumed this terrific responsibility all by himself. While thinking that he was throwing the onus on the consciences of the senators, he was in fact throwing a large share of the onus upon his own bent shoulders.

VIII

What were the reactions of our recent brothers in arms on the other side of the Atlantic?

The British viewed the Senate debacle with mixed emotions. The result had been a foregone conclusion, and there was some relief in having an end to senatorial uncertainty—at least this stage of it. Some journals were inclined to blame the two-thirds rule; others, the unbending doctrinaire in the White House. The London *Times* sorrowfully concluded that all the processes of peace would have to be suspended pending the outcome of the November election.

The French were shocked, though hardly surprised. The Paris *Liberté* aptly referred to the state of anarchy existing between the executive and the legislative in America. Other journals, smarting under Wilson's recent blast against French militarism, blamed the autocrat in the White House. "At the most troubled moment in history," gibed the Paris *Matin,* "America has a sick President, an amateur Secretary of State, and no Treaty of Peace. A President in the clouds, a Secretary of State in the bushes, and a treaty in the cabbage patch. What a situation!"

But the French did not completely abandon hope that America might yet honor her commitments. Meanwhile they would keep their powder dry and pursue the militaristic course which widened the growing rift between Britain and France, and which proved so fatal to the peace of Europe in the 1930's. The French finally became disgusted with German excuses (which were probably encouraged by America's defection), and in April, 1920, the month after the Senate rejected the treaty, their tanks rumbled into the Ruhr and occupied several German cities as hostages for reparations payments. Bullets were fired, and some blood was shed. This was but a dress rehearsal for the catastrophic invasion of the Ruhr in 1923.

The action—or rather inaction—of the United States had other tragic consequences. It encouraged German radicals in their determination to tear up the treaty: they were finding unwitting collaborators in Senator Borah and President Wilson. It delayed by many months, as British Foreign Secretary Curzon openly charged, the treaty with Turkey, thus giving the "Sick Man of Europe" (Turkey) a chance to prove that he was the "Slick Man of Europe." It held up the economic and moral rehabilitation of the Continent, and even hampered the work of relief then going forward. It further disillusioned the liberals of Europe and others who had clung to Wilson as the major prophet of a new order. It gave new comfort to the forces of disorder everywhere. It left the United States discredited, isolated, shorn of its prestige, and branded as a hypocrite and renegade. It marked the first unbridgeable rift in the ranks of the victorious Allies, a coalition that might have kept the peace. Instead they now went their separate ways, perhaps not as enemies, but certainly no longer as close friends. The United States was the first to break completely away.

America—and the world—paid a high price for the collapse of the treaty-making process in Washington. We are still paying it.

IX

One final question. Who won after all these months of parliamentary jockeying?

Lodge the master parliamentarian had not won—that is, if he really wanted the treaty with his reservations. As in November, he was unable to keep the "irreconcilables" in line on the crucial vote, and he was unable to muster a two-thirds majority. He finally had to confess failure of leadership, except in so far as he prevented a schism.

The Republican party had not won. Lodge had avoided a serious split with the "bitter-enders" by knuckling under when they laid down the law.

But the Republican leaders did not really want the issue in the campaign, and they had made strong efforts to keep it out. Now it was on their hands to cause them no end of embarrassment.

Wilson had not won. He has been praised for having kept the party ranks intact, and for having retained undisputed leadership of his following. But the Democrats in the Senate split 21 for the treaty to 23 against it, and that is hardly holding one's followers in line. Wilson lost irreparably because he did not get his treaty, even with reservations, and because he was doomed to lose again by insisting on a referendum where there could be no referendum.

The Democrats had not won. The treaty issue had caused a serious rift in the Senate, and Bryan, who was still a great leader, was on the rampage. Except for Wilson and some of his "yes men," there were few Democratic leaders who wanted this troublesome issue catapulated into the campaign. Yet there it was.

The United States had not won. It had won the war, to be sure; but it was now kicking the fruits of the victory back under the peace table. We had helped turn Europe into a scrap heap, and now we were scrapping the treaty. We were going to stand by the Allies—with our arms folded. We were throwing away the only hope of averting World War II.

The real victor was international anarchy.

V

Prohibition: Product of Hidden Urges or of Cultural Conflict?

INTRODUCTION

From January 16, 1920, when the Volstead Act went into effect, until December 21, 1933, when the Eighteenth Amendment was supplanted by the Twenty-first, the American people could not legally manufacture, sell, or transport intoxicating beverages containing more than ½ of 1 per cent of alcohol. The prohibition movement antedated the Civil War, but it was not until the era of World War I that its advocates were able to impose their will on the nation at large.

Two striking and contrasting interpretations of the motivation of those who launched what President Hoover was later to characterize as "a great social and economic experiment, noble in motive and far-reaching in purpose" are contained in the selections that follow. Andrew Sinclair, an English-born historian and novelist, regards the study of prohibition as "a study of social excess." He recognizes that there were "reasonable moral and economic and medical reasons for supporting prohibition," but, at the same time, he believes that the prohibitionists "exploited many irrational motives within themselves and their followers." In the following chapter from his study Prohibition: The Era of Excess, *Sinclair is concerned with the "hidden urges" that influenced supporters of the Prohibition cause, white Southerners, and foreign missionaries.*

In contrast to Sinclair's psychological interpretation of prohibition, Joseph R. Gusfield offers us a sociological interpretation. Gusfield, who is interested in the problem of moral reform from a sociological perspective, is critical of Sinclair's "moralistic condemnation of moralism." Gusfield sees moral reform as "one way through which a cultural group acts to preserve, defend or enhance the dominance and prestige of its own style of living within the total society." The history of the temperance movement is conceived of in this context as "a reflection of clashes and conflicts between rival social systems, cultures, and status groups."

Central to the understanding of Gusfield's analysis is the distinction that he draws between "assimilative reform" and "coercive reform." The advocate of assimilative reform regards the drinker as part of a social system in which the culture of the reformer is dominant, and he invites the intemperate person to alter his habits and adopt the reformer's ways. The coercive reformer, by contrast, sees the drinker as one who rejects the dominance and the style of life of the reformer and therefore seeks by law to compel him to affirm the reformer's values and culture.[1] In the following selection, Gusfield traces the development of coercive reform through the Prohibition party, Populism, and especially the Anti-Saloon League to the ratification of the Eighteenth Amendment and the establishment by law of the social dominance of one culture over another.

---

[1] Joseph R. Gusfield, *Symbolic Crusade: Status Politics and the American Temperance Movement* (Urbana: University of Illinois Press, 1963), pp. 3, 6–7, 11.

The Psychology of Prohibition

Andrew Sinclair

All we have to do is to think of the wrecks on either bank of the stream of death, of the suicides, of the insanity, of the ignorance, of the destitution, of the little children tugging at the faded and withered breast of weeping and despairing mothers, of wives asking for bread, of the men of genius it has wrecked, the men struggling with imaginary serpents, produced by this devilish thing; and when you think of the jails, of the almshouses, of the asylums, of the prisons, of the scaffolds upon either bank, I do not wonder that every thoughtful man is prejudiced against this damned stuff called alcohol.

Robert G. Ingersoll
The Commoner, July 11, 1913

Recent research on the nature of prejudice has made a momentous discovery. The cognitive processes of prejudiced people are different in general from the cognitive processes of tolerant people. In fact, a person's prejudice is not usually a particular attitude to a particular question; it is more often a whole pattern of thinking about the world.[1] The prejudiced person is given to simple judgments in general, to assertions, to definite statements, to terms of black and white. Ambiguity is an evil to him because set truth is the good. He thinks in stereotypes, in rules, in truisms, in the traditional folkways of his environment. Such education as he receives merely gives him more reasons for his old beliefs. Indeed, he is the man who was found frequently in the dominant middle class of the small town, on the Western farms, and in the Southern shacks, where no complex clamor of urban life unsettled the mind and brain and eyes from the easy pairings of right and wrong. He is the man who was the backbone of the dry cause.

The Eighteenth Amendment could not have been passed without the support of the psychologically tolerant, made temporarily intolerant by the stress of war. But when the moderates deserted the drys in time of peace, the hard core of the movement was revealed. The main areas of prohibition sentiment were the areas where the Methodist and Baptist churches had their

[1] See G. Allport, *The Nature of Prejudice* (Cambridge, Mass., 1954), pp. 174–175.

greatest strength. These were the areas that fathered the bigot crusade of the Ku Klux Klan, which supported prohibition, among other moral reforms. Although many sincere drys were not bigots at the beginning of the campaign for the Eighteenth Amendment, they became bigots or left the cause by the time of repeal. Prohibition, an extreme measure, forced its extremes on its supporters and its enemies. Its study becomes a study of social excess.

Although there were reasonable moral and economic and medical reasons for supporting prohibition, the drys themselves exploited many irrational motives within themselves and their followers. Among the leaders of the cause, there was hysteria in their passion to wean the human race from alcohol. There was what one leader of the Anti-Saloon League found in another, "an almost revengeful hatred of the liquor traffic . . . a dogmatic and consecrated prejudice against organized wrong." [2] There was an element of sadism and undue persecution in the drys' legislative pursuit of the sinner, and in the flogging of prostitutes and bootleggers by the Ku Klux Klan. There was a thirst for power, which revealed itself in the savage struggles for position and prestige within the dry organizations, and in the sixteen-hour days worked year after year for no profit except self-satisfaction by such men as Wayne B. Wheeler, the great lobbyist of the dry cause. There was also a deliberate exploitation of prejudiced mentalities among their listeners by revivalist preachers such as Billy Sunday. Above all, until the failure of the World League Against Alcoholism, there was a feeling that prohibition was a winning global crusade, and that those first on the wagon would be first in the promised land of earth and heaven.

Among the followers of prohibition, there were other blind motives. There was the release from tension offered by the crusade against wrong. One "chastened crusader" confessed after the Women's Crusade against the saloons in Ohio in 1873, "The Crusade was a daily dissipation from which it seemed impossible to tear myself. In the intervals at home I felt, as I can fancy the drinker does at the breaking down of a long spree." [3] Allied with this release was an unreasoning fear of hard liquor, instilled by decades of revival sermons. As a female supporter of beer and wine wrote in 1929, "It is not love of whisky which makes real temperance impossible in this year of grace. It is the fear of it, the blinding, demoralizing terror felt by good people who have never tasted anything stronger than sweet communion wine." [4] This terror drove the extreme drys into a stupid and obnoxious pursuit of the drinker during prohibition, which made the whole dry cause stink in the nostrils of the moderate. The Durant and Hearst prize contests

---

[2] E. Cherrington, *History of the Anti-Saloon League* (Westerville, Ohio, 1913), pp. 76–77. He is commenting on the character of the leader of the League at that time, Purley A. Baker.

[3] Quoted in S. Unger, *A History of the National Woman's Christian Temperance Union* (Ph.D., Ohio State Univ., 1933), p. 25. This is good treatment of the subject.

[4] A. Cullen in F. Tietsort (ed.), *Temperance—Or Prohibition?* (New York, 1929), p. 166.

for a solution to the prohibition problem revealed its distorted importance in the minds of certain drys and gave them wide publicity. One woman suggested that liquor law violators should be hung by the tongue beneath an airplane and carried over the United States. Another suggested that the government should distribute poison liquor through the bootleggers; she admitted that several hundred thousand Americans would die, but she thought that this cost was worth the proper enforcement of the dry law. Others wanted to deport all aliens, exclude wets from all churches, force bootleggers to go to church every Sunday, forbid drinkers to marry, torture or whip or brand or sterilize or tattoo drinkers, place offenders in bottle-shaped cages in public squares, make them swallow two ounces of castor oil, and even execute the consumers of alcohol and their posterity to the fourth generation.[5]

This extremism was only prevalent among a small group of the drys, but it was enough to damn all drys as fanatics. They were not so, although their spokesmen often were. Yet, living in a time before Freud and psychology were widely understood, they did not question their own motives. It was a time when "the figure of God was big in the hearts of men," and the drive of personal frustration was put down to divine guidance.[6] Men were not aware of the subconscious motives which made them prohibitionists; but these motives were none the less real. Behind the crusade against the saloon lurked the tormented spirits of many people.

Freud's masterpiece, *Civilization and Its Discontents,* suggests some of the unconscious forces that drove on the drys. The childish, the immature, those who had least recovered from the ignorant certainties of youth sought consolation in an authoritarian crusade, in the same way that those who cannot bear life without a father often make a father of God. Refuge from the ambiguities and difficulties of modern life was, for many of the drys, only to be found in total immersion in clear-cut moral reform. The saloon was a sufficient Satan to become the scapegoat of the devil in man. Abolition of the saloon was interpreted by the prohibitionists as a personal victory over doubt and sin in their own lives. With a terrible faith in equality, the prohibitionists often wanted to suppress in society the sins they found in themselves. G. K. Chesterton put the matter well:

> When the Puritan or the modern Christian finds that his right hand offends him he not only cuts it off but sends an executioner with a chopper all down the street, chopping off the hands of all the men, women and children in the town. Then he has a curious feeling of comradeship and of everybody being comfortable together. . . . He is after all in some queer way a democrat, because he is as much a despot to one man as to another.[7]

---

[5] *Ibid.,* pp. 251, 255.
[6] S. Anderson, *Winesburg, Ohio* (New York, 1919), p. 55.
[7] *New York Herald,* February 24, 1924.

It was in this wish to extend their own repressions to all society that the drys felt themselves most free from their constant inward struggle. Indeed, they defended their attacks on the personal liberty of other men by stating that they were bringing these men personal liberty for the first time. According to one dry leader, personal liberty reached its highest expression where the strongest inhibitions were invoked and enforced.[8] Moreover, personal liberty was only possible once prohibition had freed the slaves of alcohol. Of course, in reality the drys were trying to bring personal liberty to themselves, by externalizing their anguished struggles against their own weaknesses in their battle to reform the weaknesses of others. The conflict between conscience and lust, between superego and id, was transferred by the drys from their own bodies to the body politic of all America; and, in the ecstasy of that paranoia which Freud saw in all of us, they would have involved the whole earth.

Freud, whose own life was hard, considered intoxicants a great blessing in the human struggle for happiness and in the warding off of misery.

> It is not merely the immediate gain in pleasure which one owes to them, but also a measure of that independence of the outer world which is so sorely craved. Men know that with the help they can get from "drowning their cares" they can at any time slip away from the oppression of reality and find a refuge in a world of their own where painful feelings do not enter.[9]

Freud saw that the moderate use of liquor was necessary for driven men, who could not find other interests or gratifications against the miseries of the world. The prohibitionists, however, presumed that a man who was denied the bottle would turn to the altar. They were wrong. They closed the saloons, but the churches did not fill. Luckily, drugs, radios, motion pictures, automobiles, proliferating societies, professional sports, paid holidays, and the relaxed sexual ethics of the flaming twenties provided new outlets for the libidos of deprived drinkers. Without these new outlets, the drys might have had to deal with a psychological explosion.

Yet extremism was not confined to the ranks of the drys. If the moderate drys were shamed by the excesses and motives of the extreme drys, so the moderate wets were damned by the millions of heavy drinkers and alcoholics on their side. If some prohibitionists were compulsive in their craving for water for everybody, some drinkers were even more compulsive in their craving for an excess of liquor for themselves. Alcoholics may suffer from many inadequacies—emotional immaturity, instability, infantilism, passivity, dependence, pathological jealousy, oral eroticism, latent homosexuality, isola-

---

[8] E. Cherrington at San Francisco in 1930, quoted by Senator J. Reed, *The Rape of Temperance* (New York, 1930), p. 31.

[9] S. Freud, *Civilization and Its Discontents* (New York, 1930), p. 31.

tion, narcissism, and masochism.[10] People who possess such defects are not to be deprived of their liquor by respect for the law of the land. They need understanding, not prohibition, which merely drives them into drinking any murderous substitute for liquor rather than no liquor at all. For the compulsive drinker drinks because he is compulsive by nature, as is the fanatical reformer. To deprive the compulsive drinker of his drink does not cure him. He is merely forced into the search for substitutes. Equally, the prohibition of a reform to a reformer would not make him give up all reforms. He would merely turn his neuroses onto another brand of reform.

The real tragedy of the prohibitionist ideology was that it left no room for temperance. The dry crusade slipped slowly from a moderate remedy for obvious evils into a total cure-all for society. The creed of the dedicated dry would not admit the existence of the moderate drinker. By definition, all drinkers were bound to become alcoholics. The moral of the famous propaganda piece *Ten Nights in a Bar-Room* was that the first sip of beer always and inevitably led to a drunkard's grave. So believing, the Anti-Saloon League could not attract moderate support by allowing the sale of light wines and beers. National prohibition had to be total. Yet if prohibition had been confined to prohibition of ardent spirits, as the early nineteenth-century temperance associations had recommended, the Anti-Saloon League might have had the support of the brewers, the winegrowers, and the majority of the American people to this day. A survey conducted in 1946 in America showed that fewer than two-fifths of the adult population ever drank spirits, either regularly or intermittently.[11]

---

[10] See H. Mowrer, "A Psychocultural Analysis of the Alcoholic," *American Sociological Review*, August, 1940. There is a good résumé in this article of the history of psychiatric interest in alcohol problems. *Also see* D. Gerard, "Intoxication and Addiction," *Quarterly Journal of Studies on Alcohol*, December, 1955. Both of these articles have been reprinted in R. McCarthy (ed.), *Drinking and Intoxication* (New Haven, Conn., 1959), an excellent collection of articles embodying the latest research on the question of alcohol. Especially brilliant is the article of A. Lee on "Techniques of Social Reform: an Analysis of the New Prohibition Drive."

The centennial edition of the *National Temperance Almanac* in 1876 put the illogic of the dry position very succinctly:

> The first sin is drinking the first glass. If the drunkard is a sinner—and the Bible plainly declares it—then he was a sinner when he took the first glass just as much as the thief or the murderer when he took the first step in the downward course. One glass has been known to produce drunkenness. It is continual sin from the first glass down to the drunkard's grave. No drunkard shall inherit the kingdom of God.

The *Almanac* also prints a charming verse of what the drys thought were the reasons of the drinker:

> If on my theme I rightly think,
> There are five reasons why men drink;
> Good wine, a friend, because I'm dry,
> Or lest I should be by-and-by,
> Or any other reason why.

[11] J. Reiley, Jr., and C. Marden, "The Social Pattern of Alcoholic Drinking," *Quarterly Journal of Studies on Alcohol*, September, 1947.

In the early days of their counterattack, the brewers and distillers matched the hysteria of the drys in their denunciations. They accused the prohibitionists of being cranks and crackpots, "women with short hair and men with long hair." According to the wets, America was less threatened by the "gentlemanly vices" than by "perfidy and phariseeism in public and private life." Many men "marked the distinction between moderation and intemperance," and rich red blood, rather than ice water, flowed in their veins.[12] The drys were accused of being

> . . . more critical of each other, more self-conscious . . . harder, drabber in speech. Iced water, ice cream, icy eyes, icy words. Gone the mellowness, generosity, good humor, good nature of life. Enter the will-bound, calculating, material, frigid human machine. Strange that the removal of this thing, supposed to pander to the animal in us, makes one feel less a man and more an animal, above all, an ant. . . . Although—who knows?—ants may drink.[13]

The doctrine of prohibition appealed to the psychology of excess, both in its friends and in its foes. They could find only evil in each other. Extremes conjure up extremes. The fight against the devil carries another devil in its exaggerations. With a consecrated prejudice on the part of the drys opposed to an unenlightened self-interest on the part of the wets, there was little room left for compromise. Indeed, the drys were proud of their prejudice. It seemed to them a holy sentiment. With Robert Ingersoll, they did not believe that any person could contemplate the evils of drink "without being prejudiced against the liquor crime." [14]

THE SPECTER OF THE SOUTH

The extremes of dry psychology were well suited to white Southerners. They had a special use for prohibition. It offered them a moral refuge from their guilty fear of the Negro, as well as a method of controlling one of his means of self-assertion. Liquor sometimes gave the Negro the strength to repudiate his inferior status. It also encouraged him to loose his libido on white women, incited, so it was said, by the nudes on the labels of whisky bottles.[15] Thus the Negro should be prevented from drinking alcohol. To a lesser degree, the same rule should be applied to white men, although this reform was not so urgent. Congressman Hobson, from Alabama, made this clear in the House of Representatives in 1914, while speaking on his resolution for a prohibition amendment to the Constitution. "Liquor will actually

---

[12] *Address of Colonel Henry Watterson at the Blue Grass Fair, Lexington, Ky.,* August 12, 1907.

[13] F. Tuohy, "Adventures of a British Investigator in 'Dry' New York," *Literary Digest,* January 17, 1920.

[14] L. Beman (ed.), *Prohibition, Modification of the Volstead Law* (New York, 1924), p. 54.

[15] W. Irwin, "More About 'Nigger Gin,'" *Collier's,* August 15, 1908.

make a brute out of a negro, causing him to commit unnatural crimes. The effect is the same on the white man, though the white man being further evolved it takes longer time to reduce him to the same level."

In the same debate, Congressman Pou, of North Carolina, although he opposed Hobson's resolution on account of the sacred doctrine of states' rights, did not question the need for racial control. He reminded Congress gently that the South had been forced to take away the ballot from the Negro "as the adult takes the pistol from the hand of a child." [16]* Since the ballot and alcohol were the two means of assertion given to the Negro, they must be denied to him. By the time of the Hobson resolution, all the Southern states had discriminated against the Negro voter and all but two had adopted prohibitory laws against liquor. The first measure had allowed the second. Congressman Quin, of Mississippi, stressed this in reference to the South. "Prohibition itself gained a foothold there and was made possible only after the restriction upon the suffrage of the negro." [17] To Northern drys, even if the South was in the rout of democracy at the polling booth, it was in the van of reform at the saloon. If it denied the Fifteenth Amendment, it was rabid in support of the Eighteenth.

This paternalism among the responsible Southern leaders and the denial of the principle of equality was not confined to the white race. Professor Councill, the principal of the Negro school in Huntsville, Alabama, spoke out for the abolition of the saloon as the first step in the emancipation of his own race. J. F. Clark agreed with him, although from a position of racial superiority:

> The saloon is a place of rendezvous for all classes of the low and vulgar, a resort for degraded whites and their more degraded negro associates, the lounging place for adulterers, lewd women, the favorite haunt of gamblers, drunkards and criminals. Both blacks and whites mix and mingle together as a mass of degraded humanity in this cesspool of iniquity. Here we have the worst form of social equality, but I am glad to know that it is altogether among the more worthless of both races.[18]

Booker T. Washington was of much the same opinion. Prohibition would be a blessing to the Negro people second only to the abolition of slavery. "Two-thirds of the mobs, lynchings, and burnings at the stake are the result of bad whisky drunk by bad black men and bad white men." [19] Negro and white leaders could join together in the crusade against the saloon, which often incited the racial fears of the South to the pitch of murder.

Two other forces drove the Southerners towards prohibition. The first

---

[16] *Cong. Record,* 63 Cong., 3 Sess., pp. 507, 605.

* As Mr. Dooley pointed out, the South did actually allow the Negro to vote, "only demandin' that he shall prove that his father an' mother were white."

[17] *Ibid.,* 63 Cong., 1 Sess., Appendix, p. 467.

[18] Quoted in J. Sellers, *The Prohibition Movement in Alabama, 1702 to 1943* (Chapel Hill, N.C., 1943), p. 101.

[19] See B. Washington, "Prohibition and the Negro," *Outlook,* March 14, 1908.

was patriotism. The South was once again the moral leader of the nation in this reform, and in this reform lay the chance of revenge. If the North had abolished chattel slavery in the South, the South would retaliate by abolishing rum slavery in the North. The second force was the monolithic structure of the Democratic party in the South. Traditionally, the Negroes voted Republican and the whites Democratic. The elimination of Negro ballots at the polls left the Democratic party solidly in control of Southern patronage. The only chance for the Republicans to regain some form of political power lay in the proper enfranchisement of the Negroes, which was impossible, or in the wresting of the moral leadership of the South from the Democrats. To do so, they had to find a popular cause which was both moral and an instrument of racial control. Prohibition was such a cause. Fear that the Republicans might seize the leadership of the prohibition movement, or that the Prohibition party, founded in 1869, might split the Democratic vote and let in the Republicans, drove the Democrats into the dry column in the South.[20] Thus the anomaly of a party based on the wet cities of the North and the dry rural counties of the South was emphasized. The quarrel over prohibition brought into the open a deep fissure among the Democrats that made them ineffective as a party for a decade.

Other forces conspired to give alcohol a special position in the psyche of the South. Although white rural Southerners shared in the nationwide economic and moral drives towards prohibition, they also suffered from the peculiar compulsions given to them by their environment. In the Southern character, an overwhelming need to master the Negro was coupled with a split between Puritanism and hedonism. This split made the Southerner seek the forbidden as a necessary part of his greatest pleasure, while a sense of guilt drove him into dependence on the absolution of violence or of orgiastic religion.[21] The ambivalent attitude of the Southern country white toward the Negro, his emotional cocktail of fear shaken up with lust, was also his attitude toward liquor. It is no coincidence that Mississippi, the most deeply rural of all states, is the last state in the Union to keep to the Southern trinity of official prohibition, heavy liquor consumption, and an occasional lynching. When Will Rogers commented that Mississippi would vote dry as long as the voters could stagger to the polls, he was too kind to mention that they would also lynch Negroes as long as they could stagger to the rope.*

---

[20] This aspect of prohibition in the South is dealt with by D. Whitener, *Prohibition in North Carolina, 1715–1945* (Chapel Hill, N.C., 1946), pp. 133–147. Both of these studies by Whitener and Sellers fill gaps in the study of prohibition in the South.

[21] W. Cash, *The Mind of the South* (Anchor ed., New York, 1941), pp. 231–232. Cash's work is an intuitive tour de force on the motivations of the South.

* There were 573 recorded lynchings in Mississippi between 1882 and 1944. During this period, Georgia came second with 521 lynchings and Texas third with 489. After the Second World War, the number of lynchings declined dramatically, since more severe legal action was taken against those who were responsible for the murders.

The drys deliberately exploited this darkness in the Southern mind. Fundamentalist religion often attracted large audiences by the very emphasis on vice and iniquity, violence and rape, which the mass media and the yellow press adopted in the twentieth century. An example can be taken from the work of the Reverend Wilbur Fisk Crafts. He was very influential, being president of the International Reform Bureau at Washington, a prolific writer and speaker, and a pastor at different times in the Methodist Episcopal, Congregational, and Presbyterian churches. His favorite sermon on prohibition began with a description of a man in seventeenth-century Bavaria who confessed on the rack that he had eaten thirteen children, after being changed into a wolf by the devil's girdle. The man was then sentenced to be put on the wheel and beheaded, once he had been pinched in twelve places on his body with red-hot irons. His dead body was burned, and his head was set for many years on a wooden wolf as a warning.

After this edifying start, the preacher continued,

> So runs the old chronicle. Has it any parallel in present-day life? The next time you open your newspaper and read the scare heads describing the latest lynching horror in the black belt of the United States, ask yourself what devil's girdle has changed so many negroes into sensual hyenas. Remember that during the four years of the Civil War the whole white womanhood of the South, in the absence of husband and brother, in the death grapple of battle, was at the mercy of the black population of the plantations.

Yet there was no rape at that time. What, then, had changed the Negroes? Was it emancipation or education, or the possession of the suffrage? Or was it the fact, "which for all rational men is a sufficient answer," that 75 per cent of all liquor sales in the South Carolina dispensaries were to Negroes? Naturally, it was liquor which was the devil's girdle and brought about the punishment reserved for those who wore the devil's girdle. "The souls of the black men are poisoned with alcohol and their bodies in due course drenched in petroleum and burned." [22]

Of course, lynching was only the extreme manifestation of the Southern urge to violence in the same way as hoggish drunkenness and ecstatic shakes were extreme reactions to the saloon and the revival meeting. There was a responsible and moderate leadership in the Deep South, composed of such people as Senator Oscar Underwood, of Alabama, who opposed prohibition and the excesses of his countrymen with conviction and dignity. But unfortunately, the very conditions which made the Western farms and small towns susceptible to the Manichaean doctrines of the drys were present in an exaggerated form in the South. There were few large cities. The hold of the primitive Methodist and Baptist churches and of the fundamentalist sects

---

[22] Dr. and Mrs. W. Crafts, *World Book of Temperance* (Washington, D.C., 1909), pp. 57–58.

was widespread and powerful. Little industry existed below the Potomac. Conquest by the North and memories of Reconstruction lived on. And the cult of purity and white womanhood allied with the fact of miscegenation and Negro mistresses produced in the white Southerner a strange discrepancy between stressed morality and denied fact. In this interval between ideal and reality, the cant of the drinker who voted dry flourished like a magnolia tree.

INTERNATIONAL MISSION

The South adopted prohibition to protect itself against its poor and its Negroes and its own sense of guilt. Those American missionaries who supported prohibition at home and abroad had like motives. The poor and the colored people of the earth were dangerous when drunk. Moreover, as the greed of Southern planters was held responsible for the existence of the Negro problem in the South, so the greed of white traders was usually held responsible for the corruption of the native races overseas. Early American imperialism imitated the European pattern of traders who corrupted the local people with rum and firearms and diseases, followed by clergymen who tried to save those people from that corruption. In America itself, the defeat of the red Indians had been made easy by their introduction to rum; once they had been defeated, they were immediately protected from the consequences of rum by the federal government.

A similar process took place in the Pacific islands. In 1901, Senator Henry Cabot Lodge had a resolution adopted by the Senate to forbid the sale by American traders of opium and alcohol to "aboriginal tribes and uncivilized races." [23] These provisions were later extended to cover "uncivilized" elements in America itself and in its territories, such as Indians, Alaskans, the inhabitants of Hawaii, railroad workers, and immigrants at ports of entry.

The evil which the American missionaries were trying to eradicate was real enough. As they said, Christian nations were making ten drunkards to one Christian among backward peoples.[24] Prohibition of rum traders was obviously a good thing in those areas controlled by the colonial powers. But when the same paternal attitude was applied within the home ground of the colonial powers to "handle the hundreds of thousands of God's weak children, who are being ruined and destroyed through the oppressions of the liquor traffic," the missionaries ran into trouble.[25] They could say with truth, "Let no one think we are neglecting saloons on our own shores in this crusade for the defense of native races at a distance." [26] But the fact

---

[23] E. Cherrington, *The Evolution of Prohibition in America* (Westerville, Ohio, 1920), pp. 270–272.

[24] Dr. and Mrs. W. Crafts, *Intoxicating Drinks and Drugs in All Lands and Times* (rev. ed., Washington, D.C., 1911), p. 15.

[25] L. Banks, *The Lincoln-Lee Legion* (New York, 1903), p. 231.

[26] Dr. and Mrs. W. Crafts, *Intoxicating Drinks*, etc., *op. cit.*, p. 27.

that the colonial power itself was often a democracy made this missionary attitude objectionable at home. No American workingman liked to be classified with those "uncivilized" peoples, whom he was taught to consider an inferior species. He also objected to the attitude of the missionary, who claimed to know what was good for labor better than labor knew itself. Moreover, there was a suspicious similarity between the views of the employers, who said that prohibition was good for the efficiency of workingmen, and those men of God, who said that prohibition was necessary for the salvation of their souls.

The idea of world-wide prohibition was contemporaneous with the idea of America as the Messiah of mankind and the Savior of the degenerate world. The ideology of salvation, which was once applied by middle-class reformers only to backward races and the American poor, was applied to the whole globe, after the First World War seemed to prove to many Americans that their country was the last refuge of peace and virtue. In addition, the spate of prohibition legislation adopted by the belligerent powers seemed to herald a world-wide prohibition revolution. Canada and Russia forbade liquor during the war; Britain and France and Germany severely regulated liquor. The Moslem and Buddhist world was also officially under religious prohibition. In fact, over half the area of the earth seemed behind the dry banners, and that area was growing. It is small wonder that William Jennings Bryan could prophesy that "alcohol as a beverage has been indicted as a criminal, brought up to the bar of judgment, condemned, and executed. Our nation will be saloonless for evermore and will lead the world in the great crusade which will drive intoxicating liquor from the globe." [27]

The mentality of war and the fantastic hopes of a millennial peace encouraged the drys' sense of international mission. As the leader of the Anti-Saloon League said to its assembled delegates in 1919, "The President said to make the world safe for democracy. Now, it is your business and mine, it is the business of the church of God, to make a democracy that is safe for the world, by making it intelligent and sober everywhere." [28] The reason for converting the world was simple. It was the same reason, incidentally, that the Bolsheviks gave for insisting on the world-wide Communist revolution. As long as a dry America was surrounded by wet nations, or a Communist Russia by capitalist nations, neither prohibition nor Communism would be safe. How, in the opinion of the drys, could prohibition be enforced when the United States was bounded "on the north by hard liquor, on the south by liquor, on the west by rum and on the east by no limit?" [29] The best

---

[27] Quoted in W. Williams, *William Jennings Bryan: A Study in Political Vindication* (New York, 1923), p. 110.

[28] *Proceedings of the Nineteenth National Convention of the Anti-Saloon League,* 1919, p. 35.

[29] Dr. S. Hubbard, "Why Does Not Prohibition Prohibit?" *New York Medical Journal,* July 18, 1923.

hope of prohibition, like the best hope of communism, lay in the conquest of the world.

Of course, the drys saw themselves as the sworn enemies of the Bolsheviks and of communism. They said that they were the defenders of the law and the Constitution, where the Eighteenth Amendment was enshrined. But they did not mention their revolutionary destruction of the vast property interests of the liquor trade without compensation. There were further curious similarities between the Anti-Saloon League and the Bolshevik party. Both organizations were founded at much the same time. Both were small, successful, well-organized minority groups who knew what they wanted. Both exploited a condition of war to put themselves in power. Although the drys used propaganda while the Bolsheviks used revolutionary warfare, both used the methods most likely to succeed in their societies. Both groups expected through historical necessity to be the leaders of a global revolution in the habits of human society. The expectations of both groups were quickly disappointed. While Russia settled down under Stalin to "Socialism in one country," the United States settled down to prohibition in one country. Both revolutions failed in their immediate social objectives, although the names and the language of the Russian revolution lingered on.

But the analogy can be taken too far. The fact that the drys relied on the Christian churches and on democratic procedures limited their success. The methods of the World League Against Alcoholism could not be the methods of international subversion of the Comintern.[30] When Bishop Cannon demanded of the Anti-Saloon League, "Shall It Live or Die?" and came to the conclusion that it should live to lead in the international crusade against alcohol, his suggested methods of conquest were the usual propaganda methods of the League. "It must carry to every nation its testimony for Prohibition, by printed page, by cartoon, poster, in every language, and by trained workers and speakers who will be veritable apostles of Prohibition truth." [31] That such a crusade was hardly likely to be effective in Mediterranean countries, long used to drinking wine, did not deter the leaders of the League. For, as long as the crusade against liquor lasted at home and abroad, they kept their power and their jobs and their hopes and their satisfaction in the good fight well fought. It is the habit of revolutionaries never to be content with the limits of their gains, and of moral reformers rarely to accept less than the conversion of the human race.

The hidden urges behind dry leaders and white Southerners and foreign missionaries made them adopt prohibition as a panacea for themselves and for their fellow men. The dry cause brought them peace from their inner

---

[30] A full account of the foundation and constitution of the World League Against Alcoholism may be found in E. Cherrington, *op. cit.*, pp. 365–374.

[31] Pamphlet, Widener Library, Harvard. There is an extensive contemporary pamphlet collection catalogued under "PROHIBITION" in the library. Where possible, fuller information on pamphlet sources will be given.

struggles and fears and guilts. They sought to extend this peace to races and classes which they considered inferior and eventually to the whole earth. The freedom of the globe from the evil of liquor would bring the condition of liberty for the first time to all mankind. In this battle for the good of all, the drys would use any means to win. For the liquor enemy was evil and could only be fought by evil. In their exploitation of the fears and weaknesses of their fellow Americans, the drys were guilty of many questionable methods, which could hardly be justified by the purity of their intentions.

Coercive Reform and Cultural Conflict

Joseph R. Gusfield

The coercive reformer does not perceive the subjects of his reform with sympathy or warmth. They are not victims who can be assimilated into his communities or converted to his culture. Coercive reform is a reaction to a sense of declining dominance. The violators of norms are now enemies, who have repudiated the validity of the reformer's culture. They are beyond repentance or redemption. Coercive reform is nurtured by a context in which groups hold contrasting norms. In this context each group challenges the power and prestige of the other. The coercive reformer has begun to feel that his norms may not be as respected as he has thought. He is less at home and somewhat more alien to his own society.

There is a similarity between the orientation of political radicalism and the orientation of coercive moral reform. Both stem from a polarized society in which the radical and the coercive reformer are both alienated from social and political dominance. By *polarization* we mean a process in which groups within the society are sharply separated from each other. They hold different values, live in different areas, are affiliated with different organizations, and hold different political orientations. There is little cross membership. As a result the lines of group differentiation are clearly drawn. Cultural polarization refers to the process in which cultural groups—ethnic communities, religious groups, status groups of other kinds—are sharply separated. Polarization implies a situation of conflict rather than one of dominant and subordinated groups. In a polarized society there is little middle ground. Each class or status group feels alien to the other. In this sense,

From Joseph R. Gusfield, *Symbolic Crusade: Status Politics and the American Temperance Movement* (Urbana: University of Illinois Press, 1963), pp. 87–110. Reprinted by permission.

the radical, like the coercive reformer, cannot see his problems solvable within the frame of existent institutions. The middle ground of common agreement or of accepted domination between political or economic groups has disappeared. Both types are in a critical posture toward the existent situation.

These orientations of both political radicalism and coercive reform existed in the Temperance movement during the late nineteenth century in both the WCTU and in the Prohibitionist wing of the movement. The politically radical elements in Temperance contributed to the growing polarization of cultural forces in the United States which culminated in the drive for constitutional Prohibition. That drive for political enforcement was an attempt to defend the position of social superiority which had been stabilized during the nineteenth century but was threatened during the first two decades of the twentieth. . . .

POLITICAL RADICALISM AND THE WCTU

Under the leadership of Frances Willard, a determined attempt was made to ally the WCTU to a wide range of radical movements. Woman's suffrage was only one of the unpopular causes which gained Miss Willard's attention. While it was an unsuccessful attempt, it had two effects upon the organization: (1) it laid the basis for the critical attitude toward American institutions which united the Populistic and the more conservative wings of the movement in the Prohibition campaigns of the early twentieth century, and (2) it united political forces of conservatism, progressivism, and radicalism in the same movement.

CRITICISM OF AMERICAN INSTITUTIONS

Before the late 1880's, Willard's speeches were characterized by a general tone of assimilative welfare, couched in a concern for the underdog and the underprivileged. During the 1880's, however, she was deeply influenced by the criticism of the capitalistic industrial economy expressed in agrarian and Christian Socialism. During visits to England and the Temperance leaders there she had formed a number of friendships among the British Fabians. She was an associate editor of the American journal of the Society of Christian Socialists, to which she frequently contributed.[1]

---

[1] In 1889 she joined the staff of *The Dawn*, the journal of the Nationalists, as the Society of Christian Socialists were also called. The motif of this group was that of the Socialist utopia inspired by Edward Bellamy's *Looking Backward* (Boston: Houghton Mifflin Co., 1889). A lengthy stay in England led to a close friendship with Lady Somerset, leader of the British Temperance movement and a member of the Fabian Society. Through her, Willard was influenced by Fabian Socialism.

These associations led her to try to commit the WCTU to a program of radical economic and political reconstruction. The program which she advocated was one version of the then common Socialist proposals to utilize government as the vehicle of economic justice and moral reform. In speeches to the WCTU national conventions she demanded the triumph of Christ's law and the abolition of competition in industry; a minimum wage for labor and an equivalent of a guaranteed wage; collective ownership of the means of production; public ownership of newspapers as a way to end obscenity; and the nationalization of amusements as a way to insure standards of decency.[2] She was all for ending the rule of "Capitalists in control." Henry George and the Single Tax, Samuel Gompers and the Universal Federation of Labor, Sidney Webb and the Fabians, Keir Hardie and Tom Mann were all subjects of her great approval. She told audiences that in some future day humanity will declare itself one huge monopoly, the New Testament will be the basis for regulating human behavior, and "all men's weal is made each man's care *by the very construction of society and the constitution of government.*" [3]

This explicit support for the tenets of Christian Socialism contradicted the ameliorative conservative and progressive strands in the movement. Although it was still an assimilative perspective, marked by sympathy toward the urban, immigrant worker, it placed Temperance in a framework of multiple social problems, rather than visualizing it as the cornerstone of all social reform. In placing her stress on institutional reforms of a wide character, Willard implied that Temperance was itself a consequence of the economic and social structure. An immoral society produced immoral people. In her addresses between 1892 and 1898 she was quite clear that individual moral imperfection was not the root of social evils. It was institutions that brought about imperfect human beings. Crime and prostitution, she declared, are not only matters of human choice; they are also matters of the low wages paid to men and women. She took a most heretical step for the advocate of Temperance; she maintained that intemperance is itself a result of social conditions: "We are coming to the conclusion—at least I am—that we have not assigned to poverty at one end of the social scale and idleness at the other those places of prominence in the enumeration of the causes of intemperance to which they are entitled." [4]

Willard's views were never the "official" doctrine of the WCTU or of any other Temperance organization. Some members were shocked by her Socialism. For many reasons, as well as ideology, there was a brief movement to unseat her. Nevertheless Willard's radicalism succeeded in drawing into the WCTU many women who were attracted by its identification with the

---

[2] See the *Annual Reports of the NWCTU* for 1892–94.

[3] *Ibid.* (1889), p. 117.

[4] *Ibid.* (1894), p. 334.

new and the daring.[5] She was moderately successful in developing a Department of the Relation of Temperance to Labor and Capital which sought to aid the development of the Labor movement.

UNION OF CONSERVATIVE, PROGRESSIVE, AND RADICAL CHRISTIANITY

What is so outstanding about the WCTU in this period (1870–1900) is the union of the diverse strands in social Christianity. Populists and anti-Populists, Suffragists and non-Suffragists, pro-Labor and anti-Labor views were all represented in the WCTU.[6]

Despite the generally Republican support which Temperance people displayed in national politics, the WCTU did develop backing for Prohibitionist candidates. Although legislative measures were not as dominant as education in their arsenal of weapons against alcohol, the organization did provide an audience for Prohibitionist speakers and a source of actual workers in local and state campaigns. In 1884 Willard even claimed that the Prohibitionists, and with them the WCTU, were responsible for the balance of power. By withholding potential Blaine votes they permitted Cleveland to become President.[7]

During the 1890's Willard also tried to forge an alliance with the Populist Party, especially in its formative stage. She was chairman of the first Populist Party convention. During the campaigns of 1892 and 1894 she used the WCTU committee system as a device for gathering Populist petition names. This attempt to place the WCTU in the orbit of sponsors of Populism failed, partly because the urban orientation of the organization was indifferent to the rural problems of Populism and partly because the Populists were unwilling to risk the loss of immigrant votes which Temperance support would have endangered.

Relationships to political radicalism were merely one element in the WCTU. They were an important part of the total Temperance movement and make up the ideological and social basis of the coercive strain in Temperance.

---

[5] Thus Josephine Goldmark, looking for some vehicle through which to press her concerns for social welfare work, turned to "Frances Willard's WCTU."

[6] Again and again, one finds in accounts of reformers a display of a syndrome of movements including Temperance. People in Temperance were not likely to make it their sole outlet for reform. In Boston, for example, Vida Scudder and Mary Livermore were active in Feminism and Temperance. Often a special committee of the WCTU was headed by some women who had a prior and continued interest in another reform. In 1881, Wendell Phillips listed among the great social questions of the age feminism, temperance, and prison reform, a very common WCTU "package." Arthur Mann, *Yankee Reformers in the Urban Age* (Cambridge, Mass.: Harvard University Press, 1954), p. 105.

[7] *Annual Report of the NWCTU* (1884), pp. 65–69.

POPULISM AND COERCIVE TEMPERANCE REFORM

All forms of radicalism have at least one element in common: they are united by their critical posture toward the existing social order. Whether they are trying to resurrect an earlier form or to fashion a new plan, radical movements see the present as distasteful and preach the necessity of deep and fundamental changes. It is just this lack of identification with present social and political dominance which marks the coercive strain in Temperance doctrine. The Populist component in Temperance contributed to coercive reform in two respects. It provided a general expression of alienation from the urban and industrial culture and it directed attention toward the institutions of business as targets of reform. Its orientation to social problems was clearly not assimilative. The goal of Temperance through direct prohibition of sales was more in common with Populism and radical social Christianity than it was with conservative and progressive reforms.

AGRARIANISM AND TEMPERANCE

Some historians have suggested that the Prohibition Party of the nineteenth century was one arm of the leftist movements elsewhere manifested by the Greenbackers, the Non-Partisan League, the Populist Party, and the agrarian elements of the Socialist Party.[8] There is some truth in this assertion but it must be carefully qualified.

The emergence of an organized political party dedicated to national Prohibition occurred in 1869, in response to the reawakened Temperance movement which produced the WCTU. The 1872 and 1876 platforms of the Prohibition Party read like many manifestoes of the agrarian radicalism of the time. The Prohibitionists advocated a federal income tax, woman's suffrage, the regulation of railroad rates, the direct election of United States senators, free schools, and an inflationary monetary policy.[9] Their platforms also contained planks which advocated the use of the Bible in public schools and the national observance of restrictions on Sunday business and amusements. The economic and political measures were similar to those of the Greenbackers and the National Grange. They were the sentiments of farmers who saw themselves oppressed by urban financial institutions, manufacturing interests, and the political machines.

We would be misled, however, if we interpreted Temperance as a logical

---

[8] Paul Carter, *Decline and Revival of the Social Gospel: Social and Political Liberalism in American Protestant Churches, 1920–1940* (Ithaca, N.Y.: Cornell University Press, 1956), pp. 32–33.

[9] D. L. Colvin, *The Prohibition Party in the United States* (New York: George H. Doran Co., 1926), Chs. 5–6.

outcome of agrarian economic discontents. The union between Populistic, agrarian sentiment and Prohibitionist doctrine was more adventitious than that. During the 1880's, when the state Dry campaigns were most intense and agrarian movements less striking, these planks were dropped from the Prohibitionist platforms or replaced by general statements of an anti-monopolist nature. In 1892, in the wave of Populist state elections, the plat-form again reflected agrarian economic ideas. In 1896 we would have ex-pected the most forceful statement of Populist sentiments, both because such sentiments were at their height and because they would have been politically necessary to counteract the appeals of the Bryanites. Indeed, within the party the "broad gaugers" sought just such a platform. They were defeated by the "narrow gaugers," who restricted the party to the single issue of Prohibi-tion.[10] At no time from 1872 to 1896 were non-Prohibition issues given much attention in the speeches of the Prohibitionist leaders.

The platform inclusions and exclusions of the Prohibition Party suggest that party leaders saw Populist territory as a major center of Prohibitionist support. They felt it necessary to counteract the possible appeals of other third parties and of the major parties to the economic and political inter-ests of this social base. These were neither dominant nor significant appeals to Prohibitionists, however. There was no concern with the range of urban social problems which we have encountered in the WCTU. Labor, for exam-ple, was treated in very general terms or exhorted to follow abstinent stand-ards.[11] While Prohibition was not a part of the economic and political response of the farmer to his conflicts with industrialism, it did have a spe-cial appeal to the rural segment of the population, where Populist sentiments were also strong.

Agrarian discontent was at its height in the same parts of society where Prohibition made its greatest state gains in the 1880's—Kansas, Iowa, and Ohio. The Grange lent active support to the Woman's crusades in 1874 and often helped the WCTU in its local and state campaigns for liquor restric-tions. At the state levels, the Populist Party often included Prohibition as one of its aims, although it balked at including it in the national platform. The immigrant vote was considered too important to be alienated. The affinity between Prohibitionist sentiment and Populist support was close enough so that a delegate to the People's convention in 1892 could remark that a "logical Populist" was one who had been a Granger, then successively a Greenbacker, a Prohibitionist, and a Populist.[12]

---

[10] *Ibid.*, Chs. 7–9, 14.

[11] For example, the 1884 platform of the Prohibition Party contained a plank addressed to Labor and Capital. It called attention to "the baneful effect upon labor and industry of the needless liquor business." No position was taken toward unions or strikes. It was claimed that Prohibition was the greatest thing that could be done to insure the welfare of la-borers, mechanics, and capitalists. *Ibid.*, p. 160.

[12] Fred Haynes, *Third Party Movements* (Iowa City: State Historical Society of Iowa, 1916); Solon Buck, *The Granger Movement* (Cambridge, Mass.: Harvard University Press, 1933), pp. 121–168.

The Prohibitionist appeal was not based on any effort to convert the sufferers, as was the conversionist doctrine of the WCTU. Prohibition, both in the usage of the party and as an element in the other Temperance organizations, assumed that its views represented moral righteousness and that the drinkers could not be converted by means other than legislation and force. It is just this that Prohibition had in common with Populism. Both movements were nourished by a sense of conflict with the urban, industrial communities of the United States. What Populism contributed to the Prohibitionist spirit was the confrontation of one part of the society with another. On one side were the manufacturer, the banker, the director of railroads, with their urban culture from which homey virtues of church and family were absent. On the other side were the farmer and the small-town businessman, in debt to the monopolies of transport, finance, and manufacture but committed to the culture of Protestant, temperate America. In this cultural confrontation, unlike the urban progressivism of the WCTU, the native American, Protestant, sober man was the underdog. The assimilative appeal tried to redeem the urban alienated. The coercive appeal was an attempt of the alienated rural population to strike back against the urban powers.

PROHIBITION AND THE RHETORIC OF ALIENATION

What this contributed to the coercive strain in Temperance was a sense of economic and political powerlessness which formed the ideological justification for Prohibitionist doctrine. Richard Hofstadter has detailed the manner in which Populist appeals were based on a theory of conspiracy.[13] That theory held that evil men of the commercial cities of the East manipulated currency, tariffs, and national policy for their selfish advantage. Politics, too, was suspect as the area in which the monopolist bribed legislatures and rigged elections. The "people" were cheated and preyed upon by the business interests that rendered them powerless to use their constitutionally developed political institutions. The primary, the referenda, and the direct election of senators were devices to return government to "the people."

This bridge between Populist and Prohibitionist ideology is crucial for the later development of the Prohibitionist cause. In assimilative doctrines, the drinker is the subject of Temperance reform. He must be persuaded to take on Temperance habits. The Populist assumption of business malevolence is a very different point of view with distinct consequences. It leads quite easily to the assertion that institutional forces of the business quest for profits are at the root of intemperance. It was logical to link together, as Prohibition orators did, the forces of "grogshops and monopolies" as the prime enemies of total abstinence.

Populist sentiment and rhetoric made it easy to focus attention on the liquor industry as the dominant cause of drinking. The leading Prohibition-

---

[13] Richard Hofstadter, *The Age of Reform* (New York: A. A. Knopf, 1955), pp. 70–81.

ists of the 1880's manifested a Populist commitment. John B. Finch called his collected speeches *The People versus the Liquor Traffic.* John P. St. John, 1884 presidential candidate of the Prohibition Party, was the former Populist governor of Kansas. Both men spoke of the enemies of Temperance largely as "the organized liquor interests." [14]

If the liquor "trusts" were opposed to Temperance, it was difficult to see that anything short of coercion could appeal to them to stop their immoral trade. The liquor lords were seen as absolute political autocrats who tried to dictate the nominations of both Democratic and Republican parties. This sense of malevolence and power put the liquor interests outside the moral norms through which men might persuade each other, and outside the middle-class appeals to social mobility by which the dominant might impress the subjugated.

The coercive strain in Temperance orientations was thus a response to cultural confrontations which took place in an atmosphere of conflict and threatened alienation. As the economic and political dominance of agrarian society was undermined by the urban, industrial capitalism of the late nineteenth century, the cultural differentiation between rural and urban, native and immigrant, sacred and secular was given an added dimension of meaning. The failure of Temperance forces to have brought about a sober, temperate, and well-behaved society was more than the failure of a dominant culture to have implanted its style of life as the ruling style. It was tantamount to the failure of that culture to continue as the dominant source of values.

Nevertheless the Temperance issue remained in the orbit of a general stream of conservative, progressive, and radical movements expressive of dominance or alienation in the American social structure. Only as the cultural confrontations widened and the economic struggle lost some of its politically separating tendencies did Prohibition emerge as a vital and politically dominant issue.

POLARIZATION AND THE PROHIBITION CAMPAIGNS

By the turn of the century Temperance was a movement which combined both assimilative and coercive appeals within and among the various wings. Because of this mix of appeals and subsidiary movements Temperance had a pluralistic rather than a superimposed following These terms—pluralistic and superimposed—refer to the degree of political diversity and isolation which characterize social groups. Groups that differ in political outlook on almost all questions with little overlapping are in a posture of superimposition. The situation is pluralistic when the opposite is the case, when outlooks are not sharply related to group affiliation. When the rural, Protestant,

---

[14] For the speeches of St. John see Colvin, *op. cit.,* Ch. 8.

native American is almost always in favor of Prohibition, and the urban, Catholic, immigrant almost always opposed, the situation is one of super-imposition. Each element of group identity reinforces the other. The more an issue represents a constellation of superimposed social forces, the more likely is it that the issue becomes one of sharpened group loyalties and com-promise is less feasible. In a pluralistic structure there is a middle ground, pulled in both directions by the competing forces. Under conditions of superimposition the political sides are more sharply polarized.

The campaign for national Prohibition had a polarizing effect on the Temperance movement. It maximized the cultural differences between pro- and anti-Temperance forces while minimizing the class differences. In this fashion it promoted an atmosphere in which the meaning of Prohibition as a symbol of Protestant, middle-class, rural supremacy was enhanced. This process was a necessary stage in the development of Prohibition as a test of the prestige of the old middle classes in a period of industrial growth, urban development, and Catholic immigration.

The polarizing effects of the campaign for national Prohibition were un-wittingly expressed in an editorial of the Anti-Saloon League journal: [15] "The liquor issue," wrote the editor of *The American Issue*, "is no longer one of 'wet' and 'dry' arguments. Henceforth it is to be a question of 'wet men' and 'dry men.'" In effect, the issue of Prohibition posed a question of cultural loyalties in explicit terms. Attack on the saloon, rather than the drinker, located the problem of drinking in contexts which accentuated the conflict of cultures represented by the divergent sides.

The formation of the Anti-Saloon League, in 1896, has a symbolic impor-tance for the Temperance movement. Tactically, the organization led the fight to gain state and national Prohibition. Symbolically, the very title of the League suggests the movement away from the assimilative approaches of the WCTU or the political party approaches of the Prohibition Party. Both the singleness of purpose represented in the idea of the League and the sense of opposition suggested by the "anti" character of its name are dom-inant features of the Temperance movement in the period between 1900 and the passage of the Prohibition Amendment in 1920.

The saloon was pre-eminently an urban institution, a substitute for the less anonymous entertaining of the *salon,* from which it derived its name. For the small-town native American Protestant, it epitomized the social habits of the immigrant population. To the follower of the Progressive movement, the saloon was a source of the corruption which he saw as the bane of political life. Accustomed to moralizing about politics, the Progres-sive reacted against the ethics of personal reciprocity on which machine poli-tics was built. Increasingly alienated from political power, the native Amer-ican, urban middle class found a partial solution to its problems in the

---

[15] *The American Issue,* 20 (January, 1912), 4.

Progressive movement. It made common union with the already fixed alienation of the Populist. The growth of urban communities, so ran this argument, would wreck the Republic. It would lead to the segregation of an
element responsible for corruption, "which gathers its ideas of patriotism
and citizenship from the low grog shop." [16]

Within the context of Populist antipathy to urban and Catholic communities, the saloon appeared as the symbol of a culture which was alien
to the ascetic character of American values. Anything which supported one
culture necessarily threatened the other. "The Anglo-Saxon stock is the best
improved, hardiest and fittest . . . if we are to preserve this nation and the
Anglo-Saxon type we must abolish [saloons]." [17]

AGRARIAN SENTIMENTS AND THE PROHIBITION DRIVES

A new wave of Prohibition campaigns broke out in the United States after
1906. As a result of it, national Prohibition was achieved. During its spread,
the rural nature of Temperance was enhanced and it became a dominant
political issue, separated from the wider net of movements current at the
same time. The agrarian nature of the movement and the isolation of the
movement from other political issues are major characteristics affecting its
symbolic appearance.

Between 1843 and 1893, 15 states had passed legislation prohibiting state-
wide sale of intoxicants. Only in three states, Iowa, Kansas, and Maine,
was Prohibition still in force. Between 1906 and 1912 seven states passed
Prohibition laws. By 1919, before the passage of the Eighteenth Amendment,
an additional 19 states had passed restrictive legislation, some through referenda. Most of these shifts into the Dry column had occurred by 1917,
before the amendment seemed possible or probable in the near future.[18]

The active work of the Anti-Saloon League and the Methodist Board of
Morals of course had a great deal of influence on such victories. They did
bring to bear the power and influence of the Protestant churches behind
candidates and legislation of Dry aims. But the churches had long ago taken
a staunch Temperance stand. Temperance sentiment had existed for a long
time.

Several changes appeared in drinking habits during the first 20 years of
the twentieth century which reflected the decrease in the legitimacy and
dominance of Temperance norms in the American society. For one thing,
the consumption of alcohol was higher than at any time since 1850.[19] After

[16] *Ibid.*, 21 (June, 1913), 4.

[17] *Ibid.*, 20 (April, 1912), 1.

[18] For a year-by-year chronology of the Prohibition movement see Ernest H. Cherrington,
The Evolution of Prohibition in the United States (Westerville, Ohio: American Issue Publishing Co., 1920).

[19] See the statistics on consumption of alcoholic beverages, corrected for age composition
of population, collected by Mark Keller and Vera Efron and printed in Raymond McCar-

1900 it began to rise and reached its peak in the period 1911–15. Also, the increase in consumption appears to have involved more persons as drinkers. The rise in alcohol consumption was accompanied by a decrease in consumption of distilled spirits but a large increase in beer drinking, a situation which suggests both a rise in moderate rather than excessive drinking, and immigrant populations as a source of a large percentage of the rise.[20]

That the cities were probably the source of much of the increase is also suggested by two other facts. First, local option appeared to have been evaded in the cities but in the small towns and rural areas it was well enforced.[21] Second, despite the fact that by 1914 there were 14 Prohibitionist states, all predominantly rural, the national drinking rates, based on legal sales, were at their all-time high in 1915. A change was taking place in American drinking norms.

The rise of Prohibition strength owed a great deal to the sense of cultural change and prestige loss which accompanied both the defeat of the Populist movement and the increased urbanization and immigration of the early twentieth century. During the initial decade of the twentieth century, the domination of American life, thought, and morality by the ethics of Protestant theology was waning. It was far from a period of serenity, despite the lack of the flamboyant issues of 1896. Assimilative tactics had not succeeded in curtailing the drinking habits of the cultures nor in winning assent to ascetic norms.[22] The assimilative response made little sense when the dominant culture felt its dominance slipping away.

The radicalism of the coercive approach to drinking bears a remarkable resemblance to the geographical distribution of agrarian radicalism. Areas of the country which demonstrated state support for Populist candidates in

thy (ed.), *Drinking and Intoxication* (Glencoe, Ill.: The Free Press, and New Haven, Conn.: Yale Center of Alcohol Studies, 1959), p. 180.

[20] This interpretation is consistent with recent studies of the drinking habits of ethnic and religious groups in the United States. Such studies show that a bimodal drinking pattern is more typical of native American Protestants than of first- and second-generation Americans, both Catholics and Jews. The bimodality implies that both abstainers and hard drinkers are more numerous among Protestants than among non-Protestants, where the moderate drinker is the more frequent case. In studies of college drinking, for example, the Mormons had the highest percentage of abstainers of any religious group and Jews the lowest percentage. Mormons who did drink, however, showed patterns of excessive drinking more frequently than did Jews. Robert Straus and Selden Bacon, *Drinking in College* (New Haven, Conn.: Yale University Press, 1953), p. 143. Other studies with supportive findings are Robert Bale, "Cultural Differences in Rates of Alcoholism," *Quarterly Journal of Studies on Alcohol*, 6 (March, 1946), 480–498, and Charles Snyder, *Alcohol and the Jews* (Glencoe, Ill.: The Free Press, and New Haven, Conn.: Yale Center of Alcohol Studies, 1958).

[21] Joseph Rowntree and Arthur Sherwell, *State Prohibition and Local Option* (London: Hodden and Stoughton, 1900), using both systematic observations of small towns and cities and the payment of federal liquor sale licenses, concluded in 1899: "Local prohibition has succeeded [in the United States] precisely where state prohibition has succeeded, in *Rural and thinly peopled districts* and in certain small towns . . . local veto in America has only been found operative outside the larger towns and cities" (p. 253).

[22] Norton Mezvinsky, "Scientific Temperance Education in the Schools," *History of Education Quarterly*, 1 (March, 1961), 48–56.

the 1892 or 1894 elections were prone to adopt state Prohibition in the 1906–19 period. Table I provides the data to support this.

TABLE I. PROHIBITIONIST STATUS (NUMBER OF STATES) IN 1919 AND
POPULIST VOTE (1892–94) [23]

Populist Vote (1892–94)	Dry (statewide Prohibition)	Wet (no statewide Prohibition)	Total
Above 30 Per Cent	13	4	17
15–30 Per Cent	4	3	7
Below 15 Per Cent	7	14	21
Total	24	21	45

By no means do we imply that Prohibtion is explainable as an extension of Populism. Both, however, express increased tension between parts of the social structure and between divergent cultures. The centralization of opposition to Prohibition within the Eastern, urban, states, where large percentages of Catholics and immigrants were to be found, is a fact which a great many observers and analysts have noted. Major urban and industrial areas like Illinois, New York, and Pennsylvania were the last to ratify the Eighteenth Amendment. Table II indicates that there was a very close relation between rural status and Prohibitionist sentiment. It shows that where the ratio of rural to urban population was high, the likelihood that the state had gone Prohibitionist in areas affecting more than 50 per cent of its population was also high. Rural states were more likely to support Prohibitionist sentiment than were urban states.

TABLE II. URBAN-RURAL POPULATION RATIO AND PERCENTAGE OF STATE
POPULATION UNDER PROHIBITION BY STATE OR LOCAL LAWS IN 1913 [24]

Ratio of Urban to Rural Population	Number of States		Total
	More than 50 Per Cent of Population Under Prohibition	Less than 50 Per Cent of Population Under Prohibition	
Less than 50 Per Cent	19	5	24
More than 50 Per Cent	6	18	24
Total	25	23	48

[23] Populist vote based on data reported in *The World Almanac and Encyclopedia—1894* (New York: The Press Publishing Co., 1894), pp. 377 ff.
[24] Compiled from data in *Anti-Saloon League Yearbook, 1913* (Westerville, Ohio: American Issue Publishing Co., 1913), p. 10.

The areas of national Prohibition sentiment were thus Protestant, rural, and nativist. They were more likely to be found in the South and the Midwest, although New Hampshire, Maine, and Vermont were strong supporters of Prohibition. While states with high percentages of foreign-born were likely to oppose Prohibition, this was less true where the foreign population was Protestant and rural. In South Dakota, where 22 per cent of the population were foreign-born, 68 per cent lived under Dry conditions. In Illinois, where 20.1 per cent of the population were foreign-born, only 33 per cent were in Dry areas.[25]

More significant, perhaps, was the fact that within the individual state it was the urban areas that provided the greatest opposition to Dry laws. Here was the greatest source of votes against Dry legislation and for the repeal of such laws as did exist. Even in rural states, it was in the cities that the state or local laws were most often and openly evaded. In Alabama, where Prohibitionist sentiment was strong, the ten strong Wet counties were the dominant political, industrial, and financial centers of the state. The same was true in North Carolina and the other Southern states, where the Catholic population was small and the percentage of foreign-born almost nil.[26]

The polarization of population into distinct cultural and geographical areas was a salient aspect of the Prohibition campaigns. The campaign for Prohibition in California is a striking example of polarities around which the issue was drawn. Here the cultural distinctions were formed around regional differences, to an even greater degree than was true of urban-rural differentiation. Northern California was cosmopolitan, secular, Catholic, and Wet. Southern California was fundamentalist, Protestant, and provincial in its loyalty to the ideals of rural America. Although Los Angeles County was the second largest county in California in 1892, it polled approximately 14 per cent of its presidential vote for the Populist candidate (Weaver) and 4 per cent for the Prohibitionist (Bidwell). At the same time, San Francisco County, largest in California, polled 5 per cent of its vote for the Populists and 1 per cent for the Prohibitionists. The state returns were below those of the Los Angeles vote: approximately 9 per cent for the Populists and 3 per cent for the Prohibitionists.[27] The Populist campaign in California in 1894 displayed a marked Prohibitionist strain. This continued during the Anti-Saloon League and Progressive campaigns of 1909–13.[28] The League placed its organization at the use of the California Progressives. Temperance, nativism, and Progressivism were linked. It was the North that

---

[25] Based on data in *ibid., passim.*

[26] James Sellers, *The Prohibition Movement in Alabama, 1702–1943*, James Sprunt Studies in History and Political Science, 26 (1943); Daniel Whitener, *Prohibition in North Carolina, 1715–1945, ibid.,* 27 (1945). (Both published at Chapel Hill by the University of North Carolina Press.)

[27] *The World Almanac and Encyclopedia—1894, loc. cit.*

[28] This account is based on Gilman Ostrander, *The Prohibition Movement in California, 1848–1933,* University of California Publications in History, 57 (1957).

represented the greatest opposition to this triad, rather than the city per se. Southern California was Protestant and Progressive. "Los Angeles is overrun with militant moralists, connoisseurs of sin, experts on biological purity." [29] The saloon was identified as the major deterrent to the good government sought by the political reformers. In the Populist vein, it was against railroads and railroad control that the Southern Californians directed their political animosities. In all these issues, the lines of political opposition were drawn along cultural attributes even though the urban-rural dimension was subordinated. The North-South distinction had cultural as well as geographical implications.

The cultural distinction between Dry and Wet areas was even revealed in the period following Repeal in the South. In Alabama, South Carolina, and Mississippi in the 1930's the Dry vote was strongest in those areas which had been Populist in the late 1890's, were fundamentalist in religion, and where the farmholdings and the percentage of Negroes were small.[30] It was not a simple urban-rural split that Prohibition touched off in these essentially rural states.

The polarities were also related to the cultural distinctions between the plantation areas of the delta and the poor white farmer of the inland regions.[31] Some writers have interpreted the rise of state Prohibition campaigns in the South after 1906 as an effort to control the Negro.[32] Our interpretation is quite different. After 1900 whatever political power the Negro had had was broken by effective legal disenfranchisement.[33] As long as the Negro had been anti-Prohibitionist and had voting influence, there was fear among Southern politicians that Prohibition questions were likely to bring about appeals by the Wets for Negro votes. It was the disenfranchisement of the Negro which made the political movement for Prohibition feasible in the South.

The Prohibitionists understood and were conscious of the conflict of cultures which both produced the issue and characterized the opponents. Dry men were native Americans; they were Protestants who took their religion

---

[29] A statement by Willard Huntington Wright, quoted in *ibid.*, p. 65.

[30] In Alabama, Mississippi, and South Carolina, the counties most likely to have voted Dry in the post-Repeal period were those which were rural but where the percentage of Negroes was well below the state average. These were generally counties which had also been the basis of support for Populist candidates in the 1890's. This analysis is derived from county voting data in *The World Almanac and Encyclopedia—1894*, loc. cit., and Alexander Heard and Donald Strong, *Southern Primaries and Elections* (University: University of Alabama Press, 1950).

[31] C. Vann Woodward, *Origins of the New South, 1877–1913* (Baton Rouge: Louisiana State University Press, 1951), Ch. 9; V. O. Key and Alexander Heard, *Southern Politics* (New York: A. A. Knopf, 1949), Ch. 11.

[32] Sellers, *op. cit.*, pp. 46–48; Preston Slosson, *The Great Crusade and After, 1914–1928,* Vol. 12 in Arthur Schlesinger and Dixon Ryan Fox (eds.), *A History of American Life* (New York: Macmillan, 1931), Ch. 4.

[33] C. Vann Woodward, *The Strange Career of Jim Crow* (New York: Oxford University Press, 1955), Chs. 1–2.

with seriousness; they were the farmers, the small-town professionals; and their sons and daughters, while they had migrated to the big city, kept alive the validity of their agrarian morals. Wet men were the newcomers to the United States; the populations that supported the political machines of Boston, New York, and Chicago; the infidels and heathen who didn't keep the Sabbatarian laws of Protestantism; and the sophisticated Eastern "society people." All these were perpetuating and expanding the modes of life which the Dry had been taught to see as the mark of disrepute in his own local social structure. The outnumbering of the rural population by the urban, wrote an Anti-Saloon League editor, has been the cause of the wreckage of republics. "The vices of the cities have been the undoing of past empires and civilizations." [34]

The attack on the saloon emerged in urban areas as a link between elements of Progressivism and the Temperance movement. It made it easier to depict Prohibition as a move toward good government and the end of political corruption. In the same fashion, nativism carried with it connotations of positive progressive reform. It guaranteed the end of machine politics by limiting the power of groups who were felt to have no respect for American political principles. The sources of this reform were as much religious in origin as they were political. The California Voters League could declare that its objective was "a management of public offices worthy of an enlightened, progressive and Christian country." [35]

Before the Prohibition drives of the early twentieth century, the Temperance movement had played an important role in local, state, and national politics. Often the Temperance vote had been a decisive balance of power. Nevertheless, state Prohibition was usually not enacted and usually repealed when it had been in force for several years. It is true that the organized movement led by the Anti-Saloon League and the Methodists was more efficient in rallying and focusing Temperance sentiment than previous organizations had been. It is true, however, that after 1906 Temperance forces in the United States made a more concerted political effort than they had ever done before, that this effort was largely the activity of rural populations, and that it occurred in a period when the United States was more urbanized than it had ever been. The strength and vibrancy of Temperance as a political force is the dominant attribute of the movement in the period between 1906 and the passage of the Prohibition Amendment.

The great movement toward national Prohibition was not the long-awaited outcropping of a slowly developing movement over 90 years of agitation. It was the result of a relatively short wave of political organization supported by the new enthusiasm of church members in the Presbyterian, Methodist, Baptist, and other "evangelical" Protestant congregations. It is certainly true, as Virginius Dabney has pointed out, that "when the move-

---

[34] *The American Issue,* 21 (June, 1913), 4.
[35] Ostrander, *op. cit.,* p. 105.

ment for nation-wide Prohibition was approaching its climax in 1917, the political center of gravity of the country was not in New York or Chicago or San Francisco but in Junction City and Smith's Store and Brown's Hollow." [36] But this was not a new feature of American state politics. If anything it was changing as urban populations grew larger by the addition of immigrants and rural migrants.

In striving to obtain Temperance by legislative controls of liquor and beer sales, one part of the American population was trying to coerce another part. The areas of the country where Temperance norms were most respected, where alcohol sales were most easily controlled, and where the Prohibition vote was strongest were demanding that the other areas be subject to the ways of life which were most legitimate to the total abstainer. The opponents of Prohibition were no longer sufferers to be helped but enemies to be conquered. "This battle is not a rose-water conflict. It is war—continued, relentless war." [37]

. . . From a number of standpoints the drive for national Prohibition, which began in 1913, was an inexpedient movement. The Dry areas appeared to have been fairly successful in restricting liquor sales in the areas where Dry sentiment was strongest. In many urban areas, to be sure, the laws against sale were openly evaded. In the areas where sentiment was strongest against prohibitive legislation, urban parts of rural states and the urban states, laws had not been passed. By 1913 an equable arrangement appeared to have developed. Temperance sentiment was recognized where it was strong by both law and behavior. Where such sentiments were weak, the populace continued to act in accordance with their sense of what was culturally legitimate. Enforcement in urban areas where cultural support was small had been tried and had been shown to be at best a doubtful possibility. Contemplated in areas such as New York and Boston, it should have seemed an impossible task to the reformer. Instead of deepening the enforcement of the law in areas already dry, the movement aimed at expanding its status as a recognized legal norm, as an ideal if not a behavioral reality.

It is in this characteristic of cultural conflict that the disinterested nature of coercive Temperance reform is manifest. Assimilative reform diminished as the Temperance advocates sought to coerce the nonbeliever to accept an institutional framework in which drinking was no longer socially dominant. What we have shown in this chapter is that this facet, the coercive side of Temperance, emerged in a context in which the bearer of Temperance culture felt that he was threatened by the increasing strength of institutions and groups whose interests and ideals differed from his. He took a radical stand toward his society when he began to feel that he was no longer as dominant, as culturally prestigeful as he had been in an earlier period.

The development of Prohibition as a political measure focused these cul-

---

[36] Virginius Dabney, *Dry Messiah* (New York: A. A. Knopf, 1949), p. 128.
[37] *Anti-Saloon League Yearbook, 1911*, p. 4.

tural conflicts in a form which maximized struggle. Elections and legislative contests are fights; somebody opposes somebody else. One group tries to bring force to effectuate what another group detests, even though the force may be more potential than actual. The unwillingness of the potentially assimilable to follow the lead of the assimilative reformer is not a blow to the reformer's domination. The political victory of the norm-violator is, however, a blow to belief in one's domination, in his right to be followed in cultural and moral matters. It is the threat to domination which the existence of drinking on a wide scale implied, both as a moral and legal norm and as a norm of recurrent behavior. It became necessary to settle the issue by establishing social dominance through political measures, even if unenforceable.

Prohibition was an effort to establish the legal norm against drinking in the United States. It was an attempt to succeed in coercive reform. But in what sense can a legal norm, which is probably unenforceable, be the goal of a reform movement? If the drinking behavior which the movement sought to end occurred in communities in which the Temperance advocates were unlikely to live and the laws were not likely to be enforced, what was the rationale for the movement? We have shown that Prohibition had become a symbol of cultural domination or loss. If the Prohibitionists won, it was also a victory of the rural, Protestant American over the secular, urban, and non-Protestant immigrant. It was the triumph of respectability over its opposite. It quieted the fear that the abstainer's culture was not really the criterion by which respectability was judged in the dominant areas of the total society.

VI

*The Literature of the 1920's:
A Trivial Literature or a
Literature of "Useful Innocence"?*

INTRODUCTION

In an article dealing with the "Shifting Perspectives on the 1920's" Professor Henry F. May has pointed out that "Like the Civil War itself, the cultural battles of the twenties have been fought again and again. Successive writers have found it necessary either to condemn or to praise the decade, though what they have seen in it to condemn or praise has differed." [1] In the 1930's progressives and New Dealers among the historians and literary critics viewed the 1920's scornfully as a decade of reaction and spoke disparagingly of its literature as well. The outbreak of World War II in Europe and the subsequent involvement of the United States in the struggle led some to an even harsher view of the culture and literature of the 1920's. To the literary critics and literary historians Archibald MacLeish, Van Wyck Brooks, and Bernard DeVoto, most of the prominent literary figures of the 1920's were "irresponsibles" whose mordant and biased view of American society actually impaired the nation's morale. Today, by contrast, the literature of the 1920's is widely regarded as one of the decade's greatest achievements, and it is praised for its freshness, its insights, and its technical skill.

Two contrasting views of the literature of the 1920's are presented in the selections that follow. The first piece is taken from a series of lectures delivered by Bernard DeVoto at Indiana University in 1943 and published in 1944. DeVoto, with the events of World War II very much on his mind, argues that it was not American civilization that was "bankrupt" in the 1920's "but the literary way of thinking about it." He dismisses "the official literature" of the 1920's as "a trivial literature" because littérateurs in their works rejected "democracy" and failed to recognize the dignity of man.

Frederick Hoffman, a professor of English, wrote his superb study of the literature of the 1920's, published in 1955, out of a conviction that "the 1920's had not so far been fairly portrayed." [2] Hoffman contends that critics of the literature of the 1920's, like DeVoto, have not shown "respect for the values of literature." He defends the artist's right to have "a private view of public affairs," and he praises the writers of the decade for their "useful innocence."

---

[1] Henry F. May, "Shifting Perspectives on the 1920's," *Mississippi Valley Historical Review*, XLIII (December 1956), 405.

[2] Frederick J. Hoffman, *The Twenties: American Writing in the Postwar Decade* (New York: The Viking Press, 1955), p. ix.

Waste Land

Bernard DeVoto

. . . I cannot take you through the literature of a decade in one lecture. I propose merely to examine the evidence of certain illustrations which seem to me to exhibit a relationship and a rough kind of harmony. They are all from the main current of the decade's literature, the official literature, the literature praised by writers themselves. They are also, whether consciously or unconsciously, within the final limitations imposed by the literary fallacy.*

Sinclair Lewis will be remembered as the author of four novels, *Main Street, Babbitt, Arrowsmith,* and *Elmer Gantry.* Our purpose would permit us to approach them in a number of ways. We might say that their rationale shows a progressive shift from the ideas of Mr. Van Wyck Brooks to those of Mr. H. L. Mencken. We might say that their description of America is considerably more sociological than anything we have previously considered. We might say that although they show an energetic repudiation of American experience it is not an irreconcilable repudiation or even a fundamental one. We certainly ought to say that they have a greater gusto than any other fiction of the period. They are first-rate novels, and Mr. Lewis may well be the best novelist of the decade. But I have time only to inquire whether something which they lack may not be a common, and significant, lack in the literature of the period as a whole. I propose merely to inquire what Mr. Lewis's novels praise.

The critics have never been sure whether Mr. Lewis was trying to truly represent the life of his time or to caricature it, and it seems likely that Mr. Lewis has shared their uncertainty. Satire, however, has an important prerogative. So long as we understand what a satirist is driving at, we cannot ask him to tell the whole truth about it. The faithful representation of reality which other kinds of novelists hold to be their highest duty lays no

From Bernard DeVoto, *The Literary Fallacy* (Boston: Little, Brown and Company, 1944), pp. 95–123. Reprinted by permission.

* Editor's note: As defined by DeVoto, "the literary fallacy assumes: that a culture may be understood and judged solely by means of its literature, that literature embodies truly and completely both the values and the content of a culture, that literature is the highest expression of a culture, that literature is the measure of life, and finally that life is subordinate to literature" (p. 43).

obligation on him. But also there is a touchstone to satire: it has points of reference which make its values clear. Thus the spirited portraiture in *Main Street* withholds you from asking whether some aspects of life in Gopher Prairie may not have been distorted or ignored until you wonder what the town is being held against for reference. You discover that the reference is to certain adolescent ideas of Carol Kennicott. And suddenly it appears that the Village Virus which has poisoned America consists of the failure of small towns to support productions of the one-act plays of Eugene O'Neill, to provide candlelight at dinner, and to sanction lounging pajamas as evening wear for housewives. The superb evocation of the city of Zenith in *Babbitt* distracts one from values until one comes to consider the side of George F. Babbitt with whom Mr. Lewis finally developed a warm friendship and to consider the few inhabitants of the city who are held to be living the good life. Whereupon there appears so trivial an imagination of deep experience, so shallow and unsophisticated a conception of emotional relationships and intellectual activity, that one sees at once what has been left out of Zenith. What has been left out is human profundity, whether admirable or base.

Finally, when a novelist creates heroes he comes out into the open. Mr. Lewis's understanding is illuminated for us by *Arrowsmith*. Here he not only undertakes to make a sociologist's survey of the entire field of medicine in America; he also undertakes to exalt the scientific ideal and to praise a way of life which he thinks of as heroic. We may dismiss the survey as within the prerogatives of satire, though Mr. Lewis's virtuosity blinds one to the ferocious injustice done to the Public Health Service, institutions like the Rockefeller Foundation, medical research in general, and the customary life of doctors. It is not that Mr. Lewis's Jacques Loeb, Professor Gottlieb, is contained altogether in a solution of romantic tears, or that his Metchnikoff, Dr. Sondelius, is a sophomore scientist seen sophomorically. It is rather that these characters show his conception of scientific inquiry to be debased. And in Martin Arrowsmith, the details of his career, his mind and thinking and emotions, his science and the larger science it is bound to, are romantic, sentimental, and above all trivial. Himself an adolescent whose experience is never mature or complex, he is portrayed in an adolescent conception of what he stands for. As a mind Martin suffers from arrested development, as a scientist he is a fool. Mr. Lewis does indeed picture certain genuine absurdities of scientific research in the book, but never the really dangerous absurdities. And the austerity, complexity, illuminations, frustrations, methods, goals, and conditions of scientific thinking never get into the book at all. The realities of science, worthy or unworthy, the great world of science in its entirety, are altogether passed by.

Is not the same true of Mr. Lewis's characters in general? Leora Arrowsmith is emotionally undeveloped. Ann Vickers is an immature mind and her emotions are childlike. Dodsworth is so simple a personality that one doubts if he could have managed a corporation. His wife Fran, who is

Lewis's most developed character, is not developed past a simple statement of frigidity, a statement which does not disclose either the content or the roots of frigidity. Maturity of mind, maturity of emotion, complexity of character or experience, profundity of aspiration, despair, achievement, or failure—they are not discoverable in these books. They are not present in America so far as these books try to be an index to America. Mr. Lewis is not at ease when he is on the side of his characters, he is at ease when he is deriding them, when they are his butts. But his attack on them consists of showing that they are without complexity, sophistication, true power, or genuine depth. Select whatever you will, love, lust, family affection, courage, meditation, fantasy, childhood, religion, socialism, education, friendship, villainy, pain—and you find it shallow. The lives explored are uncomplicated, the experience revealed is mediocre.

Again there is no point in asking whether some part of this may be a defect of the novelist, for even if any be, a greater part certainly originates in the literary fallacy. In Mr. Lewis's work a sizable portion of our literature went out to answer questions whose answers it had worked out as assumptions in advance. The rationale existed beforehand as a chart, and when literature inquired what American life was like, it knew in advance that American life would turn out to be trivial, shallow, and mediocre. It is a short step from mediocrity to contemptibility. In the mood to which Mr. Lewis brought more energy, talent, enjoyment, and even affection than anyone else, novelists for a long time conceived of fiction as an exercise in expressing the contemptibility of American life. True to the pattern of fads, fiction began to develop specific types. There was the farm novel: frustration, cretinism, bastardy, and the squalor of the soul. A current folkway of writers was to seek the good life on little farms in Connecticut, whence frustrate peasants had been driven out, but the novel of farm life as unspeakably degraded moved all across our geography till the Pacific Ocean put a boundary to it. There was the novel of Prohibition, the novel of the repressed high school teacher, the novel of the American male as an unskilled lover, the novel which daringly denounced the courthouse gang— but a more studious mind than I has made a list. An admirer of this fiction, which he called the novel of protest, once set out to name its principal themes, with no apparent knowledge that he was writing humor:—

> the American passion for "bigness" and success, high pressure salesmanship, shoddy commercial products, poor housing conditions in urban areas, the narrow, lethargic, platitudinous, and often hysterical mob mind, corruption in government, labor injunctions, racketeering, standardization in education, industry, and art, the deportation of radicals, the abridgment of our constitutional liberties, the contract system of prison labor, militarism, the subsidizing of large corporations, political patronage, blue laws, nationalism, the legalized extortion of big business, sweat shops in the needle trades, racial prejudice,

the stretch system in factories, inelastic marriage statutes, capital punishment, the entrance of religion into politics, imperialism, profiteering,
a nation half boom and half broke, jingoism, rate inflation by public
utilities, law evasions, our present jury system, election frauds, bigotry,
child labor, the Ku Klux Klan, and wage slavery of every kind.

Of this sort of thing criticism has lately been saying that fiction had
turned from experience to data, and that is true. But such a list merely
names some of the ways in which fiction was finding the Americans mediocre
or contemptible. One observes an omission: the list makes no finding that
literary persons are mediocre or may be considered contemptible. However,
in due time Mr. Hemingway was ·to close that gap.

By process of critical rationale, by dedication, by fashion, by a variety
of other avenues, writers have come to occupy the site chosen for them by
Mr. Brooks, for which Mr. Cabell found a suggestive name, the High Place.
Biography has become a study of mediocrity and contemptibility in our past,
apparently to excuse us by accusing our ancestors. Like fiction and criticism,
it is a withdrawal to the High Place. Some writers, following Harold
Stearns's manifesto,* are making a literal withdrawal. In American society
there is no joy nor light nor hope, no dignity, no worth; reality cannot be
found there and art cannot live. So the Artist will seek societies where art
can live, finding joy and hope and beauty, experience deep in the grain,
Paris, the French Riviera, Cornwall, the Mediterranean islands, Russia.
What life in America abundantly lacks exists abundantly in such places.
Thought is free there, art is the universal goal of human effort, writers are
universally respected, and human life has a claim on the interest of literary
men which in America it assuredly has not. But whether physical or only
spiritual, the withdrawal to the High Place has become an established mode
of literature and this mode dominates the literature to which the generality
of writers acknowledge allegiance. The dedication of the High Place may
be granted easily, but the illumination of its inhabitants seems to consist of
perceiving the inferiorities of their countrymen. Few writers ever spoke of
themselves in print as a superior class. The assumption is implicit in the
critical rationale, but it is customary to speak not of superiority but of
leadership. The superiority of the caste is the inferiority of the life withdrawn from. From the High Place, the Americans are the fall guys of the
world, sometimes dangerous as a mob, less often pitiful as well-meaning
boobs, but most often tawdry, yokelish, acquisitive, coarse, an undifferen-
tiated mass preyed on by mass passions and dominated by mass fears.

Turn now to Mr. Ernest Hemingway's fiction for evidence to carry us a
little farther. Here are memorable portraits of racketeers, thugs, hunters of

---

* Editor's note: After editing *Civilization in the United States* (1922), which deplored the state of American culture, Stearns concluded that the wise thing for a young
man to do was to leave the country.

big and small game, prizefighters, bullfighters, poolroom hangers-on, prostitutes, expatriate idlers, soldiers, a miscellany of touts, sportsmen, entertain-
ers and the like, and some millionaires and writers of whom the principal
assertion is that they are sexually impotent. Mr. Hemingway's themes are
death, the fear of death, the defiance of death, and the dangers to which
male potency is exposed—and it is easy to see what he praises. He praises ag-
gressiveness, courage, male wariness, male belligerence, the instinctual life,
war and fighting, sexual intercourse, and a few primary loyalties immediately associated with them. It is also easy to say what life is not, as his fiction
represents life. Life, so far as it can be desired or respected, does not exist
above the diaphragm. It is activated by digestion, the surge of adrenalin into
the bloodstream at crises of danger or defiance, and the secretion of the testi-
cles. His hero is a pre-Piltdown stage of man, a warily aggressive anthropoid
who goes down fighting. Intellectual life does not exist even in rudimentary
form, except that the contempt heaped on it grants it a kind of existence.
There is no social life, there is not even a society. Pithecanthropus Erectus
prowls a swamp so sown with danger that the honors, constraints, bonds,
prohibitions, and decencies of men living together merely add another, extreme form of danger to it. They are weaknesses of less perfect animalities
who have risen to the ethical and social development of, say, Cro-Magnon
man; the superior, more primitive anthropoid merely uses them to destroy
him. There is hardly even love, though Mr. Hemingway has written many
love stories, one of which may well be the best of his period. Piltdown man
couples with his female and the physical mating is clean, but the beauty of
this function is corrupted when love tries to add spiritual associations to it.
They are decadent—anything is decadent which may diminish male vigor
or deflect its functioning. Life has grandeur in that it may aggressively defy
violent death, and it has tragedy in that the defiance may be vain.

In short, the world most of us live in and the qualities by which we try
to live are unrecognized in Mr. Hemingway's fiction. True, criticism has
decided that the progress of world disorder finally led him to a great affirmation, and Mr. Geismar, whom I have quoted before, seems honestly to believe that the doom of civilization was averted and hope came back to the
Western world when Mr. Hemingway found a cause he could believe in.
Still, it does not appear that the dying murderer of *To Have and Have Not*
has altered Mr. Hemingway's basic values when he has learned that adrenalin spurts in vain into the bloodstream of one man alone. Nor, after
prayerful search, can I find that the values by which the life of men is to
be judged have been altered in the novel to which Mr. Hemingway so pre-
sumptuously prefixed a quotation from John Donne. It is true that Mr.
Hemingway's constant preoccupation with belligerence, cruelty, and inflicted death has contrived to associate itself with symbols in which the
rest of us find values that ennoble life. But in the novel life is not ennobled
by those symbols. The emphasis still suggests that though the sexual act

171

may be very fine, the act of killing is an orgasm far surpassing it in intensity. The world for which Robert Jordan faithfully sacrifices his life appears to be, in prospect, still a swamp which men who are mere bowels and auto-nomic nervous systems will prowl to the same ends, though perhaps this time in bands of gangsters rather than as lonely killers. The novel is not aware, even in vision, of society as civilization or of life as something affected by the fore-brain.

From the beginning up to now, both implicitly and explicitly, with a vindictive belligerence, Mr. Hemingway has always attacked the life of the mind, the life of the spirit, and the shared social experience of mankind. Certainly he finds them contemptible; it is a legitimate guess that they scare him. The point is, however, that his disdain of intelligence, contempt of spirituality, praise of mindlessness, and adoration of instinct and blood-consciousness have many connections with other literary values held else-where in the general movement. They are related to the cult of pure es-thetics, to the mystical cult of which D. H. Lawrence was the most gifted exponent in English, to the manias of doom that obsess Mr. Faulkner (who has much else in common with Mr. Hemingway), and to such clotted phobias as those that distinguish the work of Robinson Jeffers. If some areas of literature made a thesis of the inferiority of Americans, other areas exalted the thesis to make men inferior to the animals. It is a short step from thinking of the mob to thinking of the wolf pack, from the praise of instinct to war against reason, from art's vision of man as contemptible to dictatorship's vision of men as slaves. Such considerations, however, do not concern us. We have merely to repeat that Mr. Hemingway's fiction is separated from our common experience. By a different path he has come to the High Place. He is uncomfortable there for he finally comes to use the word "writer" as an epithet of contempt, as folklore has the wounded snake striking its fangs into its own body. But there he is and love, work, decency, achievement, aspiration, and defeat, as people know them who are neither writers nor bullfighters nor anthropoids, do not come within his awareness. Or, if they sometimes intrude on him, they only press the trigger of his scorn.

I think that we have enough clues now and may let the rest of the period's literature go undescribed, coming forthwith to the symbols which this litera-ture agreed to accept as comprehending the whole. What this generation had to say about life, it was generally agreed, found final expression in Mr. Eliot's poem, "The Waste Land." I do not propose to add to the thousands of pages that have analyzed it, but only to mention the passage in which Tiresias, "Old man with wrinkled female breasts," is present at the tawdry seduction of the typist home at teatime by the young man carbuncular, the small house agent's clerk on whom assurance sits as a silk hat on a Bradford millionaire. Here thirty concentrated lines of verse render life in the modern world as a cheap inanity, love as a vulgar ritual without feeling or significance, and mankind as too unimportant to justify Mr. Eliot's hatred of Apeneck Sweeney.

It is a crucial passage, crucial not only in Mr. Eliot's poetry but in the literature of our time. All Mr. Eliot's other perceptions support it, down to the time when his forehead was crossed with ashes on the first day of a later Lent. In it an entire literary movement makes a final judgment. Literature looks at human beings and says that this is what their experience amounts to. It commits itself. Then, having made the commitment, Mr. Eliot went on to prophesy. He was right to do so. For if personality and experience in our time were justly rendered in this passage, then there could be little doubt that life must come out as he predicted.

> This is the way the world ends
> This is the way the world ends
> This is the way the world ends
> Not with a bang but a whimper.*

It happens that Mr. MacLeish had a moment of sharing this vision, and he envisaged the end of the world coming down upon a gaudy circus performance when "The armless ambidextrian was lighting A match between his great and second toe," and then above the white faces and dazed eyes of the audience

> There in the sudden blackness the black pall
> Of nothing, nothing, nothing—nothing at all.†

Literature, I say, had committed itself. It had made a final judgment. It had reached the end of a road. In homelier words, it had got out on the end of a limb. So then the end of the world arrived.

Who are the people to whom Mr. MacLeish has been appealing so passionately—on behalf of whom he has accused writers of being as irresponsible as common criminals? They are only that audience of white faces and dazed eyes whom even judgment day could not stir to an awareness of anything at all. And when the end of the world came no whimpering was to be heard, except perhaps a literary whimpering, but the typist home at teatime and young man carbuncular decided that the world should not end. Nothing whatever changed in the typist and the house agent's clerk when the bombers came over London or the shock of Pearl Harbor traveled across this country. But war provided an appeal of judgment. The typist and the clerk had fortitude, sacrifice, fellowship; they were willing to die as an act of

---

* From *Collected Poems 1909–1962* by T. S. Eliot, copyright, 1936, by Harcourt Brace & World, Inc. and reprinted with their permission; from *Collected Poems 1909–1962* by T. S. Eliot with the permission of Faber and Faber, Ltd., London.

† From "The End of the World" by Archibald MacLeish. Reprinted by permission of Houghton Mifflin Company.

faith for the preservation of hope. They were hope, the soul and body of hope. They were staunchness, resolution, dedication. In fact they were incommensurable with what Mr. Eliot's poem had said they were. In "The Waste Land," I remarked, an entire literary movement made a final judgment on mankind. It committed itself. It got out on the end of a limb. But mankind turned out to be otherwise. It was not what literature had said it was. Furthermore, literature is now, temporarily at least, willing to accept the reversal of judgment. It has, temporarily at least, agreed to accept courage, fortitude, sacrifice, dedication, fellowship, willingness to die for the sake of the future—it has agreed to accept such attributes as a norm by which mankind shall be judged.

But perhaps it was the business of literature all along to take account of such attributes. It was not the typist and the young man carbuncular who were trivial. It was not their experience nor their emotions nor the realities they lived by that were trivial. It was the imagination of writers who passed judgment on them.

Return to the question I asked toward the beginning of these lectures. If one who was ignorant of American life during the 1920's, say Mr. Geismar, were to consult the books of, say, Mencken, Lewis, Hemingway, Dos Passos, and Wolfe in an effort to understand it, could he trust their description? I answered no. We have come far enough to turn that answer into an inquiry.

Consider the work of Mr. Dos Passos. No insincerity can be alleged against him, no malice, no kind of irresponsibility, especially the kind which Mr. MacLeish charges against the generation. Mr. Dos Passos has an austere conception of the responsibility of a novelist. All his fiction proceeds from a vision of life in America since the turn of the twentieth century, a vision of the time and the society as a whole. It is conceived with great power. It is worked out with a technical mastery which no contemporary has excelled. It is never suffered to depart from his vision.

One might, of course, hold that this vision is sometimes mistaken. Thus the damage done to our society by his Ward Moorehouses and Charley Andersons would indeed have been insignificant if such men had been what they seem to Mr. Dos Passos—if they had been just feeble timeservers or drunken lechers, antlike creatures carried crazily on chips by a great flood. But they were able to damage our society because that is precisely what they were not. Because Ward Moorehouse had a powerful intelligence which he employed in clearly calculated operations with effectively mastered tools. Because Charley Anderson, as a class, did not spend his time in debauchery but instead with an ascetic sobriety and an undeviating single-mindedness operated a mastered technology in his own service, toward ends which he did not in the least misconceive.

Specific inaccuracies, however, are less important for our study than the enveloping conditions in which Mr. Dos Passos's characters exist. They are always held to his vision with complete fidelity. But, ferocious as the injuries inflicted on them are, they do not move us much. These half-drugged men and women marching past milestones of indignity toward graceless deaths do not engage us to share their pain. The truth is that they hardly seem to suffer pain. Nothing theoretical or ideological is missing. Art has not failed to put any of its instruments at the service of life. Nevertheless these creatures, these integrations of behavior, are removed so far from us that they seem to be seen through a reducing glass. They lack a vital quality, they seem like automatons. It is as if, shall I say, the doom they meet is merely a literary doom.

If one sets against them the characters of the most considerable American novelist developed during the 1930's, James Farrell, one sees at once what the vital lack is. Mr. Dos Passos and Mr. Farrell conceive the function of fiction identically. But when a Farrell character is injured he bleeds, and when society wrongs one the reader is wronged with him, and this fails to happen in the Dos Passos novels. Certainly Mr. Dos Passos does not lack anger or compassion—nor the irony and pity which Mr. Hemingway found so funny when a bigger man than he praised them. But he remains on the High Place when looking at his people. His vision is afar off, from the mountain top. Whereas the monstrous cruelties inflicted on Studs Lonigan and the O'Neills, the monstrous brutalities they are forced to commit, are indeed monstrous precisely because they are not seen from the mountain top. They are monstrous because we feel that they are an intolerable impairment of human dignity. Precisely because human life is thought of as having inherent worth, things done to men may indeed be intolerable. Precisely because the experience of men has dignity there may be tragic experience. Precisely because men are not contemptible the cruelty and injustice inflicted on them can move us to say this must not be borne.

With Mr. Farrell for illustration, however, I have come outside the decade. It is proper to consider some who in that decade stood outside the official doctrines and made the affirmation I have found in him. But first let me a little generalize what we have said so far.

We have examined a system of ideas which held that American culture was barren and American life malformed, tawdry, and venal. From this the next step, soon taken, was to find the cultural traditions actively evil and the life they expressed vile. It is easy to say that from this literature was gone a sense of the heroic in our past. It is easy to say that American literature had lost all feeling of the greatness of America, whether past or present, and of its place in the Western world and its promise to civilization. It is easy to say that belief in the future, the very feeling of hope, was gone. But to say this is superficial, for much more was gone.

Not only heroes are scarce in this literature. In books which leading writers wrote and leading critics praised, the gospel of the established church, nothing is so rare as merely decent people. Where in the literature of the 1920's is the man or woman who lived a civilized life dedicated to the mature values of civilization? Where is the man who accepts the ordinary decencies and practises them with good will, meeting with self-respect and courage the human adventure of birth, growth, education, love, parenthood, work, and death? The man who is loyal to his friends, believes in his country, is a good citizen, loves his wife, works for his family, brings up his children, and deals resolutely with the vicissitudes, strains, anxieties, failures, and partial successes that compose our common lot? In the official Scriptures that man either does not exist at all or exists as an object of derision. Mr. Dos Passos overlooks him, he is beyond the concern of Mr. Faulkner, Mr. Hemingway says that he lacks maleness, and when Mr. Lewis abandons his amiable or occasionally dangerous fools he is unable to conceive that man above the level of a high school boy.

Here criticism usually demurs. The final phase of finance capitalism, the cynicism of an inflationary boom, Prohibition, racketeering, the decay of politics, the Scopes trial, the Sacco-Vanzetti case, innumerable other data of the same kind—such evidence as this, we are told, appalled writers, who were right to dissociate themselves from it altogether. With an odd pride Mr. Edmund Wilson has remarked that this generation of writers attacked their culture more unanimously and more continuously than any other known to history. Even so, a vagrant mind wonders why orthodox dogma was unable to perceive in America any will to oppose these things except among literary folk. One goes on to point out, moreover, that not only decency and righteousness are gone from the people whom this literature exploits but, as well, the simple basis of humanity. And that, one decides, makes merely silly the distress which criticism tells us was behind the exploitation. If man is a predatory animal, then surely it is silly of writers to blame him when he acts according to his nature. The wolf may not be hated for wolfishness nor the boob for stupidity: the anger of literature would be idiotic. But the idea that writers might be idiotic is abhorrent and so, summing up, one turns from it to say instead that literature's dissociation from common experience, achieved by systematic logic, results in a fundamental judgment, and a false judgment, on the nature of man. . . .

Let us, however, turn from what I have called the official literature of the 1920's—the body of writing which was accepted by most writers as composing the movement, and which was conscious of itself as representing the age. Nothing about the period is more remarkable than the fact that second-rate writers were commonly less susceptible to the literary fallacy than their betters. But I propose to speak of certain first-rate writers who stood outside the movement.

To name only a few, when one comes to Carl Sandburg, E. A. Robinson, Willa Cather, Stephen Vincent Benét, and Robert Frost one enters a world quite different from that of the poets and novelists I have discussed and the critics who made out work-sheets for them. It is certainly not a world sugary or aseptic, washed clean of evil, or emptied of hate, injustice, cruelty, suffering, failure, or decay. No one in the generation has written with fiercer

anger of the exploitation of men than Mr. Sandburg. No one in the generation has more witheringly rebuked the ebbing from our consciousness of
certain elements of greatness in our tradition than Miss Cather or Mr.
Benét. In Mr. Frost's poetry there is a resentment of indignities inflicted on
men so fierce that compared to it Mr. Lewis's protest seems no more than a
rowdy bellow and Mr. Hemingway's a rather craven sob. The difference is
not that these writers fail in any way to be aware of evil or that any of
them fail to understand the indecencies of life. It is only a difference of
opinion—a difference of opinion about the dignity of man. That is all but
it is a final difference, one that can never be resolved.

The poetry of Robert Frost affirms what the orthodox literature of the
1920's denies: that human experience has dignity. Human feeling has
finality. Grief may be hopeless and rebellion may be futile but they are real
and so they are tragic. Tragedy may be immitigable but it *is* tragedy. The
integrity of experience is common to us all and is sacred in us all. Life *has*
sanctity; whether fulfilled or unfulfilled, it *is* worthy, it *can* be trusted, it *has*
a dignity that cannot be corrupted. The experience of men has a fundamental worth which neither other men, nor God, nor a hostile fate can
destroy. Hold the poems to any light, look at any edge or angle of them,
and they always come to the same focus. A worthless hired man comes back
to an adopted home to die with people who know his worthlessness. A
woman once mad washes her dishes beside Lake Willoughby in the knowledge of what made her mad and the knowledge that she will be mad again.
A lover of forest orchids whom the acquisitive society has crippled signs a
legal release, knowing exactly what it was that cut off his feet. In them all is
an infrangible dignity. On that infrangible dignity of man Frost's poetry
stands foursquare and in Frost's poetry American literature of our time
makes its basic affirmation. Man is the measure of things. Man's experience
is the measure of reality. Man's spirit is the measure of fate.

The literature we have glanced at lacks this basic acknowledgment of the
dignity of man. That is why it is a trivial literature—why the Waste Land
of Mr. Eliot and the Solutrean swamp of Mr. Hemingway are less than
tragedy, smaller than tragedy. Bulls and male sharks may die in agony, and
perhaps there is beauty in the moment of total aggressive force going down
before superior force, but though the pain they suffer may shock our nerves
we cannot possibly feel their death as tragic. The diminished marionettes
of Mr. Dos Passos do not move us to either pain or protest. Conceived as
aggregations of reflexes, they lack the humanity which alone gives significance to suffering or cruelty. The frustration of an animal cannot be tragic.
The accusation that any man is base or has done evil means nothing at all,
unless baseness and evil are defections from the spirit of man. Injustice is
an empty word unless man is the measure of justice. There can be no sin
unless sin robs man of a state of grace.

That is why so many literary attitudes of our time led eventually to
cynicism, heartbreak, or neurotic collapse. Out of them has come much

penitence and much of that penitence is merely absurd. It was always possible to inquire "What art?" when someone told us long ago that a spirit bruised by the mediocrity of the life round it intended to seek healing in dedication to beauty. The same question disposes of several dozen literary confessions which have told us that the penitents found no life whatever in beauty, that the palace of art proved to be a house of the dead. Again, those who fled the culture of America, which stifled thought and forbade art and made war on freedom, were presently back from various European Utopias strangely shocked because something Utopian, something which clearly could not be charged against America, had interfered with thought and art and freedom. Another group were betrayed into a more painful bewilderment. They undertook to identify themselves with the workers of the world, only to perish of a dilemma. The blue jeans of the Noble Worker were ceremonial vestments by definition and yet, by earlier definition, the bodies they covered had been denied immortal souls. Three quarters of a literary movement died of internal friction.

Such fragile attitudes are unimportant. They merely move one to inquire whether the lack of intelligence observed was in the culture complained of or in the writers complaining. What counted was not the fragility of small attitudes but the falsity of the fundamental literary attitude. As the catastrophe of our time moved on to its last act, it became clear that literary thinking had got caught in a steel trap of its own making. Literature now found itself summoning men to die for institutions, traditions, possibilities, and hopes which it had lately described as either nonexistent or contemptible. And the men whom it summoned to die for them were the inferior creatures who had lately been incapable even of perceiving, still more of understanding, the values which could make them consent to die.

For it is clear to you that I have been talking about something which need not necessarily be phrased in literary jargon. I have been talking about democracy, I have been talking, in fact, about a very specific form of democracy which first became a faith, first established the tenets and developed the energy of a faith, and first brought that faith to the problems of men living together in society, here in America. It is true that not many writers of the 1920's formally or even consciously opposed democracy. It is proper to remember that a few did. There were some who formally analyzed democracy as a mob of inferior men, dominated by mob lusts and mob panics and conditioned by the swinishness of the average man. Such writers opposed democracy, and so did a number of the period's least stable minds, prettily coquetting with notions of American monarchy and various other lightly literary lunacies, though of course the stampede of literary men to formidable absolutisms, whether communist or fascist, was a phenomenon of the next decade. However, the sum was small and the effect unnoticeable even in the coterie press.

Apart from these, it is just to say that the writers of the period avowed an honest respect for the word "democracy." A word is only a word, however. American democracy is not a word but American men and women, the beliefs they hold about themselves and one another, institutions they maintain to safeguard their beliefs and to fulfill their hopes, and the goals, ideals, constraints, and prohibitions they share and mutually acknowledge. It was precisely these people and these ideas, feelings, institutions, traditions, and culture which the literature of the period rejected. For these people and their culture the orthodox writers of the period had, as their books prove, an antipathy ranging from mere disillusionment or mere distaste, through hatred, to contempt. No wonder, then, that when judgment day came so incomparably otherwise than Mr. Eliot had predicted, the ideas of many literary men became schizophrenic. Ordinary man must now save the democratic way of life. But one earlier premise held that that way of life was not worth saving. And another earlier premise held that those who must save it could not save it. Either premise seemed to make it impossible to take a stand.

But this merely repeats what I have just said in other words. The Christian view of life holds that men are entitled to primary respect because they are all the children of God—"inasmuch as ye have done it unto one of the least of these my brethren ye have done it unto me." The view of life, Christian or non-Christian, which in all ages is called humanistic holds that man is entitled to primary respect because only in man's consciousness can the universe be grappled with. And the democratic view of life holds quite simply that the dignity of man is unalienable.

But respect for this unalienable dignity is precisely what had been drained from the literature of the 1920's. Mr. MacLeish's indictment of modern American literature which I began by quoting says that writers failed to safeguard our democracy between the two great wars. There can be no appeal from that judgment. But they failed to safeguard it because they failed in primary respect for democratic man and primary understanding of his experience.

I have remarked that for several years now literature has been confessing its errors. The confession of such an error as this is a confession of betrayal. It amounts to a confession that what truly was bankrupt was not American civilization but the literary way of thinking about it. That way of thinking, it is now quite clear—it is temporarily clear even to writers—was not competent to bring in trustworthy findings. It was not an adequate, an accurate, or a dependable instrument. It would not give results that could be used. The principal effort of literature has, by its own confession, failed. It has failed because of the insufficiency of its means. It has failed because a people, a culture, and a civilization cannot be held to literary values.

179

Some Perspectives on the 1920's

Frederick J. Hoffman

1. THE SNOW OF 1929

Not long after October 1929 people began to regret the 1920's, to renounce the sins of a "wasted decade"; they admitted they had had a good time while "the gaudiest spree in history" had lasted, but they were ready now to assume the roles of adult, mature persons. No more pathetic reminder of the reformed playboy exists than Charlie Wales of Fitzgerald's story, "Babylon Revisited" (written in 1931). Wales returns to Paris, after an exile, to reclaim his life. He is properly humble, regretful, resolved; he has become "a new man," learned his lesson, and will his sister-in-law please restore his daughter Honoria to him? He will now be able to take care of her: sober, restrained, solvent, and anxious to identify himself with the human race, he feels that she will secure him in his new conviction. He now believes "in character"; he wants "to jump back a whole generation and trust in character again as the eternally valuable element."

Paris, the Babylon to which he has made his journey of contrition, is itself suffering a depression of the spirit. The streets are almost empty of tourists, where a few months before they had been gay and colorful. "The Poet's Cave had disappeared, but the two great mouths of the Café of Heaven and the Café of Hell still yawned—even devoured, as he watched, the meager contents of a tourist bus—a German, a Japanese, and an American couple who glanced at him with frightened eyes." Looking upon the waste, reflecting upon the pathos, Charlie Wales suddenly realizes "the meaning of the word 'dissipate'—to dissipate into thin air; to make nothing out of something."

The "waste" is both a moral and a dramatic problem. There are those who soberly endured the antics of their American contemporaries during the 1920's; now they have become their judges. But the morally correct do not enjoy their role; they have a sense not so much of wickedness resisted as of their having been cheated out of something. Marion Peters, the sister-in-law who has kept Charlie's daughter from him, "was a tall woman with worried eyes, who had once possessed a fresh American loveliness." Between

From *The Twenties* by Frederick J. Hoffman. Copyright 1955 by Frederick J. Hoffman. Reprinted by permission of The Viking Press, Inc. Pp. 371–391.

the two a quiet but intense struggle develops, a struggle of two equally strong determinations, for Honoria, the prize. If he should prove that one can morally survive the 1920's, the prize is his; if not, if there is the slightest doubt of his having fully reformed, Honoria remains with the "good woman," the woman who has sacrificed her "American loveliness" so that character might return to the American personality after an absence of at least ten years. Slowly, arduously, Wales works to regain her confidence. But the stain of the 1920's is hard to remove. Two of his friends reappear from out of the past; and, though Wales tries to keep them away, to prevent their violating the temple of his humble resolve, they do just that. The 1920's cannot be put away. The terrible crime of irresponsibility, which had led to the death of his wife, haunts the atonement at the very moment of forgiveness, and Wales is once more back at the beginning, without the reward he had wished for his patient efforts to redefine himself as a responsible human being:

> Again the memory of those days swept over him like a nightmare— the people they had met traveling; then people who couldn't add a row of figures or speak a coherent sentence. The little man Helen had consented to dance with at the ship's party, who had insulted her ten feet from the table; the women and girls carried screaming with drink or drugs out of public places—
> —The men who locked their wives out in the snow, because the snow of twenty-nine wasn't real snow. If you didn't want it to be snow, you just paid some money.

On January 2, 1950, *Life* magazine summarized the five decades of our century in one hundred pages of pictures and comment. As is usual on such occasions, the 1920's figured prominently, and there was nothing new or unexpected in the display. From Gilda Gray to Grover Whalen, the celebrities of the time were exhibited; and the brief preface reflected upon their meaning:

> When the 1920's ended in the crash it became fashionable (and merciful) to forget them, and they have been buried beneath recovery, war, and a new boom. It is startling to find the old headliners still looking as chipper as they do in these pictures taken in the past few months— startling, and pleasant. They were the life of the party and everyone loves them, even though it was not a party that the nation can afford to throw again.

What distinguishes this quotation from the Luce "capsule" is the quality of its metaphor; the 1920's were a "party" that resulted in a serious hangover. We still talk about the party but are properly repentant and resolved not to have another. The same metaphor is encountered in a collection called *The Pleasures of the Jazz Age* (1948), edited by William Hoddap: "Here is a ten-year-long weekend party in which they all participated and whose hangover never really started till the stock-market crash." These people had founded "an uncharted colony of freedom—even license—for refugees from reality." In other characterizations the 1920's were called "The Era of Wonderful Nonsense," the time of the "lost generation," the "Jazz Age," the age of Freud, Ziegfeld, and Coolidge.[1]

In a very real sense Fitzgerald, who had been in the vanguard of those establishing this image of the twenties, helped to make it a permanent view. When the decade died in the last months of 1929 Fitzgerald "tightened his belt"; and in subsequent years he wrote a series of pieces, for *Scribner's, Esquire,* and other magazines, in which he described both the pleasures and the agonies of atonement since undergone. Fitzgerald's Charlie Wales perhaps best symbolizes the crowd who "went to the party" and had to pay the check.[2]

The "golden boom," the "gaudiest spree in history," required in 1931 "the proper expression of horror as we look back at our wasted youth." In the 1930's Fitzgerald wrote about his "wasted youth," dwelling again and again upon its glamour and its misguided energy. The pages of *Tender Is the Night* (1934) are filled with judgments delivered upon the waste, the triviality, the pathetic effort to realize what in the decade had seemed hopelessly beyond realization.[3] The hero, Dr. Dick Diver, sacrifices his every talent, his last ounce of energy, to keep alive an illusion that has been doomed from the start. His struggle is not with the 1920's but with a complex of enemies who, in Fitzgerald's view, had made the decade what it was: easy wealth; the falsely sentimental view of life symbolized in the Rosemary Hoyt of the film *Daddy's Girl*; the inner weaknesses and tensions of its most gifted person; above all, its indifference to human responsibility—its inability to define the terms on which men *become* responsible. In the end

---

[1] See a recent "handbook" (*Backgrounds of American Literary Thought* by Rod W. Horton and Herbert W. Edwards, 1952): The 1920's "in reality . . . presented the rather sad spectacle of irresponsible youth having its last fling." Elsewhere it speaks of "the whoopie mentality of the happy-talking twenties" and employs the usual clichés concerning "national adolescence" and other reflections that recall Fitzgerald's remarks in the early 1930's. The authors do admit that there was talent in those years, that the young men "gave the nation the liveliest, freshest, most stimulating writing in its literary experience."

[2] Since the Depression had followed immediately upon the end of the decade, "perspectives" upon it were quickly achieved. But Fitzgerald had his personal reasons for looking back in such a way. It is of some interest to note that Nick Carraway, in the midst of the wild clamor of charge and countercharge at the Plaza Hotel, suddenly and sadly remembers that he has reached "the thirtieth year of his age."

[3] If one examines the history of the composition of this novel (begun almost immediately after *The Great Gatsby* was published in 1925), one can understand its pertinence as a commentary upon the decade. It began as an account of planned murder, in essentials exploiting the most sensational contemporary "copy." Gradually this quality of American life was toned down; and Fitzgerald moved toward the use of a hero who is endowed with the most affectingly "charming" good will and is (in his profession) a scientific minister to the decade's ills as well. See Arthur Mizener's *The Far Side of Paradise* for the story of the several plans that led to the novel of 1934.

Diver, on his "way out," his wife gone away with another man, pauses for a final "benediction" of that "prayer-rug" of Riviera beach that had been the scene of his greatest triumphs and his most painful defeats:

> "I must go," he said. As he stood up he swayed a little; he did not feel well any more—his blood raced slow. He raised his right hand and with a papal cross he blessed the beach from the high terrace.

In the quiet blasphemy of this gesture Diver dismisses the decade and himself; he had been identified with it and his talents and charm were exhausted to preserve in it a quality it had not wanted. He is through with it, and it with him.

In spite of the indifferent reception of *Tender Is the Night*, Fitzgerald's identification with the 1920's persisted. The two were indistinguishable in the public mind. A man of great talent, he had fought a losing battle with the temptations and the frivolities of the time. In loving them for their own sakes, he had forfeited his full right to judge them incisively. But Dr. Diver's final gesture is ironically a farewell to something pathetically lost when the decade ended. "Now once more the belt is tight," he said in November 1931 (*Scribner's Magazine*), "and we summon the proper expression of horror as we look back at our wasted youth."

> Sometimes, though, there is a ghostly rumble among the drums, an asthmatic whisper in the trombones that swings me back into the early twenties when we drank wood alcohol and every day in every way grew better and better, and there was a first abortive shortening of the skirts, and girls all looked alike in sweater dresses, and people you didn't want to know said 'Yes, we have no bananas,' and it seemed only a question of a few years before the older people would step aside and let the world be run by those who saw things as they were— and it all seems rosy and romantic to us who were young then, because we will never feel quite so intensely about our surroundings any more.[4]

Nevertheless the image of the twenties that remained most clearly in the public mind in 1950 was that established by Fitzgerald in 1920, exploited and all but exhausted by him in the following years, and then reassimilated in terms of a moral view of wistful regret in the 1930's.

---

[4] Fitzgerald's wife, Zelda, gave her own version of the 1920's in her only novel, *Save Me the Waltz* (1932). The heroine has to suffer the disadvantages of marriage to a celebrity; she turns to ballet dancing for salvation, as Mabel Dodge Luhan might have turned to Gurdjieff's rhythmic ceremonials. This tedious novel is valuable only for its annotations upon the Fitzgerald perspective: "They were having the bread line at the Ritz that year"; "People were tired of the proletariat—everybody was famous"; "Nobody knew the words to 'The Star-Spangled Banner'"; the expatriates sought "stimulation in the church and asceticism in sex." These are *New Yorker* captions; the conflict in "Alabama's" soul concerning allegiances and loyalties is patently contrived. The strongest impression one gets from reading this novel in 1953 is that the Fitzgeralds did have a "rough time" and that the violence of their hysterias must have disturbed his every paragraph and altered the punctuation of his every sentence.

It required more than Fitzgerald, however, to fix that impression upon the public mind. The crash of 1929 was, after all, not only a sign of moral collapse. It was a fact of economic history, and in the 1930's economic facts were also moral facts. The sturdy and persistent men of Marx watched the collapse of Wall Street with ill-concealed pleasure and began the 1930's with a determination to wipe the previous decade entirely off the record. "Social responsibility," all but absent from the American scene for ten years, according to the leftists, now became the major concern. The sad young men were welcomed back to America, on probation, and were asked to renounce their sinful past and promised reward for their assumption of doctrinal saintliness. The men who had made a pilgrimage to Moscow instead of indulging themselves in Babylon-on-the-Seine prepared themselves for the roles of moral spokesmen. A haunting sense of missed opportunities for "social good" overwhelmed the men and women of the 1930's, who looked back upon the "nation that for a decade had wanted only to be entertained." The apostles of social responsibility used the decade as a grim reminder: there but for the grace of Marx go I. The antics of the 1920's were "cute but horrible." Never had a more suitable demonstration appeared of the tragedy of social and moral dissipation. It was ideally suited to the Marxist text, which exploited it with great ease and convincing persuasion.

Mr. Roosevelt's liberals toned down the criticism a bit, but only because they wanted it to be less Marxist, more native to the grain of American social thought. The *New Republic* and the *Nation* regained their confidence and addressed themselves to the review of a tradition they thought had been lost when Sacco and Vanzetti were destroyed. The men who had begun their careers in the 1920's revised their points of view, addressing themselves eagerly and respectfully to great "social forces." John Dos Passos, whose John Andrews had risked and suffered all for art, now, in *U.S.A.*, relegated the aesthetic conscience to that corner of his trilogy called "The Camera Eye." Hemingway sought and found a social objective in the streets of Madrid, and later had his Robert Jordan defend the line that Lieutenant Henry had deserted. They were cured, or seemed to be. They came back to see what they had earlier ignored; and what they had previously seen they now ignored.

It was the leftists of the 1930's who were the first to count the cost, and they outlined the terms of payment in phrases of economic liability, which invariably had overtones of moral judgment. The early years of the *New Masses* (1926–1929) had anticipated the pattern of criticism: a pitiful waste of great talent and promise, because these people had not the slightest respect for society. They were pathetically unable to go beyond a childish "revolution" against the bad taste of their elders, ignoring in their rebellion the really disastrous sins committed by the older generation, the sins of capitalism. There was no doubt about it: the failure to understand the social economy was a consequence of the disrespect for any sensible tradition, American or Russian.

This view of the 1920's has not yet been entirely corrected or revised. In the 1940's the perspective was changed a bit, but it was just as much distorted by current moral and social urgencies. To the men who fought in World War II and survived it, the 1920's seemed either a period of amusing but stupid gaiety or a horrible and expensive example of what the "irresponsibles" could cost a nation with moral and military commitments to the world. In the 1950 reviews of the half-century provided in radio broadcasts and popular magazines, the 1920's appeared a grotesque world, remembered for sophomoric behavior and ingenious evasions of serious responsibility. The popular mind saw the decade only in the figure of the musical revue, in Hollywood's strange version of Jay Gatsby, or in the revival of Anita Loos's Lorelei.

The work of Van Wyck Brooks, Archibald MacLeish, Bernard DeVoto, and the editors of the *Saturday Review of Literature* sounded another kind of alarm. Their arguments combined a search for a creditable American past and an appeal for a sensible atomic future: according to them, the irresponsibles of the 1920's had either not known or not respected the American tradition. A simple formula was set up: personal responsibility is above all responsibility to one's neighbor, to one's group, and to the world at large. An explosion at Hiroshima, or anywhere, accelerates that sense of responsibility, should make man more vitally concerned than ever over the men who killed and the men who were killed. Isolationism of any kind was immoral. The historical event must hereafter be the constant locus of literary reference. Above all, one must respect one's America, as had Whittier and Twain and Whitman. There was no such respect in the 1920's; writers had given a distorted view of American life, mocking what was pardonable in it, ignoring what was admirable. When they dismissed H. G. Wells as a "Fabian schoolma'arm," spoke condescendingly of John Dewey, and welcomed the dismal historical metaphors of Spengler, they were committed to a grievous violation of literary proprieties—a violation that could lead only to the fascism of Ezra Pound and the solemnly obedient acceptance and defense of his unhappy views.

Such a judgment of the 1920's was a complex of both leftist and liberal views; the "Marxist" condemnation, relieved of its economic emphasis, became wholly moral and wholly traditional. Perhaps we could no longer claim that the writers of the twenties were responsible for the collapse of the American economy, but we could accuse them of having failed to provide a sufficient moral "readiness" for World War II; and we could also say that they gave us no clue to the awful responsibilities of the "atomic age."

Invariably these attacks upon the decade were the product of one form or another of moral disposition and prejudice. Fitzgerald's Charlie Wales recognized only the difficulties of atonement for serious human errors; Mike Gold described the "hollow men" (1941) as guilty entirely on the grounds of their indifference to the "right" issues or the right interpretation of them; Brooks, having earlier condemned the American past for its failure to meet his moral demands, in the late 1930's and the 1940's condemned those who had thus renounced the past; DeVoto accused writers of having committed the unpardonable sin of attending to their writing, to the neglect of certain subject matters that he thought indispensable to a proper understanding of our tradition; MacLeish called his own fellow writers of the 1920's irresponsibles for similar reasons. These critics, in their emphasis on what they thought was primarily important, in their insistence upon *their* reading of human nature and of its relationship to literature, almost invariably shared the special moral dispositions of their age.

In his lectures at Indiana University (*The Literary Fallacy*, 1944), De Voto passed many remarkable judgments upon the literature of the twenties. The principal accusation was contained in the phrase "the literary fallacy"; that is, the notion that evaluations of American life "as a whole" can be seen and realized exclusively in literary terms. Most of the writers whom DeVoto condemned "begin with the study of literature; most of them employ literary data exclusively. Practically all of them who extend their inquiry beyond literary data extend it by means of primarily literary ideas." This would not be a serious error, were it not that they also speak of such matters as "culture" and "civilization." But they do not know what these terms mean; they have confined their interests to form, to a narrow reading of human and cultural matters, and they have not studied the "things that matter." As a result they commit the error of assuming that what they have found within the range of their limited interests is generally or exclusively true. This is why we need not, or should not, take them seriously; their literature lacks a "basic acknowledgment of the dignity of man. That is why it is a trivial literature—why the Waste Land of Mr. Eliot and the solutrean swamp of Mr. Hemingway are less than tragedy, smaller than tragedy."

None of these critics showed respect for the values of literature, only a persistent attempt to command and direct the perceptions of literary artists in terms of an "extra-literary" set of moral imperatives. This was in part due to the "emergency" in which much of this criticism was written; during World War II almost nothing mattered but a "literature of crisis," a literature that reaffirmed what Brooks called "primary" values; and they found little or none of this "primary" literature in the 1920's. Having discovered that the writers of the 1920's were "indifferent" to the causes that led to World War II, they accused them of being irresponsible: that is, of having neglected their roles as spokesmen of a culture and thus having encouraged the public to remain indifferent and irresponsible.

All these critics were able to cite texts. The flapper of Fitzgerald's novels

and stories, for example, repeated endlessly and apparently without variation her gestures of tired sophistication. " 'You see I think everything's
terrible anyhow.' " Daisy Buchanan says in *The Great Gatsby,* "in a convinced way. 'Everybody thinks so—the most advanced people. And I *know.*
I've been everywhere and seen everything and done everything.' " Through
Fitzgerald and his imitators, every place seemed to take on the character of
an undergraduate campus, and every person either to be living on one or in
the memory of his having lived there.

Another text might be found in the pose of bright cynicism affected by
Ben Hecht's newspaperman, Erik Dorn. The business of bootlegging, in
which fortunes were quickly made by evading the law, was a background
of *The Great Gatsby* and Dos Passos' *Manhattan Transfer.* Daisy's "advanced people" also wrote and published gloomy estimates of the melancholy results of World War I for a nation that had won it. Americans were
better out of the "international gamble," which had been so patently exposed by the war (Dos Passos' *One Man's Initiation* and *Three Soldiers;*
Hemingway's *A Farewell to Arms*). It was best to make "a separate peace";
desertion from public affairs was the only means of salvaging private dignity
(*Three Soldiers, A Farewell to Arms, In Our Time*). Since the war had
proved that the men in charge could not command respect, one was left
with a problem of personal adjustment, deprived of past securities (*The Sun
Also Rises*).

But no real tragic insight into the nature of man was possible in a time
when the war had destroyed certain necessary illusions and the march of
science had served to reduce all remaining ones. Beginning with Harold
Stearns' *America and the Young Intellectual* (1921) and ending with Joseph
Wood Krutch's *The Modern Temper* (1929), the decade offered one "proof"
after another of moral and social incapacity. Both the village and the small
city were riddled by prejudice, stupidity, callousness (Sinclair Lewis's *Main
Street* and *Babbitt;* Carl Van Vechten's *The Tattooed Countess*). The clergy
were transparently ridiculous and ungodly (Lewis's *Elmer Gantry;* Menck-
en's "Americana"). Political morality and intelligence had never reached
so low a level, at least not since Mark Twain's Gilded Age (Lewis's *The
Man Who Knew Coolidge;* weekly editorials in the *Nation,* the *New Republic;* Walter Lippmann in *Vanity Fair*). Numerous suggestions were offered
for easy solutions of the human distress. Doctor Coué performed his
"miracles" on one level of human response with as much effectiveness as
Doctor Freud did on another. Edith Wharton's Mrs. Manford (*Twilight
Sleep*) enjoyed an almost daily change of cult and "vision"; and the middle-
aged ladies of Lewis's Zenith vied with Helen Hokinson's suburbanites in
their search for the very latest word from the decade's multiple heaven.

The new social symbolism included many strangely acute designations
of the period of adjustment: what Malcolm Cowley described as "significant
gesture" became in the eyes of Hemingway's Count Mippipopolous the

"values" of the good life, for his Nick Adams the right restraint in the use of the senses, for Jake Barnes the "pure line" of the matador artist. Fitzgerald's brooding ex-Yale man, Tom Buchanan, nibbled "at the edge of stale ideas" and invoked white supremacy as a means of explaining his own boredom and tension. His more sensitive and pathetic Abe North had "a code": he was against the burning of witches. The more articulate of the expatriates believed their social behavior to be closely associated with art, even when it was concerned entirely with the destruction of art. Dada was significantly concerned with destruction—the most vulgar gesture might be the most significant or the most effective. The aim was to invert the scale of decorum, to exalt vulgarity and explode convention. Mr. Babbitt was found daily in a thousand pieces in Montparnasse and Greenwich Village.

2. "SPIRITS GROWN ELIOTIC"

Of the general images the literature of the decade impressed upon us, two are especially vivid as "classical" reminders of the time: the "pathos of the adolescent" and the "unregenerate bohemian." For the first there is the evidence of many occasions. It is contained usually in a gesture, the very vagueness of which served to thrill its readers. Undoubtedly the great early success of Fitzgerald's *This Side of Paradise* was due to its appeals to the mind of the younger generation. Its most popular gesture comes in the last two pages: Amory Blaine speaks up for the new generation, endowing it with the privileges of its immaturity. This new generation, "grown up to find all Gods dead, all wars fought, all faiths in man shaken," was to be more brilliantly and more fully characterized in other texts; but no other work was able to endow it with quite the glamour of lonely defiance to be found in the novel's last lines:

> He stretched out his arms to the crystalline, radiant sky. "I know myself," he cried, "but that is all."

Again, at the beginning of the decade, the moment of adolescent awareness was shown in Sherwood Anderson's *Winesburg, Ohio,* whose George Willard experiences for the first time "the sadness of sophistication":

> With a little gasp he sees himself as merely a leaf blown by the wind through the streets of his village. He knows that in spite of all the stout talk of his fellows he must live and die in uncertainty, a thing blown by the winds, a thing destined like corn to wilt in the sun.

This shock of realization is like a birth into a new world. Cynicism has not set in, nor has a philosophy grown. The protections accorded normal experience are removed, and the young man is forced into a world he can never really understand. This insistence upon the youth of the generation, upon its perilous freedom, proved a strong incentive to those who could claim to belong to the generation; it made those who didn't qualify wish to belong as well. In its many variations, it sounded a note of individual rebellion, of a determination to work outside conventional securities: Hemingway's Nick Adams makes a "separate peace"; Dos Passos' John Andrews calmly accepts the penalties of desertion; Floyd Dell's heroes and heroines run the gamut, from Iowa to Chicago to Greenwich Village; and Lieutenant Henry speaks for them all:

> That was what you did. You died. You did not know what it was about. You never had time to learn. They threw you in and told you the rules and the first time they caught you off base they killed you.

The range of experience varies, the definition achieves different shades and degrees of meaning. But the prevailing impression is that of the very young, frightened and puzzled and defeated at the start, but determined to formulate a code that both justifies and utilizes that defeat. This was part of the tone of the 1920's: a rhetorical quality quite different from the gestures made by Frank Norris's trapped superman or Theodore Dreiser's Hurstwood. It was a pathos realized too early, with neither the setting nor the incentive to give it the quality usually associated with "tragedy."

As for the attitude of the "unregenerate bohemian," it was even more roundly condemned by those who later criticized the decade, because it apparently ignored altogether what was usually recognized as "social experience." Far from being depressed by the period of his birth, the bohemian preferred to ignore it, except in satirical acknowledgment of its absurdity. The individual became an uncompromising anarchist, a radical of a kind that has almost vanished from the American scene since 1930. There were two variations of this attitude: one assumed that the aesthetic and the social conscience were the same; the other assumed there was no such thing as a social conscience, that there was no history but only persons. It was natural enough that this latter view should condemn the type of middle-class person Cummings had scornfully called the "official." Upton Sinclair proved to be the sole active survivor of progressive liberalism in the twenties, and Cummings was almost alone in his active sponsorship of aesthetic radicalism in the thirties. To affirm the value of the non-social personality was a difficult and unpopular task after 1929; even Maxwell Bodenheim marched in proletarian parades up Fifth Avenue in the thirties. But the basic point of view stated and dramatized in *The Enormous Room* was never altered thereafter by Cummings, except in details and kinds of reference.

Throughout the twenties writers shifted their ground uncomfortably with respect to the question of their debt to society. Of this maneuvering we have abundant evidence in Joseph Freeman's *An American Testament* and in the early history of the *New Masses*. But the position taken by Cummings is a partial sign of what in the decade was thought to be a most important privilege: that of aesthetic self-determination. From this point of view, most attacks were launched, trivial or profound or both, upon the restrictions and conventions of the world. The aesthetic radical retained a free and independent mind, refusing to permit any interference with his freedom. He was flattered to think that his views might be explained "scientifically," but he rejected without qualification the basic requirements of a scientific method. More often than not the "unregenerate bohemian" rejected philosophy as such altogether, thought himself possessed of finer instincts than the "prurient philosophers" of Cummings' poem.

The unregenerate bohemian was an extreme form of what has been an important contribution to modern culture: the emphasis, the *insistence,* upon the value of personal vision. The 1920's were one of a very few times when one could be respected for having a private view of public affairs. This private view applied not only to actual headline copy but to systems of philosophical thought, to scientific discoveries, to investigations of the nature of man and his world, and to theories of the writing and value of literature.

Much of the activity thus sponsored was of course reckless and irresponsible in its neglect of logic and in its sporadic enthusiasms. Nevertheless the literary activity of the decade stressed the very defensible assumption that the artist's sensibility is a legitimate means of gaining insight and knowledge that are indispensable to our total view of a culture. Since the artists of the decade realized the importance of their gift, they gave a special quality of insight into facts often unchallenged or misunderstood by others. For one thing, they pointed, not to the gifts of science, but to its dangers. They risked being called frivolous and ignorant, so that they might point out that science was not wholly good, that material progress may even be quite harmful, that an entirely satisfactory religious experience was all but impossible in a world that had "educated" itself beyond the need of it.

Perhaps their strongest (at any rate their loudest) activity consisted of their documentation of human absurdities. This criticism of the modern world, in spite of its frequent triviality, was both a profound and a necessary contribution to the knowledge we must have of our society. We realize now that for the most part it was correct and shrewd. Its value can be seen in several ways. One is its treatment of history, the act of taking the straight line of liberal prophecy and twisting it—rejecting the linear view of H. G. Wells for the cyclical view of Spengler. Another is the valuable distinction often drawn between scientific data and aesthetic—which suggested that mere science omitted much from what Ransom called "the world's body," and warned that a too narrow concern with abstract principle is almost as bad for life as it is for art. Again, this generation of critics described what they called a loss of taste in contemporary life. Vulgarity was clearly defined as a frantic and amoral desire to accumulate and to own goods; further, as the feeling that taste might be bought and did not need to be a responsible part of experience as a whole. The absurdities of the bourgeois mind and soul, the deformities of its architecture and its conscience, were never so fully documented. Perhaps the most valuable criticisms of the decade, and the most profound, were those which made it clear that defections of taste were not merely surface phenomena but betrayed an underlying inadequacy in our tradition and our culture.

These criticisms could not, after all, have remained effective had they pointed merely to superficial issues. The 1920's could make no more important contribution than is contained in their most jealously guarded thesis: that history and society are and remain abstractions until they are associated with personal experience. As Arthur Mizener has said (*Kenyon Review,* Winter 1950):

> . . . the situation, the moment in history, is not in itself tragic; it only provides the occasion on which the aware individual suffers the experience of unavoidable moral choices. No matter what the occasion, there is no tragedy where the forces of circumstance are not transmuted into personal experience.

If the twenties in America can be condemned seriously for a fault it is not for their vulgarity (there is vulgarity of some sort in any time) or for their immorality (immorality in any period is ordinarily a characteristic of the move toward moral redefinition). The greatest fault was their naïveté. Men and women were often quite literally and self-avowedly ignorant of tradition. They had chosen to be; they had rejected both sound and unsound generalities and thought. As a result they were open to every new influence that came along; in most cases there was no intellectual experience to use as a measure of validity. That is undoubtedly the reason so much of the discussion of ideas in the decade seemed the talk of an undergraduate newly and overly impressed by his introductory course in philosophy.

Perhaps the young men and women of the 1950's are immensely more sophisticated, learned, and disingenuous. The theories of Freud have been greatly extended, and the attitude toward them lacks the naïve enthusiasm of an earlier generation. The French masters of literature are now not only thoroughly known; they are being revaluated and their influence upon a handful of American poets now seems a part of ancient literary history. The mood in which bulletins from Moscow were received in the offices of the *Liberator* now seems incredibly naïve. Marxism has not only undergone numerous shifts in interpretation; there have been great changes of heart regarding the "crusade that failed." It is no longer possible to imagine (one no longer has the naïve expectancy to await) a doctrine's role in saving the world. The new generation is much wiser, much less likely to be taken in— one may say, less *capable* of being taken in. But in a very real sense the assertions so often made in the twenties now seem more sensible than they did in their own time. Certainly in our own postwar world we now are convinced (and not especially shocked to find) that evil actually does exist. We are aware of the peculiar failures of scientific research and suspicious of its direct application to human affairs.

It is perhaps unfortunate that we know so much and are so helpless at the same time. In looking back upon the 1920's perhaps we ought not to be worried about the "party we cannot afford to throw again," but rather about our loss of confidence in free, if erratic, inquiry, which we seem to have abandoned along with our naïveté. Our knowledge seems to lack the strength of will that accompanied the ignorance and the errantry of the 1920's. We become more sophisticated and more inflexible with each passing year. We are competent scholars, writers, thinkers, voters; we are properly shocked when one of our fellows commits an especially noticeable error against good taste and good manners. Why, then, are we restless, uncertain, and unhappy? Why is our literature not first-rate? Why are the majority of our critical essays written about the literature of the 1920's and not about that of our own time? Something must be true of that decade that has nothing to do with the big party they were supposed to have had. Perhaps they were more sane, less frivolous, than we have been led to believe.

The most intelligent and the most sensible attitude we can have toward the 1920's, as well as toward our own time, is to accept the saving grace of an irony directed at both. They are, both of them, times of war and of the effects of war. In neither time is it possible unqualifiedly to admire or simply to repudiate man's responsibility for what has happened. That irony is expressed with an especial relevance in Allen Tate's "Ode to Our Young Pro-Consuls of the Air" (1943)*. . . . The times, the poet says, have once more come round to war; and each citizen is again called upon "to take/His modest stake." We have responded to the call with full patriotism and with angry mechanical force. Once again humanity is simply divided into friend and foe; the enemy is "The puny Japanese" and "the German toad." Observing these demonstrations of moral and military might, the poet reflects upon what he had done (or might have done) to prevent these "enemies of mind" from resuming their quarrel.

There follows an ironic survey of the attacks upon the irresponsibles. The poet tries to recall past wars to present memory: the "Toy sword, three-cornered hat" of "York and Lexington"; the "Toy rifle, leather hat/Above the boyish beard" of the Civil War; then the "disorder" of Versailles, when

> Proud Wilson yielded ground
> To franc and pound,
> Made pilgrimage
> In the wake of Henry James

and its aftermath, when France "Opened the gate/To Hitler—at Compiègne." "In this bad time" the poet had no role, nor took any responsibility:

> He studied Swift and Donne,
> Ignored the Hun,
> While with faint heart
> Proust caused the fall of France.

Literature thus irresponsibly caused, or permitted, the disaster to happen. Yet, when our fortunes were most desperate, the critics rushed to the rescue of a faltering republic:

> Yet all that feeble time
> Brave Brooks and lithe MacLeish
> Had sworn to thresh
> Our flagging spirit
> With literature made Prime!

And, in response, our culture has revived, sprung to the defense of American ideals:

> Nursing the blague that dulls
> Spirits grown Eliotic,
> Now patriotic
> Are: we follow
> *The Irresponsibles!*

This is the spectacle of a nation aroused from its "Eliotic" sloth, cured of "the blague that dulls," transformed almost as if overnight by the magic of the "responsible word" from "Spirits grown Eliotic" to efficient and confirmed patriots. The poet ironically salutes the young men who have gone off to "win the world" on such short notice and after such a treacherous, defeatist past: with "zeal pro-consular," these "partisans/Of liberty unfurled!" will (once reminded of their duty) resume the task of civilizing the world.

The "Ode" concludes with a vision of the "saviors," the young men who have (because of "Brave Brooks and lithe MacLeish") thrown aside their indifference and resumed the traditional role, with the aid of "literature made Prime." The planes in which they travel on their liberating missions impress the poet with their "animal excellence," and he bids them success in finding their targets:

> Swear you to keep
> Faith with imperial eye:
>
> .   .   .
>
> Upon the Tibetan plain
> A limping caravan,
>   Dive, and exterminate
>   The Lama, late
> Survival of old pain.
> Go kill the dying swan.

The full, rich irony of this message to the "Young Pro-Consuls" comes simply from a shrewd penetration of certain falsely moral readings of American culture: first, that there is necessarily a direct relationship between literature and public life; second, that the moral responsibility for a present emergency can quickly and easily be ascribed to a literature that had not anticipated or prepared for the crisis; further, that the crisis can be met by searching for a "literature made Prime," by ignoring the totality of a culture and selecting only that part of it that is suitable to the occasion; finally, that the instruments of a war, which are the consequences of a total history and not just servants of an "ideal," can be used to return the world to sanity and rescue it from "the puny Japanese" and "the German toad."

The irony is addressed primarily to those who accused the writers of the 1920's of "the literary fallacy"—the critics who have been guilty of a larger "moral fallacy." For, as the poem suggests, literature is not maneuverable; a culture cannot be one thing at one time and its opposite immediately thereafter. An extreme neurosis of "social conscience" has led the judges of the 1920's into a trap of false criticism; it has assumed that the literature produced in the decade was cynically or irresponsibly (and thus dishonestly) engaged in corrupting an entire nation. These judgments suffer from a serious loss of perspective. The critics who made them have chosen to make what they need (what they will) out of the 1920's. They have insisted that literature should serve a moral objective of an extraordinarily narrow and limited kind. Since it has not seemed to do so, they have condemned it for not meeting their terms. This is not the way to a just or accurate estimate; it is a victim of its own narrowness of vision, and it cannot or should not endure beyond the limits of its occasion.

3. THE USES OF INNOCENCE

The positive values of the 1920's may perhaps best be suggested in the phrase "useful innocence." In the decade two generations collaborated in an exhaustive review of America's past greatness and present status. The one, the "old generation," contemporary with the Old Gang, surveyed the weaknesses of a tradition that had culminated in a war and an uneasy peace. The other generation, young in 1920 but old enough to have attended or participated in the ceremonies of 1914–1918, assumed the task of renewing that culture, of making it over according to new principles and what seemed newly acquired insights into human nature.

Of necessity, many of the writings of the decade were either important variants of old forms or new and original forms. No one can overemphasize the value of formal experiment in the 1920's. DeVoto and Brooks have complained about "moral failure" and the "literary fallacy." The truth is that the writers of the 1920's, finding a world that seemed cut free of the past, had to invent new combinations of spirit and matter and new forms of expressing the human drama. They were not aided by any secure ordering of social or religious systems. They were novelists of manners in a society distrustful of past definitions, poets of formalized insight into moral chaos. Their restless desire for the new was always motivated by their distrust of the old. *Form,* then, was a major concern, a major necessity. The careers of all important writers who began publishing in the decade are marked by a restless concern with literary form. Since the forms of the past had been generally associated with a tradition now abhorred, the new forms had perforce to be different, newly inspired, and newly seen.

When Gertrude Stein lectured on method, when Ezra Pound fulminated against softness and weakness of speech, they were speaking for a formal revolution that was also a moral revolution. The concern with form was basically a concern over the need to provide an aesthetic order for moral revisions. It is true that the best of our writers were preoccupied with literature; they were "whole men" in the genuine sense of being profoundly concerned with the moral value of literary form. Essential to the enlightenment the decade gave us was that sense of the significance of the aesthetic, of its essential nature. Such a preoccupation appears on the surface to be morally irresponsible; actually it is truly moral in the sense of its earnest desire to communicate the variants of the modern condition.

The great strength of the decade lay in its useful and deliberate innocence. Ideas habitually lose their vitality as the employment of them alters or is too closely aligned with social expediency. Naïve, innocent demonstrations of wrath over smugness, indolence, or hypocrisy are outward expressions of moral revision. The language communicates these ideas; when they descend from the level of genuine moral judgment to that of comfortable journalism, the language and the forms must be changed. The writers of the 1920's, concentrating on literary form, went about the business of morally redefining the function of the language and its association with present realities. To begin with the "new"—which is to say, the raw, unformed, unsupported, and unexplained present literary condition—is to begin innocently afresh, to explore "the thing seen" in terms of the "way it is seen."

Having rejected all precedents, the writers of the 1920's themselves became precedents for the literature of future decades. But it was in their literary, their aesthetic, successes that future writers saw merit. The narrator of Budd Schulberg's *The Disenchanted* (1950) wishes that he could accept the brilliant literary successes of Halliday and ignore the *man* who had achieved them. This narrator is a *naïf* of another decade, unable to see the tragic artist whole or judge him from any point of view other than the documentary morality of the 1930's. It is almost beyond the capacity of those who look at the 1920's, however carefully, to understand the close rapport between literary concentration and moral insight. The writers of the 1920's—or many of them——had both to *see* a world as it frankly was and to *re-establish* that world in their literary formulations. The very matter of Fitzgerald's moral extravagances (which are the substance of Halliday's past) is incorporated into his art; however imperfectly, that art formalized what would otherwise have been merely a series of sensational and superficial dissipations. The writers of the 1920's believed in everything, those of the 1930's in only one thing, those of the 1940's in nothing. The second and third groups borrowed from the first the means of formulating their one thing and their nothing. This fact startlingly, enduringly remains: the 1920's were an opportunity and a challenge offered to a group of persons who were freshly and naïvely talented, anxious to learn *how* to restate and redramatize the human condition, morally preoccupied with the basic problem of communicating their insights into their present world.

But the weight of tradition is always heavy upon the individual talent. The important truth of the decade is not that its artists rejected the past but that they looked at the past from an orientation psychologically different from that of previous decades. They did not borrow from tradition so much as they forced tradition to give to them precisely what they needed from it. They refused to accept without question the formal systems of judging and dramatizing the moral values of the human race, preferred to select what they would, and on their own terms, from what the past had to offer. As a result the literary history of the decade, like its moral history, is a mélange of contrivance, experiment, and revolt.

Invariably didactic precedent interferes with a genuine moral appraisal of such a time and such a phenomenon. The literary heroes of the time assist in perpetuating the confusion: they recant, they are "converted," they rebel against their rebellion, they grow old and do not dare to face impeachment. They cannot see, or do not wish to see, that what they did and were at one time was of the utmost importance for the state of their own health and of that of society at large.

This fact, that they do not now wish to see and that no one cares truly to see for them, remains of all the important positive legacies of the decade: the fact of useful innocence. They were truly, recklessly, innocently, rawly, tenaciously naïve. The emperor had worn no clothes after all. The world had not been saved. The health of society was not after all good. The Bridge did not lead us to Cathay. They therefore made—formally, aesthetically, and morally—what they could of the thing that they had seen. They often crossed the Atlantic in an attempt to see it from another perspective, to disengage themselves from its immediate nature only to see it more closely. They went to masters of French poetry, of seventeenth-century British drama, of nineteenth-century German philosophy and psychology, and took from them what "influences" they needed. But the best of them were from the beginning, and remained, endowed with talent, with reserves of irony, satire, and intelligent respect for the "right word." The best of them preserved in their work the exact *rapprochement* of experience with the act of experiencing, of action with the moral comedy of man acting.

196

When, as almost always, men complain of the 1920's that there was no steady adherence to the morally proper, they are narrowly right but fundamentally wrong. This was no time for Edith Wharton, as she admitted; in a genuine sense the opportunity for a formalized comedy of social manners had passed, and with it the opportunity to employ a fixed, traditional mode of moral examination. François Mauriac once said that if one were asked what is the most genuinely real human experience of personal agony, he would have to answer that it is the time immediately preceding his death, when the full weight of tradition and personal past bears upon an uncertain future, immediately foreseen. The moment of one's death is of such primary importance that the history of an entire culture can be relevant to it. This crisis in human experience requires all moral strength to meet it. But no one has sufficiently explored the role that form plays at such a time. The "comforts" that a culture offers then are either extremely reassuring or vaguely disturbing. When, as occurs so often in the literature of the 1920's, men say that "it does not mean anything to die," they would like to suggest that the agony of death is not attended by the solaces of a public moral security. It is indispensable to the health of any culture that this security be constantly examined, naïvely questioned, explosively rejected, and finally re-established and re-formed.

The "best of them" who did not die in 1914–1918, who came back to "frankness as never before," were possessed of a useful innocence in their approach to the world that was left them. They explored the corridors of history, inspected the meaning of a religion temporarily discredited; they formulated in several brilliant ways the most important of all symbolic figurations of our century—that of isolation, of the single, dispossessed soul whose life needs to be re-established in terms specifically new and unencumbered. They did not always succeed in defining this symbol, for themselves or for others. Many of their works suffered from intellectual colloquialism—which, like all other forms of colloquialism, loses its value as it loses its fresh relevance. But the great contributions to our ways of speaking about our ways of feeling have—in a manner still and always valuable—preoccupied themselves with the proper answers to the question Eliot's Gerontion put to himself at the beginning of the decade: "After such knowledge, what forgiveness?" After such experiences, what forms remain of meeting, defining, and sensibly tolerating the human condition?

VII

*Herbert Hoover and
the Great Depression:
Inflexibility or Innovation?*

INTRODUCTION

When Herbert Hoover, on March 4, 1929, became the president of the United States, prosperity still reigned in the nation, and few Americans were troubled about their country's economic future. Hoover, himself, in accepting the Republican nomination for the nation's highest office, had optimistically predicted that "given a chance to go forward with the policies of the last eight years, we shall soon with the help of God be in sight of the day when poverty will be banished from this nation." Before 1929 had come to an end, however, economic boom had given way to economic bust, and the United States was beginning to experience what was to become the longest and most severe depression in its history. By the end of 1932 the national income had fallen by more than half as compared with 1929, and about 24 per cent of the nation's civilian labor force were unemployed.

The Great Depression, as it came to be known, was the dominating event of the Hoover administration and was, as Hoover later said, the "nightmare" of his presidential years. In their analyses of the Hoover administration, historians have been particularly concerned with the President's reaction to the events of the depression and with the measures he devised to combat the downward swing of the business cycle. It is clear that Hoover did not pursue a policy of laissez faire with regard to the depression, but the scope and effectiveness of his actions and programs have been the subject of much controversy.

In the initial selection that follows, taken from the first volume of his The Age of Roosevelt, *Pulitzer prize-winning historian Arthur M. Schlesinger, Jr., concedes that Hoover "breached the walls of local responsibility as had no President in American history," but his stress in dealing with Hoover's depression policies is on the shortcomings of the President's program. He dwells on the inadequacies of Hoover's relief policy and his public works program and sharply criticizes the President for his "infatuation with the balanced budget" and for the "contradictions" in his internationalism. He contends that Hoover became increasingly inflexible the longer the depression continued and that he was limited by ideological considerations from taking the steps necessary to cope with the business decline.*

Writing in the year before Hoover's death, historian Carl N. Degler, like Schlesinger, is aware that Hoover operated "within a very rigid framework of ideology," but it is the innovating character of the Hoover depression policies that particularly engages his attention. He sees Hoover as one of the nation's "truly activist presidents" who broke with precedent "to grapple directly with the Depression." He contends that Hoover's Democratic opponents shared some of the beliefs for which he was later to be sharply criticized and notes the continuity between the Hoover depression policies and the New Deal.

The Valley of Darkness

Arthur M. Schlesinger, Jr.

I

But the President was somewhat more apprehensive. He feared that the crash might induce a general wave of contraction and panic; and he conceived it his duty to assume leadership in checking downward tendencies. "Liquidate labor, liquidate stocks, liquidate the farmers, liquidate real estate," the Secretary of the Treasury had said; his only cure was to let economic forces run their downward course as they had in '73.[1] But Hoover, convinced that the economy was basically sound, saw no reason for bringing misery to every sector of society. Where laissez-faire policy would call for putting the whole structure of prices and costs through the wringer, the New Era philosophy called for the maintenance of price levels and of spending. If this could be done, Hoover reasoned, then the stock market crash could be contained.

He unfolded his program in a series of conferences with business and community leaders in the next weeks. Through voluntary pledges from industry, he hoped to maintain wage rates and stabilize industrial prices. Through understandings with industry and local governments, he hoped to continue capital expansion and public building at a normal pace. Through Federal Reserve policy, he planned to make credit abundant for business borrowers. Through the Federal Farm Board, he aimed to prop up the agricultural sector. Through an upward revision of the tariff, he could protect American industry against foreign competition. And, with these policies under way, he hoped through persuasive exhortation and wise counsel to restore business confidence.

Of these policies, only tariff revision required new legislation. The special session of 1929 having failed on the tariff, the preparation of a new bill became the main business of Congress in the months immediately after the crash. The task was in the charge of two fervent protectionists, Senator Reed Smoot of Utah and Congressman Willis C. Hawley of Oregon, determined to attain for the United States "a high degree of self-sufficiency"

The selection from Arthur M. Schlesinger, Jr., *The Age of Roosevelt: The Crisis of the Old Order, 1919–1933* (1957) is reprinted by permission of and arrangement with Houghton Mifflin Company, the authorized publishers. Pp. 163–165, 169–174, 230–247, 506–507, 515–517.

[1] Hoover, *Memoirs*, III, 30–31.

(Smoot), to make the nation "self-contained and self-sustaining" (Hawley). In many respects, it was an audacious effort. When Paul Douglas drafted a statement denouncing the bill, he was able to obtain the signatures of a thousand members of the American Economic Association in ten days. But academic disapproval could not embarrass the protectionist faith. "If this bill is passed," said the Republican leader of the Senate, Jim Watson of Indiana, "this nation will be on the upgrade, financially, economically and commercially within thirty days, and within a year from this date we shall have regained the peak of prosperity." When Congress enacted the Smoot-Hawley law, President Hoover signed it with six gold pens, saying that "nothing" would so retard business recovery as continued agitation over the tariff.[2]

II

As the first months passed after the crash, the administration viewed the future without visible alarm. At the turn of the year Secretary Mellon observed, "I see nothing in the present situation that is either menacing or warrants pessimism." In late January President Hoover announced that the unemployment trend had already been reversed; and early in February Secretary Lamont said that production and distribution were at normal levels; "there is nothing in the situation to be disturbed about." At the same time the Employment Service declared that "within the next sixty or ninety days the country will be on a normal employment basis," and Dr. Julius Klein exulted in the *American Magazine,* "It's Great To Be a Young Man Today." On March 4 Lamont, in a meteorological mood, was certain that "as weather conditions moderate, we are likely to find the country as a whole enjoying its wonted state of prosperity." On March 7, in his most detailed statement on the economic situation, the President declared that unemployment, such as it was, was concentrated in twelve states; that "employment had been slowly increasing" since the low point in December; that business and the state governments were spending more for construction even than in 1929. *"All* the evidences," he said, "indicate that the worst effects of the crash upon unemployment will have been passed during the next sixty days." [3]

---

[2] Reed Smoot, "Why a Protective Tariff?" *Saturday Evening Post,* Sept. 10, 1932; W. C. Hawley, "The New Tariff: A Defense," *Review of Reviews,* July 1934; statement of F. W. Fetter, *American Economic Review,* June 1942; D. C. Roper, *Fifty Years of Public Life* (Durham, N.C., 1941), 236; *Nation,* July 1, 1931; Hoover, *State Papers,* I, 318.

[3] J. T. Adams, "Presidential Prosperity," *Harper's,* Aug. 1930; "The Hoover Happiness Boys," *Nation,* June 18, 1930; "Prophet Lamont," *New Republic,* Nov. 5, 1930; Julius Klein, "It's Great To Be a Young Man Today," *American Magazine,* Feb. 1930. For Hoover's March 7 statement (my italics) *New York Times,* March 8, 1930; this important statement is oddly not included in Hoover's collected *State Papers* nor mentioned in the other semi-official accounts of the Hoover administration.

Hoover's position was not an easy one. He had rightly decided he could not indulge in a public pessimism that would only feed the panic. His fault lay not in taking an optimistic line, but in bending the facts to sustain his optimism,[4] and then in believing his own conclusions. For, despite the presidential exhortations, private spending was simply not maintaining 1929 levels. Despite the presidential cheer, unemployment was increasing. The leaders of business, for all their pledges, were finding it impossible to collaborate in pegging the economy. The solemn meetings of the fall, with their professions of common purpose, had turned out to be exercises in ceremonial—"no-business meetings," in J. K. Galbraith's phrase. "There has been more 'optimism' talked and less practiced," said Will Rogers, "than at any time during our history." Some Republican leaders even began to scent conspiracy in business reactions. "Every time an administration official gives out an optimistic statement about business conditions," complained Senator Simeon Fess of Ohio, chairman of the Republican National Committee, "the market immediately drops." [5]

The crucial period when a small amount of spending might have checked the cumulative forces of breakdown had already slipped by. But Hoover found in pledges an acceptable substitute for actions; assurances given took the place of dollars spent. "Our joint undertaking," he said, on May 1, 1930, before the United States Chamber of Commerce, "has succeeded to a remarkable degree." The intensity of the slump "has been greatly diminished." "I am convinced," Hoover said, "we have now passed the worst and with continued unity of effort we shall rapidly recover." [6]

III

. . . This was 1930; it was, in Elmer Davis's phrase, the Second Year of the Abolition of Poverty. And it introduced thousands of Americans to a new and humiliating mode of existence—life on the relief rolls. Most of the unemployed held out as long as they could. But, with savings gone, credit exhausted, work unobtainable, there seemed no alternative save to subdue pride and face reality.

The system was, in the main, one of local poor relief, supplemented by the resources of private welfare agencies. Even in 1929 public funds paid three-quarters of the nation's relief bill; by 1932, the proportion rose to four-fifths. In larger cities, the social workers had had some success in improving standards of relief care, replacing the old "overseers of the poor" by

---

[4] For example, in Aug. 1930, Professor Charles E. Persons resigned from the Census Bureau in protest against statistical techniques designed to minimize and obscure the number of unemployed (*New York Times,* Aug. 16, 1930).

[5] J. K. Galbraith, *The Great Crash* (Boston, 1955), 144; Will Rogers, *The Autobiography of Will Rogers,* Donald Day, ed. (Boston, 1949), 232; Gilbert Seldes, *The Years of the Locust* (Boston, 1933), 63.

[6] Hoover, *State Papers,* I, 289–96.

public welfare departments. But in smaller communities, there was often no alternative to the poorhouse. And the whole patchwork system had an underlying futility: it was addressed to the care of unemployables—those who could not work in any condition—and not at all to the relief of mass unemployment.[7]

No other modern nation had in 1930 such feeble and confused provisions for the jobless. But the President had no doubt about the adequacy of the system for the winter of 1930–31. He told the American Federation of Labor in October that his antidepression policies had had astonishing success, and that workingmen should find inspiration in the devotion "of our great manufacturers, our railways, utilities, business houses, and public officials." Later in the month, rebuking those who were demanding a special session of Congress, the President reaffirmed his confidence that the nation's "sense of voluntary organization and community service" could take care of the unemployed.[8]

Yet, a week before, he had appointed an Emergency Committee for Employment under the direction of Colonel Arthur Woods, who had been active in the relief field during the depression of 1921. Hoover was reluctant to do even this, fearing that such action would magnify the emergency; and he informed the Committee that unemployment was strictly a local responsibility.[9] The Committee's function in consequence became that of advice and exhortation. Colonel Woods, a man of vigor, wanted to do more. He submitted to the President a draft message to Congress calling for a public works program, including slum clearance, low-cost housing, and rural electrification. Woods and his Committee also favored Senator Robert F. Wagner's bills proposing the advance planning of public works and setting up a national employment service. But the President, rejecting the Woods program, addressed Congress with his usual optimism. Getting nowhere, Woods saw the Committee through the winter and resigned in April 1931.[10]

Other events began to define the President's position. In the summer of 1930 a prolonged drought killed cattle and crops throughout the Southwest. This was Hoover's sort of problem—Belgium all over again, so much more concrete than the irritating and intangible issues of depression. "To overcoming the drought," reported Mark Sullivan, Hoover's intimate among the

[7] J. C. Brown, *Public Relief, 1929–1939* (New York, 1940), 429.

[8] Hoover, *State Papers*, I, 391, 395, 405.

[9] For Hoover's reluctance, see "Formation of Committee," interview with E. P. Hayes and E. L. Bernays, Feb. 26, 1931, Hopkins Papers. The local theory of unemployment was carried to an absurd extent. On Aug. 25, 1931, T. T. Craven, the Chief Coordinator of the Federal Coordinating Service, sent a directive to All Area Coordinators, reminding them: "All reference to the Federal business associations, the Federal Coordinating Service and to the Federal Government should be avoided, both directly and by implication. As stated before, the problem of relief is local and personal and this service is being used as a channel of communication only." (Hopkins Papers)

[10] E. P. Hayes, *Activities of the President's Emergency Committee for Employment* (Concord, N.H., 1936), 43, 141–44; H. L. Hopkins, *Spending to Save* (New York, 1936), 21–25.

newspapermen, "President Hoover turned with something like a sense of relief, almost of pleasure." [11] With echoes of his old confidence, he organized a program of assistance and asked Congress to appropriate money for government loans to enable farmers to buy seed, fertilizer, and cattle feed.

Democratic senators promptly sought to apply the Hoover program to human beings as well as livestock. Thus the old Wilsonian, William G. McAdoo, now senator from California, suggested that wheat purchased by the Farm Board be distributed to the unemployed. But Hoover reaffirmed his unwavering opposition to such proposals. The opposition, fighting back, taunted the President without mercy. He considered it wise to feed starving cattle, they said, but wicked to feed starving men, women, and children. He had fed the Belgians and the Germans, but would not feed his own countrymen. Hurt and distressed, the President, in February 1931, issued a deeply felt statement. If America meant anything, he suggested, it meant the principles of individual and local responsibility and mutual self-help. If we break down these principles, we "have struck at the roots of self-government." Should federal aid be the only alternative to starvation, then federal aid we must have; but "I have faith in the American people that such a day shall not come." [12]

IV

And so the nation staggered into the second winter of the depression, and unemployment began to settle into a way of life. The weather was glorious much of the winter—clear, light air, brilliant sunlight, dry, frosty snow. But the cold was bitter in unheated tenements, in the flophouses smelling of sweat and Lysol, in the parks, in empty freight cars, along the windy waterfronts. With no money left for rent, unemployed men and their entire families began to build shacks where they could find unoccupied land. Along the railroad embankment, beside the garbage incinerator, in the city dumps, there appeared towns of tarpaper and tin, old packing boxes and old car bodies. Some shanties were neat and scrubbed; cleanliness at least was free; but others were squalid beyond belief, with the smell of decay and surrender. Symbols of the New Era, these communities quickly received their sardonic name: they were called Hoovervilles. And, indeed, it was in many cases only the fortunate who could find Hoovervilles. The unfortunate spent their nights huddled together in doorways, in empty packing cases, in boxcars.

At the breadlines and soup kitchens, hours of waiting would produce a bowl of mush, often without milk or sugar, and a tin cup of coffee. The vapors from the huge steam cookers mingling with the stench of wet clothes and sweating bodies made the air foul. But waiting in the soup kitchen was

---

[11] Mark Sullivan, "The Case For the Administration," *Fortune,* July 1932.
[12] Hoover, *State Papers,* I, 496–99.

better than the scavenging in the dump. Citizens of Chicago, in this second winter, could be seen digging into heaps of refuse with sticks and hands as soon as the garbage trucks pulled out. On June 30, 1931, the Pennsylvania Department of Labor and Industry reported that nearly one-quarter of the labor force of the state was out of work. Clarence Pickett of the Friends found schools where 85, 90, even 99 per cent of the children were under-weight, and, in consequence, drowsy and lethargic. "Have you ever heard a hungry child cry?" asked Lillian Wald of Henry Street. "Have you seen the uncontrollable trembling of parents who have gone half starved for weeks so that the children may have food?" [13]

And still unemployment grew—from 4,000,000 in March 1930 to 8,000,000 in March 1931. And, more and more, the community found the relief problem beyond its capacity to handle. Local fiscal sources were drying up; local credit was vanishing; towns and counties found they could tax or borrow less and less. Some states had constitutional prohibitions against the use of state funds for home relief. And states too were on the verge of exhausting their tax possibilities; the general property tax had almost reached its limit, and, as income fell, the income tax, for the few states that had it, brought in declining amounts.

The burdens of private charity were meanwhile falling ever more heavily on the poor themselves. Emergency relief committees talked virtuously of the staggering of work and the "sharing" of jobs. But men working a day less a week to provide jobs for other workers were obviously contributing a portion of their own meager wages to relief while their employers contributed nothing. And, even when employers joined in company campaigns of voluntary donations, it was too often under the principle used in the Insull group, by which all, whether top executives or unskilled workers, threw in one day's pay a month. The real recipients of the dole, wrote Professor Sumner H. Slichter of Harvard, were not the men lining up to receive a nickel from the Franciscan Fathers, but "the great industries of America," paying part of their labor overhead by taxing the wages of their employees.[14]

As the number of unemployed grew, the standards of relief care declined. More and more it seemed as if the burden was too great for individual communities to carry longer. In the fall of 1931 Governor Franklin D. Roosevelt of New York established a state emergency relief administration; other states followed this example. Effective relief, said William Allen White in September 1931, would be "the only way to keep down barricades in the streets this winter and the use of force which will brutalize labor and impregnate it with revolution in America for a generation." [15]

---

[13] Congressional hearings; Hugo Johanson, "Bread Line," *Atlantic*, Aug. 1936; Edmund Wilson, *Travels in Two Democracies* (New York, 1936), 30–31; C. R. Walker, "Relief and Revolution," *Forum*, Aug. 1932; R. L. Duffus, *Lillian Wald* (New York, 1938), 287–88, 349–50.

[14] S. H. Slichter, "Doles for Employers," *New Republic*, Dec. 31, 1930.

[15] White to William Green, Sept. 1, 1931, in W. A. White, *Selected Letters . . . 1899–1943*, Walter Johnson, ed. (New York, 1947), 317.

V

But President Hoover announced that a nation-wide survey had convinced him that state and local organizations could meet relief needs in the coming winter. Giving ground slightly, he then appointed a new committee to supersede the old Woods committee. This was the President's Organization on Unemployment Relief, headed by Walter S. Gifford, president of the American Telephone and Telegraph Company. Gifford accepted the thesis of local responsibility with far more enthusiasm than Woods; and his main contribution was an advertising campaign designed to stimulate private charity. "Between October 18 and November 25," said Gifford and Owen D. Young in a joint statement, "America will feel the thrill of a great spiritual experience." Charity, the campaign hopefully suggested, could even inspire a new love between husband and wife.

On matters which might have fallen more directly within his responsibility, Gifford displayed indifference. Early in January 1932, after nearly five months in office, Gifford appeared before a committee of the Senate. There, under the incredulous questions of Robert M. La Follette, Jr., of Wisconsin and Edward P. Costigan of Colorado, Gifford disclosed imperturbably that he did not know how many people were idle, that he did not know how many were receiving aid, that he did not know what the standards of assistance were in the various states, that he did not know how much money had been raised in his own campaign, that he knew nothing of the ability of local communities to raise relief funds either through borrowing or taxation, that he did not know what relief needs were either in urban or rural areas, that he did not consider most of this information as of much importance to his job; but that, just the same, he had no question in his mind as to the capacity of the communities to meet the relief problem. "I hope you are not criticizing me for looking at life optimistically," he said plaintively. And, when Costigan asked him to supply the committee with the reports on which his optimism was based, Gifford replied, "I have none, Senator."

But on one question Gifford was clear: he was against federal aid. Should we not be concerned, asked La Follette, if the people in Philadelphia were receiving inadequate aid? As human beings, yes, said Gifford, adding incoherently, "but whether we should be concerned in the Federal Government officially with it, unless it is so bad it is obviously scandalous, and even then we would not be obliged to be concerned. I think there is grave danger in taking the determination of these things into the Federal Government." Federal aid, he said, would lessen the sense of local responsibility; it would reduce the size of private charity. His "sober and considered judgment" was that federal aid would be a "disservice" to the jobless; "the net result might well be that the unemployed who are in need would be worse instead of better off." [16]

---

[16] Senate Manufactures Committee, *Unemployment Relief: Hearings*, 72 Cong., 1 Sess. (1932), 311–31.

And so, through the winter of 1931–32, the third winter of the depression, relief resources, public and private, dwindled toward the vanishing point. In few cities was there any longer pretense of meeting minimum budgetary standards. Little money was available for shoes or clothing, for medical or dental care, for gas or electricity. In New York City entire families were getting an average of $2.39 a week for relief. In Toledo the municipal commissary could allow only 2.14 cents per meal per person per day. In vast rural areas there was no relief coverage at all. "I don't want to steal," a Pennsylvania man wrote Governor Pinchot, "but I won't let my wife and boy cry for something to eat. . . . How long is this going to keep up? I cannot stand it any longer. . . . O, if God would only open a way." [17]

VI

. . . The American system remained essentially a presidential system: in the end, all things came to the man in the White House. "His is the vital place of action in the system, whether he accept it or not," Woodrow Wilson once wrote, "and the office is the measure of the man—of his wisdom as well as of his force." And Herbert Hoover, as President, had far more definite ideas than most members of Congress about the cause and the cure of the economic crisis.

The depression was caused, Hoover said repeatedly in 1929 and 1930, by uncontrolled speculation in the securities market leading to an "inevitable crash." Still, if the crash was inevitable, the securities speculation, in Hoover's view, was not. It had been a gratuitous indulgence by an economy of whose "fundamental correctness" Hoover remained as convinced as on the day of his acceptance address in 1928. If the system of production and distribution was sound, then there was obviously no point in basic reform. The need, as he first saw it, was simply to seal off the rest of the economy from the shock effects of the Wall Street crash. The problem was, not to reorganize a defective structure, but to correct a healthy one.[18]

Hence his program of 1929: the support of purchasing power through attempts to peg wage rates and farm prices; the stimulus of credit through Federal Reserve open-market operations and the reduction of the discount rate; and, most important of all, the expansion of private and public construction. This, the President said, was the "greatest tool which our economic system affords for the establishment of stability"; and he placed the responsibility for its use on government at all levels, as well as on private industry. Appealing in late 1929 to governors to increase state programs, Hoover pledged that "the Federal Government will exert itself to the utmost within its own province." [19]

---

[17] Senate Manufactures Committee, *Federal Cooperation in Unemployment Relief: Hearings,* 72 Cong., 1 Sess. (1932), especially 7, 136–37.

[18] Hoover, *State Papers,* I, 145, 181, 290; Herbert Hoover, *The New Day* (Stanford University, 1928), 30.

[19] Hoover, *State Papers,* I, 137, 182.

For months the verbal encouragement of public works remained Hoover's chief weapon. In January 1930, he said that total construction spending for the year would be larger than in the boom year of 1929. In May he said that the acceleration of the construction program had been "successful beyond our hopes." But, while the President and other officials were making their cheerful forecasts, private outlays for construction actually fell off in 1930 by over $2 billion, and public outlays rose by a bare $400 million. In 1931 private outlays declined another $2 billion; by 1932, they were down almost to one-quarter of what they had been in 1926. And, while the federal contribution to construction expenditures steadily increased, reaching half a billion dollars in 1932, the total of public construction steadily declined, as state and local governments ran out of money. In 1932 total public construction was nearly a billion dollars less than it had been in 1930.[20]

There were several reasons for the collapse of the public works effort. Despite all the talk about the "construction reserve" ever since the Unemployment Conference of 1922 [1921] * nothing had been done, in Hoover's Department of Commerce or elsewhere, to establish a reserve fund or to work out a shelf of projects. Nor was there now the executive energy in the administration to push a public works program through. Mellon had always scoffed at the idea, and Hoover himself became at crucial moments a victim of his own optimism. In June 1930, a delegation headed by Dr. John A. Ryan of the National Catholic Welfare Council and Amos Pinchot urged on the President immediate expansion of federal public works. Hoover, listening with the exasperation of a man who knew the situation far better than his visitors, told the group that the interview was unnecessary. The tide had turned. Unemployment was declining. Business was expanding its activities. The government had the situation fully under control. Public works? "Gentlemen," the President said, "you have come sixty days too late. The depression is over." [21]

VII

Most important, the public works theory was fighting a losing battle in Hoover's mind against his mounting concern for the budget. For a time, this internal debate led to a dizzying alternation between presidential statements calling for more public works and presidential statements warning against

---

[20] *Historical Statistics,* Ser. H 1–26, H 33–35.

* Editor's note: The President's Conference on Unemployment was called by President Harding in 1921, in the midst of the post-war recession, at the behest of Secretary of Commerce Hoover.

[21] Amos Pinchot, "We Met Mr. Hoover," *Nation,* Jan. 14, 1931; testimony of J. A. Ryan, Senate Banking and Currency Committee, *Further Unemployment Relief Through the Reconstruction Finance Corporation: Hearings,* 72 Cong., 2 Sess. (1933), 144; Mellon to W. L. Jones, June 18, 1929, in Federal Employment Stabilization Board Papers, National Archives; W. T. Foster, "The Bill for Hard Times," *Survey Graphic,* April 1936; Senate Education and Labor Committee, *Establishment of Administration of Public Works: Hearings,* 72 Cong., 1 Sess. (1932), especially 107–15.

more public expenditures. But as national income continued to sink through 1930, so did tax collections. Though the Treasury could still report a surplus of nearly $200 million for 1930, it was evident that the nation was headed for a deficit in 1931. As the deficit came nearer, Hoover became increasingly preoccupied with what he actually defined as "the primary duty of the Government, that is, to hold expenditures within our income." More and more, the growing federal debt seemed the primary threat to recovery. "For the Government to finance by bond issues," Hoover declared in December 1930, "deprives industry and agriculture of just that much capital for its own use and for employment. Prosperity cannot be restored by raids upon the public Treasury."

Tax revenues continued to fall in 1931; and the federal deficit that year was almost a billion dollars—the largest peacetime deficit in American history. With national income still going down, the prospect for 1932 was even more dismal; the deficit might well end up three times as great. Hoover now redoubled his efforts. He demanded the most rigid retrenchment in government. He called for an increase in taxes. He denounced proposals for public spending. "Nothing," he said flatly in November 1931, "will contribute more to the return of prosperity than to maintain the sound fiscal position of the Federal Government." In December 1931 he formally repudiated the contention, once his own, that further expansion of public works would aid recovery.[22]

Fear of the deficit became an obsession in 1932. When Wagner and Garner urged Congress to increase public spending, Hoover harshly questioned their motives and assailed their programs—"the most gigantic pork barrel ever proposed to the American Congress," "an unexampled raid on the public Treasury." Vetoing the Garner–Wagner relief bill, he wrote, "Never before has so dangerous a suggestion been seriously made to our country." Others pointed out that his own policy of raising taxes and cutting government spending could only reduce purchasing power still further; but the President replied in a crescendo of statements—twenty of them from December to May alone—reiterating what was becoming his single theme. "The absolute necessity of a balanced budget" (March 25) was "the most essential factor to economic recovery" (May 5), "the imperative and immediate step" (May 13), "indispensable" (May 21), "the first necessity of the Nation" (August 11), "the foundation of all public and private financial stability" (August 11).[23]

VIII

The infatuation with the balanced budget thus destroyed the major plank of Hoover's first antidepression program—the expansion of public works.[24]

---

[22] Hoover, *State Papers*, I, 240, 578; II, 28, 459–60; W. S. Myers and W. H. Newton, *The Hoover Administration: A Documented Narrative* (New York, 1936), 156–57.

[23] Hoover, *State Papers*, II, 106, 148, 149, 175, 189, 194, 196, 232.

[24] The act setting up the Reconstruction Finance Corporation in 1932 authorized a new

In the meantime, the President was moving toward a radically new diagnosis of the depression. The theory of 1929—that the breakdown was the inevitable result of uncontrolled domestic speculation—was perhaps coming to seem irksome, possibly because it fixed responsibility too squarely on the American business community. In October 1930, Hoover suddenly discovered that the roots of the depression lay "only partly in the United States." The major cause, he now felt, had been the over-production of raw materials abroad, leading to lower prices and reduced buying power in foreign countries and thus to reduced foreign purchases in America. The actual decline of the foreign trade balance in 1930 was less than $60 million, a sum which hardly explained the collapse of the American economy; but, despite statistics, the President grew rapidly more confident of his new thesis. In December he said that "the major forces of the depression now lie outside of the United States," and by June 1931, that "the main causes . . . came not from within but from outside the United States." [25]

Events in Europe soon gave a touch of plausibility to the new Hoover line. The failure of the Kreditanstalt in Vienna in June 1931 put the international gold standard under intense strain. Hoover's debt moratorium that summer was no more than a palliative, and in September it became evident that the City of London could no longer defend the pound. By January 1932 about forty nations—though not America or France—had gone off gold. The world financial crisis increased the pressure on the American economy.

For Hoover the restoration of the gold standard now became almost as indispensable as balancing the budget. Gold, he said, was a metal "enshrined in human instincts for over 10,000 years," and he did not mean to abandon it. John Maynard Keynes predicted that the curse of Midas would fall on the countries which clung to gold—that they would suffer the disadvantages of costs fixed in terms of gold, while their competitors in the world market could enjoy the benefits of devaluation. The United States, said Keynes, was setting "the rest of us the problem of finding some way to do without her wheat, her copper, her cotton and her motor-cars"; it was willing the destruction of its own export industries. But Hoover identified America's economic future with gold. Indeed, he later claimed that the nation had been within two weeks of being driven off the gold standard early in 1932 when it was saved from incalculable disaster by the swift action of his administration. "Never," he subsequently recalled—perhaps a strong word for a century and a half of American history—"was our nation in greater peril." [26]

There remained crucial contradictions in Hoover's new internationalism.

---

public works effort, based on self-liquidating loans; but the administration spent only a small portion of the sums available under the act. See pp. 217–18.

[25] *Historical Statistics,* Ser. M 55; Hoover, *State Papers,* I, 376, 429, 574.

[26] J. M. Keynes, *Essays on Persuasion* (London, 1931), 292–93; Herbert Hoover, *Addresses Upon the American Road, 1933–1938* (New York, 1938), 30. For the gold crisis controversy, see Myers and Newton, *Hoover Administration,* 79, 159–73, and Rixey Smith and Norman Beasley, *Carter Glass* (New York, 1939), 317–20.

His attitude toward foreign debts and convertibility showed a genuine concern for the world financial community. But the world financial community seemed to him somehow separate from the world trading community. He never quite put the two ideas together. Even when he spoke, in the same sentence, of the American economy both as "self-contained" and as vulnerable to "shocks and setbacks from abroad," he apparently saw no inconsistencies. The result was that his gold and tariff policies worked at cross-purposes. While with one hand he tried to maintain convertibility, with the other he raised American tariffs, evidently not understanding that exchange depreciation and import duties might be alternative means of achieving the same end.

The gold standard which Hoover sought so earnestly to protect in 1932 he had in fact already gravely wounded when he signed the tariff of 1930. Denied the opportunity to earn dollars in the American market, many nations had no choice but to protect themselves against American exports. Thus Italy, Spain, France, Britain, Canada were quick to raise barriers against American goods. The drift toward economic nationalism threatened not only the world trading community but the world financial community as well. Yet 1932 found Hoover combining his international theory of depression with a stout defense of protective tariffs. The suggestion of reciprocal trade agreements he rejected as "a violation of American principles." [27]

IX

By 1932 Hoover had moved from the New Era philosophy, with its emphasis on maintaining purchasing power in the American economy, toward something much closer to old-fashioned laissez faire, where faith in a balanced budget and the gold standard was tempered only by a commitment to protectionism. This evolution was assisted by the growing influence of the Undersecretary of the Treasury, Ogden L. Mills of New York, who became Secretary in February 1932, when Hoover finally induced Mellon to go to London as Ambassador. But it was evident to Hoover and Mills that the balanced budget and the gold standard, while primary, were not enough by themselves. Something also had to be done to protect the business of the nation against threatening bankruptcy and liquidation.

One possible approach was that suggested by Gerard Swope and H. I. Harriman.* There were reasons for supposing that the President might look

---

[27] Hoover, *State Papers*, II, 46, 397.

* Editor's note: The Swope plan, named after Gerard Swope, the president of General Electric, called for the organization of interstate firms with more than fifty employees into trade associations which could co-ordinate production and consumption and stabilize prices. The companies concerned would adopt pension and unemployment insurance plans which would be financed and managed by both the employers and the employees. A national economic council was to be established at the apex of the system.

Henry I. Harriman, the president of the United States Chamber of Commerce, believed in the cartelization of the economy and the concomitant suspension of the antitrust laws.

with favor on industrial planning. After all, no one had done more in the twenties to foster the trade association and to advocate self-government in industry than Hoover, and few men had seemed to care less about the Sherman Act. Even as President, he had questioned "destructive competition," suggested the revision of the antitrust laws, and called for "the development of cooperative spirit and responsibility in the American business world . . . such that the business of the country itself could and should assume the responsibility for the mobilization of the industrial and commercial agencies." "Self-government outside of political government," he told the American Banking Association in 1930, "is the truest form of self-government." But perhaps the Swope and Harriman proposals implied too much in the way of reorganizing the fundamentally sound economic system. In any case, he dismissed the Swope plan as "the most gigantic proposal of monopoly ever made in history" and the Chamber of Commerce plan as "sheer fascism." [28] Evidently self-government outside of political government could be carried too far.

If the structure of business was not to be reorganized, the alternative was to guarantee the existing structure. The President was disappointed in his early hope that the New York banking community might bolster the credit system on its own, as it had in previous crises. Only twice during the depression, as he saw it, had the New York bankers come together for organized cooperation in an important way—once to save the reichsmark, once to save the pound. Counting on similar action in support of American business, Hoover summoned leading bankers to secret meetings in the fall of 1931, and invited them to pool their funds in order to provide a credit reserve for their weaker brethren. To his chagrin, most of the group insisted that this was the government's responsibility. "I returned to the White House after midnight," Hoover later wrote, "more depressed than ever before." After consideration, the bankers did agree to try the National Credit Association idea. But their hearts were not in it; and a few weeks later the project was an evident failure.[29]

In the meantime, Eugene Meyer, whom Hoover had appointed governor of the Federal Reserve Board in 1930, had been advocating a new plan. Meyer wanted to revive his old War Finance Corporation in the guise of a Reconstruction Finance Corporation, empowered to make loans to banks, railroads, and insurance companies. With the National Credit Association fiasco behind him, Hoover now reluctantly accepted the Meyer proposal. He still objected to an ambitious lending program, but he hoped that the passage of the legislation would by itself reassure the credit system and restore confidence. "I look upon it," Ogden Mills said of the RFC, "as an in-

---

[28] Hoover, *State Papers*, I, 136, 382, 394, 437; Hoover, *Memoirs*, III, 334, 420; Myers and Newton, *Hoover Administration*, 119, 155.

[29] Mark Sullivan, "Storm Over Washington," *Saturday Evening Post*, April 1, 1933; Hoover, *Memoirs*, III, 84–88, 97.

surance measure more than anything else. I think its very existence will have a great effect psychologically, and the sooner it is created, the less use we will have to make of it." [30]

X

The RFC thus became in 1932 the administration's new weapon against the depression. It faced an increasingly critical situation. Banks were closing their doors—nearly 2300 suspended in 1931 alone, and anxious depositors were beginning to withdraw their savings from banks that were still open. In the meantime, the flight of gold from the country, as foreign investors threw their American securities on the market and took gold in exchange, drew further on the metallic reserve. When the RFC went into operation in February 1932, the total reserves of the Federal Reserve member banks had fallen to within $50 million of the lowest amount allowed by law.[31]

But the RFC leadership—Eugene Meyer as chairman, Charles G. Dawes as president—were not ready for vigorous action. During the year, the agency succeeded in disbursing only about $1.5 billion of its $2 billion, and the great bulk of this money went to banks and trust companies. Even this transfusion was not as effective as it should have been; for the RFC was authorized only to make loans to banks, not to purchase their stock; and the great need for banks was not more indebtedness but more capital. "For a fatal year and a half," Russell Leffingwell of Morgan's later observed, "the Reconstruction Finance Corporation continued to lend money to the banks on adequate collateral security and gradually bankrupted them in the effort to save them." [32]

For the first five months, RFC operations were kept secret—to some extent, even from the Democrats whom the RFC law required to be appointed to the board of directors. "Several months passed," Jesse Jones of Texas, the dominant Democrat in RFC, wrote later, "before Chairman Meyer and Secretary Mills seemed to think it necessary to regard the Democratic directors as their equals. . . . Apparently they expected us blindly to do their bidding." And, if it was bad to tell things to the Democratic directors, it was even worse to tell them to the people. In particular, Hoover objected to the publication of RFC loans on the ground that publicity might invite the very disasters—the run on the bank, for example—which the loans were intended to prevent. Jones, however, received this argument with skepticism. And the President did not strengthen his case by using secrecy to obscure the character of RFC loan policy.

In signing the bill, Hoover had declared that RFC was "not created for

---

[30] Senate Banking and Currency Committee, *Creation of a Reconstruction Finance Corporation: Hearings,* 72 Cong., 1 Sess. (1932), 40.

[31] J. H. Jones, *Fifty Billion Dollars* (New York, 1951), 14–15.

[32] Leffingwell to Alexander Sachs, Jan. 4, 1935, Roosevelt Papers.

the aid of big industries or big banks." Statements issued in the first months of operation conveyed the impression that the agency was concentrating on help for the little fellow. But in July 1932, John Garner secured the passage of an amendment compelling the RFC to report its loans to Congress. An analysis of the loans outstanding now put a different face on the official statements. Thus Hoover's claim in April that the RFC had loaned $126 million to banks in 45 states took on a less virtuous aspect when it was discovered that over half this sum had gone to three large banks.

Charges of favoritism in the distribution of loans increased criticism of the RFC. In June Dawes suddenly resigned, announcing that he must return to Chicago to take charge of the affairs of the Central Republic Bank. A few weeks later the RFC loaned Dawes's bank $90 million; this was at a time when its total deposits amounted to only $95 million. Even this loan could not save the bank, which soon was forced into reorganization, though in time, and after litigation, the loan was repaid to the RFC. The circumstances by which Dawes's bank received prompt assistance from the agency he had just left while the unemployed were denied federal aid roused natural speculation. So too did the disclosure that Atlee Pomerene, Dawes's successor, had authorized a loan of $12 million to a Cleveland bank of which he was director. When John T. Flynn published these facts early in 1933, President Hoover's secrecy policy seemed to many wholly disreputable. And, to support this impression, the loans to big banks were tapered off as soon as the secrecy provisions were ended.[33]

XI

The administration's special concern for business was natural enough. "The sole function of government," Hoover said in the fall of 1931, "is to bring about a condition of affairs favorable to the beneficial development of private enterprise." Let business recover, Hoover believed, and recovery for the rest of the nation—the worker, the farmer, the unemployed—would come in due course.

Thus the plight of labor received little direct attention. By September 1931 the President was forced to abandon his early effort to maintain wage rates. When the Norris–La Guardia bill outlawing yellow-dog contracts came up in 1932, the administration greeted it without enthusiasm. Republicans denounced it in Congress; and Hoover's Secretary of Labor, in a meeting with the counsel of the National Association of Manufacturers, even offered Donald Richberg a federal judgeship if he would abandon support of the measure. Richberg spurned the suggestion, and Congress finally passed the bill, Hoover appending a glum signature. In August 1932, when Hoover called

---

[33] Hoover, *State Papers*, II, 106; Jones, *Fifty Billion*, 517, 72–83; J. T. Flynn, "Inside the RFC," *Harper's*, Jan. 1933.

together Business and Industrial Committees from the twelve Federal Reserve Districts to organize "a concerted program of action along the whole economic front," he did not think to ask labor representatives.[34]

At the start, the farmers received somewhat more attention. Depression suddenly brought into prominence what had been a peripheral part of the original Farm Board program—that is, the stabilization corporations, designed to support farm prices by holding temporary crop surpluses off the market. This stabilization system, however, had been intended as a means of ironing out minor crop variations, not of dealing with major surpluses. Any effect the Board's purchases of wheat and cotton had in maintaining prices in 1930 was quickly offset by the encouragement stiffening prices offered to new production, as well as by the continuing decline in demand. It became rapidly clear that price support could not work without production control.

In January 1930 the Board began to warn that it could not "protect farmers when they deliberately over-plant." By midsummer Alex Legge, president of International Harvester, whom Hoover had made chairman of the Board, and Secretary of Agriculture Arthur Hyde launched a campaign for voluntary acreage reduction. To cotton farmers, the Board suggested that they plow up every third row. To wheat farmers, it urged reduced sowing. But most farmers, having no assurance that their neighbors would reduce their planting, or perhaps thinking that they would, went on producing in the hope of cashing in on prospective higher prices.

"I believe," said Hyde, "in controlled production." But, he hastily added, "such control, in my judgment, must come about by voluntary action of the farmers themselves, and not by mandate of law." Yet in a few months the Board itself conceded that voluntary methods would not work because of the "individualistic character" of the American farmer. "While there are still a few of the agricultural leaders who lower their voices when they speak of production control," Legge told Hoover, "yet practically all of them have accepted the principle as essential."

But the President hated the idea of federal surplus control. He disliked almost as much the tentative experiments in stabilization permitted under his act of 1929. "Even indirect purchase and sale of commodities," he said, "is [sic] absolutely opposed to my theory of government." And so the Hoover farm policy declined into self-inflicted impotence. By mid-1931, the Board abandoned its price support efforts and devoted itself to the task of disposing of its holdings. Thereafter the administration watched farm prices fall with helpless defeatism.[35]

[34] Hoover, State Papers, II, 8–9; New York Times, Oct. 19, 20, 1932; Myers and Newton, Hoover Administration, 242.

[35] Federal Farm Board, Second Annual Report, 492, 514, 526; Legge to Hoover, March 5, 1931, in Forrest Crissey, Alexander Legge (Chicago, 1936), 206; A. M. Hyde, "The Agricultural Teeter Board," Review of Reviews, Oct. 1931; Hoover, State Papers, II, 312; O. H. Kile, The Farm Bureau Through Three Decades (Baltimore, 1948), 166–68; Lawrence Sul-

XII

The same belief that government should concentrate on aid to business led the President to continue to resist proposals for federal action on behalf of the unemployed. As the third winter of the depression approached, Hoover's principle began to receive new challenges. "We shall help the railroad; we shall help the financial institutions; and I agree that we should," said Senator Wagner. "But is there any reason why we should not likewise extend a helping hand to that forlorn American, in every village and every city of the United States, who has been without wages since 1929? Must he alone carry the cross of individual responsibility?" Nor was the argument that relief was a local problem as persuasive as it had been in 1929 or 1930. The administration did not tell General Dawes, noted Edith Abbott, the social worker, that he should seek assistance for his bank from the Chicago city council.[36]

The La Follette–Costigan bill, with its provisions for federal grants to states for relief purposes, was beaten in February 1932. But Senator Wagner and Congressman Henry T. Rainey, the Democratic leader in the House, began a new fight in the spring for alternative forms of federal aid. When Joseph T. Robinson of Arkansas, the Democratic leader in the Senate, proposed in May a federal bond issue of over $2 billion to subsidize self-liquidating public works, and Al Smith, Bernard Baruch, and Owen D. Young promptly backed the project, Hoover, his hand forced, came up with a counterproposal of his own, making the RFC the instrumentality of federal assistance.[37]

The first result of the jockeying between the Democrats and White House was the passage of the Wagner–Garner bill, which added to its spending proposals a provision enlarging the lending authority of the RFC by $300 million for loans to supplement local relief in needy states. Though Hoover favored this provision, as well as a provision enabling the RFC to undertake a program of self-liquidating loans, he objected to other aspects of the bill and vetoed it. When these provisions were enacted in a slightly different form a week later, the President accepted them, thereby approving the Emergency Relief Act of 1932. The use of loans, repayable with interest in July 1935, maintained to his satisfaction the pretense of local responsibility. It was evident in any case that the administration proposed to construe its new powers as narrowly as possible.

"These loans," the President said, "are to be based upon absolute need and evidence of financial exhaustion. I do not expect any state to resort to it except as a last extremity." From the White House viewpoint, the RFC was

---

livan, "The Curse of Plenty," *Outlook*, Sept. 3, 1930; Russell Lord, "The Forced March of the Farmers," *Survey Graphic*, April 1936; Theodore Norman, "The Federal Farm Board" (Ph.D. Thesis, Harvard University).

[36] Wagner in the Senate, *Congressional Record*, 72 Cong., 1 Sess. (Jan. 15, 1932); Edith Abbott, "The Fallacy of Local Relief," *New Republic*, Nov. 9, 1932.

[37] *New York Times*, May 12, 13, 1932.

to discharge a banking function. When Governor Pinchot of Pennsylvania, pointing out that the expenditure of $60 million among the more than one million jobless in his state would give each of them only 13 cents worth of food per day for a year, applied for the sum of $45 million, the RFC, after due deliberation, made about $11 million available. By the end of the year, only $30 million of the $300 million was allotted for relief, and even less for public works.[38]

XIII

The President stood manfully by his principles. But it remains unclear both from his statements at the time and from his subsequent recollections what his actual picture was of the state of his nation. Years later he wrote, "Many persons left their jobs for the more profitable one of selling apples." This sentence perhaps epitomized the presidential incredulity before the depression. If people sold apples on the street corners, it must have been because they could make more money doing that than doing something else. What jobs there were which offered even less security than apple-selling did not rouse his curiosity.

From time to time, the President produced letters from his Surgeon-General affecting to show that the state of public health was better in depression than it had been in prosperity; "no greater proof could be adduced," he liked to say, "that our people have been protected from hunger and cold." When the United Hospital Fund of New York City replied with statistics showing an "abnormal and progressive" increase in sickness, when the Pennsylvania Secretary of Public Health reported alarming increases in malnutrition and tuberculosis, when the daily newspaper contained items demonstrating the effects of privation, the President brusquely rejected them. "Nobody is actually starving," he told newspapermen. "The hoboes, for example, are better fed than they have ever been. One hobo in New York got ten meals in one day." [39]

As there could be nothing basically wrong with conditions, so there could be nothing basically wrong with the economic mechanism. The problems thus lay in the area of psychology, not economics. As Ogden Mills put it, "There is more to fear from frozen minds than from frozen assets." Something of this feeling undoubtedly lay behind the optimistic exhortations of 1930. When the economy failed to respond to pep talks, the President looked for other stimulants. "What the country needs," he told Raymond Clapper

---

[38] Hoover, *State Papers*, II, 236; Senate Banking and Currency Committee, *Unemployment Relief: Hearings*, 72 Cong., 1 Sess. (1932), 18; Alfred E. Smith, "The New Outlook," *New Outlook*, Oct. 1932; Abbott, "Fallacy of Local Relief"; J. C. Brown, *Public Relief, 1929–1939* (New York, 1940), 126.

[39] Hoover, *Memoirs*, III, 195; Hoover, *State Papers*, I, 608, II, 45, 101; Sen. Man. Com., *Unemployment Relief*, 116–17; O. E. Clapper, *Washington Tapestry* (New York, 1946), 3–4.

in February 1931, "is a good, big laugh. There seems to be a condition of hysteria. If someone could get off a good joke every ten days, I think our troubles would be over." He said the same thing to Weber and Fields. In 1932 he asked Will Rogers to think up a joke that would stop hoarding. To Rudy Vallee, the crooner, he said, "If you can sing a song that would make people forget their troubles and the Depression, I'll give you a medal." And to Christopher Morley: "Perhaps what this country needs is a great poem. . . . I keep looking for it, but I don't see it. Sometimes a great poem can do more than legislation." [40]

No President ever worked harder. Up at six, he threw on old clothes for his only bout of exercise—his seven-o'clock session with his "medicine ball cabinet." For thirty or forty minutes he fired the ball hard back and forth with a group of friends; then breakfast; and he was in his office by eight-thirty. It was characteristic that he was the first President to have a phone on his desk. From breakfast until bedtime at eleven, he labored without stint, smoking long, thick cigars as worry etched new lines into his gray face and his eyes became strained and bloodshot. "I am so tired," he sometimes said, "that every bone in my body aches." His manner grew increasingly preoccupied and dour. As he walked about the White House, he rarely spoke to the servants; "never a good-morning or even a nod of the head," said Ike Hoover, the White House usher. If someone addressed him, a low murmur came in reply, almost as if dragged out by force. He rarely looked at people in conversation, instead shuffling papers on his desk and doodling on blank sheets. He had no capacity for relaxation and was irritated by interruption. "There was always a frown on his face and a look of worry," said Ike Hoover; he "never laughed aloud." One of his secretaries remonstrated with him over his lack of small talk. Said the President sternly, "I have other things to do when a nation is on fire." [41]

XIV

Hoover was, as William Allen White said, "constitutionally gloomy, a congenital pessimist who always saw the doleful side of any situation." "He worried more than any President," said Ike Hoover. The Secretary of State, Henry L. Stimson, regretted his chief's fatal preference for "seeing the dark side first." Stimson, noting "the ever present feeling of gloom that pervades everything connected with the administration," could not remember a single joke cracked in a year and a half of Cabinet meetings. One private session

---

[40] S. J. Woolf, "Mills Weighs Our Problems," *New York Times Magazine,* Feb. 28, 1932; Clapper, *Washington Tapestry,* 3–4; Will Rogers, *The Autobiography of Will Rogers,* Donald Day, ed. (Boston, 1949), 275; *Time,* April 4, 1932; Christopher Morley, "What the President Reads," *Saturday Review of Literature,* Sept. 24, 1932.

[41] T. G. Joslin, *Hoover Off the Record* (New York, 1934), 4, 6, 55, 318, 194; I. H. Hoover, *Forty-Two Years in the White House* (Boston, 1934), 184, 233, 250, 267, 323; Donald Richberg, *My Hero* (New York, 1954), 149–50.

with the President seemed to the Secretary of State "like sitting in a bath of ink." [42]

XV

. . . The gloom and insecurity communicated itself to the nation. A people looking for leadership could not but respond with resentment. Hoover became the butt of a thousand bitter jokes. One told of Hoover's request to Mellon for the loan of a nickel to call up a friend, and of the Mellon reply: "Here's a dime, call up all your friends." Another asserted that there was no question about Hoover's being the world's greatest engineer: "in a little more than two years, he has drained, ditched and damned the United States." Vaudeville comedians, on being told that business was turning up, asked, "Is Hoover dead?"

Furtive books began to appear, investigating Hoover's years in the Far East and in high finance, accusing him of crimes ranging from British citizenship to cheating the Chinese government, oppressing coolie labor, engaging in the slave trade, making money out of Belgian relief, and even bringing about the execution of Edith Cavell. The very word "Hoover" became a prefix charged with hate: not only "Hoovervilles," but "Hoover blankets" (newspapers wrapped around for warmth), "Hoover wagons" (broken-down automobiles hauled by mules), "Hoover flags" (empty pockets turned inside out), "Hoover hogs" (jackrabbits).

The sense of popular hatred wounded the President. "It is a cruel world," he remarked at one point; and, again, "My men are dropping around me." And it also, perhaps, helped confirm his intellectual rigidities. The White House usher noted that, where Theodore Roosevelt and Wilson liked to send for people who took views different from their own, Hoover preferred to discuss matters with people whom he knew in advance would agree with him. Looking back twenty years later in his *Memoirs*, Hoover himself could see no mistakes committed during his presidency, no opportunities missed, no wrong guesses, nothing to regret. And at the time, criticism began to seem to him, not just the give-and-take of politics, but a dangerous threat to the American way of life. "He regarded some of it," Theodore Joslin, his faithful secretary, said, "as unpatriotic." He felt himself fighting, not just for the established order, but for the survival of American institutions.[43]

The ideological issue emerged with increasing clarity in the second half of his administration. He felt, no doubt, genuine indignation at the behavior of leading businessmen. William Allen White reported that in private he

---

[42] W. A. White, *Autobiography* (New York, 1946), 515; Hoover, *Forty-Two Years*, 267; H. L. Stimson and McGeorge Bundy, *On Active Service in Peace and War* (New York, 1948), 196, 197, 205.

[43] Joslin, *Hoover*, 91, 182, 34; J. N. Leonard, *Three Years Down* (New York, 1939), 215–16; Hoover, *Forty-Two Years*, 232.

grumbled at their perfidy and complained of their greed. "But also," White added, "because he had worked for thirty years with men of wealth, he could not publicly scold a million dollars, much less a hundred million." This was the America he respected, whatever its faults, and this America had to be preserved. His anger was directed rather at those who threatened to change this America, especially by enlarging the power of the federal government.

Hoover had, he admitted, "no taste" for emergency powers. To avoid the drift toward a superstate, he wanted "to solve great problems outside of Government action." Victory over depression must be won "by the resolution of our people to fight their own battles in their own communities." For the federal government to assume what had been local obligations would be to undermine "the very basis of self-government." The question for the future, he believed, was whether history should be written in terms of individual responsibility or of the "futile attempt to cure poverty by the enactment of law." Depression, he said, could not be ended "by legislative action or executive pronouncement. Economic wounds must be healed by the action of the cells of the economic body." [44]

Yet the same man who could invoke the healing processes of nature and warn with passion against centralization could also, in another mood, boast of "the most gigantic program of economic defense and counterattack ever evolved in the history of the Republic." For all his faith in individualism, he brought great areas of the economy—the banks, the railroads, the insurance companies, the farmers, even, toward the end, the unemployed—into the orbit of national action. No doubt, he entered on these programs grudgingly, and did as little as he could to develop their possibilities. Yet he breached the walls of local responsibility as had no President in American history.

How could he be so certain where the exact line of demarcation was drawn between beneficent intervention and limitless evil? Senator Norris's project for the government ownership and operation of Muscle Shoals seemed to him, for example, "the negation of the ideals upon which our civilization has been based." [45] Yet his own projects seemed equally Bolshevistic, for example, to James M. Beck. In the end, Hoover, dragged despairingly along by events, decided that wherever he finally dug in constituted the limits of the permissible. Doctrinaire by temperament, he tended to make every difference in degree a difference in kind and to transform questions of tactics into questions of principles.

As his term wore on, the ideological obsession grew. He had himself done unprecedented things to show the potentialities of national action; but anyone who went a step beyond transgressed the invisible line and menaced the

---

[44] W. A. White, "Herbert Hoover," *Saturday Evening Post*, March 4, 1933; Hoover, *State Papers*, II, 189, I, 470, 502–3, 504, 582, II, 251, I, 430–31.

[45] Hoover, *State Papers*, II, 249, I, 527; Alfred Lief, *Democracy's Norris* (New York, 1939), 395.

American way of life. His was the tragedy of a man of high ideals whose intelligence froze into inflexibility and whose dedication was smitten by self-righteousness.

The Ordeal of Herbert Hoover

Carl N. Degler

In 1958 Herbert Hoover published a book about his old chief entitled *The Ordeal of Woodrow Wilson*. Wilson's struggle for the League was short and his part in it has gained lustre with passing years. Not so with the ordeal of Herbert Hoover. The Great Depression was considerably longer and his reputation has never been free from the memory of that ordeal. Today, in fact, there are two Hoovers. The first is the living man, the former President who has unstintingly and very capably served Democratic and Republican Administrations alike. He is the Hoover of nation-wide birthday celebrations, of rhapsodic editorials, of admiring Republican national conventions. That conception bears almost no relation to the second, the historical Hoover. In the history books his Administration is usually depicted as cold-hearted, when not pictured as totally devoid of heart, inept, or actionless in the face of the Great Depression. Simply because of the wide gulf between the two Hoovers it is time to try to answer the question William Allen White posed over thirty years ago. Writing an evaluation of Hoover's Administration in the *Saturday Evening Post* of March 4, 1933, White closed his piece with [the] following words: "So history stands hesitant waiting for time to tell whether Herbert Hoover . . . by pointing the way to social recovery . . . is the first of the new Presidents . . . or whether . . . he is the last of the old."

The notion of two Hoovers should never have grown up; his life and views were too consistent for that. During Hoover's tenure of office, Theodore Joslin, his press secretary, undertook to examine closely all the President's utterances and writings of the preceding ten or eleven years. "In all of those million-odd words, dealing with every important subject," Joslin reported in 1934, "the number of times he reversed himself or modified an important position could be counted on the fingers of one hand." And so it has remained even after March 4, 1933.

Nor were those principles, to which Hoover held so consistently, simply

From *The Yale Review*, LII (June 1963), 563–583. Copyright by Yale University Press. Reprinted by permission.

conservative ones, as has so often been assumed. In 1920, for example, when Hoover's political career began, he was the darling of the progressives who still clustered about the figure of the fallen Wilson. College and university faculties were calling upon Hoover to run for president that year—on either ticket. Indeed, his silence as to which party he belonged to, for a time caused his name to figure as prominently in Democratic primaries as in Republican. For example, he received the most votes by far in the Michigan Democratic primary that year. That year, too, Franklin Roosevelt, who was also a member of Woodrow Wilson's Administration, wrote Josephus Daniels that Herbert Hoover "is certainly a wonder, and I wish we could make him President of the United States. There could not be a better one." (Nor did Roosevelt's enthusiasm cool until much later. In 1928 he refused to write an article against Hoover's candidacy because Hoover was "an old personal friend.")

Hoover's principles were distinctly and publicly progressive. In 1920, for example, he defended the principle of collective bargaining and the right to strike—two very unpopular principles at that date—before a frosty Chamber of Commerce in Boston. As Secretary of Commerce in the Harding Administration he opposed the sweeping federal injunction against the railroad strikers and worked with Harding to have the steel industry abandon the twelve-hour day. In his book of guiding principles, *American Individualism*, which he published in 1922, he was careful to distinguish his views from laissez-faire capitalism. The American way, he insisted, "is not capitalism, or socialism, or syndicalism, nor a cross breed of them." It did include, though, government regulation in order to preserve equality of opportunity and individual rights. "This regulation is itself," he pointed out, "proof that we have gone a long way toward the abandonment of the 'capitalism' of Adam Smith. . . ." While Secretary of Commerce in the 1920's he instituted much needed regulations for the burgeoning radio and airplane industries. It was Herbert Hoover who said in 1922 at the first conference on radio that "the ether is a public medium and its use must be for the public benefit. The use of radio channels is justified only if there is public benefit. The dominant element of consideration in the radio field is, and always will be, the great body of the listening public, millions in number, country-wide in distribution." In the same address, he said, "It is inconceivable that we should allow so great a possibility for service to be drowned in advertising chatter." In 1928 he was recommending that a three billion dollar reserve of public works be built up to serve as an economic stabilizer in times of recession.

In short, though he served both Harding and Coolidge, Herbert Hoover was not of their stripe. As he himself said later in his memoirs, "Mr. Coolidge was a real conservative, probably the equal of Benjamin Harrison. . . . He was a fundamentalist in religion, in the economic and social order, and in fishing." (The last because Coolidge, the fishing tyro, used worms for bait.) Moreover, unlike Coolidge, Hoover did not publicly ignore the scandals that rocked the Harding Administration. In June 1931, while dedicating the Harding Memorial at Marion, Ohio, Hoover went out of his way to speak of the tragedy of Warren Harding and of the enormity of the betrayal of a public trust by Harding's friends.

Hoover's record as president contains a number of truly progressive achievements. Although he cannot take credit for initiating the Norris-La Guardia Act of 1932, the fact remains that one of the most important prolabor acts in the whole history of American labor was signed by Herbert Hoover. Like other progressives, he sponsored legislation for conservation like the giant Boulder Dam project and the St. Lawrence Seaway.

But perhaps the most striking example of Hoover's willingness to recognize the new role of government in dealing with the complexities of an industrial economy was his breaking precedent to grapple directly with the Depression. From the outset Hoover rejected the advice of his Secretary of the Treasury, Andrew Mellon, who, as Hoover himself said, was a country-banker of narrow social vision. Mellon believed the crash should be permitted to run its course unmolested. His simple formula in a depression, as he told Hoover, was "Liquidate labor, liquidate stocks, liquidate farms, liquidate real estate." A panic, he told the President, was not so bad. "It will purge the rottenness out of the system. High costs of living and high living will come down. People will work harder, live more moral lives. Values will be adjusted, and enterprising people will pick up the wrecks from less competent people."

In contrast, Hoover's anti-depression action was swift in coming. Within a matter of weeks after the great crash of the stock market at the end of October, Hoover called a meeting of prominent business, labor, and farm leaders to work out plans for preventing the market crash from adversely affecting the rest of the economy. A week later he met for the same purpose with railway presidents. The economic leaders agreed to his plan of holding the line on wages and encouraging industrial expansion. In his annual message to Congress in December 1929, Hoover proudly told of these and other efforts his Administration had made to stem the economic decline. These efforts, he said, "must be vigorously pursued until normal conditions are restored." In January he continued to expand public works on Boulder Dam and on highway construction. By the end of July 1930, the Administration had got underway $800 million in public works, and the President called upon the states and local units of government to follow the national government's example in order to provide as much employment as possible.

The President was well aware of the unprecedented character of his swift anti-depression action. He said as much in his message to Congress in December 1929; he made the same point more explicitly at the Gridiron dinner in April 1930. The country, he said, had avoided the dole and other unsatisfactory devices to meet unemployment by "voluntary cooperation of industry with the Government in maintaining wages against reductions, and the intensification of construction work. Thereby we have inaugurated one of the greatest economic experiments in history on a basis of nation-wide cooperation not charity."

At first Hoover was optimistic about the effects of his program. Several times during the first year he compared the economic decline with that of 1921–22, usually with the observation that the earlier one was the more difficult. As he told the Chamber of Commerce in May 1930, the amount of public works contracted for was already three times the amount in the corresponding period of the previous "great depression."

Yet his optimism did not keep him from action. One thing he emphasized was the necessity of learning from this Depression about the prevention of future ones. He advocated better statistical measures and reform of the banking structure to prevent the drain of credit from productive to speculative enterprise, such as had led to the stock market boom and crash. Moreover, although he emphasized from the beginning that the Depression was "worldwide" and that its "causes and its effects lie only partly in the United States," he did not use this as an excuse for inactivity. There was no need simply to wait for the rest of the world to recover, he said. "We can make a very large degree of recovery independently of what may happen elsewhere." In October 1930 he told the American Bankers Association that depressions were not simply to be borne uncomplainingly. "The economic fatalist believes that these crises are inevitable and bound to be recurrent. I would remind these pessimists that exactly the same thing was once said of typhoid, cholera, and smallpox." But instead of being pessimistic, medical science went to work and conquered those diseases. "That should be our attitude toward these economic pestilences. They are not dispensations of Providence. I am confident in the faith that their control, so far as the cause lies within our own boundaries, is within the genius of modern business."

Hoover also told the bankers that he could not condone the argument which had been reported from some of them that the people would have to accept a lower standard of living in order to get through the Depression. Such a suggestion, he said, could not be countenanced either on idealistic or on practical grounds. To accept it would mean a "retreat into perpetual unemployment and the acceptance of a cesspool of poverty for some large part of our people." Several times during the Depression Hoover made it clear that the government had a responsibility to employ as many as possible as its contribution to the mitigation of the unemployment which was growing alarmingly.

The failure of the economy to respond to treatment and the loss of many Republican seats in the elections of 1930 caused Hoover for a while to place new emphasis upon the foreign sources of the Depression. At the end of 1930 he told the Congress that the "major forces of the depression now lie outside of the United States." In fact, though, the real collapse of the European economy was still almost six months away. Hoover was most fearful that the growing Congressional demands for new expenditures would throw the budget out of balance. His concern about the budget and his hostility toward the Congress were both measured in his tactless remark at a press conference in May 1931 that "I know of nothing that would so disturb the healing process now undoubtedly going on in the economic situation" as a special session of Congress. "We cannot legislate ourselves out of a world economic depression; we can and will work ourselves out."

The last sentence, because it was obviously too sweeping to be accurate, was to plague him for years. More important, he quite clearly did not believe it himself, since he later advocated legislation for just the purposes he said it could not serve. In the very next month, for example, he explained at some length to a group of Republican editors just how much the Administration had been doing to extricate the country from the Depression. "For the first time in history the Federal Government has taken an extensive and positive part in mitigating the effects of depression and expediting recovery. I have conceived that if we would preserve our democracy this leadership must take the part not of attempted dictatorship but of organizing cooperation in the constructive forces of the community and of stimulating every element of initiative and self-reliance in the country. There is no sudden stroke of either governmental or private action which can dissolve these world difficulties; patient, constructive action in a multitude of directions is the strategy of success. This battle is upon a thousand fronts." Unlike previous administrations, he continued, his had expanded, instead of curtailing, public works during a depression. Public works expenditures, both by the federal and state governments, he said, continued to increase. Some two billion dollars were being spent, and a million men were employed on these projects. Aid was also being given to farmers in the drought areas of the South and the Middle West.

That Hoover truly favored action over patient waiting for the storm to lift was further shown in his elaborate twelve-point program for recovery presented in his annual message in December 1931. Among his recommendations was the Reconstruction Finance Corporation, which would become one of the major agencies of his Administration and of the New Deal for stabilizing banks and aiding recovery. At a press conference the same month he emphasized anew the desirability of domestic action. "The major steps we must take are domestic. The action needed is in the home field and it is urgent. While reestablishment of stability abroad is helpful to us and to the world, and I am convinced that it is in progress, yet we must depend upon ourselves. If we devote ourselves to these urgent domestic questions we can make a very large measure of recovery irrespective of foreign influences." By early February 1932 the Reconstruction Finance Corporation was in operation. That same month he persuaded the Congress to enact the Glass-Steagall banking bill, which increased the bases for Federal Reserve bank reserves and thus expanded credit and conserved gold. The purpose of the RFC was to shore up failing banks and other financial institutions caught in runs upon their deposits. With the permission of the Interstate Commerce Commission, the RFC could also extend financial aid to railroads.

Beyond these operations, though, the President would not let the lending agency go. Especially did he resist federal aid to the unemployed, although the demands for it were growing monthly. He even opposed Congressional appropriations to the Red Cross on the ground that they would dry up private sources of relief funds. A dole, he said in 1931, must be avoided at all costs because "the net results of governmental doles are to lower wages toward the bare subsistence level and to endow the slacker." He did urge the citizenry generously to support, as he did himself, private charities, like the Red Cross, which were carrying so much of the burden of unemployment relief. At no time, of course, did Hoover object to helping the unemployed; he was no Social Darwinist arguing for the survival of only the fittest. Again and again, using the most idealistic language, he called upon Americans to extend a hand to those fellow citizens in need. But as much as he publicly and privately deplored the suffering which the economic crisis brought, he feared and deplored even more the effects which would be sure to follow if the federal government provided relief to the unemployed. Nowhere was the rigidity of Hoover's highly trained, agile, and well-stocked intellect more apparent than in this matter. Throughout his years as president, despite the cruelest of sarcastic barbs in the press and from the public platform, he held to his position.

Yet surprising as it may seem today, for a long time the country was with him. This was true even during 1931 and early 1932 when it was becoming increasingly evident that private charities, municipal relief funds, and even the resources of the states were inadequate to meet the costs of providing for ten or eleven million unemployed. Already in August 1931 Governor Franklin Roosevelt had told the New York legislature that unemployment relief "must be extended by government—not as a matter of charity but as a matter of social duty." Yet, as late as February 1932 the country was still following Hoover's view of relief and not Roosevelt's. This was shown by the fate of a bill sponsored by liberal Senators Robert M. La Follette, Jr. of Wisconsin and Edward F. Costigan of Colorado to provide federal money to the states for relief. The bill was defeated by a vote of 48 to 35. Democratic Senators made up some forty percent of the votes which killed the measure.

By May 1932, though, the pressure for some federal assistance in relief matters was building up fast. The National Conference of Social Workers, which in the previous year had refused to endorse the principle of federal relief, now switched to supporting it. More important from Hoover's standpoint was the announcement by Senator Joseph Robinson, the conservative Democratic leader in the Senate, that he was joining the liberals in favoring federal relief. Within two days the President announced, after consultation with Robinson, that the RFC would hereafter lend money to the states if their resources for relief were exhausted. The next day the President defended the extraordinary powers of the RFC as necessitated by the economic emergency. In words which sound in retrospect like those of his successor, he said, "We used such emergency powers to win the war; we can use them to fight the depression, the misery and suffering from which are equally great."

Soon thereafter, though, the President demonstrated that he would not take another step toward putting the federal government into the relief field. Two bills by Democrats which went beyond his limits were successfully vetoed. After Congress had adjourned in July 1932, he issued a nine-point program for economic recovery, but most of the items on it were old and the rest were only recommendations for exploratory conferences. By the summer of 1932, then, the Hoover program for recovery had been completed; his principles would permit him to go no further.

As one reviews the actions which Hoover took it is impossible to describe him as a do-nothing president. He was unquestionably one of the truly activist presidents of our history. But he was an activist within a very rigid framework of ideology. Of all American presidents, Herbert Hoover was probably the most singlemindedly committed to a system of beliefs. His pragmatism was well hidden and what there was of it emerged only after great prodding from events. To a remarkable degree, one can observe in his acts as president those principles of individualism which he set forth so simply in his book ten years before. The very same principle, for example, which prevented his sanctioning federal relief to the unemployed, dictated the tone and content of his veto of the bill to create a government corporation to operate Muscle Shoals. The government, he said, should not compete with private enterprise. Moreover, such a project, by being run by the federal government, abrogated the basic principle that all such enterprises should be "administrated by the people upon the ground, responsible to their own communities, directing them solely for the benefit of their communities and not for the purposes of social theories or national politics. Any other course deprives them of liberty." It was this same belief in individual freedom and cooperation which kept him from accepting a governmental system of old age and unemployment insurance. He advocated such measures only when undertaken voluntarily and through private insurance companies.

Even the Reconstruction Finance Corporation, perhaps his most enduring anti-depression agency, was created to assist private business, not to supplant it. True, it was a credit agency in competition with private enterprise, but it was designed to perform tasks which no private institution dared risk; the competition was therefore minimal if not nonexistent. Moreover, although it has been frequently alleged that the RFC lent money to corporations while the Administration denied relief to the unemployed, in Hoover's mind the distinction was crucial and real. The RFC was making loans which would be repaid—and most were—when the banks got back on their feet; it was not making grants. Even when Hoover did permit the RFC to lend money to the states for relief purposes he still insisted that no grants of federal funds be made.

But there was an even more important social justification for agencies like the RFC and the Federal Home Loan Board, which Congress created in July 1932 at the President's request. Hoover recognized as no president had before that the welfare of society was dependent upon business and that government, therefore, must step in. He did this, not because, as some critics said, he favored business over the common people, but because he recognized that if the banks failed the economy would collapse, savings would be lost, and jobs destroyed. The RFC and the Federal Home Loan Board, in effect, socialized the losses of financial institutions by using government to spread their obligations through society. Hoover was not prepared, though, to socialize the losses of the unemployed. That step in ameliorating the impact of the Depression was undertaken by the New Deal through the WPA and other relief agencies. In this respect Hoover was a transitional figure in the development of the government as an active force in the economy in times of depression. He was the first to smash the old shibboleth of government unconcern and impotence.

Perhaps his long-term role was even greater. In the face of great opposition and much outright hostility, he made a determined and even courageous effort to give the business community and voluntary private agencies a chance to show whether they could bring the nation out of a depression. Their failure to do so gave a moral as well as a political impetus to the New Deal. Just as after Munich no one could say the West had not done its utmost to meet Hitler halfway, so after Hoover's Administration no one could say that government had rushed in before other social or economic agencies had been given a try. That this was so goes a long way toward explaining the remarkable consensus among Americans ever since the 1930's that government has the prime responsibility for averting or cushioning the effects of a depression.

A second principle which stopped Hoover from permitting the federal government to provide relief was his conviction that the budget must not be unbalanced. As early as February 1930 he warned the Congress against extravagance and told of his own efforts to economize. Economy was essential, he emphasized, in order to avoid increasing taxes. But as decreasing revenues began to fall behind expenditures, Hoover's concern to keep the budget in balance overcame his reluctance to increase taxes. On July 1, 1931 the deficit was almost $500 million—an astronomical figure in those days when the total federal budget was less than $4 billion. In December of that same year Hoover recommended an increase in taxes. When Congress proved dilatory he told a press conference in March 1932 that a balanced budget "is the very keystone of recovery. It must be done." Anything less would undo all the recovery measures. "The Government," he warned, "no more than individual families can continue to expend more than it receives without inviting serious consequences."

Hoover recommended a manufacturers' sales tax as the chief new revenue device, in which suggestion he was joined by the new Democratic Speaker of the House, John Nance Garner of Texas. Garner enjoyed a reputation for being hostile to business and something of a radical in the old Populist tradition, but in the matter of bringing the budget into balance he stood foursquare with the President. Congress did not pass the sales tax, but it did pass one of the largest peacetime tax increases in American history.

Today it seems incredible that in a time of economic slump when consumer purchasing power was the principal requirement for recovery, the nation should elect to take money out of the hands of consumers. Yet this was precisely what the bill, recommended and signed by the Republican President and passed by the Democratic House, entailed. In fact, when in the course of the debate the House seemed hesitant about increasing taxes, the Democratic Speaker, John Garner, could not contain his anxiety. Conspicuously forsaking the Speaker's chair, Garner advanced to the well of the House to make an earnest plea for more taxes. At the conclusion of his speech, he asked "every man and every woman in this House who . . . is willing to try to balance the budget to rise in their seats." Almost the whole House, with its majority of Democrats, rose to its feet, to a growing round of applause. When he asked those who did not want to balance the budget to rise, no one did. The overwhelming majority of the newspapers of the country strongly commended the Congress in June 1932 for its efforts to balance the budget through increased taxes.

During the campaign of 1932 the Democrats continued to equal or even outdo Hoover in their slavish adherence to the ideal of a balanced budget. Franklin Roosevelt, for example, unmercifully attacked the Administration for its extravagance and its unbalanced budget, calling the fifty percent increase in expenditures since 1927 "the most reckless and extravagant past that I have been able to discover in the statistical record of any peacetime government anywhere, any time." He promised a cut of 25 percent in the budget if he were elected. Nor was this simply campaign oratory. As Frank Freidel has observed in his biography, Roosevelt was perfectly sincere in his dismay at the Hoover deficit and he would continue to be regretful about deficits until well after 1933.

From the record, then, it is evident that Democrats were in no better theoretical position to deal with the Depression than Hoover. Leaders of both parties thought of the government as a large household whose accounts must be balanced if national bankruptcy were to be avoided. Neither party could conceive of the central role which government must play in the economy in an industrial society in time of depression. It would take the whole decade of the New Deal and the continuance of the Depression before that fact would be learned by leaders and people alike.

Despite his fixation on the question of the budget, Hoover's conception of the Depression was sophisticated, rational, and coherent; the remedies he suggested were equally so, given his assumptions. In trying to find a way out, Hoover placed most reliance on what modern economists would call the "expectations" of businessmen. If businessmen feel that times are good or at least that they are getting better, they will invest in new plant and equipment, which in turn will employ men and create purchasing power. In substance, the remedies Hoover offered were designed to raise the expectations of businessmen and to maintain purchasing power until the economy picked up again. His first step was securing agreement among businessmen to hold the line on wages in order to keep purchasing power from falling. (And, by and large, as a result of his efforts, wage rates did not fall until the middle of 1931, but employment did, with, unfortunately, the same effect.) A second step in his program was to use government to help out with public work projects and, when private agencies proved inadequate, to provide credit through agencies like the RFC and the Home Loan Board. Finally, as a third arrow in his anti-depression quiver, Hoover sought, through the prestige of his office, to create that sense of confidence and approaching good times which would encourage businessmen to invest. As it turned out, though, he gambled and lost. For with each successive ineffectual statement, the value of his words dropped, until, like the worthless coins of a profligate monarch who debases his own coinage, they were hurled back at his head by a disenchanted press and people.

The Hoover recovery program failed, but probably no government program then thought permissible could have been any more successful. Certainly the New Deal with its more massive injection of government money into the economy succeeded little better. It ended the decade with 9.5 million still unemployed, and industrial production remained below the 1929 level throughout the 1930's except for a brief period in late 1936 and early 1937. On the other hand, most of the countries of Western and Central Europe regained the 1929 level of production by early 1935.

Part of Hoover's ordeal during the Great Depression undoubtedly derived from his personality, which, for a president, was unusual. Indeed, until he became President he had rarely been connected with government other than in an office which was nonpartisan or which he soon made so. Outwardly, at least, he was far removed from the stereotype of the politician; he could not slap a back or utter a guffaw. He appeared shy in public, though stolid was a more accurate description. A bulky man of over 200 pounds, standing almost six feet when he entered the White House, he gave a paradoxical impression of conservative solidity and beaming youth at the same time.

His public speech, like his writing, was formal, often stiff, and sometimes bordered on the pedantic. Early in Hoover's Administration, soon after the stock market crash, William Allen White, a Hoover supporter, spotted the new President's weakness. "The President has great capacity to convince intellectuals," he wrote. "He has small capacity to stir people emotionally and through the emotions one gets to the will, not through the intellect." Even Hoover's press secretary recognized that he "experienced the greatest difficulty in interpreting himself and his acts to the public." Indeed, it was characteristic of Hoover that though he found speech writing one of the most laborious of his tasks, he insisted upon writing all his own speeches. The compulsion could be at least enervating, and at worst dangerous to his health. Often he traded sleep for time to work on his speeches and at least once, at St. Paul in the campaign of 1932, he was on the verge of collapse from fatigue. His method of writing was tedious and incredibly time-consuming, involving innumerable drafts, meticulously gone over by himself, only to have still further proofs run off for more rewriting. Yet, after all this effort, his final draft usually was dry, too long, and ponderous.

In view of his poor public image, it is not surprising that for most of his presidency, Hoover's relations with the press were strained when not downright painful. Although he continued the press conferences which Wilson had begun, they were formal affairs with written questions; many reporters were convinced that the President concealed more than he revealed in the meetings. But it was probably Hoover's sensitivity to criticism that worked the real damage. His annual addresses to newspapermen at the Gridiron Club, which, as was customary, mercilessly lampooned his administration, often carried an edge, betraying his sensitivity to the press corps' jibes. Only occasionally did his private wit break through in public. At the Gridiron Club dinner in December 1932, after his defeat for reelection, he puckishly said, "You will expect me to discuss the late election. Well, as nearly as I can learn, we did not have enough votes on our side. During the campaign I remarked that this Administration had been fighting on a thousand fronts; I learned since the campaign that we were fighting on 21 million fronts." (The size of the Democratic vote.) This was one of the rare times that Hoover poked fun at himself in public.

Yet, despite his difficulties as a public figure, in private Hoover was neither phlegmatic nor shy. In fact he was extremely convivial, seeking constant company, whether at the White House or at his retreat on the Rapidan in the Blue Ridge Mountains. His wife told Joslin that the President could not be happy without numbers of people around him. His friends cherished his constant flow of stories and he delighted in his cigars and pipe. He was an outdoor type of man, reveling in fishing and hiking. Although he liked a joke, he rarely laughed out loud, though his friends knew well his soft chuckle. His own brand of humor could be heavy-handed. Thus in January

1931, when addressing the National Automobile Chamber of Commerce, he observed, with a smile, that 3.5 million cars had been sold in the first year of the depression and that consumption of gasoline was up five percent. "This certainly means," he twitted, "that we have been cheerful in the use of automobiles; I do not assume they are being used for transportation to the poorhouse. While I am aware that many people are using the old automobile a little longer it is obvious that they are still using it and it is being worn out. Altogether the future for the industry does not warrant any despondency." Will Rogers was not so sure. Some months later in a radio broadcast, he drawled, "We are the first nation in the history of the world to go to the poorhouse in an automobile."

Part of the reason Hoover resented the barbed comments of the press was that he worked so hard. It was as characteristic of Herbert Hoover that he was the first president to have a telephone on his desk as it was characteristic of Calvin Coolidge that he refused to have one. Hoover rose at 6 a.m. each morning, joined a group of his friends for a brisk half-hour session with a five pound medicine ball on an improvised court on the White House grounds, then went in to breakfast. He was at his desk by 8:30. He worked steadily all day, smoking incessantly, and usually well into the night. Often he would wake up in the middle of the night and pore over papers or write for an hour or two before going back to sleep. Nevertheless, he rose at the same early hour. Subordinates were not always able to keep up with his pace; some had to be dispatched to rest, but Hoover, miraculously, never succumbed to his self-imposed regimen. His secretary reports that he was not sick a single day of the four years he spent in the White House. A few days at the camp on the Rapidan or a short trip usually sufficed to restore his energies and his will to work. But toward the end of his tenure, even the optimism and strength of a Hoover faltered, at least once. He told his secretary, "All the money in the world could not induce me to live over the last nine months. The conditions we have experienced make this office a compound hell."

Aside from the circumstances in which he found himself as President, one of the reasons the office was "hell" was that Hoover was a poor politician. Often it is said that he did not like politics, or even that he was above politics. Both statements describe the image he held of himself, but many of Hoover's actions while in office are clearly partisan and political. If, for example, he could objectively recognize the weaknesses of the Harding Administration once he was elected president, he could also say during the campaign of 1928 that "the record of seven and one [-half] years" of Coolidge and Harding "constitutes a period of rare courage in leadership and constructive action. Never has a political party been able to look back upon a similar period with more satisfaction." In December 1931, when some voices were calling for a coalition government to deal with the worsening depression, Hoover made it clear that he would have nothing to do with Democrats. "The day that we begin coalition government you may know that our democracy has broken down," he told newspapermen at a Gridiron Club dinner. On the other hand, he could appoint Democrats to office, as he did former Senator Atlee Pomerene to head the RFC when he wanted that office to win support from Democrats. Nor was he devoid of political dramatics. In September 1931 he made a quick descent upon the American Legion Convention in Detroit in a successful effort to stop the Legion from going on record in favor of a bonus for veterans. By going all the way to Detroit, speaking for eleven minutes, and then immediately leaving for Washington again, he demonstrated the importance of his message and the weight of the schedule of work he pursued in Washington. Moreover, as the account written by his Press Secretary Joslin makes clear, he was no more above benefiting from parliamentary trickery in Congress than the next politically-minded president. As Joslin wrote, "It was characteristic of the President to hit back when attacked." Hoover suffered deeply when attacked, and he did not turn the other cheek. As William Allen White, who supported and admired the President, wrote in 1933, "he was no plaster saint politically. He had, during his three years, rather consistently and with a nice instinct chosen to honor in public office men of a conservative type of mind." Moreover, the behind-the-scenes circumstances of his nomination in 1928 and his renomination in 1932, both of which were steam-roller operations, should remove any doubts about his willingness and ability to use devices and tactics quite customary in politics.

No, it was not that he was above politics or that he really despised the operations of politicians. His difficulty was that he was temperamentally incapable of doing what a politician has to do—namely, to admit he could be wrong and to compromise. In the whole volume of his memoirs devoted to the Depression there is not a single mention of a major error on his part, though his opponents are taxed with errors in every chapter. Over a hundred pages of the volume are devoted to the answering of every charge of Franklin Roosevelt in 1932. Nowhere, though, does he notice that in 1932, he himself in his speech at Detroit incorrectly quoted Roosevelt and then proceeded to criticize at length his opponent for something he never said. This inability to admit error, to compromise, William Allen White recognized in 1931 as Hoover's undoing. After all, White wrote, "Politics . . . is one of the minor branches of harlotry, and Hoover's frigid desire to live a virtuous life and not follow the Pauline maxim and be all things to all men, is one of the things that has reduced the oil in his machinery and shot a bearing. . . ." Hoover's inability to admit error and the seriousness with which he viewed himself are both illustrated in another incident during the campaign of 1932. One of the Democrats' favorite sports that year was recalling, with appropriate sounds of derision, Hoover's remarks in 1928 to the effect that the United States was well on the way to abolishing poverty. Hoover, instead of admitting he had been somewhat optimistic, once again donned his hair shirt and stolidly endorsed the earlier statement because, as he said, it expressed the ideals for which Americans stood. Yet this was in the middle of the Depression and he was running for reelection.

In good times, Herbert Hoover's humble birth might have been an asset, but in the Great Depression it was not. Left an almost penniless orphan at nine, Hoover became a world figure and a millionaire before he was forty-five. With such spectacular success behind him it was understandable that he should think, albeit mistakenly, that anyone could achieve at least half as much as he. Undoubtedly his own experience fostered his insistence, throughout his life, that individual initiative was the prime motive force in a good society. What to other men appear as obstacles or handicaps, to the self-made man appear, at least in retrospect, as goads or incentives. Like most such men, Hoover attributed his success to will. When Theodore Joslin once asked him what had been his boyhood ambition, he replied without hesitation, "to be able to earn my own living without the help of anybody, anywhere." To such a man individual effort seems capable of moving mountains unaided; he is loath to see it shunted aside by collective action even in times of economic dislocation. The self-made man can indeed be the wrong man at such times.

Nor was it an accident that the other prominent self-made politician of the time, Alfred E. Smith, was also doubtful about the virtues of government aid to the unemployed, that he should attack Franklin Roosevelt for accusing the Hoover Administration of aiding the corporations and ignoring the poor. "I will take off my coat and vest," Smith vowed in the spring of 1932, "and fight to the end against any candidate who persists in any demagogic appeal to the masses of the working people of this country to destroy themselves by setting class against class and rich against poor." In a short time, Smith's views, like Hoover's, would bring him to outright opposition to the New Deal. It is not without significance in this respect that Roosevelt, who came to represent government benevolence toward the unemployed, was no self-made man, but lived securely and unadventurously on inherited wealth.

The differences in social origins of Roosevelt and Hoover, of course, are only one facet of the divergence between the Hoover Administration and the New Deal. Indeed, since the 1930's it has become commonplace to see Hoover and Roosevelt as opposites. Certainly there are differences—and important ones—between the administrations of the two Presidents, but we are now far enough removed from both to recognize also the real continuity between them that William Allen White was prescient enough to foresee dimly. When the two administrations are seen against the backdrop of previous administrations and earlier social attitudes, the gulf between them shrinks appreciably. Both men, it is worth recalling, were protégés of Woodrow Wilson; both of them, therefore, accepted a role for government in the economy which added up to a sharp departure from laissez-faire. Both, in the course of their respective administrations, drew upon their experiences in the First World War, where they had seen government intervening in the economy. Hoover's RFC, for example, was frankly modeled, as he said, after the War Finance Corporation. Both saw big business standing in need of controls, and, for a while, both believed that cooperation between business and government was the best way to achieve that control. Hoover, for instance, cited the Federal Reserve System as the ideal kind of business and government cooperation for purposes of regulating the economy; Roosevelt in the NRA also placed his trust in controls worked out through business and government cooperation. Moreover, both Roosevelt and Hoover took the view that it was government's responsibility to do something about a depression; neither man was willing to subscribe to the view which prevailed before 1929—namely, that economic declines were simply natural phenomena through which the nation struggled as best it could and that government could not be expected to do much about them.

Finally, it is also worth noticing that the temperament of the two men, their conceptions of America and of its future are much closer than the conventional picture paints them. (It was Roosevelt, during the campaign of 1932, who created the erroneous image of Hoover as the man without faith or hope in the future.) All through the Depression, Hoover's unvarying theme was that all this would pass and the essential vigor of the American economy would reassert itself. Undoubtedly he counted too heavily on the influence of his words to overcome the lack of business confidence, but there is no question of his optimistic outlook. One measure of it was the shock he received when he read Roosevelt's address to the Commonwealth Club in San Francisco. That was the speech in which Roosevelt talked about the frontier being ended and opportunities for economic growth being limited. Hoover took up the challenge, denying "the whole idea that we have ended the advance of America, that this country has reached the zenith of its power, the height of its development. That is the counsel of despair for the future of America. That is not the spirit by which we shall emerge from this depression." The important point is that such pessimism was really not expressive of Roosevelt's thought, either. Although historians have frequently referred to the Commonwealth Club address as the one clear indication during the campaign of 1932 of the philosophy behind the New Deal, we now know that the speech was neither written by Roosevelt, nor read by him before he appeared before his audience. As Rexford Tugwell has pointed out, the Commonwealth Club address, which Berle and he wrote, did not reflect Roosevelt's true attitude toward the American economic future. Indeed, its very singularity among Roosevelt's campaign speeches demonstrates how foreign it was to Roosevelt's feelings and convictions. The speech belied his abundant enthusiasm for the future, and his deep faith in the country and its capacities. Moreover, he soon contradicted its import in his Inaugural Address, when he electrified the country with the cry, "All we have to fear is fear itself."

How ironical that these words of Roosevelt should be so well known, when it was Herbert Hoover who all along had been saying the same thing —in less graphic and less credible language, to be sure—but saying it nonetheless. That fact, too, contributed to the ordeal of Herbert Hoover.

VIII

The New Deal and the American Reform Tradition: How New Was the New Deal?

INTRODUCTION

There seems little question that a greater amount of significant reform legislation was enacted during the years of the New Deal (1933–1938) than during any other five-year period of American history. Indeed, it may very well be that more significant social and economic legislation was placed on the federal statute books during the New Deal era than during the entire history of the United States prior to 1933. What has intrigued historians, however, has not been the sheer bulk of this legislation but rather whether the reforms of the New Deal were consonant with the American tradition of reform or departed from that tradition.

Eric Goldman and Richard Hofstadter, authors of two of the most provocative books written on the subject of modern American reform, have taken opposite positions on this question. In his brilliantly written Rendezvous with Destiny, *Professor Goldman relates the principal reforms of the New Deal to the New Freedom of Woodrow Wilson, the New Nationalism of Theodore Roosevelt, and the so-called "Associational Activities" of the 1920's. Although he notes that not all New Deal legislation can be neatly fitted into this framework, he nevertheless regards the statutes of the New Deal as basically within the confines of the reform tradition.*

Although Professor Hofstadter concedes in his Pulitzer-Prize winning Age of Reform *that "absolute discontinuities do not occur in history," what seems to him noteworthy about the New Deal is "the drastic new departure that it marks in the history of American reformism." He finds the New Deal different from Progressivism in the basic problems with which it attempted to deal and "in its ideas and its spirit and its techniques."*

The New Deal and Its Antecedents

Eric F. Goldman

SECOND HONEYMOON

The day after the Inaugural the new President proclaimed a four-day bank holiday, summoned Congress into special session, and started day-and-night White House conferences on emergency banking legislation. The bill was ready seventy-two hours later. The House of Representatives debated it thirty-eight minutes. The Senate debated it three hours. That night the President signed it. The Hundred Days were under way, the most controlled, directed, overpowered period in all the history of Congress.

Many of the bills whisked through Congress bespoke the central idea common to both principal reform traditions, the New Freedom and the New Nationalism—the belief that the best solution for economic and social ills was action by the federal government under strong executive leadership. The powerful leadership of Franklin Roosevelt set up federal protections for bank depositors and for all investors in stocks. Federal credit eased the burden of debt on farmers and householders, and federal guidance reorganized the railroads. A variety of federal devices made phony bankruptcy proceedings more difficult, imposed excess-profit and dividend taxes, created the Civilian Conservation Corps for the youthful unemployed, and raised prices by taking the country off the haloed gold standard. "Liberal" measures, the country called them, and quite clearly liberalism had come to mean not the Mencken-type emphasis of the Twenties but a full-blown revival of economic and social reformism. Talk of liberty in reform circles now was likely to produce a yawn, if not a scowl; opportunity, at least opportunity for the millions to have jobs, was the point.

The New Deal handling of the desperate unemployment problem produced the most sweeping reaffirmation of general progressive doctrine. For three years Herbert Hoover and the conservative press had been arguing that the use of large-scale federal funds for unemployment relief would bring about a dangerous political centralization, tear down the character of the recipients, and violate the economic law that the national debt cannot go beyond a fixed point without bankrupting the government. To these arguments, liberals of a dozen schools of thought made substantially one set of replies. Unemployment on its 1933 scale was too big a problem for the states and cities; environment shaped human character, and federal relief funds, by helping to remove squalor, would build character rather than injure it. The conservative appeal to economic laws was met by a barrage of Reform Darwinism,* even by a fresh Reform Darwinian formulation of economics. Well before the depression began, a number of economists had been developing theories which brushed aside the alleged economic law standing in the way of large-scale public spending. During the Thirties the long-time leader in world reform thinking, John Maynard Keynes, was rapidly developing these ideas into a persuasive system. The supposed economic law, Keynes argued in the authentic manner of Reform Darwinism, was simply the rationalization of upper-income groups who did not want to pay heavy taxes. There was nothing dangerous about running up a government debt. On the contrary, when private expenditures of money fell off, a sensible government would start "compensatory spending."

Franklin Roosevelt, together with a large segment of the liberal movement, distrusted the Keynes-type argument in the early New Deal days. At heart they hankered for a balanced budget. Yet the idea of large-scale federal spending on relief, with its implied contempt for rigid economics, its assignment of a key role to the national government, and its promise of quick alleviation of human distress, was a natural for the President and his following. Amid the roar of the Hundred Days, Congress passed a half-billion-dollar relief bill, and the President gave the administration of the money to a *de facto* Keynesian whose economics consisted largely of an urge "to feed the hungry, and Goddamn fast."

Harry Hopkins had always been in a hurry. He was already in a hurry when his father, a convivial jack-of-all-trades, finally settled the family in Grinnell, Iowa, and the homely youngster hustled his way to the title of "Big Man of the Class" at Grinnell College. On graduation, Hopkins almost took a job on a Montana newspaper; he almost did a dozen things; and somewhere in the middle of it all, a professor urged him to sign up as counselor in a boys' camp in New Jersey. A charitable boys' camp sat well with the son of a pious Methodist mother, who had bundled her five children off to church every Sunday and made them repeat the minister's points afterward. A boys' camp sponsored by influential people and near New York City had special attractions for the ne'er-do-well's son who was determined to find a place for himself in the exciting world of power. The professor did not have to urge long.

---

* Editor's note: Reform Darwinism, as Goldman defines it, was the faith of thoroughgoing evolutionists who believed that institutions "could and should change rapidly." They stressed the importance of environment and believed in man's ability to manipulate the environment in order to bring about a "better world."

Nor did Hopkins remain long in the camp organization. Quickly he was off to a series of successes in the social-work profession. By 1933 Hopkins had attained the number-one social worker's position in the nation, director of emergency relief in New York State, and a striking if somewhat mixed reputation. Associates knew him as a man who thought more swiftly than anyone working for, with, or against him, a first-class administrator with a habit of cutting through red tape like so much confetti, a wraith of quick cigarettes, frayed suits, curt sarcasms, and a highly developed ability to confuse advancing mankind with advancing Harry Hopkins.

Transferred to Washington to direct the New Deal relief program, Hopkins sat down at his desk before the workmen had moved it out of the hallway and in two hours spent more than five million dollars. During the ensuing months Hopkins's shabby little office in the old Walker-Johnson Building, with the faded paint and the water pipes up and down the walls, became the most swift-acting agency in all frenzied Washington. When somebody brought in a plan that "will work out in the long run," Hopkins snapped: "People don't eat in the long run—they eat every day." When inspectors from the Budget Bureau came around to see the "organizational chart," they heard that Hopkins had ordered: "I don't want anybody around here to waste any time drawing boxes. You'll always find that the person who drew the chart has his own name in the middle box." Out of the fury came striking new practices of unemployment relief, a devil for conservatives to flay, and an application of liberal doctrine so personal that its effects sank deep into the national mind.

The level-headed businessman, Frank Walker, discovered just how personal the application was when Roosevelt sent him on a tour to inspect the workings of the relief program. In his home state of Montana, Walker found former businessmen laying sewer pipes in their old business clothes because they had no money to buy overalls. And one of the ditch-diggers spoke for millions when he told Walker: "I hate to think what would have happened if this work hadn't come. . . . I'd sold or hocked everything I could. And my kids were hungry. I stood in front of the window of the bake-shop down the street and wondered just how long it would be before I got desperate enough to pick up a rock and heave it through that window and grab some bread to take home."

In the White House the lights burned late six or seven nights a week. Wearing out assistants by his energies, amazing intimates by his ability to toss off worries, Roosevelt kept prodding, brain-picking, quipping, politicking the Hundred Days ahead. Federal relief would alleviate distress; it could hardly cure a depression.

There was no lack of advice on the cure. The president of the Chamber of Commerce, a charwoman from Butte, the head of the AFL, Harvard classmates of Roosevelt, the third vice-president of Kiwanis, and some five thousand other people all brought or sent the President sure-fire remedies. Immediately around the President was the group of brilliant and contentious minds that the country had been calling the Brain Trust since the campaign of 1932. Yet amid all the babble, the proposals from informed and responsible people revealed a striking fact. Many business leaders and labor officials, Farm Bureau men and liberals, Brain-Trusters and Kiwanians, agreed on certain fundamentals of a recovery program.

Some concurrence from supposed ideological opposites was not surprising. Although the New Nationalism and the Associational Activities* outlook had important differences, they agreed on encouraging the formation of large economic units and on an important role for government in economic life. The depression of 1929, by presenting free enterprise in its most chaotic and inhumane form, brought an onrush of converts to the general idea of national planning of national economic units. New Freedomite reformers, who had so long battled any program that accepted the concentration of industry, now forgot their old battle in their concern with getting government controls over the existing situation. Businessmen who had railed at any system restricting their independence besought the government to tell them how to avoid bankruptcy. As the banks closed and the abyss seemed near in March 1933, free enterprise virtually abdicated. "There was hardly an industrial, economic, financial, commercial, reform, or agricultural leader who did not advance some idea of governmental intervention," the Washington insider Hugh Johnson has recalled. "A snowfall of paper plans drifted about the Capitol, and there was not one of them that would not, in some measure, have modified the Anti-Trust Acts."

The merger of Associational Activities ideas and New Nationalist thinking in a demand for national planning was plain in the Brain Trust. Raymond Moley, chief of the group, perfectly represented the coalescence in his own amiable, hardheaded self. As a boy in Berea, Ohio, Moley wept at the 1896 defeat of William Jennings Bryan, and as a young man he made a hero of Tom Johnson. Then, while the trust-busters kept on thundering and the trusts kept on growing, Moley began to wonder whether moralistic anti-big-business agitation was not trying to change the tides of economic development. As a professor of political science, first in the Midwest and then at Columbia, Moley sought solutions of the nation's ills that assumed the necessity of a battle against "ignorance" rather than against "sin." The nature of the proper enlightenment was not always clear. But the Moley who became important in the Roosevelt circle was a man who talked easily with people of an Associational Activities persuasion and who cited approvingly the Crolyite book that Theodore Roosevelt had quoted to the Bull Moose convention, Van Hise's *Concentration and Control*. The essential,

---

* Editor's note: The phrase is used by Goldman to connote the view of Herbert Hoover and others that government should assist the formation and activities of trade associations.

Moley was sure, was to end "the thoughtlessness and aimlessness" of free competition.

The merger of the New Nationalism and Associational Activities was no less striking in the relations of two important figures who gathered around Moley in the Brain Trust. No human beings could have seemed more different than Hugh Johnson and Rexford Tugwell. Johnson learned to spell to the whinnying of cavalry horses and the bawling of top sergeants at Fort Scott, Kansas, yelling to anyone who would listen to him: "Everybody in the world is a rink-stink but Hughie Johnson and he's all right!" Tugwell, the son of a prosperous farmer and cannery-owner in Sinclairville, New York, was raised to a genteel tradition of concern with community problems, almost to a Rooseveltian *noblesse oblige*. West Point remembered Johnson as the most talented hazer and the possessor of the biggest nose in the history of the school. The University of Pennsylvania recalled Tugwell as a handsome, smartly dressed ideologue, a gourmet with a special pride in his elaborate salads, who was given to practicing his sharp wit on bourgeois America and was more than likely to steer his date to a reform soirée. While Johnson was doing a hell-roaring border patrol along the Rio Grande, Tugwell was showing intimates a poem that included the lines:

> *I am sick of a Nation's stenches*
> *I am sick of propertied Czars. . . .*
> *I shall roll up my sleeves—make America over!*

The mature careers of the two men showed no more similarities. Johnson swashbuckled his way to a brigadier general's star, interrupting his military life only for tossing off children's books that were chock-full of carnage and last-minute touchdowns. Somewhere along the line, the Army discovered that its leathery-faced cavalryman, a perfect Captain Flagg in his tough talk and his sentimentality, also had a mind, a quick, perceptive instrument that expressed itself in curiously effective off-beat phrases. The Army sent Johnson to law school, then made him its principal representative on the War Industries Board of World War I. After the Armistice, Johnson resigned from the Army and entered business, first as an officer of the Moline Plow Company, later as one of the men who helped Bernard Baruch manage his web of interests. Still clattering across any room in a roar of Army attitudes, deeply involved with large-scale business, Johnson in 1933 seemed a caricature of the traditional reform type. Tugwell was close to being a typecase of the liberal professor. Settled at Columbia, he was entrancing classes by his iconoclasm and making a national reputation as a heretical agricultural economist. It was hardly surprising that at early Brain Trust sessions the relations between Tugwell and Johnson were a study in hostility, Tugwell holding Johnson off with witticisms, Johnson snapping and snarling at his debonair torturer.

Yet with the passage of a few months, Tugwell and Johnson were soon bending happily over the same charts and memoranda. Johnson had emerged from his service with the War Industries Board and his work with Baruch an ardent advocate of Associational Activities, though he added to Hoover's reliance on co-operation between government and economic units the belief that some degree of governmental compulsion should be used. Tugwell had emerged from his books and his indignation a highly involved economic thinker but fundamentally a New Nationalist. The line between Johnson's planning by partial co-operation and Tugwell's planning by over-all compulsion was a wavering one, much too wavering not to be pushed aside by the impact of depression. The common denominator of their thinking in 1933, and of his own, was described by Moley when he wrote of the Brain Trust's "rejection of the traditional Wilson-Brandeis philosophy. . . . We believed that any attempt to atomize big business must destroy America's greatest contribution to a higher standard of living for the body of its citizenry—the development of mass production. . . . We recognized that competition, as such, was not inherently virtuous; that competition . . . created as many abuses as it prevented." So the Brain-Trusters, Moley summarized, turned "from the nostalgic philosophy of the 'trust busters,'" turned to national economic planning.

This was the kind of thinking swirling around the President during the Hundred Days, and it did not disturb him. In the period immediately pre-ceding his election Roosevelt had begun to submerge the New Freedom element in his own thinking; he too could find little in trust-busting liberal-ism that seemed to apply to the emergency at hand. The real question for him, the real quarrel among his advisers, was not national planning versus free competition. The issue was: should the planning hew closer to the Associational Activities pattern, with its emphasis on noncompulsory rela-tions between the government and economic life, or should it follow more the New Nationalist pattern of powerful federal controls?

Next to feeding the hungry, the most urgent problem was agriculture. Another good crop was on its way and, with farm prices already perilously low, another good crop could mean disaster.

Even during the campaign of 1932, while most of his program was still a cloud of generalities, Roosevelt edged toward a specific idea of national planning for agriculture. Shortly before the nominating convention, Tug-well began urging on Moley a plan that was the product of many minds but had been most actively propagandized by Professor Milburn L. Wilson, of the Montana State College. Wilson's proposal assumed that the Ameri-can farmer could no longer depend on the foreign market. Instead of call-ing on the government to arrange dumping abroad, as the McNary-Haugen bill had done, Wilson argued that the government should plan crop-control at home by an elaborate procedure known as the "Domestic Allotment Plan." The Wilson program appealed to the planner in Moley; when Moley arranged a conference between Roosevelt and Tugwell, the plan appealed no less to the planner in Roosevelt. Roosevelt wanted to know more, and just as the convention was about to vote on the nomination, Tugwell wired Wilson to meet him in Chicago. The two men talked for a day in a hotel room; then Tugwell reported to Hyde Park on the long-distance phone. Roosevelt was sufficiently impressed to slip into his acceptance speech an endorsement of the basic Wilson principle that the federal government should make itself responsible for getting rid of farm surpluses without resorting to attempts at dumping abroad.

But just how was the responsibility to be fulfilled? Advocates of an Asso-ciational Activities tendency—most notably Hugh Johnson's friend George Peek—urged as little compulsion as possible. Peek argued long and ably that the chief mechanism for raising farm income should be a payment to the farmer for whatever money he lost by having to sell at a low price in foreign markets; only in years of superabundant yield should the actual size of his crop be curtailed, and then not until the crop was actually in growth. Professor Wilson, backed by a group including Tugwell, proposed crop curtailment, even in normal years and before planting, by offering attractive rentals to farmers on acreage taken out of production. The final legislation, the bill establishing the Agricultural Adjustment Administra-tion, made the execution of either or both plans possible. But the Triple A plainly contained ample provisions to make it one of the boldest uses of national agricultural controls in the history of Western civilization.

The next week or so, the already famous Roosevelt smile was especially radiant. The President was busy with the final stages of a bill which, of all the New Deal legislation, was his labor of love. The idea of a Tennessee Valley Authority lit fires in a dozen cubicles of Roosevelt's mind. A TVA would provide a yardstick for power costs; it would mean a giant stride in conservation, an enthusiasm of Franklin no less than of Theodore Roosevelt; it would chain a capricious, destructive river to the development of one of the most depressed areas in the country.

Shortly before the bill went to Congress, its chief sponsor, Senator George Norris, came to dinner at the White House, and the two men, the Dutchess County patrician and the son of a Nebraska dirt farmer, sat talking en-thusiastically over TVA's possibilities.

"What are you going to say when they ask you the political philosophy behind TVA?" Norris laughed.

"I'll tell them it's neither fish nor fowl," Roosevelt laughed back, "but, whatever it is, it will taste awfully good to the people of the Tennessee Valley."

Until midnight that evening the President squeezed dry his interlude, talking of forests and schoolhouses and the future, far away from the nag-ging present of hungry men and warring policies.

The next day the present returned with the jarring report that Congress was about to rush through a kind of industrial-recovery legislation which Roosevelt thoroughly disapproved. The President had not wanted to hurry industrial-recovery legislation. He felt that, though there was general agreement on the need for national planning, too much disagreement over key points still existed among important economic leaders. One school believed that industrial reorganization alone would bring recovery; another school insisted that industrial reorganization had to be accompanied by a pump-priming public-works program. There were also serious differences over the degree of governmental compulsion that should be involved. The President was reluctant to force the decisions. But now, with Congress getting out of hand, Roosevelt could wait no longer. He summoned the proponents of the more important plans among his aides, listened to them wrangle, then told them to go lock themselves in a room until they could agree on one bill.

After two days the conferees produced a bill, and the President accepted it with only minor modifications. With respect to the pump-priming issue, the National Industrial Recovery Act compromised, providing for public works but appropriating for them a sum much smaller than the ardent pump-primers wanted. The heart of the bill, the machinery for industrial planning, was less of a compromise. The codes were to be originally drafted by representatives of industry, which meant the trade associations in most cases; the antitrust laws were suspended; no prohibition was placed on price-fixing. All of these provisions had been major goals of business-minded planners since George Perkins's day. But the terms concerning hours, wages, and conditions of competition were to be written under the supervision of a federal administrator; they had to be approved by the President; and, once given White House approval, they carried the force of federal law. Herbert Hoover, speaking up from the deepest oblivion any living ex-President had ever known, was horrified. "Fascism, pure fascism," the advocate of Associational Activities called the enormous governmental powers granted to the National Recovery Administration.

Raymond Moley was jubilant. His Brain-Trusters, representing quite different approaches, had joined in giving the nation blueprints for both industry and agriculture which brushed aside the Wilsonian hostility to large-scale economic units and brought into actual fact a government-sponsored national planning. To the program of Associational Activities had been added the idea of federal compulsion, which men like Croly and Van Hise had long been advocating. The appointments of the top personnel of the Triple A and the NRA emphasized the way in which the New Deal was sweeping Associational Activities into a bolder pattern. None other than Baruch's assistant on the War Industries Board of World War I, George Peek, accepted the post as head of the Triple A. Another Baruch protégé, Hugh Johnson, not only moved into the top position of the NRA; he promptly began talking federal power in a way that made businessmen feel like so many captured peasants herded before the Czar.

Happily, Moley worked away on the draft of the Fireside Chat in which Roosevelt was to present the Triple A and the NRA to the public, working into the speech a huzza to the coming era of national planning. The President seemed to like the passage, and Moley pressed his advantage.

Did the President, Moley asked, realize to its fullest significance the "enormous step" he was taking? Did he realize that the Tripe A and the NRA were committing him to a sharp break not only with the conservative adulation of free enterprise but with the appeal for a return to free enterprise of New Freedom liberalism? Did he really approve, in its deepest meaning, this passage extolling national planning?

Roosevelt paused thoughtfully, then replied: "I never felt surer of anything in my life than I do of the soundness of this passage."

Uncle Ted, thrashing out his last years in impotent fury at Woodrow Wilson, had died too soon. For in the clear import of basic legislation and in the mind of the President of the United States, the nation was close to the repudiation of trust-busting and the dependence on compulsory federal planning which Theodore Roosevelt had appealed for under the name of the New Nationalism. . . .

LIBERALISM, AND THEN SOME

"Hugh," said Harry Hopkins, "your codes stink."

Hugh Johnson's face reddened, partly in anger, even more in surprise. When he took the job as NRA Administrator, Johnson knew that he was in for a rough time, but he did not expect sharp criticism from New Dealers, especially from so loyal a New Dealer as Harry Hopkins. Now, when the NRA was scarcely six months old, Hopkins proved only the first of many reformers who denounced the codes, and the criticism was increased by groups that liberals had long considered two of their prime concerns, the small businessmen and labor. Seven Cleveland grocers spoke for thousands of small businessmen when they wired the President: "NRA is the worst law ever passed by Congress." A Baltimore picket line expressed a common labor feeling with placards reading: "NRA means National Run Around."

By March 1934 the discontent was so great that President Roosevelt set up a National Recovery Review Board, under the chairmanship of Clarence Darrow. The seventy-six-year-old veteran of reform threw himself into the task as if it were his first case in Ashtabula. For four months, in the cramped heat of a Washington hotel suite, he drove his board through hearings on some three thousand complaints, only the infrequency of the old man's quips suggesting that this was to be his final important effort. And when Darrow sent his bulky three reports to the President, Hugh Johnson knew full well that he had lost much of liberal America.

"[In] virtually all the codes we have examined," the final Darrow report stated, "one condition has been persistent. . . . In Industry after Industry, the larger units, sometimes through the agency of what is called an Institute [a trade association], sometimes by other means, have for their own advantage written the codes, and then, in effect and for their own advantage, assumed the administration of the code they have framed. . . . To deliver industry into the hands of its greatest and most ruthless units when the protection of the anti-trust laws had been withdrawn was a grave error. It may safely be said that not in many years have monopolistic tendencies in industry been so forwarded and strengthened."

. . . The wrathful Darrow reports contained many overstatements or inaccuracies, and Hugh Johnson immediately boomed corrections across the nation. But the General's loudest roars could not drown out the fact that Darrow's basic contention was correct. Most of the codes had been written primarily by big business and were decidedly advantageous to big business. As a matter of fact, Darrow overlooked one choice subject for his sarcasm: in most important respects, the cotton, woolen, carpet, and sugar codes were copies, down to the last comma, of the trade-association agreements written during the Administration of Herbert Hoover.

The story of Triple A was less clear-cut. Industry was more completely dominated by large-scale producers than was agriculture, and the trade associations were more prepared, by their experience and by the nature of their field, to bend national planning to their own purposes. Yet the Triple A revealed the same tendency as the NRA. From the beginning of its operation, big-scale processors and distributors saw to it that their interests were generously protected. During the first three years of the New Deal, the total earnings of farmers leaped up, twenty-five per cent in 1933, fifteen per cent more in 1934, an additional sixteen per cent in 1935. But the new prosperity was not evenly spread. Large-scale farmers, organized in powerful associations, had their crops placed on the list for curtailment on highly favorable terms, while smaller and more weakly organized producers often were not on the lists at all or, if they were, benefited little from the program. Moreover, the Triple A assumed most of the risks of production for the landowner, but did not provide safeguards to prevent the landowner from passing on to tenants any unfavorable effect of the reduced acreage. "Proportionately at least," the historian Dixon Wecter has commented, "the principle—or application—of the AAA seemed to be: to him that hath it shall be given."

More and more, liberals who were concerned with agriculture began to sound like the Darrow Reports in their comments on the Triple A. Their indignation climaxed in the spring of 1935, when a group resignation removed from the Triple A some of its most devoted reform figures. To the liberal journals like the *Nation* this was a "purge" which spelled "the defeat of the social outlook in agricultural policy." The Triple A had succumbed to the "triumphant greed of the processors, distributors, and big producers." The *Christian Century,* an organ of liberal Protestantism, added: "What it all boils down to is that the old divergence between the NRA and the AAA—a matter of much conservative criticism a year or so ago—has been done away with. Both now . . . represent recovery programs . . . controlled by the big corporations involved, giving a subsidiary attention to the interests of the labor element, and hoping that the consumer will be satisfied with a few kind words and a seat out in the alley."

. . . Clarence Darrow, called before a Senate committee investigating the NRA, was melancholy and confused. "The concentration of wealth is going on," he told the Senators, "and it looks almost as if there were nothing to stop it. . . . I think this movement is going on faster than it ever did before, much faster. . . . If we do not destroy it there will be nothing but masters and slaves left before we get much further along." Darrow implied that the antitrust laws should be restored in full force; he also argued that "something like a socialistic system" was necessary. What the old warrior said was obviously contradictory, and it was obviously the struggle of a liberal caught in liberalism's worst domestic trouble.

The liberal in the White House was disturbed too. Though Roosevelt brushed aside the Darrow reports, he soon moved to bar price-fixing from future industrial codes; to set up an Industrial Appeals Board, which was to hear the complaints of small businessmen; and to get under way studies directed toward helping the low-income farmer. But the discontent with the NRA and the Triple A, particularly the irritation at the NRA, did not quiet. Worse still, the perversion of the purpose of New Deal planning meant that the whole structure was adding little to the nation's purchasing power, and recovery was stalling. Suddenly fate, in the form of a Brooklyn chicken-dealer, intervened. The Schechter poultry firm wanted to know what happened to its Constitutional rights if the Live Poultry Code told it how much it had to pay chicken-killers and which chickens were fit to sell. In May 1935 the Supreme Court answered by unanimously decreeing the NRA unconstitutional. Seven months later the Court knocked the other leg from under Roosevelt's New Nationalism by invalidating the crop-control sections of the Triple A. . . .

In the White House, testiness had long since disappeared. Only a short while after the invalidation of the NRA, Roosevelt was musing to Secretary of Labor Frances Perkins: "You know the whole thing is a mess . . . [and] we have got the best out of it anyhow. Industry got a shot in the arm. Everything has started up. . . . I think perhaps NRA has done all it can do. . . . I don't want to impose a system on this country that will set aside the anti-trust laws on any permanent basis." The President was back to his old self, impatient at the thought of permanence for the New Nationalism or any other ism, happily playing by ear.

Roosevelt could hardly improvise on the keyboard of American reform thought without hitting one chord constantly. Use the power of the federal government to smash concentrated wealth and to restore free enterprise;

use it simultaneously to lift the standard of living of the country's less favored groups; and, by both these moves, make opportunity more abundant —in short, the reform program conceived in the depression of 1873, erected into a powerful political force by decades of agitation, given effectiveness and respectability by the early Theodore Roosevelt and by Woodrow Wilson, kept alive even during the complacent Twenties. When Uncle Ted's New Nationalism failed, there was always the Jeffersonian New Freedom of the Chief.

Even in the middle of Roosevelt's New Nationalist period, two quite different facts had been reopening his mind to the New Freedom. The Roosevelt of the early Thirties had considerable sympathy for big business, and thought of government controls less as a crackdown than as a partnership between government and business. But during the NRA period the President discovered that corporation executives could prove highly unsatisfactory partners. Many openly flouted or skirted around all provisions of the NRA which were not entirely favorable to them, assailed most of the other New Deal measures, and spent millions of dollars trying to convince the country that Roosevelt was an egomaniacal Communist. By the time the President had to consider substitutes for the NRA, his irritation with big-business men had reached the point where he was remarking to intimates: "I get more and more convinced that most of them can't see farther than the next dividend."

Simultaneously, the President's mind was being moved in an anti-big-business direction by a push from the left. The shrewd, unscrupulous Senator Huey Long, clawing his way toward the Presidency, was not asking his audiences to wait for the workings of elaborate reforms, or to understand that there might be some point in co-operating with trust magnates. He was flailing his arms, pointing to his pockmarked face as evidence of the way the rich ground the poor, and announcing that after the election of 1936 "your Kingfish, Huey, asittin' in the White House, will know how to handle them moguls." By late 1935 the Kingfish had demagogued himself to a political strength which, if it could not move him into the White House, might possibly move Roosevelt out. A secret poll taken by the Democratic National Committee indicated that Long at the head of a third-party ticket would poll three to four million votes. This strength was not confined to the area around Louisiana but reached into pivotal Northern states—including a potential one hundred thousand votes in New York State, which could swing that big group of electors to the Republicans. Before the election an assassin's bullet ended the Long threat. But Roosevelt had learned to worry about what could happen to a reform President who did not reckon sufficiently with the anti-big-business feeling rooted in decades of American agitation. From the demagogic left and from the uncooperative right, the Jeffersonian reformer in Roosevelt was being pushed to the fore.

The New Deal never did pass over to a strict New Freedom pattern. The

Social Security Act, one of the most important bills passed after the invalidation of NRA, was no more Jeffersonian than it was New Nationalist; if it belonged to either pattern, it probably fitted better the Crolyan conception of the protective state. Nor did any one date or action mark the transition from the New Nationalism to the New Freedom. The shift came, in a blurred gradualism, after the invalidation of the NRA and the Triple A in 1935.

The change was marked by a slow turnover in the President's Brain-Trusters. By 1938 Washington was saying: "Moley is in opposition; Tugwell is in the city-planning business; and Hugh Johnson is in a rage," and the place of the early Brain-Trusters was being filled by a much larger group who shared an enthusiasm for New Freedom liberalism. Some of these men had been in the Administration almost from its start—most importantly, Harold Ickes and Harry Hopkins—and were now moving into the inner circle. Others were new figures, working together in shifting combinations, rising and falling in importance, men like Robert H. Jackson, Leon Henderson, Isador Lubin, and a half-dozen or more brilliant young graduates of Harvard Law School who had been placed in New Deal posts through the influence of the day's leading Jeffersonian legalist, Felix Frankfurter.

Early in the Hundred Days, one of these young lawyers showed up at a White House reception, maneuvered a friend into asking him to perform, and enchanted the President for two hours by singing Irish ballads, sea chanteys, and mountain laments. "You certainly stole the show, Tommy," the friend congratulated him. "I always steal the show," said Tommy Corcoran, and he always did. Springing somehow from a humdrum Rhode Island merchant family, Corcoran left Brown University loaded with prizes and then proceeded to equal Brandeis's record at Harvard Law School, a record that had seemed about as vulnerable as Babe Ruth's sixty home runs. The Hundred Days were not over before Corcoran was the unquestioned leader of Frankfurter's protégés, ranging airily through the government bureaus, making droves of friends and bringing the friends together for a session of songs and denunciations of big business, calling them all "my kids" from the senescence of his thirty-three years.

By 1934 Corcoran began admitting that one of his kids was his full equal, and at first friends were amazed at the choice. The anointed of the handsome, ebullient Tommy was a pale, shy ascetic, completely oblivious of pleasure or even comfort, who was shepherded around by Corcoran like a child at his first visit to an Automat. But Ben Cohen, Corcoran kept telling everyone, was something special, and everyone soon agreed. Cohen's legal powers aroused an admiration akin to worshipfulness, and his selfless absorption in public service won for the Corcoran-Cohen team a respect that Corcoran's pyrotechnics could never have achieved alone.

The team enjoyed a moment of importance in early New Deal days when, through Frankfurter's recommendation, Corcoran and Cohen were called on to draft the Securities and Exchange Act and the Securities Tax Bill. The President was impressed with their skill but these were not the days for militant Wilsonians. Corcoran and Cohen gained their real admission to the inner circle in 1935, when Roosevelt made one of the first important moves of his New Freedom period, the attack on holding companies in the power utilities field. The President asked the long-time trust-buster, Secretary of the Interior Harold Ickes, to supervise the working out of a bill, and, through Ickes's office, Corcoran and Cohen were assigned the detailed work.

The pair went at the task in a manner that was soon to be famous—all-night furies of work, with endless cups of sticky-sweet black coffee—and the bill that went to Congress would have delighted the heart of any trust-hating Populist. All holding companies in the power field, the "death sentence" clause provided, had to prove their social usefulness within five years or dissolve. When the provision provoked a savage battle in Congress, Corcoran bobbed up in the middle of the fight, artfully explaining and defending, dangling patronage before the eyes of reluctant Congressmen, rushing back and forth to the White House for reports and instructions. The holding companies were partially reprieved before Congress passed the bill, but the Corcoran-Cohen team was made. From then on, few important White House conferences did not include one or both of the men, at least four key laws were products of their legal wizardry, and "Tommy the Cork," as the President was soon affectionately calling the front man of the team, emerged as one of the two or three most inside New Deal insiders.

Shortly after the Holding Company Act went to Congress, Roosevelt sent to Congress a tax bill that was truculently anti-corporation. The President's "State of the Union" address of January 1936 bristled with phrases about the men of "entrenched greed" who sought "the restoration of their selfish power." All suggestions to revive the New Nationalist aspects of the NRA and the Triple A were brushed aside. Instead, the Administration pressed ahead with key legislation that bore the unmistakable New Freedom stamp. It went along with the Wagner-Connery Labor Act, probably the most bluntly anti-corporation legislation the United States has ever accepted, and pressed the Fair Labor Standards Act, with its ironclad provisions of minimum wages and maximum hours. A modified Triple A and other agricultural legislation, dropping much of the national-planning aspect of the original Triple A, aimed directly to improve the economic position of farmers and took especial care to promote the interests of the lowest-income group.

Amid this churn of legislation, the most symbolic of all New Freedom moves was made. In October 1937 a recession declared itself to the roar of crashing stocks, and the Corcoran group, attributing the recession to greedy price-fixing by monopolistic combines, urged on the President a series of bold steps, among them a general trust-busting campaign. Roosevelt was a willing listener, but the New Nationalist in him had not entirely disappeared. For the moment, the President decided, he would ask for a new housing act, hoping that this would stimulate employment. Beyond that, he would sit tight.

But Tommy Corcoran had no intention of sitting tight. The Administration was now being assailed on all sides, by conservatives for having caused the recession and by liberals for not ending it. To Corcoran it seemed as if the whole New Deal was on the run and something had to be done quickly. In a council of war instigated by Corcoran, a group of the new Brain-Trusters decided to gamble. They would go ahead on their own trust-busting campaign, hoping to stir the President into joining them but leaving him free to repudiate them at any time.

Assistant Attorney General Robert Jackson opened the campaign. In a radio speech written by Corcoran and Cohen, Jackson charged: "By profiteering, the monopolists and those so near monopoly as to control their prices have simply priced themselves out of the market, and priced themselves into the slump." In the excitement that followed, Corcoran asked Harold Ickes to speak and the Secretary responded with two blistering assaults on big capital. Washington was in a tumult. Conservative Senators demanded that Roosevelt immediately repudiate Jackson and Ickes. Ickes told his friends he slept with his hat hanging ready on the bedpost.

But the business indices were fighting on the side of the New Freedom trust-busters. As the recession worsened in the spring of 1938, Uncle Ted's New Nationalist nephew was overwhelmed by the Chief's disciple; Roosevelt, too, became convinced that the whole New Deal was threatened by selfish and shortsighted big capital. In March he reinvigorated the antitrust division of the Justice Department, naming as its chief the able, combative Thurman Arnold. The next month the President sent to Congress a strong message urging "a thorough study of the concentration of economic power in American industry and the effect of that concentration upon the decline of competition."

The New Nationalism and then the New Freedom—in a very real sense the New Dealers were right when they insisted that what they were doing hitched on to long-running American ideas. Yet there was something more to New Deal liberalism in both its New Nationalist and New Freedom phases, and the something more, as always, was connected with the climate of national opinion.

The New Deal, though it had given the country a way of coping with fear, had not entirely conquered it, and the common attitude was to go along with the New Deal enthusiastically but warily. If it could produce, fine; but there was always the reservation, accentuated by the recession of 1937, that the New Deal might not solve the problem. "Here we come, WPA!" the college boys wise-cracked, and millions beyond college age smiled understandingly.

The depression not only created a continuing uneasiness that another crash was round the corner; it brought into frightening focus a number of long-time trends that also spelled insecurity. Every year of increased urbanization and mechanization left thousands of individuals feeling more like an easily replaceable cog in the wheel, more alone in the impersonal crowd. By the late Thirties students of American society were also writing of "the specter of insecurity" raised by the steadily mounting percentage of the population who depended on someone else for a job, the growing proportion of women supporting themselves or contributing a vital portion to the family income, the ineluctable decline in independent farming. At the same time, the average age of the population was rapidly changing, with the age curve moving ever farther beyond the confidence of youth. It was the 1930's that, poignantly, kept Walter Pitkin's *Life Begins at Forty* at or near the top of the best-seller list for two solid years.

The general sense of insecurity was accompanied by a special restiveness among America's minority groups. They were not only, in fact, the least secure—the "last hired, the first fired," as the Negroes put it. By the 1930's the Negroes were more than half a century from slavery, and thousands of the newer immigrant families were raising a second or third generation on American soil. Often these later products of minority origins had the education and the manner to compete successfully for higher prestige positions and to move in higher-status circles, and the general liberal atmosphere of the Thirties encouraged their aspirations. Just because of this encouragement and the increased adaptation to the ways of the dominant groups, the enormous obstacles still standing in the way were the more frustrating.

Despite these developments, there is little evidence that any considerable part of the population gave up the faith in America as the land of opportunity. Too many generations had rooted their whole way of life in the belief; too many facts still proclaimed that the United States, more than any other country, did actually throw open the road for ambition. What happened was that millions of Americans were supplementing the credo of opportunity with a demand for laws that would guarantee them greater economic security and more equality in the pursuit of economic and social status. In case—just in case—economic opportunity did not knock, they wanted to be sure that the mailman would be around with a social-security check. In case—just in case—the social ladder proved too steep, they wanted laws which would guarantee that they would not be left on too humiliating a rung.

These trends showed themselves plainly in liberal thinking. Previous generations of reformers had been little concerned with security or equality brought about by law. The emphasis had been simply on creating a situation in which men could compete on reasonably even terms. Now, during both the New Nationalist and the New Freedom phases of the New Deal and increasing in intensity, a drive was being made to bring about greater security by legislation. The President himself laid down the line in 1934 when he placed "the security of the men, women and children of the Nation" first among the objectives of his Administration. The Social Security Act of 1935, of course, was the keystone of the Administration's security legislation, but a similar purpose marked a variety of New Deal legislation, ranging from the creation of the Home Owner's Loan Corporation in 1933 to the establishment of the Farm Security Administration in 1937. How far New Deal liberalism was ready to go in guaranteeing security was far from clear. Conservatives could only gloomily note the portents. The President spoke of a security program "which because of many lost years will take many future years to fulfill"; both the Farm Security and Resettlement Administrations were bringing group security ideas even into that sanctuary of individual relations, the medical field; and many powerful New Dealers were ready to agree with Eleanor Roosevelt when she declared: "In the nineteenth century . . . there was no recognition that the government owed an individual certain things as a right. . . . Now it is accepted that the government has an obligation to guard the rights of an individual so carefully that he never reaches a point at which he needs charity."

The New Deal made no concrete moves toward enforced equality, unless it was in its none too vigorous steps against segregation in public housing and against discrimination in employment on government contracts, but it smiled sympathetically on a liberal movement that was hurrying in that direction. The very tone of the New Deal was far more aggressively equalitarian than that of either Populism or progressivism. It was the New Dealer's President who told the Daughters of the American Revolution: "Remember, remember always that all of us, and you and I especially, are descended from immigrants." It was his wife who gladly permitted herself to be photographed while escorted by two Negro R.O.T.C. cadets.

Over much of previous progressivism had hung an air of patronizing the unfortunate, of helping the group that reformers often called "the little people." The attitude of the new liberalism was spoken with classic tartness when Joseph Mitchell presented his stories of "McSorley's Wonderful Saloon." The phrase "little people," Mitchell declared, was "repulsive. . . . There are no little people in this book. They are as big as you are, whoever you are." The point was carried to its further significance by a discerning, upper-income liberal, who added: "For quite a while I have lived in a commuter community that is rabidly anti-Roosevelt and I am convinced that the heart of their hatred is not economic. The real source of the venom is that Rooseveltism challenged their feeling that they were superior people, occupying by right a privileged position in the world. I am convinced that a lot of them would even have backed many of his economic measures if they had been permitted to believe the laws represented the fulfillment of their responsibility as 'superior people.' They were not permitted that belief. Instead, as the New Deal went on, it chipped away more and more at

257

their sense of superiority. By the second term, it was pressing hard on a vital spot and the conservatives were screaming."

To many liberals, it was just these variations in reform that gave the New Deal its great strength. "This isn't a do-gooder tea club, patching things up here and there," one of the President's close associates exulted. "This is a real people's movement getting at the heart of the great modern problem, insecurity—insecurity in jobs and insecurity in feelings." Other liberals were not so confident. Even with the new concerns over economic security and social equality, American liberalism of the late Thirties was still fundamentally the New Freedom, and once it was tested over any considerable period of time, it could easily develop all the serious difficulties inherent in the New Freedom.

The New Deal was to have time only to begin the test of its variety of the New Freedom. For just as it was really swinging into its new phase, frenetic men across the oceans, whose interest in liberalism had always been minimal, decided to shove a different issue to the fore.

From Progressivism to the New Deal

Richard Hofstadter

THE NEW DEPARTURE

The Great Depression, which broke the mood of the twenties almost as suddenly as the postwar reaction had killed the Progressive fervor, rendered obsolete most of the antagonisms that had flavored the politics of the postwar era. Once again the demand for reform became irresistible, and out of the chaotic and often mutually contradictory schemes for salvation that arose from all corners of the country the New Deal took form. In the years 1933–8 the New Deal sponsored a series of legislative changes that made the enactments of the Progressive era seem timid by comparison, changes that, in their totality, carried the politics and administration of the United States farther from the conditions of 1914 than those had been from the conditions of 1880.

It is tempting, out of a desire for symmetry and historical continuity, to see in the New Deal a return to the preoccupations of Progressivism, a re-

Reprinted from *The Age of Reform: From Bryan to F.D.R.*, Vintage Edition, by Richard Hofstadter, by permission of Alfred A. Knopf, Inc. Copyright 1955 by Richard Hofstadter. Pp. 300–325.

sumption of the work of reform that had begun under Theodore Roosevelt and Woodrow Wilson, and a consummation of the changes that were proposed in the half-dozen years before the first World War. Much reason can be found for yielding to this temptation. Above all, the New Dealers shared with the Progressives a far greater willingness than had been seen in previous American history to make use of the machinery of government to meet the needs of the people and supplement the workings of the national economy. There are many occasions in its history when the New Deal, especially in its demand for organization, administration, and management from a central focus, seems to stand squarely in the tradition of the New Nationalism for which such Progressives as Herbert Croly had argued. Since it is hardly possible for any society to carve out a completely new vocabulary for every new problem it faces, there is also much in the New Deal rhetoric that is strongly reminiscent of Progressivism. Like the Progressives, the New Dealers invoked a larger democracy; and where the Progressives had their "plutocrats," the New Dealers had their "economic royalists." F. D. R., asserting in his first inaugural address that "The money changers have fled from their high seats in the temple of our civilization. We may now restore that temple to the ancient truths," sounds very much like almost any inspirational writer for *McClure's* in the old days.[1] On a number of particular issues, moreover, like the holding-company question, monopoly, and public power, one feels as though one is treating again, in the New Deal, with familiar problems—just as, in the crucial early days of 1933, the formation of a strong bloc of inflationist Senators from the West seemed to hark back to the Populist movement.

Still, granting that absolute discontinuities do not occur in history, and viewing the history of the New Deal as a whole, what seems outstanding about it is the drastic new departure that it marks in the history of American reformism.[2] The New Deal was different from anything that had yet happened in the United States: different because its central problem was unlike the problems of Progressivism; different in its ideas and its spirit and its techniques. Many men who had lived through Progressivism and had thought of its characteristic proposals as being in the main line of American traditions, even as being restoratives of those traditions, found in the New Deal an outrageous departure from everything they had known

---

[1] Naturally there was also some continuity in personnel, for F. D. R. himself was only one of a considerable number of American leaders who had been young Progressives before the war and were supporters of the major reforms of the thirties. However, one could draw up an equally formidable list—chiefly Republican insurgents of the Bull Moose era, but also many Democrats—who had supported Progressive measures and later became heated critics of the New Deal.

[2] Here I find myself in agreement with the view expressed by Samuel Lubell (op. cit., p. 3): "The distinctive feature of the political revolution which Franklin D. Roosevelt began and Truman inherited lies not in its resemblance to the political wars of Andrew Jackson or Thomas Jefferson, but in its abrupt break with the continuity of the past."

and valued, and so could interpret it only as an effort at subversion or as the result of overpowering alien influences. Their opposition was all too often hysterical, but in their sense that something new had come into American political and economic life they were quite right.

Consider, to begin, the fundamental problem that the New Dealers faced, as compared with the problems of the Progressives. When Theodore Roosevelt took office in 1901, the country was well over three years past a severe depression and in the midst of a period of healthy economic development. Its farmers were more prosperous than they had been for about forty years, its working class was employed and gaining in living standards, and even its middle class was far busier counting the moral costs of success than it was worrying about any urgent problems of family finance. When F. D. R. took his oath of office, the entire working apparatus of American economic life had gone to smash. The customary masters and leaders of the social order were themselves in a state of near panic. Millions were unemployed, and discontent had reached a dangerous pitch on the farms and in the cities.

Indeed, the New Deal episode marks the first in the history of reform movements when a leader of the reform party took the reins of a government confronted above all by the problems of a sick economy. To be sure, the whole nineteenth-century tradition of reform in American politics was influenced by experience with periodic economic breakdowns; but its political leaders had never had to bear responsibility for curing them. Jefferson in 1801, Jackson in 1829, and after them T. R. and Wilson—all took over at moments when the economy was in good shape. While each of them had experience with economic relapse—Jefferson in 1807 as the consequence of his embargo policies, the Jacksonians briefly in 1834 and again after 1837, T. R. briefly during the "bankers' panic" of 1907, and Wilson with a momentary recession just before the wartime boom—their thinking, and the thinking of the movements they reprsented, was centered upon sharing an existing prosperity among the various social classes rather than upon restoring a lost prosperity or preventing recurrent slumps.

The earlier American tradition of political protest had been a response to the needs of entrepreneurial classes or of those who were on the verge of entrepreneurship—the farmers, small businessmen, professionals, and occasionally the upper caste of the artisans or the working class. The goal of such classes had generally been to clear the way for new enterprises and new men, break up privileged business, big businesses, and monopolies, and give the small man better access to credit. The ideas of this Progressive tradition, as one might expect, were founded not merely upon acceptance but even upon glorification of the competitive order. The Jeffersonians, the Jacksonians, and after them most of the Progressives had believed in the market economy, and the only major qualification of this belief they cared to make stemmed from their realization that the market needed to be policed and moralized by a government responsive to the needs of the economic beginner and the small entrepreneur. Occasionally, very occasionally, they had argued for the exercise of a few positive functions on the part of the national government, but chiefly they preferred to keep the positive functions of government minimal, and, where these were necessary, to keep them on the state rather than put them on the national level. Their conceptions of the role of the national government were at first largely negative and then largely preventive. In the Jeffersonian and Jacksonian days it was to avoid excessive expenditure and excessive taxation, to refrain from giving privileged charters. Later, in the corporate era, it was to prevent abuses by the railroads and the monopolists, to check and to regulate unsound and immoral practices. It is of course true that some of the more "advanced" thinkers of the Populist and Progressive movements began to think tentatively of more positive functions for government, but it was just such proposals—the subtreasury scheme for agricultural credits and the various public-ownership proposals—that provoked the greatest opposition when attempts were made to apply them on a national scale.

The whole reformist tradition, then, displayed a mentality founded on the existence of an essentially healthy society; it was chiefly concerned not with managing an economy to meet the problems of collapse but simply with democratizing an economy in sound working order. Managing an economy in such a way as to restore prosperity is above all a problem of organization,[3] while democratizing a well-organized economy had been . . . in some important respects an attempt to find ways of attacking or limiting organization. Hence the Progressive mind was hardly more prepared than the conservative mind for what came in 1929. Herbert Hoover, an old Bull Mooser, while more disposed to lead the country than any president had been in any previous depression, was unprepared for it, and was prevented from adjusting to it by a doctrinaire adherence to inherited principles. F. D. R.—a fairly typical product of Progressivism who had first won office in 1910—was also unprepared for it in his economic thinking, as anyone will see who examines his career in the 1920's;[4] but he was sufficiently opportunistic and flexible to cope with it somewhat more successfully.

Hoover, an engineer born in Iowa, represented the moral traditions of native Protestant politics. An amateur in politics who had never run for office before he was elected President in 1928, he had no patience with the politician's willingness to accommodate, and he hung on, as inflexibly as the situation would permit, to the private and voluntary methods that had

---

[3] The closest thing to an earlier model for the first efforts of the New Deal was not the economic legislation of Progressivism but the efforts of the Wilson administration to organize the economy for the first World War. Hugh Johnson in the NRA and George Peek in the AAA were in many ways recapitulating the experience they had had in the War Industries Board under Bernard Baruch.

[4] See Frank Friedel's *Franklin D. Roosevelt: the Ordeal* (Boston, 1954), and his forthcoming volume on F. D. R.'s governorship.

always worked well in his administrative career.[5] F. D. R., a seasoned professional politician who had learned his trade straddling the terrible antagonisms of the 1920's, was thoroughly at home in the realities of machine politics and a master of the machine techniques of accommodation. Unlike Hoover, he had few hard and fast notions about economic principles, but he knew that it would be necessary to experiment and improvise. "It is common sense," he said in 1932, "to take a method and try it. If it fails, admit it frankly and try another. But above all, try something."

To describe the resulting flood of legislation as economic planning would be to confuse planning with interventionism. Planning was not quite the word for the New Deal: considered as an economic movement, it was a chaos of experimentation. Genuine planners like Rexford Guy Tugwell found themselves floundering amid the cross-currents of the New Deal, and ended in disillusionment. But if, from an economic standpoint, the New Deal was altogether lacking in that rationality or consistency which is implied in the concept of planning, from a political standpoint it represented a masterly shifting equipoise of interests. And little wonder that some of the old Republican insurgents shuddered at its methods. If the state was believed neutral in the days of T. R. because its leaders claimed to sanction favors for no one, the state under F. D. R. could be called neutral only in the sense that it offered favors to everyone.

Even before F. D. R. took office a silent revolution had taken place in public opinion, the essential character of which can be seen when we recall how little opposition there was in the country, at the beginning, to the assumption of the New Dealers that henceforth, for the purposes of recovery, the federal government was to be responsible for the condition of the labor market as a part of its concern with the industrial problem as a whole. Nothing revolutionary was intended—but simply as a matter of politics it was necessary for the federal government to assume primary responsibility for the relief of the unemployed. And, simply as a matter of politics, if the industrialists were to be given the power to write enforceable codes of fair practice, labor must at least be given some formal recognition of its right of collective bargaining. Certainly no one foresaw, in the first year or two of the New Deal, that the immense infusions of purchasing power into the economy through federal unemployment relief would be as lasting or as vital a part of the economy of the next several years as they proved in fact to be. Nor did anyone foresee how great and powerful a labor movement would be called into being by the spirit and the promise of the New Deal and by the partial recovery of its first few years. But by the end of 1937 it was clear that something had been added to the social base of reformism. The demands of a large and powerful labor movement, coupled with the interests

---

[5] Characteristically, also, Hoover accepted what might be called the nativist view of the Great Depression: it came from abroad; it was the product, not of any deficiencies in the American economy, but of repercussions of the unsound institutions of Europe.

of the unemployed, gave the later New Deal a social-democratic tinge that had never before been present in American reform movements. Hitherto concerned very largely with reforms of an essentially entrepreneurial sort and only marginally with social legislation, American political reformism was fated henceforth to take responsibility on a large scale for social security, unemployment insurance, wages and hours, and housing.[6]

Still more imposing was the new fiscal role of the federal government. Again, none of this was premeditated. Large-scale spending and unbalanced budgets were, in the beginning, a response to imperative needs. While other schemes for recovery seemed to fall short of expectations, spending kept the economy going; and it was only when F. D. R. tried in 1937 to cut back expenditures that he learned that he had become the prisoner of his spending policies, and turned about and made a necessity into a virtue. His spending policy never represented, at any time before the outbreak of the war, an unambiguous or wholehearted commitment to Keynesian economics. Here only the war itself could consummate the fiscal revolution that the New Deal began. In 1940 Lord Keynes published in the United States an article in which he somewhat disconsolately reviewed the American experience with deficit spending during the previous decade. "It seems politically impossible," he concluded, "for a capitalistic democracy to organize expenditure on the scale necessary to make the grand experiment which would prove my case—except in war conditions." He then added that preparations for war and the production of armaments might teach Americans so much about the potentialities of their economy that it would be "the stimulus, which neither the victory nor the defeat of the New Deal could give you, to greater individual consumption and a higher standard of life." [7] How remarkably prophetic this was we can now see. There had been under peacetime conditions an immense weeping and wailing over the budgets of F. D. R.—which at their peak ran to seven billion dollars. Now we contemplate budgets of over eighty billion dollars with somewhat less anguish, because we know that most of this expenditure will be used for defense and will not be put to uses that are politically more controversial. But, above all, we have learned things about the possibilities of our economy that were not dreamed of in 1933, much less in 1903. While men still grow angry over federal fiscal and tax policies, hardly anyone doubts that in the calculable

---

[6] As the counsel for the National Association of Manufacturers put it: "Regulation has passed from the negative stage of merely preventing unlawful and improper conduct, to the positive stage of directing and controlling the character and form of business activity. The concept that the function of government was to prevent exploitation by virtue of superior power has been replaced by the concept that it is the duty of government to provide security against all the major hazards of life—against unemployment, accident, illness, old age, and death." Thomas P. Jenkin: *Reactions of Major Groups to Positive Government in the United States* (Berkeley, 1945), pp. 300–1.

[7] J. M. Keynes: "The United States and the Keynes Plan," *New Republic*, Vol. CIII (July 29, 1940), p. 158.

future it will be the fiscal role of the government that more than anything else determines the course of the economy.

And what of the old Progressive issues? They were bypassed, sidestepped, outgrown—anything but solved. To realize how true this was, one need only look at the New Deal approach to those two *bêtes noires* of the Progressive mind, the machines and the trusts.

Where the Progressives spent much of their energy . . . trying to defeat the bosses and the machines and to make such changes in the political machinery of the country as would bring about direct popular democracy and "restore government to the people," the New Deal was almost completely free of such crusading. To the discomfort of the old-fashioned, principled liberals who were otherwise enthusiastic about his reforms, F. D. R. made no effort to put an end to bossism and corruption, but simply ignored the entire problem. In the interest of larger national goals and more urgent needs, he worked with the bosses wherever they would work with him—and did not scruple to include one of the worst machines of all, the authoritarian Hague machine in New Jersey. As for the restoration of democracy, he seemed well satisfied with his feeling that the broadest public needs were at least being served by the state and that there was such an excellent rapport between the people and their executive leadership.[8]

The chief apparent exception to this opportune and managerial spirit in the field of political reform—namely, the attempt to enlarge the Supreme Court—proves on examination to be no exception at all. F. D. R.'s fight over the Supreme Court was begun, after all, not in the interest of some large "democratic" principle or out of a desire to reform the Constitutional machinery as such, but because the Court's decisions had made it seem impossible to achieve the managerial reorganization of society that was so urgently needed. His first concern was not that judicial review was "undemocratic" but that the federal government had been stripped, as he thought, of its power to deal effectively with economic problems. Nor was this fight waged in the true Progressive spirit. The Progressives, too, had had their difficulties with the judiciary, and had responded with the characteristically principled but practically difficult proposal for the recall of judicial decisions. In short, they raised for reconsideration, as one might expect of principled men, the entire question of judicial review. F. D. R. chose no such method.[9] To reopen the entire question of the propriety of

---

[8] Of course to speak of democracy in purely domestic terms is to underestimate the world-wide significance of the New Deal. At a time when democracy was everywhere in retreat, the New Deal gave to the world an example of a free nation coping with the problems of its economy in a democratic and humane way.

[9] Indeed, in his message calling for reorganization Roosevelt declared that his proposal would make unnecessary any fundamental changes in the powers of the courts or in the Constitution, "changes which involve consequences so far-reaching as to cause uncertainty as to the wisdom of such a course." It remained for the leading senatorial opponent of the bill, Senator Burton K. Wheeler, to advocate an amendment to the

judicial review of the acts of Congress under a representative democracy would have been a high-minded approach to what he felt was a Constitutional impasse, but it would have ended perhaps even more disastrously than the tactic he employed. F. D. R. avoided such an approach, which would have involved a cumbersome effort to amend the Constitution, and devised a ";gimmick" to achieve his ends—the pretense that the age of the judges prevented them from remaining abreast of their calendar, and the demand for the right to supplement the judiciary, to the number of six, with an additional judge for each incumbent who reached the age of seventy without retiring.

Students of the Court fight are fond of remarking that Roosevelt won his case, because the direction of the Court's decisions began to change while the fight was in progress and because Justice Van Devanter's retirement enabled the President to appoint a liberal justice and decisively change the composition of the Court.[10] It seems important, however, to point out that a very heavy price had to be paid for even this pragmatic attempt to alter a great and sacrosanct conservative institution. The Court fight alienated many principled liberals and enabled many of F. D. R.'s conservative opponents to portray him to the public more convincingly as a man who aspired to personal dictatorship and aimed at the subversion of the Republic.

If we look at the second of the two great foes of Progressivism, big business and monopoly, we find that by the time of the New Deal public sentiment had changed materially. To be sure, the coming of the depression and the revelation of some of the less palatable business practices of the 1920's brought about a climate of opinion in which the leadership of business, and particularly of big business, was profoundly distrusted and bitterly resented. Its position certainly was, in these respects, considerably weaker than it had been twenty-five years before. Still, by 1933 the American public had lived with the great corporation for so long that it was felt to be domesticated, and there was far more concern with getting business life on such a footing as would enable it to provide jobs than there was with breaking up the larger units. The New Deal never developed a clear or consistent line on

---

Constitution permitting Congress to override judicial vetoes of its acts. Charles A. and Mary R. Beard: *America in Midpassage* (New York, 1939), Vol. I, p. 355.

[10] Presumably it will always be debated whether the new harmony between Congress and the Supreme Court that developed even while the Court fight was going on can be attributed to Roosevelt's Court reform bill. Merlo Pusey in his *Charles Evans Hughes* (Vol. II, pp. 766 ff.) argues that the change in the Court's decisions was not a political response to the legislative struggle. He points out, among other things, that the New Deal legislation that came before the Court after the NRA and AAA decisions was better drafted. It is beyond doubt, however, that the resignation of Van Devanter was precipitated by the Court fight. Ibid., Vol. II, p. 761. The fact that advocates of both sides can go on arguing about who won the fight is the best evidence that the issue was satisfactorily settled. It aroused so much feeling that an unambiguous victory for either side would have been unfortunate.

business consolidation, and New Dealers fought over the subject in terms that were at times reminiscent of the old battles between the trust-busters and the trust-regulators. What can be said, however, is that the subject of bigness and monopoly was subordinated in the New Deal era to that restless groping for a means to bring recovery that was so characteristic of Roosevelt's efforts. The New Deal began not with a flourish of trust-busting but rather, in the NRA, with an attempt to solve the problems of the business order through a gigantic system of governmentally underwritten codes that would ratify the trustification of society. One of the first political setbacks suffered by the New Deal arose from just this—for it had put the formation of its codes of fair practice so completely in the hands of the big-business interests that both small businessmen and organized labor were seriously resentful. Only five years from the date of its passage, after the NRA had failed to produce a sustained recovery and had been declared unconstitutional by the Supreme Court, did the administration turn off and take the opposite tack with its call for an inquiry into corporate consolidation and business power that led to the Temporary National Economic Committee's memorable investigation.[11] Although at the time many observers thought that the old Progressive trust-busting charade was about to be resumed, the New Deal never became committed to a categorical "dissection" of the business order of the sort Wilson had talked of in 1912, nor to the "demonstration" prosecutions with which T. R. had both excited and reassured the country. The New Deal was not trying to re-establish the competitive order that Wilson had nostalgically invoked and that T. R. had sternly insisted was no longer possible. Its approach, as it turned out, was severely managerial, and distinctly subordinated to those economic considerations that would promote purchasing power and hence recovery. It was, in short, a concerted effort to discipline the pricing policies of businesses, not with the problem of size in mind, nor out of consideration for smaller competitors, but with the purpose of eliminating that private power to tax which is the prerogative of monopoly, and of leaving in the hands of consumers vital purchasing power.

History cannot quite repeat itself, if only because the participants in the second round of any experience are aware of the outcome of the first. The anti-trust philosophers of the closing years of the New Deal were quite aware that previous efforts to enforce the Sherman Act had been ceremonial demonstrations rather than serious assaults upon big business. Thurman Arnold, who was put in charge of the anti-trust program, was well known for his belief that earlier interpretations of the Sherman Act had actually concealed and encouraged business consolidation. In his account of the contemporary function of anti-trust prosecution Arnold put his emphasis

---

[11] There had been in the meantime, however, the assault upon the holding companies embodied in the so-called "death sentence" of 1935.

upon benefits for the consumer and repudiated the earlier use of the Sherman Act: "Since the consumers' interest was not emphasized, such enforcement efforts as existed were directed at the punishment of offenses rather than the achievement of economic objectives. Indeed, in very few anti-trust prosecutions was any practical economic objective defined or argued with respect to the distribution of any particular product. In this way the moral aspects of the offense, and that will-o'-the-wisp, corporate intent, became more important considerations than economic results. Anti-trust enforcement, not being geared to the idea of consumers' interests, became a hunt for offenders instead of an effort to test the validity of organized power by its performance in aiding or preventing the flow of goods in commerce. The result was that although the economic ideal of a free competitive market as the cornerstone of our economy was kept alive, no adequate enforcement staff was ever provided to make that ideal a reality. Such, broadly speaking, was the state of the Sherman Act from 1890 down to the great depression." [12]

But if such a position as Thurman Arnold's can be legitimately distinguished from the Progressive type of anti-trust, as I think it can, there are men today whose political thinking was forged in the service of the New Deal who go beyond him in repudiating anti-trust action as a mere attack upon size, and who take, on the whole, an acquiescent attitude toward big business. A few years ago John Kenneth Galbraith made quite a stir with his book *American Capitalism,* whose central thesis was that the process of business consolidation creates within itself a "countervailing power"—that is, that it brings about the organization not merely of strong sellers but of strong buyers as well, who distribute through large sectors of the economy their ability to save through organization.[13] In Galbraith's book, as in most recent literature in defense of bigness, it is not the effort at disorganization but the effects of counter-organization, in labor, agriculture, and government and within business itself, that are counted upon to minimize the evils of consolidation. More recently David Lilienthal, another graduate of the New Deal administrative agencies, has written a strong apologia for big business that followed Galbraith in stressing the technologically progressive character of large-scale industry in language that would have horrified Brandeis and Wilson.[14] It is not clear whether the attitudes of men like Galbraith and Lilienthal represent dominant liberal sentiment today—

---

[12] Thurman Arnold: *The Bottlenecks of Business* (New York, 1940), p. 263.

[13] This is a rather simplified statement of the thesis of Galbraith's *American Capitalism* (Boston, 1952). Students of the history of anti-trust ideologies will be particularly interested in Galbraith's strictures on the TNEC Report (pp. 59–60).

[14] Galbraith argues that "the competition of the competitive model . . . almost completely precludes technical development" and that indeed "there must be some element of monopoly in an industry if it is to be progressive." Ibid., pp. 91, 93, and chapter vii, *passim.* Cf. David Lilienthal: *Big Business: a New Era* (New York, 1953), chapter vi. For another such friendly treatment by a former New Dealer, see Adolph A. Berle: *The Twentieth Century Capitalist Revolution* (New York, 1954).

though it may be pertinent to say that their books brought no outpouring of protest from other liberal writers. The spectacle of liberals defending, with whatever qualifications, bigness and concentration in industry suggests that that anti-monopoly sentiment which was so long at the heart of Progressive thinking is no longer its central theme. The generation for which Wilson and Brandeis spoke looked to economic life as a field for the expression of character; modern liberals seem to think of it quite exclusively as a field in which certain results are to be expected. It is this change in the moral stance that seems most worthy of remark. A generation ago, and more, the average American was taught to expect that a career in business would and should be in some sense a testing and proving ground for character and manhood, and it was in these terms that the competitive order was often made most appealing.[15] Contrariwise, those who criticized the economic order very commonly formed their appeals within the same mold of moral suasion: the economic order failed to bring out or reward the desired qualities of character, to reward virtue and penalize vice; it was a source of inequities and injustices. During the last fifteen or twenty years, however, as Galbraith observes, "the American radical has ceased to talk about inequality or exploitation under capitalism or even its 'inherent contradictions.' He has stressed, instead, the unreliability of its performance." [16]

THE NEW OPPORTUNISM

The New Deal, and the thinking it engendered, represented the triumph of economic emergency and human needs over inherited notions and inhibitions. It was conceived and executed above all in the spirit of what Roosevelt called "bold, persistent experimentation," and what those more critical of the whole enterprise considered crass opportunism. In discussing Progressivism I emphasized its traffic in moral absolutes, its exalted moral tone. While something akin to this was by no means entirely absent from the New Deal, the later movement showed a strong and candid awareness that what was happening was not so much moral reformation as economic experimentation. Much of this experimentation seemed to the conservative opponents of the New Deal as not only dangerous but immoral.

The high moral indignation of the critics of the New Deal sheds light on another facet of the period—the relative reversal of the ideological roles of conservatives and reformers. Naturally in all ideologies, conservative or

---

[15] See, for instance, the touching letter quoted by Lilienthal (op. cit., p. 198), from a university graduate of the twenties: "We were dismayed at the vista of mediocre aspiration and of compartmentalized lives. The course of a big business career was predictable and foreclosed. It was also, as the personnel department pointed out, secure. The appeal of graduated salary raises and retirement on a pension was held out as the big lure. But in my high school days the appeal had been to ambition, a good deal was said about achievement and independence."

[16] Galbraith, op. cit., p. 70.

radical, there is a dual appeal to ultimate moral principles and to the practical necessities of institutional life. Classically, however, it has been the strength of conservatives that their appeal to institutional continuities, hard facts, and the limits of possibility is better founded; while it has usually been the strength of reformers that they arouse moral sentiments, denounce injustices, and rally the indignation of the community against intolerable abuses. Such had been the alignment of arguments during the Progressive era. During the New Deal, however, it was the reformers whose appeal to the urgent practical realities was most impressive—to the farmers without markets, to the unemployed without bread or hope, to those concerned over the condition of the banks, the investment market, and the like. It was the conservatives, on the other hand, who represented the greater moral indignation and rallied behind themselves the inspirational literature of American life; and this not merely because the conservatives were now the party of the opposition, but because things were being done of such drastic novelty that they seemed to breach all the inherited rules, not merely of practicality but of morality itself. Hence, if one wishes to look for utopianism in the 1930's, for an exalted faith in the intangibles of morals and character, and for moral indignation of the kind that had once been chiefly the prerogative of the reformers, one will find it far more readily in the editorials of the great conservative newspapers than in the literature of the New Deal. If one seeks for the latter-day equivalent of the first George Kennan, warning the people of San Francisco that it would do them no good to have a prosperous town if in gaining it they lost their souls, one will find it most readily in the 1930's among those who opposed federal relief for the unemployed because it would destroy their characters or who were shocked by the devaluation of the dollar, not because they always had a clear conception of its consequences, but above all because it smacked to them of dirtiness and dishonesty. In the past it had been the conservatives who controlled the settlement of the country, set up its great industrial and communications plant, and founded the fabulous system of production and distribution upon which the country prided itself, while the reformers pointed to the human costs, the sacrifice of principles, and drew blueprints to show how the job could be better done. Now, however, it was the reformers who fed the jobless or found them jobs, saved the banks, humanized industry, built houses and schools and public buildings, rescued farmers from bankruptcy, and restored hope—while the conservatives, expropriated at once from their customary control of affairs and from their practical role, invoked sound principles, worried about the Constitution, boggled over details, pleaded for better morals, and warned against tyranny.

Lamentably, most of the conservative thinking of the New Deal era was hollow and cliché-ridden. What seems most striking about the New Deal itself, however, was that all its ferment of practical change produced a very slight literature of political criticism. While the changes of the Progressive era had produced many significant books of pamphleteering or thoughtful analyses of society—the writings of such men as Croly, Lippmann, Weyl, Brooks Adams, Brandeis, the muckrakers, Socialist critics like W. J. Ghent and William English Walling—the New Deal produced no comparable body of political writing that would survive the day's headlines. In part this was simply a matter of time: the Progressive era lasted over a dozen years, and most of the significant writing it engendered came during its later phases, particularly after 1910; whereas the dynamic phase of the New Deal was concentrated in the six hectic years from 1933 to 1938. Perhaps still more important is the fact that the New Deal brought with it such a rapid bureaucratic expansion and such a complex multitude of problems that it created an immense market for the skills of reform-minded Americans from law, journalism, politics, and the professoriat. The men who might otherwise have been busy analyzing the meaning of events were caught up in the huge expanding bureaucracy and put to work drafting laws that would pass the courts, lobbying with refractory Congressmen, or relocating sharecroppers.

To this generalization there is one noteworthy exception: in his two books, *The Symbols of Government* and *The Folklore of Capitalism,* Thurman Arnold wrote works of great brilliance and wit and considerable permanent significance—better books, I believe, than any of the political criticism of the Progressive era.[17] But what do we find in these works, the most advanced of the New Deal camp? We find a sharp and sustained attack upon ideologies, rational principles, and moralism in politics. We find, in short, the theoretical equivalent of F. D. R.'s opportunistic virtuosity in practical politics—a theory that attacks theories. For Arnold's books, which were of course directed largely against the ritualistic thinking of the conservatives of the 1930's, might stand equally well as an attack upon that moralism which we found so insistent in the thinking of Progressivism.

Arnold's chief concern was with the disparities between the way society actually works and the mythology through which the sound lawyers, economists, and moralists attempt to understand it. His books are an explanation of the ritualistic and functionally irrational character of most of the superficially rational principles by which society lives. At the time his books were written, the necessity of coping with a breakdown in the actual workings of the economy had suddenly confronted men with the operational uselessness of a great many accepted words and ideas. The language of politics, economics, and law had itself become so uncertain that there was a new vogue of books on semantics and of works attempting to break "the tyranny of words," a literature of which Arnold's books were by far the most important. The greater part of Arnold's task was to examine, and to satirize,

---

[17] Thurman W. Arnold: *The Symbols of Government* (New Haven, 1935), *The Folklore of Capitalism* (New Haven, 1937). By 1941 the first of these works had gone through five printings; the second, fourteen.

the orthodox conservative thinking of the moment. This is not our main concern, but what is of primary interest here is the extent to which Arnold's thinking departs from, and indeed on occasion attacks, earlier Progressivism. The deviation of Arnold's system of values from the classic values of American Progressivism was clear from his very terminology. I noted, in discussing the Progressive climate of opinion, the existence of a prevailing vocabulary of civic morals that reflected the disinterested thinking and the selfless action that was expected of the good citizen. The key words of Progressivism were terms like *patriotism, citizen, democracy, law, character, conscience, soul, morals, service, duty, shame, disgrace, sin,* and *selfishness*—terms redolent of the sturdy Protestant Anglo-Saxon moral and intellectual roots of the Progressive uprising. A search for the key words of Arnold's books yields: *needs, organization, humanitarian, results, technique, institution, realistic, discipline, morale, skill, expert, habits, practical, leadership*—a vocabulary revealing a very different constellation of values arising from economic emergency and the imperatives of a bureaucracy.

Although primarily concerned with the conservatives of the present, Arnold paid his respects to the reformers of the past often enough to render a New Dealer's portrait of earlier Progressivism. He saw the reformers of the past as having occupied themselves with verbal and moral battles that left the great working organizations of society largely untouched. "Wherever the reformers are successful—whenever they see their direct primaries, their antitrust laws, or whatever else they base their hopes on, in actual operation—the great temporal institutions adapt themselves, leaving the older reformers disillusioned, like Lincoln Steffens, and a newer set carrying on the banner." [18] Respectable people with humanitarian values, Arnold thought, had characteristically made the mistake of ignoring the fact that "it is not logic but organizations which rule an organized society"; therefore they selected logical principles, rather than organizations, as the objects of their loyalties. Most liberal reform movements attempt to make institutions practice what they preach, in situations where, if this injunction were followed, the functions of the institutions could not be performed. [19] Where the Progressives had been troubled about the development of institutions and organizations, Arnold's argument often appeared to be an apotheosis of them.

At one point or another, Arnold had critical observations to make on most of the staple ideas of Progressive thinking. *The Folklore of Capitalism* opened with a satire on "the thinking man," to whom most of the discourse of rational politics was directed; and the thinking man was hardly more than a caricatured version of the good citizen who was taken as the central figure in most Progressive thinking. While Progressive publicists had devoted much of their time to preachments against what they called "lawlessness,"

---

[18] *The Symbols of Government,* p. 124.   [19] *The Folklore of Capitalism,* pp. 375, 384.

one of the central themes of Arnold's books was an analysis of law and legal thinking showing that law and respectability were so defined that a good many of the real and necessary functions of society had to go on outside the legal framework.[20] Similarly anti-Progressive was his attack on the anti-trust laws—a source of some amusement when he was later put in charge of the enforcement of these laws. But Arnold did not deny that the laws, as they had been interpreted by reformers, had had some use. Their chief use, as he saw it, had been that they permitted the organization of industry to go on while offering comfort to those who were made unhappy by the process. They had, then, a practical significance, but a far different one from that which the reformers had tried to give them. The reformers, how-ever, had had no real strategy with which to oppose the great trusts: "The reason why these attacks [against industrial organizations] always ended with a ceremony of atonement, but few practical results, lay in the fact that there were no new organizations growing up to take over the functions of those under attack. The opposition was never able to build up its own commis-sary and its service of supply. It was well supplied with orators and econ-omists, but it lacked practical organizers. A great cooperative movement in America might have changed the power of the industrial empire. Preaching against it, however, simply resulted in counterpreaching. And the reason for this was that the reformers themselves were caught in the same creeds which supported the institutions they were trying to reform. Obsessed with a moral attitude toward society, they thought in Utopias. They were inter-ested in systems of government. Philosophy was for them more important than opportunism and so they achieved in the end philosophy rather than opportunity." [21]

Arnold professed more admiration for the tycoons who had organized American industry and against whom the Progressives had grown indignant than he did for the reformers themselves. He spoke with much indulgence of Rockefeller, Carnegie, and Ford, and compared John L. Lewis with such men as examples of skillful organizers who had had to sidestep recog-nized scruples. "Actual observation of human society . . . indicates that great constructive achievements in human organization have been accom-plished by unscrupulous men who violated most of the principles which we cherish." [22] The leaders of industrial organization ignored legal, humani-tarian, and economic principles. "They built on their mistakes, their action was opportunistic, they experimented with human material and with little

---

[20] Cf. *The Symbols of Government*, p. 34: "It is part of the function of 'Law' to give recognition to ideals representing the exact opposite of established conduct . . . the function of law is not so much to guide society as to comfort it. Belief in fundamental principles of law does not necessarily lead to an orderly society. Such a belief is as often at the back of revolt or disorder."

[21] *The Folklore of Capitalism*, p. 220.   [22] *The Symbols of Government*, p. 5.

regard for social justice. Yet they raised the level of productive capacity beyond the dreams of their fathers." [23]

Not surprisingly Arnold also had a good word for the politicians, who, for all their lack of social values and for all the imperfections in their aims and vision, are "the only persons who understand the techniques of government." One would prefer a government in the hands of disinterested men, to be sure, but such men are so devoted to and satisfied with the development of good principles that they fail to develop skills, and hence fail to constitute "a competent governing class." Hence society is too often left with a choice between demagogues and psychopaths on one side, or, on the other, "kindly but uneducated Irishmen whose human sympathies give them an instinctive understanding of what people like." [24] Several pages of *The Folklore of Capitalism* were given to a defense of the political machines for the common sense with which they attack the task of government and for the humanitarian spirit in which their work is conducted.[25]

Taken by itself, Arnold's work, with its skepticism about the right-thinking citizen, its rejection of fixed moral principles and disinterested rationality in politics, its pragmatic temper, its worship of accomplishment, its apotheosis of organization and institutional discipline, and its defense of the political machines, may exaggerate the extent of the difference between the New Deal and pre-war Progressivism, but it does point sharply to the character of that difference.[26]

---

[23] Ibid., p. 125.   [24] Ibid., pp. 21–2.

[25] *The Folklore of Capitalism*, pp. 367–72; cf. pp. 43, 114–15; cf. *The Symbols of Government*, pp. 239–40.

[26] There are many points at which Arnold yields to the need to seem hard-boiled and at which (rather like F. D. R. himself) he becomes flippant over serious questions. While such lapses have a good deal of symptomatic importance, I do not wish to appear to portray his writing as an attack upon political morality as such: it was not an effort to destroy political morality, but to satirize a particular code of morality that he considered obsolescent and obstructive, and to substitute for it a new one, the precise outlines of which were obviously vague. In my judgment, Arnold did not even successfully pose, much less answer, the very real and important questions that were suggested by his books concerning the relations between morals and politics, or between reason and politics. For a searching criticism see the essay by Sidney Hook in his *Reason, Social Myths, and Democracy* (New York, 1950), pp. 41–51 and the ensuing exchange between Hook and Arnold, pp. 51–61, which to my mind succeeds only in underscoring Arnold's philosophical difficulties. The great value of Arnold's books lies not in the little they have to say about political ethics, but in their descriptive, satirical, and analytical approach to the political thinking of his time, and in their statement of the working mood of a great many New Dealers.

I should perhaps add that my own comments in this area are not intended to be more than descriptive, for there are large questions of political ethics that I too have not attempted to answer. In contrasting the pragmatic and opportunistic tone of the New Deal with the insistent moralism of the Progressives, it has not been my purpose to suggest an invidious comparison that would, at every point, favor the New Deal. Neither is it my purpose to imply that the political morals of the New Dealers were inferior to those of their opponents. My essential interest is in the fact that the emergency that gave rise to

To emphasize, as I have done, the pragmatic and "hard" side of the New Deal is not to forget that it had its "soft" side. Not all its spokesmen shared Arnold's need to pose as hard-boiled.[27] No movement of such scope and power could exist without having its ideals and its ideologies, even its sentimentalities. The New Deal had its literature of inspiration and indignation, its idealistc fervor, its heroes and villains. The difference I hope to establish is that its indignation was directed far more against callousness and waste, far less against corruption or monopoly, than the indignation of the Progressives, and that its inspiration was much more informed by engineering, administration, and economics, considerably less by morals and uplift. For the New Deal not only brought with it a heartening rediscovery of the humane instincts of the country; it also revived the old American interest in practical achievement, in doing things with the physical world, in the ideal that had inspired the great tycoons and industry-builders of the Gilded Age but that afterwards had commonly been dismissed by sensitive men as the sphere only of philistines and money-grubbers.

At the core of the New Deal, then, was not a philosophy (F. D. R. could identify himself philosophically only as a Christian and a democrat), but an attitude, suitable for practical politicians, administrators, and technicians, but uncongenial to the moralism that the Progressives had for the most part shared with their opponents. At some distance from the center of the New Deal, but vital to its public support, were other types of feeling. In some quarters there was a revival of populistic sentiment and the old popular demonology, which F. D. R. and men like Harold Ickes occasionally played up to, chiefly in campaign years, and which Harry Truman later reflected in his baiting of Wall Street. Along with this came another New

---

the New Deal also gave rise to a transvaluation of values, and that the kind of moralism that I have identified with the dominant patterns of thought among the Progressives was inherited not so much by their successors among the New Dealers, who tended to repudiate them, as by the foes of the New Deal.

[27] I have been referred to David Lilienthal's *TVA: Democracy on the March* (New York, 1944) as an illustration of the idealism and inspirational force of the New Deal, and as a work more representative of its spirit than the writings of Thurman Arnold. Lilienthal's book is indeed more unabashedly humanitarian, more inspirational, more concerned with maintaining democracy in the face of technical and administrative change, more given to idealization of the people. It also shows, however, a dedication to certain values, readily discernible in Arnold, that would have been of marginal importance to all but a few of the Progressives. Like Arnold, Lilienthal is pleading the cause of organization, engineering, management, and the attitudes that go with them, as opposed to what he calls the "fog" of conventional ideologies. He appeals to administrative experience, technology, science, and *expertise,* finds that efficient devices of management "give a lift to the human spirit," and asserts that "there is almost nothing, however fantastic that (given competent organization) a team of engineers, scientists, and administrators cannot do today." (Pocket Book ed., New York, 1945, pp. ix, x, 3, 4, 8, 9, 79, 115.) In the light of this philosophy it is easier to see that Lilienthal's more recent defense of big business does not represent a conversion to a new philosophy but simply an ability to find in private organization many of the same virtues that as TVA administrator he found in public enterprise.

Deal phenomenon, a kind of pervasive tenderness for the underdog, for the Okies, the sharecroppers, the characters in John Steinbeck's novels, the subjects who posed for the FSA photographers, for what were called, until a revulsion set in, "the little people." With this there came, too, a kind of folkish nationalism, quickened no doubt by federal patronage of letters and the arts, but inspired at bottom by a real rediscovery of hope in America and its people and institutions. For after the concentration camps, the Nuremberg Laws, Guernica, and (though not everyone saw this so readily) the Moscow trials, everything in America seemed fresh and hopeful, Main Street seemed innocent beyond all expectation, and in time Babbitt became almost lovable. Where Progressivism had capitalized on a growing sense of the ugliness under the successful surface of American life, the New Deal flourished on a sense of the human warmth and the technological potentialities that could be found under the surface of its inequities and its post-depression poverty. On the far fringe there was also a small number of real ideologues, aroused not only by the battle over domestic reform but by the rise of world fascism. Although many of them were fellow travelers and Communists, we stand in serious danger of misunderstanding the character of the New Deal if we overemphasize the influence of this fringe either upon the New Deal core or upon the American people at large. It has now become both fashionable and, for some, convenient to exaggerate the impact of the extreme left upon the thinking of the country in the 1930's. No doubt it will always be possible to do so, for Marxism had a strong if ephemeral impact upon many intellectuals; but the amateur Marxism of the period had only a marginal effect upon the thought and action of either the administrative core of the New Deal or the great masses of Americans.[28] For the people at large—that is, for those who needed it most—the strength of the New Deal was based above all upon its ability to get results.

---

[28] Granville Hicks, in his *Where We Came Out* (New York, 1954), chapter iv, makes a sober effort to show how limited was the Communist influence even in those circles which were its special province. A complementary error to the now fashionable exaggeration of the Communist influence is to exaggerate its ties to the New Deal. Of course Communists played an active part in the spurt of labor organization until the experienced labor leaders expelled them, and in time Communists also succeeded in infiltrating the bureaucracy, with what shocking results we now know. But it was the depression that began to put American Communism on its feet and the New Deal that helped to kill it. The Communists, as consistent ideologues, were always contemptuous of the New Deal. At first they saw fascism in it, and when they gave up this line of criticism during the Popular Front period, they remained contemptuous of its frank experimentalism, its lack of direction, its unsystematic character, and of course its compromises.

IX

The United States Enters World War II: Did the U. S. Maneuver Japan into the Attack on Pearl Harbor?

INTRODUCTION

As Wayne S. Cole has pointed out in an able analysis of the literature dealing with American entry into World War II, the controversy among historians regarding this question is to some extent a continuation of the debate that raged before Pearl Harbor between "interventionists" and "non-interventionists." The arguments employed between 1939 and 1941 by defenders and opponents of the administration's foreign policy have reappeared in the works of scholarship dealing with these years. As a matter of fact, some of the authors who have written on this subject were personally involved in the pre-Pearl Harbor controversy regarding the relations of the United States with the belligerent nations.[1]

The historians who have defended the foreign policy of the Roosevelt administration in the two years before Pearl Harbor (Cole uses the term "internationalist" to describe them) view the Axis powers as having constituted a threat to the security of the United States and have taken the position that the question of American entry into the war was by 1941 really beyond our power to control. In their opinion, the policies pursued by Roosevelt in 1940 and 1941 vis-à-vis Germany and Japan were, on the whole, the only policies consistent with our security and our principles. Regarding Germany as the greater threat to the United States, American policy-makers, they contend, hoped to avoid war with Japan, provided that this could be accomplished without jeopardizing our security and our interests and without abandoning our friends in the Far East. In the end, they assert, this proved impossible, and although the administration was aware that Japan would strike somewhere, it was genuinely surprised when the blow fell on Pearl Harbor.

The revisionists, by contrast, do not believe that the Axis powers were a threat to the security of the United States and contend that the decision for war or for peace was the administration's to make. Failing to provoke Germany into war despite a series of unneutral acts, Roosevelt, the revisionists argue, led the United States into the war through the back door by maneuvering Japan into the attack on Pearl Harbor. The United States, in their view, was unprepared for this attack because of the incompetence, or worse, of its civilian and military leaders in Washington.

The revisionist and the internationalist positions regarding American entry into World War II are represented here by Charles C. Tansill and Herbert Feis, respectively. Professor Tansill is the author of an impressive number of books in the field of American diplomatic history, including America Goes to War *(1938), generally regarded as the best of the revision-*

---

[1] Wayne S. Cole, "American Entry into World War II: A Historiographical Appraisal," *Mississippi Valley Historical Review*, XLIII (March 1957), 600–601.

ist books dealing with World War I. Tansill's revisionist interpretation of
Japanese-American relations between 1937 and 1941, which follows, is taken
from his Back Door to War: Roosevelt's Foreign Policy, 1933–1941 and his
essay in Perpetual War for Perpetual Peace (this essay is a somewhat con-
densed version of the treatment of the same subject in Back Door to War).

Herbert Feis, who like Tansill has contributed importantly to the field of
American diplomatic history, served as an economic advisor in the Department of State between 1931 and 1943 and as special consultant to the secretary of war from 1944 to 1946. His The Road to Pearl Harbor (1950) is a
study of the relations between the United States and Japan from 1937 to
December 7, 1941. In the selection that follows Feis responds to some of the
revisionist arguments concerning the events preceding the Japanese attack
on Pearl Harbor.

The United States Moves to
War Against Japan

Charles C. Tansill

1. PRESIDENT ROOSEVELT DELIVERS
A QUARANTINE SPEECH DIRECTED
AGAINST JAPAN

Grew's dispatch* reached the Department of State on October 5. On this
same day President Roosevelt made a famous address in Chicago in which
he advocated a quarantine against aggressor nations.[1] His words of criticism
and warning were directed chiefly against Japan and their baleful effect was
all that Grew had feared. It was really big talk in a high key. He was
actually far more worried about party reverses at home than about Japanese
movements in Manchuria. An economic recession in the United States had
made it clear that the big ballyhoo of New Deal politicians had suddenly

---

From *Perpetual War for Perpetual Peace*. Edited by Harry Elmer Barnes. Published
by The Caxton Printers, Ltd., Caldwell, Idaho. Used by special permission of the copyright owners. Pp. 289–307, 310–313.

* Editor's note: A dispatch by Grew of September 15, 1937, advising against American
action that might antagonize Japan.

[1] *Foreign Relations: Japan, 1931–1941*, I, 379–83.

turned very sour. The Morgenthau diaries give indisputable proof of the deep concern the administration felt with regard to the wide break in the economic structure of the nation.[2]

Joined with this bad news from the economic front was the hostile reaction in the press over the appointment of Senator Hugo Black to the Supreme Court. In September it was made known that Mr. Black had once hidden his face under the wide hood of a Klansman. In dismay he fled to Europe and President Roosevelt found it convenient to make a hurried trip to the Far West. It was highly expedient for him to make some address that would divert public attention from the widespread effects of economic recession and to cover the flight of the nimble Justice Black. A sharp denunciation of the Japanese advance in North China would draw a big herring across a noisome trail and, if it led to eventual war, there was the bright consolation that the war powers of the President are so indefinable and far-reaching that they would insure a long period of dictatorship.

The quarantine speech of October 5 had many macabre overtones designed to frighten the American people. Many parts of the world were experiencing a "reign of terror," and the "landmarks and traditions which have marked the progress of civilization toward a condition of law, order and justice" were being "wiped away." "Innocent peoples and nations" were being "cruelly sacrificed to a greed for power and supremacy" which was "devoid of all sense of justice and humane consideration." If this sad condition of affairs existed in other parts of the world it was vain for anyone to "imagine that America will escape, that it may expect mercy, that this Western Hemisphere will not be attacked, and that it will continue tranquilly and peacefully to carry on the ethics and the arts of civilization."

This attempt to frighten the American people and thus make them forget conditions at home was only partly successful. It is true that Justice Black was soon a "forgotten man" but business conditions grew so steadily worse that they could not escape notice. Moreover, a large part of the American press expressed the view that, if conditions abroad were so bad, it would be wise for America to adopt an isolationist attitude and stay away from trouble. There is no doubt that the President was "disappointed by the failure of the people to respond to his Chicago speech."[3] It was a bit of globaloney with such a strong smell that it took some years for American nostrils to get accustomed to it.

It is true, nonetheless, that the President's challenge to Japan marked a tragic turning point in our relations with that country. He had inaugurated a policy of pressure that eventually pushed America down the road to Pearl Harbor. Japan erected the first milestone along this road by the bombing of the *Panay* on December 12, 1937. A prompt apology and a large in-

---

[2] "The Morgenthau Diaries," *Collier's*, CXX (October 4, 1947), 20; *ibid.*, CXX (October 25, 1947), 85.

[3] James F. Byrnes, *Speaking Frankly* (New York: Harper & Brothers, 1947), p. 6.

demnity indicated that the Foreign Office was still anxious for peace, but the fact that such an incident had occurred gave support to the President's program of pressure upon Japan.

2. THE PRESIDENT PUSHES A PROGRAM
OF PRESSURE UPON JAPAN

The first item in this new program aimed at Japan was the sending of Admiral Royal E. Ingersoll to London in the latter part of December, 1937, with instructions to "explore with the British what we could do if we both found ourselves involved in war in the Far East with Japan." [4] When asked why he was sent to London in 1937 the Admiral replied that "everybody knew" that "sooner or later, we were all going to be involved in a war in the Pacific which would include the Dutch, the Chinese possibly, the Russians, the British, and ourselves." The only tangible result of these Anglo-American conversations in London was a "distribution of codes and ciphers." [5] It should be remembered, in this regard, that similar secret conversations between British and French officials in 1905 constituted the first link in the chain that bound the British to a policy of war with Germany in 1914.

While Admiral Ingersoll was engaged in conversations in London, the President had a press conference on January 8, 1938, in which he expressed the significant opinion that the time had arrived for "Congress to enact legislation aimed at the equalization of the burdens of possible war so that the whole nation will engage in war if we unfortunately have one." [6] Congress did not follow this suggestion. A majority of the members of both houses were still thinking of peace, not war. But the martial mood of the President and Secretary of State became apparent on July 1 when the Chief of the Office of Arms and Munitions Control sent a letter to "148 persons and Companies manufacturing airplane parts" stating that the "Government of the United States is strongly opposed to the sale of airplanes or aeronautical equipment which would materially aid or encourage" the practice of "bombing civilian populations from the air." The Japanese had been guilty of such a practice and therefore the Department of State would "with great regret issue any licenses authorizing exportation, direct or indirect, of any aircraft, aircraft armament, aircraft engines" or aircraft accessories to

---

[4] Testimony of Admiral R. E. Ingersoll during the *Hearings Before the Joint Committee on the Investigation of the Pearl Harbor Attack,* 79 Cong., 2 sess. (39 parts; Washington, D. C.: Government Printing Office, 1946), IX, 4272–73. (The *Hearings* will hereinafter be designated *Pearl Harbor Attack.*)

[5] *Ibid.,* pp. 4274–77.

[6] *The Public Papers and Addresses of Franklin Delano Roosevelt;* edited by Samuel I. Rosenman (13 vols.; New York: Random House, Inc., 1941), VII, 67.

Japan.[7] This "moral embargo" invoked against Japan led to further measures that forged an iron ring around that island empire and pushed it
strongly in the direction of war with the United States.

In September, 1938, the President was so sure that the United States
would soon "get into war" that he sent Harry Hopkins on a tour of airplane factories to see how production could be expedited. When Hopkins
returned to Washington he was visited by Brigadier General George C.
Marshall, who was later made Chief of Staff through the influence of Hopkins and Pershing. Marshall quickly caught the belligerent mood of the
circle close to the President and it was not long before "several millions of
dollars of WPA funds were transferred (secretly) to start making machine
tools for the manufacture of small arms ammunition." [8]

While America was thus secretly preparing for what the President regarded as an inevitable war, the Japanese government was making pacific
overtures to the United States. On May 16, 1939, a prominent Japanese made
an important approach to Ambassador Grew concerning an improvement
in Japanese-American relations. If the "democratic nations, especially the
United States, could indicate to Japan that restoration of good relations
with Japan is desired and that the way is open for Japan to align herself
with the democratic nations, . . . those Japanese who are working for precisely those objectives would have their hand greatly strengthened." [9] On
the following day the Japanese Minister of Foreign Affairs, Hachiro Arita,
commented upon the dangerous activities of the Soviet government and the
negotiations then going on in Moscow for an alliance between Britain,
France, and the Soviet government. He then remarked that "there had been
a suggestion that he give Mr. Grew an assurance that Japan would withhold any action to 'strengthen the Anti-Comintern Pact' until Mr. Grew
returned to Washington and had an opportunity to discuss with his Government the possibility of making to Japan some 'gesture of welcome.' " Arita
stressed the fact that Japan was "very anxious to avoid involvement in the
affairs of Europe," but it was impossible to ignore the fact that "Russia
straddled Europe and Asia, and that, whether Japan liked it or not, its
[Russia's] policies and actions form a bridge by which events in the Far
East and in Europe act and react on each other." It was possible that the
danger of a tripartite pact between Britain, France, and Russia might compel Japan to enter into some arrangement with Germany and Italy. He
could assure Mr. Grew, however, that the agreement under discussion with

---

[7] Joseph C. Green, Chief of the Office of Arms and Munitions Control, to 148 Persons
and Companies Manufacturing Airplane Parts, July 1, 1938, *Foreign Relations, Japan:
1931–1941*, II, 201–2.

[8] Robert E. Sherwood, *Roosevelt and Hopkins* (New York: Harper & Brothers, 1948),
pp. 100–101.

[9] Eugene H. Dooman to Secretary Hull, Tokyo, June 7, 1939, *Pearl Harbor Attack*,
Part XX, pp. 4144–64.

Germany and Italy "would contain no military, political or economic clauses." [10]

On May 18, 1939, Grew had a long talk with Arita who once more insisted that an alliance between Britain, France, and Russia would probably push Japan into a closer understanding with Germany and Italy. He was equally insistent that Japan, in joining hands with Germany and Italy, had "no other purpose than to combat the destructive activities of the Comintern." If the United States, "not understanding the true position of Japan on this point, should base her future policies on such misunderstanding, it would bring about a deplorable situation not only respecting the relations between the United States and Japan but also in respect of the peace of the world." [11]

The next step by the Japanese government was an invitation to the United States to adopt a program whereby the two nations would jointly attempt to find a peaceful solution of the political differences that were leading to war in Europe. In discussing this matter with Prime Minister Hiranuma, Mr. Dooman, the American chargé d'affaires in Tokyo, asked the pertinent question whether the head of the Japanese cabinet "believed it likely that the American people would look with favor on American collaboration with Japan in approaching the difficulties in Europe when Japan herself was considered to be guilty of the same acts of which Germany and Italy stood condemned." Hiranuma replied that "if the Powers could come together to find by negotiation a solution of the world's troubles these issues involving American rights in China could be disposed of without difficulty." With reference to the conflict in the Far East he expressed the hope that "the American Government at least realized that Japan had not intended or expected to engage in war with China." [12]

Secretary Hull's answer, which did not arrive in Tokyo until the end of July, was negative and tart. Japan was advised to use its "influence toward discouraging among European governments, especially those governments with which your Government may have special relations, the taking of any action, or the pursuance of any policy, that might endanger the general peace." The establishment of world peace was made more difficult by "the continuance of armed conflict" in the Far East. The intimation was clearly given that if Japan was sincere in her desire to help the cause of peace in Europe she should give a better example in eastern Asia.[13]

In order further to emphasize the hostile attitude of the United States

---

[10] *Ibid.*, pp. 4148–50.

[11] Ambassador Grew to Secretary Hull, Tokyo, May 18, 1939, *Foreign Relations, Japan: 1931–1941*, II, 1–5.

[12] Mr. Dooman to Secretary Hull, Tokyo, May 23, 1939, *Pearl Harbor Attack*, Part XX, p. 4139.

[13] The Secretary of State to the Japanese Prime Minister, *Foreign Relations, Japan: 1931–1941*, II, 6–8.

toward Japan, the Department of State, on July 26, 1939, gave notice to the Japanese government that, after six months, the treaty of February 21, 1911, would expire.[14] This action was a severe blow to a Japanese cabinet that was desperately striving to arrive at some understanding with the United States. But Prime Minister Hiranuma disregarded this sharp rebuff and made another attempt to effect more friendly relations between Japan and the United States. On August 26, 1939, the Japanese ambassador (Horinouchi) had a long conversation with Secretary Hull. He gave assurances that his government "had decided to abandon any further negotiations with Germany and Italy relative to closer relations under the anti-Comintern Pact to which they have been parties for some time." After this conciliatory statement, he reiterated his "personal desire to clear up any misunderstanding or differences between our two countries and to restore the friendly relations heretofore existing." Mr. Hull's answer was one more example of his usual moral platitudes and the Japanese gestures of good will were in vain.[15]

While Secretary Hull was prating of peace, President Roosevelt was constantly thinking of war with Japan. Ambassador Grew saw this fact clearly in September, 1939. During the course of a conference with the President he took pains to point out that, if America placed an embargo upon oil exports to Japan, the result might be a Japanese effort to take the Dutch East Indies and thereby control the rich oil resources of Borneo. The President's reply showed that he was already thinking of war. If Japan decided upon such a step, American naval forces could "easily intercept her fleet." [16]

But Grew wished to prevent rather than provoke war with Japan. While the President was talking this belligerent bombast, Grew was confiding to his diary that the Department of State should "offer the Japanese a *modus vivendi*" and then commence negotiations for a new commercial treaty. In Japan the Shidehara policy of conciliation had once existed: "It can exist again." [17] To Grew the Japanese program, with its insistence upon "strategic protection against a future attack by Soviet Russia," did not appear too unreasonable. If America wished to change this program it should not try to do so through the employment of sanctions: "There must be no tone of threat in our attitude." [18]

It is evident that Grew did not appreciate the fact that the President's dislike of Japan had gone so deep and spread so far that it would lead inevitably to war. In defiance of Grew's advice against sanctions, a White House statement was issued once more invoking a moral embargo upon the

---

[14] Secretary Hull to the Japanese Ambassador, July 26, 1939, *Peace and War*, p. 475.

[15] Memorandum of a conversation between Secretary Hull and the Japanese ambassador (Horinouchi), August 26, 1939, *ibid.*, pp. 480–82.

[16] Herbert Feis, *The Road to Pearl Harbor* (Princeton, N. J.: Princeton University Press, 1950), p. 41, quoting from the manuscript diary of Ambassador Grew.

[17] *Ibid.*, p. 42.   [18] Grew, *Ten Years in Japan*, pp. 296–303.

shipment to Japan of "airplanes, aeronautical equipment and materials essential to airplane manufacture." [19] This statement of December 2 was followed by another one of December 20. This later pronouncement issued from the Department of State and contained the significant formula that "national interest suggests that for the time being there should be no further delivery to certain countries of plans, plants, manufacturing rights, or technical information required for the production of high quality aviation gasoline." [20] In 1940 there was a series of statements issued by the Administrator of Export Control which indicated a drastic curtailment of exports to Japan.[21] If embargoes could produce war the administration was determined to overlook no opportunity to exert pressure upon Japan along that line.

3. BRITAIN AND FRANCE ADOPT A POLICY OF APPEASEMENT TOWARD JAPAN

American pressure upon Japan was followed by Japanese pressure upon Britain and France. On March 30, 1940, Japan set up a "new Central Government of China" to be headed by Wang Ching-wei. Secretary Hull immediately announced that the Department of State would continue to recognize the government of Chiang Kai-shek "as the Government of China." [22] But the British Foreign Office was more conciliatory. On March 28, Sir Robert Craigie, the British ambassador in Tokyo, delivered an address in which he stated that Britain and Japan were "striving for the same objective, namely, a lasting peace and the preservation of our institutions from extraneous, subversive influences." [23] This address keynoted British policy. On July 17 the Burma Road was closed to shipments of war matériel to China.[24] France had already acceded to demands for a similar embargo upon supplies going to Chiang Kai-shek through Indochina. The Nationalist government in China was being effectively shut off from aid that was essential to her continuance in the war against Japan.

4. JAPAN CONCLUDES AN ALLIANCE WITH THE ROME–BERLIN AXIS

While Japan was exerting pressure upon Britain and France she was making overtures to the Rome-Berlin Axis. An alliance with these European dictatorships had been long in the making. Its most important Japanese sponsor was General Hiroshi Oshima, the Japanese ambassador to Germany. He and Ribbentrop were on intimate terms. In the summer of 1938 Ribbentrop in-

---

[19] *Foreign Relations, Japan: 1931–1941*, II, 202.   [20] *Ibid.*, pp. 203–4.   [21] *Ibid.*, 807–8.
[22] *Ibid.*, pp. 59–60.   [23] London *Times*, March 29, 1940.
[24] *Documents on American Foreign Relations, 1940–1941;* edited by S. Shepard Jones and Denys P. Myers (Boston: World Peace Foundation, 1941), III, 270–71.

quired if Japan would be willing to sign a treaty aimed at all the potential enemies of the proposed Rome-Berlin-Tokyo triangle.[25] Tokyo rejected this broad proposal [26] and in February, 1939, Prince Ito was sent to Berlin to acquaint Ribbentrop with the decision that Japan wished to limit the proposed treaty to action against Russia alone.[27]

In order to speed a decision by Japan to enter into an alliance with the Rome-Berlin Axis, Heinrich Stahmer hurried to Tokyo and insisted that the prime purpose in effecting the new political alignment was to keep America out of war.[28] Stahmer succeeded in silencing all Japanese opposition to the tripartite pact which was signed with great pomp in Berlin on September 27, 1940.[29] Article III pointed straight at the United States: "Japan, Germany and Italy . . . undertake to assist one another with all political, economic and military means when one of the Contracting Parties is attacked by a power at present not involved in the European War or in the Sino-Japanese Conflict." [30] There is evidence, however, that Japan extracted from Stahmer a secret oral understanding that she retain for herself the right to decide whether the *casus foederis* existed in any situation that might arise.[31]

5. JAPAN IS READY TO SACRIFICE HER POSITION
IN CHINA FOR THE SAKE OF PEACE
WITH THE UNITED STATES

But this tripartite pact of September 27, 1940, did not mean that Japan had abandoned all hope of a satisfactory arrangement with the United States. Quite the contrary! In November, 1940, Foreign Minister Matsuoka asked Bishop James E. Walsh, Superior General of the Catholic Foreign Mission Society of Maryknoll, New York, and Father J. M. Drought, of the same order, to undertake a special mission to Washington in order to impress upon the President and Secretary Hull the fact that the Japanese government "wished to negotiate a peace agreement: (1) an agreement to nullify their participation in the Axis Pact . . . (2) a guarantee to recall all military forces from China and to restore to China its geographical and political integrity." Other conditions bearing upon the relations of Japan and the United States were to be explored and agreed upon "in the conversations that it was hoped would ensue."

Bishop Walsh and Father Drought then had a conference with General

---

[25] Interrogation of General Oshima, February 4, 1946, *Record of Proceedings of the International Military Tribunal for the Far East* (Washington, D. C.: Department of State, 1946), Exhibit No. 497, pp. 6050–54.

[26] *Ibid.*   [27] *Ibid.*, pp. 6063–71.   [28] *Ibid.*, Exhibits Nos. 549, 550, 553, pp. 6323–93.

[29] William L. Shirer, *Berlin Diary* (New York: Alfred A. Knopf, 1941), pp. 532–37.

[30] *Foreign Relations, Japan: 1931–1941*, II, 165–66.

[31] H. L. Trefousse, *Germany and American Neutrality, 1939–1941* (New York: Bookman Associates, 1951), p. 71.

Muto, the director of the Central Bureau of Military Affairs, who assured them that "he and his associates in the Japanese Army were in accord with the efforts to reach a peace agreement."

Bishop Walsh and Father Drought hurried to Washington where (on January 23, 1941) they placed the whole matter before President Roosevelt and Secretary Hull during a long conference of more than two hours. They were told that the matter would be "taken under advisement," [32] and thus ended an anxious effort on the part of the Japanese government to find a path to peace, even though this path led to a renunciation of Japan's objectives in China and a tremendous loss of face.* It seems quite possible that the Far Eastern Military Tribunal brought to trial the wrong persons. It might have been better if the tribunal had held its sessions in Washington.

6. BLUEPRINT FOR ANGLO–AMERICAN CO-OPERATION
IN THE WAR ON JAPAN

Instead of acting upon the proposals of Bishop Walsh and Father Drought, the President and Secretary Hull initiated Joint Staff conferences in Washington from January to March, 1941. Delegations from Britain, Australia, Canada, and New Zealand surveyed with American representatives the many questions involved in the defense of the Pacific area against Japanese attack. During the session, which resulted in the ABC-1 Staff Agreement, the British delegation ardently argued that the defense of Singapore was so essential that the United States should be willing to divide the Pacific Fleet for that purpose. Although this proposal was rejected, the agreement did outline for American task forces some important operations that would be beneficial for Britain in the event both powers were involved in war with Japan.

The ABC-1 Staff Agreement was promptly approved by the Secretaries of the Navy and War; the President gave it no explicit approval.[33] It was soon apparent, however, that American military plans were profoundly affected by it.[34] The changes made in them were far more than mere technical details: they indicated a close community of thought and proposed

---

[32] *International Military Tribunal for the Far East*, Exhibit No. 3441, pp. 32979–85.

* Editor's note: It was decided at the January 23, 1941, conference that Bishop Walsh and Father Drought "should continue their informal contact with the Japanese Embassy" and, through the Postmaster General, with Secretary of State Hull. It was also decided to delay negotiations until the new Japanese ambassador, Admiral Nomura, arrived in Washington. Discussions with Nomura began in March "but the proposed Japanese concessions were gradually withdrawn or whittled away until they were unacceptable to the United States." William L. Langer and S. Everett Gleason, *The Challenge to Isolation, 1937–1940* (New York: Harper & Brothers, 1952), pp. 314–15, 320–21, 467–70; Julius W. Pratt, *A History of United States Foreign Policy* (New York: Prentice-Hall, Inc., 1955), p. 650.

[33] *Pearl Harbor Attack*, Part V, p. 2391.

[34] Admiral H. R. Stark to the Commanders in Chief of the U. S. Pacific Fleet; the Asiatic Fleet; and the Atlantic Fleet, April 3, 1941, *ibid.*, Part XVII, pp. 2462–63.

action between Britain and the United States. A blueprint had been drawn for an Anglo-American parallel policy. It would be carried out as soon as the President could find a pretext for doing so.

7. JAPAN PRESSES FOR PEACE WITH THE UNITED STATES

As Hitler moved toward war with Soviet Russia he began to think more and more of Japanese assistance in this projected struggle. In March, 1941, Ribbentrop strongly argued that Japan, in its own interest, should enter the war "as soon as possible." This intervention would not only destroy England's key position in the Far East but it would also "keep America out of the war." [35] On March 26 Matsuoka, the Japanese Foreign Minister, arrived in Berlin. On the following day Ribbentrop plied him with the usual Nazi line of argument. It would be "very advantageous if Japan should decide as soon as possible to take an active part in the war upon England." Japanese intervention would be "most likely to keep America out of the war." When Matsuoka bluntly inquired about the attitude of Germany toward America after Britain was defeated, Ribbentrop quickly answered that "Germany did not have the slightest interest in a war against the United States." [36]

Japan also did not have the "slightest interest in a war against the United States." The appointment of Nomura as ambassador to the United States was an indication of this fact. Admiral Nomura had been the Japanese naval attaché in Washington during the first World War and had formed a friendly relationship with Franklin D. Roosevelt, then serving as the Assistant Secretary of the Navy. His reception at the White House was cordial but the President frankly referred to the fact that relations between Japan and the United States were steadily "deteriorating." [37] At the State Department he soon discovered a studied policy of "coolness toward the Japanese."

On March 8 Hull and Nomura had their first conversation on Japanese-American relations. Subsequently they met more than forty times in vain endeavors to find some firm ground on which to build a new structure of friendship. Hitler viewed these negotiations with frank alarm. As Ribbentrop later remarked:

> The Fuehrer . . . saw the attitude of the United States "short of war" and he was worried . . . about groups in Japan who wanted to come to an arrangement with America. He was afraid that if an arrangement would be made between the United States and Japan, this would mean, so to speak, the back free for America and the ex-

[35] *Nazi Conspiracy and Aggression* (Washington, D. C.: Government Printing Office, 1946), P-S 1834, IV, 469–75.

[36] Memorandum of a conversation between Ribbentrop and Matsuoka, March 28, 1941, *Nazi-Soviet Relations, 1939–1941* (New York: Didier Publications, 1948), pp. 298–303.

[37] Memorandum by Secretary Hull, February 14, 1941, *Foreign Relations, Japan: 1931–1941*, II, 387.

pected attack or entry into the war by the United States would come quicker.[38]

Japan paid little attention to this pressure from Berlin and Nomura carried on his talks with Hull without much thought of the desires of the Rome-Berlin Axis. The Japanese government was willing to give two important pledges: (1) to use only peaceful measures in the southwest Pacific; (2) to go to the support of Germany only in the event that she was the object of aggression. In return for these pledges Japan wished America (1) to restore normal trade relations between the two countries; (2) to assist Japan to secure access to basic raw materials in the southwest Pacific area; (3) to exert pressure upon Chiang Kai-shek so that he would consent to certain peace terms; (4) if Chiang refused to yield to this pressure the American government would withdraw support from his regime; (5) and, finally, to lend friendly diplomatic assistance aimed at the removal of Hongkong and Singapore as doorways "to further political encroachment by the British in the Far East." Secretary Hull countered with a memorandum emphasizing the following points: (1) respect for the territorial integrity and the sovereignty of each and all nations; (2) support of the principle of noninterference in the internal affairs of other countries; (3) support of the principle of equality, including equality of commercial opportunity; (4) nondisturbance of the *status quo* in the Pacific except as the *status quo* may be altered by peaceful means.[39]

The discussion of these bases for a friendly accord was not helped by occasional verbal pyrotechnics on the part of Matsuoka. On May 14 he had a conversation with Ambassador Grew during the course of which he sharply criticized the attitude of the United States toward Germany. American attacks upon German submarines might bring into action Article III of the tripartite pact of September 27, 1940.[40]

This conversation was the subject of comment by Sumner Welles during a conference with the British ambassador. Lord Halifax inquired as to the progress of the Hull-Nomura talks. Was there any chance that they would have a successful outcome? Welles thought that the "chances might not be better than one in ten." He then handed to Halifax a copy of a letter Matsuoka wrote to Grew immediately after their conversation on May 14. It was written in such a rambling style that Halifax thought it "bore evidences of lunacy." Welles shared this impression but finally came to the conclusion that "it might be due to the fact that Mr. Matsuoka was understood to be drinking extremely heavily at this time and the mental state apparent

---

[38] Testimony of Ribbentrop at Nuremberg, September 10, 1945, *Nazi Conspiracy and Aggression,* Supplement B, pp. 1200–1201.
[39] *Foreign Relations, Japan: 1931–1941,* II, 407.
[40] Ambassador Grew to Secretary Hull, May 14, 1941, *ibid.,* pp. 145–48.

in the writing of this letter might be momentary rather than permanent." [41]

It is apparent that Matsuoka's belligerent state of mind was a result of the pressure from Berlin. Hitler would soon launch his attack upon Russia and he was particularly anxious that America remain neutral. But this Japanese threat failed to restrain Roosevelt. On June 20 an announcement was made in Washington that no more oil would be exported from American eastern ports (including the Gulf of Mexico) except to the British Empire and the Western Hemisphere. Two days later, Hitler's armies crossed the Russian frontier and the German offensive began to roll. When the news reached Tokyo, Matsuoka rushed to the Emperor and strongly argued that Japan should support Germany by immediately attacking Russia. He readily admitted that his program implied possible war with the United States.[42]

Although Konoye wished to apply a brake to the forward tactics of Matsuoka, the Japanese army leaders were restive, and liaison conferences on June 25 and July 2 mapped a new and dangerous program: (1) Japan should not rush into a conflict with the Soviets; (2) the triple alliance should not be abandoned; (3) Japan should move south into Indochina.[43] Knowledge of this decision reached Washington during the first week in July. The Japanese code had been broken and from July to December, 1941, the President and Secretary of State could read the instructions from the Japanese Foreign Office to Ambassador Nomura.[44] The projected Japanese drive to the south was soon familiar in all its details.

8. ROOSEVELT FREEZES JAPANESE FUNDS
IN THE UNITED STATES

On July 16 the Japanese cabinet resigned. When Konoye was asked to form a new cabinet he dropped Matsuoka and named Admiral Toyoda as the new Foreign Minister. Toyoda was particularly fearful of further American embargoes upon the export of essential commodities to Japan. In the third week in July he sent an ominous instruction to Nomura in Washington: "Should the U. S. . . . take steps at this time which unduly excite Japan (such as . . . the freezing of assets), an exceedingly critical situation may be created. Please advise the United States of this fact and attempt to bring about an improvement in the situation." [45]

The efforts of Nomura to this end were in vain. On July 26 an order was

---

[41] Memorandum of a conversation between Sumner Welles and Viscount Halifax, May 17, 1941. 711.94/2207, MS, Department of State.

[42] "Memoirs of Prince Konoye," *Pearl Harbor Attack*, Part XX, p. 3993; see also the diary of the Marquis Koichi Kido in *International Military Tribunal for the Far East*, Exhibit No. 635.

[43] "Memoirs of Prince Konoye," *op. cit.*, pp. 4018–19.

[44] These intercepted decoded messages from Tokyo are given in detail in *Pearl Harbor Attack*, Part XII, pp. 1–316.

[45] Japanese Foreign Office to Ambassador Nomura, July 23, 1941, *ibid.*, pp. 4–5.

issued freezing Japanese funds in the United States. This meant an end to the export of oil to Japan. When Nomura called at the Department of State to inquire about the situation, Welles received him in his best frigid manner. Nomura expressed the hope that this restriction would not mean any "further deterioration in the relations of our two countries," but Welles parried this indirect query by remarking upon the extraordinary patience "which the United States had demonstrated in its relations with Japan during recent years." The Japanese ambassador quietly stated that he believed the best thing under the circumstances was to adopt some "compromise solution which would prove acceptable to both sides." Welles crisply replied that there was not the "slightest ground for any compromise solution." [46]

9. THE ATLANTIC CONFERENCE PUSHES AMERICA CLOSER TO A BREAK WITH JAPAN

Any thought of a compromise solution of Japanese-American difficulties was made more difficult by the decisions of the Atlantic Conference between Churchill and President Roosevelt. On August 9, 1941, in the Newfoundland harbor of Argentia, the first conference between these two statesmen was held. It was soon apparent that Britain was deeply disturbed about conditions in the southwest Pacific. According to a British suggestion, America was to state very frankly to Japan that any "further encroachment" in the direction of Malaya or the Netherlands East Indies would compel the United States to take measures that might lead to war. Welles wished to broaden the scope of American action. He would have the United States play the role of policeman in a very wide area in the Pacific. American forces should be ready to repel any Japanese thrust whether it was directed "against China, against the Soviet Union or against British Dominions or British colonies, or the colonies of the Netherlands in the Southern Pacific area." Churchill and Roosevelt were in hearty agreement with this wider formula, but the President was too cautious to broadcast it to the American public.[47]

Churchill did not secure at Argentia all the items in his program but he at least secured pledges that relieved many of his fears. In a speech in Parliament, January 27, 1942, he remarked: "The probability, since the Atlantic Conference . . . that the United States, even if not herself attacked, would come into a war in the Far East, and thus make final victory sure, seemed to allay some of these anxieties. . . . As time went on, one had greater as-

---

[46] Memorandum of a conversation between Sumner Welles and Ambassador Nomura, July 28, 1941, *Foreign Relations, Japan: 1931–1941*, II, 537–39.

[47] Memorandum of conversations at Argentia between President Roosevelt, Prime Minister Churchill, Sir Alexander Cadogan, Harry Hopkins, and Sumner Welles, *Pearl Harbor Attack*, Part IV, pp. 1784–92.

surance that if Japan ran amok in the Pacific, we should not fight alone."⁴⁸

10. ROOSEVELT REFUSES TO MEET PRINCE KONOYE

In a statement he handed to the Japanese ambassador on August 17, Roosevelt carried out his pledge to Churchill. It was phrased in language that carried a definite warning against Japanese expansion:

> If the Japanese Government takes any further steps in pursuance of a policy . . . of military domination by force or threat of force of neighboring countries, the Government of the United States will be compelled to take immediately any and all steps which it may deem necessary toward safeguarding . . . the safety and security of the United States.⁴⁹

A new issue now came up with reference to a meeting between Roosevelt and Prince Konoye. As early as August 7 the Japanese government had asked for such a meeting. It was now informed (August 17) that if it was ready to "suspend its expansionist activities" the Department of State would "endeavor to arrange a suitable time and place to exchange views."

In Tokyo Ambassador Grew was deeply impressed with the importance of a meeting between Konoye and Roosevelt. In a dispatch to Secretary Hull he thought such a conference would present an opportunity for "the highest statesmanship."⁵⁰ In the State Department, however, there was little enthusiasm for a Konoye-Roosevelt conference. In the Division of Far Eastern Affairs a memorandum was prepared which flatly stated: "The holding of the meeting between the President and the Japanese Prime Minister on the basis of the present status of the discussions between this country and Japan would result in more of disadvantage than of advantage as regards this country's interests and policies."⁵¹

Ambassador Grew strongly contested this viewpoint and cogently argued against a firm stand by the Department of State upon an inflexible program of principles in advance of a meeting between Roosevelt and Konoye. Political differences could be expressed in subtle shades that would not affront sensitive nations that objected to the conventional pattern of black and white. It would be best to go to such a meeting in a spirit that welcomed adjustment of existing difficulties; not in a spirit of challenge.⁵² But Secre-

---

⁴⁸ Winston Churchill, *The End of the Beginning* (Boston: Little, Brown & Company, 1943), p. 33.

⁴⁹ *Foreign Relations, Japan: 1931–1941*, II, 556–59.

⁵⁰ Ambassador Grew to Secretary Hull, Tokyo, August 18, 1941, *ibid.*, pp. 565.

⁵¹ Memorandum of the Division of Far Eastern Affairs, September 23, 1941. 711.94/2344, *Strictly Confidential*, MS, Department of State.

⁵² Ambassador Grew to Secretary Hull, September 29, 1941, *Foreign Relations, Japan: 1931–1941*, II, 645–50.

tary Hull paid little attention to these admonitions from Grew. On October 2 he handed to Ambassador Nomura a statement that vetoed any idea of a Roosevelt-Konoye meeting. Before such a conference could be agreed upon there would first have to be a definite meeting of minds upon the agenda.[53] Sir Robert Craigie, the British ambassador in Tokyo, was sharply critical of the Hull attitude:

> By pursuing a policy of stalling, the United States is arguing about every word and every phrase on the grounds that it is an essential preliminary to any kind of an agreement. . . . It would be very regrettable indeed if the best opportunity for the settlement of the Far Eastern problem since I assumed my post here, were to be lost in such a manner. . . . Both the U. S. Ambassador in Japan and I are firmly of the opinion that it would be a foolish policy if this superb opportunity is permitted to slip by by assuming an unduly suspicious attitude.[54]

11. GENERAL MARSHALL AND ADMIRAL STARK OPPOSE AN ULTIMATUM TO JAPAN

When Hull insisted upon a continued "unduly suspicious attitude" toward Japan, the Konoye Ministry resigned (October 16). In the new cabinet General Hideki Tojo assumed the post of Prime Minister, with Shigenori Togo as the new Minister of Foreign Affairs. The story of the attempts of the Tojo cabinet to find some path to peace is a twice-told tale that does not have to be repeated here.[55] It has long been equally obvious that the highest officers in the American Army and Navy were deeply concerned about the rapid drift toward war and wanted to postpone the conflict for at least three months. But Chiang Kai-shek began a drive to hasten American intervention. On November 2 the Generalissimo wrote to Roosevelt that a new Japanese offensive against Yunnan might shake the morale of the Chinese Army and the Chinese people "to its foundation." For the first time in "this long war a real collapse of resistance would be possible" if the Japanese drive succeeded in taking Kunming.[56] But General Marshall and Admiral Stark resisted this Chinese pressure to push America immediately into the war. On November 5, after a review of the situation in the Far East, they strongly recommended that "no ultimatum be delivered to Japan." [57]

---

[53] Oral statement handed by Secretary Hull to Ambassador Nomura, October 2, 1941, *ibid.*, pp. 656–61.

[54] *Pearl Harbor Attack*, Part XII, p. 51.

[55] Feis, *The Road to Pearl Harbor*, pp. 282–325; Charles A. Beard, *President Roosevelt and the Coming of the War, 1941* (New Haven, Conn.: Yale University Press, 1948), pp. 496–516; Frederic R. Sanborn, *Design for War; a Study of Secret Power Politics, 1937–1941* (New York: Devin-Adair Company, 1951), pp. 377–425.

[56] *Pearl Harbor Attack*, Part XV, pp. 1476–78.   [57] *Ibid.*, Part XIV, pp. 1061–62.

12. JAPAN IS "MANEUVERED" INTO FIRING
THE FIRST SHOT AT PEARL HARBOR

The rejection of the Konoye-Roosevelt meeting was a real ultimatum to Japan, and after October 16 tension in Tokyo rapidly mounted. On November 5 instructions were sent to Nomura that November 25 would be the deadline in the negotiations in Washington.[58] This deadline was repeated in instructions on November 11.[59] From the intercepted Japanese radiograms, Secretary Hull knew all about this deadline. On November 15 Hull handed Nomura another one of his long oral statements. He knew that it could not be accepted by Japan. The bases for an agreement were a challenge. Complete control over "its economic, financial and monetary affairs" should be restored to China, and Japan should abandon any thought of preserving in China a "preferential position." [60]

Japan realized that this was really a challenge, but a last attempt was made to preserve peace. Saburo Kurusu was sent to Washington to assist Nomura. He had served as consul in Chicago and New York, and his happy marriage to an American girl had given him a personal interest in finding some road to accommodation. But Hull was hell-bent for war. The constant needling by Chiang Kai-shek had gotten under his skin and President Roosevelt felt pressure from his administrative assistant, Lauchlin Currie, also a warm admirer of Soviet Russia. At this point Owen Lattimore, American adviser to Chiang-Kai-shek, sent a strongly worded cablegram against any *modus vivendi* or truce with Japan: "Any *modus vivendi*" now arrived at with Japan would be "disastrous to Chinese belief in America." [61] For a week Currie had been "terribly anxious" because he feared that "Hull was in danger of selling China and America and Britain down the river." [62] In Chungking, Madame Chiang Kai-shek became "unrestrainedly critical" of the American government for its failure to "plunge into the war" and thus aid China.[63] From London word came from Churchill with reference to the situation in China: "There is only one point that disquiets us. What about Chiang Kai-shek? Is he not having a very thin diet?" [64]

Under the impact of these cablegrams Hull became hysterical. During a

---

[58] Japanese Foreign Office to Ambassador Nomura, November 5, 1941, *ibid.*, Part XII, p. 100.

[59] Japanese Foreign Office to Ambassador Nomura, November 11, 1941, *ibid.*, pp. 116–17.

[60] Oral statement handed by Secretary Hull to Ambassador Nomura, November 15, 1941, *Foreign Relations, Japan: 1931–1941*, II, 734–37.

[61] Owen Lattimore to Lauchlin Currie, November 25, 1941, *Pearl Harbor Attack*, Part XIV, p. 1160. See also *Hearings Before the Sub-Committee to Investigate the Administration of the Internal Security Act* (McCarran Committee), United States Senate, 82 Cong., 1 sess., Part I, pp. 156–57.

[62] *Hearings, ibid.*, pp. 157–58.

[63] Ambassador Gauss to Secretary Hull, Chungking, December 3, 1941. 711.94/2600, MS, Department of State.

[64] *Pearl Harbor Attack*, Part XIV, p. 1300.

telephone conversation with Secretary Stimson he remarked that he had just about made up his mind about any thought of a *modus vivendi* or truce with Japan—he "would kick the whole thing over." [65] This is just what he and President Roosevelt did on the following day, November 26. On that afternoon Hull handed to the Japanese diplomatic representatives a ten-point proposal which amounted to a sharp ultimatum: "The government of Japan will withdraw all military, naval, air and police forces from China and Indochina." [66] Both Hull and the President knew the Japanese government could not accept such a proposal: it was an invitation to war. It was not long before that invitation was accepted.

On* the morning of December 4, the Navy radio receiving station at Cheltenham, Maryland, intercepted a Japanese overseas news broadcast from Station JAP in Tokyo, in which there was inserted a false weather report, "east wind rain." On November 19 the Japanese Government had instructed its ambassador in Washington that such a weather forecast would indicate imminence of war with the United States.[67] After intercepting this Japanese instruction the radio receiving stations of the American armed forces were on the alert for the "east wind rain" message. As soon as it was translated, Lieutenant Commander Kramer handed it to Commander Safford with the exclamation: "This is *it*." Safford got in touch immediately with Rear Admiral Noyes who telephoned the substance of the intercepted message "to the naval aide to the President." [68]

According to the testimony of Captain Safford [in 1941 a Commander], the

> "winds" message and the change of the [Japanese] naval operations code came in the middle of the week: two days to Saturday and three days to Sunday. It was unthinkable that the Japanese would surrender their hopes of surprise by delaying until the week-end of December 13–14. This was not crystal-gazing or "intuition"—it was just the plain, common sense acceptance of a self-evident proposition. Col. Sadtler saw it, and so did Capt. Joseph R. Redman, U.S.N., according to Col. Sadtler's testimony in 1944. . . . The Japanese were going to start the war on Saturday, December 6, 1941, or Sunday, December 7, 1941.[69]

---

[65] Stimson diary, November 26, 1941; *Pearl Harbor Attack*, Part XI, p. 5434.

[66] Oral statement handed by Secretary Hull to Ambassador Nomura and Mr. Kurusu, November 26, 1941, *Foreign Relations, Japan: 1931–1941*, II, 766–70.

* Editor's note: The remainder of the text is reprinted, by permission, from *Back Door to War* by Charles C. Tansill, copyright 1952 by Henry Regnery Company. Pp. 650–652.

[67] Japanese Foreign Office to Ambassador Nomura, Tokyo, November 19, 1941. *Pearl Harbor Attack*, pt. 12, p. 154.

[68] George Morgenstern, *Pearl Harbor* (New York, 1947), p. 206.

[69] *Ibid.*, p. 211. The testimony of Captain Safford is given in detail in *Pearl Harbor Attack*, pt. 8, pp. 3555–3814.

For the next three days Commander Safford and Lieutenant Commander Kramer tried in vain to get some action out of their superior officers with regard to the implications of the "east wind rain" message. When they induced Captain McCollum to exert some pressure upon Admiral Stark he was given a sharp rebuke which so infuriated him that he later poured the whole story into the receptive ears of Admiral Kimmel. This disclosure led Kimmel to press for the Pearl Harbor investigations.

The unaccountable failure of high naval officers to convey a warning to Honolulu about the imminence of war was given additional highlights on the evening of December 6 when the Japanese reply to the American note of November 26 was sent secretly to Ambassador Nomura. It was intercepted by Navy receiving stations and decoded. When the President read this message to Nomura he at once exclaimed: "This means war!" He tried to get in touch with Admiral Stark but was informed that the chief of naval operations was at the National Theatre enjoying the delightful strains of *The Student Prince*.[70] The next day the Admiral's ears would be assailed by the crashing echoes of the attack upon Pearl Harbor.

It would ordinarily be assumed that the President, after reading this intercepted Japanese message, would hurriedly call a conference of the more important Army and Navy officers to concert plans to meet the anticipated attack. The testimony of General Marshall and Admiral Stark would indicate that the Chief Executive took the ominous news so calmly that he made no effort to consult with them.[71] Did he deliberately seek the Pearl Harbor attack in order to get America into the war? What is the real answer to this riddle of Presidential composure in the face of a threatened attack upon some American outpost in the faraway Pacific? This problem grows more complicated as we watch the approach of zero hour. At 9:00 A.M. on December 7, Lieutenant Commander Kramer delivered to Admiral Stark the final installment of the Japanese instruction to Nomura. Its meaning was now so obvious that Stark cried out in great alarm: "My God! This means war. I must get word to Kimmel at once." [72] But he made no effort to contact Honolulu. Instead he tried to get in touch with General Marshall, who, for some strange reason, suddenly decided to go on a long horseback ride. It was a history-making ride. In the early hours of the American Revolution, Paul Revere went on a famous ride to warn his countrymen of the enemy's approach and thus save American lives. In the early hours of World War II, General Marshall took a ride that helped prevent an alert from reaching Pearl Harbor in time to save an American fleet from serious disaster and an American garrison from a bombing that cost more than two thousand lives. Was there an important purpose behind this ride? This question looms constantly larger as we look further into the Pearl Harbor hearings.

---

[70] In this regard the testimony of Commander Lester B. Schulz is pertinent and colorful. *Ibid.*, pt. 10, pp. 4662–63.

[71] *Ibid.*, pt. 3, pp. 1049–1541; pt. 5, pp. 2096–2477.   [72] Morgenstern, *op. cit.*, p. 269.

When Colonel Bratton, on the morning of December 7, saw the last part of the Japanese instruction to Nomura he realized at once that "Japan planned to attack the United States at some point at or near 1 o'clock that day." [73] To Lieutenant Commander Kramer the message meant "a surprise attack at Pearl Harbor today." [74] This information was in the hands of Secretary Knox by 10:00 A.M., and he must have passed it on to the President immediately.

It was 11:25 A.M. when General Marshall returned to his office. If he carefully read the reports on the threatened Japanese attack (on Pearl Harbor) he still had plenty of time to contact Honolulu by means of the scrambler telephone on his desk, or by the Navy radio or the FBI radio. For some reason best known to himself he chose to send the alert to Honolulu by RCA and did not even take the precaution to have is stamped, "priority." As the Army Pearl Harbor Board significantly remarked: "We find no justification for a failure to send this message by multiple secret means either through the Navy radio or the FBI radio or the scrambler telephone or all three." [75] Was the General under Presidential orders to break military regulations with regard to the transmission of important military information? Did he think that the President's political objectives outweighed considerations of national safety? Was the preservation of the British Empire worth the blood, sweat, and tears not only of the men who would die in the agony of Pearl Harbor but also of the long roll of heroes who perished in the epic encounters in the Pacific, in the Mediterranean area, and in the famous offensive that rolled at high tide across the war-torn fields of France? New cemeteries all over the world would confirm to stricken American parents the melancholy fact that the paths of military glory lead but to the grave.

But the President and Harry Hopkins viewed these dread contingencies with amazing equanimity. In the quiet atmosphere of the oval study in the White House, with all incoming telephone calls shut off, the Chief Executive calmly studied his well-filled stamp albums while Hopkins fondled Fala, the White House scottie. At one o'clock, Death stood in the doorway. The Japanese had bombed Pearl Harbor. America had suddenly been thrust into a war she is still fighting.

---

[73] *Ibid.*, p. 275. See also the testimony of Colonel Rufus S. Bratton in *Pearl Harbor Attack*, pts. 9–10, pp. 4508–4623.

[74] *Ibid.*, p. 276.

[75] *Pearl Harbor Attack*, pt. 39, p. 95; Robert E. Ward, "The Inside Story of the Pearl Harbor Plan," United States Naval Institute *Proceedings*, LXXVII, No. 12 (December 1951), 1271–83.

War Came at Pearl Harbor:

Suspicions Considered

Herbert Feis

Ten years after victory, we look ruefully at the way the world has gone. It is right and natural to search out any errors of judgment or faults of character that have led us to our present pass. But such self-scrutiny can go awry if governed by a wish to revile rather than a wish to understand. Unless we are alert, that could happen as a result of the suspicions that have come to cluster around the way in which the United States became engaged in the Second World War—torch-lit by the Pearl Harbor disaster.

The more recently available sources have added but little to our knowledge of the events that led to our entry into the war. The books of memoirs written by Japanese witnesses have told us something more, especially about the struggle within the Japanese Government. But in my reading, while they may improve our knowledge of details, they do not change the fundamental view of this experience or its main features. In American and British records still kept secret there may be information or explanations that would do so. But even this I doubt. With no new great revealing facts to display, and no great new insights to impart, the most useful service would seem to be to act as caretaker of what is known, and in particular to deal with certain warped comments and inferences that seasonally must feel the straightening edge of evidence.

Of all the accusations made, the one most shocking to me is that Roosevelt and his chief advisers deliberately left the Pacific Fleet and base at Pearl Harbor exposed as a lure to bring about a direct Japanese attack upon us.

This has been diffused in the face of the fact that the Japanese High Military Command conference before the Imperial Throne on September 6, 1941, resolved that "If by the early part of October there is no reasonable hope of having our demands agreed to in the diplomatic negotiations mentioned above, we will immediately make up our minds to get ready for war against America (and England and Holland)." This is September 6. The plan for the attack on Pearl Harbor was not approved and adopted until

---

From *The Yale Review*, XLV (March 1956), 378–390. Copyright by Yale University Press. Reprinted by permission.

October; and Secret Operation Order #1, the execution of the plan, was not issued until November 5. The presence of the Pacific Fleet at Pearl Harbor was not a lure but an obstacle.

The literature of accusation ignores or rejects the real reasons why the Pacific Fleet was kept in Hawaii. It must do so, since one of the main reasons was the hope that its presence there would deter the Japanese from making so threatening a move south or north that American armed forces might have to join in the war. It scorns the fact that the American military plans —to be executed in the event that we became engaged in war—assigned vital tasks to this Pacific Fleet. A mind must indeed be distracted if it can believe that the American Government could, at one and the same time, use the Pacific Fleet as a target and count on having it as part of its main defending force.

A variant of this accusation, which at least does not require such a willingness to believe the worst, might also be noted—that despite ample knowledge that Pearl Harbor was about to be attacked, the American Government purposefully left it exposed and allowed the event to happen.

Those who do not find such an idea at odds with their view of the sense of duty and regard for human life of President Roosevelt and his chief advisers can find striking points about the occurrence that may be construed to correspond with this conception. How they glare out of the record in hindsight: Ambassador Grew's warnings; Secretary Hull's acute gleam put into words at least three times in Cabinet Councils in November that the Japanese attack might come "at any moment, anywhere"; the intercepted Japanese messages telling of the Japanese effort to secure minute information as to the location of the ships of our Pacific Fleet in the Harbor; carelessness in checking up on the protective measures taken by the local commanders; failure to use the chance to give an effective last-minute warning to Hawaii. How else, it is asked, can these be explained except in terms of secret and conscious purpose?

However, just as hindsight makes the failure of perception plain, so it also makes it understandable—but only by bringing back to mind the total circumstances. That can be done here only in the barest way. Up to then Japanese strategy had been wary, one small creeping step after another, from Manchuria to North China into China and down into Indo-China. American military circles came to take it for granted that it would go on that way. Then there was the fact that Japan's basic objectives lay to the south and southeast; there and there only it could get what it needed—raw materials, oil, and island bases to withstand the attack from the West. Expectation already set in that direction was kept there by impressive and accurate intelligence reports of movements under way. Against this flow of preconception, the signs pointing to Pearl Harbor were not heeded.

Such features of contemporary thinking within the American Government explain, though they do not excuse, the failure to discern that Pearl

Harbor was going to be attacked. To think the contrary is to believe that the President and the heads of the American Army, Navy, and Air Force were given to deep deception, and in order to have us enter the war were ready to sacrifice not only the Pacific Fleet but the whole war plan for the Pacific. This, I think, is the difference between history and police court history.

I have taken note of these accusations that have been built about the disaster at Pearl Harbor because they appeal to the sense of the sinister which is so lively in our times. But I am glad to turn to ideas and interpretations of broader historical import.

The first of these is that Roosevelt and the Joint Chiefs of Staff were obligated by secret agreements with Churchill and their British colleagues to enter the war at some time or other, in one way or other. Therefore, it is further supposed, the American authors of this agreement had to cause either Germany or Japan, or both, to attack us.

This view derives encouragement from the fact that the American Government *did* enter into a secret agreement about strategy with the British. The accord, known as ABC-1 Staff Agreement, adopted at Washington in March, 1941, set down the respective missions of the British and American elements in the event that the United States should be at war with Germany or Japan, or both; and subsequently the American basic joint war plan, Rainbow-5, was adjusted to fit this combined plan of operations. An attempt was made at a similar conference in Singapore soon after to work out a more detailed United States-British-Dutch operating plan for the Pacific. This attempt failed; but the discussion that took place there left a lasting mark on American official thinking, for the conferees defined the limits on land and sea beyond which Japanese forces could not be permitted to go without great risk to the defenders.

The ABC-1 agreement did not place the Roosevelt Administration under *political* obligation to enter the war against either Germany or Japan, not even if Japan attacked British or Dutch areas in the Far East. Nor did Roosevelt give a promise to this effect to Churchill when they met at Newfoundland in August, 1941. Up to the very eve of the Japanese assault the President refused to tell the British or Dutch what we would do. In short, the Government kept itself officially free from any obligation to enter the war, certainly free of any obligation to thrust itself into the war.

But I do think this accord conveyed responsibilities of a moral sort. After ABC-1 was adopted, production of weapons in the United States and the British Commonwealth took it into account; and the allocation of weapons, troops, ships, and planes as between threatened areas was based on the expectation that the United States would carry out the assignments set down in the plan.

Thus, it may be fairly thought, Roosevelt and his administration were obligated to try to gain the consent of Congress and the American people to play the part designated in the joint plans if Japanese assaults crossed the land and sea boundaries of resistance that were defined at these joint staff conferences. In the last November weeks when the end of the diplomatic talks with Japan came into sight, and General Marshall and Admiral Stark were asked what measures should be taken in face of the threatened Japanese advances, they advised the President to declare the limits defined at Singapore, and to warn the Japanese that we would fight if these were crossed. There is much reason to think this would have been done even had the Japanese not struck at Pearl Harbor and the Philippines, and this boundary would have been the line between peace and war. But this re-affirmation was made not as a measure required to carry out a secret accord, but because it was believed to be the best course.

A variant explanation of the way we dealt with Japan runs somewhat as follows: that Roosevelt was determined to get into the war against Germany; that he had to find a release from his public promises that the United States would not enter "foreign wars" unless attacked; that his efforts to do so by unneutral aid to Britain and the Soviet Union had failed because Hitler had refused to accept the challenge; and so he sought another door into war, a back door, by inviting or compelling the Japanese attack.

This interpretation, with its kick at the end, twists the record around its own preconception. The actions taken did not flow from a settled wish to get us into war. They trailed along the rim of necessity of the true purpose —which was to sustain resistance against the Axis. How many times the American Government refused to do what the British, French, Chinese, Russians, Dutch asked it to do, because it might involve us in actual combat!

This slant of reasoning about American action passes by the course of Japanese conduct which aroused our fears and stimulated our opposition: the way in which, despite all our pleas and warnings, Japan pressed on. By not recognizing that these Japanese actions called for American counter-action, it excuses them. Thus our resistance is made to appear as nothing else but a deceitful plot to plunge us into war. Furthermore, it dismisses as insincere the patient attempt to calm Japan by diplomatic talks, by offers to join in safeguarding its security.

There were influential individuals in the Roosevelt Administration who wanted to get into the war and indifferent as to how we got into it. Of these, Secretary of the Interior Ickes was, I believe, the most candid, at any rate in his diary entries. Secretary of the Treasury Morgenthau and his staff also had a positive wish that we should engage in war—but against Germany, not against Japan, for that might have brought a diversion of forces to the Pacific. Secretary of War Stimson thought that it would not be possible for Great Britain to sustain the fight unless we entered it; but toward the very end, particularly as it was becoming plain that the Soviet Union was going to survive the Nazi assault, he began to wish for delay. However, time and time again the memoirs and diaries record the impatience of these officials, and those who thought like them, with Hull's caution and Roosevelt's watchful indirection.

The most genuine point made by those who dissent, one that merits thorough analysis, is that the American Government, in conjunction with the British and Dutch, refused to continue to supply Japan with machines and materials vital to it—especially oil. It is contended that they thereby compelled Japan to resort to war, or at least fixed a time period in which Japan was faced with the need of deciding to yield to our terms or go to war.

In reflecting upon this action, the reasons for it must not be confused with the Japanese response to it. Japan showed no signs of curbing its aggressive course. It paid no heed to repeated and friendly warnings that unless it did, the threatened countries would have to take counter-measures. As when on February 14, 1941, while the Lend-Lease Act was being argued in Congress, Dooman, Counselor of the American Embassy in Japan and known to be a firm and straightforward friend of that country, carried back from Washington the message for the Vice-Minister for Foreign Affairs: that the American people were determined to support Britain even at the risk of war; that if Japan or any other country menaced that effort "it would have to expect to come in conflict with the United States"; and that the United States had abstained from an oil embargo in order not to impel Japan to create a situation that could only lead to the most serious outcome. Japan's answer over the following months had been to force its way further into Indo-China and threaten the Dutch East Indies.

This sustained proof that Japan was going on with its effort to dominate Asia, and the alliance pledging it to stand by Germany if that country got into war with the United States, made a continuation of trade with Japan an act of meekness on our part. Japan was concentrating its foreign purchases on products needed for war, while reducing civilian use by every means, and was thus accumulating great reserve stocks. These were enabling it to maintain its invasion of China without much strain, while continuing to expand its war-making power. Had *effective* restraints—note that I do not say *total* restraints—not been imposed, the American Government would have been in the strange position of having declared an unlimited national emergency, of calling upon the American people to strengthen their army, navy, and air force in great urgency, while at the same time nourishing the opponent that might have to be met in battle. This was a grave, if not intolerable, responsibility.

It is hard to tell how squarely the American and British Governments faced the possible consequence of their restrictive measures. My impression is that they knew the danger of war with Japan was being increased; that Japan might try to get by force the means denied it. The Japanese Government served plain warnings that this game of thrust and counterthrust might so end. These were soberly regarded, but did not weaken the will that Japan was not to have its way by threat.

Mingled with the anxiety lest these restrictive measures would make war more likely, there was a real hope that they might be a deterrent to war. Conceivably they would bring home to the Japanese people that if it came to war, they might soon run out of the means for combat, while the rapid growth of American military strength would make it clear that they could not in the end win. And, as evidence of these probabilities became plain, the conciliatory elements in the Japanese Government would prevail over the more militant ones.

This almost happened. But the reckless ones, those who would rather court fatality than accept frustration, managed to retain control of Japanese decision. The pressure applied by us did not prevent war, and may have brought the time of decision for war closer. The valid question, however, is not whether the American Government resorted to these restrictions *in order* to drive Japan to attack; it is whether the American Government failed to grasp a real chance, after the restraints had begun to leave their mark in Japanese official circles, to arrive at a satisfactory understanding that would have averted war. Twice, in the opinion of some qualified students of the subject, such a chance emerged, or at least appeared on the horizon of diplomacy. Were they real opportunities or merely mirages or decoys?

The first of these was the occasion when in the autumn of 1941, the Japanese Prime Minister, Prince Konoye, sought a personal meeting with the President. It is averred that the President's failure to respond lost a chance to avert the war without yielding any American principle or purpose. Some think the reason was that American diplomacy was inflexible, dull in its insight, and too soaked in mistrust. Others, more accusatory, explain the decision by a lack of desire for an agreement that would have thwarted the design for war.

Since there is no conclusive evidence of what Konoye intended to propose or could have achieved, comment on this subject must enter into "the boggy ground of what-might-have-been." Some observers, including Ambassador Grew, believe that Konoye could have made a real, and an irreversible, start toward meeting American terms. It will always be possible to think that this is so. But to the Americans in authority, the chance seemed small. Konoye was a man who in every past crisis had allowed himself to flounder between criss-cross promises; hence there was good reason to fear an attempt at deception. Such glimpses as we have of what he might have proposed do not support the view that he could have offered a suspension or end of the fight against China. His freedom to negotiate would have been subject to the conditions stated by those who had controlled Japan's course up to then —their price for allowing him to go to meet the President.

Even so, to repeat, it is possible that skilled and more daring American diplomacy might have handled the meeting so as to get a satisfactory accord;

or, failing that—and this is the more likely chance—to bring about so deep a division within the Japanese circle of decision as to have prevented war-like action. These alluring historical queries will continue to roam in the land of might-have-been.

But the risks were great. The echoes of Munich and its aftermath were still loud. The American Government might have found itself forced to make a miserable choice: either to accept an accord which would have left Japan free to complete its conquest of China and menace the rest of Asia, or to face a deep division among the American people. Any understanding with Japan that was not clear and decisive would have had unpredictable consequences. The Chinese Government might have felt justified in making a deal following our own. The Soviet Union, at this time just managing with the greatest effort and agony to prevent German victory, might also have chosen to compromise with Hitler rather than to fight it out. Specula-tions such as these must leave the subject unsettled. But in any case I think it clear that the American decision was one of judgment, not of secret intent. Konoye was not told that the President would not meet with him; he was told that he would not do so until more progress had been made toward defining what the Japanese Government was prepared to propose.

The same basic question had to be faced in the final crisis of negotiation in November, 1941: whether to relax restraints on Japan and leave it in a position to keep on trying to control much of Asia in return for a promise not to press on farther for the time being.

The opinion that the Japanese truce offer made at this last juncture ac-cepted the main purposes and principles for which the American Govern-ment had been standing may be summarily dismissed. It was ambiguously worded, it was silent about the alliance with Germany, and it would have required the American Government to end its support of China—for the last of its numbered five points read: "The Government of the United States undertakes to refrain from such measures and actions as will be prejudicial to the endeavors for the restoration of general peace between Japan and China." This scant and unclear proposal was at once deemed "entirely un-acceptable." Furthermore, there seemed little use and much possible dam-age in making a counter truce-offer of the same variety. The intercepted Japanese messages stated flatly that this was Japan's last and best offer. They told of the swift dismissal of a much more nearly acceptable one that Nomura and Kurusu asked their superiors in Tokyo to consider. A dead-line had been set. Thus it was all but sure that the reduced counter-offer which had been patched together in Washington would be unheeded. But it might shake the coalition to which by then the opponents of the Axis had pledged their lives and national destinies.

This seems to have been the thought uppermost in Hull's mind in recom-mending to the President that the counter truce-offer be withheld. As set down in this historic memo of November 26, he had been led to this conclusion by the opposition of the Chinese, the half-hearted support or actual opposition of the British, Dutch, and Australian governments, and the further excited opposition to be expected because of lack of appreciation of the importance and value of a truce. This I believe to have been the true determining reason for a decision reluctantly taken. Even if by then Japan was genuinely ready for reform, the repentance had come too late. The situation had grown too entangled by then for minor measures, its momentum too great. Germany-Italy-Japan had forced the creation of a defensive coalition more vast than the empire of the Pacific for which Japan plotted. This was not now to be quieted or endangered by a temporary halt along the fringe of the Japanese advance.

Even though these reasons for dropping the idea of a truce may seem sufficient, they leave the question why the American Government could not have given a softer and less declaratory answer. Why had it to give one so "bleakly uncompromising"? It could have said simply that the Japanese offer did not convey the assurances that would warrant us and the alliance for which we spoke to resume the shipment of war materials to Japan and end our aid to China. Why was it deemed advisable or essential at this juncture to state fully and forcibly our maximum terms for a settlement in the Pacific? Was it foreseen that, scanned with mistrust as it would almost surely be, this would be construed as a demand for the swift abandonment of Japan's whole program? Was it done, as the accusation runs, with the deliberate intent of banning any last chance for an accord? Of propelling the Japanese attack?

That this was not the reason I am as sure as anyone can be on a matter of this sort; but I can offer only conjecture as to what the inspiring purposes were. Perhaps to vindicate past actions and decisions. Perhaps a wish to use the dramatic chance to put in the record a statement of the aims for which the risk of war was being accepted, and of the basis on which the Americans would found the peace when the time came. Such an idea was in accord with the usual mode of thought of the men in charge of the Executive Branch of the Government and of most of the American people. It gave vent to the propensity exemplified in Hull to find a base in general principles meant to be at once political standards and moral ideals. After long caution, it appealed as a defiant contradiction of the Axis program. All this, however, is surmise rather than evidenced history.

But I think it is well within the realm of evidenced history that the memo of November 26 was not in any usual sense of the word an ultimatum. It did not threaten the Japanese with war or any other form of forceful punishment if our terms were not accepted. It simply left them in the state of distress in which they were, with the prospect that they might later have to submit to our requirements. The Japanese Government could have, as

Konoye and Nomura pleaded with it to do, allowed the situation to drag along, with or without resuming talks with the American Government. Its power to make war would have been depleted, but neither quickly nor crucially. The armed forces and even the position in China could have been maintained.

Notably, the final Japanese answer which ended negotiations on December 7, 1941, does not accuse the American Government of confronting it with an ultimatum, but only of thwarting the larger Japanese aims. Part 14—the clinching part of this note—reads: "Obviously it is the intention of the American Government to conspire with Great Britain and other countries to obstruct Japan's efforts toward the establishment of peace through the creation of a New Order in East Asia, and especially to preserve Anglo-American rights and interests by keeping Japan and China at war. This intention has been revealed clearly during the course of the present negotiations. Thus, the earnest hope of the Japanese Government to adjust Japanese-American relations and to preserve and promote the peace of the Pacific through coöperation with the American Government has finally been lost."

This is a more nearly accurate description of the purposes of the American Government under Roosevelt than those attributed to it by hostile and suspicious American critics. Our Government did obstruct Japanese efforts, believing them to be unjust, cruel, and a threat to our national security, especially after Japan became a partner with Hitler's Germany and Mussolini's Italy and bent its efforts toward bringing the world under their combined control.

This determination stood on the proposition that it was better to take the risks of having to share in the suffering of the war than of finding ourselves moved or compelled to fight a more desperate battle against the Axis later on. The American Government, I believe, knew how serious a risk of war was being taken. But in its addresses to the American people it chose to put in the forefront the perils we would face if the Axis won, and to leave in the background, even to camouflage, the risks of finding ourselves plunged into wars which during the election campaign it had promised would not occur. Whether any large number of Americans were fooled by this, or whether most of them, in reality, were content to have the prospect presented that way rather than in a more blunt and candid way, I do not know.

This essay in interpretation has compelled me to recall and stress the aggressive Japanese assault—though I should have been glad to let that slip into the past. The passage of time does not alter facts, but it can bring a fuller and calmer understanding of them. It frees the mind for fairer appreciation of the causes and circumstances which impelled Japan along its tragic course and which impelled us to resist it. For both countries there are many common lessons. One of them is that continued friendliness requires mutual effort to relieve the other, to the extent it can, of deep cause for anxiety—the Japanese people of their anxiety over the means of living decently, the American people of anxiety about their security and power to defend the free world. Another is that they must both feel, speak, and act so honestly and steadily that their view of each other will be cleared of mistrust, and brightened by trust.

The Yalta Agreements: Surrender to Russia or Wartime Realism?

INTRODUCTION

Of the various Allied diplomatic conferences during World War II, the most significant was the Yalta conference of February, 1945. It was the Yalta conference, as Paul Clyde has pointed out, that "cemented the military victory and shaped the broad outlines of the future." [1] *Far-reaching decisions were made with respect to Germany, Poland and eastern Europe, the Far East, and the United Nations. The initial reaction to the conference in the United States, before all the terms of the agreements were made public, was highly favorable; but as the Soviet Union extended its power and influence in Europe and Asia and as Soviet-American tension grew, the Yalta agreements were subjected to increasing criticism. To some of the more rabid critics of the Roosevelt and Truman administrations, Yalta became part of a gigantic conspiracy whose object was the promotion of international Communism.*

The journalist William Henry Chamberlin looks upon Yalta as a "moral and diplomatic debacle," "the climax of a gravely mistaken course in foreign affairs." He finds fault with all phases of the agreements and rejects the contentions of the defenders of Yalta. Professor John L. Snell and his associates take the other side of the argument. They assert that the Yalta agreements can only be understood in the context of the times and in the light of the emergence of a new balance of world power. They find the agreements on the whole reasonable and repudiate the charge that the Soviet view invariably triumphed at Yalta.

---

[1] Paul H. Clyde (Foreword), John L. Snell (Editor), *The Meaning of Yalta: Big Three Diplomacy and the New Balance of Power* (Baton Rouge: Louisiana State University Press, 1956), p. viii.

Appeasement at Yalta

William Henry Chamberlin

Morally, politically and militarily the Yalta Conference of February 4–11, 1945, was held under unfavorable conditions. The Soviet armies had recently launched a successful offensive. The memory of what proved to be the last German offensive, in the Ardennes region, was still fresh. The speed with which Germany would crumble before Eisenhower's offensive in the spring was not anticipated. Singularly faulty intelligence work had conveyed the impression that Japan still possessed large and effective forces in Manchuria.

The two leading figures in the American delegation, Roosevelt and Hopkins, were in very poor health and were committed by past attitudes to the policy of trusting Stalin and hoping for the best. The newly appointed Secretary of State, Edward R. Stettinius, possessed no visible qualifications for this office except an impressive shock of white hair, an adulatory attitude toward Roosevelt and a naive faith that all international problems could be solved by a determined application of good will and optimism.

A measure of the political judgment of Mr. Stettinius is furnished by his expression of opinion, four years after Yalta, that the Soviet Union at this conference made greater concessions than the United States, and that Yalta was an American diplomatic triumph.[1]

In his record of the Yalta proceedings Mr. Stettinius is effusive in his praise of one of his subordinates whose name inspires little confidence in most American minds today. Alger Hiss, according to Stettinius, "performed brilliantly" at Yalta, as in the Dumbarton Oaks conversations where preliminary details of the United Nations organization were worked out, at the San Francisco conference and the first meeting of the UN Assembly.[2] When Roosevelt asked Stettinius to get a lawyer to consult with him on the Polish boundary statement Stettinius promptly called for this "brilliant performer." [3]

---

[1] Edward R. Stettinius, *Roosevelt and the Russians* (Doubleday), p. 295.   [2] *Ibid.*, p. 31.   [3] *Ibid.*, p. 270.

Of the other members of the American delegation only two, Averell Harriman, Ambassador to the Soviet Union, and Charles E. Bohlen, assistant to the Secretary of State and a Russian language expert who acted as translator, possessed a background of Soviet experience. There is nothing in the records of the conference to indicate that either Harriman or Bohlen did anything to avert moral and diplomatic debacle. Years later Harriman and Bohlen, nominated Ambassador to the Soviet Union by the Eisenhower Administration, were stubbornly maintaining that nothing was wrong with the Yalta Agreement except Soviet nonobservance of its provisions.

The principal decisions at Yalta, some revealed in a communiqué after the end of the meeting, some kept secret for a year or longer, dealt with the following subjects.

Poland. It was agreed that the eastern frontier of Poland should follow substantially the so-called Curzon Line, with minor digressions in favor of Poland. This was a ratification, for Stalin, of the spoils of his pact with Hitler. Poland was to receive accessions of German territory not precisely specified.

The existing Provisional Government of Poland was to be reorganized on a broader democratic basis, "with the inclusion of democratic leaders from Poland itself and from Poles abroad." The new government was to be called the Polish Provisional Government of National Unity and was to receive diplomatic recognition from the Big Three powers. This government was to be pledged to "the holding of free and unfettered elections as soon as possible on the basis of universal suffrage and secret ballot."

Germany. "We are determined to disarm and disband all German armed forces, break up for all time the German General Staff, remove or destroy all German military equipment, eliminate or control all German industry that could be used for military production, bring all war criminals to swift and just punishment and exact reparation in kind for the destruction wrought by the Germans; wipe out the Nazi Party, Nazi laws, organizations and institutions, etc." It was specified in the protocol of the conference that German labor might be used as a source of "reparations." A commission with American, Soviet and British representatives was set up to study the question of dismemberment of Germany.

The Far East. According to an agreement that was kept strictly secret at the time and that was published a year later, on February 11, 1946, the Soviet Union promised to enter the war against Japan "two or three months after Germany has surrendered and the war in Europe has terminated" on the following conditions:

That the status quo in Outer Mongolia be preserved. (Outer Mongolia, nominally a part of China, had been a Soviet protected state since 1921.)

That the southern part of Sakhalin with adjacent islands be returned to the Soviet Union.

That the commercial port of Dairen be internationalized, "the pre-eminent interests of the Soviet Union in this port being safeguarded, and the lease of Port Arthur as a naval base of the Soviet Union restored."

That the Chinese Eastern Railway and South Manchuria Railway (the principal railways of Manchuria) be operated by a joint Soviet-Chinese company, "it being understood that the pre-eminent interests of the Soviet Union shall be safeguarded and that China shall retain full sovereignty in Manchuria.

"That the Kurile Islands shall be handed over to the Soviet Union."

Declaration on Liberated Europe. There was to be mutual agreement between the three powers to concert their policies "in assisting the peoples of the former Axis satellite states of Europe to solve by democratic means their pressing political and economic problems." Interim government authorities were to be formed "broadly representative of all democratic elements in the population and pledged to the earliest possible establishment through free elections of governments responsive to the will of the people."

It was agreed that a conference to prepare the Charter of the United Nations should meet in San Francisco in April and that two of the affiliated Soviet Republics, the Ukraine and Byelorussia, should have individual seats in the UN Assembly. An agreement on Yugoslavia substantially confirmed the establishment of Tito's dictatorship, with one or two facesaving reservations, which, in practice, proved quite meaningless.

A separate important compact at Yalta, signed by Major General John R. Deane, chief of the United States military mission in Moscow, and Major General A. A. Gryzlov, on behalf of the Soviet Government, provided that all Soviet citizens liberated by the United States and all United States citizens liberated by the Soviet Union should be segregated from enemy war prisoners and maintained in separate camps until they had been handed over to their respective military authorities.

Here, in brief summary, is the factual content of the Yalta agreements. What is their moral and political significance?

First, the principle of self-determination for all peoples, emphasized in the first three clauses of the Atlantic Charter, was clearly scrapped, although professions of respect for the principles of the Atlantic Charter are sprinkled through the Yalta Declaration. The Soviet annexation of Eastern Poland, of Koenigsberg and past of East Prussia and the Polish authorized seizure of ethnic German territory were clearly against the will of the vast majority of the peoples concerned. There was no pretense in any of these changes of an honestly conducted plebiscite. These decisions created millions of homeless, embittered refugees and drew frontier lines that were unjust and unnatural and a very probable cause of future conflicts.

Second, the independence and territorial integrity of Poland were sacrificed. The legitimate Polish government in London, composed of representatives of all the leading political parties in pre-war Poland, was thrown over. A made-in-Moscow, communist dominated government which had come to

Poland in the wake of the Red Army, received the prestige of promised diplomatic recognition by the western powers. (In actual practice the "enlargement" of this government by the addition of Poles in Poland and abroad made no change in its domination by Moscow puppets.)

The Polish government in London was not a phantom. It had the undivided allegiance of hundreds of thousands of Poles who were fighting for the allied cause in the West, on land, on sea and in the air. It guided one of the most effective underground resistance movements in Europe.

It should not have been difficult to foresee how the pledges of "free unfettered elections" would work out, with Soviet-trained communists in charge of the police, the Red Army in occupation of the country and no safeguards for honest voting, such as the presence of foreign inspectors and American and British troop units, to counterbalance the effect of the Red Army. The effect of this abandonment of Poland was certain to be profound throughout Eastern Europe. For of all the countries in this area Poland had much the strongest legal and moral claim to American and British support. Polish resistance to Hitler's aggression had been the original occasion of the war. Poland had concluded an alliance with Great Britain on the eve of the outbreak of hostilities.

The treatment of Poland at Yalta offers a remarkably close parallel with the treatment of Czechoslovakia at Munich in 1938. If one substitutes Poland for Czechoslovakia, Stalin for Hitler, Roosevelt and Churchill for Daladier and Chamberlain the likeness is complete. Publicists of the Left showed (and sometimes still show) the same complacency about Yalta that some publicists of the Right displayed about Munich. There were the same distorted and irrelevant arguments to justify a shabby and dishonorable transaction, about Sudeten Germans in Czechoslovakia and Ukrainians in Eastern Poland. There was the same eagerness to find excuses for the rapacious dictator and there was the same impatient distaste with the protests of the victim against being murdered.

Harry Hopkins who, next to Roosevelt, bears the principal American responsibility for the Great Betrayal which reached its climax at Yalta, brushed the moral issue off with the remark: "The Poles are like the Irish. They are never satisfied with anything anyhow." And a junior diplomatic official in the United States told the Polish Ambassador that the Polish problem had to be settled because it had become "an intolerable headache"! [4]

Like Munich, Yalta must be set down as a dismal failure, practically as well as morally. For Hitler was not satiated by his acquisitions at Munich and Stalin was not appeased at Yalta. The human and industrial resources of Czechoslovakia became an asset for the Nazi war machine. Poland also, under its communist rulers, is being organized systematically against the West.

---

[4] Jan Ciechanowski, *Defeat in Victory* (Doubleday), pp. 383–84.

Third, the Yalta Agreement, besides foreshadowing the enslavement of tens of millions of people in Eastern Europe, represented, in two of its features, the endorsement by the United States of the principle of human slavery. One of these features was the recognition that German labor could be used as a source of reparations. This gave implied American sanction to the retention of large numbers of German war prisoners, years after the end of hostilities, as forced laborers in the Soviet Union, Great Britain and France. And the agreement that Soviet citizens who were found in the western zones of occupation should be handed over to the Soviet authorities amounted, for the many Soviet refugees who did not wish to return, to the enactment of a fugitive slave law.

Fourth, the secret clauses of the Yalta Agreement which offered Stalin extensive territorial and economic concessions in the Far East as the price of Soviet participation in the war against Japan were immoral, unnecessary and unwise. These secret clauses were immoral because they gave away effective control of Manchuria, the most industrialized part of China, without consulting with or even informing the Chinese Government, an ally since Pearl Harbor. They were unnecessary because Stalin would almost certainly have entered the war without any bribe.

Moreover, it was a case of paying Stalin a second time for something he had already agreed to do, presumably in consideration of lend-lease aid and the second front, without any bribe. When Cordell Hull visited Moscow in October, 1943, Stalin proposed to enter the war against Japan after the defeat of Germany. According to Hull, this offer was unsolicited and had no strings attached to it.[5]

Stalin repeated this promise at Teheran. But Roosevelt, without waiting for a request, suggested that the Soviet Union should have access to the key Manchurian port of Dairen.[6] Finding Roosevelt so eager to anticipate his wishes, Stalin began to raise his price.

During Churchill's visit to Moscow in October, 1944, the Soviet dictator consented to take the offensive against Japan three months after the defeat of Germany, but on two conditions. The United States was to build up reserve lend-lease supplies for the operation and the "political aspects of Russian participation" were to be clarified.[7]

It was typical of the Soviet attitude toward obligations that, although there were repeated promises of bases for the American air force in Eastern Siberia, no such bases were ever made available. The United States, however, continued unusual efforts to build up the Soviet military reserve stocks in Eastern Siberia.[8]

Finally, the invitation to the Soviet Union to take over the Kurile Islands, South Sakhalin and an economic stranglehold on Manchuria was unwise,

---

[5] *The Memoirs of Cordell Hull* (Macmillan), p. 1310.
[6] Robert Sherwood, *Roosevelt and Hopkins* (Harper's), p. 792.
[7] John R. Deane, *The Strange Alliance* (Viking), p. 247.   [8] *Ibid.*, p. 254.

from the standpoint of American national interests. To increase what was already a prospective formidable predominance of Soviet strength in the Far East after the war by giving the Soviet Union take-off points for threatening Japan (South Sakhalin and the Kuriles) and economic domination of Manchuria was not a demonstration of farsighted statesmanship.

Even now Yalta has its defenders. They are to be found mainly among the unreserved admirers of Franklin D. Roosevelt's foreign policy and among those who, because of wartime association with the Administration, feel that their personal prestige is bound up with the vindication of this conference. Their four principal arguments are:

(1) That Yalta gave Stalin nothing that he was not in a position to take, or had not taken, anyway.

(2) That there was moral value in obtaining such Soviet promises as "free unfettered elections in Poland" and "democratic processes" in the "liberated countries."

(3) That the Yalta concessions were necessary to keep the Soviet Union in the war against Germany and to bring about Soviet intervention in the war against Japan.

(4) That the only alternative to the Yalta Agreement was the politically impossible one of going to war with the Soviet Union.

The first of these arguments misses the political and moral heart of the Yalta issue. The question was not what Stalin might have taken by military force in Eastern Europe and the Far East, but what he could take with the approval of the western powers. The difference is extremely important. In the case of Poland, for instance, it would have been far more difficult to maintain a Soviet satellite regime if this regime had not received the endorsement of the western powers. Nor was there anything inevitable about the Soviet domination of Manchuria and North Korea. It is a reasonable assumption that a peace treaty could have been concluded with Japan months before the end of the war if there had been enough farsighted statesmanship to propose the same terms which were finally signed in San Francisco in 1951. Had this been done before the Soviet Government was able to intervene in the Far Eastern war the Korean-Manchurian door could have been bolted against Soviet intrusion.

Argument two seems to be on a par with praising a man as a financial genius because he accepted a number of bad checks from a fraudulent bankrupt. The Yalta promises were not the first international obligations on which Stalin defaulted.

The third argument is based on the assumption that Stalin's own interests did not prompt him to seek to deliver a knockout blow against the two powers which were the greatest potential checks against his ambitions, in Europe and in Asia, Germany and Japan. There was no reason to bribe him to continue a war in Europe or to start a war in Asia so clearly prompted by his own sense of interest.

Was there an alternative to the appeasement of Yalta, besides war? Of course there was. Suppose the United States and Great Britain before Yalta and at Yalta had committed themselves to a firm, uncompromising declaration that they would neither use the war as a means of territorial gain themselves nor recognize any annexations carried out by other powers in violation of the principles of the Atlantic Charter. The Soviet frontiers of 1939 (frontiers with which the Soviet Government before the war often expressed itself as entirely satisfied) and not one square foot of Polish, Latvian, Estonian, Lithuanian, Finnish, Rumanian, German, Chinese or Japanese territory beyond these frontiers would have been acknowledged as legal and valid.

Behind such a declaration would have stood the mightiest concentration of sea and air power the world had ever seen, a highly mechanized army and an American war economy capable of almost unlimited further achievement. On the other side would have been a Soviet Union devastated by invasion and bled white in manpower, dependent in the final drive to victory on American trucks, field telephones, canned food and other lend-lease supplies.

Moreover, at the time of Yalta the hope of a genuine liberation from Nazi tyranny was still high in Poland and other countries of Central and eastern Europe. Except in Czechoslovakia the communist parties in these lands were tiny minority groups, with no appreciable popular following. So hated was the very name communist in Poland that the revived Polish Communist Party, which had been written off as a bad fifth column investment by Moscow in the late thirties, tried to conceal its real nature by calling itself the Workers' Party.

In view of these circumstances, in view of Stalin's habitual caution in foreign affairs, the Soviet dictator might well have renounced his designs of conquest and been satisfied with the preservation of his original realm. And if Stalin had taken a tough and negative attitude the date of the cold war would have been advanced,—very much to the advantage of the West. For at the time of Yalta the power relation was less favorable to the Soviet Union than it became later, when the Soviet Union repaired its war damage, crushed all semblance of open dissent in the satellite countries and swung China against the West. It was not the least of the sins of Yalta that it helped to blind American and British public opinion to the threat of Soviet expansion and contributed to the mood of recklessly hasty demobilization as soon as the shooting war with the Axis was over. There was no corresponding demobilization on the Soviet side.

Yalta should not be regarded as an isolated accident or a piece of black magic. It was a consequence, as well as a cause, a consequence of the dry rot of appeasement which was already well advanced at the time of the Teheran Conference, if not earlier. But Yalta will be remembered as the climax of a gravely mistaken course in foreign affairs. It was the supreme example of giving Stalin an unlimited diplomatic blank check, of deserting friends and favoring enemies in the vain hope of appeasing a regime which, by its nature and philosophy, is unappeasable.

The Meaning of Yalta

John L. Snell et al.

GERMANY AND THE MEANING OF YALTA*

Some of the Yalta decisions affecting Germany were summarized in a press report on February 12. This public proclamation embraced certain decisions on which there was such general agreement that they required little or no discussion at Yalta; it included other statements which camouflaged the extent of the Soviet retreat on German matters at Yalta. In it the Big Three announced:

> It is our inflexible purpose to destroy German militarism and Nazism and to ensure that Germany will never again be able to disturb the peace of the world. We are determined to disarm and disband all German armed forces; break up for all time the German General Staff that has repeatedly contrived the resurgence of German militarism; remove or destroy all German military equipment; eliminate or control all German industry that could be used for military production; bring all war criminals to just and swift punishment and exact reparation in kind for the destruction wrought by the Germans; wipe out the Nazi Party, Nazi laws, organizations and institutions, remove all Nazi and militarist influences from public office and from the cultural and economic life of the German people; and take in harmony such other measures in Germany as may be necessary to the future peace and safety of the world. It is not our purpose to destroy the people of Germany, but only when Nazism and militarism have been extirpated will there be hope for a decent life for Germans, and a place for them in the comity of nations.

In a moderate bid for German action to shorten the war, the Big Three proclaimed: "The German people, as well as the German soldiers, must

From John L. Snell, editor, *The Meaning of Yalta: Big Three Diplomacy and the New Balance of Power* (Baton Rouge: Louisiana State University Press, 1956), pp. 70–74, 119–126, 152–166, 186–187, 205–208. Reprinted by permission.

* Editor's note: By John L. Snell.

realize that the sooner they give up and surrender, by groups or as individuals, the sooner their present agony will be over." [1]

This proclamation veiled the vast indecision of the great Allies in questions concerning Germany. They could not agree, and as long as Germany fought on they could not afford to disagree. But the prospects of Germany's early collapse had brought the western statesmen face to face at last with the greatest European dilemma of the twentieth century: how can the threat of German power be eliminated from Europe without leaving Soviet power dominant throughout the continent? Therein lies the essential meaning of Yalta so far as Germany—and much of Europe—is concerned.

Roosevelt was no conscious advocate of the balance-of-power concept but, like other American statesmen since Wilson, he supported a principle which was its corollary: that it was not in the interest of the United States for any one state in Europe to dominate the whole. Churchill, on the other hand, consciously followed a balance-of-power policy in his negotiations with the Russians concerning the future of Germany. Thus it came about that the discussions of Germany questions at Yalta revealed beneath the verbiage of conciliation toward Russia the hard rock of Anglo-American solidarity and moderation toward Germany. The Russians failed to win full satisfaction on a single one of the demands they raised at Yalta concerning Germany's future.

The credits and debits of Yalta concerning the German problem read as follows: Stalin demanded a decision to dismember Germany; Churchill and Roosevelt postponed any specific plans, though they agreed in principle to the possibility of dismemberment. Stalin demanded a decision to deindustrialize Germany and rebuild the U.S.S.R. with German equipment; the President and the Prime Minister refused to agree to deindustrialization and postponed consideration of reparations. The Russians hoped that the western boundary of Poland might be drawn by Big Three agreement at the Western Neisse River and that the Ruhr and Saar would be separated from Germany; both Roosevelt and Churchill were opposed. The single set of demands concerning Germany which were met fully at Yalta were those which Roosevelt and Churchill advanced there: France was to have a zone of occupation and to participate in the integrated administration of Germany through the Control Council.

The positive material reconstruction of Germany was not desired at Yalta by any of the participants, nor could it possibly have been planned there; Roosevelt and Churchill avoided committing themselves to the permanent destruction of Germany only at the risk of alienating their Moscow colleague. This situation, so unfavorable for Germany, was of Germany's own creation. Adolf Hitler had sought to conquer Europe while posing as

---

[1] *Yalta Papers*, 969–71; United States, Department of State, *The Axis in Defeat, a Collection of Documents on American Policy toward Germany and Japan* (Washington, n.d.), 8–9.

its savior against Bolshevism.[2] Hitler himself had offered Europe its choice of mistresses: Nazism or Bolshevism. But he had shown the opportunistic motivation of his egocentric ideology by outlawing his own nation against the western community. In February, 1945, it seemed certain that Europe would soon be rid of the ruthless and insatiable mistress whom Hitler had forced upon it; the era of German hegemony in European history was almost over, having been desperate in character but brief in duration. Was the second mistress which Hitler had offered, Russian communism, to be the only choice left after the debauchery into which Hitler had led Europe? This was the verdict of the Nazi newspaper *Völkischer Beobachter*, which headlined the Yalta communiqué as the "DEATH SENTENCE FOR EUROPE" and insisted that conference unity had been preserved only by the surrender of Roosevelt and Churchill to every demand Stalin raised.[3]

Ultimately a combination of American and British military and economic power broadened the choices facing Europe, but only after Germany and Japan were defeated and after it became crystal clear that Stalin thought in terms of the same two crude alternatives which Hitler had presented. In February, 1945, this was not fully apparent, and Hitler's Germany still held the Big Three together as it had made them "strange allies" in the first place. "We separated in the Crimea," Churchill has recalled, "not only as Allies but as friends facing a still mighty foe with whom all our armies were struggling in fierce and ceaseless battle." [4]

The Yalta negotiators had not solved "the German problem." But they had done an essential job of "papering over the cracks" in an alliance which could not be sacrificed until victory was won. This, in essence, was the best the Big Three at Yalta could do when they turned intermittently from the profound problem of Germany to consider the more immediately pressing difficulties which had been created by the Red Army's occupation of central-eastern Europe. . . .

EASTERN EUROPEAN EPILOGUE *

Early in the war Poland had emerged as the roughest testing ground of the possibility of maintaining amicable relations between East and West. Harry Hopkins once told Stalin that "the question of Poland *per se* was not so important as the fact that it had become a symbol of our ability to work out problems with the Soviet Union." [5] Uppermost in the American delegation's thoughts was winning Soviet acceptance of the United Nations blueprint and Russian participation in the Pacific war. Churchill declared at

---

[2] Paul Kluke, "Nationalsozialistische Europaideologie," *Vierteljahrshefte für Zeitgeschichte* (Tübingen and Munich), III (July, 1955), 240–75.

[3] Munich *Völkischer Beobachter*, February 13–16, 1945.

[4] Churchill, *Triumph and Tragedy*, 510.

* Editor's note: By Charles F. Delzell.   [5] Sherwood, *Roosevelt and Hopkins*, 898.

Yalta that his country "had no material interest in Poland." Britain's interests, he said, was "only one of honor" toward an allied state whose invasion had precipitated the war.[6] Stalin, on the other hand, took the uncompromising stand that for his country the Polish problem was not just a "symbol," nor a "question of honor," but one of "security." [7] Because of the relative weight which each of the Big Three assigned to the Polish issue, the nature of their prior agreements, and the realities of Russian military power in eastern Europe, there was little room at Yalta for successful bargaining against the U.S.S.R.

Nonetheless, Churchill and Roosevelt argued the Polish problem with Stalin for six days and nights. Obviously, it was not a question of what they would permit him to do but what they could persuade him to accept. In the protracted, exhausting discussions, Churchill, whose previous diplomatic engagements involved him in this region much more deeply than was the case with Roosevelt, doggedly carried the burden of western argumentation. He marshaled his points carefully and often eloquently, and in the drafting of the final agreements he endeavored, insofar as the limited time permitted, to weigh the import of every word. President Roosevelt preferred to play the role of moderator, but in the showdowns he usually aligned himself with Churchill. Roosevelt's exposition was not always so skillful, energetic, or persistent as that of the Briton, but it fully evidenced his concern for a really independent Poland as well as for lasting world peace. For his part, Stalin set forth with bluntness Soviet Russia's strategic interests, and he cleverly seized upon the weak points in the westerners' case. He reminded them that they should not expect him to be any less Russian than Clemenceau and Lord Curzon; he skillfully equated the legitimacy of his Lublin regime with that of de Gaulle in France; and employing the same arguments that Churchill had used recently in Greece to justify British measures, he argued persuasively that nothing must be allowed to jeopardize the security of the Soviet armies in Poland. The Russian leader was impervious to arguments based either on "high moral" principles or on the need for placating Polish-American voters. But sometimes he was willing to accept phraseology that enabled the West to "save face," especially if he felt certain that in the execution of the agreements he could have his own way.

Thus Roosevelt and Churchill were able to win a moral victory when they persuaded Stalin to agree with minor changes to the pledges contained in the somewhat loosely phrased Declaration on Liberated Europe. Certainly there was nothing reprehensible in the terms of this American-sponsored document, which called for "free" and "democratic" regimes in eastern Europe. But the present-day observer is inclined to marvel at the optimism of the Big Three when they declared: "We reaffirm our faith in

---

[6] *Yalta Papers,* 678–79.   [7] *Ibid.,* 679–81.

the principles of the Atlantic Charter, our pledge in the Declaration by the United Nations, and our determination to build in cooperation with other peaceloving nations a world order under law, dedicated to peace, security, freedom and general well-being of all mankind." [8] At the time of the Crimea conference there was still reason to hope that Stalin might honor his promises. Had he not scrupulously refrained from criticizing the British military operations in Greece, in accordance with his recent bargain with Churchill? When the evidence of Soviet lack of good faith in Rumania and other eastern countries was forthcoming a few weeks after Yalta, the United States and Britain were in an excellent position, thanks to the "Yalta Declaration," to make it clear to the world who was at fault.

On the subject of the Yugoslav agreements between Tito and Prime Minister Šubašić, the British were able to win Soviet acceptance of pledges for a more parliamentary and constitutional type of government than then existed under Tito. What was regrettable in this was not the Yalta agreement but its violation.

The discussions of the perplexing Polish territorial problem ended by assigning to Soviet Russia the land east of the Curzon Line, except for minor rectifications in favor of Poland. No plebiscites were called for, and the action was taken without the consent of the Polish government in exile, although hardly to its surprise. The agreement thus violated the spirit of the Atlantic Charter. But it is impossible to see how the western statesmen could have prevented Soviet acquisition of this land, short of armed conflict with Russia, for the military balance of power in eastern Europe had shifted entirely in her favor by 1945. To ratify the shift or to repudiate the eastern ally? Therein lay the meaning of Yalta so far as the Polish problem was concerned.

Because of firm western opposition to "overstuffing the German goose" with millions of displaced people from Silesia, Stalin was forced to agree to leave the western frontier of Poland undefined. But in assenting to this, he undoubtedly foresaw that he could at a later time unilaterally assign a wide strip of the Soviet zone in Germany to Poland, thereby tightening his grip on a grateful Polish government. This he did a few months later, when he handed to Poland the territory east of the Oder and Western Neisse rivers.

On the issue of the Polish government, Churchill and Roosevelt could barely budge Stalin, in view of the Soviet recognition of the Lublin-Warsaw Committee of National Liberation a month before Yalta. There seems to be no reason to dispute the contention of Charles E. Bohlen, who was present at the conference, that on this subject only three courses of action were open to the western leaders: (1) they could have accepted the *fait accompli*,

---

[8] The Declaration on Liberated Europe is quoted in its final version in the Appendix of this volume.

doing nothing, which is what Stalin doubtless would have preferred; (2) they could have stood uncomprisingly behind the Polish government in exile, in which case probably no member of it would have returned to Poland; or (3) they could have attempted to get as many members as possible of the London group into a "reorganized" government.[9] Realistically, they chose the third course.

The crux of the negotiations was whether the Lublin-Warsaw regime should simply be "enlarged," as the Russians insisted, or completely "reorganized," as the West demanded. After six days of haggling, the agreement that emerged on paper was ambiguous at best. In deference to Stalin, no mention was made in the document of the government in exile, but reference repeatedly was made to the "Provisional Government which is now functioning in Poland." On the other hand, the western phrasemakers were able to insert a clause explaining that this provisional government would be "reorganized on a broader democratic basis . . . with the inclusion of democratic leaders from Poland itself and from Poles abroad." [10]

Admiral William D. Leahy commented to the President at the time that the Polish agreement was so elastic that the Russians could "stretch it all the way from Yalta to Washington without ever technically breaking it." Roosevelt readily conceded this. "I know, Bill—I know it. But it's the best I can do for Poland at this time." [11] Upon his return from the 14,000-mile trip, the President, in his last personal report to Congress, endeavored to put forth the best possible interpretation of the Polish compromise, but he scarcely concealed from his listeners that it was not entirely to his liking.[12] In the House of Commons Churchill was confronted with a full-dress debate on the Crimea conference between February 27 and March 1, and vigorous opposition was raised by some three dozen members who regarded the agreements as inconsonant with Britain's written and moral obligations to her Polish ally.[13] Most of the Poles abroad were in a rage, and on the Italian front General Anders threatened for a time to pull his Polish forces out of the line.[14] A great number of his soldiers decided to live permanently in western Europe.

From the vantage point of hindsight and an absolute standard of morality, one can readily concede the cogency of many of the criticisms levied against the agreements. But a fairer historical approach has been suggested

---

[9] United States Senate, 83rd Congress, 1st Session, *Hearings before the Committee on Foreign Relations: Nomination of Charles E. Bohlen, March 2, and 18, 1953* (Washington, 1953), 2–113.

[10] *Yalta Papers*, 973–74. [11] Leahy, *I Was There*, 315–16.

[12] For the text of President Roosevelt's speech, see Leland M. Goodrich and Marie J. Carroll, *Documents on American Foreign Relations, 1944–45*, VII (Boston, 1947), 18–28.

[13] Churchill, *Triumph and Tragedy*, 401–402. Excerpts from the debate in the House of Commons are reprinted in R. Umiastowski, *Poland, Russia, and Great Britain, 1941–1945: A Study of the Evidence* (London, 1946), 509 *et seq.*

[14] Anders, *An Army in Exile*, 247–54.

by Churchill, notwithstanding the fact that he was an "interested party." He has reminded the world to judge the actions of statesmen on the basis of the limited knowledge available to them at the moment of their decisions and the over-all objectives that they considered to be pre-eminent.[15]

If the western leaders cannot escape responsibility for certain miscalculations, neither can many of the Polish politicians abroad. The war had left them "men without a country," yet they unrealistically and stubbornly insisted that virtually no political or territorial changes could be acknowledged in a region in which a great change in power relationships had, in fact, occurred. Clearly they could not hope to maintain an independent, viable state between the U.S.S.R. and the Soviet zone of Germany unless they were willing to collaborate with their all-powerful neighbor. Still, it is hard to blame the Poles for having been reluctant to give up a vast portion of their prewar state without a plebiscite and in the mere hope that the Communists would not attempt to subvert a fusion government. Churchill has stoutly insisted that if the Poles had been willing in 1941 or even as late as the autumn of 1944 to agree to the Curzon Line, Stalin might have been persuaded to permit the establishment of a truly independent but friendly government, much as he did in the case of Finland. This may be true, but the historian can not write in the subjunctive case.

Like the other decisions, the Yalta agreement on the Polish government rested on the assumption that the Kremlin would honor it. Instead, the dispute over "reorganization" as opposed to mere "enlargement" resumed almost at once, bedeviling the last weeks of Franklin D. Roosevelt's life and adding to the headaches of Harry S. Truman's first months in office. From Moscow, Ambassador Harriman in March informed Washington that Molotov refused to live up to the Yalta agreements regarding the future Polish government; and on April 7 Stalin protested to Roosevelt that the United States and British ambassadors in Moscow had departed from the principles of Yalta.[16] Just before his death in April, 1945, Roosevelt cabled Churchill with respect to the Polish controversy: "We must be firm . . . and our course thus far is correct." [17] However, the "reorganized" Polish government that eventually was formed and recognized by the Great Powers retained a majority of the cabinet seats for former members of the pro-Soviet Lublin committee. The elections which Stalin had promised within a few weeks after Yalta were postponed until January, 1947, and were of course neither "free" nor "unfettered." [18]

---

[15] Cf. Churchill, *Triumph and Tragedy*, 402.

[16] See *Yalta Papers*, 989–93, for the exchange of Russian and American protests of bad faith during March and April, 1945; cf. Harry S. Truman, *Year of Decisions* (Garden City, 1955), 15–16, 23–26, 37–39, 50, 71–79, 84–86, 107–109, 254–55, 263, 280–81, 320–22, 347–410, and *passim*.

[17] Churchill, *Triumph and Tragedy*, 454.

[18] Mikolajczyk, *Rape of Poland*, 180–202; Arthur Bliss Lane, *I Saw Poland Betrayed* (Indianapolis, 1948), 276–88.

The Meaning of Yalta

The Soviet Union failed to live up to the Yalta agreements concerning central-eastern Europe, and western statesmen, especially Roosevelt, have been denounced as traitors or bemoaned as babes in the diplomatic woods for having accepted Stalin's promises. But the historical moment must be remembered and Yalta agreements on eastern Europe must be viewed as part of an entire complex of wartime problems. The fact that Roosevelt and Churchill had blocked Soviet pretensions in Germany made it difficult for them to resist all of Stalin's Polish demands and neither was ready to let the Polish problem rupture western relations with the Soviet Union; Japan remained to be defeated even after Nazism was crushed. Consideration of strategic problems in the Far East undoubtedly conditioned the Yalta bargaining of the West on all European questions. By the time the final agreements on central-eastern Europe were signed, Stalin had delighted both Roosevelt and Churchill by promising to enter the war against Japan. Diplomacy has ever been a "give-and-take proposition," and the global proportions of the Yalta give-and-take must be considered if the historical meaning of Yalta is to be understood. . . .

YALTA AND THE FAR EAST *

. . . in February, 1945, the secret Far Eastern agreement seemed "very reasonable." Indeed, to some it appeared to usher in "the dawn of the new day we had all been praying for and talking about for so many years." Shortly after the Yalta conference General MacArthur was quoted as having stated that Russian seizure of Manchuria, Korea, and possibly part of northern China was inevitable, and that to deny Port Arthur to Russia would be impractical. Less than a decade later the Yalta agreement was branded not only as a betrayal of American principles, but as downright "treason," and General MacArthur in 1955 characterized as "fantastic" concessions which in 1945 seemed "inevitable." [19] In 1948 and especially in 1952 the Far Eastern agreements at Yalta became major issues in American presidential elections.

The controversy over these agreements may well last as long as the Far East remains important in world affairs; it is likely to be reopened whenever the careers of Roosevelt, Churchill, and Stalin are evaluated. The whole controversy hinges on two basic questions, one of power and one of morality. The first: Was Russian entry into the war against Japan neces-

---

* Editor's note: By George A. Lensen.

[19] Leahy, *I Was There*, 318–19; Sherwood, *Roosevelt and Hopkins*, 870; Felix Wittmer, *The Yalta Betrayal: Data on the Decline and Fall of Franklin Delano Roosevelt* (Caldwell, 1953), 76; Letter from Col. Paul L. Freeman, Jr., to General Marshall (February 13, 1945), and memorandum from General George A. Lincoln to General Marshall (March 8, 1945), as cited in Department of Defense, "The Entry of the Soviet Union into the War against Japan," 50–52; statement of General MacArthur, New York *Times*, October 21, 1955.

sary? The second: Did Roosevelt and Churchill willfully and lightly sacrifice the interests of a third power and a friend, China?

Did defeat of Japan depend on Russian help? . . . Suffice it to state here that in February, 1945, no one could count upon the effective use of the atomic bomb in the war against Japan,[20] and that American planners estimated that eighteen months of fighting after the not yet attained German surrender and at least 500,000 American casualties—perhaps one million—might be required to subdue the Japanese, even with Russian help.[21] In the circumstances it is understandable that United States and British military strategists sought the destruction or at least the diversion of the Japanese forces on the Asian continent by Russian action. As late as July 24, 1945, the Combined Chiefs of Staff recommended Russian entry into the war against Japan "to assist in the execution of the over-all strategic concept." Roosevelt's successor, Harry S. Truman, has stated emphatically in his memoirs that even on this date, seven days after he had received news of the successful test explosion of the A-bomb, it was still of great importance to the United States to secure Soviet participation in the war against Japan.[22] In February, 1945, it was up to the President and the Prime Minister to make the political arrangements which the military needs seemed to require, and this they did. This may have been a mistake; quite clearly it was not "treason."

Had the Joint Chiefs of Staff and the President decided that Russian entry into the war against Japan was not desirable, would the Soviets have come to the same conclusion? Admiral William H. Standley, upon his return from ambassadorial duties in Moscow in October of 1943, had told Roosevelt: "I don't think you can keep Stalin out." During World War I Japan had invoked the Anglo-Japanese Alliance ostensibly to come to Britain's aid, but actually to conquer the former German possessions in China for herself. In 1945 Russia was America's ally in Europe; she might well have entered the Pacific war uninvited to help herself, with or without the pretext of aiding the United States. Then the sky would have been the limit. The conditional entry, negotiated at Yalta, put at least a paper restraint on Russian ambitions, and this was the only restraint anyone could have put on Stalin at Yalta in February, 1945.

The alternative to refusal of Russian help or failure to bargain for it would not simply have been to fight without Russian assistance; the exclusion of Russia would have aroused Russian apprehension if not hostility.

---

[20] Churchill, *Triumph and Tragedy*, 388–89; *Yalta Papers*, 383; Stettinius, *Roosevelt and the Russians*, 90.

[21] Churchill, *Triumph and Tragedy*, 388–89; Sherwood, *Roosevelt and Hopkins*, 867; Stettinius, *Roosevelt and the Russians*, 8–9; Harry S. Truman, *Year of Decisions* (Garden City, 1955), 265.

[22] Walter Millis (ed.), with the collaboration of E. S. Duffield, *The Forrestal Diaries* (New York, 1951), 51; Department of Defense, "The Entry of the Soviet Union into the War against Japan," 90–91; Truman, *Year of Decisions*, 236, 265, 381–82, 411.

Stalin was in a stronger bargaining position than the Joint Chiefs of Staff or Roosevelt realized, for Japan was ready to offer much to keep Russia neutral. As Japan's position grew more desperate during the war, so did the plans of her leaders. Expecting the co-operation of Communist Russia and the capitalist states to deteriorate if not end upon the defeat of Germany, Japanese admirals wanted their diplomats to negotiate a coalition or alliance with the Soviet Union and "apparently also hoped eventually to draw the Soviet Union into the Japanese war effort as a fighting member in good standing." Marquis Koichi Kido, the Lord Keeper or the Privy Seal, whose duty it was to advise the Emperor, looked to Russia for a possible alignment because she was "Oriental" in outlook. As Stalin had said to Matsuoka in April, 1941, "You are an Asiatic. So am I." Other Japanese felt that "the Soviet Union would want to see Japan retain a fairly important international position so that the two countries could ally themselves in the future against America and Britain." Stalin had asserted in 1941 that "the whole world can be settled" if Japan and Russia co-operate. In June, 1945, Koki Hirota, a former prime minister and onetime ambassador to Moscow, suggested to Jacob A. Malik, then Soviet ambassador to Japan, that "if the Soviet Army and the Japanese Navy were to join forces, Japan and the Soviet Union together would become the strongest powers in the world." [23]

The Japanese were prepared to make substantial concessions to Russia in order to bring her into the war on their side or, if this were not possible, to restrain her from taking up arms against Japan. Foreign Minister Shigenori Togo, for example, went so far as to suggest that Japan might have to return to her pre-1904 boundaries. Others would have given up even more. In the words of a former Japanese diplomat, the Japanese military leaders were "frightened out of their wits" at the thought of a new war with Russia and were willing to pay a heavy price to avoid one. After all, "If a ship is doomed what matters its cargo, however precious? Jettison the cargo as fast as possible, if only doing so may save the ship." [24]

Having been promised what they wanted at Yalta, the Russians rebuffed Japanese overtures. Had their conditions been rejected at Yalta, Stalin conceivably might have made his bargain with the Japanese instead of with Roosevelt. True, Russian entry into the war against Japan enabled Soviet historians to boast that "the Armed Forces of the Soviet Union played the decisive role in the crushing of the Japanese imperialism, in the final liberation of China from the Japanese usurpers," but had Russia chosen

---

[23] William H. Standley and Arthur A. Ageton, *Admiral Ambassador to Russia* (Chicago, 1955), 499; Robert J. C. Butow, *Japan's Decision to Surrender* (Stanford, 1954), 77, 86–87, 121–22; Toshikazu Kase (David Nelson Rowe, ed.), *Journey to the Missouri*, 131; Otto D. Tolischus, *Tokyo Record* (New York, 1943), 107.

[24] Kase, *Journey to the Missouri*, 169; Butow, *Japan's Decision to Surrender*, 84; Tolischus, *Tokyo Record*, 107.

to attain her ends by acting as a peace-loving mediator, her propaganda stock in these days of smiling imperialism would have been even higher in the Far East.[25]

There are other questions. Granted that Russian entry into the war against Japan was desirable, was the price paid for Soviet help too high? Were the concessions justified? Did Roosevelt "sell out" Nationalist China? Did Yalta pave the way for Russian domination of China? The best way to answer these questions is to take a closer look at the agreements.

The stipulation in the Yalta agreement that "the *status quo* in Outer-Mongolia (The Mongolian People's Republic) shall be preserved" implied Soviet domination of this area. This was contrary to the Sino-Soviet Treaty of 1924, which recognized Chinese sovereignty over Sovietized Outer Mongolia. But this sovereignty ceased to exist in the middle 1920's, and by the time of Yalta the Soviet Union had exercised *de facto* control there for about twenty years. The parenthetical inclusion of "the Mongol People's Republic" in the Yalta agreement merely strengthened later Russian arguments vis-à-vis the Chinese for Outer Mongolia's formal "independence." [26]

The provision that "the southern part of Sakhalin as well as all the islands adjacent to it shall be returned to the Soviet Union" provoked no American discussion. Professor Hugh Borton, then of the State Department, recommended that southern Sakhalin be treated as an international trusteeship, in view of its importance to both Russia and Japan. But somehow his memorandum had not been included in the Yalta Briefing Book.[27] Postwar disillusionment in America in the Yalta agreements led to the devaluation of experts, particularly professors. Actually, the Yalta records show that it was not the advice of the academicians which was taken that caused trouble, but that which was ignored.

The agreement that "the commercial port of Dairen shall be internationalized, the preeminent interests of the Soviet Union in this port being safeguarded and the lease of Port Arthur as a naval base of the USSR restored" has been criticized severely as a reversion to nineteenth-century imperialism. Harriman has tried to meet these objections by pointing out that "there is no reason from the discussions leading up to the Yalta agreements to presume that the safeguarding of the 'pre-eminent interests of the Soviet Union' should go beyond Soviet interests in the free *transit* of exports and

---

[25] G. Efimov, *Ocherki po novoi i noveishei istorii Kitaia* [Account of the Modern and Contemporary History of China] (Moscow, 1951), 401; V. Avarin, *Bor'ba za Tikhii Okean* [The Struggle for the Pacific Ocean] (Leningrad, 1947), 419; E. M. Zhukov (ed.), *Mezhdunarodnye otnosheniia na Dal'nem Vostoke (1870–1945)* [International Relations in the Far East (1870–1945)] (Moscow, 1951), 610–11.

[26] Gerald H. Friters, *Outer Mongolia and its International Position* (Baltimore, 1949), 149; State Department, *United States Relations with China*, 113, n. 2, and 117, n. 7; Charles Patrick Fitzgerald, *Revolution in China* (New York, 1952), 235.

[27] *Yalta Papers*, 385–88; Ernest J. King and Walter Muir Whitehill, *Fleet Admiral King, A Naval Record* (New York, 1952), 591–92.

imports to and from the Soviet Union," and that "President Roosevelt looked upon the lease of Port Arthur for a naval base as an arrangement similar to privileges which the United States has negotiated with other countries for the mutual security of two friendly nations." Be that as it may, the Russian desire to get back from the Japanese what they had lost in the Russo-Japanese War seemed on the whole reasonable[28]

The provision that the Chinese-Eastern Railroad and the South Manchurian Railroad, which provides an outlet to Dairen, should be jointly operated by a Soviet-Chinese company—with the understanding that "the pre-eminent interests of the Soviet Union shall be safeguarded and that China shall retain full sovereignty in Manchuria"—has encountered less criticism. China had never recognized Russia's sale of the Chinese-Eastern Railroad to Japan in 1935 and still clung to the Sino-Soviet agreement of 1924, which provided that the manager of the railway be a Soviet citizen. Furthermore, the curious geographical conformation of Russia's Maritime Province made joint operation highly logical. Last but not least, Roosevelt and other Allied leaders were still preoccupied with the thought of future security against Japanese aggression. Japan had put down roots in southern Manchuria that could not be destroyed by military defeat alone. China did not seem strong enough to neutralize this area. As one historian has put it: "To recognize Russia's legitimate economic and strategic stake in Manchuria under conditions that specified 'that China shall retain full sovereignty' was a solution far more conservative than to abandon the 'cradle of conflict' to the winds of fate." [29] It must also be remembered that Roosevelt was not "giving away" any Chinese territory which he or even the Chinese actually held, but what the Japanese had in fact conquered. The concessions at Yalta seemed the most effective way of winning Manchuria back for the Chinese, at least politically.

But whatever historical arguments there may have been for the cession of southern Sakhalin, Dairen, and Port Arthur, there were none to justify the transfer of the whole Kurile Archipelago to the Soviet Union. A State Department memorandum by Professor George H. Blakeslee, which unfortunately, like the memorandum by Professor Borton, was not included in the Briefing Book, recognized that Russia had "a substantial claim" to the northern Kurile Islands and a strategic interest in the central group. "There would seem, however, to be few factors which would justify a Soviet claim to the southern islands," the memorandum continued. "This transfer to the Soviet Union would create a situation which a future Japan would find difficult to accept as a permanent solution. It would deprive Japan of islands which are historically and ethnically Japanese and of waters which are

---

[28] State Department, *United States Relations with China*, 114, n. 3, 4; Leahy, *I Was There*, 318–19; Werner Levi, *Modern China's Foreign Policy* (Minneapolis, 1953), 240–41.

[29] William Appleman Williams, *American-Russian Relations, 1781–1947* (New York, 1952), 277.

valuable for fishery. If the southern islands should be fortified they would be a continuing menace to Japan." In view of the proximity of the Kurile Islands to the Aleutians and their consequent importance to the United States as a land bridge between Japan and Alaska, the memorandum recommended that the northern and central Kuriles should be placed under the projected international organization.[30] The advice of Professor Blakeslee was not considered at Yalta, where Stalin was assured that all the Kurile Islands "shall be handed over to the Soviet Union."

The Roosevelt-Stalin agreement qualified the provisions concerning Outer Mongolia, Dairen, Port Arthur, and the railroads by making them subject to concurrence by Chiang Kai-shek, but then proceeded to nullify this qualification by stating that "these claims of the Soviet Union shall be unquestionably fulfilled." Was this a "sell-out" of the Chinese government?

It is relevant to remember in this connection that Chiang Kai-shek's own policy from the middle of 1943 on was directed toward a *rapprochement* with the Soviet Union. For this he sought American mediation, suggesting to Vice-President Henry A. Wallace in June, 1944, that Roosevelt act as "middleman" between China and the U.S.S.R. Chiang was willing to go "more than halfway" to obtain a friendly understanding with the Soviet Union, partly because he hoped that this might induce the Russians to continue recognizing his government as *the* government of China and deprive them of incentive to support the Chinese Communists, and partly because he felt that obligating Russia to something by a treaty was better than leaving her a free hand.[31] It was only in later years, when the Nationalist government began to shift the blame for its own shortcomings upon the shoulders of the United States, that Nationalist officials "demanded American support as an atonement for the betrayal at Yalta." [32]

Postwar accusations of betrayal ignored the stipulation in the Yalta agreement that "the Soviet Union expresses its readiness to conclude with the National Government of China a pact of friendship and alliance between the USSR and China." The pact of friendship and alliance was not intended to betray China, but to strengthen it. As a Briefing Book paper stated, "The American Government's long-range policy with respect to China is based on the belief that the need for China to be a principal factor in the Far East is a fundamental requirement for peace and security in that area." And another paper, considering the "political and military situation in China in the event the U.S.S.R. enters the war in the Far East," recommended that the British and American governments "should make every effort to bring about cooperation between all Chinese forces

---

[30] *Yalta Papers*, 379–83.

[31] Levi, *Modern China's Foreign Policy*, 243–44; State Department, *United States Relations with China*, 550; Max Beloff, *Soviet Policy in the Far East, 1944–1951* (London, 1953), 29; "Statement of W. Averell Harriman," 3339.

[32] Levi, *Modern China's Foreign Policy*, 244.

and the Russian military command in order to prevent military developments from further widening the gap between the Communists and the Chinese Government and increasing the possibility of a disunited China after hostilities." In point of fact, the treaty which eventually was concluded between Nationalist China and the U.S.S.R., the Soong-Stalin agreements of August, 1945, was heralded by so pro-Nationalist a magazine as *Life* as a promise of "genuine peace" in the Far East.[33]

It was a weak China, unable to fill the power vacuum which the defeat of Japan would create, that the United States government dreaded. Stalin's recognition of the Nationalist government as the central authority in China was most reassuring, therefore, and subsequent Soviet statements were even more encouraging. Thus in June, 1945, the new President, Harry S. Truman, could inform his special representative in China, Patrick J. Hurley, that:

> 1. Stalin has made to us a categorical statement that he will do everything he can to promote unification under the leadership of Chiang Kai-shek.
>
> 2. That this leadership will continue after the war.
>
> 3. That he wants a unified stable China and wants China to control all of Manchuria as a part of a United China.
>
> 4. That he has no territorial claims against China, and that he will respect Chinese sovereignty in all areas his troops enter to fight Japanese.
>
> 5. That he will welcome representatives of the Generalissimo to be with his troops in Manchuria in order to facilitate the organization of Chinese administration in Manchuria.
>
> 6. That he agrees with America's "open door" policy in China.
>
> 7. That he agrees to a trusteeship for Korea under China, Great Britain, the Soviet Union, and the United States.[34]

Certainly this seemed to offer that promise of "a strong, stable, and united China" which was the objective set forth in the President's Briefing Book for the Yalta negotiations when it stated: "We regard Sino-Soviet cooperation as a *sine qua non* of peace and security in the Far East and seek to aid in removing the existing mistrust between China and the Soviet Union and in bringing about close and friendly relations between them." [35]

The same outlook underlay American-Soviet relations. "President Roosevelt and I saw alike with regard to Russia," wrote Cordell Hull. "We both realize that the path of our relations would not be a carpet of flowers, but we also felt that we could work with Russia. There was no difference of opinion between us that I can recall on the basic premise that we must and could get along with the Soviet Government." [36]

---

[33] *Yalta Papers*, 352, 356; *Life*, XIX (September 10, 1945), 42.
[34] Truman, *Year of Decisions*, 269.   [35] *Yalta Papers*, 356–57.
[36] Hull, *Memoirs*, II, 1467.

No one could have expected the Russians to enter the war against Japan for the sole purpose of saving American lives. It is understandable that some territorial agreement was reached. It is less understandable, however, that there was almost no discussion of Russian claims. It is by no means impossible that the Russians would have satisfied themselves with only the northern and central Kurile Islands. But nobody ever raised the question. Nor did anybody counter the other Russian demands. The Americans might have reminded Stalin that his demands violated not only Russia's treaty with Japan of 1925 but also her treaty with China of 1924. In the former she had declared that the treaty ending the Russo-Japanese War "remains in full force," and in the latter she had renounced "the special rights and privileges relating to all concessions in any part of China acquired by the Tsarist Government under various Conventions, Treaties, Agreements, etc." Probably Roosevelt felt that Stalin could not be swayed and that nothing would be gained by antagonizing him. But by agreeing that in 1904 Japan had been the aggressor, Churchill and Roosevelt put the finger on their own countries, for it was with English and American moral and financial support that Japan ventured to challenge Russia in apparent defense of the Open Door.

Roosevelt and Churchill missed a golden opportunity to remind Stalin of earlier Communist condemnations of the czarist government's role in the Russo-Japanese War and to accuse him, tongue in cheek, of "deviationism." But perhaps it was just as well, for when Churchill had reminded Stalin at Teheran in another connection of the old Communist slogan "no annexations and no indemnities," Stalin had only replied with a broad grin: "I have told you that I am becoming a Conservative." Stalin asserted at the end of the war that the Russian people had been looking forward to the defeat of Japan to liquidate the blemish cast upon their country in 1904, that "for forty years we the people of the older generation have waited for this day." This was contrary not only to the traditional party line but also to current Russian feelings. General Deane observed in Moscow that Russia's entry into the war against Japan evoked relatively little enthusiasm or interest.[37]

Yet, when all this has been said, it must be remembered that the United States did not "give away" at Yalta anything that it was within her power to withhold except by making war against her Russian ally. In the words of Secretary of War Henry L. Stimson, the concessions to Russia on Far Eastern matters which were made at Yalta were "generally matters which are within

[37] Harriet L. Moore, *Soviet Far Eastern Policy, 1931–1945* (New York, 1945), 159, 175; Iosif V. Stalin, "Obrashcheniia tovarishcha I. V. Stalina k narodu" [Speech of Comrade Joseph V. Stalin to the People], as cited by B. A. Romanov, *Ocherki diplomaticheskoi istorii russko-iaponskoi voiny 1895–1907* [Outlines of the Diplomatic History of the Russo-Japanese War, 1895–1907] (Moscow, 1947), 3; Winston S. Churchill, *Closing the Ring* (Boston, 1951), 398–99; Deane, *The Strange Alliance*, 311.

the military power of Russia to obtain regardless of U. S. military action short of war. The War Department believes that Russia is militarily capable of defeating the Japanese and occupying Karafuto [Sakhalin], Manchuria, Korea and Northern China before it would be possible for the U. S. military forces to occupy these areas. Only in the Kuriles is the United States in a position to circumvent Russian initiative. If the United States were to occupy these islands to forestall Russian designs, it would be at the direct expense of the campaign to defeat Japan and would involve an unacceptable cost in American lives." [38] Stimson's statement points to the essential meaning of Yalta, so far as American interests in the Far East were concerned. Yalta enabled the United States virtually to ignore the Japanese forces on the mainland of Asia and thus to concentrate upon the Japanese home islands. This was an asset which facilitated the exclusive postwar occupation by the United States of the real heart of Far Eastern industry—Japan.

It was not the Yalta agreement, but failure to live up to the agreement that furthered postwar conflict. Perhaps the breakdown in Russo-American co-operation was inherent in the amorality of Communism; perhaps it was due to the age-old inability of comrades-in-arms to remain comrades-in-peace. As Stalin said at Yalta: "It is not so difficult to keep unity in time of war since there is a joint aim to defeat the common enemy, which is clear to everyone. The difficult task will come after the war when diverse interests tend to divide the Allies." [39]

The Yalta agreements were not faultless, but their imperfections lay in the limitation of the human mind, in man's inability to gaze into the future. Churchill summed this up when, on the eve of Yalta, in one of his more humble moments, he wrote to Foreign Secretary Eden concerning the difficulty of long-range planning for a postwar world: "Guidance in these mundane matters is granted to us only step by step, or at the utmost a step or two ahead." [40] The Far Eastern sequel to Yalta has borne out Churchill's statement, and additional verification has been provided by the appearance of flaws in the plans for world order which the Big Three drafted there. . . .

THE BIG THREE AND THE UNITED NATIONS *

. . . [By agreeing to permit the Soviet Union to have three seats in the U. N. Assembly], Roosevelt saddened many liberal supporters, who felt that he had weakened his moral position vis-à-vis the Soviet Union. A few weeks after the conference, in explaining his position to the American dele-

---

[38] Department of Defense, "The Entry of the Soviet Union into the War against Japan," 70. See also *ibid.*, 20.

[39] James F. Byrnes, *Speaking Frankly* (New York, 1947), 44.

[40] Churchill, *Triumph and Tragedy*, 351.   * Editor's note: By Forrest C. Pogue.

gation to the San Francisco conference, the President stressed the fact that he had talked the Russians into taking fewer votes than they had demanded and into agreeing to an equal number of votes for the United States. He said that American delegates to the United Nations conference were free to vote as they pleased on the issue, but that he had told Stalin that if he were a delegate he would vote for the extra seats for the U.S.S.R. Senator Vandenberg, the leading Republican on the delegation, commented: "This will *raise hell*." [41] (Italics in the original.)

But, in the final analysis, Roosevelt's U. N. policy at Yalta must be praised or damned in terms of the desirability of obtaining British and Russian co-operation in the world organization. Without their support no U. N. could be founded or could work effectively; to get their support, compromise was essential. Therein lay the essential meaning of Yalta in the history of man's search for world order. Furthermore, it should be remembered that the Russians and British had accepted the American voting procedure, and that Roosevelt's strong stand against sixteen votes for the Soviet Republics held the Russians to the minimum number they would settle for. While the concession was something Roosevelt did not care to defend, it was not a serious blow to the U. N. Charter and it gave the Russians no great increase in power in the Assembly, as events have fully shown. Moreover, Roosevelt at Yalta won approval of pre-April negotiations regarding the troublesome question of territorial trusteeships for the U. N. . . .

Most important of all, Roosevelt won from Churchill and Stalin an agreement to call the United Nations Conference on World Organization before the war's end. At Yalta the President demanded that agreement be reached on details of the organization before the territorial concessions were made. He may have hoped, like Wilson, that such peace machinery might help remove injustices of the peace settlement. Had he lived to hear Vandenberg's defense of the U. N. Charter in June, 1945, just before the United States Senate overwhelmingly accepted membership in the United Nations, Roosevelt might have felt that the Republican senator from Michigan was speaking for him. Vandenberg declared that the United Nations organization served the intelligent self-interest of the United States; that it offered "our only chance to keep faith with those who have borne the heat of battle." And he added:

> I have signed the Charter with no illusions regarding its imperfections and with no pretensions that it guarantees its own benign aims; but with no doubts that it proposes an experiment which must be bravely undertaken in behalf of peace with justice in a better, happier, and safer world.

---

[41] Arthur H. Vandenberg, Jr. (ed.), with the collaboration of Joe Alex Morris, *Private Papers of Senator Vandenberg* (Boston, 1952), 159–60.

> Within the framework of the Charter, through its refinement in the
> light of experience, the future can overtake our errors. But there will
> be no future for it unless we can make this start. . . .[42]

Critics of the U. N. compromises at Yalta must ask whether the postwar
world has been better or worse for having had the United Nations to help
keep a semblance of East-West order in the midst of the "Cold War." After
ten years of U. N. contributions to world peace, the answer can hardly
remain in doubt. . . .

YALTA IN RETROSPECT *

. . . The meaning of Yalta cannot be grasped unless the conditions under
which the conference leaders worked are remembered. In February, 1945,
the Allied peoples generally agreed that Germany and Japan must be
severely punished and cured of aggressive tendencies. Agreement was widespread that Germany and Japan must be effectively disarmed and their
heavy industries restricted in order to prevent them from making war in
the future. The western powers generally acknowledged that the U.S.S.R.
had suffered terribly in the war and should receive compensation from the
common enemies. Thoughts of the postwar era were pervaded by a desire
to counterbalance the power of Germany and Japan by the force of the
"world policemen" who had co-operated to win the war. Roosevelt certainly
hoped, and probably believed until the last weeks before his death, that
he could sit down at a table with Stalin and Churchill and work out solutions to the problems of the world. The Big Three tended, as a result, to
give smaller states little opportunity to shape their own futures. The President strongly believed that Soviet expansive tendencies would be allayed
when the U.S.S.R. won security on its European and Asian frontiers.

Other assumptions likewise encouraged Roosevelt to overestimate the
possibilities of postwar co-operation with the Soviet Union. Knowledge
that Russia had been severely damaged in the early years of the war with
Germany led him to surmise that the U.S.S.R. might require a generation
to recover. Some Washington officials believed that the Soviet Union would
be dependent upon postwar economic aid for her recovery, and that for this
reason Stalin could be counted upon to maintain good relations with the
United States. In short, one must remember both the war-born opportunism and the hopes and fears of 1945: concessions which would shorten
the war and save lives would be acceptable to the people of the West; the
formation of a workable United Nations organization held hope for the
correction of any basic errors which might have been made in the various
peace arrangements; and, more realistically, it was feared that the Soviet

---

[42] United States House of Representatives, 79th Congress, 1st Session, *Congressional Record*, XCI, 6981–82.

* Editor's note: By Forrest C. Pogue.

Union might become the center of opposition to the West unless bound as closely as possible to its wartime allies.

All these factors powerfully asserted themselves when the Big Three met in the Crimean palace of the czar in February, 1945. But yet another factor loomed large in the conference at Yalta. The disintegration of Germany meant that the force which had dominated central Europe since 1938 was gone and that its place in central-eastern Europe would be taken by the Soviet Union. A disarmed Italy and a weakened France could not be expected to balance the enormous power of the Red Army. Britain, seriously drained of her capital wealth by the heavy exactions of the war and lacking the manpower reserves to challenge a potential enemy of Russia's strength, could not hope to redress the balance of Europe as she had for two centuries. The people of the United States viewed their exertions in Europe as temporary and hoped for their early termination; they were in no state of psychological readiness to take up Britain's traditional role. The approaching defeat of Japan threatened to create a power vacuum in the Far East like that which Hitler's defeat would leave in Europe. Thus concessions at Yalta inevitably reflected the powerful position of the Soviet Union in Europe and its potential power in the Far East. Personal diplomacy at Yalta came to grips with the basic realities of a new balance of power in the world at large, and the freedom of action of the individual statesman was greatly restricted by these impersonal forces. Therein lies the overriding fact about the conference; without its comprehension, the meaning of Yalta is sure to be missed.

Several courses were open to the western leaders at Yalta in dealing with the new set of power relationships. It was possible to make minimum concessions to Stalin and hope for Russian co-operation and goodwill; it was possible to break off discussions at the first sign of demands which would ratify the new power relationships or create a greater imbalance in world politics than already existed; and it was possible to state certain moral positions in indignant and ringing Wilsonian phrases. Roosevelt and Churchill selected the first course, believing and hoping that it would bring victory and at the same time save the peace. They gained something by forcing the Russians to put their promises on record; but they could not make Stalin keep his word. The United States and Great Britain have at least the moral right and, technically, the legal right to use Soviet violations as the basis for repudiation of Allied concessions at Yalta, for it was the Soviet breach of contract that started the "Cold War."

XI

*The Decision to Drop
the Atomic Bomb:
Tragic Error or
Military Necessity?*

INTRODUCTION

Persuaded by a small group of scientists who advised him of the potentialities of atomic energy for military purposes, President Franklin D. Roosevelt provided in 1939 for the initiation of a small-scale government atomic research program. The first controlled chain reaction in unseparated uranium was produced on December 2, 1942, opening the way to the development of an atomic bomb. The task of actually producing the bomb was entrusted on May 1, 1943, to the Manhattan District of the Army Engineer Corps, headed by Brigadier General Leslie R. Groves. Secretary of War Henry L. Stimson explained to General Groves that his mission was "to produce [the bomb] at the earliest possible date so as to bring the war to a conclusion." [1]

By the time an atomic bomb was ready for military use the war in Europe had already come to a close, but Japan was still continuing the struggle in the Pacific. On July 25, 1945, General Carl A. Spaatz, Commanding General of the United States Army Strategic Air Forces in the Pacific, received orders to drop a bomb on Hiroshima, Kokura, Niigata, or Nagasaki as soon after August 3 as weather permitted. Hiroshima was the target actually selected, and it became on August 6 the first city ever subjected to atomic attack. Three days later a second bomb was dropped on Nagasaki. On August 14 the Japanese government formally accepted the terms of the Potsdam Declaration, and the Emperor prepared an Imperial Rescript ordering the surrender of the Japanese forces.

The wisdom of the American decision to use the atomic bomb against Japan and the extent to which it hastened the final victory in the Pacific are contrastingly viewed in the following selections. Hanson W. Baldwin, the military analyst of The New York Times, *regards the utilization of the bomb as one of several "great mistakes" made by the United States in World War II. Victory, he believes, was near when Hiroshima and Nagasaki were bombed, and the use of the bomb hastened Japan's decision to capitulate by little more than a few days, a month or two at the most. The price paid for this small gain, as Baldwin sees it, was the loss of the "pre-eminent moral position" once occupied by the United States. The political scientist Harold Stein, who expresses his views on the subject in a review of Herbert Feis's* Japan Subdued: The Atomic Bomb and the End of the War in the Pacific, *disagrees with Baldwin and argues that it was the atomic bombing of Hiroshima and Nagasaki that caused Emperor Hirohito to issue the Imperil Rescript that was required to bring the war to a close. In Stein's view, had the bomb not been utilized, an invasion of Japan that would have produced staggering American and Japanese casualties might very well have been necessary to induce a Japanese surrender.*

---

[1] Cited in Elting E. Morison, *Turmoil and Tradition: A Study of the Life and Times of Henry L. Stimson* (Boston: Houghton Mifflin Co., 1960), p. 621.

The Atomic Bomb—
The Penalty of Expediency

Hanson W. Baldwin

The utilization of the atomic bomb against a prostrate and defeated Japan in the closing days of the war exemplifies . . . the narrow, astigmatic concentration of our planners upon one goal, and one alone: victory.

Nowhere in all of Mr. [Henry L.] Stimson's forceful and eloquent apologia for the leveling of Hiroshima and Nagasaki is there any evidence of an ulterior vision; indeed, the entire effort of his famous Harper's article, reprinted and rearranged in his book, *On Active Service* is focused on proving that the bomb hastened the end of the war. But at what cost!

To accept the Stimson thesis that the atomic bomb should have been used as it was used, it is necessary first to accept the contention that the atomic bomb achieved or hastened victory, and second, and more important, that it helped to consolidate the peace or to further the political aims for which war was fought.

History can accept neither contention.

Let us examine the first. The atomic bomb was dropped in August. Long before that month started our forces were securely based in Okinawa, the Marianas and Iwo Jima; Germany had been defeated; our fleet had been cruising off the Japanese coast with impunity bombarding the shoreline; our submarines were operating in the Sea of Japan; even inter-island ferries had been attacked and sunk. Bombing, which started slowly in June, 1944, from China bases and from the Marianas in November, 1944, had been increased materially in 1945, and by August, 1945, more than 16,000 tons of bombs had ravaged Japanese cities. Food was short; mines and submarines and surface vessels and planes clamped an iron blockade around the main islands; raw materials were scarce. Blockade, bombing, and unsuccessful attempts at dispersion had reduced Japanese production capacity from 20 to 60 per cent. The enemy, in a military sense, was in a hopeless strategic position by the time the Postdam demand for unconditional surrender was made on July 26.

Such, then, was the situation when we wiped out Hiroshima and Nagasaki.

From Hanson W. Baldwin, *Great Mistakes of the War* (New York: Harper & Brothers, 1949), pp. 88–107, 113–114. Reprinted by permission of Willis Kingsley Wing. Copyright 1949, 1950 by Hanson W. Baldwin.

Need we have done it? No one can, of course, be positive, but the answer is almost certainly negative.

The invasion of Japan, which Admiral Leahy had opposed as too wasteful of American blood, and in any case unnecessary, was scheduled (for the southern island of Kyushu) for Nov. 1, 1945, to be followed if necessary, in the spring of 1946, by a major landing on the main island of Honshu. We dropped the two atomic bombs in early August, almost two months before our first D-Day. The decision to drop them, after the Japanese rejection of the Potsdam ultimatum, was a pretty hasty one. It followed the recommendations of Secretary Stimson and an "Interim Committee" of distinguished officials and scientists, who had found "no acceptable alternative to direct military use." [1]

But the weakness of this statement is inherent, for none was tried and "military use" of the bomb was undertaken despite strong opposition to this course by numerous scientists and Japanese experts, including former Ambassador Joseph Grew. Not only was the Potsdam ultimatum merely a restatement of the politically impossible—unconditional surrender—but it could hardly be construed as a direct warning of the atomic bomb and was not taken as such by anyone who did not know the bomb had been created. A technical demonstration of the bomb's power may well have been unfeasible, but certainly a far more definite warning could have been given; and it is hard to believe that a target objective in Japan with but sparse population could not have been found. The truth is we did not try; we gave no specific warning. There were almost two months before our scheduled invasion of Kyushu, in which American ingenuity could have found ways to bring home to the Japanese the impossibility of their position and the horrors of the weapon being held over them; yet we rushed to use the bomb as soon as unconditional surrender was rejected. Had we devised some demonstration or given a more specific warning than the Potsdam ultimatum, and had the Japanese still persisted in continued resistance after some weeks of our psychological offensive, we should perhaps have been justified in the bomb's use; at least, our hands would have been more clean.

But, in fact, our only warning to a Japan already militarily defeated, and in a hopeless situation, was the Potsdam demand for unconditional surrender issued on July 26, when we knew Japanese surrender attempts had started. Yet when the Japanese surrender was negotiated about two weeks later, after the bomb was dropped, our unconditional surrender demand was made conditional and we agreed, as Stimson had originally proposed we should do, to continuation of the Emperor upon his imperial throne.

We were, therefore, twice guilty. We dropped the bomb at a time when Japan already was negotiating for an end of the war but before those negotiations could come to fruition. We demanded unconditional surrender, then

---

[1] Henry L. Stimson and McGeorge Bundy, *On Active Service* (New York: Harper and Brothers, 1948), p. 610.

dropped the bomb and accepted conditional surrender, a sequence which indicates pretty clearly that the Japanese would have surrendered, even if the bomb had not been dropped, had the Potsdam Declaration included our promise to permit the Emperor to remain on his imperial throne.

What we now know of the condition of Japan, and of the days preceding her final surrender on Aug. 15, verifies these conclusions. It is clear, in retrospect (and was understood by some, notably Admiral Leahy, at the time), that Japan was militarily on her last legs. Yet our intelligence estimates greatly overstated her strength.

The background for surrender had been sketched in fully, well before the bombs were dropped, and the Strategic Bombing Survey declares that "interrogation of the highest Japanese officials, following V-J Day, indicated that Japan would have surrendered . . . even . . . if the atomic bombs had not been dropped." [2] "Even before the large-scale bombing of Japan was initiated, the raw material base of Japanese industry was effectively undermined. An accelerated decline of armament production was inevitable." [3]

Admiral Chester W. Nimitz, in a talk to the National Geographic Society on January 25, 1946, declared, "I am convinced that the complete impunity with which the Pacific Fleet pounded Japan at point-blank range was the decisive factor in forcing the Japanese to ask the Russians to approach us for peace proposals in July.

"Meanwhile, aircraft from our new fields in the Okinawa group were daily shuttling back and forth over Kyushu and Shikoku and B-29's of the Twentieth Air Force were fire-bombing major Japanese cities. The pace and the fury were mounting and the government of Japan, as its official spokesmen have now admitted, were looking for a way to end the war. At this point the Potsdam Ultimatum was delivered and the Japanese knew their choice.

"They were debating that choice when the atomic bomb fell on Hiroshima. They were debating that choice when our ships shelled installations within less than 100 miles of Tokyo. . . .

"The atomic bomb merely hastened a process already reaching an inevitable conclusion. . . ."

There can be no doubt that this conclusion of Admiral Nimitz will be the verdict of history. Militarily, we "killed" Japan in many different ways: by crushing defeats at sea and on land; by the strangulation of the blockade of which the principal instrument was the submarine; by bombing with conventional bombs. After the seizure of Okinawa—probably even before that—the blockade alone could have defeated Japan; was, indeed, defeating her. Admiral Leahy was right; invasion was not necessary.

---

[2] "Air Campaigns of the Pacific War," Strategic Bombing Survey, Government Printing Office, Washington, D.C., 1947, p. 53.

[3] "The Effects of Strategic Bombing on Japan's War Economy, Appendix A B C," Strategic Bombing Survey, Government Printing Office, Washington, D.C., 1946.

By the time "intensive strategic bombing" of the home islands began in March, 1945, production of military supplies in Japan "was already 20 per cent below its peak." And this drop reached 50 per cent by July, 1945. Lack of steel and other minerals, and the inherent industrial weakness of Japan relative to her enemies, doomed the Japs. Japan was just too weak for the war she waged; her ambitions exceeded her capacity.

"Aircraft production from 1942 on (long before either blockade or bombing had become effective) never reached a level sufficient to allow the Japanese to obtain air superiority in any of the contested areas. . . .

"Production of weapons and ammunition for ground troops was not sufficient to keep line troops supplied, to fill the long sea lines, and to maintain adequate stocks in reserve. . . .

"Motor vehicles were never in sufficient supply. . . ." [4]

In the words of a well known Japanese correspondent, Masuo Kato, who was in Washington for the Domei News Agency when the war started: "The thunderous arrival of the first atomic bomb at Hiroshima was only a *coup de grâce* for an empire already struggling in particularly agonizing death throes. The world's newest and most devastating of weapons had floated out of the summer sky to destroy a city at a stroke, but its arrival had small effect on the outcome of the war between Japan and the United Nations." [5]

It is therefore clear today—and was clear to many even as early as the spring of 1945—that the military defeat of Japan was certain; the atomic bomb was not needed.

But if the bomb did not procure victory, did it hasten it?

This question cannot be answered with equal precision, particularly since the full story of the Japanese surrender attempts has not been compiled. But a brief chronology of known events indicates that the atomic bomb may have shortened the war by a few days—not more.

The day before Christmas, 1944 (two months *before* the Yalta conference), U. S. intelligence authorities in Washington received a report from a confidential agent in Japan that a peace party was emerging and that the Koiso cabinet would soon be succeeded by a cabinet headed by Admiral Baron Suzuki who would initiate surrender proceedings. [6]

The Koiso cabinet *was* succeeded by a new government headed by Suzuki in early April, 1945, but even prior to this significant change, the Japanese—in February, 1945—had approached the Russians with a request that they act as intermediary in arranging a peace with the Western powers. The Russian Ambassador, Malik, in Tokyo, was the channel of the approach. The Russians, however, set their price of mediation so high that the Japa-

---

[4] "Japanese War Production Industries," Strategic Bombing Survey, Government Printing Office, Washington, D.C., 1946, pp. 1, 61.

[5] Masuo Kato, *The Lost War* (New York, Alfred A. Knopf, 1946).

[6] Ellis M. Zacharias, "The A Bomb Was Not Needed," *United Nations World*, August, 1949.

nese temporarily dropped the matter. The United States was not officially informed of this approach until after the end of the war.

Prior to, coincident with, and after this February attempt, ill-defined peace approaches were made through the Japanese Ambassadors in Stockholm and Moscow, particularly Moscow. These approaches were so informal, and to some extent represented to such a degree the personal initiative of the two Ambassadors concerned, that they never came to a head.

But after a meeting with Stalin in Moscow on May 27, before the trial A-bomb was even tested in New Mexico, Harry Hopkins cabled President Truman that:

"1. Japan is doomed and the Japanese know it.

"2. Peace feelers are being put out by certain elements in Japan. . . ." [7]

In April, 1945, as the United States was establishing a foothold on Okinawa, the Russians in effect denounced their neutrality agreement with Japan, and from then until July 12, the new cabinet was moving rapidly toward surrender attempts.

On July 12, fourteen days before we issued the Potsdam Proclamation, these attempts reached a clearly defined point. Prince Konoye was received by the Emperor on that day and ordered to Moscow as a peace plenipotentiary to "secure peace at any price." [8] On July 13, Moscow was notified officially by the Japanese foreign office that the "Emperor was desirous of peace." [9]

It was hoped that Moscow would inform the United States and Britain at the Potsdam conference of Japan's desire to discuss peace. But instead of an answer from the "Big Three," Ambassador Sato in Moscow was told by Molotov on August 8 of Russia's entry into the war against Japan, effective immediately.

However, since early May—well before this disappointing denouement to the most definite peace attempts the Japanese had yet made—the six-man Supreme War Direction Council in Japan had been discussing peace. On June 20, the Emperor told the (Supreme War Direction) Council that it "was necessary to have a plan to close the war at once as well as a plan to defend the home islands." [10]

The Council was deadlocked three to three, and Premier Suzuki, to break the deadlock, had decided to summon a Gozenkaigi (a meeting of "Elder Statesmen," summoned only in hours of crises) at which the Emperor himself could make the decision for peace or further war. Suzuki knew his Emperor's mind; Hirohito had been convinced for some weeks that peace was the only answer to Japan's ordeal.

---

[7] Sherwood, *op. cit.*, p. 903.

[8] "The Summary Report on the Pacific War," Strategic Bombing Survey, Government Printing Office, Washington, D.C., 1946, p. 26. *See also* "Japan's Struggle to End the War," same source.

[9] Kato, *op. cit.*

[10] *Ibid.*, p. 26, *n.*

The first atomic bomb was dropped on Hiroshima on August 6; Russia entered the war on August 8; and the second atomic bomb was dropped on Nagasaki on August 9. The dropping of the first bomb, and the Russian entry into the war, gave Suzuki additional arguments for again putting the issue before the Supreme War Direction Council, and, on August 9, he won their approval for the Gozenkaigi. But neither the people of Japan nor their leaders were as impressed with the atomic bomb as were we. The public did not know until after the war what had happened to Hiroshima; and even so, they had endured fire raids against Tokyo which had caused more casualties than the atomic bomb and had devastated a greater area than that destroyed at Hiroshima. The Supreme War Direction Council was initially told that a fragment of the Hiroshima bomb indicated that it was made in Germany (!), that it appeared to be a conventional explosive of great power, and that there was only one bomb available. When the Gozen-kaigi actually was held on August 14, five days after the second bomb was dropped, War Minister Anami and the chiefs of the Army and Navy General Staff—three members of the War Council who had been adamant for continuation of the war—were still in favor of continuing it; those who had wanted peace still wanted it. In other words, the bomb changed no opinions; the Emperor himself, who had already favored peace, broke the deadlock.

"If nobody else has any opinion to express," Hirohito said, "we would express our own. We demand that you will agree to it. We see only one way left for Japan to save herself. That is the reason we have made this determination to endure the unendurable and suffer the insufferable." [11]

In the words of Harry F. Kern, managing editor of *Newsweek,* who had made a special study, with the assistance of *Newsweek* correspondents, of the events surrounding the Japanese surrender:

"I think it's fair to say that the principal effect of the atom bomb on the Japanese surrender was to provide Suzuki with the immediate excuse for setting in motion the chain of events which resulted in the surrender." (An "excuse" was necessary—as the attempted military coup, following the Gozenkaigi of August 14, showed—if the leaders of the "peace party" were to avoid assassination at the hands of the rabid militarists of the "war party.")

"However, I think it is also a reasonable surmise that the Russian declaration of war would have served the same purpose, and that the dropping of the bomb was therefore unnecessary. In no case was the dropping of the bomb the reason for the Japanese surrender, and I don't think we can say that it acted as anything more than a catalyst in advancing the plans of Suzuki and his supporters." [12]

Or, as the Strategic Bombing Survey puts it, "it is the Survey's opinion that certainly prior to December 31, 1945, and in all probability prior to November 1, 1945, Japan would have surrendered even if the atomic bombs

[11] *Ibid.*
[12] From a letter to the author, January 5, 1949.

had not been dropped, even if Russia had not entered the war, and even if no invasion had been planned or contemplated." [13]

This seems, in the light of history, a reasonable judgment, and, in view of our available intelligence estimates, one that we could have then made. It is quite possible that the atomic bombs shortened the war by a day, a week, or a month or two—not more.

But at what a price! For whether or not the atomic bomb hastened victory, it is quite clear it has not won the peace.

Some may point to the comparative tranquility of Japan under Mac-Arthur in the postwar period as due in part to the terror of American arms created by the bomb. This is scarcely so; Japan's seeming tranquility is a surface one which has been furthered by a single occupation authority and the nature of the Japanese people. But I venture to estimate that those who suffered at Hiroshima and Nagasaki will never forget it, and that we sowed there a whirlwind of hate which we shall someday reap.

In estimating the effect of the use of the bomb upon the peace, we must remember, first, that we used the bomb for one purpose, and one only: not to secure a more equable peace, but to hasten victory. By using the bomb we have become identified, rightfully or wrongly, as inheritors of the mantle of Genghis Khan and all those of past history who have justified the use of utter ruthlessness in war.

It may well be argued, of course, that war—least of all modern war—knows no humanity, no rules, and no limitations, and that death by the atomic bomb is no worse than death by fire bombs or high explosives or gas or flame throwers. It is, of course, true that the atomic bomb is no worse qualitatively than other lethal weapons; it is merely quantitatively more powerful; other weapons cause death in fearful ways; the atomic bomb caused more deaths. We already had utilized fire raids, mass bombardment of cities, and flame throwers in the name of expediency and victory prior to August 6, even though many of our people had recoiled from such practices.

Even as late as June 1, 1945, Stimson "had sternly questioned his Air Forces leader, wanting to know whether the apparently indiscriminate bombings of Tokyo were absolutely necessary. Perhaps, as he [Stimson] later said, he was misled by the constant talk of 'precision bombing,' but he had believed that even air power could be limited in its use by the old concept of 'legitimate military targets.' Now in the conflagration bombings by massed B-29's, he was permitting a kind of total war he had always hated, and in recommending the use of the atomic bomb he was implicitly confessing that there could be no significant limits to the horror of modern war." [14]

---

[13] Strategic Bombing Survey, "The Summary Report on the Pacific War," *op. cit.*, p. 26.
[14] Stimson, *op. cit.*, pp. 632–33.

If we accept this confession—that there can be no limits set to modern war—we must also accept the bitter inheritance of Genghis Khan and the mantles of all the other ruthless despoilers of the past.

In reality, we took up where these great conquerors left off long before we dropped the atomic bomb. Americans, in their own eyes, are a naively idealistic people, with none of the crass ruthlessness so often exhibited by other nations. Yet in the eyes of others our record is very far from clean, nor can objective history palliate it. Rarely have we been found on the side of restricting horror; too often we have failed to support the feeble hands of those who would limit war. We did not ratify the Hague convention of 1899, outlawing the use of dumdum (expanding) bullets in war. We never ratified the Geneva Protocol of 1925, outlawing the use of biological agents and gas in war. At the time the war in the Pacific ended, pressure for the use of gas against Japanese island positions had reached the open discussion stage, and rationalization was leading surely to justification, an expedient justification since we had air superiority and the means to deluge the enemy with gas, while he had no similar way to reply. We condemned the Japanese for their alleged use of biological agents against the Chinese, yet in July and August, 1945, a shipload of U. S. biological agents for use in destruction of the Japanese rice crop was en route to the Marianas. And even before the war, our fundamental theory of air war, like the Trenchard school of Britain, coincided, or stemmed from, the Douchet doctrine of destructiveness: the bombardment of enemy cities and peoples.

Yet surely these methods—particularly the extension of unrestricted warfare to enemy civilians—defeated any peace aims we might have had, and had little appreciable effect in hastening military victory. For in any totalitarian state, the leaders rather than the peoples must be convinced of defeat, and the indiscriminate use of mass or area weapons, like biological agents and the atomic bomb, strike at the people, not the rulers. We cannot succeed, therefore, by such methods, in drawing that fine line between ruler and ruled that ought to be drawn in every war; we cannot hasten military victory by slaughtering the led; such methods only serve to bind the led closer to their leaders. Moreover, unrestricted warfare can never lay the groundwork for a more stable peace. Its heritage may be the salt-sown fields of Carthage, or the rubble and ruin of a Berlin or Tokyo or Hiroshima; but neither economically nor psychologically can unrestricted warfare—atomic warfare or biological warfare—lead anywhere save to eventual disaster.

During the last conflict we brought new horror to the meaning of war; the ruins of Germany and Japan, the flame-scarred tissues of the war-wounded attest our efficiency. And on August 6, 1945, that blinding flash above Hiroshima wrote a climax to an era of American expediency. On that date we joined the list of those who had introduced new and horrible weapons for the extermination of man; we joined the Germans who had first utilized gas, the Japanese with their biological agents, the Huns and the Mongols who had made destruction a fine art.

It is my contention that in the eyes of the world the atomic bomb has cost us dearly; we have lost morally; we no longer are the world's moral leader as in the days of the Wilsonian Fourteen Points. It is my contention that the unlimited destruction caused by our unlimited methods of waging war has caused us heavy economic losses in the forms of American tax subsidies to Germany and Japan. It is my contention that unrestricted warfare and unlimited aims cost us politically the winning of the peace.

But it is not only—and perhaps not chiefly—in public opinion or in the public pocketbook or even in public stability that we have suffered, but in our own souls. The American public is tending to accept the nefarious doctrine that the ends justify the means, the doctrine of exigency. What we have done to ourselves—and Hiroshima and Nagasaki were heavy blows to a weakening moral structure—can best be expressed in the words of the following editorial from the Bulletin of the Atomic Scientists:

> In the first World War, American public opinion was shocked by the sinking of passenger-carrying ships by German submarines; in the second World War, American submarines sank all Japanese ships on sight, and even the revelation that one of these ships was carrying American prisoners of war, has brought no belated wave of indignation at home. The Germans began the terror bombing of cities. The American propaganda long stuck to the pretense that we bombed only "military objectives" (with "pin-point" accuracy). Probably, this was done out of consideration for public opinion; but this concern proved to be excessive. Public opinion in America as well as elsewhere has long since accepted terror bombing of whole cities as legitimate means of warfare. So conditioned, it was able to "take" the news of the destruction of Hiroshima and Nagasaki almost without qualms. Is it not legitimate to predict that if another war comes, no public indignation will meet an announcement of a successful use of psitaccosis virus, or of the wiping-out of enemy crops by chemicals, or poisoning of drinking water in the enemy's capital by radioactive poisons?
>
> In mass fire and bomb raids on German and Japanese cities, America has won the leadership in this form of terror warfare; in the atomic bombardment of Hiroshima (arranged so as to inflict the maximum number of civilian casualties), we have compounded the terror of aerial war a thousandfold.[15]

The use of the atomic bomb, therefore, cost us dearly; we are now branded with the mark of the beast. Its use may have hastened victory—though by very little—but it has cost us in peace the pre-eminent moral position we once occupied.

---

[15] *Bulletin of the Atomic Scientists*, September, 1948, p. 259.

The Rationale of Japanese Surrender

Harold Stein

I

*Japan Subdued** is the last of the five admirable studies in which Herbert Feis has set forth the diplomatic history of the United States from the events that led to Pearl Harbor to the surrender ceremony on the U.S.S. Missouri. "Diplomatic history" in the conventional sense is actually an inadequate description, for *Japan Subdued* is not limited to the doings of the diplomats; it follows the actions of the extraordinary group of men in the United States government concerned with winning and ending the war, using or not using the atomic bomb; it describes, in sharp contrast, the doings of the unhappy group of vacillating and conflicting statesmen, military and civilian, who surrounded the Emperor of Japan and the Emperor himself. To Feis diplomacy encompasses the actions of scientists, politicians, and generals and is never limited to diplomatic negotiations and the formal interchange of diplomatic messages.

In the opening chapters of the book, Feis lays out with brilliant clarity the three separate but overlapping plans for securing Japanese surrender that our government had decided on in the spring of 1945:

(1) *Combined Assault.* This was the direct military approach, with an initial landing on Kyushu, followed by a final attack on Honshu. The plans for this were given final approval, and our armed forces were turned in this direction immediately after V-E Day. Originally it was in support of this plan that Russian entrance into the war seemed so important; by May 1945 neither Marshall nor King regarded Soviet participation as essential, but Marshall particularly, mindful of the losses that we might well sustain, wanted Russian help to reduce our burden and speed up the end.

There is no doubt that an American invasion would have brought about total Japanese defeat; and it is hard, almost impossible, to believe, regardless of the Japanese military code (*Dulce et decorum est pro patria mori!*) and the honorable status of military suicide, that at some point the Emperor would not have stepped in and insisted on surrender. Otherwise—if, for example, the Emperor had been killed in an air raid—the consequences

From *World Politics*, XV (October 1962), 138–150. Reprinted by permission.

* Editor's note: This article is a review of the book by Herbert Feis entitled *Japan Subdued: The Atomic Bomb and the End of the War in the Pacific* (Princeton, N.J.: Princeton University Press, 1961).

might have been appalling: without the Imperial Rescript, the Emperor's personal order to surrender, Japanese unit commanders might still be waging guerrilla warfare on islands in the Pacific. The basic assumption, however, was reasonable: whatever the process of decision-making, sooner or later some one in the Japanese government would speak for the nation and surrender, but the time of decision might easily have been (in our thinking) insanely late.

(2) *Inducement.* The inducements we had in mind were mercy and tolerance, not compromise. From the Japanese standpoint, our inducements were not *per se* appealing. We were insisting on the defeat of Japan: Japan's total withdrawal to its home islands, demilitarization under our surveillance, Allied trials of those we considered war criminals. All we were willing to offer was the promise that total defeat would not include the annihilation of Japan and the Imperial family. Obviously inducement of this limited scope would have no value until Japan was ready to accept defeat. Nor can one see much persuasive power in promises that Russia would not enter the war and that we would abstain from dropping the atomic bomb—possible alternatives that might be described as inducements in reverse. As Feis notes, Stalin presumably would never have agreed to the first, nor is there serious reason to believe that a threat of the bomb would have brought the agonies of decision in Tokyo to the necessary climax, since even the bomb itself caused surrender only after the passage of time. One can add that the Japanese army was staking all on the defense of the home islands and would have pretended—and did in fact—that the turn of the tide would come then, and only then. Therefore, since the Japanese generals prophesied partial victory and a compromise peace, a merciful defeat was no substitute.

(3) *Shock: The Atomic Bomb.* It was the hope of Truman and Stimson, those most directly responsible, that the atomic bomb would bring a quick end to hostilities. It did, and it did so (for reasons set forth below) in the only way that could cause an immediate surrender of all Japanese armed forces on the mainland, on the home islands, and on hundreds of scattered islands in the Pacific—the Imperial Rescript. The carefully measured account that Feis gives of the last days in Tokyo shows that the shock of the bomb was the spur that caused the Emperor to take his unprecedented action. Whether the second bomb, the one dropped on Nagasaki, was also essential is less certain, though probable, and those who doubt should remember that after the Emperor ended the Council meeting on August 10 (after Hiroshima) with his flat decision to surrender, the military were still trying to avoid surrender by reversing the irreversible on August 14 (after Nagasaki).

There was a further alternative not given serious consideration at the time: continued bombing and blockade without invasion. The staff of the Strategic Bombing Survey, having seen the devastation of Japan, concluded that Japan would have "surrendered" probably before November 1, 1945, and "certainly" before December 31. Feis sets this aside as an unrealistic alternative because of the burning desire of all American leaders for a far quicker termination of the holocaust that had been going on so long; and of course he is right. Beyond that, it should be noted that while a prediction of the timing of the devastating consequences of strangulation is reasonable, the same assurance cannot be given to predictions of the act of governmental surrender. What American can say how much suffering—death as well as misery—the Japanese government might have permitted or required its people to undergo before it gave up the fight?

There is more substantial foundation for speculation in respect to the consequences of a more realistic alternative—invasion without the bomb as a way of winning and ending the war. The American casualties, as our military leaders calculated in 1944 and 1945, would have been substantial, perhaps up to a million men, with, conceivably, half a million dead. The Japanese military losses can be more easily estimated. Assuming the same kind of defense that the Japanese forces adopted in the Philippines, which led to 475,000 dead out of 630,000 troops, the home army of 1,500,000 men in 1945 would have lost in *killed* about one million and a quarter. But the civilian casualties would have continued simultaneously, and these would also have been staggering. The fire bomb raid on Tokyo in March 1945 had killed and wounded more men, women, and children than the atomic bomb on Hiroshima. By July the civilian population of Japan was on short rations; fire bombing of the rice fields would have been able to destroy the new crop. Death and disease of thousands, perhaps hundreds of thousands, perhaps millions of civilians were not far off unless the war ended in the very near future. Such a fate as a substitute for Hiroshima and Nagasaki would have made Japan a nation killed with kindness.

II

Why could we not persuade Japan to surrender? Why did the atomic bomb accomplish so quickly what evident defeat and continually increasing civil and military losses and devastation could not do? The answer lay in the workings of the Japanese government. Ordinarily predictions of what would cause a government, or its armed forces, to surrender are based on assumptions about governmental "rationality." In this case, predictions of early surrender were based, as our Acting Secretary of State, Grew, once put it, on the assumption that "all sensible Japanese" would recognize inevitable defeat after the fall of Okinawa and that therefore we could then persuade Japan to surrender. It was quite true that any "sensible" Japanese would or should have known after the loss of Okinawa that Japan could not win the war; but the *ergo* does not necessarily follow. Quite possibly most of the French people and certainly Hitler and his chief assistants looked on Churchill's great speech after Dunkirk as a form of suicidal nonsense; all the quantitative advantages seemed to lie with the Nazis. But England, like Japan, was an island nation and ardent patriots give up slowly. One can say that Churchill's rationality was not Hitler's; and rationality in the eyes of the Japanese military was far different from ours. Feis's account of the slow, painful, stumbling movement of the Japanese government toward surrender reveals why the atomic bomb could precipitate a decision that the continuing abominations of a losing war could not. In summary, the events can be set down as follows:

The ending of the dreadful fighting on Okinawa was announced by us on June 22, and there seems to have been a widespread agreement within the Japanese government that the Japanese armed forces could no longer keep us from entering the seas around Japan. Yet it took two weeks and the Emperor's personal intercession before the Japanese government would agree to seek any means at all of surcease from continued fighting. Then at last, on July 7, the Japanese government decided to send an envoy to Moscow to seek Soviet mediation. This belated, mishandled, and unrealistic move on the part of the Japanese is usually described as a "peace feeler." The meaning of the phrase is uncertain; more precisely, the Japanese plan was an attempt to make a deal. Even the most realistic of the Japanese leaders, including the Emperor himself, thought quite vaguely that a rescinding of the Treaty of Portsmouth (but of course not the liberation of Korea) or some such promise would persuade the Russians to somehow persuade us to stop fighting. (It is worth noting that the retention of the Emperor was not a matter of concern at this point; this shadowy deal would obviously not have permitted Allied occupation of Japan.) Sato, Japanese ambassador in Moscow, perhaps stimulated by the grim but hopeful atmosphere of his abode, unlike the phantasmagoria in which his superiors were living in Tokyo, warned them—again and again, and with great courage—that their proposal was preposterous.

This unrealistic attempt to use the Soviet Union as a shield originated with the civilian members of the Cabinet. When, on July 16, "the Emperor was emerging from his isolated seclusion and making an active effort to arrange a peace," his support of the proposal was based on the advice he received from Marquis Kido. The military, whose veto power over Cabinet decisions was absolute, accepted the proposal only after it was agreed that Prince Konoye, who was to be the envoy to arrange the deal, was to be accompanied by high-ranking army and navy officers who would protect the military interests. One is reminded of our own famous Defense-State Department deal on NATO: an American commander plus American troops *plus* German rearmament. Admiral "One Package" Robbins shepherded Secretary Acheson to New York to the meeting with our allies in order to enforce the agreement; but our allies recalcitrantly accepted the honey of American participation and rejected the vinegar of German rearmament. The Admiral could do no more than stand by when the knots on his package came untied;

the role of the military in our democracy is frequently difficult. In Japan, the military did not suffer from such disadvantages.

The Japanese military developed an alternative proposal at this time, which was composed of equal parts of rational planning and pure wishful thinking. As Feis says, ". . . the heads of the Japanese military organization that was doomed to extinction, still avowed [just before Hiroshima] that they would be able to repel the invasion of Kyushu with great losses to the attacking ships and men, and that when this happened the President and the American military commanders would lose face, and the will of the enemy to accept great losses would break, and thus the American government would be receptive to the idea of a compromise peace" (p. 108).

At least to an American, the notion that the Americans would abandon the fight because of heavy losses seems sheer fantasy. Yet the conviction of the Japanese that they could inflict grievous losses on us if we did invade was thoroughly realistic. "There were over a million and a half men in the Japanese Home Army. Of these, a ground force of about seventeen able and determined divisions were being assembled in Kyushu, but with barely enough oil and ammunition for one great battle. . . . Thousands of planes, mostly of a sort that could be used only for suicide attacks, were being hoarded—as a special assault armada that was to be launched from hundreds of secret small airstrips in the interior" (p. 107). The Japanese, therefore, however profound their misreading of American character, were on solid ground when they promised to cause serious losses to the invading forces; but partly from understandable ignorance, partly from willfulness, they refused to read the handwriting on the wall: Russia's obvious move toward war and our ominous threat in the Potsdam Declaration, "prompt and utter destruction." The Japanese military leaders had no reason to doubt the substantial reality of "utter destruction" even if based merely on a continuation of our conventional air raids. These they expected; and they well knew also that their anti-aircraft defenses were practically destroyed. Whatever the weight of the kamikaze attacks against our ships, whatever the valor of their ground forces imbued so deeply with the Bushido Code, their cities and their people were bound to suffer destruction almost unparalleled in history. Even if a compromise peace had been conceivable, its price would have been appalling.

There were three characteristics of Japanese governmental behavior that prevented any early or orderly moves toward surrender:

(1) The interrelations of the Japanese leaders were characterized by double-dealing and dishonesty so standardized that many individuals probably used dishonesty as an ambiguous cloak to avoid decision; similarly, agreement was of no more than fleeting significance. Thus Suzuki became Prime Minister by promising "that he would comply with the judgment of the Army" and by assuring the Emperor "that . . . he would implicitly carry out the Emperor's wishes." And again, the Cabinet agreed that there

should be no comment on the Potsdam Declaration about surrender terms for Japan, pending word from Russia, but merely publication of a censored version which omitted those promises that would have had the greatest appeal to the Japanese people. Yet on the following day at a press conference Suzuki said, under military pressure and without warning Togo, the Foreign Minister, that the Declaration was "nothing but a rehashing of the Cairo Declaration," so there was no "recourse but to ignore it entirely and resolutely fight for the prosecution of the war."

(2) The second aspect of Japanese governmental behavior that conditioned the course of Japanese actions toward surrender was the strange role, both constitutional and traditional, of the military leaders and their own attitudes toward war and peace. Under the Japanese constitution, a Cabinet fell automatically if either the War or Navy Minister resigned. Thus in our terms it might be said that the civilian members of the Cabinet and of the Supreme Council could argue with the military, could request and even be granted limited concessions, but could never bargain on equal terms. Using their position of power, the almost unanimous military leaders ("almost," since Admiral Yonai, Navy Minister, wanted to end the war and always voted with the almost unanimous civilians—but then the navy had entered the war against the United States with reluctance) consistently rejected any practical actions that would lead to surrender, basing all on the suicidal defense of the home islands. The extent of their commitment to this objective was illustrated by their unwillingness to permit Suzuki even to abstain from public rejection of the Potsdam ultimatum, described above. Again, the day after Hiroshima, August 8 in Tokyo, when Suzuki tried to "convoke an immediate meeting of the Supreme Council, some of the military members said they could not be present." Even in the prolonged meetings of the Supreme Council and the Cabinet that were held on August 9 just after they had learned of the Russian declaration of war and the fall of the bomb on Nagasaki, the military leaders insisted that any reply to Truman's new ultimatum should not only require that the national polity and Imperial family be preserved, but also that the Japanese forces should disarm themselves, that there be no Allied occupation, and that all war criminals be prosecuted by the Japanese government itself.

Any "sensible" Japanese knew that these terms would not be accepted, save for the protection of the polity and the Imperial family, which was implicit in the Declaration: why then did the military leaders demand a policy that would mean more atomic bombs, more napalm bombs, more shells from the Allied battleships and cruisers, partial or total starvation, hundreds of thousands or millions of deaths, even on the absurd assumption that we would not have carried the invasion on to total victory? Feis gives what is at least a partial answer: "For them surrender meant at least humiliation and loss of career, at most disgrace and condign punishment—death" (p. 119).

(3) The position of the Emperor was the third decisive element in the governmental process. The Emperor customarily had a role that was looked on both by him and by his governing officials as reigning, not ruling. Imperial intervention in the affairs of state was almost as unthinkable as royal intervention in the United Kingdom—almost, but not quite. On June 18, after the Supreme Council decided (1) that the invasion battle ought to be risked and (2) that Kido's plan for trying to secure Soviet intervention should proceed, Kido, who knew that the Emperor agreed with him, had to "persuade" the Emperor to let the military know that he wanted an approach to the Soviets—lest the military renege in characteristic fashion on that half of the agreement. On June 22, our government announced the completion of the Okinawa campaign and on the same day the Emperor urged six members of the Council to seek an end of the war by negotiation. But it was not until two weeks later, on July 7, that the Emperor, again following Kido's advice, proposed to Suzuki that the Soviets be told openly of Japan's desire for Soviet mediation and of the Emperor's intention to send a special envoy. Yet on July 11, Togo cabled Sato telling him *not* to reveal the Japanese desire for Soviet intervention, although expressly stating that that was exactly what was wanted, a vivid example of Japanese governmental double-talk. Presumably the Emperor pursued his efforts, for on the next day Togo sent another message stating the Emperor's desires and his intention to send Konoye as emissary. And then the Emperor, as Feis puts it, "having taken one weak initiative, was quiescent."

The day after the bomb fell on Hiroshima, the Emperor argued with Togo and Suzuki that there should be a quick termination of the war, but the essential action was delayed until the meeting that began on August 9—after Soviet entry into the war and the bombing of Nagasaki. After fifteen hours of debate, with the military and a few civilian Cabinet ministers still holding out for the impossible, at 2:00 in the morning Suzuki finally called on the Emperor to decide, "in an act unprecedented in modern Japanese history." The Emperor had previously expressed his willingness to act on Suzuki's request, and now at long last he issued the absolute command: the Voice of the Sacred Crane, the ultimate expression of the Imperial mystique.

The Cabinet meeting ended at 4:00 in the morning on August 10, Tokyo time. The Foreign Office promptly drafted the authorized message, which fully accepted the terms of the Potsdam Declaration so long as it did not "comprise any demand which prejudices the prerogatives of His Majesty as Supreme Ruler." This message, which showed that the Japanese government now finally realized that the war was lost, was transmitted by the Swedish and Swiss legations, a clear indication that the message meant surrender and not some shadowy negotiated compromise like the previous appeals to Russia.

Nonetheless, on the following day the Minister of War was still calling on the army "to fight doggedly to the end in this holy war." When the Allied reply which accepted the Japanese condition was received on August 12, the anguished debate was resumed. Once again the military and their supporters opposed acceptance; even Suzuki vacillated. On August 13, there was more debate. On August 14, Kido brought to the Emperor one of the American leaflets (in Japanese) dropped on Tokyo which told the Japanese people of the Japanese acceptance of the Potsdam terms and of our reply. Kido warned the Emperor that since this information was now known, he must act immediately to prevent action by extremists. Once again the Emperor accepted Kido's advice, convoked with his Imperial authority an immediate meeting of the Supreme Council: this time the military had to come, and the Emperor ordered them to accept the Allied offer. This was the end.

III

These developments in Japan are now known to all; in 1945 the American authorities were working partly in the dark, though they did have some light. Grew, Acting Secretary of State during most of this period, and Dooman, his chief adviser on Japanese matters, had an intimate knowledge of Japan. They interpreted the significance of the new Japanese Cabinet in April correctly: Suzuki and several of the others were indeed sane enough and open-minded enough to seek an escape from the do-or-die trap that the Japanese army imposed—that is, they wished to escape if they could. Grew and Dooman also understood the religious meaning of the Imperial role and rightly predicted that surrender would come only if the Japanese were allowed to retain the Emperor. On this crucial point they were victors over opponents in the State Department who assumed, wrongly, that the Emperor was the keystone in the arch of Japanese militarism.

Further light was cast by the intercepts of Japanese messages. The President and his chief advisers knew of the clumsy Japanese efforts to secure Soviet mediation for the sake of ensuring some kind of compromise peace, efforts which went on until August 8 when Molotov informed Sato of the Russian declaration of war. From these messages it could be deduced that Japanese recognition of loss and destruction was real, but recognition or admission of total defeat was still rejected. The much maligned phrase "unconditional surrender" was cited in these intercepts incorrectly, because President Truman had made it clear in his statement on May 8 that the words applied only to the armed forces. But it was obviously not the phrase that bothered Togo; he was rejecting the demands he anticipated before they were fully stated not because he misunderstood them but because he understood them only too well. What Togo was not prepared to accept were such requirements as the giving up of Korea and Formosa, the forbidding of military activities, and American occupation of the home islands. It is thus surprising, in retrospect, that at the beginning of May such extremely knowledgeable people as Grew thought that surrender could be induced by making our terms clearer and by promising that we would not seek to eliminate the Imperial dynasty.

Grew and some of his colleagues were unduly optimistic; their optimism seems to have reflected a kind of unwillingness to recognize what was well known, the ultimate military monopoly of power in the Japanese Cabinet and Supreme Council—save only for unprecedented intercession by the Emperor. The inarticulate premise was that if sane men desire peace, they can persuade or outvote the bitter-enders. Recent historians have taken a similar position. Thus Feis quotes Ehrman's *Grand Strategy* about the situation on August 2: "It was indeed as reasonable to deduce from the latest developments that an atomic bomb might now enable the peace party to force surrender on its opponents as it was to deduce that the two parties would together accept defeat without it. Togo and the Emperor were desperate; but they still could not prevail. The situation seemed to have reached the point where the bomb—and perhaps the bomb alone—would have the required effect" (p. 104). Ehrman is thinking in terms of persuasion, when the situation required something quite different.

The basic conclusion—that a quick ending turned on the bomb alone—is shared regretfully by Feis and seems undebatable; but the reason for this conclusion may be put in a slightly different way from his stated rationale. The "peace party"—Togo and his variably vacillating colleagues—could not force surrender on the "war party," because the war party's spokesman, Anami, the War Minister, had the power of *liberum veto*. Nor was there any visible chance of persuading Anami. He was not immune from assassination, that dark portent that hung over all the Japanese politicians. More important, his conduct was governed by a code in which death for the fatherland was as honorable as victory and surrender for any reason dishonorable. The Minister of War could hardly be persuaded to seek peace by the prospect of hundreds of thousands of military deaths, even less by the prospect of the deaths of millions of civilians.

Seen in these terms, the peace-party-war-party explanation is hardly fitting, for what was needed was not a stimulant for intellectual reconsideration, for persuasion, for arousing the people, for encouraging the opposition: it was an act that would cause the Emperor to perform his unprecedented act to speak with the Voice of the Sacred Crane.

IV

Feis gives us not only this vivid description of the Japanese government in action, but also an account of the doings of our own government. Most significant perhaps is the extraordinary contrast between the dismal days in Tokyo and the worrisome but reasoned meetings that preceded the decision to drop the atomic bomb on Hiroshima and Nagasaki.

It should be unnecessary to note that the development of the atomic bomb in the United States was not set in motion by a "power elite." The original proposal was made by scientists moved by a burning desire to destroy Hitler and Nazism: the man who carried the message to Roosevelt was Einstein, greatest of living scientists, most loving and kind-hearted of men. The victory in Europe caused a questioning. Feis gives a fascinating account of a group of atomic scientists in Chicago known as the Franck Committee who in early June 1945 suggested that even "the saving of American lives achieved by the sudden use of atomic bombs against Japan may be outweighed by the ensuing loss of confidence and wave of horror and revulsion sweeping over the rest of the world and perhaps even dividing public opinion at home" (pp. 41–42). Presumably, if the bomb had been ready a year earlier, the same group of eminent and public-spirited scientists who raised these questions in June 1945 would have urged the military on to use it without hesitation to wreak vengeance on Hitler and destroy the Nazi power. This guess, however, is parenthetical. The group in fact knew quite well that no American president could toss aside a weapon that would bring a quick termination of the war and save American lives; he might, however, accept an alternative which could be tried without abandoning the possibility of ultimate recourse. Their proposed alternative was a demonstration of the bomb before a group of UN observers, followed up by various further steps, such as an ultimatum to Japan either to surrender or to evacuate a named area, or a sharing of responsibility for the decision with "public opinion" at home and with other nations.

These views were not lightly rejected. On the recommendation of Stimson, President Truman had earlier appointed what was known as the Interim Committee, composed of Stimson as chairman, Byrnes representing the President, Bard and Clayton for Navy and State, and the three eminent scientists who were leaders in our wartime research, the President of Harvard, the President of MIT, and the President of the Carnegie Institution of Washington; as Feis emphasizes, the absence of military members was deliberate. (The contrast with the processes of decision-making in Tokyo is dramatic.) The Committee was to consider (1) the whole range of questions which would be raised by the eventual disclosure of the existence of the bomb, and (2) the use of the bomb. The Committee wisely set up a Scientific Advisory Panel composed of four physicists who had been making major contributions to the devising of the bomb: Robert Oppenheimer, and three Nobel Prize winners, Arthur H. Compton, E. O. Lawrence, and Enrico Fermi.

When the Franck Committee was reaching its conclusions, the Panel was considering what to recommend to the Interim Committee; it delayed making its final report until after it had studied the Franck Committee recommendations. It then proposed (1) that talks be initiated with the United Kingdom, Russia, France, and China immediately about cooperation in "making this development contribute to improved international relations";

but (2) on the basic question, the reluctant advice was "We can see no alternative to direct military use." Feis, who has pondered over these questions long and deeply, has come to agree with this advice, though he suggests that we should have announced to Japan what our terrible weapon was and what it would do. Feis feels that such an announcement might have influenced the Japanese government to surrender, but his own description of the proceedings in Tokyo makes this conclusion seem, to this reviewer, so improbable as to be impossible. On the other hand, Feis's opinion that an announcement would have been prudent "for the record," as they say, is hard to dispute.

Misconceptions from 1945 to the present day on what would have caused Japan to surrender seem to have been partly created by a distaste for the horror of historical fact and partly by an underlying assumption that all nations surrender for the same reasons and in the same way. Yet, as even a cursory glance at World War II surrenders will show, the same factors that lead one country to surrender do not apply to others. During World War II, the first surrender problem facing us was in North Africa; here, after no substantial battle at all, the French surrendered because their officers accepted Darlan's claim of legitimacy in ordering them to surrender; Petain's actual public statements of denial were overlooked either because the officers thought that Darlan represented the "true" Petain, or because the excuse was all they really sought.

In the case of Italy, surrender depended on (1) the displacement of Mussolini and (2) our assurance that we would protect the new government. The Italians long since had had no need for proof of their own military incapacity. The Italian navy, which had remained intact, followed orders and surrendered *en masse;* the ground forces merely disintegrated.

Germany was quite different. Here surrender was a consequence of vast military defeat. What was notable was the speedy and effective execution of surrender with no real central government capable of ordering surrender. (Doenitz's legitimacy was not taken seriously.) The German military tradition did not envisage the hopeless continuation of fighting and the German field marshals saw no virtue in mass suicide. They were quite capable of surrendering whole armies even without Hitler's approval.

In Japan we faced a different situation. Officers and men would not surrender unless ordered to do so; no one in the Japanese government could serve as surrogate for the Emperor, as Darlan did for Petain; and there could be no overthrow of military dominance by popular uprising or by vote of the Cabinet or Council (as with Mussolini). The only way was to force the Emperor not only to want peace rather than victory, as he did in April—and probably even earlier—but to enforce his want by command. Without the Imperial Rescript there was no effective means of surrender. What we needed was not mere additional Japanese defeats, but something that would somehow serve as justification for the Emperor in an unprecedented fashion to end the fighting. And that was what the use of the atomic bomb accomplished.

V

There is one more tormenting question for which a speculative answer can be suggested:

By the spring of 1945 Pandora's box was open; the knowledge of how to make an atomic bomb could not be unlearned; used or not used against Japan, its potential danger was equally real. What then was the effect of actual use of the bomb on postwar attempts to secure international control? Feis supplies a persuasive answer: "But the mind . . . may wonder whether, if the exterminating power of the bomb had not been actually displayed, the nations would have been impelled to make even as faltering an effort as they have made to agree on measures to save themselves from mutual extinction by this ultimate weapon" (p. 187).

XII

The Korean War: Who Was Right, Truman or MacArthur?

INTRODUCTION

When the Chinese Communists entered the Korean War in force, United Nations Commander General Douglas MacArthur, who but a few days previously had launched a general offensive to end the war, announced that "we face an entirely new war." In order to achieve victory in this "new war," the general proposed a naval blockade of the Chinese coast, the air bombardment of selected targets in China, the reinforcement of the U.N. troops in Korea by the soldiers of Chiang Kai-shek, "diversionary action" by the Chinese Nationalists against the Chinese mainland that might lead to "counter-invasion," and, apparently, the use of atomic weapons to seal off Korea from China. The Truman administration, which from the beginning of the Korean War had sought to keep the fighting limited lest Russian intervention be provoked and World War III initiated, refused to institute any of General MacArthur's suggestions. Unwilling to accept the limitations imposed upon his forces by the administration, MacArthur, in defiance of orders, publicly sought to promote his own views regarding the proper conduct of the war. The result was that on April 10, 1951, President Truman relieved the general of his various commands.

The constitutional right of the president as commander-in-chief to remove a general from his post is, of course, not subject to dispute, but this still "leaves unanswered the question of whether the government waged the [Korean] war in the most effective manner consistent with the limitation of war." [1] In short, was the Truman administration correct in limiting the war to the extent that it did, or would it have been wiser for it to have adopted General MacArthur's recommendations in the hopes that this would have led to total victory in Korea? Beyond this question, the Truman-MacArthur controversy points up a whole congeries of questions concerning the ability of the American democracy to fight a limited war.

The two selections that follow present conflicting points of view regarding the wisdom of MacArthur's proposals to enlarge the Korean War beyond the limits set by the Truman administration. Alvin J. Cottrell and James E. Dougherty criticize the Truman administration's conduct of the war, defend MacArthur's proposals for expanding the war, and stress what the United States lost by failing to win a decisive victory in Korea. The Korean War, in their opinion, "revealed the inadequacy of Western democratic governments to deal with a conflict situation which is protracted and kept indecisive."

The position of the Truman administration as it was presented at the

---

[1] Robert Endicott Osgood, *Limited War: The Challenge to American Strategy* (Chicago: University of Chicago Press, 1957), p. 173.

joint hearings of the Senate Foreign Relations and Armed Services Committees following General MacArthur's return to the United States is summarized in a chapter taken from Professor John W. Spanier's book, The Truman-MacArthur Controversy and the Korean War. *The military and political reasons for the administration's rejection of MacArthur's proposals are set forth in this selection, and the gains that the administration believed accrued to the United States because of the manner in which the war was fought are indicated. Spanier, it is clear from other chapters of his book, is by no means uncritical of the Truman administration's conduct of the war, but he has considerably more sympathy for the administration's position than for that of MacArthur.*

The Lessons of Korea: War and the Power of Man*

Alvin J. Cottrell and James E. Dougherty

The Korean War represented a crucial turning point in the struggle between the communists and the Free World. The manner of the American response to the North Korean attack demonstrated to the communists the West's ability to react swiftly and decisively to an act of outright aggression. But more important still, the Korean War revealed the inadequacy of Western democratic governments to deal with a conflict situation which is protracted and kept indecisive. It was the experience of this war, more than any other single factor, which has given rise, during the last two years, to the debate over the readiness of the United States to wage so-called "limited wars." This debate, insofar as it has centered upon the size and the mobility of American tactical forces on the periphery of the Sino-Soviet bloc, completely misses the crucial point: namely that the problem of waging "limited war" is essentially not one of military power but of political will.

Through the years 1950–1953, the United States was, in terms of sheer military power, the superior contestant. Narrow limits were indeed imposed

From Orbis, II (Spring 1958), 39–65. Reprinted by permission.

* This article has been adapted from research materials utilized in the preparation of the *Study on Protracted Conflict,* to be published in fall 1958 by Frederick A. Praeger under the auspices of the Foreign Policy Research Institute of the University of Pennsylvania.

upon the Korean conflict, but "it was obviously the stronger Power which imposed them and made them stick." [1] It is fair to ask whether the United States, if it had in being all of the elaborate force levels called for by contemporary proponents of the "limited war" doctrine, would even now be able to avoid a repetition of Korea. Since the memory of the Korean War, with all its bitter frustrations, continues to permeate American thinking in the present discussion on weapons policy,[2] a review of United States strategy in that war may serve to remind us that mere possession of the requisite military power does not provide, by itself, an answer to our problem: namely how to meet the intermediate—"limited"—challenges of the communists.

IMPOSED LIMITATIONS ON THE WAR

The Korean War has been the only military conflict directly involving the United States and members of the communist bloc. The conflict was limited in several ways: The hostilities were confined to a precise geographical area. The nearby territory of Formosa was "neutralized" and the territory north of the Yalu River was declared off limits. The war was limited with regard to the nationality of the forces eligible to participate, for the armed forces of the Nationalist Chinese Government, a member of the Security Council, which urged U. N. members to resist the aggression, were not allowed to take part in the action. Furthermore, the war was limited as to weapons employed, types of targets selected and kinds of supplementary operations undertaken. Thus, weapons of mass destruction were not used; the rail and supply lines of the Chinese communists were not hit; and long range American aerial reconnaissance was ruled out.

It is significant that none of these limitations were or could have been forced upon the United States by the enemy. They all were voluntarily assumed by the United States. The reasons given for accepting these limitations were various, but practically all of them were reducible to fears of one sort or another: fear that the United States would alienate its European allies by prosecuting too vigorously a war in Asia; fear of antagonizing the Asian neutrals if Chiang's forces were utilized; and, above all, fear that the war, if it was not rigidly localized, would become general and global.

The difficulties encountered by the United States during the Korean War sprang in the first instance from a failure to view the struggle against the total strategic background. Probably the communists themselves did not foresee the full strategic implication of the border crossing on June 24,

---

[1] Bernard Brodie, "Nuclear Weapons: Strategic or Tactical," *Foreign Affairs,* XXXII (January 1954), 228.

[2] Cf., e.g., Henry A. Kissinger, *Nuclear Weapons and Foreign Policy* (New York, 1957), and Robert E. Osgood, *Limited War: The Challenge to American Strategy* (Chicago, 1957).

1950, and they may not have anticipated the prompt response of the United States and the U. N. Security Council. The United States entered the war for definite enough a purpose: the defense of a free nation against flagrant communist aggression. At the outset, the United States and its friends in the United Nations were under no misapprehension as to the fundamental issues, political and moral, raised by the attack on South Korea.

Some of the countries who later assumed a neutralist posture voted in the U. N. to resist the North Koreans. By October of 1950, when U. N. forces began their offensive to the Yalu, the General Assembly went beyond the original objective of merely defending South Korea and defined the U. N.'s goal as the establishment of a "unified, independent and democratic government in the sovereign state of Korea." This policy statement was intended and interpreted as an authorization for General MacArthur to move northward to the Yalu River.[3] In the same month, the situation changed ominously when the Chinese communists began to pour into Korea. Then the Korean War began to assume a different meaning: MacArthur called it an "entirely new war." The West was slow to evaluate the strategic consequences of the conflict with Communist China. Since the war had started over the Korean question, Western diplomats and commentators persisted in regarding it as a war over Korea, in which the additional features of Chinese communist intervention now had to be taken into account. A mental block obscured the full significance of the fact that the war was now between Communist China and the United States. It took the communists four months—from June to October 1950—to develop a novel strategy for turning Korea to their own strategic advantage.

Once the Chinese were in the fight, the unity of purpose of the United States and its allies in the U. N. began to flag. While India began to view Korea as an arena of the Cold War in which she vowed to be neutral, Great Britain "became anxious to minimize her responsibility for sponsoring the decisive resolution" concerning MacArthur's authority to cross the 38th Parallel.[4]

Once it was known that China was the antagonist, what were the decisions to be made by the United States? Some of these decisions, by their very nature, could not even be faced unless the United States formulated for itself a reasonably clear picture of the over-all Sino-Soviet strategy in Asia. Policy-making flows from analysis, and analysis hinges on framing the right questions. Several questions had to be asked, and at least hypothetical answers had to be given to them. There is some cause for wondering whether American policy-makers did pose the right questions in October 1950. Why did Communist China enter the Korean War? Did she come in

---

[3] Cf. *U. S. Policy in the Korean Conflict,* Department of State Publication 4263, Far Eastern Series 44, 1951, p. 17. The vote in the General Assembly was 47–5. India, fearing that action in North Korea would bring in Communist China, abstained.

[4] "The Record on Korea," *The Economist,* March 10, 1951, p. 526.

enthusiastically to defend herself against an American-U.N.-dominated Korea on her border, or did she come in somewhat reluctantly and fearfully as a result of Soviet cajolery, pressure and promises? Was Mao Tse-tung confident of his estimate of the Korean situation before committing himself? Or did he use the gradual build-up of "volunteer" forces during October to probe his enemy and thus to gauge the Western reaction to his move? Was Stalin prepared to divert sizable and much-needed resources from the Soviet Union to support the Chinese in the event of large-scale fighting? Were the communists prepared to face atomic conflict? What were the strategic implications of China's move for American interests in Japan, Formosa, Indochina, and elsewhere? What did the communist bloc really stand to gain in Korea? How great and how genuine was the danger that the Korean tinderbox would spark a world conflagration? What was the relation of American objectives in the Far East to American objectives in the NATO community? These and similar questions impinged upon the decisions which had to be made in the fall of 1950, particularly those concerning the role of Chiang's army, the application of an economic and naval blockade to China, going beyond the Yalu and using atomic weapons.

The gravest American error in Korea was the failure to respond decisively during the first few days of the Chinese communist intervention. Since the United States temporized in the face of Mao Tse-tung's probingly cautious, "unofficial" entry into the war, Mao was able gradually to build up his ground forces in North Korea. The initiative passed out of American hands, and the war became prolonged. The longer the war dragged on, the more often the debate within the United States over the Korean War raised the specter of general war. Whenever it was suggested that the United States take steps to regain the military initiative, the proposals were invariably rejected on the grounds that they involved the danger either of provoking general war or of offending the friends of the United States. The major proposals put forth for regaining the initiative concerned the use of Chiang Kai-shek's Nationalist forces on Formosa, the application of a blockade against China, operations beyond the Yalu River and the introduction of atomic weapons.

THE USE OF CHIANG'S FORCES

There may have been justification for the neutralization of Chiang's forces on Formosa by executive order of June 27, 1950, under which the Seventh Fleet was to protect Formosa and thus restrain Chiang from carrying out air or sea attacks against the mainland. Secretary of State Dean Acheson had argued that if Chinese troops from Taiwan were to join the U. N. forces in Korea, the Red Chinese might decide to enter the conflict precisely to weaken Chiang's army and thus diminish his capability of defending the island against a potential communist assault.[5] Another and perhaps the most important reason for the U. S. refusal to permit Chiang's participation was, in a sense, a political one, imposed upon the United States by foreign sentiment and by its own reluctance to offend that sentiment. It was summed up succinctly by W. Averell Harriman in the report which he gave to President Truman on his meeting with General MacArthur in early August 1950:

> He [General MacArthur] did not seem to consider the liability that our support of Chiang on such a move would be to us in the Far East. I explained in great detail why Chiang was a liability and the great danger of a split in the unity of the United Nations on the Chinese-Communist-Formosa policies; the attitude of the British, Nehru and such countries as Norway, who, although stalwart in their determination to resist Russian aggression, did not want to stir up trouble elsewhere.[6]

This decision to hold Chiang "under wraps" should have come in for review and modification as soon as Chinese intervention loomed seriously on the horizon. The argument about non-interference in the Chinese Civil War, if it ever had any validity, lost all its effectiveness in October 1950. When intelligence reports were received through Indian and British diplomatic channels concerning an impending Chinese military move into Korea, "intelligence reports" should have immediately been filtered through the same channels to the communists concerning an impending "deneutralization" of Formosa. Had this been done, Mao may well have reconsidered his policy of introducing "volunteers," who could conceivably have been recalled and publicly "chastised" for unauthorized activities. The pretext of "volunteers" reflected Mao's extreme caution. October and November 1950 were doubtless the critical months in the Korean War, when Mao scanned carefully American responses to his moves and took the measure of the U. N.'s firmness of purpose. The U. S. might at this point have blocked China from entering the war, and Mao could have recalled the "volunteers" with a minimum loss of face. General MacArthur, at the time of his dismissal, proposed that restrictions be removed from the deployment of Chiang's forces and that these forces be given substantial American logistical support against China. Regardless of how helpful Chiang's army may have been on the Korean peninsula, it is not mere hindsight to conclude that, had the Chinese Nationalists been poised for action across the Formosa Straits, the communists would not have felt free to remove sizable forces from the Fukien area for use in Korea. In his testimony to the Senate on the military situation in the Far East, General MacArthur stated:

---

[5] Harry S. Truman, *Years of Trial and Hope*, II (Garden City, 1956), 343.
[6] *Ibid.*, p. 352.

I believe that the minute you took off the inhibitions from the Generalissimo's forces it would result in relieving the pressure on our front in Korea. I believe that they would have tended to shift the center of gravity of their military mobilization down further south than they are at the present time.[7]

Among the arguments often advanced against accepting Chiang's offer of troops was that the United States might unwittingly commit itself to deploying American ground forces to achieve Chiang's major objective: reestablishing the Nationalist Government on the mainland.[8] This reasoning would have us believe that America could not have controlled the scope of its operations on the Chinese mainland, even though it had demonstrated its ability to impose precise limits on its Korean actions. The U. S. certainly could have supplied Chiang with enough material to allow him to carry out diversionary attacks against the Chinese communists without running the risk of being drawn into the morass of China. The United States could have reduced or cut off the aid to Chiang if and when his operations conflicted with American strategic objectives.[9] There is no need to conclude that Chiang's ambitions were bound to prevail over American interests. American policy-makers pondered all the possible alternatives before them and assumed fatalistically that, once a decision had been made, all its possible consequences, pleasant and unpleasant, would come to pass by some mysterious process over which they had no control.

ECONOMIC SANCTIONS

The question of invoking economic warfare measures against China raised problems of coalition diplomacy for the United States. There can be little doubt that an intensified application of economic sanctions against Communist China, reinforced by a naval blockade against communist shipping along the coast of China, would have greatly reduced the strength of the Chinese armies in Korea. Admiral Forrest Sherman, Chief of Naval Operations, made this statement during the Senate hearings:

A naval blockade by the United Nations would substantially reduce the war potential of Communist China. . . . China is not capable of taking countermeasures that could appreciably reduce the effectiveness of such a blockade.

A naval blockade by the United Nations would be advantageous

---

[7] Hearings, Senate Armed Services Committee, 82d Congress, 1st Session, 1951, *The Military Situation in the Far East,* Part I, pp. 266–267.

[8] Cf., for example, Harold M. Vinacke, *Far Eastern Politics in the Postwar Period* (New York, 1956), p. 240.

[9] General MacArthur told the Senate: "I have said that I can conceive of no condition in which I would attempt to land United States ground forces in continental China." Hearings, *cit. supra.,* Part I, p. 267.

from a psychological standpoint. It would demonstrate to the Chinese Communists, and to the neighboring Asian peoples, the power of the forces against communism—it would demonstrate the effectiveness of sea power, a power that the Chinese communists can do little to thwart.[10]

The general arguments against economic weapons were reducible to one, namely that they could have little effect because of the agricultural character of the Chinese economy and because China would still be able to receive goods from the Soviet bloc. *The Economist* stated its position in this way:

> It is and should remain the British argument that economic sanctions will do more harm than good. Because the main strategic materials from all sources—oil, for example—are already under embargo, very little of vital importance is going into China from the Western world. A greatly increased effort at control would produce only small additional results, which could have little effect on the slender war potential of Peking. . . . What is more, the strict application of sanctions means sooner or later that an American warship stops on the high seas ships bearing Indian jute to China. . . .[11]

American allies were firmly opposed to boycott and blockade, because such policies would have hurt their Far East trade, which totals several hundred shiploads per year. Britain, moreover, was concerned over the precarious position of Hongkong. Consequently, the United States was unable to expect its allies to favor General MacArthur's proposal for applying economic sanctions. Nevertheless, the failure to apply sanctions enabled China to protract the conflict without suffering any unusual economic strains. The fact that China was an underdeveloped agrarian nation made her almost totally dependent upon imports for the success of her first five-year plan. Every shipload of goods received in the eastern ports helped to lessen China's need for making demands upon her Soviet ally or the East European satellites. The supply lines from the Soviet Union to Korea, some 4,000 miles in length, were already operating under a heavy strain.[12]

---

[10] Hearings, *cit. supra.*, Part II, p. 1514. Admiral Sherman said that a blockade could seriously interefere with several war commodities, including rubber, petroleum, industrial chemicals, pharmaceuticals, machine tools, spare parts and electrical equipment. He pointed out that 78 million tons of shipping enter Chinese ports every year in about 2,500 foreign ships. *Ibid.*, p. 1512. See also the testimony of Admiral Turner Joy: "I believe the United Nations could have defeated the communists, or at least caused them to withdraw from the Korean Peninsula, had not the commander-in-chief of the Far East been restricted in the use of his forces, and had an effective United Nations (naval) blockade of Red China been established as soon as the Chinese entered the war." "The Korean War and Related Matters," *op. cit.*, pp. 22–23. For an account of the effective naval blockade against North Korea, see M. W. Cagle and F. A. Manson, *The Sea War in Korea* (Annapolis, 1957), pp. 299–300.

[11] "Korean Stalemate," *The Economist*, February 10, 1951, p. 298.

[12] According to Admiral Sherman, "practically all material from Russia to China must be transported via the Trans-Siberian Railway, which is known to be already overtaxed

Had the United States been able to persuade all the U. N. members who had branded China as an aggressor to cut off trade with her, the impact of an embargo upon Communist China's economy and war effort would have proved considerable. Mao was, no doubt, agreeably surprised to see that he was free to make strategic moves in Korea without being forced entirely to rely upon his own meager resources and those of his Soviet ally, who was ill-prepared to increase aid shipments. Central to the Chinese communist leader's concept of protracted war is the notion of altering the relative power distribution between oneself and the enemy, strengthening the former and weakening the latter by every available means.[13]

OPERATIONS BEYOND THE YALU

There were two principal suggestions for extending operations beyond the Yalu River. The first was to reconnoiter Manchuria and the Chinese coastal areas. As early as July 1950, the Air Force had contemplated flying high-level photo missions over Dairen, Port Arthur, Vladivostok and the Kuriles. When President Truman heard about these proposed flights over Soviet-controlled territory, he instructed Secretary of the Air Force Finletter not to allow his Far East commanders "to engage in activities that might give the Soviet Union a pretext to come into open conflict with us." [14] This decision to refrain from sweeping reconnaissance over Soviet areas on the Pacific coast may have been justified at the time, although such restraint precluded our gaining the very intelligence needed to corroborate the Central Intelligence Agency estimate that the U.S.S.R. did not intend to intervene on a large scale in the Far East. Certainly, official policy on reconnaissance should have undergone review when it became apparent that General MacArthur's post-Inchon offensive would take U. N. forces into North Korea or, at the very latest, when the State Department learned through Indian and British diplomatic channels that the Chinese communists had made a definite threat to intervene. Had reconnaissance been conducted, the request for authority to bomb the Yalu bridges could have been made in time to hinder the Communist Chinese build-up of massive ground armies in the Korean peninsula. The continued failure to reconnoiter the area above the Yalu even after MacArthur reiterated the need for such operations in the spring of 1951 was indefensible.

The second suggestion for going beyond the Yalu related to actual offensive operations in Manchuria, including "hot pursuit" of communist fighter

---

. . . inadequate and vulnerable. . . . Traffic along that railroad is particularly subject to easy disruption." Hearings, *cit. supra.*, p. 1513.

[13] *On the Protracted War* in *Selected Works of Mao Tse-tung*, II (London, 1954), 189.

[14] Harry S. Truman, *op. cit.*, p. 346. For the validity of this assumption—that the Soviets needed or wanted a "pretext" to become directly embroiled in the war—see below, pp. 501–2.

planes and the bombing of enemy supply routes and industrial centers. It should be made clear that at no time were ground force operations by American forces north of the Yalu contemplated. Air components alone could have executed whatever additional measures the Chinese intervention made imperative.

The limitations which the United States placed upon itself with respect to the use of air power along the Yalu not only prevented the carrying of the war into Manchuria but, furthermore, prevented the U. N. forces from holding their line of farthest advance because it deprived them of maximum effective air support. Air Marshal Sir John Slessor wrote as long ago as 1936: "The airplane is not a battlefield weapon—the air striking force is not as a rule best employed in the actual zone in which the armies are in contact." [15] Later, Slessor applied this maxim to the military situation which obtained in Korea:

> One of the strongest reasons for my dislike at the time of our advance to the Yalu in 1950 was that to do so would deprive the United Nations armies of the massive support of air power, unless we were prepared to spread the war into Manchuria, which for political reasons we were not prepared to do (whether or not those political reasons were good is irrelevant to this military point). And I am on record as being sure, when our armies were subsequently in retreat toward the thirty-eighth parallel, that as soon as they had come back far enough to restore to us the depth in the enemy's rear to enable the air to act freely again, the effect would be to retard and finally to arrest the communist advance.[16]

The communists held a unique advantage in being able to use Manchuria as a privileged sanctuary into which their MIG's could retreat after attacking American forces in Korea. On November 13, 1950, the State Department wired instructions to its embassies in six nations to inform the allied governments

> that it may become necessary at an early date to permit U. N. aircraft to defend themselves in the air space over the Yalu River to the extent of permitting hot pursuit of attacking enemy aircraft up to 2 or 3 minutes' flying time into Manchuria air space.
>
> It is contemplated that U. N. aircraft would limit themselves to repelling enemy aircraft engaged in offensive missions to Korea.
>
> We believe this would be a minimum reaction to extreme provocation, would not in itself affect adversely the attitude of the enemy toward Korean operations, would serve as a warning, and would add greatly to the morale of U. N. pilots. . . .[17]

---

[15] J. C. Slessor, *Air Power and Armies* (New York, 1936), p. 213, quoted by the same author in *Strategy for the West* (New York, 1954), pp. 127–128.

[16] J. C. Slessor, *Strategy for the West*, p. 128.   [17] Hearings, Part III, p. 1928.

The instructions made it clear that the United States was not seeking the concurrence of the governments concerned. Nonetheless, in the face of the "strongly negative responses" received from those governments, the State and Defense Departments decided that the plans for "hot pursuit" ought to be abandoned.[18] On this issue, too, coalition diplomacy came into conflict with tactical operations which were considered necessary or desirable from a military point of view.

After the United States' allies reacted unfavorably to the "hot pursuit" proposals, it was practically a foregone conclusion that General MacArthur's recommendations for more ambitious operations beyond the Yalu, i.e., bombing Manchuria, would be received with even less enthusiasm in the NATO capitals. General MacArthur frequently stressed the fact that his objective was not to extend the scope of ground operations into China itself, but rather to force China to remove herself from the Korean War by the continued application of added pressure on the Chinese supply lines in Manchuria.[19] Nevertheless, Canada's Lester Pearson publicly expressed doubts that his government could participate in any program in Asia involving commitments on the mainland of China, and the British House of Commons carried on a long discussion about war on the Chinese mainland if MacArthur's policies were adopted. Secretary of State Acheson testified to the Senate that he deemed it "highly probable" that the Sino-Soviet agreement of 1950 included a Soviet promise to assist China if the Manchurian Railway were subjected to a bombing attack by a foreign power.[20] Secretary Acheson did admit, however, that his views on the risk of direct Russian intervention were based on an analysis of Russian self-interest and treaty obligations, not on specific information from intelligence and diplomatic sources concerning Soviet intentions.[21]

THE USE OF ATOMIC WEAPONS

There is no question that of all the proposals advanced for regaining the initiative the suggestion to introduce atomic weapons in Korea was the one fraught with the most serious implications. Despite the fact that by the end of November 1950 approximately 400,000 Chinese had poured into Korea,[22] there were some credible reasons why atomic weapons should not have been used at that time. The American atomic stockpile was then earmarked primarily for use by the Strategic Air Command. The diversion of atomic weapons to Korea might have retarded the build-up of the West's far-flung system of atomic air bases, on which Western deterrent power hinged. Moreover, the technology of tactical atomic weapons and delivery systems had not been developed beyond its earliest stages when the fighting

---

[18] *Ibid.*, p. 1723.   [19] *Ibid.*, Part I, p. 259.   [20] *Ibid.*, Part III, pp. 1877–1878.
[21] *Ibid.*, Part I, p. 1859.
[22] *United States Policy in the Korean Conflict, cit. supra.*, pp. 22–23.

in Korea was at its peak; experiments with low-yield atomic weapons for use against troop concentrations in the immediate battle-zone had scarcely begun. Consequently, Americans and their allies, with the disturbing image of atomic bombs dropped by strategic aircraft on Hiroshima and Nagasaki still vivid in their minds, were unable or unwilling to distinguish between the tactical use of nuclear weapons against enemy armies in the field and their strategic use against urban populations deep in enemy territory.[23]

The West, therefore, cavilled at any suggestion that atomic weapons should or could be used in Korea. In particular the European allies of the United States, more vulnerable to atomic attack than the American Continent, took a less sanguine view of the atomic risks than some American policy-makers. On November 30, 1950, President Truman, perhaps in an effort to bring United States nuclear capability into close support of American diplomacy, hinted at a press conference that the introduction of atomic weapons into the Korean conflict was being discussed. "Naturally, there has been consideration of this subject since the outbreak of the hostilities in Korea, just as there is consideration of the use of all weapons whenever our forces are in combat. Consideration of the use of any weapon is always implicit in the very possession of that weapon." [24] If this guarded reference was intended to frighten the Chinese communists, the effort backfired. Before the news could have any impact on the strategic thinking of the Chinese communist leadership, the British Labour Government reacted to this veiled threat with open concern, and Prime Minister Clement Attlee hurried to Washington in order to obtain Mr. Truman's assurance that the Korean War would remain "conventional." Domestic critics voiced misgivings to the effect that, since the atom bomb had become a popular symbol of cataclysmic destruction, its use under any circumstances would set off an uncontrollable chain of events which would propel the world into an unwanted total war. Others argued that, even if global war would not be touched off by atomic warfare in Korea, the peoples of Asia would be even more deeply offended by a new exhibition of "American contempt for Asian lives" than they had been five years earlier at the time of Hiroshima and Nagasaki.

In retrospect, the American decision to forego the actual use of atomic weapons in Korea was the most defensible of all the negative decisions made in Washington. The "atomic question," in a sense, was a false one, for probably it would never have been raised had other conventional alternatives, which were available for dealing with Communist China's aggression, been adopted with vigor and determination.[25] It was one thing, however, to

---

[23] Cf. Raymond Aron, "Europe and Air Power," *The Annals of the American Academy of Political and Social Science*, CCIC (May 1955), 95.

[24] Harry S. Truman, *op. cit.,* pp. 395–396.

[25] The feasibility of the most important of these alternatives was lucidly expressed by Senator Ralph Flanders during the Senate hearings in June 1951: ". . . General Mac-

Alvin J. Cottrell and James E. Dougherty

decide that the United States would not bring to bear its most powerful military weapon upon a given conflict situation; it was quite another thing to forfeit the psychological and political value inherent in the possession of the atomic bomb by communicating such a decision baldly to the enemy. The disclosure of our intentions may well have served to reassure our allies or to placate an ill-informed public incited by irresponsible party politicians and segments of the press. But however much the Western public may have wished to ignore the fact, the Korean War was fought in the atomic age, and one of the contestants in this war was an atomic power. Hence atomic weapons had a role to play in the strategy of the war, even if they were never actually employed.

Today, when nuclear weapons constitute such an important component of the Western defense establishment, it is essential that we read correctly the lessons of the Korean War with regard to the American decision not to use the atomic bomb. For some Americans, who for the first time had occasion to pass prior judgment upon the potential use of atomic weapons, the problem was a moral one. For others the problem was political, since they conceived of it in terms of Asian sentiments or NATO solidarity. These objections were, at least in the context of the Korean War, more logical than those which sprang from a fear that the use of atomic weapons was certain to touch off World War III. There are weighty reasons for concluding that the Soviet Union was willing to be drawn, in 1950–51, into a general war with the West neither in Korea nor, as some people feared, in Europe. In either case, the question confronting the Russians was identical: Were they ready for general war? It is clear now that the time was not at all appropriate for the Kremlin to risk large-scale conflict with the West had the latter applied additional pressure upon Communist China. Stalin was in no position to enter the Korean War openly. His Far East air force was not strong enough to stand a contest of attrition and replacement production with the United States. The Soviet Union, moreover, would have encountered serious logistic difficulties in attempting to establish and supply operational bases in North Korea, some 4,000 miles from the locus of Russian industrial power. Had the United States increased military pressure in Korea, one wonders how long the communist bloc would have attempted to match the West in a war in which technical equipment and material

---

Arthur's proposals on bombing Manchuria can be interpreted and executed in a way which involves a minimum risk of starting World War III. . . . All that would seem to be required would be that we have in Manchuria the same freedom of maneuver in the air, and perhaps in the air alone, not on land, to make our protection of the whole of Korea possible. . . .

"It seems to me to be foolish to talk about invading the mainland of China when the military objectives can be stated in so much more limited terms . . . (or) to assume that such a limited undertaking would start World War III. . . .

"It strikes me we are in a rather silly position, and that more resource and enterprise would diminish the serious risk of a war of attrition to which we are presently subjected without materially increasing the risk. . . ." Hearings, Part III, pp. 1945–46.

resources (rather than manpower, which was far more expendable for the communists) were being devoured at a steadily increasing rate. The Soviets, had they attempted to intervene massively against the United States in the Far East or launched an attack against Western Europe, could not have avoided the type of war which has long been the nightmare both of the Tsarist and bolshevik strategists: a two-front all-out war against a powerful enemy. During World War II, the Kremlin had been at pains to avoid a showdown with the Japanese while holding off the Germans in the West. By contrast, the United States, between 1942 and 1945, was strong enough to take on two powerful enemies on opposite sides of the globe.

Most important of all, Russian atomic stockpiles and strategic delivery capabilities were distinctly inferior to those at the disposal of the U. S. Communist conflict doctrine prescribes the postponement of the all-out, decisive engagement until overwhelming victory is assured. It is, therefore, unlikely that the Soviet Union would have allowed itself to be drawn into a war beyond its borders under circumstances as unfavorable as those surrounding the Korean War. When asked whether the bombing of Manchurian air bases would bring the Soviets into the conflict and thereby touch off World War III, General Mark Clark replied to the Senate Subcommittee investigating the War: "I do not think you can drag the Soviets into a world war except at a time and place of their own choosing. They have been doing too well in the Cold War." [26]

WAR BY TRUCE: PANMUNJOM

Despite the limitations which the United States imposed upon itself, it was the consensus of Western observers at the scene that the U. N. forces were on the verge of breaking through the communists' lines in June 1951. At this point, the communists feared that the United States was about to mount a tactical offensive in Korea, supported by the extension of air operations into Manchuria. They switched to a strategy of protracted truce negotiations to prevent being driven out of Korea and to demoralize the West by weakening its will to take up the fight again later. This was the second crucial junc-

---

[26] "The Korean War and Related Matters," *op. cit.*, p. 6. Yuri A. Rastvorov, former Lieutenant Colonel of the MVD, wrote that as time went on "it became apparent that the whole Korean adventure had been one of Stalin's worst blunders. Soviet army leaders realized that China was not prepared for a long war with a major power and could not be so prepared on short notice. Indeed, some of us wondered why the U. S. did not push the Korean war to a victorious conclusion. Had it done so, I believe that Stalin would have relinquished the entire peninsula without further Soviet intervention. . . . *At the end of 1950 Soviet atomic strength was as much bluff as reality. Moscow's ambiguous announcements about atomic explosions we discounted as mainly propaganda. For us in Japan, news of the U. S. atomic activities had highest priority. Moscow got some tips that A bombs from the U. S. were being shipped to Korea and many Soviet leaders feared that they might suddenly be used.*" "Red Fraud and Intrigue in Far East," *Life*, Dec. 6, 1954, p. 176 (editors' italics).

ture of the war. Just as the circumspect use of "volunteers" had enabled Mao's forces to enter the war with a minimum risk of provoking a commensurate action by the United States against China, the changeover to truce talks in June 1951 eliminated, for all practical purposes, any further danger that Mao's forces might suffer a serious military reversal. Thus the negotiations provided a perfect alibi for a Chinese withdrawal from the shooting war—with their major units intact and well-trained and with the prestige of having fought the United States to a stalemate. The first American strategic mistake had been the failure to act swiftly in November 1950 to counter the stealthy Chinese entrance into the war; the second major blunder by the United States was the virtual decision to accept the communist demand for a cessation of hostilities prior to the opening of truce negotiations.

Had the U. S. followed the World War I example of continuing the offensive until the armistice was actually signed, the Korean War might well have ended by mid-summer of 1951 on much more favorable terms for the Free World and for Korea. Instead, the United States gave the communists an invaluable breathing spell. . . .

KOREAN BALANCE SHEET

In the light of the contemporary debate over U. S. military strategy, it is important to review the after-effects of the Korean War. The Chinese communists used the war as a training school in which the most up-to-date technical weapons were available. Thus Korea helped them transform their ill-equipped revolutionary forces into a modern army.[27] Meanwhile, the "Resist America, Aid Korea" campaign conducted by Peking helped considerably to consolidate the new regime at home and to stiffen the political loyalty of the Chinese people.[28] China won and the United States lost considerable prestige in Asia, for this was the first time in history that an Oriental nation held the technically superior West at bay. The Korean War, moreover, gave tremendous impetus to the international communist campaigns for propagating pacifism, especially through such devices as the Stockholm Peace Appeal,[29] and strengthening neutralism throughout the

---

[27] Several thousand fighter pilots, both Chinese and Russian, had an opportunity to be tested under combat conditions. At the end of the war, China had an air force rated the world's third largest, primarily on the strength of 1,500 MIG's which were made available by the Soviet Union. Cf. Charles J. V. Murphy, "Defense and Strategy," special reprint from *Fortune*, Headquarters, Air Force ROTC, Air University, Maxwell Air Base, December 1954, pp. 21–23.

[28] Richard L. Walker, *China Under Communism: The First Five Years* (New Haven, 1955), p. 92.

[29] "No operative contradiction exists between pacifist propaganda and the launching of aggressive war. In Soviet thinking, pacifist propaganda cannot hit home unless the targets of that propaganda are actively engaged in fighting and unless, by their physical sufferings and psychological experiences, they are convinced of the absolute necessity of peace." Stefan T. Possony, *A Century of Conflict* (Chicago, 1953), p. 356.

Arab-Asian world. Neutralist India, originally a supporter of the U.N. decision to counter North Korean aggression, began to sound a strident note of hostility against the United States as soon as Communist China became a contestant; the defense of a small republic then became, in Indian eyes, a case of American intervention in Asian affairs. When, in mid-1951, the Soviet Union espoused the role of peacemaker, the Asians seemed to forget entirely that the war had been instigated by a puppet government armed by the Soviets. By manifesting a willingness to settle for a draw in Korea, the West virtually admitted that Communist China's right to intervene in the peninsula was equal to that of the United Nations.

The United States, by waging the kind of war it did in Korea from November 1950 on, allowed the strategic initiative to pass into the hands of an enemy leader who had frequently stressed in his military writings that an army, once it can be forced into a passive position or deprived of its freedom of action, is on the road to defeat. Mao Tse-tung fully realized that the side which enjoys superiority at the outset of the conflict need not retain the initiative throughout the campaign:

> In the course of a struggle, a correct or incorrect command may transform inferiority into superiority or passivity into initiative, and vice versa. . . . The inferior and passive side can wrestle the initiative and victory from the side possessing superiority and the initiative by securing the necessary conditions through active endeavour in accordance with actual circumstances.[30]

One of the most suitable means of achieving superiority and seizing the initiative from the enemy, Mao wrote, is to create illusions in the mind of the enemy, including the illusion that he is up against overwhelming strength. Mao applied his superior understanding of strategic principles in Korea to compensate for the overwhelming superiority of American technological power. Throughout 575 truce meetings, the communist leaders stalled for time. The Chinese communists built up their military power and international support, while the United States suffered all the "internal and external contradictions" which Mao had forecast for all his enemies: mounting casualty lists, consumption of war material, decline of troop morale, discontented public opinion at home and the gradual alienation of world opinion.[31]

The United States imposed upon itself a number of severe limitations in conducting the Korean War. The motivation for these restraints was largely a political one. American policy-makers hoped that, with a war policy of forbearance unprecedented in modern history, the United States would earn the respect both of its new Atlantic allies and the uncommitted peoples. This hope, unfortunately, proved to be an illusory one. The United States built up very little credit either in Europe or in Asia: Americans, in fact,

---

[30] Mao Tse-tung, *On the Protracted War, op. cit.,* II, 215.   [31] *Ibid.,* p. 189.

found themselves in the incredible position of having to defend themselves against charges of waging "germ warfare," forestalling the "natural integration" of Formosa with the Chinese Mainland, and preventing the restoration of peace in the Far East by keeping Red China out of the United Nations. While Europeans placed little credence in communist propaganda, most were inclined to blame the United States for placing too much emphasis on the conflict in Korea. Finally, few people in Europe and Asia believed that the United States deserved any praise for limiting the war—for American political leaders, in their efforts to justify the Korean policy, argued frequently that any extension of the war would lead to general war and risk of communist retaliation against the United States. American motives, consequently, were taken to be more selfish than altruistic.

The decision to meet communist aggression in Korea in June 1950 was both courageous and wise. But the United States failed to foresee the future implications of the outcome of the Korean War—that popular political support for all subsequent responses to communist peripheral attacks would to a large extent hinge upon the success of the first direct encounter between American and communist forces.

There can be little question but that Secretary of State Acheson was confronted by serious political problems during the course of the Korean War. The United States had scarcely begun to construct a defense of Europe through the North Atlantic Treaty Organization when the Korean War broke out. The Europeans, especially the British, were inclined to dissociate the crisis in the Far East from their security interests and feared that an American emphasis of Asia might slow down the development of the Atlantic Alliance. The United States, on the other hand, had historically been oriented more towards Asia than Europe, and emerged from World War II as the dominant power in the Pacific. Whereas Great Britain was in the process of reducing her political commitments in Asia, the United States, which had borne the greatest burden among the Western powers in fighting the Axis on both fronts, realized its growing strategic responsibilities in both theaters. This divergence of basic interests in the Western Alliance was aggravated by Mao's entry into the war.

There is no doubt, however, that the success of Communist China was in large measure due to Mao's strategy of delay and attrition. Had the United Nations been able to conclude the war with MacArthur's Inchon offensive, America would have been spared many a diplomatic dilemma. Mao, by entering the Korean War, shored up the faltering regime of North Korea and denied the U. N. a decision with finality. Then, by switching in June 1951 to "attritional" truce talks which lasted for two years, the communists were able to camouflage their flagging capabilities and resources and, at the same time, to wear down the American will to resume the kind of energetic initiative needed to bring the war to a successful conclusion.

The Lessons of Korea: War and the Power of Man

The American people were increasingly dissatified with the conduct of the Korean War, which they found both frustrating and pointless. After the experience, in the twentieth century, of two world wars, both of which had ended in climactic, overwhelming victories, it was difficult for Americans to readjust their thinking to the notion of a war which, for two years, had to be fought out along the "line of scrimmage." What Americans objected to was not the fact that the war was kept limited, or waged at a level lower than that of a general war, but rather the fact that its limitations whittled down the real superiority of the United States. Since American policy-makers had posed a false dilemma—either a protracted stalemate or all-out war—popular opinion within the United States tended to conclude that American conventional forces had been misused in Korea. Perhaps the most serious effect of this was to inhibit the freedom of action of U. S. policy-makers when confronted by subsequent crises in so-called peripheral areas.

The communists, doubtless realizing to what an extent the Korean War had served as a conditioner of the American mind, were able to parlay their psychological gains in Korea into a swift victory in Indochina. A successful prosecution of the war in Korea by the United States might have either convinced the Chinese communists that a new adventure in Indochina should not be risked or, failing this, prepared the American people for intervention in Indochina.

In recent years, far too much criticism has been hurled at the Dulles policy of "massive retaliation" on the grounds that it did not prevent the loss of North Vietnam.[32] Such criticism, unfortunately, does not go to the root of the problem. Most of the critics of the declaratory policy of "massive retaliation" imply that statements of this sort are relatively worthless in meeting the intermediate range of communist military threats and that, first and foremost, the United States needs to increase its tactical force levels to fight limited wars in any part of the globe. Yet the experience of Korea shows clearly that the possession of forces "in being" does not of itself assure an effective defense against communist aggression. . . .

In the current quest for a sound military policy, the need for many different types of weapons is recognized as a matter of course. But, as Korea amply attested, hardware without courage and firmness of purpose is of little value. Mao Tse-tung, who now must be ranked with the great classical strategists, long ago warned against the fallacy of the mechanistic assumption that "weapons mean everything." He wrote that the view of the communists differs from that of the capitalist: "We see not only weapons, but also the power of man. Weapons are an important factor in war but not the decisive one; it is man and not material that counts." [33]

---

[32] Secretary Dulles made his statement concerning the possibility of retaliating "at times and places of our own choosing" on January 11, 1954. The communist assault on Dienbienphu was launched on March 13, 1954.

[33] Mao Tse-tung, *On the Protracted War* (Foreign Languages Press, 1954), p. 54.

The Administration's Defense:

The Meek Shall Inherit

John W. Spanier

MacArthur had condemned the Administration's Korean and Chinese policy in forthright and unequivocal terms. "I was operating in what I call a vacuum. I could hardly have been said to be in opposition to policies which I was not aware of even. I don't know what the policy is now." No doubt MacArthur overstated his case somewhat for dramatic effect, but his words illustrate the intensity of his frustration after Communist China's intervention. Washington was fighting an accordion war—up and down—at a "staggering" cost. "It isn't just dust that is settling in Korea . . . it is American blood." [1] His own plan, he maintained, would be decisive, and it would quickly achieve the desired results—victory in the field, a united Korea, and an end to hostilities. His only requirement was that the restrictions imposed upon him by the politicians in Washington should be lifted. It is to these two themes—the Administration's indetermination and his own resolution—to which MacArthur constantly returned. His course was positive; Truman's negative. He stood for victory; the President for stalemate. The choice was clear, the alternatives simple.

The Truman Administration, not unnaturally, saw MacArthur's strategy in a different light. It would, as Secretary of State Acheson emphasized, accept the "large risk of war with China, risk of war with the Soviet Union, and a demonstrable weakening of our collective-security system—all this in return for what? In return for measures whose effectiveness in bringing the conflict to an early conclusion are judged doubtful by our responsible military authorities." [2] The United States could not, therefore, allow its field commander's desire to achieve military victory in a local area to govern its

---

Reprinted by permission of the publishers from **John W. Spanier**, *The Truman-MacArthur Controversy and the Korean War*. **Cambridge, Mass.: Harvard University Press, Copyright, 1959, by The President and Fellows of Harvard College. Pp. 239–256.**

[1] *Military Situation in the Far East*, Hearings before the Committee on Armed Services and the Committee on Foreign Relations, United States Senate, 82d Cong., 1st Sess. (Washington, 1951), p. 30. This document will hereafter be referred to as *Senate Hearings*.

[2] *Ibid.*, pp. 325, 351, 354.

entire global foreign policy, particularly since his strategic recommendations were militarily unfeasible and politically undesirable.

To clarify these points, to emphasize them, and then once more to re-emphasize them, the Administration brought an impressive array of witnesses before the committee: Secretary of Defense Marshall, the Joint Chiefs of Staff, the Secretary of State, and ex-Secretary of Defense Louis Johnson. Altogether, they testified for almost a month, from May 7 to June 7 [1951]. MacArthur had testified for three days.

During his days on the witness stand, MacArthur had argued that his military program to defeat Communist China had received the endorsement of the Joint Chiefs of Staff, and that the limitations imposed upon him were political. The Joint Chiefs quickly denied both of these notions. They made it quite clear that they had opposed an extension of the war on strictly military grounds; in other words, their professional opinion was that MacArthur's program was militarily impracticable. Perhaps the most important military testimony in this respect came from the Air Force Chief of Staff. His testimony has suffered from gross neglect, partly no doubt, because it came near the end of the hearings when public interest was rapidly waning. Nevertheless, what General Hoyt Vandenberg had to say remains significant because he dismissed once and for all the notion that the Joint Chiefs had allowed their views to be colored by considerations not strictly professional.

In declaring his opposition to the bombing of Manchuria, General Vandenberg prefaced his remarks with the comment that the role of air power was not well understood in the United States. Strategic air power, he said, should be employed only for the destruction of the enemy's industrial centers. He did not doubt that the air force could lay waste the cities of Communist China and Manchuria, but the result might not be conclusive. In war, there could first of all be no guarantee, no certainty. More important, Communist China's arsenals lay in the Soviet Union; despite large-scale bombing of Manchuria and continental China, therefore, the Russians would still be in a position to supply the weapons of war from across the Manchuria border.[3]

Destruction of Red Chinese and Manchurian cities would, in addition, require "full" application of the Strategic Air Command's power. Anything less would be unable to achieve the task, since the rate of attrition would be too high. The air force would lose planes and crews more quickly than they could be replaced. The resulting loss would deprive the air arm of its capacity for "massive retaliation" against the Soviet Union. ". . . The United States Air Force, if used as a whole, can lay waste Manchuria and

---

[3] *Ibid.*, pp. 1378, 1402, 744, 887, 943.

[the] principal cities of China, but . . . the attrition that would inevitably be brought about upon us would leave us, in my opinion, as a Nation, naked for several years to come . . ." The bombing of Manchuria would require twice the number of bombers then available to the Strategic Air Command. Under present circumstances, therefore, the air force could not afford to "peck at the periphery." SAC must be kept ready for its principal role—to deter the Soviet Union from attack and to preserve the global balance of power; or, if it did not succeed in this task, to destroy the heart of international Communism's power, the Soviet Union's industrial complex. "While we can lay the industrial potential of Russia today [to] waste, in my opinion, or we can lay the Manchurian countryside [to] waste, as well as the principal cities of China, we cannot do both, again because we have a shoestring Air Force [87 wings]. We are trying to operate a $20 million business with about $20,000." [4]

It was, therefore, better to concentrate on the 200 miles of supply line in North Korea—"we can exercise very concentrated attacks on that supply line. If you extend the length another hundred miles back into Manchuria, you can get certain other bases, but with the same air power you would thin out your present attacks against the 200 miles of supply line that is Korea." [5]

Not only could the country not afford to attack Manchuria because the rate of attrition which the air force would suffer would undermine its deterrent capacity, but "going it alone" would seriously affect its over-all strength in another way. If we "went it alone" in Asia, we probably would have to "go it alone" in Europe. This would deprive the United States of its bases in both Europe and North Africa. The advantages of keeping these bases were obvious: bombers stationed near to the Soviet Union would have to load less gasoline and would be able to carry more bombs than planes flying in from farther away. Bombers striking from the continental United States would have to be refueled two or three times per mission. At that rate, a plane could render only two to three missions per month; from Europe and North Africa, the same plane could carry out fifteen to twenty missions every thirty days. Vandenberg estimated that minus its overseas bases, the United States would require an air force five to six times the size it at present possessed. European bases, while not therefore "absolutely essential," were "highly desirable." [6]

An economic blockade too would be limited in its effectiveness in bringing enough pressure to bear upon Communist China to quickly end the war. The limitation was, according to Admiral Sherman, dictated by two factors. The first consideration was the nature and stage of Communist China's economic development. This was still sufficiently lacking in indus-

---

[4] *Ibid.*, pp. 1398, 1399, 1379, 1385, 1393.   [5] *Ibid.*, pp. 887, 744, 507.
[6] *Ibid.*, pp. 1386, 884.

trialization and specialization that a blockade would not have the same immediate impact as it would on a more highly industrialized country. A blockade could only be an effective long-run weapon. . . .[7]

The second consideration limiting the effectiveness of a blockade of Communist China was the thoroughness with which China could be cut off from the essential supplies she had to import. The long Sino-Russian border would make any blockade incomplete. Admiral Sherman stressed that the loss of imports enforced by a naval blockade would force Communist China to rely more upon the Soviet Union, and thereby place an increasing drain on both the Soviet economy and the Trans-Siberian railroad. This long railway, which was subject to easy disruption by bombing, sabotage, or naval raiding parties, was already overtaxed and could not therefore adequately replace the supplies stopped on the sea; moreover, it could attempt to do so only at the expense of supplying the Soviet Union's own forces in the Far East.[8] The other members of the Joint Chiefs were less optimistic than Admiral Sherman. General Bradley, the chairman of the Joint Chiefs, qualified Sherman's analysis: the Trans-Siberian railroad could handle 17,000 tons a day in addition to its own tonnage-maintenance requirements. Russia had also built up supply depots and certain war industries to relieve the railway of some of its load during wartime. The implication was clear: Russian forces in the Far East had a "considerable military capacity": they could for a time get along with fewer supplies. This available tonnage could be switched to supply Communist China.

A blockade by itself could not, therefore, speedily terminate hostilities. A blockade could necessarily yield only slow results since it relied for effects principally on starvation and attrition. Only if combined with other military measures, such as air bombardment, could a naval blockade yield immediate results; short of such supplementary means, a blockade could not seriously hamper China's capacity to continue its conduct of the war. The Admiral also emphasized that the key to an effective United Nations naval blockade would be the wholehearted cooperation of our allies. Any effective blockade must include Port Arthur and Dairen, over which the Soviet Union exercised certain military rights and privileges under the Sino-Soviet treaty. The Russians would "very probably" demand unimpeded access to both ports; stopping her ships might provoke her entry into the war.[9] "If the United Nations should declare a naval blockade, the Russians would probably respect it, as they did the United Nations blockade of Korea. If the United States should declare a blockade unilaterally, the Russians might not respect it, and it is conceivable that they might oppose it by force." [10]

The implication of Admiral Sherman's words is clear: a unilateral blockade by the United States would signify the isolation of this country from

---

[7] *Ibid.,* pp. 1512–13. [8] *Ibid.* [9] *Ibid.,* pp. 1525, 1518, 1521, 1189.
[10] *Ibid.,* pp. 1514, 1517, 742.

its allies. Since this would for all practical purposes neutralize the United States Air Force, Moscow might be tempted to break the blockade of Dairen and Port Arthur. With NATO's massive retaliation nonexistent, the Strategic Air Command could, in the event of war, operate at only 15 to 20 per cent of its effectiveness. If, on the other hand, the United States imposed the blockade in cooperation with its Atlantic allies, any Soviet counteraction would risk the possibility of an immediate reaction by NATO, or more specifically, American strategic air power based on Western European and North African soil. "The fact is that our allies have been unwilling to join in a naval blockade of China, and have been slow to establish a tight economic blockade." [11]

Another reason for the need of a United Nations blockade was equally obvious; most of the strategic imports and ships carrying goods to Communist China bore the flags of non-Communist United Nations members. Sherman recommended that greater effort be concentrated on increasing the effectiveness of the economic blockade. In recent weeks, he said, United States efforts along these lines had been successful. The British government had prohibited any further sales of rubber for the rest of the year,[12] and the General Assembly had on May 18 by a vote of forty-five to four approved a resolution calling for an embargo on arms, ammunition, petroleum, and other materials of war, although as Secretary Acheson stressed, "Many countries were already doing this . . . ; others were not."

In expanding this point, Acheson emphasized that as early as 1948 the United States had agreed with its allies to draw up a number of lists of such items as arms, ammunition, implements of war and atomic energy whose export to the Soviet bloc would be restricted. These lists were expanded in 1949, so that by the end of that year the participating European nations had embargoed shipments to the Soviet bloc of about two-thirds of the industrial items which American experts then regarded as being of primary strategic significance. In both of the following years, the number of categories of goods not to be exported to the Communist sphere was augmented by approximately 50 per cent, and the total number of items restricted, or closely supervised to prevent excessive shipment, was increased threefold. The result was that by early 1951 about 90 per cent of the items the United States considered to be of strategic importance were already on the embargo lists. Since late 1949, moreover, certain specialized petroleum products, such as aviation gasoline and special lubricants, had also been embargoed to the Sino-Soviet bloc by the United States, England, and other governments. Acheson stressed that ever since the Chinese Communists consolidated their grip on the Chinese mainland, for many months before the outbreak of the Korean War, the British government had cooperated with the United States and the principal American and British oil com-

---

[11] *Ibid.,* pp. 1523, 1570, 1514, 882.   [12] *Ibid.,* pp. 1515–16.

panies in restricting shipment of petroleum products to those types and quantities clearly intended for civilian use. Immediately after the Communist attack in Korea, the British Admiralty had taken over all British oil stocks in the Far East and secured agreements by British companies to follow a sales policy parallel to that of American companies. The Hong Kong government had reinforced this policy by closely supervising the bunkering of vessels in Hong Kong and rationing shipments to Macao to prevent leakage to Communist China, by numerous seizures of illicit cargoes, confiscation of the ships involved, and the levying of severe fines on smugglers. It was possible that despite these measures small amounts of petroleum products may have been smuggled into the mainland, but, Acheson said, it "can be stated flatly, however, that . . . no significant shipments of petroleum products of military usefulness have been exported to Communist China from or through any place in the free world." Thus the "facts show there already exists on the part of the major industrial countries of the free world an economic embargo with respect to materials of primary strategic significance." The economic blockade made the naval blockade much less important. "I think it is clear that we cannot get nations to go further in regard to a naval blockade than they are willing to go on an economic blockade, since it is a more drastic sanction." [13]

Thus the Administration, particularly its military advisers, doubted the efficacy of winning the Korean War through the application of air power and the imposition of a naval blockade. MacArthur had always denied that his prescription would need few [many?] extra ground troops. General Collins, Army Chief of Staff, did not agree. The successful implementation of MacArthur's strategy would require the United States to send "considerably" more troops to Korea.[14] General Bradley, indeed, thought that a decision could be effected only if American troops were actually sent into China proper.

> Chairman Connally . . . if we have an all-out war, and the war should expand to include China, would it not almost inevitably follow that at some time in the future development of that, we would have to put ground troops on Chinese soil?
>
> General Bradley. To get decisive results, in my opinion you would . . . if you go to an all-out war with China, I think you would have to do something like the Japanese did. Go in and try to get a decision. I do not believe you could get any decision by naval and air action alone.
>
> Chairman Connally. Well, naval and air action as against China without ground troops would mean just sort of a holding proposition, would it not?
>
> General Bradley. Well, I think it would be a rather long-drawn-out affair in which you would try to knock out their centers of communi-

---

[13] *Ibid.*, pp. 1726–27. [14] *Ibid.*, p. 1219.

cation and knock out as much of their industry as possible, possibly try to limit on supplies and food without taking any positive action inside China itself.[15]

The Communist army in Korea could be decimated; but it could not be defeated without hitting its center of power. The air force and navy could hamper China's capacity to fight; but they could not destroy it. If there were no alternative to military victory, there could also be no substitute to military invasion and occupation. MacArthur had himself recognized at the time of the North Korean aggression that air and naval forces alone would not suffice to halt the Communist attack; ground troops would be needed. If this was true for a Soviet satellite, it was certainly true for Communist China.

In any case, even if it were not necessary to employ American troops inside continental China, large reinforcements would be needed. An all-out war with Communist China would require "substantially" more naval, air, and ground power, as well as an increase in supply and service troops to support the forces at the front. These could not, however, be furnished without a more intensive program of mobilization and greater effort to produce the ammunition and other implements of war.[16]

Could these troops not be supplied by Nationalist China? The Joint Chiefs thought not. Chiang would need his troops to safeguard Formosa; and his soldiers were anything but first-class. General MacArthur's mission to Formosa had "indicated a state of readiness which didn't seem to be conducive of successful action by those troops . . ." The Nationalist troops "had very limited capabilities, particularly for offensive action. As General MacArthur himself had pointed out, they would have to have almost complete logistical support from ourselves, transportation furnished . . . their leadership, equipment, and training were all of such a state that they would be of limited use in offensive operations." [17] Any diversionary action against continental China would, in addition, require excessive United States naval and air support—excessive, that is, to the returns that could be expected from such an investment.[18] Nor was the reason purely the military's unfavorable estimate of Chiang's troops. Of greater importance, although not explicitly stated during the hearings, was the Administration's evaluation of Chiang Kai-shek's political prospects on the continent. The only circumstances under which Nationalist troops might reconquer vast portions of China, if not the whole mainland, would be if upon their landing, the Chinese Communist army rallied to Chiang Kai-shek as the French people and the Bourbon army had rallied to Napoleon upon his return to French soil from Corsica. In the Administration's opinion, it was precisely this confidence of the masses which Chiang lacked; its loss had accounted

---

[15] *Ibid.*, p. 745.   [16] *Ibid.*, pp. 882–883.   [17] *Ibid.*, pp. 619, 337, 673–674, 742, 886, 903.
[18] *Ibid.*, pp. 1584, 1620.

for his defeat in the first place, for his fall in four short years from "the undisputed leader" of the Chinese people to a "refugee" on a small island off the coast of China. It was extremely doubtful that a year's absence had restored the Chinese people's affection for their old leader.

There was, in short, no substitute for American troops. But concentrating American armed power in Korea meant stripping other areas of their forces, lowering the deterrent to Soviet intervention in these parts of the world, and increasing their vulnerability to attack. In fact, the attrition of American military strength, particularly air and ground strength, might well deprive the United States of its ability to counter emergencies elsewhere, and perhaps even weaken the United States sufficiently to attract a Soviet attack. This country could not therefore afford to engage "too much of our power in an area that is not the critical strategic prize." Yet, this is precisely what MacArthur's strategy would entail; nothing would probably delight the Kremlin more. It would, in General Bradley's famous phrase, "involve us in the wrong war, at the wrong place, at the wrong time, and with the wrong enemy." [19]

Indeed, it might also involve us with the right enemy, since bombing Communist China and inflicting a severe defeat upon the Soviet Union's closest and strongest ally would probably leave the Kremlin no alternative but to intervene. As Secretary Acheson said:

> We know of Soviet influence in North Korea, of Soviet assistance to the North Koreans and to Communist China, and we know that understandings must have accompanied this assistance. We also know that there is a treaty between the Soviets and the Chinese Communists. But even if this treaty did not exist, China is the Soviet Union's largest and most important satellite. Russian self-interest in the Far East and the necessity of maintaining prestige in the Communist sphere make it difficult to see· how the Soviet Union could ignore a direct attack upon the Chinese mainland.

To be sure, General MacArthur had argued that the Soviet Union would not intervene if the United States and its allies acted with determination and without hesitation; the Administration, however, remembered that he had said the same thing just before Communist China had entered the battle. (It might have added that MacArthur's foresight had proven itself equally fallible on other occasions. In 1939, he had declared Japan would not attack the Philippines; proponents of such a view, he had said, failed to understand "the logic of the Japanese mind." If Japan did covet the islands, however, his Filipino forces would prove themselves more than a match for the invading army. In early 1941, he had doubted that the Japanese would commit suicide by attacking as mighty a naval power as the United States, but if Japan should launch such an attack, American,

---

[19] *Ibid.*, pp. 731–732, 1219.

British, and Dutch forces could handle her with half the forces they then had in the Far East!) Admittedly, the Administration had shared MacArthur's mistaken estimate of Peking's intentions before November 24; but it was unwilling to take a second chance. "I cannot accept the assumption," said Secretary Acheson, "that the Soviet Union will go its way regardless of what we do. I do not think that Russian policy is formed that way any more than our own policy is formed that way. This view is certainly not well enough grounded to justify a gamble with the essential security of our Nation."

There were a number of courses the Russians could follow. Acheson believed that "They could turn over to the Chinese large numbers of planes with 'volunteer' crews for retaliatory action in Korea and outside. They might participate with the Soviet Air Force and the submarine fleet." Or, the "Kremlin could elect to parallel the action, taken by Peiping and intervene with a half million or more ground-force 'volunteers'; or it could go the whole way and launch an all-out war. Singly, or in combination, these reactions contain explosive possibilities, not only for the Far East, but for the rest of the world as well." [20]

Hostilities with the Soviet Union at the present time had, however, to be avoided. Not only was a war unnecessary because Soviet imperialism had been contained and denied the fruits of its aggression; it was also undesirable because the United States might have to fight such a war alone. Our allies, as Secretary Acheson said,

> are understandably reluctant to be drawn into a general war in the Far East—one which holds the possibilities of becoming a world war —particularly if it developed out of an American impatience with the progress of the effort to repel aggression, an effort which in their belief offers an honorable and fair less catastrophic solution.
>
> If we followed the course proposed, we would be increasing our risks and commitments at the same time that we diminished our strength by reducing the strength and determination of our coalition.
>
> We cannot expect that our collective-security system will long survive if we take steps which unnecessarily and dangerously expose the people who are in the system with us. They would understandably hesitate to be tied to a partner who leads them to a highly dangerous short cut across a difficult crevasse.
>
> In relation to the total world threat, our safety requires that we strengthen, not weaken, the bonds of our collective-security system.
>
> The power of our coalition to deter an attack depends in part upon the will and the mutual confidence of our partners. If we, by the measures proposed, were to weaken that effort, particularly in the North Atlantic area, we would be jeopardizing the security of an area which is vital to our own national security.[21]

[20] *Ibid.*, pp. 1719, 741, 751.   [21] *Ibid.*, p. 1719.

The Administration's Defense: The Meek Shall Inherit

Allied fears of a large-scale war in the Far East and a corresponding shift of American power from Europe to the opposite side of the world—or World War III, which would probably see the Russians occupying their countries—were not the only reason for Washington's reluctance to test MacArthur's opinions about Soviet intentions. Even if the United States were willing to "go it alone" and alienate its allies, it had to resist this temptation for one simple reason—the United States was unready to fight a global war.

> Senator Johnson. General, from an over-all standpoint of the disposition of our forces throughout the world, are we sufficiently strong to fight a successful holding action in the event the Soviet Union attacks at an early date?
>
> General Collins. Not as of the moment; no, sir. That applies particularly to Europe. I think that we have sufficient forces out in the Far East to hold there. I think that we have sufficient forces in Alaska to hold there. I do not think we have sufficient forces in Europe.

General Bradley was even more emphatic: "I would not be a proponent of a policy which would ignore the military facts and rush us headlong into a showdown before we are ready." [22]

Even in Asia, the Russians possessed the capacity to intervene and put up a good fight; contrary to General MacArthur's opinion, Administration witnesses considered Soviet power in the Far East "a very serious matter." They had "many thousands of planes in the other areas of Vladivostok, Dairen-Port Arthur, in Harbin, Manchuria, and troop concentrations at Sakhalin near to Japan." The Russians had over the past few years also been building up their Far Eastern industries, and they had "undoubtedly" been accumulating sufficient supplies to sustain their divisions "for a considerable length of time." [23]

Refusal to accept MacArthur's military program did not, therefore, in the opinion of the chairman of the Joint Chiefs, constitute "appeasement."

> There are those who deplore the present military situation in Korea and urge us to engage Red China in a larger war to solve this problem. Taking on Red China is not a decisive move, does not guarantee the end of the war in Korea, and may not bring China to her knees. We have only to look back to the five long years when the Japanese, one of the greatest military powers of that time, moved into China and had almost full control of a large part of China, and yet were never able to conclude that war successfully. I would say from past history one would only jump from a smaller conflict to a larger deadlock at greater expense. My own feeling is to avoid such an engagement if possible because victory in Korea would not be assured and victory over Red China would be many years away . . .

---

[22] *Ibid.*, pp. 1212, 1188, 1218, 732, 742, 745, 883–884, 896.
[23] *Ibid.*, pp. 360, 743, 1002–03, 1588.

Some critics of our strategy say if we do not immediately bomb troop concentration points and airfields in Manchuria, it is "appeasement." If we do not immediately set up a blockade of Chinese ports—which to be successful would have to include British and Russian ports—it is appeasement. These same critics would say that if we do not provide the logistical support and air and naval assistance to launch Chinese Nationalist troops into China it is "appeasement."

These critics ignore the vital questions:

Will these actions, if taken, actually assure victory in Korea?

Do these actions mean prolongation of the war by bringing Russia into the fight?

Will these actions strip us of our allies in Korea and in other parts of the world?

From a military viewpoint, appeasement occurs when you give up something, which is rightfully free, to an aggressor without putting up a struggle, or making him pay a price. Forsaking Korea—withdrawing from the fight unless we are forced out—would be an appeasement to aggression. Refusing to enlarge the quarrel to the point where our global capabilities are diminished, is certainly not appeasement but is a militarily sound course of action under the present circumstances.[24]

Did the rejection of MacArthur's program mean that the Administration would continue to "go on as before"? Would it continue to sacrifice American lives, as MacArthur had charged, "without justified purpose"? The answer to the first question was "yes," to the second "no." American lives in Korea had not been sacrificed in vain.

The operation in Korea has been a success. Both the North Koreans and the Chinese Communists declared it to be their purpose to drive the United Nations forces out of Korea and impose Communist rule throughout the entire peninsula. They have been prevented from accomplishing their objective.

It has been charged that the American and allied forces in Korea are engaged in a pointless and inconclusive struggle.

Nothing could be further from the fact. They have been magnificent. Their gallant, determined, and successful fight has checked the Communist advance and turned it into a retreat. They have administered terrible defeats to the Communist forces. In so doing, they have scored a powerful victory.

Their victory has dealt Communist imperialist aims in Asia a severe setback.

The alluring prospect for the Communist conspiracy in June 1950—the prospect of a quick and easy success which would not only win Korea for the Kremlin but shake the free notions of Asia and paralyze the defense of Europe—all this has evaporated.

---

[24] *Ibid.*, p. 733.

But the achievements gained by the United States and her friends were not simply negative:

> Instead of weakening the rest of the world, they have solidified it. They have given a more powerful impetus to the military preparations of this country and its associates in and out of the North Atlantic Treaty Organization.
>
> We have doubled the number of our men under arms, and the production of material has been boosted to a point where it can begin to have a profound effect on the maintenance of the peace.
>
> The idea of collective security has been put to the test, and has been sustained. The nations who believe in collective security have shown that they can stick together and fight together.
>
> New urgency has been given the negotiation of a peace with Japan, and of initial security arrangements to build strength in the Pacific area.
>
> These are some of the results of the attack on Korea, unexpected by —and I am sure most unwelcome to—the Kremlin.[25]

Korea had thus been a success. But how could fighting now be ended? Could this really be achieved without carrying the war into China as General MacArthur had recommended? Could the hostilities actually be concluded without risking the dire consequences pointed out by the government's witnesses? Their testimony seemed to suggest that the United States would continue to fight indefinitely, that is until Communist China finally tired of the war; this impression, needless to say, was not welcome to the American public, and must be attributed largely to the Administration's inability to clarify the nature of previous cold-war clashes and their relationship to the present war in Korea.

A comprehensive presentation of Administration policy would have clarified that in each of the East-West conflicts which had preceded Korea, both sides had aimed only at limited objectives and pursued these aims by limited means. The Soviet rulers had in no case aimed at a knock-out blow of the Western powers, since this purpose could have been achieved only by means of total war. Each Communist challenge had been met by the Western powers, particularly the United States, with an equally limited response; the West, too, had been reluctant to resort to global hostilities.

Each side had been unwilling to precipitate atomic warfare. The almost equal distribution of power between them and the very destructiveness of modern weapons had limited the objectives which they could safely seek. Both blocs had therefore surrendered the notion that they could impose their respective wills upon one another; neither pursued total military victory nor unconditional surrender.

---

[25] *Ibid.,* pp. 1716–17.

The means, in short, had limited the end, and necessity had become the mother of moderation. Consequently, the Administration believed: first, that the United States must restrain its efforts to counter expansionist Soviet moves to the restoration of the *status quo;* and second, that the Soviet government acted upon the assumption that if the Western nations resisted its thrusts successfully, it was safest to break off the engagement and accept the pre-crisis situation. In this context, the American government viewed the intermittent American-Soviet trials of strength as a series of conflicts whose aim it was to determine the precise location of the boundary which divided the Communist states from the free world; American containment would allow no further Russian encroachment beyond this line, and Soviet imperialism could satisfy its ambitions only at the risk of all-out war.

Berlin was an obvious case in point. The Russians had hoped to drive the Western allies out of the former German capital, and they had expected to achieve their objective by a land blockade of the city. The Western allies had refused to be intimidated, since they could have not withstood the political and psychological consequences of Berlin's fall. At the same time, the Atlantic allies had shared the Soviet Union's reluctance to pay the price of a full-scale war for a limited aim. Consequently, they had not tried to reopen the corridor into Berlin by sending tanks and troops to challenge the Red army; instead, they had limited themselves to the air lift. The Soviets had not challenged this effort, for they had realized that to have done so would have precipitated the total war which both sides hoped to avoid. The United States and the Soviet Union had been unwilling to take a risk of this magnitude in order to achieve a decisive result in Berlin. Consequently, the issue had been settled on the basis of the *status quo.* Neither side had won a victory in the traditional sense of the word; instead, both sides had accepted the stalemate.

Nor had the blockade been settled quickly; it had taken fifteen months for the crisis to pass. Patience, firmness, and determination had been needed to execute this policy, since it had required the application of just enough pressure to achieve its objective, but not so much pressure that it would have precipitated a world war. As Secretary Marshall explained, "We have brought to bear whatever has been necessary, in money and also manpower, to curb the aggressor; and we have sought in every possible way to avoid a third World War." Berlin had been an expensive operation; nevertheless, it had been a better alternative than a total war and the vast destruction which such a holocaust would have inflicted upon all sides.[26]

Korea fell into the same category as Berlin. It was "only the latest challenge in this long, hard, continuing world-wide struggle. We are applying there the same policy that has been successfully applied in the attempted aggressions that preceded it elsewhere in the world." [27] This war, too, was

---

[26] *Ibid.,* pp. 365–366, 731.   [27] *Ibid.,* p. 366.

being fought under certain ground rules. The Chinese Communists possessed a "privileged sanctuary" in Manchuria, but the United States possessed a similar sanctuary in Japan, Okinawa, and South Korea, particularly around the main port of Pusan. "They are not bombing our ports and supply installations," said General Bradley, "and they are not bombing our troops." [28]

The objective too was limited. The purpose of the fighting was to restore the situation that had existed before the North Korean attack on June 25, 1950. When Senator Alexander Smith said that he was "a little bit confused" by the idea of "stopping where we began," Acheson replied:

> Senator, if you accomplish what you started out to do, I don't think that is synonymous with saying you stopped where you began.
> We started out to do two things. One is repel the armed attack and the other is to restore peace and security in the area.
> Now, if we do these two things, we have done what we started out to do, and I should think that is success.

Thus, without admitting outrightly that the Administration had abandoned the goal of a militarily unified Korea, the Secretary of State informed the Communists that it was willing to call a cease-fire on the 38th Parallel. The price for a united Korea was too high; the *status quo* was therefore acceptable.[29]

To be sure, Acheson had always insisted that the United States had never harbored any other aim, but this explanation will not withstand critical examination. That the attempt to unify Korea by force had been made, but that circumstances had necessitated acceptance of the present solution, is evident from General Bradley's testimony:

> General Bradley . . . as we went farther north and the United Nations again came out with a resolution to establish a unified Korea, united and free Korea; that was the mission they gave to General MacArthur in late September. [Actually the United Nations resolution was approved on October 7, though Bradley is correct when he says that the mission was originally assigned to MacArthur by Washington in late September.]
> Senator Cain. And yet to carry out that mission from a military point of view or that objective from a political point of view, it will, before we are through, if we do not change that mission, be required to defeat the enemy and to repel him, not from South Korea but we must repel the enemy from Korea, or otherwise, sir, how can we make Korea a free, independent, and democratic nation?
> General Bradley. Well, I think we could have an intermediate military objective . . .[30]

---

[28] *Ibid.*, pp. 751, 892.   [29] *Ibid.*, p. 1786.   [30] *Ibid.*, p. 955.

In late September and early October, the Administration had argued that the parallel had to be crossed to safeguard South Korea's security; for if North Korea were not defeated, South Korea might be subjected to a further attack at some future date when the enemy had recovered his strength and reorganized his army. Administration witnesses did not repeat this argument after Communist China's intervention, even though the threat to South Korea's future existence remained—only, of course, on a more potent scale. This time they explained that although a cease-fire on the 38th Parallel would only reaffirm the position that had existed at the time of the initial challenge, it could be made to contain safeguards to deter another invasion. Why such an arrangement had not been considered in October of 1950 was not said; but the implication was that it had not then been a question of accepting such a cease-fire or nothing. The opportunity for a militarily united Korea had been rendered possible by the destruction of the North Korean army. Circumstances had now changed. The *status quo* had been restored at the 38th Parallel and the Administration was willing to call an end to the fighting on this line.[31]

There remained only one question: would the Chinese Communists, as the Russians before them, settle on the basis of the 38th Parallel, the line from which the North Korean advance had originally started? Secretary Acheson believed they would, although he could not predict the time when this would happen. But Berlin had taken fifteen months to settle; Greece eighteen months; Korea was then in its tenth month. Hope for an early finish of the fighting, however, was good for several reasons. First, "the offensives of the enemy have been broken and thrown back with enormous enemy casualties. These defeats . . . present grave problems for the Communist authorities in China. While the manpower resources of China are vast, its supply of trained men is limited. They cannot cover up their casualties. They cannot gloss over the draft of more and more men for military service." Second, the "Chinese Red leaders have betrayed their long-standing pledge of demobilization and the military demand for man power has, instead, been increased." And third, "Peiping has also broken its promises of social and economic improvement. In the great cities, dependent on imported materials, unemployment increases. The regime has not lightened the burdens of the people. It has made them heavier." The dissatisfaction caused by this increasing toll of dead and injured, as well as by the broken pledges, were already "reflected in a sharp increase in repressive measures, and in propaganda to whip up the flagging zeal of their own people. In the light of all these factors," Acheson concluded, "I believe that the aggression can best be brought to an end with a minimum risk and a minimum loss, by continuing the punishing defeat of the Chinese in Korea." The infliction of heavy casualties on the Chinese army, the destruc-

---

[31] *Ibid.*, pp. 1053–54.

tion of its morale and "trained fabric" would, in other words, bring the Chinese Communists to negotiate an end to hostilities without the risk of World War III.[32]

Shortly after Acheson made this statement, the Communists made their first move to end the war. On June 23, 1951, the Russian delegate to the United Nations, Jacob Malik, intimated that the Soviet Union was ready for a cease-fire in Korea. The Communists, therefore, having also tried unsuccessfully to conquer the entire Korean peninsula, had finally decided to incorporate the stalemate on the 38th Parallel into the almost global stalemate along the line determined in previous engagements.

The meek had inherited; they had restored the Republic of Korea to its prewar boundaries; they had managed to avoid an enlarged war and its attendant dangers in the Far East; they had preserved the unity of the Atlantic community and through the rearmament program increased their power several times; and they had husbanded their strength to balance Russian power and to create "unassailable barriers" in the path of Soviet expansion. They had refused to dissipate their military power on the periphery of the Communist empire, but had conserved it for its primary function, the continued denial of Communist ambitions and the encouragement of trends within the Soviet political and social system which would so increase its strains and stresses that they would moderate the ambitions of its leaders.

It was this article of faith upon which the Administration's case, in the final analysis, rested: Soviet imperialism could be contained without the horror of another global conflict, that the indefinite frustration of the Kremlin's appetite could cause the regime to become more accommodating and negotiate outstanding issues, and to accept a live-and-let-live attitude based upon the realities of military strength and the necessity of compromising with power. "For no mystical, Messianic movement—and particularly not that of the Kremlin," George Kennan had predicted, "can face frustration indefinitely without eventually adjusting itself in one way or another to the logic of that state of affairs." United States containment policy, therefore, "has it in its power to increase enormously the strains under which Soviet policy must operate, to force upon the Kremlin a far greater degree of circumspection than it has had to observe in recent years, and in this way to promote tendencies which must eventually find their outlet in either the break-up or the gradual mellowing of Soviet power." [33] Or, as Secretary Acheson expressed it during the hearings: ". . . what we must do is to create situations of strength, then I think that the whole situation in the world begins to change so far as the potentialities of the Soviet Union being able to achieve its present purposes is concerned; and with that change there comes a difference in the negotiating positions of

[32] *Ibid.*, pp. 1717–18.   [33] Kennan, pp. 127–128.

the various parties, and out of that I should hope that there would be a willingness on the side of the Kremlin to recognize the facts which have been created by this effort of ours and to begin to solve at least some of the difficulties between east and west." [34] Time, in short, *was* on the side of the United States and her allies—if the Western powers could remain united, contain further Communist expansion, and preserve the balance of power on the basis of the *status quo.*

---

[34] *Senate Hearings,* p. 2083.

XIII

*A Catholic Is Elected
President: Did Kennedy Win
Because of or in Spite of
His Religion?*

INTRODUCTION

Twenty years of Democratic occupancy of the White House came to an end when Dwight D. Eisenhower decisively defeated Adlai E. Stevenson in the presidential election of 1952. Although Eisenhower repeated his victory in 1956, the Democrats apparently remained the majority party throughout the years of his presidency. In the election of 1960 Richard M. Nixon, Eisenhower's vice-president, was the Republican candidate; and John F. Kennedy, the second Catholic nominated for the presidency by his party, was the Democratic choice. The contest proved to be the closest in terms of the popular vote of any presidential election since 1884: Kennedy's popular vote exceeded that of Nixon by only 112,881.

Both of the following selections stress the importance of the religious issue in the 1960 election, but they reach diametrically opposite conclusions concerning its effect on the outcome. Writing soon after the election, Louis H. Bean, an expert in the study of American elections, contends that all the signs had pointed to a close contest and that the Catholic vote was the deciding factor in Kennedy's favor. The religious issue, he argues, gave Kennedy more electoral votes than it took away from him as Catholic pride won over Protestant prejudice.

The authors of the second selection, all of them associated with the University of Michigan's Survey Research Center, which has conducted many significant studies of American voting behavior, agree with Bean that the religious issue was the most important factor in determining the outcome of the 1960 presidential election. The question they seek to answer, however, is why Kennedy, as the representative of the majority party, did not win by a margin more indicative of the strength of his party. Concentrating on the popular vote, they conclude that Kennedy's religion substantially reduced his vote and accounts for the narrowness of his triumph.

Why Kennedy Won

Louis H. Bean

Before I explain why I think the election of Senator Kennedy is the result of Catholic pride winning over Protestant prejudice, let me set the political stage as it appeared at the beginning of 1960 in the months before the conventions. A close election was then already in prospect. With the nomination of Senator Kennedy to oppose the Vice President, the Catholic issue became a reality. It was commonly believed that this presumed handicap, added to the Republicans' allegation that in Nixon and Lodge they had a team of maturity and experience, made it fairly certain that the country would again turn down a Catholic Democrat as it did in 1928. The whole election process from conventions through the TV debates was an effort to equalize the "images" of the two teams, thus making more certain that the outcome would be close. But a careful reading of the 1928 experience applied to the prospect of a close election, and ample evidence that in 1960 the number of Catholics voting for a Catholic would outweigh the number of non-Catholics voting against him, indicated to me that we would find Kennedy on the winning side.

What was the evidence of a close election in 1960? And did voters in 1960 behave as they did in 1928 on the religious issue?

Early this year [1960] it was reasonably clear that the two parties were more evenly divided than in 1956. The Democrats rated 42 per cent in the 1956 popular vote for Stevenson, but at least two major factors which contributed to Stevenson's defeat would play no role in 1960. These factors were Eisenhower's popularity and the Suez crisis. On the basis of the evidence described below, I concluded that the 1960 Democratic potential strength was probably about 50–52 per cent instead of the 42 per cent of 1956, and that even though this represented an 8 to 10 percentage-point gain over Democratic strength in 1956, it foreshadowed a close election, with considerable doubt as to the winner. Before 1948, we used to figure that a Democratic candidate had to have at least 52 per cent of the popular vote to win.

The basic evidence consisted in the fact that Stevenson's 45 per cent vote in 1952 fell short by about 5 percentage points of the vote he should have had in view of the total vote cast for Congressional candidates. This shortage I attribute primarily to the complex of Republican advantages in 1952 which may be summed up in the phrase "Eisenhower popularity." In the 1956 election, Stevenson's 42 per cent fell short by about 10 percentage

From *The Nation*, CXCI (November 26, 1960), 408–410. Reprinted by permission.

points of what he should have had in view of the Democratic vote for Congressmen. From the Gallup and other polls during the last few days before the 1956 election, we know that Eisenhower's curve against Stevenson jumped by about 5 percentage points with the development of the Suez crisis. Thus 5 points for Eisenhower's popularity plus another 5 points for the impact of the international situation on the course of the campaign meant that Stevenson's potential strength in 1956 was 50 to 52 per cent instead of 42. Economic prosperity like that of 1956 was expected to last well through 1960. Even though the unemployment rate might tend to be somewhat above that of 1956, the fact did not alter the general appraisal of a close election. Furthermore, a 10-point Democratic gain for 1960 was also indicated in polls I had occasion to conduct in March of this year on the probable strength of a Stevenson-Kennedy ticket that might arise out of a convention deadlock.

The convention choices of Nixon and Kennedy did not alter the prospect of a close election. Kennedy chose Johnson to make sure of carrying the Southern states, while Nixon countered by selecting Lodge to present the voters with a ticket of "maturity and experience." The first impact of these choices appeared to be a gain for the Republican ticket, especially in California, New York and in the North Central industrial areas, where anti-Johnson feeling prevailed. But the national and local public-opinion polls showed no major shift in either direction and corroborated the prospect of a close election by revealing that political sentiment was divided evenly in all major regions.

Kennedy did not succeed in cutting down the Republican claim of greater maturity and wisdom in international affairs until the first TV debate. This and the subsequent debates made it quite clear that each party had chosen a relatively young man of ability and great intellectual capacity. The net effect of domestic and international issues raised in the debates, and the way they were repeated and handled many times in speeches all over the country, was to equalize the standing of the two candidates in nearly all respects, leaving the one major difference that could not be removed: religious affiliation.

The farm belt was supposed to be in revolt against Secretary Benson's efforts to lower farm price supports, organized labor and "organized" management were supposed to be very active in getting voters to register and vote, and the Negro voters were expected to shift to Nixon because they were supposed to dislike Senator Johnson, and dollar-minded people were supposed to be frightened by the threat of inflation if Kennedy were elected. Nevertheless the polls kept on showing close races in practically all states, and all public-opinion pollsters were of necessity careful to indicate that they could not tell what the final outcome would be.

In spite of efforts by both candidates to remove the religious issue from the campaign, there was ample and continuing evidence that the issue was dividing voters in much the same way as it had done in 1928, and that many more voters than usual were undecided chiefly because of it. Yet this very issue, it was clear to me, was the key to the election.

For a long while, in fact ever since James A. Farley indicated a willingness to oppose Roosevelt's third term in 1940 and was advised that a Catholic couldn't be elected, I have held the view that in a close election a Catholic Democratic candidate could win. This conclusion was based on my statistical study of the impact of the religious issue in the voting in 1928, state by state. While most people still believe that Al Smith lost because of his religion, my findings showed that his being a Catholic brought him more votes in the Northeast than turned away from him in the South and Midwest. Religion gave him a net advantage, but not enough to offset the fact that in 1928 the country as a whole was only about 45 per cent Democratic. Had the two parties rated about 50–50 in 1928, I believe Al Smith would have won. The reasoning behind this is that if the national vote is evenly divided, Northern states will tend to be Republican and Southern states Democratic, but the net advantage of Catholic support would have put more Northern states in Al Smith's column than the one state of Massachusetts which he gained. The simple fact is that a 10–15 point gain in some of the populous Northeastern states, where most Catholic voters are located, far outweighs 20 to 30 point losses in Southern states with fewer votes, popular as well as electoral.

As students begin digging into the details of the 1960 results, they will find many facts on which they will say the outcome depended. For example, it has already been suggested that Kennedy obtained the election by winning Texas because of Southern reaction against the rough treatment given to Mrs. Lyndon Johnson by Dallas hoodlums.

In all states where the election was won or lost by narrow margins, similar specific episodes will be cited. But the overriding feature in this election is extremely similar to that of 1928: states where Catholics are relatively numerous gave Kennedy more support than he would have had were he not a Catholic. In other states his support was reduced.

The accompanying table may be taken as a tentative illustration of the way the religious issue affected the vote. It should be borne in mind that the vote figures used are subject to change as final tabulations become available. The figures on the Catholic segment of church membership are those of the National Council of Churches, and while not quite up to date are usable as a rough measure of Catholic concentration if not as a measure of actual voting strength. The pluses and minuses in the middle column represent in percentage points by how much the Democratic vote exceeded or fell behind what one would normally expect when the national vote divides 50–50 as it did this year.

Note that in Rhode Island, where Kennedy received 65 per cent of the vote, I estimate a plus of about 18 percentage points. In Massachusetts, he received 61 per cent of the vote and a plus of about 18 points. In Connecticut, where he received 54 per cent, the plus amounted to about 9 points; in New York, where he received 53 per cent, it totaled 6.

Kennedy pluses also show up in New Jersey, Pennsylvania, Illinois and California * where, on the basis of latest counts, he received approximately 50 to 51 per cent of the votes cast. Here the pluses range between 2 to 7 percentage points. The fact that these pluses occur in states with the heav-

DEMOCRATIC PERCENTAGE OF POPULAR VOTE FOR KENNEDY
AND CATHOLIC PROPORTION OF CHURCH MEMBERSHIP
IN SELECTED STATES

	% Vote for Kennedy	% Points Above or Below Normal [1]	Catholic % in Total Church Membership
N.C.	52	−14	2
Tenn.	46	−15	3
Okla.	41	−15	8
Va.	47	−20	8
Ky.	47	− 8	20
Kan.	40	− 4	23
Ind.	45	− 5	27
S.D.	42	− 5	29
Mo.	51	− 4	31
N.D.	44	− 3	34
O.	47	0	41
Wis.	48	+ 1	46
Pa.	51	+ 2	46
N.Y.	53	+ 6	50
Ill.	50[2]	+ 7	50
Mich.	51	+ 9	52
Calif.	50[2]	+ 2	54
Conn.	54	+ 9	62
N.J.	50[2]	+ 5	64
Mass.	61	+18	72
R.I.	65	+18	78

[1] For any national Democratic percentage there are corresponding state percentages. The plus and minus figures are based on state percentages corresponding to a 50 per cent Democratic vote nationally.

[2] Approximate.

iest Catholic concentrations definitely suggests that at least a number of these would today be in the Nixon column were it not for the additional support from Catholic voters. With the latest count giving Kennedy 300 electoral votes and a popular vote of only 50.1 per cent,** it is clear that

* Editor's note: The final California totals put the state in the Nixon column. Kennedy received 49.5 per cent of the state's vote and Nixon, 50.1 per cent.

** Editor's note: The final results gave Kennedy an electoral vote of 303 and a popular vote of 49.7 per cent.

the religious factor worked tellingly in his favor. Rhode Island, Massachusetts, Connecticut and New York supply 73 electoral votes to Kennedy's total of 300, which represents a surplus of 31 votes over the required 269. The other three states—New Jersey, Pennsylvania and Illinois—supply 75 electoral votes.

Conversely there are eleven states with relatively few Catholics where anti-Catholic bias was sufficient to reduce Kennedy's percentage below 50. These states, Florida, Virginia, Kentucky, Tennessee, Indiana, Oklahoma, Arizona, Nebraska, Utah, Montana and Oregon, represent a total of 84 electoral votes. Thus the religious issue apparently added more electoral votes to Kennedy's column than it took away. Without this net gain, Kennedy would not have had the required minimum of 269.

The relationship shown here may be summarized by pointing out that states having about 60 per cent Catholic church membership gave Kennedy approximately 10 per cent more of the popular vote than he would have received had the religious factor not been present; states having only 20 per cent Catholic church membership tended to give him 10 per cent less of the popular vote. . . .

I know that many will be surprised by the main point of this analysis —i.e., that on balance Al Smith was actually helped by the religious issue and that it was this same factor which gave Kennedy his winning electoral margin in an unusually close popular vote. The general tendency is to look upon the religious factor in terms of its most dramatic manifestation, the activities of highly prejudiced persons and groups, which came to light in this election as it did in 1928. But prejudice is only one side of the religious-issue coin, and not as important as most people think. In fact, when one balances the Protestant anti-Kennedy vote against the Protestant pro-Kennedy vote in this year's election, the net is a gain for Kennedy. According to a Gallup pre-election poll, Protestant voters were expected to go 40 per cent for Kennedy, Catholic voters 79 per cent for him, and Jewish voters, 78 per cent. This represents a 3-point gain over Stevenson's percentage among Protestants and Jews, and a 28-point gain among Catholics.

We need to sharpen our notions as to religious prejudice in politics. "Prejudice" does not cover the subject; a more important aspect is pride. When Jews vote for a Jewish candidate, it is not because they expect that David Ben-Gurion will give up his job of running Israel and move to Albany or the White House. It is a matter of pride, as it was in the case of German-Americans voting for Willkie in 1940. So I think it was pride that led many Catholics to vote for a Catholic, Kennedy, but prejudice that led those Protestants who are traditionally Democratic to vote against him. And many more, I believe, voted from pride than from prejudice.

Stability and Change in 1960:

A Reinstating Election

Philip E. Converse, Angus Campbell, Warren E. Miller,

Donald E. Stokes

John F. Kennedy's narrow popular vote margin in 1960 has already insured this presidential election a classic position in the roll call of close American elections. Whatever more substantial judgments historical perspective may bring, we can be sure that the 1960 election will do heavy duty in demonstrations to a reluctant public that after all is said and done, every vote does count. And the margin translated into "votes per precinct" will became standard fare in exhortations to party workers that no stone be left unturned.

The 1960 election is a classic as well in the license it allows for "explanations" of the final outcome. Any event or campaign strategem that might plausibly have changed the thinnest sprinkling of votes across the nation may, more persuasively than is usual, be called "critical." Viewed in this manner, the 1960 presidential election hung on such a manifold of factors that reasonable men might despair of cataloguing them.

Nevertheless, it is possible to put together an account of the election in terms of the broadest currents influencing the American electorate in 1960. We speak of the gross lines of motivation which gave the election its unique shape, motivations involving millions rather than thousands of votes. Analysis of these broad currents is not intended to explain the hairline differences in popular vote, state by state, which edged the balance in favor of Kennedy rather than Nixon. But it can indicate quite clearly the broad forces which reduced the popular vote to a virtual stalemate, rather than any of the other reasonable outcomes between a 60–40 or a 40–60 vote division. And it can thereby help us to understand in parsimonious terms why a last feather thrown on the scales in November, 1960, could have spelled victory or defeat for either candidate.

From *The American Political Science Review*, LV (June 1961), 269–280. Reprinted by permission.

I. SURFACE CHARACTERISTICS OF THE ELECTION

Any account of the election should not only be consistent with its obvious characteristics as they filtered clear from raw vote tallies in the days after the election, but should organize them into a coherent pattern of meaning as well. These characteristics are, of course, the ones that have nourished post-election speculation. In addition to the close partisan division of the popular vote, the following items deserve mention:

(1) *The remarkably high level of turnout.* About 62.7 percent of estimated adults over 21 voted in the 1952 election, a figure which had stood as the high-water mark of vote turnout in recent presidential elections. The comparable turnout proportion for the 1960 presidential election appears to have been 64.3 per cent.[1]

(2) *Upswing in turnout in the South.*[2] The South appears to have contributed disproportionately to the high level in turnout. Outside the South, the increase in total presidential votes cast in 1960 relative to the 1956 election was about 7 percent, a figure scarcely exceeding estimated population growth in this period. In the South, however, presidential ballots in 1960 increased by more than 25 per cent relative to 1956, an increase far outstripping population growth in this region.[3]

(3) *Stronger Republican voting at the presidential level.* On balance across the nation Nixon led Republican tickets, while Kennedy trailed behind many other Democratic candidates, especially outside of the Northeast. These discrepancies in the partisanship of presidential voting and ballots at other levels were not, of course, as striking as those in 1956. Nevertheless, their political significance has an obvious bearing on the future expectations of the two youthful candidates, and therefore occasions special interest.

(4) *The stamp of the religious factor in 1960 voting patterns.* While the Kennedy victory was initially taken as proof that religion had not been

---

[1] Estimates of turnout lack much meaning except as raw vote totals are stated as a proportion of the potential electorate. Whereas the number of adults over 21 in the nation is known with reasonable precision, the number of adult citizens over 21 who are "eligible" according to any of several possible definitions depends on cruder estimates, which can be quite diverse. For the 1952 figure we employ here Table No. 446 for the "Civilian Population 21 Years and Older," *Statistical Abstract of the United States* (1958 edition). The 1960 figure rests on an estimated 107 million adults over 21.

[2] The South is defined throughout this article to include 15 border and deep Southern States. Texas, Oklahoma, Arkansas, Kentucky, West Virginia and Maryland (but not Delaware) are included and form the western and nothern boundaries of the region.

[3] Population growth in areas such as Texas and Florida includes the immigration of American citizens from outside the South who are more accustomed to voting in every election than are Southerners. It seems almost certain, however, that there was a real increase in motivation among long-term Southern residents as well. The factor of population change was quite insufficient to account for the 1960 increase in Southern turnout.

important in the election, all serious students of election statistics have since been impressed by the religious axis visible in the returns. Fenton, Scammon, Bean, Harris and others have commented upon the substantial correlation between aggregate voting patterns and the relative concentration of Catholics and Protestants from district to district.

Of these surface characteristics, probably the last has drawn most attention. Once it became clear that religion had not only played some part but, as these things go, a rather impressive part in presidential voting across the nation, discussions came to hinge on the nature of its role. It could safely be assumed that Kennedy as a Catholic had attracted some unusual Catholic votes, and had lost some normally Democratic Protestant votes. A clear question remained, however, as to the *net* effect. The *New York Times*, summarizing the discussion late in November, spoke of a "narrow consensus" among the experts that Kennedy had won more than he lost as a result of his Catholicism.[4] These are questions, however, which aggregate vote statistics can but dimly illuminate, as the disputed history of Al Smith's 1928 defeat makes clear. Fortunately in 1960 the election was studied extensively by sample surveys, permitting more exact inferences to be drawn.

The national sample survey conducted by the Survey Research Center of The University of Michigan in the fall of 1960 had features which give an unparalleled opportunity to comment on the recent evolution of the American electorate. The fall surveys were part of a long-term "panel" study, in which respondents first interviewed at the time of the 1956 presidential election were reinterviewed.[5] In the fall of 1956 a sample of 1763 adults, chosen by strict probability methods from all the adults living in private households in the United States, had been questioned just before and just after the presidential election. This initial sample was constituted as a panel of respondents and was interviewed again in 1958 and twice in connection with the 1960 presidential election.[6] These materials permit the linking of 1960 and 1956 voting behavior with unusual reliability.[7]

---

[4] *New York Times*, November 20, 1960, Section 4, p. E5.

[5] Results of the 1956 survey, considered as a simple cross-section sample of the nation, are reported in Campbell, Converse, Miller and Stokes, *The American Voter* (New York, 1960). There are natural difficulties in any attempt to retain contact with a farflung national sample over periods of two and four years, especially in a population as geographically mobile as that of the current United States. Of the original 1763 respondents interviewed twice in 1956, nearly 100 had died before the 1960 interview. Others had been effectively removed from the electorate by advanced senility or institutionalization. Of the remaining possible interviews, numbering somewhat over 1600 people, more than 1100 were successfully reinterviewed in the fall of 1960. The 1956 social, economic and political characteristics of the 1960 survivors show almost no sign of deviation from the characteristics of the larger pool of original 1956 respondents. Therefore, although attrition may seem substantial, there is no evidence of alarming bias.

[6] The sequence of interviews in 1956, 1958 and 1960 was carried out under grants from the Rockefeller Foundation. The 1960 sample design provided not only contact with the 1956 panel which, due to aging, no longer gave an adequate representation of the 1960

II. THE EVOLUTION OF THE ELECTORATE, 1956–1960

The difference in presidential election outcome between 1956 and 1960 might depend upon either or both of two broad types of change in the electorate. The first includes shifts in the physical composition of the electorate over time due to non-political factors, *i.e.*, vital processes. Some adult citizens who voted in 1956 were no longer part of the eligible electorate in 1960, primarily because of death or institutionalization. On the other hand, a new cohort of voters who had been too young to vote in 1956 were eligible to participate in the 1960 election. Even in a four-year period, vital processes alone could account for shifts in the vote. In addition, changes in the electoral vote, though not in the nationwide popular vote margin, might result from voters changing their residences without changing their minds.

Secondly, there are obviously genuine changes in the political choice of individuals eligible to vote in both elections. Such citizens may enter or leave the active electorate by choice, or may decide to change the partisanship of their presidential vote.

The contribution of these two types of change to the shift in votes from a 1956 Eisenhower landslide to a narrow 1960 Kennedy margin—a net shift toward the Democrats of almost 8 percent—may be analyzed. Somewhat less than 10 percent of the eligible 1956 electorate had become effectively ineligible by 1960, with death as the principal cause.[8] Older people naturally bulk large in this category. The felt party affiliation or "party identification" expressed in 1956 by these "departing" respondents was somewhat Republican relative to the remainder of the sample.[9] Nonetheless, these people cast a vote for president which was about 48 percent Democratic, or 6 percent *more Democratic* than the vote of the 1956 electorate as a whole.

---

electorate, but also a set of additional interviews filling out an up-to-date cross-section sample of all adult citizens living in private households in 1960. Analysis of the additional interview material is being carried out under a grant from the Social Science Research Council. Both the panel and cross-section bodies of data contribute, where appropriate, to materials in this article.

[7] The longitudinal analysis of political change permitted by a panel design can only be poorly approximated in simple cross-section surveys, where deductions must rest on the respondent's recollection of his behavior in time past. Most analysts have justly felt uncomfortable with recall materials of this sort, since it has been clear that the accuracy of a vote report declines rapidly as time passes. In both 1958 and 1960, we asked our respondents to recall their 1956 vote. The results, as compared with actual reports collected just after the 1956 election, demonstrate forcefully the inaccuracies which accumulate with time.

[8] Throughout this article, the "eligible electorate" is taken to consist of those non-institutionalized citizens over 21. Negroes disqualified in many parts of the South, for example, are included in this bounding of the electorate, as well as those who had moved, too recently to have established new voting residences in 1960.

[9] The concept of party identification is treated in detail, Campbell *et al., op. cit.*, p. 120 ff.

Although this appears to be a contradiction, it is actually nothing more than a logical consequence of existing theory. The high Republican vote in 1956 depended on a massive defection to Eisenhower by many people identified with the Democratic party. Since the strength of party attachments increases as a function of age, and since defections are inversely related to strength of party identification, it follows that 1956 defection rates were much higher among younger citizens than among older.[10] The data make it clear that the group of older people voting for the last time in 1956 had cast a much straighter "party vote" than their juniors. Only about 5 percent of these older Democrats had defected to Eisenhower, as opposed to about a quarter of all Democrats in the electorate as a whole. So both things are true: this departing cohort was more Republican than average in party identification but had voted more Democratic than average in 1956. If we remove them from the 1956 electorate, then, we arrive at a presidential vote of about 60 percent for Eisenhower among those voters who were to have the option of voting again in 1960. Hence the elimination of this older group from consideration increases the amount of partisan change to be accounted for between 1956 and 1960, rather than decreasing it.

Comparable isolation of the new cohort of young voters in 1960 does very little to change the picture. Little more than one half of this new group of voters normally votes in the first election of eligibility;[11] furthermore, in 1960 its two-party vote division differed only negligibly from that of the nation as a whole. As a result, its analytic removal leaves the vote among the remainder of the electorate nearly unchanged. By way of summary, then, differences in the 1956 and 1960 electorates arising from vital processes do not explain the 1956–1960 vote change; if anything, they extend the amount of change to be otherwise explained.

We may further narrow our focus by considering those people eligible in both 1956 and 1960, who failed to join the active electorate in 1960. A very large majority of these 1960 non-voters had not voted in 1956, and represent Negroes in the South as well as persistent non-voters of other types. Among those who *had* voted in 1956, however, the vote had been rather evenly divided between Eisenhower and Stevenson. As with the older voters, removal of this group leaves an active 1956–1960 electorate whose vote for Eisenhower now surpasses 60 percent, broadening again the discrepancy between the two-party divisions in the 1956 and 1960 votes. The final fringe group which we may set aside analytically is constituted of those citizens eligible to have voted in 1956 who did not then participate, yet who joined the electorate in 1960. The fact that young voters often

---

[10] Our theoretical understanding of this net of relationships is suggested *ibid.,* pp. 161–167.

[11] Participation rates by age in 1960 follow rather nicely the rates indicated *ibid.,* Fig. 17–1, p. 494.

"sit out" their first presidential election or two indicates part of the composition of such a group. Once again, however, these newly active citizens divided their ballots in 1960 almost equally between the two major candidates, and the residual portion of the 1960 electorate changes little with their removal.

By this point we have eliminated all the fringe groupings whose entry or departure from the active electorate might have contributed to change in the national vote division between 1956 and 1960. We come to focus directly, then, on the individuals who cast a vote for Kennedy or Nixon in 1960 *and had voted for president in 1956* (Table I). As we see, paring away the fringe groupings has had the total effect of increasing the net shift in the vote division between the two years from 8 percent to 11 percent. If we can explain this shift it will be clear that we have dealt with those broad currents in the electorate which brought the 1960 election to a virtual stalemate.

Naturally, the most interesting features of Table I are the cells involving vote changers. In a sequence of elections such as the 1956–1960 series it is

TABLE I. 1956–1960 VOTE CHANGE WITHIN THE ACTIVE CORE OF THE ELECTORATE

1960 Vote for ↓	1956 Vote for		Total %
	Stevenson %	Eisenhower %	
Kennedy	33	17	50
Nixon	6	44	50
	39	61	100

Note: Since we usually think of vote shifts in terms of proportions of the total electorate, percentages in this table use the total vote as a base, rather than row or column totals.

a temptation to assume that about 8 percent of the Eisenhower voters of 1956 shifted to Kennedy in 1960, since this was the net observable change between the two years. Much analysis of aggregate election statistics is forced to proceed on this assumption within any given voting unit. However, we see that the net shift of 11 percent in the vote of the active 1956–1960 electorate in fact derived from a gross shift of 23 percent, over half of which was rendered invisible in the national totals because counter-movements cancelled themselves out.

A traditional analysis of these vote changers would specify their membership in various population groupings such as age and occupation category, union membership, race and the like. However, results of this sort in 1960 are so uniform across most of these population groupings that they seem to reflect little more than national trends, and change seems at best loosely connected with location in various of these specific categories. If we took the fact in isolation, for example, we might be struck to note that union members voted almost 8 percent more Democratic in 1960 than in 1956. However, such a figure loses much of its interest when we remind ourselves that people who are not labor union members also shifted their votes in the same direction and in about the same degree between 1956 and 1960. Such uniform changes characterize most of the standard sociological categories.

There is, of course, one dramatic exception. Vote change between 1956 and 1960 follows religious lines very closely. Within the 6 percent of the active 1956–1960 electorate who followed a Stevenson-Nixon path (Table I), 90 percent are Protestant and only 8 percent are Catholic. Among the larger group of Eisenhower-Kennedy changers, however, only 40 percent are Protestant and close to 60 percent are Catholic. In the total vote in 1956 and 1960, Protestants show almost no net partisan change. Eisenhower had won 64 percent of the "Protestant vote" in 1956; Nixon won 63 percent. Meanwhile, the Democratic proportion of the two-party vote among Catholics across the nation skyrocketed from a rough 50 percent in the two Eisenhower elections to a vote of 80 percent for Kennedy. These gross totals appear to substantiate the early claims of Kennedy backers that a Catholic candidate would draw back to the Democratic party sufficient Catholics to carry the 1960 election. Furthermore, it appears that Kennedy must have gained more votes than he lost by virtue of his religious affiliation, for relative to Stevenson in 1956, he lost no Protestant votes and attracted a very substantial bloc of Catholic votes.

The question of net gains or losses as a result of the Catholic issue is not, however, so simply laid to rest. The data cited above make a very strong case, as have the aggregate national statistics, that religion played a powerful role in the 1960 outcome. The vote polarized along religious lines in a degree which we have not seen in the course of previous sample survey studies. Moreover, the few interesting deviations in the 1960 vote of other population groupings, to the degree that they are visible at all, seem with minor exceptions to reflect the central religious polarization. That is, where a group exceeded or fell below the magnitude of the national shift to the Democrats, it is usually true that the group is incidentally a more or less Catholic group. The central phenomenon therefore was religious; the question as to its net effect favoring or disfavoring Kennedy remains open.

In a strict sense, of course, the answers to this question can only be estimated. We know how the election came out, with Kennedy a Catholic. We cannot, without major additional assumptions, know what the election returns might have been if Kennedy were a Protestant and all other conditions remained unchanged. We can make an estimate, however, if we can assume some baseline, some vote that would have occurred under "normal" circumstances. A number of such baselines suggest themselves. We might work from the 1956 presidential vote, as we have done above (42 percent Democratic); or from the more recent Congressional vote in 1958 (56 percent Democratic); or from some general average of recent nation-wide votes. But it is obvious that the simple choice of baseline will go a long way toward determining the answer we propose to the question of net religious effect. If we choose the 1958 vote as a baseline, it is hard to argue that Kennedy could have made any net gains from his religion; if we choose the 1956 presidential vote, it is equally hard to argue that he lost ground on balance.

Indeed, the most cogent arguments documenting a net gain for Kennedy —those accounts which appear to express the majority opinion of election observers—use the 1956 presidential vote quite explicitly as a baseline. Yet the second Eisenhower vote seems the most bizarre choice for a baseline of any which might be suggested. The vote Eisenhower achieved in 1956 stands out as the most disproportionately Republican vote in the total series of nation-wide presidential and Congressional elections stretching back to 1928. In what sense, then, is this extreme Republican swing plausible as a "normal vote?" Its sole claim seems to lie in the fact that it is the most recent presidential election. Yet other recent elections attest dramatically to the extreme abnormality of the 1956 Eisenhower vote. In the 1954 Congressional elections the nation's Democrats, although they turned out less well than Republicans in minor elections, still fashioned a solid majority of votes cast. The fall of 1958 witnessed a Democratic landslide. Even in 1956, "underneath" Eisenhower's towering personal margin, a Democratic popular vote majority exceeding that which Kennedy won in 1960 appeared at other levels of the ticket. Finally, if 1956 is taken as a normal baseline and if it is true that Kennedy did score some relative personal success in 1960, how can we possibly explain the fact that other diverse Democrats on state tickets around the nation tended to win a greater proportion of popular votes than he attracted?

It seems more reasonable to suggest that Kennedy did not in any sense *exceed* the "normal" vote expectations of the generalized and anonymous Democratic candidate; rather, he fell visibly below these expectations, although nowhere nearly as far below them as Adlai Stevenson had fallen. This proposition is congruent not only with the general contours of election returns in the recent period, but with the great mass of sample survey data collected in the past decade as well. With this proposition we can draw into a coherent pattern the several surface characteristics which seemed intriguing from the simple 1960 vote totals. With it, we can locate the 1960 election more generally in the stream of American political history.

III. THE BASIC VOTING STRENGTH
OF THE TWO PARTIES

We have found it of great explanatory value to think of election results as reflecting the interplay of two sets of forces: stable, long-term partisan dispositions and short-term forces specific to the immediate election situation. The long-term partisan dispositions are very adequately represented by our measures of party identification. The stability of these dispositions over time is a matter of empirical record.[12] Their partisan division over any period, as it may favor one party or the other, provides the point from which one must start to understand any specific election. This underlying division of loyalties lends itself admirably to the goal of indicating what a "normal" vote would be, aside from specific forces associated with the immediate election.

In these terms, the basic Democratic majority in the nation is scarcely subject to dispute. Year in and year out since 1952, national samples of the American electorate have indicated a preference for the Democratic party by a margin approaching 60–40. However, since no election in recent years has shown a Democratic margin of this magnitude, it would be as absurd to take a 60–40 Democratic majority for a baseline as it would be to work from the 1956 presidential vote. Actually there is little temptation to do so. Over the years large amounts of information have been accumulated on the behavior of people identifying with the two major parties, and it is clear that the realistic voting strength of the Democrats—and this is the sort of baseline which interests us—falls well short of a 60–40 majority. The fact that heavy Democratic majorities in the South are concealed by low voting turnout is but one factor which reduces realistic Democratic strength. Outside the South, as well, Democrats under the same conditions of short-term stimulation are less likely to vote than Republicans.

It is possible to manipulate the data in such a fashion as to take into account all of the significant discrepancies between nominal party identification and realistic voting strength. We thereby arrive at a picture of the vote division which could be expected in the normal presidential election, if short-term forces associated with the election favored neither party in particular, but stood at an equilibrium. In such circumstances, we would expect a Democratic proportion of the two-party popular vote to fall in the vicinity of 53–54 percent.[13] Outside of the South, such a vote would fall short of a

---

[12] The absence of any significant change in the distribution of party loyalties throughout the Eisenhower period is best illustrated by Table 6–1, *ibid.*, p. 124. Distributions drawn in 1959 and 1960 continue the same pattern. Furthermore, there is no evidence that this surface stability of party identification is concealing a great flux of compensating changes beneath the surface. There have indeed been one or two slow, modest evolutions since 1952 which do involve compensating changes and hence are not visible in simple distributions. Nevertheless, our panel data show strikingly that among all the political orientations which we measure, partisan identification is by far the most stable for individuals over the periods which our data cover.

[13] This figure should be taken to indicate a rough range. It would vary upward or downward slightly according to the assumptions made concerning the overall proportion of the electorate turning out. While the computations underlying this estimate are tedious, their rationale is entirely straightforward. Turnout rates and the two-party vote division within each of seven categories of party identifiers have shown remarkable regularities over the range of elections which we have studied. These rates are not constant

50–50 split with the Republicans; within the South there would be a strong Democratic majority exceeding a 2-to-1 division.

Short-term forces associated with a specific election may, according to their net partisan strength, send the actual vote in that election deviating to one side or the other of the equilibrium point. In 1952 and 1956 the popularity of Eisenhower constituted one such force, and this force was strongly pro-Republican. The distortions produced in the behaviors of party identifiers of different types have now become familiar. If the net partisan force is strong, as in 1956, identifiers of the favored party vote almost *en bloc*, without defection. The small group of "independents" who do not commit themselves to either party divide very disproportionately in favor of the advantaged party, instead of dividing their vote equally as in the equilibrium case. And members of the disfavored party defect in relatively large numbers, as Democrats did in 1956. A useful description of any specific election, then, is an account of the short-term forces which have introduced these strains across the distribution of party identification.

In such a description, the existing division of deeper party loyalties is taken for granted. Its current character is not to be explained by the immediate political situation. The point is made most clearly by the 1960 election. The fact that the Democrats enjoyed a standing majority was in no way a consequence of the personal duel between Kennedy and Nixon, for it was a majority created long before either candidate became salient as a national political figure, and long before most of the campaign "issues" of 1960 had taken shape. In this perspective, then, we can consider some of the forces which drew the 1960 vote away from its equilibrium state.

IV. SHORT-TERM FORCES IN THE 1960 ELECTION

Popular vote tallies show that Kennedy received 49.8 percent of the two-party vote outside of the South, and 51.2 percent of the popular vote cast in the South. The vote outside the South is almost 1 percent more Democratic than our equilibrium estimates for this part of the nation. In the South, however, the Democratic deficit relative to the same baseline approaches 17 percent. Naturally, some short-term forces may balance out so that no net advantage accrues to either party. But the comparisons between our baselines and the 1960 vote suggest that we should find some short-

---

from election to election, but do vary for each type of identifier quite dependably as a function of the net balance of short-term partisan forces characterizing the specific election. While we have observed no election which registered a perfect equilibrium of these forces, we have observed situations in which net forces were Democratic (e.g., 1958) as well as Republican (e.g., 1952 or 1956). It is therefore possible to compute the turnout rate and two-party vote division which could be expected for each type of party identifier in the intermediate case in which short-term forces are balanced. The estimate employed above derives from a summation of these computations across categories of identifiers, weighted in a fashion appropriate to represent the entire electorate.

term forces which gave a very slight net advantage to Kennedy outside of the South, and yet which penalized him heavily within the South.

As in all elections that attract a wide degree of public attention, a number of short-term forces were certainly at work in 1960. A comprehensive assessment of these forces must await further analysis. However, there can be little doubt that the religious issue was the strongest single factor overlaid on basic partisan loyalties in the 1960 election, and we have focused most of our initial analyses in this area. Fortunately we know a great deal about the "normal" voting behavior within different religious categories, and can use this knowledge to provide baselines which aid in estimating the net effect of Kennedy's Catholicism upon his candidacy.

The Catholic Vote. As we have observed, the vote division among Catholics soared from a 50–50 split in the two Eisenhower contests to an 80–20 majority in the 1960 presidential vote. However, it is hard to attribute all of this increment simply to the Kennedy candidacy. In the 1958 election, when there were mild short-term economic forces favoring the Democratic party, the vote among Catholics went well over 70 percent in that direction. Ever since our measurements of party identification began in 1952, only a small minority—less than 20 percent—of Catholics in the nation have considered themselves as Republicans, although a fair portion have typically styled themselves as "Independents." Most of what attracted attention as a Republican trend among Catholics during the 1950's finds little support in our data, at least as a trend peculiar to Catholics. To be sure, many Democratic Catholics defected to vote for Eisenhower in 1952 and 1956. So did many Democratic Protestants. As a matter of fact, the defection rate among Democratic Catholics in 1952 was very slightly less than among Democratic Protestants, and in 1956 was very slightly more. In neither case do the differences exceed sampling error. There is some long-term evidence of a faint and slow erosion in the Catholic Democratic vote; but this has been proceeding at such a glacial pace that the 1956–1960 vote trends which we are treating here dwarf it completely. There is no reason to believe that the short-term personal "pull" exerted on Democrats generally by Eisenhower had a different strength for Catholics than for Protestants. The myths that have arisen to this effect seem to be primarily illusions stemming from the large proportion of Democrats who are Catholics. Their loss was painful in the two Eisenhower votes. But they were at the outset, and remained up to the first glimmer of the Kennedy candidacy, a strongly Democratic group.

We may specify this "normal" Democratic strength among Catholics by applying the same operations for Catholics alone that we have employed for the electorate as a whole. In the equilibrium case, it turns out that one would expect at least a 63 percent Democratic margin among Catholics. The difference between 63 percent and the 80 percent which Kennedy achieved can provisionally be taken as an estimate of the increment in

Democratic votes among Catholics above that which the normal, Protestant Democratic presidential candidate could have expected.

We can readily translate this 17 percent vote gain into proportions of the total 1960 vote, taking into account levels of Catholic turnout and the like. On such grounds, it appears that Kennedy won a vote bonus from Catholics amounting to about 4 percent of the national two-party popular vote. This increment is, of course, very unequally divided between the South and the rest of the nation, owing simply to the sparse Catholic population in the South. Within the 1960 non-Southern electorate, Kennedy's net gain from the Catholic increment amounts to better than 5 percent of the two-party vote. The same rate of gain represents less than 1 percent of the Southern popular vote.

The Anti-Catholic Vote. Respondents talked to our interviewers with remarkable freedom about the Catholic factor during the fall of 1960. This is not to say that all respondents referred to it as a problem. There were even signs that some Protestant respondents were struggling to avoid mention of it although it was a matter of concern. Nonetheless, nearly 40 percent of the sample voluntarily introduced the subject before any direct probing on our part in the early stages of the pre-election questionnaire. Since this figure certainly understates the proportion of the population for whom religion was a salient concern in 1960, it testifies rather eloquently to the importance of the factor in conscious political motivations during the fall campaign.

These discussions of the Catholic question, volunteered by our respondents, will, in time, provide more incisive descriptions of the short-term anti-Catholic forces important in the election. Our interest here, however, is to estimate the magnitude of anti-Catholic voting in terms of otherwise Democratic votes which Kennedy lost. In such an enterprise, our material on the political backgrounds of our respondents is most useful.

We focus, therefore, upon the simple rates of defection to Nixon among Protestants who were identified in 1960 with the Democratic party. As Figure 1 shows, this defection rate is strongly correlated with regularity of attendance at a Protestant church. Protestant Democrats who, by self-description, never attend church, and hence are not likely to have much identification with it, defected to Nixon only at a rate of 6 percent. This rate, incidentally, is just about the "normal" defection rate which we would predict for both parties in the equilibrium case: it represents the scattered defections which occur for entirely idiosyncratic reasons in any election. Therefore, for Democrats who were nominal Protestants but outside the psychological orbit of their church, the short-term religious force set up by a Catholic candidacy had no visible impact. However, as soon as there is some evidence of identification with a Protestant church, the defection rate rises rapidly.

Although Protestant Independents are not included in Figure 1, they show the same gradient at a different level of the two-party vote division. The few Protestant Independents not attending church split close to the theoretically-expected 50–50 point. Then the Nixon vote rises to 61 percent in the "seldom" category; to 72 percent for the "often" category; and to 83 percent for the Protestant Independents attending church regularly. This increment of Republican votes above the "normal" 50–50 division for Independents matches remarkably the increment of Republican votes above the "normal" figure of 6 percent in the case of the Democrats.

We customarily find in our data certain substantial correlations between church attendance and political behavior. The correlation between church attendance and vote among Protestant Democrats and Independents is not, however, one of these.[14] The strong associations seem linked in an obvious way to the 1960 election. We need not assume, of course, that each defection pictured here represents a sermon from the pulpit and an obedient member of the congregation. Social science theory assures us that whether through sermons, informal communication or a private sense of reserve toward Catholicism, the faithful Protestant would react more negatively to the presidential candidacy of a Catholic than would more indifferent Protestants.[15] It remains notable, however, that Democrats who were at the same time regular Protestants defected to Nixon at rates far exceeding those which Eisenhower had attracted in 1952 or 1956.

We may use Figure 1, then, as a tool to estimate the magnitude of the anti-Catholic vote. It is easily argued that the area below the dotted line in Figure 1 represents "normal" defections within each category of church attendance, and that the votes represented by the triangle above the dotted line are votes which Kennedy lost on religious grounds. It is then a simple mechanical matter to convert this triangle into proportions of the popular vote for South and non-South.

On the surface, Figure 1 seems to say that the impact of the religious factor was very nearly the same, North and South, for the Southern gradient of defections is only slightly higher than the non-Southern gradient. If we think of the impact of short-term forces *on individuals* as a function of their party and religious loyalties, this conclusion is proper. Indeed, as we consider in later analyses the impact by different types of Protestantism, it may well be that the character of the impact will show no remaining regional difference whatever. However, to construe Figure 1 as suggesting that the *magnitude* of the anti-Catholic effect was about the same in votes cast

---

[14] Re-examination of earlier data shows a faint residual relationship between Republican voting and church attendance among Democratic Protestants which is not statistically significant. In 1956, the rank-order correlations involved were about 05 both within and outside the South. On the other hand, the comparable coefficient for Independents in 1956 was negative, —.04. The text ignores these variations as probably inconsequential.

[15] This is simply a special case of propositions concerning group identifications more generally, discussed in Campbell *et al., op. cit.,* ch. 12.

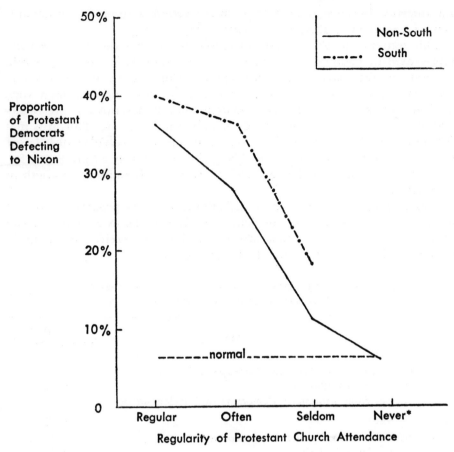

FIGURE 1. *Defections to Nixon among Protestant Democrats as a Function of Church Attendance.*

in North and South, is quite improper. The differences between the regions turn out to be substantial.

We must consider first that less than two-thirds of the active non-Southern electorate is Protestant, whereas within the South the electorate is almost completely (95 percent) Protestant. Secondly, Protestants are more faithful church-goers in the South than outside it. Quite specifically, we find that over half of the Southern presidential vote is cast by Protestants who go to church regularly, whereas less than 20 percent of the vote outside the South comes from regular, church-going Protestants. Finally, of the minority outside the South who are Protestant and attend church regularly, only a small proportion are Democratic identifiers: Republicans clearly predominate in

---

* The number of Protestant Democrats who "never" attend church in the South is too small for inclusion.

this category. In the South, the situation is reversed, with regular Protestants being far more often than not Democratic identifiers.

This conjunction of regional differences means that the defecting votes represented in Figure 1 are of vastly different sizes, South and non-South. It turns out that outside the South regular, church-going Protestants who are Democrats cast only about 5 percent of the total non-Southern vote. Within the South, however, regular church-going Protestants who are Democrats contributed over 35 percent of the total Southern vote. Thus it is that the anti-Catholic impact in the South turns out to involve a much larger share of the votes than elsewhere. The anti-Catholic vote in the South fulfills our search for a short-term force of strong net Republican strength in that region.

Summing up these apparent anti-Catholic votes as proportions of the total vote in the South, the non-South, and the nation as a whole, we can compare them with our estimations of the bonuses received by Kennedy from Catholics. Table II shows the balance sheet.

TABLE II. OFFSETTING EFFECTS OF THE CATHOLIC ISSUE,
1960 DEMOCRATIC PRESIDENTIAL VOTE

Area	% of 2-party vote in area
Outside the South, Kennedy's "unexpected" . . .	
Gains from Catholics	5.2%
Losses from Protestant Democrats and Independents	−3.6
NET	+1.6%
Inside the South, Kennedy's "unexpected" . . .	
Gains from Catholics	0.7%
Losses from Protestant Democrats and Independents	−17.2
NET	−16.5%
For the *nation as a whole,* Kennedy's "unexpected" . . .	
Gains from Catholics	4.3%
Losses from Protestant Democrats and Independents	−6.5
NET	−2.2%

There is every reason to believe that these preliminary estimates under-estimate the importance of religion in the 1960 vote and, in particular, under-estimate the magnitude of the anti-Catholic vote. We have at no point taken account, for example, of the possibility that certain Republican identifiers, exposed to short-term forces which would normally have produced defections to the Democrats, may have been inhibited from such defection by Kennedy's Catholicism. In the midwest there were signs of a "farm revolt" favoring the Democrats which failed to materialize in the presidential balloting. At lower levels on farm belt tickets one finds that major Democratic candidates consistently surpassed "normal" Democratic expectations. Yet Kennedy seems to have been peculiarly insulated from any of this profit-taking: in these areas he lagged behind other major Democrats by a rather consistent 5 percent. It is difficult not to believe that at lower levels of office net short-term forces were favoring the Democrats, and Republican identifiers were defecting at unusual rates. Analyses may show that religion was a primary force inhibiting such defections at the presidential level.

Other early glimpses of our data also suggest the estimates of anti-Catholicism in Table II are conservative. It is likely that a number of non-religious short-term forces generated by the campaign itself were favorable to Kennedy on balance. As a number of other surveys reported, Nixon held a substantial lead over Kennedy in the early stages. At the outset, Kennedy was little known to the public: he stood primarily as the Democratic candidate and a Catholic. As the campaign went on, other and non-religious aspects of the Kennedy image filled in, and the public impression was usually positive. In this crucial shift in sentiment during the campaign, the television debates probably played an important role. Although there were Democrats who reacted warmly to Nixon's performance, our materials show quite strikingly that the net response to the debates favored Kennedy, as has been commonly supposed. In case studies, a reading of interviews has already turned up numerous Protestants of varying partisanship who were much more impressed by Kennedy as a candidate than by Nixon, yet who could not bring themselves to vote for a Catholic. In the measure that Kennedy's attractiveness as a candidate exceeded Nixon's and other short-term forces apart from religion were favoring the Democrats, the total popular vote should have been drawn to the Democratic side of the equilibrium point. The fact that it stayed instead on the Republican side may represent further damaging effects of religion for Kennedy.[16]

Refined analyses at a later date will permit us to estimate more adequately the role which all the major motivational factors, including religion, played in the 1960 outcome. For the moment, however, it is impressive the degree to which the surface characteristics of the 1960 election become intelligible even when viewed simply as the result of an "ancient" and enduring division of partisan loyalties overlaid by a short-term cross-current of religious motivation.

Normally we would expect a national vote falling as close to its equilibrium point as the 1960 case to be a relatively low-turnout election. That

---

[16] Two other motivational patterns associated with religion in 1960 deserve note. There were undoubtedly broad-minded Protestants who were drawn to a Kennedy vote out of a desire to see the religious precedent broken and hence buried; and there were undoubtedly Catholics who were drawn away from a Kennedy vote out of fear that the fact of a Catholic president would keep the religious issue uncomfortably prominent. It is hard to find instances of these viewpoints in our sample, however, and it is to be assumed that their incidence was slight.

is, a vote near the equilibrium point suggests either weak short-term forces or else a balance of stronger forces creating conflict in individuals and thereby lowering their motivation to vote. It is rare that forces strong enough to compel indifferent citizens to come out and vote do not also favor one party over the other quite categorically.

In 1960, however, the motivational picture underlying the vote was somewhat different, and can best be understood by separating the Protestant South from the rest of the nation. In the South, of course, a strong and unidirectional short-term force was reflected in a sharp departure from equilibrium and a surge in turnout, as fits normal expectations. What is abnormal is that this strong Republican short-term force raised motivation in a Democratic preserve, rather than diluting it through conflict. It is likely that conflict *was* created, especially where Democratic partisanship was strong. "Strong" Democrats in our sample made virtually no contribution to the 1960 rise in Southern turnout. The increase came from weaker Democrats, whose participation increased so radically over 1952 and 1956 that their turnout even surpassed that of strong Democrats in very exceptional fashion. For these voters, it seems likely that such forces as anti-Catholic feelings rapidly overcame relatively weak party loyalties and left strong motivation to turn out.

While turnout elsewhere did not show the same remarkable surge which appeared in the South, it remained at the fairly high level characteristic of the 1952 and 1956 elections, despite a partisan division of the vote near the regional equilibrium point. Strong balancing forces appear to have been in operation which did not create much conflict within individuals. The reason is clear: to the degree that religious motivations were engaged, forces were conflicting between groups rather than within individuals. Non-Southern Catholics, predominantly Democratic, were exposed to strong unidirectional short-term forces motivating them to get out and vote for Kennedy. Non-Southern Protestants, predominantly Republican, were exposed to contrary forces, at least where Protestant religious fidelity was strong. Thus the vote fell near the equilibrium point, but there was rather high turnout as well.

The other surface characteristics of the election are equally intelligible in these terms. Despite his position as majority candidate, Kennedy very nearly lost and tended to run behind his ticket. In the northeast, where concentrations of Catholics are greatest, his relation to the rest of the ticket was not generally unfavorable. The penalty he suffered becomes visible and consistent in the Midwest, where Catholics are fewer and Protestant church attendance is more regular. In the South, and for the same reasons, the differences between the Kennedy vote and that of other Democrats become large indeed. Everywhere, if one compares 1956 vote statistics with 1960 statistics, the course of political change is closely associated with the religious composition of voting units.

There was some relief even outside the more committed Democratic circles when the Kennedy victory, slight though it was, demonstrated that a Catholic was not in practice barred from the White House. Yet it would be naive to suppose that a Catholic candidate no longer suffers any initial disadvantage before the American electorate as a result of his creed. Not only did Kennedy possess a type of personal appeal which the television debates permitted him to exploit in unusual measure, but he was also the candidate of a party enjoying a fundamental majority in the land. Even the combination of these circumstances was barely sufficient to give him a popular vote victory. Lacking such a strong underlying majority, which Al Smith most certainly lacked in 1928, it is doubtful that the most attractive of Catholic presidential candidates in 1960 would have had much chance of success. It remains to be seen how far the experience of a Catholic president may diminish the disadvantage another time.

V. THE 1960 ELECTION IN HISTORICAL PERSPECTIVE

In a publication which appeared a few months prior to the 1960 elections[17] we posed the question of "how long a party can hope to hold the White House if it does not have a majority of the party-identified electorate." We had identified the two Eisenhower victories as "deviating elections," in which short-term forces had brought about the defeat of the majority party. We had not found any evidence in our 1952 or 1956 studies that these short-term forces were producing any significant realignment in the basic partisan commitments of the electorate. We felt that unless such a realignment did occur, "the minority party [could] not hope to continue its tenure in office over a very extended period."

We now know that the eight-year Eisenhower period ended with no basic change in the proportions of the public who identify themselves as Republican, Democrat, or Independent. If there had been an opportunity in 1952 for the Republican party to rewin the majority status it had held prior to 1932, it failed to capitalize on it. The Democratic party remained the majority party and the 1960 election returned it to the presidency. It was, to extend the nomenclature of our earlier publication, a "reinstating" election, one in which the party enjoying a majority of party identifiers returns to power. The 1960 election was remarkable not in the fact that the majority party was reinstated but that its return to power was accomplished by such a narrow margin. We had recognized the possibility that "the unfolding of national and international events and the appearance of new political figures" might swing the vote away from its natural equilibrium. We now see that such a deflection did occur and that it very nearly cost the majority party the election.

---

[17] Campbell et al., op. cit., ch. 19.

It may be argued that the deficit the Democratic presidential candidate suffered from his normal expectation did not derive from damaging circumstances which were specific to the 1960 election but from a progressive weakening in the willingness of some Democratic partisans to support their ticket at the presidential level. It has been suggested that some voters who consider themselves to be Democrats and customarily favor Democratic candidates at the lower levels of office may have come during the Eisenhower period to have a perverse interest in favoring Republican candidates for president, either because of notions of party balance in government, because of local considerations in their states, or simply out of admiration for Eisenhower.

Important differences no doubt exist between voting at the presidential level and voting for a congressman. Our studies have shown, for example, that the popular vote for lesser offices is a more party-determined vote than the vote for president and varies around the normal equilibrium vote figure within a much narrower range than does the presidential vote.[18] However, the supposition that Kennedy failed to win a normal Democratic majority because of a cadre of Democrats who are covertly Republican in their presidential voting is not supported by our data.

Table I has already demonstrated that the overall shift in partisanship of the vote between 1956 and 1960 cannot be explained as a simple unilateral movement of erstwhile Eisenhower Democrats. The election did not depend, as was often supposed, upon the number of Eisenhower Democrats whom Nixon could retain as "covert Republicans." Our panel materials show that if Nixon had been forced to depend only upon the Eisenhower Democrats whom he retained, he would have suffered a convincing 54–46 defeat, assuming that other Democrats had continued to vote for Kennedy. He did not suffer such a defeat because he drew a new stream of Democratic defections nearly sufficient to put him in the White House.

The patterns of short-term forces in the 1960 election were independent of those shaping the 1956 election, then, in the sense that they affected a new set of people, on new grounds. There were Democrats susceptible to Eisenhower in 1956; there were Democrats sensitive to religion in 1960: the two sets of people do not intersect much more than one would expect by chance. In short, there is little evidence that the two Eisenhower elections had created a set of Democrats peculiarly disposed to vote for a Republican presidential candidate.

Analysis of our 1960 data is not sufficiently complete to enable us to describe the entire pattern of forces to which the electorate was reacting on Election Day. We do not know, for example, what the partisan impact of international affairs, which had favored the Republican candidate so

---

[18] Angus Campbell, "Surge and Decline: A Study of Electoral Change," *Public Opinion Quarterly*, Vol. 24 (Fall 1960), pp. 397–418.

strongly in the preceding two elections, was in the 1960 election. We do not know the effect of the Negro discrimination issues. We do not know in detail as yet how the personal attributes of the major candidates, other than their religious affiliations, were evaluated by the public. We feel confident, however, that we will not find any short-term force which moved as large a fraction of the 1960 electorate as did the issue of a Catholic president. This was the major cause of the net departure of the vote totals from the division which the comparative underlying strength of the two parties in 1960 would have led us to expect. After two consecutive "deviating" elections won at a presidential level by the minority party, the 1960 election reinstated the Democratic party. But short-term forces generated by the immediate 1960 situation once again favored the Republicans on balance, and the difference in votes which separated this "reinstating election" from a third "deviating election" was slight indeed.

XIV

The Goldwater Phenomenon:
Traditional Republicanism or
Pseudo-Conservatism?

INTRODUCTION

Between 1940 and 1960 the presidential nominee of the Republican party and the Republican platform had been largely determined by the party's "Eastern Establishment." In the 1964 Republican convention, however, Senator Barry Goldwater, the hero of the G.O.P.'s right wing, bested the internationalist and mildly reformist forces that had controlled the Republican presidential party. The victorious Goldwater did not try to conciliate his party opponents in the choice of his running mate, and he campaigned on a platform that was unacceptable to Republican moderates in several important respects. The electoral results were devastating for the G.O.P.: Goldwater's Democratic opponent, Lyndon B. Johnson, won the election by the largest margin of popular votes and the largest percentage of the popular vote received by any presidential candidate in American history.

Writing on the eve of the 1964 presidential election, H. G. Nicholas, Reader in the Comparative Study of Institutions at Oxford University and author of Britain and the United States *(1963), recognizes that the nomination of Goldwater represented a break with the consensus nature of American party politics in recent years, but he nevertheless contends that Goldwater "could claim that there was a Republican tradition behind him and that he and his policies had a place within it." Nicholas also stresses the anti-Eastern character of the Goldwater revolt, and he speculates that the rising influence in conservative politics of the West and Southwest may be a permanent factor surviving Goldwater's defeat.*

The distinguished historian Richard Hofstadter is less concerned with the relationship of Goldwater to any Republican tradition than with his "excessively sharp deviation from the pattern of American politics" and the "practical conservatism" of the post-World War II years. He sees the Goldwater movement as "almost an ideal test case for the nature of pseudo-conservatism." Pseudo-conservatives, Hofstadter had previously written, show signs of a serious and restless dissatisfaction with American life, traditions, and institutions," and "their political reactions express rather a profound if largely unconscious hatred of our society and its ways." [1]

---

[1] Richard Hofstadter, *The Paranoid Style in American Politics and Other Essays* (New York: Alfred A. Knopf, 1965), pp. 43–44, 66.

Reflections on Goldwaterism

H. G. Nicholas

It has long been the plea of lazy or perverse onlookers at the game of American politics that the content was incomprehensible because the players were indistinguishable. In Bryce's time the argument was that the two parties were like identical bottles, bearing different labels but both empty. When, with the advent of Wilsonian internationalism and Rooseveltian New Deal, it became impossible any longer to deny a clear content to the policies of at least the Democratic Party, refuge was often taken in the contention that while the parties did indeed stand for something what they stood for was essentially the same. Thus, in the 'twenties, both supported 'normalcy'; in the 'forties both supported the war, entry into the United Nations, and NATO; and in the 'fifties 'Eisenhowerism' meant a Republican President who maintained as 'interventionist' an alliance policy as his Democratic opponent, as high a level of public spending, as liberal an attitude on foreign trade, and as cautiously conciliatory a posture towards the U.S.S.R. When youth and Kennedy took the helm, there was no lurch into liberalism, still less socialism. On Cuba, China, labour, the budget, taxation, the Democrats did not sensibly depart from the Eisenhower line; indeed on foreign and civil rights, to say nothing of health insurance and housing, the Democratic Administration seemed to lag behind its own professions.

What caused puzzlement abroad caused some irritation at home, particularly among the ranks of the American Right. Theirs was a long record of frustration. In the Democratic Party they were mainly the Whites of the deep South (though on certain economic issues they could be radical, too); their long grip on the Democratic Party had, from the 'thirties onwards, steadily weakened as the urban masses (who included often the Negro fugitives from Southern states) strengthened their representation within the party, giving it a pro-labour, pro-welfare slant. Southern conservatives remained faithful to a party whose presidential leadership repeatedly flouted them, because Congress provided them with a range of pillboxes, in the form of committee chairmanships and the like, from which they could defend, at the level of the legislature, what could no longer be protected from the executive or the courts.

The Republican Right had an even less rewarding row to hoe. Congress

From *The World Today*, XX (November 1964), 465–472. Reprinted by permission of the publishers, The Royal Institute of International Affairs.

offered them comparatively little refuge since normally Democratic majorities dominated both chambers—even under an immensely popular Republican President like Eisenhower. Their party, after all, as repeated public-opinion polls demonstrated, was in a permanent minority amongst the politically committed electorate; it could only win by attracting the uncommitted or reducing the enemy, and neither piece of good fortune often came its way. Their best hope was indeed in capturing the Presidency, but here the Right were always being told that to enable Republicanism to woo the floaters or the Democrats they must agree to nominate at least a moderate or a man of the Centre.

In 1952, however, they rebelled and fought to get 'Mr Conservative', Senator Taft, the nomination. But the Eisenhower forces were too strong for them and they were outmanœuvred; 'Mr Conservative' had to yield defeat to a man who six months before had kept it a close secret whether he was a Republican or a Democrat. The Right acquiesced; one does not fight a steamroller. But for a moment before the ranks closed in outward harmony their long frustrated passions found vent. Senator Dirksen of Illinois, in accents vibrant with the Middle West's long feud with the urban East, pointed at Dewey as the arch-manipulator and cried, 'We followed you before and you took us down the road to defeat.' In that moment, though they did not know it, the television-viewers were catching the first authentic note of the Goldwaterism of 1964. The fact that what followed was not defeat but the first Republican victory for twenty-four years was of little relevance. The Republicanism that won was a Republicanism of the Eastern 'establishment', of the moderates, the internationalists, even of the 'Atlantic Firsters'. Also it was a Republicanism of the White House; in Congress the party remained generally in a minority. Consequently though the Dirksens could harry they could seldom dictate; time and time again they saw the White House policies they disliked assisted through Congress by a coalition of Eisenhower Republicans and liberal Democrats. In 1956 they had no choice but to acquiesce in another landslide of victory.

In 1960 they hoped that Nixon would not only win but, after winning, be their kind of President; his nomination represented the most they could hope for while the Eisenhower image still darkened the land. Kennedy's victory denied to both sides the opportunity to discover whether the enigmatic Nixon was in fact their kind of a Republican. But of course it did not silence the debate in the party or stop the recriminations attendant on defeat; it was Nixon's 'me-tooism' on a wide range of foreign and domestic issues that, the Right contended, had lost him the election. There was little evidence to support their contention, nor any sure way of refuting it. But it provided a rallying point for the frustrated; Senator Goldwater's *The Conscience of a Conservative* provided a gospel; his own engaging personality gave frustration a new look; and powerful industrial and financial interests provided the money. At last the Right had what they had wanted ever since Hoover—some would say since Coolidge—a candidate who offered a real alternative. At last American politics would become comprehensible to all those Europeans who could only think in terms of Left and Right. At last those American political scientists who had long advocated a clarification or a realignment of the American parties would get the 'more meaningful two-party system' they had been wanting. How odd it was that neither European observers nor American academics seemed happy with the clarification now that they had it.

NATURE OF THE AMERICAN PARTIES

Is the situation that has thus developed unique? Is it 'un-American' in the sense of portending a break with the kind of American party politics we have known and come to live with hitherto? Two schools of thought have long debated the true nature of American par es: the one has seen them as instruments of consensus, agencies which bring together the vast diversities of interest which mark the continental United States and convert a congeries of interest groups into a nation-wide, if uneasy, pair of rivals; the other school would argue that parties have arisen and perpetuate themselves in order to provide the electorate with a choice between alternative candidates and alternative policies. It is obvious that the two schools of thought are not completely antithetical; parties which create consensus may yet offer alternatives, while parties which offer alternatives may yet themselves be coalitions. Yet it is also true that the nature of parties will differ according as they incline one way or the other. The consensus type of party will have made, for the voter, many of the important choices before ever polling day comes round; in the process whereby groups negotiate to form parties, many crucial decisions will have been foreclosed. The party which emphasizes choice and clear-cut alternatives will have to run the risk of alienating substantial elements which it might have accommodated if it had been willing to blur the lines of its appeal a little more.

In general, in recent times, American parties have worn a consensus look. Especially has this been true of the Democratic Party, which has always had to accommodate two natural incompatibles—Southern rural Whites and Eastern urban poor. But the Republican Party has exemplified this character too. Was it not born, in Lincoln's day, out of a marriage of Eastern business and the Midwestern farmer? Even when it hardened, in the Gilded Age, into a mere vehicle for plutocracy, it was soon forced to broaden itself again in Theodore Roosevelt's hands into an instrument through which he could assert the continuing community of interest between the 'established' elements in American society and the great commonalty. Most recently, under President Eisenhower, it evoked an endorsement so broad that, though it might still be called the conservative party, it was a conservatism that bound together at the polls business man, farmer, trade unionist, professional man, Easterner, Westerner, and Southerner. The memories and, more important, the personalities of the Eisenhower octave are still fresh in the public mind. What has provoked the narrowing of appeal that Senator Goldwater's nomination implies? How truly revolutionary is the Senator's 'new look'?

The Eisenhower consensus, electorally impressive as it was, rested upon a shaky, temporary base, the extraordinary personal charm and glamour of one man; it was, one might almost say, composed of only two elements, the smile and the record. Whether from awareness of this fragility or, more probably, from a deep-seated reluctance, born of temperament and training, to rule as well as reign, Eisenhower made virtually no effort to institutionalize his own leadership of the Republican Party. He did not use his position to reward his friends or punish his foes, or even to make public distinction between them, much less to build bastions which would outlast his own two terms. He made no attempt to discipline party rebels or to define, in terms relevant to the needs of the mid-century, what the continuing role of the party of Lincoln ought to be. Consequently, when he stepped down from the throne and when after him Richard Nixon, failing election in 1960, passed into that condition of quasi-impotence which is reserved for defeated presidential candidates, the party lacked any sense of national direction, any leadership from above, any criterion of what constituted Republicanism. This made it comparatively easy for a determined group, well financed, operating through the state machines which were the only persistent and stable elements in the party, to win control of delegates in state after state and so, almost without the realization of press or public, to move up to a point from which they could secure for their own candidate the party's presidential nomination. At almost any stage in this process, except perhaps the very last, a decisive intervention by Mr Eisenhower could have thwarted this operation, but for him to have made it would have been to act out of character, and there was no one who could act for him or in his name. So the party gave its endorsement to a leader whom a majority of its rank and file did not want, and to policies and attitudes which its most popular living exemplar (to say nothing of its tutelary deity, Abe Lincoln of Illinois) was known to dislike, if not deplore.

REPUBLICAN TRADITION

Yet, although Senator Goldwater probably was, as his critics aver, the candidate of a minority within a minority, he too could claim that there was a Republican tradition behind him and that he and his policies had a place within it. In the battle of words which is the inevitable accompaniment to a revolutionary *coup d'état*, two epithets have been in constant employment by the Goldwaterites—'conservative' and 'radical'. *The Conscience of a Conservative* Senator Goldwater entitled his first political apologia, a title which might seem to imply a claim to the conservative mantle last worn with consistence and dignity by the last Senator Robert Taft. But as the Goldwater star rose, his followers increasingly often referred to themselves and their candidate as 'radicals'. 'Radical' is a term with some history to it in the Republican Party. It was Republican radicals in Congress who pressed and harassed Lincoln throughout the Civil War for earlier and more drastic action against slavery and the Southern 'rebels'. It was these same radicals who, after the war, pressed for a more thorough-going 'reconstruction' of the defeated South than Lincoln thought wise or fair, and who subsequently came within an ace of impeaching Lincoln's successor in the White House, Andrew Johnson. Debate raged then and since as to what this radicalism consisted in—concern for the Negro, vengefulness against the 'rebels', extremity of party spirit, hostility to great concentrations of wealth—all these interpretations have won varying degrees of acceptance. But whatever the content of this radicalism, one characteristic of its *modus operandi* is undisputed: it was Congress-bred and Congress-based. It was consistently and tirelessly suspicious of executive authority and supremely confident, even in the most critical moments of the war, of Congress's ability and right to substitute the will and wisdom of the legislature for those of the President.

As the Grand Old Party matured into the party of business, high finance, and *laissez-faire,* radicalism waned, sometimes to vanishing point. But despite certain assertions by Republican Presidents such as Theodore Roosevelt of the authority and national leadership inherent in the presidential office, suspicion of the executive branch remained a prevailing Republican attitude. Through the Republican Presidencies of Harding and Coolidge, a proper deference to Congressional wisdom marked all White House behaviour, and in the long reign of Franklin Roosevelt no charge found more eager response amongst his Republican critics than that of dictatorship. Even President Eisenhower, operating in a world and with a predominantly Democratic Congress which both equally demanded presidential leadership, sought whenever possible to wrap the inescapable assertions of his authority in the garb of deference to the legislative will.

This element in the Republican tradition finds no more enthusiastic exponent than Senator Goldwater, who comes, innocent of all executive experience, direct from his seat in the Senate to the presidential hustings. But the Goldwater radicalism goes further than this. Unlike his Civil War progenitors, he is not merely against presidential power, he is against power, organized governmental power, *as such*.

Here too he may claim to be the inheritor of a tradition. The hostility to social-welfare legislation, the pledge to cut taxes annually and progressively, the campaign to 'return' power from the federal to the state governments—these features of Goldwaterism, taken together with the emphasis on rugged individualism and unrestricted property rights, are an expression of a very old streak in the American political character, the streak of anti-governmentalism, of would-be anarchism. To speak of this as 'fascism', as some of the Senator's opponents have, is as nonsensical as it is unfair. If Senator Goldwater's philosophy were ever to be taken to its logical conclusion and given its head by the voters, the result would not be a totalitarian despotism. Far from it: it would be anarchism tempered by vigilantism, and so tempered not because Mr Goldwater is a would-be vigilante but because society abhors a vacuum, and if power is driven out of the front door it returns by the back. What he advocates is of course inconceivable and impossible, whether regarded in itself or in company with the Senator's other demands—for example a presidential drive against crime or a further strengthening of the armed forces. But the essential appeal of his credo remains powerful because rooted in a historic philosophy of revolt and 'frontierism', which survives to provide protective coverage for resistance to any government of the day that pursues policies one happens to dislike.

This irresponsible kind of protest, this yearning to cast away all the trammels of government and all the burdens of long-established commitments is not a novelty in American politics. It is rather like a subterranean river flowing through the heartland of American life, always there but only intermittently audible on the surface. It was heard in New Deal days, in the form of the Liberty League, the organization created to thwart Franklin Roosevelt's re-election in 1936, supplementing the official Republican campaign with its own passionate slogans of 'Only x more days to save the American Way of Life.' As war drew nearer, it received the tributary flow of isolationist sentiment; much of the appeal of 'America First' lay in its promise that survival could be guaranteed without the burdens and constraints that aid to the allies would impose. When war came to America it persisted in the form of a continuing resistance to almost all manifestations of government control, rationing, price limitations, allocation of scarce materials, mobilization of labour, etc.; it appeared in its most preposterous but not least typical form as the 'housewives'' contention that the Office of Price Administration's order abolishing pre-sliced bread for the duration was a blow levelled at the American Way of Life. What marks out the current Goldwater protest from these and other previous manifestations is, of course, its scale. For the first time the river has not merely rumbled; it has surfaced, as a stream broad enough to bear a candidate towards a major party's presidential nomination, if not to the White House itself.

Ideology has at last been given a free run for its money, partly because there has been a lot of money; paradoxically, prosperity has furnished the wherewithal for protest. What we have been hearing is the bark of the overdog. But ideology by itself, or even ideology plus the money-bags, could not have done the trick. Mr Goldwater has also drawn upon that regional feeling which a skilful agitator against Washington can always evoke. He is, or claims to be, the spokesman of the West. The humiliations that the Republican Right have suffered in this generation have been handed out to them by Easterners—not only Democratic Easterners like Franklin Roosevelt and John Kennedy, but Republican Easterners like Governor Dewey, Senator Lodge, and John Foster Dulles. True, Westerners and Midwesterners have been nominated by the party. Landon in 1936 came from Kansas, Wendell Willkie in 1940 from Indiana, Mr Eisenhower could claim both Kansas and Texas as his *fons et origo*, Mr Nixon was a native son of California. But, it is contended, for various reasons they all failed to make the voice of the West ring out in the nation's capital; either they were not elected or else, like Mr Eisenhower, they let wily Easterners corrupt their native virtue, substituting internationalism for Americanism and federal interference for free enterprise.

And indeed, extravagances apart, the claim is not wholly erroneous. The heartland of Republicanism has long lain in the Midwest, but the money and leadership in the party have generally been found, at election times, in the East. The tension thus created has sometimes been fruitful for the party; more often in recent years it has pulled it apart. In the postwar years, moreover, this tension has been heightened by a shift in the domestic American balance of power, consequent upon the rising wealth and population of the Far West, especially the states of California, Arizona, and Texas. The natural outlook of these states is in any case away from Washington; it is indeed, in foreign affairs, away from Europe and towards the Far East. This was reflected in the rise, during the last war, of 'Pacific Firstism', and the pressure, during the Korean crisis, from largely the same circles for an all-out Asiatic policy regardless of consequences. It has been remarked that the Pacific is the Republican ocean and the Atlantic the Democratic, and this is not untrue if by 'Republican' be understood those elements in the party which have fought against the leadership of the east coast 'Old Guard'.

The irony of the rise of the new West and Southwest is that this has largely been the consequence of policies pursued by that very government in Washington which these regions affect to deplore. It was the federal money poured into the shipyards, steel plants, and aeroplane factories of these states during the second World War, largely on account of their strategic location and their facilities for dispersal but also in response to local demands for fair shares of the pork-barrel, that provided the basic stimulus for their phenomenal economic growth. Population moved in from the South and Midwest, and private capital followed where government money (and often government housing and roads) had blazed a way. And so, despite the peacetime decline of some wartime industries, others succeeded them, notably in the fields of electronics and space exploration (again federally assisted) until the region reached a peak of ease and plenty not only new to it but serving to excite the envy of the rest of the U.S.A. and act as a magnet on other Americans from all over the Union. At last, in this present year [1964], California has attained its ambition of seeing its population exceed that of New York State and henceforth it will shine as the largest state in the Union. Can such a giant remain for ever in leading-strings?

EFFECTS OF GOLDWATER REVOLT

There is perhaps then in the Goldwater revolt a permanent element which will survive his own defeat. The old easy ascendancy of the East, of Ivy League brains and family and Wall Street capital, may no longer persist unchallenged. The significance accorded to this year's California primary, in which Governor Rockefeller staked his New York all and lost, may prove to be lasting. On the conservative side of American politics at least there may have to be a new deal, cutting the West and Southwest in on a game in which they have hitherto received less recognition than that to which the size of their investment entitled them. . . .

Goldwater and Pseudo-Conservative Politics

Richard Hofstadter

I

Goldwater's capture of the Republican nomination was the triumphal moment of pseudo-conservatism in American politics. One may say that it was an accident, in that it was out of scale with right-wing Republican strength and could happen only because of a series of failures and misadventures among moderate Republicans which are not likely to recur. But in another sense it was far from accidental: it resulted from the chronic, frustrating impotence of the minority party and from the efficient organization that the right wing had quietly built up inside it.

If Goldwater is accepted on his own terms as a conservative, he baffles understanding, but if he is taken as a product of the pseudo-conservative revolt, his ideas fall into place. Questioning his conservatism may seem gratuitous, but there is more at stake here than an empty issue or a suitable label. What is at stake, as Robert J. Donovan puts it, is whether the Republican party can learn to make "a distinction between the conservatism represented by Senator Goldwater and his supporters and the conservatism that conserves." [1]

Unquestionably Goldwater's ideas do retain some shreds and scraps of genuine conservatism, but the main course of his career puts him closer to the right-wing ideologues who were essential to his success, who shaped his tactics, who responded to his line of argument, and whose extremism he chose to defend at the vital moment of his career. Without invoking these formative affiliations, how are we to explain the character of a "conservative" whose whole political life has been spent urging a sharp break with the past, whose great moment as a party leader was marked by a repudiation of our traditional political ways, whose followers were so notable for their destructive and divisive energies, and whose public reputation was marked not with standpattism or excessive caution but with wayward impulse and recklessness?

Goldwater's brand of conservatism has its most recognizable American roots in those thinkers, quite numerous in this country, who imagine conservatism to be almost identical with economic individualism. Here he has responded more fervently to the nostalgic reveries and the pronouncements of perennial truths that mark ideological conservatism than he has to the tradition of shrewd and subtle manipulation, concession, and conciliation that has characterized American conservatism in practice. Most conservatives are mainly concerned with maintaining a tissue of institutions for whose stability and effectiveness they believe the country's business and political elites hold responsibility. Goldwater thinks of conservatism as a system of eternal and unchanging ideas and ideals, whose claims upon us must be constantly asserted and honored in full.[2] The difference between conservatism as a set of doctrines whose validity is to be established by polemics, and conservatism as a set of rules whose validity is to be established by their usability in government, is not a difference of nuance, but of fundamental substance.

---

[1] *The Future of the Republican Party* (New York, 1964), p. 127.

[2] "The laws of God, and of nature, have no date-line. The principles on which the Conservative political position is based have been established by a process that has nothing to do with the social, economic, and political landscape that changes from decade to decade and from century to century. These principles are derived from the nature of man, and from the truths that God has revealed about His creation. Circumstances do change. So do the problems that are shaped by circumstances. But the principles that govern the solution of the problems do not. . . . The challenge is not to find new or different truths, but how to apply established truths to the problems of the contemporary world." Barry Goldwater: *The Conscience of a Conservative* (New York, Macfadden ed., 1960), "Foreword," p.3. (It may be necessary to add, since Goldwater has been exceptionally candid about the extent to which his books were ghost-written, that I have used them on the assumption that he read them carefully before he signed them, and that they do indeed represent his views as of the time that they were written.)

Again: "The basic problems are no different in our times than under Lincoln or Washington. . . . We have merely changed the horse for the tractor, the hand tools for a machine." A speech before the Utah State Convention of the Junior Chamber of Commerce in 1960, quoted in *The New Republic,* March 27, 1961, p. 14.

It is instructive how far Goldwater's devotion to eternal truths brought him beyond the position of such a Republican predecessor as Eisenhower, and how far it took him even beyond the conservatism of Robert A. Taft. Many of Eisenhowers' statements both before and after his presidency could lead one to conclude that his social thinking was more similar to Goldwater's than different. Eisenhower too spoke often for the old-fashioned prudential virtues and against growing federal bureaucracy, and his cabinet incorporated at least two members, George Humphrey and Ezra Taft Benson, who fully shared the right-wing philosophy. But in practice Eisenhower was faithful to the opportunistic traditions of American conservatism. Though a mediocre politician with little enthusiasm for the political game, he was nonetheless so intuitively an "insider" in the American political tradition that he instinctively took the working politican's approach to the split mentality of American conservatism. He knew that many conservatives yearn for the days of untrammeled enterprise, uncomplicated foreign problems, and negligible taxes, but also that they can usually recognize the complexity of the contemporary world, the difficult obligations the country has taken on, and the irreversibility of the historical process that has brought us from simple agrarian conditions to the complex conditions of modern urban life and corporate organization. When Eisenhower spoke in philosophical terms, therefore, he often gave voice to their wistfulness about old ideals, but in administrative practice he usually bowed to what he thought were the necessities of the hour. . . .

In any case, to ultra-conservatives, for whom the old pieties are binding moral principles, the Eisenhower administration was worse than a disappointment, it was a betrayal. It did not repeal the New Deal reforms, do away with high taxes, kill foreign aid, or balance the budget. In fact, its primary historical function seemed to be to legitimate what had been done under Roosevelt and Truman: when it left certain domestic and foreign policies intact, it made them more generally acceptable by passing them, so to speak, through the purifying fire of eight years of Republicanism and thus confirming that they represented, after all, a bipartisan consensus. The right-wing minority saw all this not as a clue to the nature of our national problems but as further evidence that the conspiracy originally set in motion by the Democrats was being carried on by the Eastern Republicans behind Eisenhower. McCarthy, for example, had been quick to strike at Eisenhower and to change his slogan, "Twenty years of treason," to a more inflammatory one: "Twenty-one years of treason." Again, one of Eisenhower's budgets prompted Goldwater to brand his administration as "a dime-store New Deal." On a later occasion he said with fervor: "One Eisenhower in a generation is enough." [3]

Goldwater's deviation from Taft Republicanism also marks him off from the established moderate conservative wing of his party. Unlike Goldwater,

[3] *Time,* July 24, 1964, p. 27.

Taft came from a family with long seasoning in public affairs; and, again unlike Goldwater, he took an active part on Capitol Hill in framing legislation. His brand of conservatism was modified by several concessions to the demands of expediency and responsibility. Though he had a profound dislike of change and a passionate bias toward fiscal conservatism and decentralized administration, Taft accepted the idea that the federal government should concern itself with "seeing that every family has a minimum standard of decent shelter," should "assist those states desiring to put a floor under essential services in relief, in medical care, in housing, and in education," should underwrite the states in providing "a basic minimum education to every child," sustain minimum-wage laws "to give the unorganized worker some protection" comparable to that given to organized workers by the unions, persist in a steeply graduated income tax, maintain minimum farm prices, and through its social security program (which he held to be woefully inadequate) "assure to every citizen 65 years of age and over a living wage."

These commitments, made in various speeches from 1943 to 1951, accept the reality of the welfare state. They stand in sharp contrast to Goldwater's notion that economic individualism can still be ruthlessly applied to American life. Before Goldwater found it necessary to modify a few of his positions for the sake of his primary and presidential campaigns in 1964, his beliefs came straight out of nineteenth-century laissez-faire doctrine and the strictest of strict constructionism. Governmental activities in "relief, social security, collective bargaining, and public housing," he thought, had caused "the weakening of the individual personality and of self-reliance." He asked for "prompt and final termination of the farm subsidy program," declared himself against "every form of federal aid to education," denounced the graduated income tax as "confiscatory," and asserted that the country had "no education problem which requires any form of Federal grant-in-aid programs to the states." The government, he said, "must begin to withdraw from a whole series of programs that are outside its constitutional mandate," including "social welfare programs, education, public power, agriculture, public housing, urban renewal. . . ." [4] Collectively, such statements called for the dismantling of the welfare state. "My aim is not to pass laws but to repeal them," Goldwater once boasted, and on another occasion he said: "I fear Washington and centralized government more than I do Moscow." [5] These are the characteristic accents of the pseudo-conservative agitators, who are convinced that they live in a degenerate society and who see their main enemy in the power of their own government.

---

[4] *The Conscience of a Conservative*, p. 43; *Congressional Record*, 87th Cong., 1st sess. (June 21, 1961), p. 10971; ibid., 88th Cong., 1st sess. (September 3, 1963), p. 16222; statement to Senate Subcommittee on Education, Senate Committee on Labor and Public Welfare, April 30, 1963 (*Hearings*, I, 279).

[5] *Fortune*, May 1961, p. 139; *Look*, April 21, 1964; cf. *The Conscience of a Conservative*, p. 22.

Goldwater's departure from the Republican pattern was compounded by his position on civil rights. One of the oldest, though hardly the most efficacious, of the traditions of many conservatives in the North—and even to a degree in the South as well—has been a certain persistent sympathy with the Negro and a disposition to help him in moderate ways to relieve his distress. This tradition goes back to the Federalist party; it was continued by the Whig gentry; it infused the early Republican party. By adopting "the Southern strategy," the Goldwater men abandoned this inheritance. They committed themselves not merely to a drive for a core of Southern states in the electoral college but to a strategic counterpart in the North which required the search for racist votes. They thought they saw a good mass issue in the white backlash, which they could indirectly exploit by talking of violence in the streets, crime, juvenile delinquency, and the dangers faced by our mothers and daughters.

Eisenhower, like Goldwater, had been unmoved by noble visions of progress toward racial justice, but he at least gave lip service to the ideal and thought it important to enforce the laws himself and to speak out for public compliance. But Goldwater arrived at the position, far from conservative in its implications, that the decisions of the Supreme Court are "not necessarily" the law of the land.[6] Of course, the decisions of the Court have always had political content and they have often been highly controversial; there is no reason why they should suddenly be regarded with whispered reverence. But it is only in our time, and only in the pseudo-conservative movement, that men have begun to hint that disobedience to the Court is not merely legitimate but is the essence of conservatism.

It is not the authority and legitimacy of the Court alone that the pseudo-conservative right calls into question. When it argues that we are governed largely by means of near-hypnotic manipulation (brainwashing), wholesale corruption, and betrayal, it is indulging in something more significant than the fantasies of indignant patriots: it is questioning the legitimacy of the political order itself. The two-party system, as it has developed in the United States, hangs on the common recognition of loyal opposition: each side accepts the ultimate good intentions of the other. The opponent's judgment may be held to be consistently execrable, but the legitimacy of his intent is not—that is, in popular terms, his Americanism is not questioned. One of the unspoken assumptions of presidential campaigns is that the leaders of both parties are patriots who, however serious their mistakes, must be accorded the right to govern. But an essential point in the pseudo-conservative world view is that our recent Presidents, being men of wholly evil intent, have conspired against the public good. This does more than discredit them: it calls into question the validity of the political system that keeps putting such men into office.

---

[6] *The Conscience of a Conservative*, p. 37; cf. *The New York Times*, November 24, 1963.

A man like Goldwater, who lives psychologically half in the world of our routine politics and half in the curious intellectual underworld of the pseudo-conservatives, can neither wholly accept nor wholly reject such a position. He disdains and repudiates its manifest absurdities (Eisenhower as a Communist agent), but he lives off the emotional animus that gives birth to them. This ambiguity makes it more understandable why, on the night of his defeat, he so flagrantly violated the code of decorum governing the conduct of losing presidential candidates. The code requires a message of congratulation, sent as soon as the result is beyond doubt, so worded that it emphasizes the stake of the whole nation in the successful administration of the victor, and reasserts the loser's acceptance of the public verdict. In withholding his congratulations until the morning after the election, and then in hinting at Johnson's incapacity to solve the acute problems gratuitously enumerated in his telegram, Goldwater did something more than show bad manners. By complying with the code, but grudgingly and tardily, he expressed his suspicion that the whole American political system, with its baffling ambiguities and compromises, is too soft and too equivocal for this carnivorous world.

II

Although the ultras usually speak with nostalgia about the supposed virtues of our remote past, they have a disposition to repudiate the more recent past, and it was in character for Goldwater to write off as unacceptable the Republican conservatism of recent years. But in return, he and his followers were unable to win acceptance from the major centers of genuinely conservative power. Businessmen, to be sure, gave Goldwater a narrow margin of support, but they gave him far less than any other Republican in recent history. The press also broke from its normal pattern: for the first time in memory a Democrat was favored by newspapers with an aggregate circulation much larger than those endorsing his opponent. Conservative chains like the Hearst and Scripps-Howard newspapers backed Johnson, as did establishment Republican papers like the New York *Herald Tribune*. Old centers of Republican conservatism such as rural New England turned their backs on Goldwater, and he became the first Republican presidential candidate to lose Vermont. The conservative voters of the normally Republican states of the wheat belt also deserted in large numbers. Repeatedly the pollsters who found Republican voters expressing doubt about Goldwater or open opposition to him noticed a recurrent explanation: "He's too radical for me." The American public is not notably sophisticated about ideological labels, and its use of the term "radical" rarely shows much precision; but this response registers a sounder sense of the situation than that of the highbrow conservatives who acclaimed the Arizonan as their own. Whatever tag

Goldwater chose to wear, a large part of the public saw in him an excessively sharp deviation from the pattern of American politics and they found it frightening.

Goldwater's deviation is as much marked in his conduct as in his ideas. American politics is run mainly by professionals who have developed over a long span of time an ethos of their own, a kind of professional code. In emphasizing how completely Goldwater, and even more his followers, departed from the professional code, it is important to be clear that one is not making a substantive criticism of what they stood for but an attempt to compare their ways historically with our normal conservative practice. The professional code is not a binding moral imperative for anyone—not even for politicians. At one time or another most politicians have broken it. On occasion we admire them for breaking it in the interest of what they believe to be a higher principle. Finally, it should be conceded that Goldwater, at certain moments of his career, observed it handsomely, and that he too was victimized at times when the code was broken by others.[7]

The point, however, is that the professional code, for all its limitations, is an American institution embodying the practical wisdom of generations of politicians. It seems ironic that the most unqualified challenge ever made within a major party to this repository of the wisdom of our ancestors should have been made by a self-proclaimed conservative, and that Goldwater's advisers in 1964 brought him as close as any presidential candidate has ever come to subverting the whole pattern of our politics of coalition and consensus.

Professional politicians want, above all, to win, and their conduct is shaped by this pragmatic goal. Moreover, they know that if they win they have to govern; and their behavior in dealing with opposing factions in their own party, with the opposition party, and with the electorate is constantly molded and qualified by the understanding that they have to organize a government capable of coping with the problems of the moment. Both their ideas and their partisan passions are modified by the harsh corrective of reality. They are quite aware, for example, that their promises, which express rather what they think they should offer to do than what they think they can do, cannot be perfectly fulfilled. They are also aware that their denunciation of the opposing party in the conduct of election campaigns must be followed by the attempt to work with the opposition in Washington. Under the heated surface of our political rhetoric, therefore,

---

[7] For example, Goldwater observed the code conspicuously in his conduct toward Nixon in 1960 and again momentarily in 1964 when he expressed some sympathetic understanding for the position of Republicans who could not afford to be fully identified with him. His opponents broke it at the Cow Palace when they circulated the famous Scranton letter, which, in its denunciation of his ideas and alleged tactics, went far beyond the usual etiquette of intra-party dispute.

On the requirements of American coalition politics as they bear on convention behavior, and on their repudiation by the Goldwater forces, see my essay: "Goldwater and His Party," *Encounter,* XXIII (October 1964), 3–13.

there exists a certain sobriety born of experience, an understanding that what sounds good on the banquet circuit may not make feasible policy, that statements, manifestos, and polemics are very far from pragmatic programs; that these have to be *translated* into programs for the solution of our domestic and foreign problems; and that even then these programs have to undergo still further modification in the legislative mill before they can become reality.

Goldwater's career is distinguished by its lack of training for this code. Before his entry into national politics, his experience had given him responsibility for no national organization and had required an attention to administrative demands no more complex than those of his inherited department store. As a member of the Senate, he assumed no important role, involved himself with no legislation on major national problems. His main business there was simply to vote No. He made no outstanding contributions to debate or to the consideration of legislative details (as, for example, Taft had done); he was not prominent in committee work, and his busy speech-making program made him a frequent absentee. He did not, as a working senator, command the ear of fellow senators, not even of those who shared his views. In the framework of practical politics, he remained an "outsider," and as a presidential candidate he continued to make decisions that reflected the outsider's cast of mind.[8]

But to say this of Goldwater's legislative role is not to deny that he worked hard to earn his position in his party: it is simply that he rose to it not by making contributions to government but through his partisan activity, which for years was dedicated and tireless. He was chairman of the Republican Senatorial Campaign Committee. He was constantly available to fellow Republicans everywhere, giving substantial help to their campaign efforts and their fund-raising. His arduous round of speechmaking on the banquet circuit gave him a chance to bring his "conservative" message to thousands of rank-and-file party workers and to put many party leaders in his debt. His role, then, was that of the partisan exhorter and organizer, a speaker and ideologue for whom preaching a sound philosophy was more interesting than addressing himself to the problems of state. But in this role he was constantly speaking to audiences already largely or wholly converted to his point of view, unlike the legislator on Capitol Hill who must constantly deal with shrewd and informed men who differ with him. Resounding applause no doubt confirmed his conviction of the validity and importance of

---

[8] For a shrewd statement of the differences between the political mentality of the outsider and that of the insider, see the contrast drawn by Eric L. McKitrick between Andrew Johnson and Abraham Lincoln in *Andrew Johnson and Reconstruction* (Chicago, 1960), esp. Ch. 4.

Oddly enough, the externals of John F. Kennedy's senatorial career correspond with Goldwater's. However, the difference in their cast of mind, not to speak of their intellectual caliber, was beyond reckoning. It was only one aspect of these differences that JFK was, by family training, education, and social position—one suspects also, as it were, by instinct—an insider.

his "conservatism," and persuaded him that an irresistible conservative revival was astir in the country, but it did not enlarge his capacity to conciliate or persuade those who differed with him—still less to learn from an exchange of views. The habits of mind thus shaped were carried into his campaign, during which he once again brought salvation to the already converted.[9]

Goldwater, then, made up for his lack of stature as a legislative leader by his outstanding success as a partisan evangelist who particularly mobilized those Republicans whose discontent was keenest, whose ideological fervor was strongest, those most dissatisfied with the bland and circumspect Eisenhower legacy. At the grass roots large segments of the Republican party were taken over by dedicated enthusiasts, hitherto political amateurs, with a bent for unorthodox ideas and new departures. Reporters at San Francisco were impressed by the preponderance of unfamiliar faces among the Goldwater delegates.[10] Victory won with the help of these new-idea delegates was followed by the creation of a Goldwater staff in which professionals and cosmopolitans were entirely overshadowed by amateurs and provincials—a staff the press called "the Arizona Mafia."

Goldwater's advisers and enthusiasts, being new to major-party politics, found it easy to abandon the familiar rules of political conduct. Party workers raised on the professional code want above all to find winners, to get and keep office, to frame programs on which they can generally agree, to use these programs to satisfy the major interests in our society, and to try to solve its most acute problems. If they find that they have chosen a loser, they are quick to start looking for another leader. If they see that their program is out of touch with the basic realities, they grope their way toward a new one.

But Goldwater's zealots were moved more by the desire to dominate the party than to win the country, concerned more to express resentments and punish "traitors," to justify a set of values and assert grandiose, militant visions, than to solve actual problems of state. More important, they were immune to the pressure to move over from an extreme position toward the center of the political spectrum which is generally exerted by the profes-

---

[9] With one exception, and that a slip-up apparently, he held no press conferences during the campaign. When he visited the cities he generally avoided the crowds, the slums, and the ghettos and appeared only in halls filled with militant conservatives who needed no persuasion by him. There was precious little effort on the senator's part to take his case to the unconvinced." Donovan: op. cit., p. 55.

[10] Robert D. Novak remarks that these were "not merely the run-of-the-mill party workers under the command and the bidding of regular party leaders. Here was a new breed of delegate, most of whom had never been to a national convention before. . . . They were going there for one purpose: to vote for Barry Goldwater. To woo them away to another candidate would be as difficult as proselytizing a religious zealot." *The Agony of the G.O.P. 1964* (New York, 1965), pp. 345–6.

Cf. Richard Rovere: "They are a new breed. It has been said—quite proudly—by the Goldwater people that this was the first Convention for more than half of them. . . . There was youth on every hand." "Letter from San Francisco," *The New Yorker,* July 25, 1964, p. 80.

sional's desire to win. Their true victory lay not in winning the election but in capturing the party—in itself no mean achievement—which gave them an unprecedented platform from which to propagandize for a sound view of the world.

Since the major parties in the United States have always been coalitions of disparate and even discordant elements, the professional leaders of major parties have always had to forge out of their experience the techniques of consensus politics that are adapted to holding such coalitions together and maintaining within them a workable degree of harmony. The art of consensus politics, in our system, has to be practiced not only in coping with the opposition party but internally, in dealing with one's partisans and allies. The life of an American major party is a constant struggle, in the face of serious internal differences, to achieve enough unity to win elections and to maintain it long enough to develop a program for government. Our politics has thus put a strong premium on the practical rather than the ideological bent of mind, on the techniques of negotiation and compromise rather than the assertion of divisive ideas and passions, and on the necessity of winning rather than the unqualified affirmation of principles, which is left to the minor parties.

The perennial task of coalition building has resulted in a number of rituals for party conventions, which Goldwater and his followers either ignored or deliberately violated at San Francisco. A candidate who enters a convention with the preponderant and controlling strength that Goldwater had in 1964 has at his disposal a number of effective devices to conciliate and incorporate the opposition. One is to write a conciliatory platform, which makes concessions to the defeated side or which hedges on disputed matters. Party platforms are often vague, they are usually long and tedious, and they remain unread; but their significance lies precisely in showing the ability of all factions and candidates to agree at least on a statement of policy. Their very vagueness proves that party leaders do not consider it necessary to fight issues out or to reach clear statements of principle and policy. Bitter or prolonged platform fights, such as those waged by the Democrats in 1896 and 1924, are always signs of a fatal absence of basic unity.

The winning candidate has other placatory devices available. One is the choice of a running mate: he may pick his leading opponent for this role, as Kennedy did in 1960, or he may turn to someone who represents the main opposing tendency in the party. He may go out of his way to arrive at an understanding, as Eisenhower did with Taft in 1952 or Nixon with Rockefeller in 1960. In his acceptance address he will almost invariably do the graceful thing and dwell upon conciliatory themes, stressing the commitments and sentiments that unite the party rather than those that divide it. In return, some corresponding rituals are expected of the loser: he, or one of his close associates, usually presents a motion to make the nomination unanimous. If he speaks, he minimizes the issues that have divided his party, denounces the opposition party with renewed vigor, and promises to support the victor with all his might. Normally he keeps this promise, as Goldwater himself did for Nixon in 1960.[11]

This traditional placatory ritual was flouted at every point by the Goldwater organization at San Francisco. To begin, their platform in effect repudiated many recent Republican policies. Then, proposed amendments endorsing civil rights, reasserting civilian control over nuclear weapons, and condemning extremist groups were crushed, and in the debate over the last of these, Governor Rockefeller was interrupted unmercifully by booing from the galleries. (The Goldwater managers, disturbed by this outburst, were able to prevent their delegates from persisting in the demonstration but could not stop their partisans in the galleries from giving vent to their feelings.) In the choice of a running mate, Goldwater again had an opportunity to soften the conflict by taking some eminent man from the large moderately conservative middle band of the party who would have been acceptable on all sides, but he settled on an obscure provincial, William E. Miller—professional enough, to be sure, but undistinguished except by belligerent partisanship. The effects of this choice were in no way mollified by the selection of his fellow Arizonan Dean Burch as national chairman—"a politician of limited experience who had never even been a county chairman and who was a complete stranger to hundreds of eminent Republicans around the country." [12] Finally, to top it all, Goldwater's acceptance speech, far from sounding the conciliatory note so necessary after the acrimony of the proceedings, said that "those who do not care for our cause we don't expect to enter our ranks in any case," and flung his famous challenge: "I would remind you that extremism in the defense of liberty is no vice. And let me remind you also that moderation in the pursuit of justice is no virtue!"—a two-sentence manifesto approved by a dozen top members of his staff and written by a hard-core right-winger whom Goldwater found congenial and kept by his side as a speechwriter throughout the campaign.

Most presidential candidates try to look their best at the strategic moment when their party convention acclaims them. For Goldwater this was impossible. His moment of victory at the Cow Palace found him firmly in the hands of his ecstatic pseudo-conservative followers. For the past few years his own presidential prospects had done much to draw them into active politics, and it was their money and hard work which had built the Goldwater movement. In precinct after precinct and county after county they had fought

---

[11] Goldwater's break with the professional code in 1964 did not come from failure to understand its easily mastered general principles but from his constant gravitation toward the doctrinaires. "We are a big political party," he declared in a speech on September 11, 1963, "and there is all kinds of room for a difference of opinion. But in differing, we need not beat the hides off those we differ with." Novak: op. cit., p. 232. It was this message that got lost at San Francisco.

[12] Donovan: op. cit., p. 92.

and ousted old-line Republicans.[13] They were now prominent among his delegates—an official of the John Birch Society claimed that more than a hundred of the Goldwater delegates were Birchites. The Goldwater campaign had given focus to the right-wing movement, and had brought into prominence such exponents of the paranoid style as John A. Stormer and Phyllis Schlafly, whose books were sold and given away by the millions, and whose conspiratorial views articulated the mental heat behind pseudo-conservatism more fully than Goldwater's more equivocal utterances. Schlafly's *A Choice Not an Echo* expressed the animus of Midwestern Republicans against "the secret New York kingmakers" who had repeatedly stolen the Republican nomination "to insure control of the largest cash market in the world: the Executive Branch of the United States Government." It was reminiscent of the same bias which a few years earlier had inspired Goldwater to suggest that "this country would be better off if we could just saw off the Eastern Seaboard and let it float out to sea." Stormer's *None Dare Call It Treason*, which took its title from a couplet attributed to Sir John Harrington:

> Treason doth never prosper, what's the reason?
> For if it prosper, none dare call it treason,

was a masterful piece of folkish propaganda, which continued the McCarthyist and Birchite line of accusation without committing the bizarre verbal indiscretions that have caused people to make fun of Robert Welch.* It drew up a thoroughgoing indictment of Eisenhower Republicanism without in so many words calling Eisenhower a traitor.[14]

To be fully faithful to this clientele, Goldwater had to be graceless to many fellow Republicans; yet it would have been graceless too to spurn the people whose work had won his victory. But, in fact, he saw nothing wrong with them. While he could hardly take Robert Welch seriously, he had said more than once that the John Birch Society was a fine organization,[15]

---

[13] The procedure by which Goldwater and his followers conducted their campaign for delegates was not one calculated to develop their talents for conciliation. As Novak puts it, Goldwater repealed "the rule of preconvention politics that required a candidate to appease the uncommitted rather than titillate his own committed followers. . . . Rather than appease the uncommitted, Goldwater was destroying them. And this required keeping his own committed followers in a state of high titillation. . . . He was conquering, not convincing, the Republican party." Op. cit., p. 353.

* Editor's note: Founder of the John Birch Society.

[14] Phyllis Schlafly: *A Choice Not an Echo* (Alton, Ill., 1964), p. 5; John A. Stormer: *None Dare Call It Treason* (Florissant, Mo., 1964), esp. pp. 33–53, 196–8, 224–5. These young writers represent the militant younger generation of conservatives that was attracted to Goldwater. Stormer was chairman of the Missouri Federation of Young Republicans, and Schlafly president of the Illinois Federation of Republican Women and a Goldwater delegate at the Cow Palace.

[15] "A lot of people in my home town have been attracted to the [Birch] society," Goldwater said in 1961, "and I am impressed by the type of people in it. They are the kind of people we need in politics." On another occasion he called them "the finest people in my community," and still later, when it had become clear that they might be a serious cam-

and now he would neither repudiate nor offend its members. This meant that the path to the customary procedures of our politics was closed off, since the right-wingers scorned them. The convention showed the nation for the first time how well organized the right-wing movement was, but it also proved, as the subsequent campaign was to prove again, that the right wing, though brilliantly organized for *combat,* was not organized to conciliate or persuade. Having convinced themselves that the forces they were fighting were conspiratorial and sinister, not to say treasonous, they found it impossible to shake off the constricting mental framework of the paranoid style. The sudden and startling outburst of wild applause, the jeers and fist-shaking at the broadcast booths and press stands, which came when Eisenhower made a mildly hostile reference to some unidentified columnists, was a key to the prevailing mood. Animated by a profound resentment, and now at last on the verge of a decisive victory over their tormentors, the Goldwater zealots were filled with the desire to punish and humiliate, not to appease and pacify.[16] The acceptance speech showed that this desire extended upward into Goldwater's own staff.

The shock inflicted by San Francisco was so severe that some gesture seemed imperative; and for a moment it seemed that Goldwater would make the usual effort at rapprochement when the Hershey Conference * was held in August. Indeed he did say there many of the expected things, and some in strong terms; but the damage had been done, and Goldwater's announcement to reporters at the close of the conference that "this is no conciliatory speech at all. It merely reaffirms what I've been saying all through the campaign," canceled much of the conciliatory effect. The wounds had been covered over, not healed, and although Goldwater won the dutiful support of a number of moderates, including his main opponent, Scranton, he went on to conduct a right-wing campaign in which they were inevitably out of key.[17] By now it was not altogether a matter of his being unwilling to offer reassurance. What had happened was that he had been so extreme so long that neither the Republican moderates nor a

---

paign liability, he stood by them, insisting that as a group they should not be called extremists. "They believe in the Constitution, they believe in God, they believe in Freedom." *Time,* April 7, 1961, p. 19; ibid., June 23, 1961, p. 16; *The New York Times,* July 18, 1964.

[16] Cf. Richard Rovere's report from San Francisco (p. 80). For the most part, he found the Goldwater delegates young and affluent, "smartly dressed, well organized, and well spoken. And they were as hard as nails. The spirit of compromise and accommodation was wholly alien to them. They did not come to San Francisco merely to nominate their man and then rally his former opponents behind him; they came for a total ideological victory and the total destruction of their critics. . . . They wished to punish as well as to prevail."

* Editor's note: A gathering of Republican leaders designed to restore party unity.

[17] It was impossible after San Francisco to put the pieces together again. Scranton made many strong campaign speeches, as the code required, for Goldwater, and acted as his host at a great rally in Pittsburgh near the end of the campaign. In his introduction he made a casual reference to the fact that he did not always agree with Goldwater. At this he was met by such a chorus of boos from the faithful that he hurried through to a perfunctory and cool conclusion. See Novak: op. cit., p. 5.

large, strategic segment of the electorate had confidence that further reas-
surances from him would have any meaning.

Overwhelming defeat in the election—a thing which the professional politician always takes as a spur to rethink his commitments and his strategy—
had no such effect on the Goldwater camp. His enthusiasts were more disposed to see the event as further evidence of the basic unregeneracy of the
country, or worse, of the conspiracy by which they had been thwarted all
along. The old right-wing myth, that there was an enormous conservative
"silent vote" that would pour out to the polls if the party would only
nominate a proper right-winger, was exploded, but it seems to have been
replaced by a new one: that Goldwater was defeated so badly largely because he was sabotaged by the party moderates and liberals.[18] It must be
conceded that if one's underlying purpose is not to win elections or affect
the course of government but to propagandize for a set of attitudes, the right-
wing enterprise of 1964 can be considered something of a success. It was so
taken by many Goldwater ideologues, and on the far right the post-election
mood was one of cheer, if not elation. One of its spokesmen said that the
election marked "the defeat not of conservatism but of the Republican
party"—a clear confession that the fate of an ideology was taken as being
far more important than the well-being of the institution; and Goldwater
remarked in a revealing statement: "I don't feel the conservative cause has
been hurt. Twenty-five million votes are a lot of votes and a lot of people
dedicated to the concept of conservatism." [19]

If one accepts the point of view of political doctrinaires and amateurs,
whose primary aim in politics is to make certain notions more popular, this
statement has its validity: for a generation, no politician has been able to
preach Goldwater's brand of ultra-right-wing individualism and aggressive
nationalism to so wide an audience from so exalted a platform. However,
a practical conservative politician, more concerned with consequences than
with doctrine, might see the matter in a different light. He would observe
that Goldwater's overwhelming defeat and the consequent collapse of Republican party strength in Congress have smashed the legislative barriers
that for more than twenty-five years have blocked major advances in the

---

[18] As is often the case, there is a modest portion of truth in this myth: the battle with
the moderates in the primaries and at San Francisco helped to fix an image of Goldwater
in the public mind that was never erased. But after San Francisco, it was not true that
Goldwater was a loser because the moderates deserted him, but rather that the moderates,
with their survival in mind, had to desert him because he was a loser. After the Hershey
Conference, most of them were prepared to obey the professional code (as, for example,
Scranton handsomely did), but many of those who were running for office found it too
dangerous to their chances. This effect was not confined to the moderates. The ultra-
conservative senatorial candidate in California, George Murphy, also found it expedient to
keep his distance from Goldwater, and this strategy may have been an element in his
success.

[19] *The New York Times*, November 5, 1964. Goldwater's figure represented the current
state of the vote count, which was not complete.

welfare state. He would note that the preponderance in Congress has been overwhelmingly shifted toward the liberals, that legislative seniority, the makeup of the House Rules Committee, the composition indeed of all the committees, were so changed that a new flood of welfare legislation of the kind so fervently opposed by Goldwater was made possible; that medicare, a major extension of federal aid to education, a new voting-rights bill, a wider coverage for the minimum-wage act, regional aid for the Appalachian states, and a general anti-poverty program—all policies which the Goldwater forces considered dangerous in the extreme—were brought much closer to enactment; and that beyond these lay the further improved chances of a new immigration act with quota changes, urban transportation measures, the creation of a national arts foundation, even repeal of the "right to work" section of the Taft-Hartley Act.

From this point of view, liberals could be grateful to Goldwater. No other Republican could have made such a startling contribution to the first really significant and general extension of the New Deal since the 1930's. It was his campaign that broke the back of our postwar practical conservatism.